T0200844

# Shifting Mobility

## Part 1

## Transforming Planning and Design for New Human Mobility Code

**Dewan Masud Karim**

Multimodal Planning, Design and Safety Professional
Toronto, Ontario, Canada

CRC Press
Taylor & Francis Group
Boca Raton  London  New York

CRC Press is an imprint of the
Taylor & Francis Group, an **informa** business

A SCIENCE PUBLISHERS BOOK

First edition published 2024
by CRC Press
2385 NW Executive Center Drive, Suite 320, Boca Raton FL 33431

and by CRC Press
4 Park Square, Milton Park, Abingdon, Oxon, OX14 4RN

© 2024 Taylor & Francis Group, LLC

*CRC Press is an imprint of Taylor & Francis Group, LLC*

Reasonable efforts have been made to publish reliable data and information, but the author and publisher cannot assume responsibility for the validity of all materials or the consequences of their use. The authors and publishers have attempted to trace the copyright holders of all material reproduced in this publication and apologize to copyright holders if permission to publish in this form has not been obtained. If any copyright material has not been acknowledged please write and let us know so we may rectify in any future reprint.

Except as permitted under U.S. Copyright Law, no part of this book may be reprinted, reproduced, transmitted, or utilized in any form by any electronic, mechanical, or other means, now known or hereafter invented, including photocopying, microfilming, and recording, or in any information storage or retrieval system, without written permission from the publishers.

For permission to photocopy or use material electronically from this work, access www.copyright.com or contact the Copyright Clearance Center, Inc. (CCC), 222 Rosewood Drive, Danvers, MA 01923, 978-750-8400. For works that are not available on CCC please contact mpkbookspermissions@tandf.co.uk

*Trademark notice*: Product or corporate names may be trademarks or registered trademarks and are used only for identification and explanation without intent to infringe.

*Library of Congress Cataloging-in-Publication Data (applied for)*

ISBN: 978-0-367-25435-3 (hbk)
ISBN: 978-1-032-52089-6 (pbk)
ISBN: 978-0-429-28954-5 (ebk)

DOI: 10.1201/9780429289545

Typeset in Times New Roman
by Radiant Productions

*This book is dedicated to the
individuals who lost their lives
on mobility facilities across the world*

# Preface

*"No one is more hated than he who speaks the truth."*
—Plato

## A new value for urban mobility

Alongside my passion for city building, I am an adventure traveler and photographer. While traveling with my wife in new places, I must juxtapose a feeling of safety and security on the unknown places we've no previous exposure to. It's this attention to another level of detail, like a sixth sense, where unfortunately I see and feel that women's safety remains far from our surroundings. And I almost always go with my wife's 'women's' sixth sense whenever she says "I am not comfortable here" when arriving at a place or when staying the night. It has always worked to avoid her 'perceived' unsafe situations.

One day our conversation went to a different level, as we looked for deeper insights, the visible signs of safety on the street or in public places. Instead of playing a guessing game with our sixth sense, we looked for vibrant, active places, but there are very few. Maybe it's because of the cozy coffee shops, but ours is not biased criteria. Maybe it's the lack of walkable streets but for wealthy or gentrified neighbourhoods.

Our debate and observations continued for a decade as we searched for illusive visible signs of safety in the largest 'third' space in cities, in the mobility space.

Then one day while walking in the Barrio Lastarria neighbourhood in Santiago, we spotted an amazingly simple clue. It was late evening, on a very hot and steamy day. On a side street outside of a tourist area, a single woman was walking on the sidewalk. She was wearing a simple evening dress. Walking casually, showing no sign of discomfort or fear in her gestures even though it was close to midnight. It was neither an overly well-lit street. A little kid was also jumping and moving across the sidewalk, closely following the women. Maybe they were related or connected, maybe not. The woman was making passive contact with passers-by and some seniors. The child was playing, with no sign of fear in his body language. It was a simple city street scene. Nothing spectacular.

Suddenly we looked at each other with a jaw dropping realization. Dumbfounded. Flabbergasted.

We had found the mysterious missing clue! In one of the oldest symbols of a thriving human civilization.

As a passionate history lover, I know this simple clue. But I missed it: when women's place in our society is in shape, it's a most visible clue to a progressive society. When women's place in society deteriorates, it is the most visible symbol of the decline of a civilization. The horrific death at the hands of Christian extremists of Hypatia, one of the greatest personalities of the history of the human species, marked the beginning of the Dark Ages and the first visible marker of the collapse of ancient European and Middle Eastern civilizations. Her story should have been a common children's story in the 21st century's women's rights movement. But modern women are often distracted by the masculine form of femininity that has shaped the new face of unbridled Capitalism in a form of 'liquid modernity' that has already proven over the past decade to be a step in the wrong direction.

But it was not entirely my fault for missing the signs of the street's safety. I was never taught any other demography while studying engineering or planning except hidden patriarchal essentials. Neither have we but rarely considered in the process of mobility system planning and design the many other vital elements of society, nor the different types of users, nor non-vehicle modes.

Contradictions are the trademark of our new "liquid modern" society, particularly in the post-pandemic era. In an era of energy scarcity, excessive or in many cases unnecessary use of vehicles is normalized through the digital media without informing of the consequences of the high-energy lifestyle. Young generations are forced to live a "cheap" consumer product lifestyle, even though they scream in support of the 'Greta Thunberg mantra' through the glazed windows of gas guzzling cars. Climate change is on everyone's lips, but not in their hands. The sheer negative psychological impacts of our lonely car-oriented neighbourhoods are now hidden behind streaming services and spectacle entertainment. Mobility's environmental impact is too often attempted cured by medicine, meditation, and mindfulness. On the top of all these symptoms is our mega mobility infrastructures.

Over the last two centuries, our striving for high-speed mobility has inflicted numerous human sufferings, disseminated the urban fabric of public space, and exterminated human values from the true essence of mobility in favour of technological product and infinite growth. Large mobility infrastructure initiatives often sideline basic human rights and are "mitigated" through a paper-based environmental assessment process. Large mobility infrastructures have low capacity per unit, a double or more crash rate, are highly inefficient and unhealthy, with no identity and no sense of community. Moving toward the latter half of the 21st century, our finite planet will be entering a new beginning of "growth with limits" based on the boundary principles of the earth. And this new decoupling of growth and mobility will have to respect long-forgotten human values in mobility mega-infrastructure projects.

All earlier attempts to continue with the status quo of massive mobility infrastructure expansion disregarded human rights, environment, health, and social values. Any and all mobility infrastructure "megalomania"[1] perished in a sea of asphalt and concrete. If new applications of technology, new mobility and progressive city building ideas apply the same failed ideologies, any future attempts will imitate the past's futile path.

The big question we are now facing is: Are there any other alternatives to a sustainable future?

The answer is: Yes. Human resiliency has overcome many impending disasters. By not following the path of 'business-as-usual'.

Also, a different force has emerged over the last two decades, where the story of this book begins. I have seen in my days the tail end of Jane Jacobs' life in Toronto. I never met her, but her footprints are everywhere in the Toronto where she lived. And I now see today the horrific alternative path she warned us of. Her 'Nostradamus-like' vision of the city is now unfolding in real city building stories all around us and across the world.

But we can feel and smell the winds of change, as brave interventions have managed to change the street scene. Janette Sadik-Khan in New York and Gabe Klein in Washington and Chicago rode the stormy ride in the first decade of this millennium. I was lucky to meet both in MIT Media and tried to steal their fiery energy and migrate it to my hometown Toronto and region. I met some brilliant minds of shared mobility and visionaries across the globe, particularly at a Berlin gathering that surprised me with the pace of mobility change displayed after such a stagnant 20th century. I met the living legend of the human scale city proponent Jan Gehl when a Toronto downtown

---

[1] "Megalomania" puts forward an extreme reflection of the appearance of progress in the contemporary city, in terms of architecture and infrastructure (Architecture Lab).

plan was environed. I joined the forces of local leader Jennifer Keesmaat, on her North York team who quietly implemented many new mobility concepts on the ground. Their practices eventually removing invisible vehicle spaces and redesigning the unsafe and outdated facilities that had spread like wildfire across North York in less than half a decade. Even today when I walk with my wife or friends or colleagues to show them how from outright denial to widespread adoption of many of my redesign proposals it still amazes me how fast mobility has changed and continues to evolve in even better directions.

I have shared these stories on many platforms, and traveled to Europe, Asia, and Africa as an invited keynote speaker to explain the phenomenal cultural sources of my proud, lifelong mobility passion. So, it was about time to lock these stories and new concepts and implementations into a book.

The sheer gap between traditional mobility and new winds of change is the original concept of this book. The monumental mobility system-wide changes that I worked on, proposed, or implemented in many places are converted in this two-volume series into new concepts, theories, approaches, professional practices, and illustrations. Whether the discovery of new mobility code, inclusion of invisible people, invisible spaces, missing mobility users or modes, or accounting for the limits of our planetary boundary, all ideas are blended and locked into numerous sections of the two books.

I believe looking through the lens of humanity when we build our future urban mobility is the only coveted path that can stop impending planetary decline and bargain for a new resilient way to survive through volatile environmental changes. The central focus of this book is on bringing back the natural instincts of human mobility while keeping basic human rights through the wisdom of 'mobility equity', an ancient human understanding of human values that was once encrypted by ancient civilizations.[2]

---

[2] Known as Cyrus Charter (UN, 1971) in 600 BC and later revived by renowned poet Sheikh Saadi in 12th century, roughly 800 years before universal human charter of rights adopted by few modern nations. The charter is described as:
"Human beings are members of a whole
In creation of one essence and soul
If one member is afflicted with pain
Other members uneasy will remain
If you have no sympathy for human pain
The name of human you cannot retain"

# Acknowledgements

This book is a real story of creating the most enduring but ephemeral phenomena of human civilization – human mobility. After more than 25 years of honing and shining my lifelong passion for human mobility, it was to time to share the fascinating stories from my professional work, personal observations, and community reflections on the city's most visible, vibrant, and loveable public spaces. Mobility public space will remain a generator of all key characteristics of human civilization, and an integral part of the third space between our home and work or learning places. This book shares the knowledge that emerged from thousands of thought-provoking ideas that become a reality, the numerous placemaking stories contributed by people or institutions, and entities that I came across during this incredible journey.

I would like to express my deepest gratitude to the contributors who assisted me in various forms to complete this book, including the review of book contents, research analysis, modeling and coding, the creation of graphics, mapping, providing resources and raw data, and artistic sketches and drawings, and the endless number of those that helped me along this journey. It would take another book to document you all.

While I am indebted to many people for this book, my lifelong transformation from a rigid engineering professional, to a people-oriented human approach, to human mobility, would not have happened without the continuous and endless support from Mushtari Afroz, my wife. Be us experiencing human conditions in the mobility space, observing the ephemeral beauty of an ever-changing human movement, or connecting the mobility world to numerous aspects of social, cultural and environmental perspective, Mushtari's insights as an artist into a deeper meaning of life has become the core philosophical guidance of writing this book. She also assisted in translating many complex findings but beautiful ideas, into artistic representation materials, translating brand new ideas and complex phenomena into simple caricatures, and interpreting many of my research results into a simpler language other than that of traffic engineering.

Losing my one and only brother in the mobility space and seeing the shared tragedy's eternal impact on my parents' lives, has guided me through this book to be honest to myself, and be truthful in informing others of the facts, about current mobility systems reflected across the ideas, and in the approach and process developed in the two-book series.

The mobility transformation across the cities where I've worked would not have become reality without the dedicated, skillful, and open-minded professionals of the "silent majority" in Japan and Canada. They were brave to join my endless "troublesome" requests, stick together facing monumental oppositions, remain united against entire city halls or traditional practitioners' "no change" attitude, stirring the debate while sharing the success of numerous implementations and becoming personal friends and allies for the rest of my life. In both private and public sectors, professionals and collaborators extended the boundary of their limits for new planning, design and implementation approaches to test untested approaches, ideas, and concepts. During my professional service with the City of Oshawa, several planners including Margret Kish, Susan Aston, Hena Kabir, Suzanne Elston, Susan McGregor, Tom Goodeve, Warren Munro and Paul Ralph, quietly processed my numerous official and secondary sustainable mobility policy interventions, design, funding, and development requirements or modification recommendations, despite the image of Oshawa as a 'vehicle city' hanging over us due to the longtime presence of the automobile manufacturing industry. Engineers and technicians such as Bill Grylls, Anthony Ambra, Craig Kelly and managers of parking and parks departments participated and implemented unthinkable acts, including the installation of the first bike lane on Mary Street, the first protected bike lane on Ahtol Street, protected bicycle parking installations, removing vehicle lanes or closing the street to accommodate downtown institutions' needs, the first mini-roundabout installations, and currently the implementation of an active transportation and transportation master plan initiated during my worktime in Oshawa.

Besides internal collaborations, outside organizations' members participated in some of my wild endeavors. Members of the Oshawa Cycling Club assisted in organizing cycling events and in developing the active transportation master plan. Several former counselors and the mayor of Oshawa was instantly convinced by the persuasive words of former provincial minister Eleanor McMahon from Share the Road and made the case for a citywide cycling facility plan. Indeed, Oshawa has since been recognized as a "bicycle-friendly" city, helping alter its "rustbelt" city image toward an inclusive and diverse city. Pedestrian plans, workshops, features, and events with the help Mandy Johnson from 'Walkable Communities' helped get the former mayor John Henry's signature on the 'Pedestrian Charter'. Working with Donald Wiedman from Bikes and Transit .com paved the way for heightened awareness of combining bicycles with the transit and trail systems of Oshawa. With the introduction of more smart growth developments and sustainable mobility implementation, the City of Oshawa is slowly moving toward reducing vehicle dependence in their mobility systems.

The most enduring and daring implementation of my profound ideas and concepts realization happened during my work periods in the City of Toronto. Hearing that former Chief Planner Jennifer Keesmaat was looking for individuals to implement people-friendly approaches to city building, I was convinced that Toronto, having so many professionals working in such a diverse and complex urban environment, would be the ideal test breeding ground to apply many new ideas and concepts. That assumption was correct. Comically referred as #WeTheNorth, the bravest transportation planners among all Toronto district offices, a team consisting of Andrew Au, Diane Ho, Sheikh Ariful Alam enthusiastically joined up to push a new agenda of transportation. Our close collaborators were urban designers like Dawn Hamilton, Helene Iardes, Leo Desorcy, Sasha Terry, Rong Yu, Swathika Anandan, Joseph Luk, Michael Sakalauskas, and Dulini Ratnayake who listened tirelessly, constructively debated, explored, and came up with new way to apply urban design practices to accommodate my wildest ideas while rebuilding city mobility spaces from a new perspective. I am equally grateful to the many passionate planners who incorporated multimodal mobility ecosystem concepts into their development proposals, transit-oriented development studies, and secondary plans including changing or inserting policies, that were perceived as 'impossible'. Diane Silver, Cathie Ferguson, Andria Sallese Muzzatti, John Andreevski, Colin Ramdial, Vanessa Giulia, Guy Matthew, Kathryn Moore, Seanna Kerr, Allison Meistrich, Nigel Tahair to name a few. Despite skeptical view, I found many allies and partners in crime in traditional transportation services including the young and brave Daniel duo - Daniel Reynolds, Daniel Samson, ardent supporter Janet Lo in the Pedestrian section, Adam Popper in Cycling, and Sheyda Saneinejad in Vision Zero. Introducing big data was our biggest hurdle, but with a few consulting colleagues including Jesse Coleman, Streetlight data was successfully incorporated into transportation data and forecasting. And finally, I am grateful for two great leaders and visionaries who transformed Toronto over the last decade in so many ways – former Chief Planner Jennifer Keesmaat and general manager Barbara Gray of Transportation Services, particularly for including me as a key reviewer of Complete Streets initiatives, school travel safety, and brave new initiatives for redesigning Lawrence Heights neighbourhoods to tackle the stereotypical perception of priority neighbourhoods.

My unconventional style of blending institutional, professional and research inquiries would have likely never become a reality if I had not met a few great minds and visionaries in transportation.

A few turning points of my professional life came from meeting with the greatest personalities who shocked the entire mobility planning and design community. Meeting a few visionaries at the MIT Media Lab conference will remain the brightest moment of my professional life. Brief encounters with former transportation commissioner of New York Janette Sadik-Khan, former transportation commissioner of Chicago Gabe Klein, Susan Shaheen of the University of California, Berkeley, and Gereyon Meyer from VDI/VDE Innovation + Technik GmbH uplifted me with confidence that my ideas are worth spreading. Recognition of my "Innovation Master Ideas" at that conference was one my happiest of achievements. Both Susan and Gereyon later inviting me to write a chapter for "Disrupting Mobility". I was also fortunate to work with brilliant startups – realtime data source provided by the Streetlight data team (CEO Laura Schewel, Tori Clifford, Michael Bailey) and the multimodal information platform Transit Screen team (CEO Matt Caywood, Ryan Croft now with Pacto, Diana Dakik, and Colin Illar) to introduce new innovation systems and ideas into the public service. Besides this Boston intellectual crowd, I met many more at Mobility Dialogue in Berlin. Through the beautiful personalities (Juliana Obynochnaya and Alejandra Labarca Danus) who organized the wonderful event and introduced me to many more bright European minds. The brilliant artificial intelligence system to track personal mobility from MotionTag data was a game changer. With co-founder Fabien Sauthier (including his assistant Sara De Rosso), personal mobility data was prepared for my research – the basic data of Mobility code and DNA elements research conducted for this book. During the Covid-19 pandemic, Fabien's team tirelessly processed my endless data requirements, explored ideas, and passionately listened to some of the findings. Mr. Shakil Haider assisted in data digging in Python and summarizing raw data into simple charts and graphics. During my time as a public servant, I continued to work with the academic sector and supervised a number of research students to conduct research in detail in few of my concepts. As part of Toronto Metropolitan University, Sheikh Ariful Alam conducted research in active transportation modeling including increases in potential of active transportation trips when shared mobility systems are introduced appropriately. Haya Rizvi conducted research in shared mobility policy to develop a toolkit such as the "Shopping List" and its impact on the reduction of vehicle trips and parking demand. These research findings, with my additional analysis and interpretation, are included in the second volume of this two-book series.

Converting complex ideas into artistic representation was the biggest hurdle to writing this book. I have many ardent supporters, but they all wished I could find a simple way to translate complex concepts and ideas. I realized the pressing need for artistic collaboration, but it was not easy to find the right partners. During my professional life in the City of Toronto, both Swathika Anandan and Dulini Ratnayake took my requests seriously and developed numerous render models with new multimodal, street design and planning concepts in the master planning process. Later Swathika Anandan and Helene Iardes created Mobility DNA concepts and converted them into beautiful sketches. When I conceived the idea of chapter sketches, Lowell Lo came forward to develop beautiful sketches from an artistic and architectural perspective. But a major challenge remained, when Harry Olson who I met via transportation commissioner Gabe Klein to develop the first few graphics was no longer available. After searching for a few months, I came in contact with two new artists – Francisco Meija Diaz, a Mexican living in Toronto and Tamara Osses Alvarado, living in Chile. Both tireless worked with me through numerous iterations to conceptualize my new ideas into beautiful graphics throughout the book. In the end, the search for book cover design would not have been possible if Mitsuki B. Fujimoto/Nitzkhi had not stepped forward via the Book An Artist platform.

Finally, the writing of this book would have remained in my wildest dream if I had never met Donald Wiedman through a City of Oshawa bicycles, transit, and trails project. I am deeply indebted to his tireless help editing and reviewing drafts from a literature perspective, through numerous proofreads, for his artistic eye for graphics, charts, and illustrations, and for the formatting and compilation of book in its entirety.

# Contents

## Section IV: Implementation of New Mobility Code

## Chapter 6: Physical Mobility(-as-a-Place) for Everyday: Reinventing Public Realm    321

## Section V: Implementation of New Mobility

## Chapter 7: Shifting Flexible Policies for a New Mobility Ecosystem     381

# Section I

# Origin and Evolution of Human Mobility

# CHAPTER 1

## PART 1

# The Interconnected World of Mobility

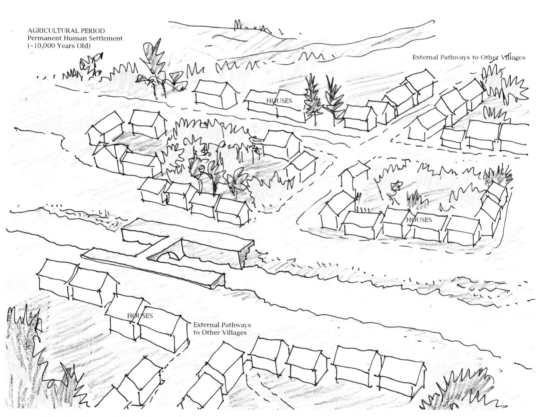

AGRICULTURAL PERIOD
Permanent Human Settlement
(~10,000 Years Old)

External Pathways to Other Villages

HOUSES

HOUSES

HOUSES

External Pathways
to Other Villages

**Fig. 1.0:** Connecting neighbourhoods through human mobility is one of the foundations of our civilization.

*"Only walking manages to free us from our illusions about the essential."*
—Frederic Gros

## Introduction

Human movement is often perceived as a synonym and symbol of our freedom. Mobility is a defining feature of basic human rights. Movement is also a visible notion of activity for all species including humans. All babies make desperate attempts to move and explore their surroundings with explosive quests. As we grow older, we move in the quest with tangible or intangible motives. As we approach the end of our life, the last thing we want to give up is mobility. We also move without moving. Staying represents why we move and when we will make our next move. Human movement is the defining symbol of our species. We are born without a blueprint, unlike other animals. This 'lack' acts as a driving force of community living. We need to socialize to survive as individuals in group or collective forms. We look together for food, resources, pleasure, and suitable places to live. Mobility gives us all remarkable abilities to shape human evolution and build our civilizations. And yet why we move and what moves us remains a mystery. The journey of writing this book started in the quest for knowledge to comprehend the hidden nature of human mobility, and to gain insights into our own mobility identity and build cities around the fundamental nature of our mobility needs, while replacing the ideology that discounted our basic desire for human movement.

*"If the government cannot create happiness for its people, there is no purpose for the government to exist."*
—Bhutan legal code, 1729

## How Mobility has Evolved: Socially and Culturally

Of all the symbols of civilization, none have evoked as much bafflement, incredulity, and conjecture as the way we move, why we move, and the mobility ecosystem that makes movement possible. The mobility system is the fundamental building block of city building and one of the important elements of public space that is often measured as key indicators of the quality of life of city inhabitants. With the growing popularity of the livable, healthy, and clean city, the topic of sustainable mobility continues to generate intense debate among all inhabitants, politicians, practitioners, and decision makers. Traditional architects, city planners and traffic engineers argue for a modern lifestyle approach to automobile-oriented city building that would continue with the infinite expansion of road infrastructure and urban sprawl[1] while pushing city boundaries out further to accommodate the rapid rate of urbanization (Squires, 2002). Whether it is low density urbanization, such as North American cities, or high-density urbanization, such as Asian cities, wider highways and more parking are believed to modernize cities and achieve an easier path to the "American Dream". Although every city plan identifies the details of its automobile-oriented vision as the most influential pillar of urbanization, the scientific discussion behind such epic policy is surprisingly scarce (Galster et al., 2001) on what research says about the nature of the relationship between automobile dependent development and the improvement of human quality of life.

---

[1] Urban sprawl is defined as a condition of land use (using eight distinct dimensions of land-use patterns: density, continuity, concentration, clustering, centrality, nuclearity mixed uses, and proximity) that is represented by low values on one or more of these dimensions (Galster et al., 2001).

Some elusive targets were achieved. Most perished in philosophical doctrine.

However, without limits, our never-ending infrastructure expansion carries the seed of civilization's decline. As has happened to all sprawling habitations in human history.

To the contrary, the supporters of livable cities have been arguing passionately over the last few decades promoting transit-oriented development and the benefits of a compact community, and to limit space and resources in cities to better manage the impacts of urbanization (Ewing et al., 2002). New evidence and results of mobility implementation in the right hands are emerging in favour of the latter approach (Jackson, 2003). In addition, the recent growth in awareness of the numerous benefits of improving and expanding active mobility such as walking and cycling is more favourable toward the sustainable developments once envisioned by the "Our Common Future" declaration (WCED, 1987). Not a flawless method, but in the wrong hands a misguided application of transit-oriented development could lead to similar consequences of the automobile-oriented approach with lesser impact (Padeiro, 2019) despite its promise of greater equitable mobility access for citizens.

The concept of equality in mobility systems however has created a deeply divided, inequal society.

All major 'modern' city building ideology has something in common. It does not clearly say why we move, what moves us or why stay at some locations for different lengths of times. Do we (or any species) have an inherent nature of movement that defines us? Where do instructions come from for when, why, and how we move or stay? Simply, what exactly is the human mobility that has guided or misguided us to build compact and organic mobility ecosystems versus mega infrastructures to move us around cities?

These simple questions or the absence of inquiry point us to an embarrassing query – did we understand our own mobility instinct from the beginning, before building the mobility systems that could have become of the genuine indicators of quality-of-life in cities?

With neither side yet to produce any direct philosophical or scientific evidence linking the nature of human mobility needs with systems, this book attempts to address this disquieting quandary from a different perspective. The endeavour of this book is not to answer all fundamental queries. It strives to begin a long overdue and much needed tour and steering of the discussion of future mobility in a sensible direction. A common approach to settle any mobility system debate is not an easy task. Faced with economic, political, and environmental challenges however, the question of the true nature of human mobility and its appropriate infrastructure sizes and design scales in a self-sustained community should be the centre of future city building and measured prosperity of its inhabitants.

Technology arrives and disappears over time. But the true desire for human mobility remains the same. When a civilization is built around one single technology, the society develops fatal cracks when that specific technology diminishes, and better competitors arrive. That's exactly what's happened with cars in cities. We built our cities around cars. Now facing a monumental challenge of finding enormous resources to move cars, we must now find a way to build cities around our true human mobility instinct and build future mobility around low-carbon or zero-emission mobility ecosystems. There are debates about the composition of a new mobility ecosystem. There are many new concepts floating around about the new face of mobility in the future city. However, one answer is very clear. The future mobility system will not be designed around the car, even if it is zero-emission and drives without a human. It will be built around our authentic human mobility code and its elements of DNAs. Many of the new concepts introduced in this book are built around the multimodal mobility ecosystem and originate from the hidden existence of our mobility DNA and how it is interconnected with the built form, context, and shape of the city.

"*Structures don't march in the street.*"
—Banner of May 1968 civil unrest in France

## Misguided Structures of Current Mobility

When it comes to defining the mobility system, confusion starts with the improper use of words. In general, the entire city building system codifies our movement into a narrow band – transporting people or goods from one place to another. A recent effort toward future mobility in the city building process attempted to define mobility (Forum for the Future, 2010).[2] While this definition broadened the narrow band of the transportation viewpoint from the utility-only perspective, the narrow viewpoint remains the 'functional' definition of our movement in cities.

Structuralism as a philosophy often refers to different schools of thought and provided a 'continuity' of many things that prevail in the mobility world of today. Structuralism favours assumed deterministic forces over people's organic and natural ability to act as a human being (Marshall, 2004). Old schools of structured thought around cars as the only way to provide mobility service in cities clashed with the very meaning of human mobility. When a mobility problem was attempted to be defined, we were told to 'focus' and isolate mobility from everything else and to focus on basic structures. But structures are rigid and spell trouble in an organic huma-oriented system where variation is common and a dominant medium (Gilcher-Holtey, 2014). The biggest problem with nature is everything is linked to everything else. And only after building massive mobility systems, we started to realize that severe inequality was created by our mobility supply. Transit-oriented corridors gentrified the local people and pushed them into the suburbs, creating a political nightmare of mobility inequality. Highways mostly cut through racially oppressed poor suburbs, but not through downtowns or posh neighbourhoods. Pollution concentrated along the highways and mega streets of suburban neighbourhoods. Chronic disease is on the rise due to our car-centric sedentary lifestyle. The volatile fossil fuel market has created a trap for the poor who need a subsidy when the price tilts slightly upward. Depression is common in the suburbs or badly planned dense areas especially among women, seniors, and predominantly among regular private vehicle commuters. Our greenwashed environmental approach is ultimately pushing local flora and fauna toward extinction, especially along polluted and divided transportation corridors. And most importantly, the mobility system works for only one demography – the adult, healthy white male, an old dominant form of social colonization rooted in European culture. We have forgotten most of the people in society – women, children, senior citizens, and people with physical abilities. The list is so long it will take another book to properly identify who and what we're ignoring in our improper definition of mobility.

The approach in this book will be to peek often outside the 'acceptable' walls of mobility systems. Many new ideas will link social, psychological, cultural aspects to mobility, and set boundary limits to our 'infinite' demand before building massive infrastructures that we cannot afford decades after their construction; simply checking whether any system is resilient enough to survive environmental, natural, or manmade disruption; prepare the city for the next low-carbon solutions or at least keeping options open to prepare for the uncertain future; and most importantly, introduce thought-provoking concepts and practically successful innovative ideas that must find their way into mainstream practice leading to needed changes in city building.

> *"In postmodernity, we no longer exist in a world of human scale."*
> —Fredric Jameson

---

[2] "'Mobility' means more than just transport. Our definition of mobility is a means of access – to goods, services, people, and information. This includes physical movement, but also other solutions such as ICT-based platforms, more effective public service delivery, and urban design that improves accessibility."

# So, What Went Wrong?

It is a long list. A few errors more pressing than others.

The art of building urban mobility and human conditions have seemed to be in direct conflict. Contradicting each other's core principles. At the heart of the quest to build mobility systems is the relationship between the nature of human mobility and finding a reasonable solution after managing the demand at sources. We seemed to forget to ask the fundamental questions. Why has the city's mobility become so insular and unresponsive to the dramatic social, historical, human changes that have occurred around us and changed over time, while mobility supply has remained constant. We are building more roads or widening the same roads repeatedly to invite more cars, adding nearly infinite parking spaces to the extent where there is less space for living or working than for the storage of cars in extreme car-oriented cities. What makes mobility system planners and decision makers build a rigid and intolerant human environment as opposed to contemporary progressive ideas that emerged in other places? On what values do we build our principles when we decide to build or expand future mobility systems in cities?

The answers were surprisingly close to nonexistent.

Technical systems around our vehicle-oriented cities do not exist independent of the ideas, ideologies, and philosophies that shape our society, politics, and culture. Currently mobility systems are a mere reflection of the conscious and unconscious objectives and biases that planners and designers are exposed to from their political and social surroundings. Instead of pointing fingers at shallow and visible causes, this book dives deeper into systematic philosophical ideas and ideologies that are now built into the daily practice and process of mobility planning and design.

## *Utilitarian and functional mobility*

The birth of urban automobility as we see it today aligned with one of the most tumultuous periods of modern human history. A few core professions, practices, and modernism in urban mobility developed and mass produced during the darkest periods of 20th century immediately before World War II. Like many of the social and cultural evolutions during this period, mobility planning and in general city building could not escape the rise of misguided 'modernism' and its three basic ideologies: the utilitarian principles of human selfishness, functionalism in infrastructure, and structural discrimination through mega streets and ugly urban highways. And this newfound 'modernism' was rooted in an underlying philosophy that laid the foundation for the industrial approach to mobility in cities. With or without knowing it, the first principle of the numerous mobility planning and traffic engineering incorporated utilitarian principles[3] is that *"people are completely selfish, and that each person ought to promote the greatest happiness, no matter whose"* (Bentham, 1789). This utilitarian principle later become human history's most destructive lethal force of European colonization by embodying "white male" ideology reproduced from the "Vitruvian man" (Stanford University, 2019) and later (mis)guided by Darwin's evolution theory through scientific racism (Dennis, 1995). The existence of human's selfish being was ignited by megastructure mobility networks under the disguise of utilitarian principle and became a root cause of congestion later uncovered through the famous "Braess Paradox" (Braess et al., 2005). Secondly, functionalism came along in the early era of fascism in the 20th century during the machine age. By mixing utility and functionalism, single purpose product or facility culture was born, which discards the possibility of doing the same thing for other purposes. The mobility system was the first victim. Building lifeless mega streets and massive parking lots for vehicles only and discarding the possibility of other mobility modes or human usage follows the utility and functional use of everyday objects by Adolf Loos (Loos, 1908). The third 'modern' principle created sprawling cities. Driven by 'modern' ideology, modernists came up with an idea that cities should be built for

---

[3] Including when predecessor Jeremy Bentham reintroduced the idea and became known as the father of modern utilitarianism.

machines, not humans. Building a high rise "tower in a park" connected by mega streets and ugly elevated highways came from another influential architect Le Corbusier (Le Corbusier, 1929). These three ideologies along with their creators and followers produced literally all basic foundations and principles of the 'modern' vehicle-oriented city planning and mobility systems that are now coming back to haunt us today with the most destructive form of city building seen in human history.

### Irrational desires of mass car culture fantasy

The industrial era brought many machines into our lifestyle. The use of machines solved many problems. Urbanization was born with machine assisted process. The steam engine brought the first mass urbanization. Electric rail and early public transport created many cities in the 20th century, and they did not require the possession of a machine for daily personal uses. The invasion of the car and its accompanying mass consumerism changed everything. Today's car culture is everywhere, but it was not a natural technology adoption. A myth of endless happiness was created, invoking utility principles. The heart of every utility made up of deceptions. Every deception needed some external forces. The use of the machine was an easy tool to achieve the target. Cars were depicted as the happiness machine to deceive and hide isolated, depressed, and lifeless suburban life. Wild unconscious human desire was evoked to promote the new technology and culture of possessions. A new corporate culture of vehicle ownership was born by misusing the human psyche indicated in Freud's famous theory of human psychology and who we are. Modern mass consumerism was born with new propaganda techniques to control mass populations. Modernism ended around 1980 but the car remains at the centre of a new post-modern mass consumer culture, making it the permissive 'master' built into the social culture of everyday life. Even though it has been identified as one of the products of mass consumerism that helped to erode the quality of life in the cities we live in today, the permissive master remains with us in an environmental and autonomous format in the 21st century.

> "*Repetition is due to the reflection in the sphere of cultural production of the standardized and repetitive processes of monopoly capitalist industry.*"
> —Theodor Adorno

### Cult of rigidity – Creative repetitions to monotonous manifesto

The initial attempt to create standards or acceptable norms for mobility infrastructures was to avoid mistakes, maintaining or creating basic services, and avoiding confusion by repeating the same product. Variations over minimum standards were available to designers or builders to create the highest possible quality of mobility facilities. Varying a system design within a safe range creates diversity in products. However, a hardline approach against variations in traffic engineering and mobility planning was adopted from the patriarchs and colonization principles of utilitarian ideology and unbridled capitalism which feed each other (Daelen and Bruneau, 2020). The underlying foundation of this ideology is a "white European male" or patriarchy approach that cuts off (Loos, 1908) any beauty, ornamentation, or cultural aspects in street and public space planning and design. Over time the variation and diversity foundations of core human-centred instinct was lost in the modern era under the banner of utilitarian ideology, 'streamlining' the process and constricting through rigid assumptions that then hardened into professional dogma and an almost religion-like belief system.

Mobility system planning in cities is a process of repetitions. Repetitions of policies, bylaws, regulations, standards, and assumptions. These functional processes are necessary to create basic safety, quality, and comfort for city residents. There is no doubt. Anarchy would replace peaceful city life without the proper regulatory frameworks that have kept cities intact over thousands of years. Rules and morality in civilization process is about taming internal irrational human behaviour (Freud, 1929) for the survival of our own species. But when these processes were applied and built over time without human context and only 'driven' by monotonous meaningless outcomes, such as the ever-increasing hyper speed world of automobiles in cities without considering the consequence on human life, creative repetitions turned into an ugly ending. Where scientific facts fall short of certainty (and they most often do) and humans are guided by ideologist assumptions, inference, and beliefs (Adams, 1995), a mobility system becomes inefficient overtime even though short-term it seems 'functional'. The slicing up of a city's historic and dense neighbourhoods by unnecessary highway building or destroying the cultural and social identity of neighbourhoods through road widening projects predicted by computer generated models based on fundamentally faulty assumptions is a burning example. Instead of creative repetitions (Adorno and Horkheimer, 1979) for context-sensitive built form, the rigid design approach turned into a monotonous manifesto (Marx, 1976). Rigid repetitions without creative attachment and diversity in design produced aesthetically unpleasant mobility places and unlivable cities even though they appear functional on the surface.

> *"The trouble with .... western liberalism generally... were their progressive, optimistic interest in maximizing happiness."*
> —Friedrich Nietzsche

## *Religion of comfortableness*

In the modern technology-rich era, how did 'one-mobility' dogma get trapped in the entire modern mobility world when technology was supposed to free us from our car monoculture? Too often we ignore the basics of the modern world to avoid an 'uncomfortable' discussion. Like many other approaches in the modern era, the modern mobility world of the last century evolved through hidden ideologies that swept through the end of the 19th century and the whole of the 20th century. Through the "Civilizing Process", it become apparent why superior technology such as 'motorization' was perceived as "civilized and superior" while older forebearers such as pedestrians or cycling or human activities were forced into being perceived as 'uncivilized' representing our 'savage' past (Linklater, 2010) particularly in western societies. Eastern societies cobbled the same path through aggressive social media colonization (Goel, 2021). In ancient and middle-age eras, only a few could afford a fast mobility machine under feudalism, i.e., a monarchy system. If drivers of faster mobility machines harmed innocent users, people could point the blame on the few rulers at the top. It was not easy to escape blame and punishment when a chariot, cart, or horse carriage driver killed someone on the street. That changed under capitalism. Capitalism made the system abstract. During economic booms-and-bursts, people tirelessly and helplessly point to the abstract figure of government (Goel, 2021). Ford's capitalism arrived in the early 20th century with the "American Dream" of standardizing product manufacturing, relying on an unskilled labour for the assembly line who were living in close proximity to the factory, with relatively higher wages to afford, and mass consume the product they manufactured (Tolliday, 1987). Now everyone owns a car and blames someone else for the pollution, degradation, and crash atrocities that have become an almost abstract process. A few practitioners took full advantage of the confusing state. Known as structuralism[4] which emerged in the 1960s (Sturrock, 1981), with a few hidden powerful authorities controlling the world view. A few of the professional institutions or groups who believed in the infinite consumption of Fordism were architects, economists, and traffic engineers who started to practice the forceful

---

[4] Structuralism is the intellectual movement and philosophical orientation often associated initially with the Western discourses of Levi-Strauss, Marx, and Althusser, for example, who claimed to analyse and explain invariant structures in and constitutive of nature, society, and the human psyche.

interjection of their own structures in everything that shaped social life including city building. Like capitalism's basic structure that requires a constant future crisis to create more and more products, traffic engineering along with planners adopted the road widening approach in response to the "future crisis" of congestion problems. A never ending cycle of "more is needed" continued every time a new round of "road improvements" was completed. These bizarre practices created a culture of comfortableness, and praise for minions and their mundane achievements. Anyone, professionals, innovators or pioneers, who would bring progressive mobility ideas would be vilified, humiliated, and labelled a troublemaker and punted out of the system defined as 'incompatible'. All this to only maintain the mass culture of a new religion of comfortableness: high-tech vehicle monoculture, a default "permissive (Traube, 1989) master" of the 21st century. A rigid invisible structure was created through hidden rules. But the rigid structure soon faced stiff resistance which gave birth to the "identity politics era" of post-structuralism after the "May 1968" civil unrest that still reverberates through life today. The oppressed become leaders of new groups formed around identity (such as women, ethnic minorities, religious groups, and sexual minorities) and the "silent majority" soon become a powerful force that would reshape conversations in city building and redefine the mobility world.

> "*The subject is not identical to itself and all attempts to think of the subject, or a group, or the human, as self-identical leads inevitably to establishing a boundary on the other side of which are those we do not like because they are not like us.*"
> —Joan Copjec

### *The rise and fall of mobility-isms*

Arriving late but over time, a few new 'mobility-isms' attempted to reshape the politics of urban mobility. On the surface, new culture promoted environmental responsibility, raised inequality issues and systematic discrimination appropriately, and introduced equity and diversity approaches to fix the default inequality that comes with the monoculture of vehicles. Some of the 'new' isms tried to separate themselves from old school car-oriented culture thought under new banners of "sustainable mobility": pedestrianism, cycling urbanism, transit urbanism, tactical urbanism, human scale urbanism, placemaking urbanism, the "Complete Streets" movement, the "Vision Zero" movement and, more recently, autonomous vehicle and shared mobility urbanism. All these attempts rightfully promoted the demise of vehicles to create a future city around low-emission mobility. Though, over time the creators' fresh ideas of new mobility-isms become isolated from original objectives and get lost in populism. Like post-structuralism, these movements got trapped under new politics and detached themselves from the fundamental underlying issues that originally created current mobility inequality problems and attempted to fix mobility's status through 'patchwork' solutions (Chua, 2018). When human desire is essentialized by inserting a subject's identity, we create boundaries and divisions (Copjec, 2020). Division distracts us from our goal. The environmental movement in mobility created 'environmentalists' who have proposed only one silver lining solution, the electric car, to solve all vehicle related environmental problems. Transit arrived with the idea to provide a mass movement alternative to vehicles, but the transit-oriented concept soon spawned into endless high-rise towers around transit stations while keeping wide roads and highways intact. New transit routes, whether the right or wrong transit technology, would be used for winning votes and support from 'disgruntled' suburbanites. Pockets of transit neighbourhoods or corridors would soon displace more people to the suburbs due to their sky-high housing prices. Pedestrianism rightfully focused on improving street design but ignored the fundamental problems of the 'add-a-lane' approach and creating an invisible wall between walkways and roads and boulevards. Pedestrian areas with expensive traffic calming measures would end up mostly in wealthy neighbourhoods. Tactical urbanism was on the right-track when identifying unused space on streets or reclaiming abandoned public spaces but trapped itself within a wall of paint or bollards or temporary spectacle murals instead of making the changes permanent or establishing systematic programming. Placemaking finally fixed the lack of access to quality public space, but it was only applied to the city's prominent corners leaving most neighbourhoods behind. The human scale movement targeted the basic issue of vehicles consuming the most city space but would be trapped by its "Nordic look" of a "too manicured and expensive" makeover even through a cheaper affordable version was demonstrated in Asia or Latin America. Shared mobility with its great benevolent cause of fixing idle assets and the wasted capacity of cars would soon turn into aggravating vehicle usage, pollution, and inequality and penetrate only a few markets, namely wealthy, educated, Caucasian-majority users. Autonomous urbanism rightfully identified the opportunity to reuse surplus lands for placemaking, but it soon become lost in "adding additional multimodal options" built around a 'car-as-the-backbone' agenda. This is nothing but Ford capitalism under the disguise of a shimmering techno-feudalism banner of technological progress. Complete Streets emerged as a new hope of fixing century-old faulty street designs, energized practitioners or professionals and enticed new millennials into active mobility but remained disturbingly silent on 10-lane wide "mega complete streets". Complete Streets, to achieve "mobility nirvana" in its philosophical core, remains incomplete in its most completeness. It ignored social and cultural space and predominantly focused on functional uses of new mobility users. Vision Zero arrived from Sweden with grand fashion to fix rising safety problems, particularly for children, seniors, and disadvantaged communities or groups. But it would soon fall victim to "zero vision", proposing only to fix eye-candy items like speed limits and signage without touching the most crash-prone and dangerous street design practices that created "uncivilized streets" in the first place. Cycling urbanism arrived with the big hope of fixing car-oriented streets with a network of bicycle facilities while shifting vehicle users to bicycles. But isolated cycling policy only achieved limited success and soon turned into the most disappointing and divisive of mobility identity politics. The new shiny and positive image of cycling soon became a hiding place for hardline cycling leaders, creating deeper wounds and division in the mobility world. Many leaders become bureaucratic staff in public agencies or media-centric personalities while approving or ripping proposed cycling routes into pieces, delaying protected lane installations using "environmental needs assessments", or ignoring suburban needs while creating facilities mostly in wealthy neighbourhoods. With an alphabet soup of mobility-ism identities, these plebes of post-modernism mobility culture created more oppression and divisions, which is defeating to their original purpose of emancipation. A diarrhea of banal speech under the banner of mobility 'isms' is still drowning out true mobility voices and blocking real progress toward low-emission sustainable mobility.

## *The silent majority and civic feudalism*

The new mass culture of mobility-isms has baffled the silent majority. But good practitioners and decision makers are the ones keeping the city running, supplying micro-packages of good planning, delivering extraordinary design, and building a competent city building culture. These frontline fighters face a harsh environment, negotiate deals with tough stakeholders, overcome red-eye reaction from their corporate or civic leaders who pretend to be the king of their constituents, while constantly asking for innovative approaches for the public good. They are silently looking for new creative solutions to the problems they face every day. There are no monuments for hardworking people, nor any public places or squares named after them, not even minimal recognition for achieving an incremental but crucial success in city building.

Multiple mobility-isms started to confuse good practitioners, asking: which 'mobility-ism' has the right answer? What vision should be followed for future city building? Confusion multiplied when it became clear that each mode 'ism' divided people and society based on their preferred mobility modes. Clashes between civic politics and supporters often disrupted the entire system, stalling the progress. Underneath the new mobility-isms politics banner lies new mobility problems. It's tried to do a constant patchwork while only "adding a new layer" of new mobility while keeping the basic vehicle system intact to satisfy base voters. Romanticisms about new environmental-friendly modes created even more complex behaviour of a new comfortable religion. Instead of honestly and passionately fixing the old problems, greenwash mobility-isms created a mass culture of a cheap and 'comfort-zone' approach.

And that would bring us back again to square one, despite some sporadic successes of the new mobility system.

Using multiple tools for different purposes is one of the greatest intelligence features of a human being. Trapping people and attaching them to a single mobility mode identity is destined to fail. This is the fundamental reason why the new politics of mobility-isms turned into troubling stories.

### The last man – Mobility Kardashians

The failure of new mobility-isms has become disturbingly visible in recent years, particularly during the Covid-19 pandemic. It brings us back to a defining fundamental trouble of modern human beings. Through the all-new mobility-ism process, we repeatedly create new mass cultures with empty values and the lack of basic skills underneath. We are too afraid to ask the fundamental questions, to keep our job, avoid ruffling feathers, and the conformist culture of the work environment. We never rock the boat in fear of sinking. Philosopher Friedrich Nietzsche reserved his most fervent fury for these empty values of the herd (Hughes, 2016) that dominate the modern mass culture of cars and new 'mobility-isms'. After a century-and-a half, we are surrounded by his "last man". These men and women, except for a bunch of 'troublemakers', who regularly turn their back on challenging ideas to solve real mobility problems. They find their banal existence only in trivial and narcissistic views on the 'new' isms of mobility with endless and empty social media posts about shallow achievements of "sustainable mobility" that do not touch even the very basic structure that has repeatedly created the failed conditions. On the contrary, there are exceptional outstanding individuals who risk their careers, or even lives, and often challenge the 'normal' status quo of the unimodal system or oppose personnel who promote timid mediocre changes in mobility systems. These overnight "future mobility experts" ultimately turn themselves into the "last man" culture who will do everything in one's power to pretend and celebrate new 'mundane' project achievements that continue the old school rigid structures around vehicles under a new shining banner. Nietzsche caricatured this mass culture as the "religion of comfortableness" a devastating portrayal of our modern mass culture of conformity. This would also be an ultimate description of our modern world and social norm that is shy of risking 'comfort' to strive for greatness in city building, which has evolved around a human-centred approach for over ten millennia.

> *"In individuals, insanity is rare; but in groups, parties, nations and epochs, it is the rule."*
>
> —Friedrich Nietzsche

### New colonization of mobility ideology

The ideological basis of building the city around machines in western countries gradually spread across the world. Mobility systems in capitalist, socialist, and communist worlds as a result all look alike. After the fall of the Berlin Wall, a new world order of monoculture spread like an infectious disease. Having no opposition, rigid Cartesian ideology (Grosholz, 1991) engulfed the postmodern society including the mobility world by constructing the notion that the subject was rational, unified, and distanced from world affairs. The footprint of Le Corbusier's city is now seen anywhere in the suburbs of Algiers, Purbachal, a new city in Dhaka, the outskirts of Shanghai, or in a disgruntled crime-prone 'tower-in-the park' neighbourhoods in Toronto or Los Angeles. Elevated highways started to divide neighbourhoods in Dhaka or Kolkata, or Bangkok or Moscow as they did in minority communities in Atlanta. Streets in Moscow are as wide as in Detroit. Dubai's sky-high towers with high-speed vehicle-only corridors resemble urban highways in Kuala Lumpur. Owning a new vehicle is as much a symbol of social status in Lagos as it is in Tehran. To remove pedestrians from the street, footbridges in Singapore and in Amman look alike. In the name of freedom and desire to have the "American Dream", consultants from the western world planted these "symbols of progress" into the developing world. Local professionals remained silent or supported these schemes, ignoring local non-motorized mobility culture. To make it worse, rich east Asian countries and world-level western financial institutions financed mega structures in poor Asian, African, and Latin American countries, accumulating for them an enormous infrastructure burden and financial debt for future generations. Social media touts the last nail in "the dead city" coffin by spreading this excessive daily lifestyle consumption into the hands of people who have little affordability, and with nonexistent human skills or resource access to maintain and operate mega substructures. Without knowing the severe impact of social and cultural space in dense cities, car culture is entrenched into every corner of the planet. And an insane foreign practice of city building without any context is now part of developing nations' professional culture.

## Green mobility inequity

The misapplication of green and transit-oriented mobility has given birth to a new platform of inequality.

The environmental movement started with the noble cause of addressing the degradation of the natural environment and a lack of awareness in 1970. From an artistic movement by Robert Rauschenberg to climate change awareness by Al Gore, the environmental agenda correctly addressed the greatest struggle of this century. Gradually, the noble cause becomes a noble pain through the green political agenda. From green whitewashing to environmental gentrification, the benevolent face of the most pressing issue of a new generation became a "business product" and was used to 'shield' the same old status quo business under a new 'green' banner (Anguelovski, 2021). Sustainable mobility did not escape the environmental hypocrisy. The 'green' car has become the silver lining method among environmentalists, scientists, and progressive thinkers who ignore the fact that the 'green' car also destroys city space and streets, like fossil-fuel cars, and just moves pollution to another medium. The transit-oriented neighbourhood has become a hidden tool of "transit gentrification", a civil rights issue often neglected and overlooked in city growth and future mobility policies (Wilson, 2020). As new transit comes in and replaces car-dominated corridors, the original vulnerable residents are pushed out to disconnected and disoriented 'cheaper' suburbs due to increased housing values and rents in regeneration areas. Vegan shops, boutiques, and expensive restaurants pop up along new transit corridors as a 'sign' of progress, albeit for few. Streets are being widened for 'transit' or "active mobility" while throwing additional lanes in to address 'congestion' and continuing the age-old 'land-grab' policy under a new "sustainable agenda". Bike lanes have become the "new ornament" for gentrified areas. Wide boulevards, green streets, and vibrant public parks are not surprisingly linked to mostly privileged neighbourhoods. Even shared mobility and new technology has shown bias, and dominant users coming from privileged neighbourhood or demography. The 'successes' of new transit became mobility and city planning tools as well as unintended or in many cases intended policy consequences in the new form of violation of human rights. Very few acknowledged this new form of discrimination and micro-aggressive behaviour amongst the professional and sustainable mobility advocacy communities. "Al Gore" syndrome became the hallmark of the new and extreme form of urban inequality, a new political nightmare giving birth to populist urban politics that created an urban vs. suburban divide. The new form of systematic discrimination was cut into pieces, sliced into thin layers, and delivered as a "quantum package". Like photons can't be separated from light, this new inequality in a micro-aggressive package is now built onto the mainstream flow of city building. Future mobility progress cannot be achieved through a new form of discrimination. It must address equitable mobility access head-on while changing the bad habit of just 'talking' about it. This book proposes new planning tools, to avoid a concentrated "mobility node" centred around key mobility locations, spread across neighbourhoods with equal and affordable access for all residents in each city neighbourhood.

## Creation of lifeless streets

Over 10 millennia of human civilization, city residents used to enjoy a greener environment on street corners, joyfully watching the wildlife activities of the natural ecosystem in street trees, enjoying cultural activity on streets or in public squares, meeting friends, neighbours, or relatives in public squares to interact socially in daily life, and trade locally produced products in public spaces. During the initial invasion of automobiles into cities in the early 20th century, mobility system planning, and design gradually became disconnected from the natural and human environments. To see green space, we now must travel, ironically by car, to the greenbelt zone or conservation areas. Culture and art are now trapped behind the four walls of theatres and art galleries where only a few can gain access and enjoy culture. Most of the city population is now disconnected from their natural ecosystem and devoid of the art and culture that used to be on the street and in public spaces before the automobile era. The creation of lifeless streets has percolated into every aspect of our urban life. We lost our rivers beneath expressways. Green parks come with lifeless massive asphalt parking lots. Street tree lines were replaced with on-street parking. We lost our building frontage and courtyards to infinite car parking. Our waterfronts are full of elevated expressways. Freeways have dissected our vibrant neighbourhoods into identity-less puzzle pieces. Road widening took down the historic buildings, vibrant retail, and the mixed-use active city life that used to flourish on city streets (Jacobs, 1985). Even our sidewalks are now often blocked by parked cars and delivery vans. Our life has become trapped inside buildings. We lost our neighbourhood identity to the same copycat lifeless streets and cookie-cutter suburban neighbourhoods everywhere (Kunstler, 1994). Human interaction has been replaced with TV screens and computer games. The absence of natural, social, and cultural activity has turned our city streets into a traffic sewer where thousands of cars and trucks either move at a high-speed or feel like a graveyard when congested with polluting cars, clogging up our "dysfunctional streets" (Sadik-Khan, 2016). To reverse the destructive trend, this book addresses the issue of equitable street planning head-on with a new formula of giving one-third of space to natural green space, one-third to human space and active mobility, and one-third to high-occupant mobility like transit or high-capacity shared mobility.

## Invasion of public space – Destruction of social and cultural life

From ancient to preindustrial periods, public space was the heart of city life. Public space was the centre of social gathering. Art and culture had no better place but public space to display new performances and visual art. Daily life needs were found in open street bazaars or in markets squares. Discussion on city governance, life, politics, innovation, and intellectual gatherings happened in public spaces. A civilization's identity, culture, and resiliency were born, grown, and thrived in its public space. Morality and ethics were born, nurtured, and flourished in these public spaces too. People found refuge in a public space when they were lonely. The public place was at the heart of most human activity, recreation, sporting events, and entertainment. Streets and squares were used for mobility flow too, to reach destinations, and not just for a utilitarian purpose. And this importance of public space was known to the automobile invaders and their supporters. The invasion of public space for high-speed cars and their storage became known as the greatest misallocation of space, resources, and energy in human history when from the 1940s to the 1960s destruction led to the disappearance of nearly all public space in cities. The result is well known today. It did not just eliminate public space, it wiped out the very heart and core fundamentals of human civilization: the social, cultural, and environmental strength that created resilient societies throughout the history of the human species. Most modern cities built around cars are unhealthy, polluted, isolated, depressed, and with a lower quality of life despite their shiny highways and sparking glass buildings. The impacts on humans are worse in developing nations due to lack of social, welfare, and healthcare access. And these destructions were accomplished through early industrial utilitarian and modern colonization philosophical ideology. We do not have to go far to find evidence. Wide streets look identical in every country. A parking lot in India looks strikingly like a parking lot in West Texas. Poor pedestrian facility, full of obstructions in Kuala Lumper, looks the same as most pedestrian fatality-prone facilities in Florida. Everywhere the primary victim of the vehicle invasion was our centuries-old public green and open spaces. When an automobility ideology is forcefully introduced through state laws, rules, and legislation without knowing its limitations, it demolishes the basic notion of culture and social bonding that defines the human species.

*"There is more to life than increasing its speed."*
—Mahatma Gandhi

## Why Things are Changing

Despite our love affair with cars, we do not celebrate our precious moments lost in dark, endless parking lots or on very wide streets where cars pass at high speeds. Nor do we gather to engage with our friends in the middle of a gigantic highway interchange or at the corner of a wide suburban intersection. To spend time with family, friends, enjoying food, culture, and experiencing social life, we tend to go back to historic human-scaled places, with green space, in vibrant and active parts of our city. Kids are allowed to run around in car-free space. Women linger longer on vibrant walkable streets. When we grow old, we look for peaceful corners of public space to rest and observe human activities. Businesses flock to active places. Street vendors sell products on neglected street corners. Our unintentional attraction to the invisible magnetic power of active places, referred herein as "human space", is simply a hint to building more human-friendly cities.

To be fair, city planning has seen dramatic changes, particularly over the last two decades. Designs of streets have started to incorporate all users, typically known as the livable city with a 'complete' streets design approach. Pockets of city areas are being redesigned. Sidewalks widened. We've planted trees in the boulevard as a buffer from cars. The separated bike lane has been brought back from its century-old ashes. Better transit planning with increased frequency and wider service coverage has been restored. The public realm has improved, but mostly in wealthier parts of the city. The unintentional side-effect of well-designed places has become another platform of an unequal society.

Islands of car-free transformations were 'nice-to-haves' but only worked for a few people.

So, what is the magic formula for mobility equity? There may be none. Some principles work for a segment of people but create a wall of separation from the rest. Commonly the triple-A formula: all users, ages, and ability, was promoted as the perfect solution. It however left out all genders, and affordability and "access for all" out of this equation.

### *Mobility megatrends*

The current rapid urbanization trend combined with demographic and social changes are leading us toward new mobility behaviour. While overall sustainable mobility demand is rising, individuals are making less trips (9% trips per person and distance travelled) compared to one or two decades ago (DoT, UK, 2019). Our society is aging fast, and seniors make less work trips and usually travel in mid-day. Senior's driving rates, however, are still high and overrepresented in vehicle and pedestrian crashes. The online society is using more cellphones for mobility, making less work trips by working from home and less daily needs trips during peak times due to on-demand delivery. Sharing vehicles, bicycles, and rides are now more common. Environmental awareness is pushing us toward cleaner and low-emission modes. Active modes such as walking, cycling, and micro-mobility are rising in popularity fast, especially in dense areas. These changes are making a serious dent in automobile ownership, particularly in the first two decades of the 21st century. A new generation of younger demography is showing less inclination toward owning a vehicle (Klein, 2017) due to single living (Potoglou, 2008), the rising cost of living, and the availability of transportation alternatives (Liu, 2020), and they are more inclined to live in cities (Oakil et al., 2016) with transit and shared mobility services (Polak, 2015). New generations, especially younger residents, are the future of cities. Understanding their mobility behaviour will provide a vital clue for transportation researchers, planners, mobility service providers, and decisions makers as to how to gradually and carefully plan cities that rely less on vehicle ownership and more on mass transit or active or micro-mobility where facilities and technologies are provided equally to all urban residents.

> *"There is racism physically built into some of our highways."*
> —Pete Buttigieg, the US transportation secretary

### *The rise and fall of the "racist highway"*

The stunning declaration of systematic discrimination through mega streets and an open call to take down racist highways in 2021 by the US government is a stern acknowledgement of the mobility discrimination inflicted by mega mobility infrastructures (McKelvey, 2021). Mobility professionals remained silent over 70 years on the larger community impact of mobility engineering and misapplication of technology in a harmful way. Ugly urban highways were intentionally inserted into neighbourhoods where minorities lived (Campanella, 2017), there was racial disparity in pedestrian fatalities (Eden, 2017) and historic communities were divided. Mega streets polluted these communities. These mega mobility structures enabled people to travel from the suburbs to the city centres, for mostly Caucasian middle-class commuters who could afford such a lifestyle. Traffic planners found two new ways to apply utilitarianism to make the case for these racist highways. The first approach was the traditional micro-ethical viewpoint in engineering ethics that tends to set the context in which engineers must work on given projects (Herkert, 2001). A micro-ethics ideology leads to bigger problems of neglecting the impact of technology on society (van de Poel, 2011). These lethal ideologies are aligned with functionalism ideology and the Cartesian method of separating items from society and focusing them on the one function of moving cars. Seven decades have shown the consequences. With billions spent every year on "future transportation improvements" such as mega street widening, highways, or regional rail projects using overly optimistic demand forecasts produced by traffic engineers. These projects use travel demand models based on the fundamentally flawed assumption that most urban trips are long, and the purpose of most of our trips is work or school. Demography has changed. People's lifestyle has changed. Our work pattern has changed toward home-based work post Covid-19 pandemic. And more people live in mixed-use neighbourhoods. These changes have altered our travel pattern. Yet not a single travel demand model corrected its data or its assumptions, despite true personal tracked data being available for the last two decades. If true data was explored it would have shown more short trips, more than half of trips non-work, and most of the trips made outside of peak hours. These facts are well established and well known. It is mind-boggling how almost all progressive planners point to wasted highway projects or traffic engineers talk about nonexistent congestion but remain silent on true human mobility DNA and relevant solutions. Politicians are now leaning toward rejecting road widening and tearing down urban highways because of community resistance. Urban expressways were torn down in every western city. It will take few more years though to undo the systematic discrimination created by the racist ideology built into our practice of city building.

*"In a society where no one is any longer recognizable by anyone else, each individual is necessarily unable to recognize his own reality."*
—Guy Debord, *The Society of the Spectacle*

## Reconnecting communities – Toward livable cities

Toward the end of the 20th century, a renewed interest in livable city planning gradually became a widespread topic among city builders. The centre of this new city building debate is an ancient philosophy of old city building. That all ancient cities come with unique characters and enormous variety in city views, landscapes, and things built for human living. But one thing is common. All these cities are walkable, and their structures are built on a human scale. These 'lovable' cities were built from simply observing everyday human life and building everything around it. In the modern day, the livable city concept started with simple and effective mobility at its heart. Transit, walking and cycling would serve to discard the failed ideological concept around vehicles. But it is deeper than just visible facilities. As part of our human 'right-to-the-city',[5] the livable city aimed to overcome commodity-oriented everyday life[6] and create city spaces for social interaction that align with our natural everyday life which is shaped by shared urban 'third' space, predominantly our streets and mobility system. Instead of a transient machine- or technology-centric life, human feelings and emotions gave birth to modern livable city ideas. The centre of this human-oriented inspiration came from the organic city building concept proposed by Jane Jacobs. Placemaking through livable streets remains at the heart of the organic city and even today remains a most influential formation of social life in cities. Today ideas are evolving around the 15-min city, aiming to have everything in daily life accessible by walking and cycling within a 15-min distance. But the key secret remains an ancient land-use technique: mixed-use, gentle density, and jobs and small-scale retail, all within a short distance. Likewise, there needs to be a protection layer to shield humans from the fast and accelerating pace of the new liquid economy[7] which is threatening to further erode basic forms of community and damage the fabric of everyday life. Though the debate and effort to build cities for everyone is far from over, this book series proposes new and creative ideas and philosophical foundations that will be shaping our city building and mobility ecosystem for the years ahead of us in the climate change era.

## Return of affordable transit form

Shared transit is the origin of public transit in cities. Over time it was lost into the rigid and mega-facility-oriented transit form. Gradually rigidity became the Achilles' heel of declining transit usage. And mega transit projects became weapons of political platforms instead of fulfilling real transit needs. Mass transit in the form of shared and improvised on-demand form was lost when single-occupant vehicle aggression had it removed in the early 20th century. Streetcars and trams gradually disappeared to make way for masses of personal vehicles. Transit moved to underground and elevated forms, making it too rigid and expensive. Dedicated spaces and priority lanes for buses and streetcars were removed to make even more space for cars and more time at traffic signals.

---

[5] The 'right-to-the-city' is an idea and a slogan first proposed by Henri Lefebvre in 1968 which influenced social movements, thinkers, and certain progressive local authorities as a call to action to reclaim the city as a co-created space: a place for life detached from the growing effects that commodification and capitalism are proposed to have had over social interaction and the rise of posited spatial inequalities in worldwide cities throughout the last two centuries.
[6] The Practice of Everyday Life is a concept coined by Michel de Certeau that examines the ways in which people individualize mass culture, altering things from utilitarian objects to street plans to rituals, laws, and language, to make them their own. It became an influential approach in pushing cultural studies away from producer/product to the consumer.
[7] The liquid economy generally refers to the arrival of the Fourth Industrial Revolution with a character of ever-expanding non-stop processes of 21st-century capitalism.

In a few places transit took a different turn. Germany reinvented and revived the streetcar in a modern light rail form. And the famous Curitiba bus experiment gave birth to the modern bus rapid transit system. Dedicated bus lanes have now become a common street scene in Latin American and Asian cities, and transit priority signals are back in many cities. New York and Australian cities took the lead in installing full-time, part-time, and dedicated bus stop and bus bump-out facilities. Flexible on-demand transit arrived with new IoT (Internet of Things) technology to make room for the missing middle in transit systems. Numerous transit real-time and navigation apps have also become common over the last decade-and-a-half. With land-use planning following the transit revival, city growth policies are now being geared toward transit corridors and nodes. Future growth is also now being linked to transit expansion instead of road widening. The struggle to bring transit up to the level of its glorious past faces numerous challenges including new forms of gentrification, and a housing affordability crisis near transit lines created by revitalization techniques that displace former residents. As on-demand transit grows, an additional shift toward transit in medium and small cities will likely stop vehicle-oriented city building once and for all.

## *Surprising comeback of small mobility*

The return of walking, cycling, and micro-mobility surprised city builders at the dawn of the 21st century. As mixed-use and non-residential development increased, particularly in downtown or dense areas, many seniors, young generations, renters, and small mobility facilities started to come back. The common mobility habits of these demography are mainly walking and transit. As transit became expensive and more bicycle networks were being formed, cycling again became a popular mode in many cities. The E-bike came next along with cargo bikes and bikeshare options. The breakthrough for new mass short trip modes came with scooters, kick scooters, mopeds, and ultra-small vehicles. But the wonderful world of micro-mobility arrived without technological help and created a supply management nightmare. While walking and cycling facility is deficient, new micro-mobility has practically no place to operate. To hide their planning and design flaws, most cities started to ban these new modes. But some moved forward with new space and lane creations making it easier to ride. City planning was and is very slow to respond. Walking and cycling facility design guidance and bike or space parking requirements are still a reluctant topic in planning. Many city planners have started to widen streets again in the name of wider and separated active mobility facilities. Green space has disappeared. The safety buffer space removed. Most cities have not found an answer for how to accommodate micro-mobility modes and their facilities into the mainstream city planning process. This book provides a comprehensive approach to reinventing the small mobility world.

## *Winds of change*

Most noticeable changes started to appear among the people who pioneered the change in the city building process. Decision makers and leading planning figures became interested in city building, particularly in the public sector. Global awareness of cities leading role in climate change brought public sector leaders and practitioners together under the same umbrella. Many mayors led the way including Enrique Peñalosa in Bogota, Bloomberg in New York, Anne Hidalgo in Paris, and Valérie Plante in Montreal. Even federal governments started to pay attention to sustainable mobility policies, notably New Zealand's prime minister Jacinda Ardern pushing green mobility as a central policy to building resiliency in systems, Canada's environment minister Catherine McKenna ending large funding for road or highway widening, and Iceland's prime minister Katrín Jakobsdóttir banning fossil fuels in cars by 2030. Mobility leaders in local city governments are even more promising, given that the city remains at the centre of mobility change. It started with a surprise appointment of a visionary leader Janette Saik Khan in New York, followed by Gabe Kelin in Chicago, Brent Toderian in Vancouver, and Jennifer Keesmaat in Toronto, who along with many more bold and brave personalities around the world started to change the gears of the mobility system in the right direction. Most encouraging is that many leaders are women, a long-overdue change needed to counter white male dominance in mobility leadership.

### *A new profession for a new mobility ecosystem*

Leadership changes also put the spotlight on rigid engineering practice and professional dogma that was repeatedly built over the last century applying a failed vehicle-oriented philosophy. Many old planning and design practices came from the high-speed military facility approach, which is not compatible with city conditions. Under intense pressure, professional engineering bodies are now reluctantly coming under the new ecosystem umbrella. The first major rift came from the new street design manual (NACTO [National Association of City Transportation Officials]) and a complete streets design that discarded many old professional habits that contain very little science behind them. New guidelines were developed for transit, cycling, walking, and micro-mobility systems. Road widening projects are not presented at conferences anymore. However, old habits die hard. Many planners still present road widening projects for transit, cycling, and autonomous vehicles. Behind a new face, many old-school mentality practitioners are attempting to insert the old utility approach into new mobility practices. This is becoming a larger concern among the most of the new progressive city practitioners. Eventually the corrupted practices behind a micro-ethical guard will fall. But it will not be easy to give up 400-year-old rigid Cartesianism, 250-year-old utilitarianism, 110-year-old functionalism, and an 80-year-old machine-oriented approach. Within the next few years, when climate changes financial burden sets in, old ideological professional practice is bound to end. History has never made any exception for those who resisted change. It will be the same for future city builders.

> *"Desire makes everything blossom; possession make everything weather and fade."*
>
> —Marcel Proust

## Infinite Mobility to a Sixth Extinction

Many underlying philosophies of ideological transformation and professional dogma built into the current mobility system are pushing our planetary system close to the brink of collapse. Infinite mobility demand requires infinite planetary resources. 'Modern' mobility needs an enormous scale of resources. To continue currently, we will need flawless and infinite resources in our hands. We will need all energy resources to continue at same capacity as today. It sounds like a fairy tale.

The planet has faced five extinctions. The human species has nearly gone extinct almost five times before. All of them were natural threats (Fig. 1.1). All indications are however that current planetary change points to a human-made impact. Many believe our innate mass consumption and reckless vehicle mobility will be the major source of our next and probably last extinction. The planet will survive but very likely without mass industrial consumption, and without humans.

Possessing anything and everything, whether we need it or not, has become the hallmark of the unbridled capitalistic world. While this started during the early industrial age, it grew on a monumental scale after WWII. Every household in the US now possesses at least 300,000 items and boundless consumption has become a symbol of the 'boom-and-burst' economy. The enormous consumption of such a human-made mass is referred to as "anthropogenic mass". Earth has overall 1.1 tera-tons of living biomass (Bar-On et al., 2018). The estimated weight today of human-made objects is about one tera-ton in which the majority is made up of buildings, bridges, and roads (Briggs, 2020). The anthropogenic mass has recently doubled and will continue to double roughly

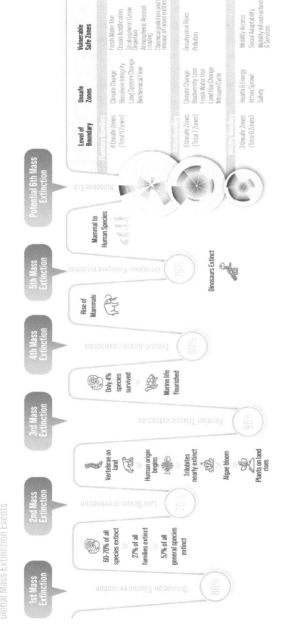

**Fig. 1.1:** Known or potential causes – past and future global mass-extinction.

every 20 years (Elhacham et al., 2020), and it will surpass all global living biomass at the crossover point in the year 2020 (± 6). On an average, more than the body weight of every person in the world in 'stuff' is now being produced each week. And among all human-made mass, the personal vehicle and its massive infrastructure is at the pinnacle of our infinite consumption culture, once glorified by Henry Ford who manipulated the "American Dream" into a car in every household. The average household now has two cars, and every car now has eight parking spaces. In both Europe and North America, roughly half of the space in cities is covered with streets and car parking lots. Automobile ownership has dramatically changed consumerism. People can carry more goods, buy bulk volume amounts, at massive stores which call themselves big boxes. Wide roads and massive impervious surfaces have become the most visible and massive symbols of our infinite consumerism culture. This toxic dream lifestyle has even been planted as a 'symbol' of progress in developing nations, making China the largest market of vehicle consumers in the world. The car continues to be displayed as more about social status and less about mobility. For all to live the American Dream, the world's population will have to acquire 18 billion cars, and eight parking spaces for each car.

But there is a limit to our growth.

Since the 1972 study "Limits to Growth" was published, it has been well known that industrial civilization was on track to collapse sometime within the 21st century, due to overexploitation of planetary resources (Meadows, 1972). One of the key premises of this projection was the inevitable consequences of exponential growth. If the growth rate is 4%, it takes but 18 years to double its size, and 7% takes only 10 years. The study was ignored, framing the authors as a bunch of outsiders. A recent updated study confirmed that we only have 10–15 years to determine the long-term fate of human civilization and pointed to a 2040 steep decline in economic and industrial growth (Branderhorst, 2020). This time the predictions came from a major mainstream accounting firm – KPMG. City planning has been running on long time-based infinite consumption, mostly using vehicles as a platform. The Keynesian theory of building infrastructures for vehicles was and is still today used as a stimulus package during an economic downtown. Realizing the limits of vehicle-based growth, city planning adopted a new approach to maintain infinite growth. This time it is transit-oriented planning. Although transit has higher capacity than vehicles, it is not infinite. But rarely has transit-oriented planning imposed any limits to growth, bending to developers' greed and allowing unsustainable 80-plus-storey buildings around transit stations. Pointed extreme density around transit stations however did not solve the problem. Indeed, it aggravated the situation. Active and micro-mobility was misused and added more growth to an area already oversaturated. Even today, large cities like Toronto or Los Angeles have no official policy directions matching transit capacity with development scale. When the author proposed linking the transit line and active mobility capacity to development growth in the City's several secondary plans, the proposal received a cold response from both planning and development sides alike. This flawed belief in infinite city growth created major overcrowding in transit, and affected sidewalk and delivery safety, not to mention the financial pressure on limited city budgets. This century however, lifestyle is taking a slight pause, and some are imagining how mobility might look like without needing to possess a vehicle or device to simply move around in cities. City building's philosophy and system wide mobility approach will as a result have to match the new reality of resources constraint, and embrace environmental, social, and good governance priorities to avoid societal risks.

We have been dreaming a long time of dealing with climate change without change.

Changing personal mobility choice toward very low-emissions and limiting or not subsidizing automobility is real change. This book focuses on how to induce those mobility changes gradually over time instead of the rhetoric-only dreamy 'car-free' or vehicular transit-oriented approach that we have practised for the last three decades without significant change in mobility behaviour.

# CHAPTER 1
## PART 2
# Sequencing New Mobility DNA

*"Status quo is more dangerous than the unknown."*
—John Kotter Harvard Business School

## Our Mobility DNA

This book explores a holistic approach to mobility planning, introduces or reintroduces a few ideas to encounter the basic underlying issues of the current automobility system and prepare for an uncertain future with a shifting mobility concept. Some approaches are new. Many are integrated from the evolution of mobility history. A few are thought-provoking and most importantly practical and feasible solutions, tested in the real world to improve quality of life for all citizens, not just for the most fortunate ones.

### *Decoupling ideology and mobility*

Mobility and human psychology are unorthodox synonyms. Human's psychological forces underlie our behaviours, feelings, and emotions (Stangor, 2010). Yet examining how human mobility evolved from an active lifestyle for thousands of years to an abrupt change to vehicle mobility in the last century is often considered untouchable. The connection between our society, culture, philosophical mindset, and urban mobility systems is considered unrelated and hence remains unexplored in the typical mobility planning process. Yet many of our current mobility problems or issues are linked to philosophical and ideological roots from our past. In the industrial era, mobility philosophy has been turned into an ideology and has produced numerous system biases. While developing the numerous concepts and solutions presented throughout this book, our systemic biases and psychology take a front seat. Unlike the incorrect use of the evolution approach that aligns with utilitarian ideology where humans are the most intelligent and the superior species, this book embraces the reality that humans are born without a blueprint. Our prematurity creates an urgency and desire to live in a community for survival. Humans' inner drive is an interface of psychic and physical dimensions of human reality. This 'drive' works as a driving force to create our language, culture, norms, and values to retain our societal form. This book is based on the premise that human movement connects these basic "human neurons" with invisible mobility DNA. Everything around us influences our mobility DNA and every human creates their own mobility form, a unique footprint in his daily life. This newly discovered mobility code and its DNA contains our instinct for using multiple modes to maximize our desired mobility goals. Our mobility blueprint is our unique movement identity which separates us from other individuals. The approach avoids creating a spectacle society where mobility modes are isolated from our basic desires and driven to become a symbol of social status and create super egos and excessive consumption. This book's intention is simple: to broaden our horizons and learn lessons from the past from what worked and what didn't go very well. A true mobility ecosystem can only be achieved in the future when all forms of mobility modes and the system work harmoniously together toward the greater goal of improving human well-being, not commercial well-being.

## Lovable city with beautiful mobility

While the livable city created a new way of rebuilding the divided and unequal community, over time it turned into the unlovable city despite having all green elements and clean mobility. The old perpetrator, classical utilitarianism, found its way into the new livable city, making it a spectacle city connected by mega structures and mega networks. Key new livable mobility features are asphalt-dominated cycling, lifeless wide concrete sidewalks, an aggressive form of "transit-vehicle only" facility, and a solutionism approach[8] to shared, electric, and autonomous mobility

| Lovable City Equation |
|---|
| **Spectacle city** = Livable – lovable |
| **Everyday city** = Livable + lovable |
| **Unlovable city** = Livable – lovable – green + asphalt + concrete + linear placemaking |
| **Lovable city** = Green space + Human space + Our desire and drive for everyday life + beautiful mobility |
| **Beautiful mobility** = Mobility DNA + Eco-energy + Eco-mobility + Mobility boundary + Human Resonance + Missing-Middle mobility + Mobility-as-a-place + Physical Mobility + Shifting mobility |

as a magic answer to all city problems. This book proposes to create a lovable city with human-oriented flavours of everyday life borrowed from ancient walkable cities. It avoids creating a 'spectacle', particularly with not any overly optimistic and aggressive technological applications. The idea proposes to beautify the mobility that we adore and love and align less with the influence of commodity. It evokes finding our origin and basic mobility instincts, adopting new mobility or technology with limits, inserting our feelings and emotions into space, movement, and environments through social interactions, and rebounding the community frame lost to industrial aggression in the mobility landscape. Land-use needs to come together with mixed-use, gentle density, and smaller block formats to regenerate mass volumes of everyday needs done with short trips. The following elaborates the key elements of 'beautiful' mobility.

## Mobility DNA

Among all new and innovative ideas and solutions provided in this book, the one underlying concept that pulls them all together is the understanding of the existence of our hidden "mobility code and its DNA elements". The underlying concept is simple. Mobility shapes who we are. We move to satisfy our internal hidden individual desire for movement. Over time we develop mobility habits that create a movability motif with a unique pattern. The question is how do we display such a unique mobility identity? First, a human is a living organism that self-organizes its own activities. Whether searching for food, reproduction, or simple recreation, we move from one place to another place. Second, the movements and stillness become part of our daily habits and develop into an internal hidden structure that dictates our daily movement habit. Other intelligence is directed by our conscious brain but our desire for movement is predominantly controlled by our unconscious sense, so it remains unknown. Our brain does not calculate our movements every day and tell us what to do. The habit of movement is ingrained into our senses, through feelings, emotions, tangible, and

---

[8] The terms 'solutionism' (proposed by Evgeny Morozov) is a belief that complex issues can be disassembled into neatly defined technical problems that can be adequately solved through technology.

intangible purposes. Finally, our movement habit starts to show an individual, group or collective mass pattern. From there we develop tools through the different mobility modes to decide how we will move in the most energy efficient and economical way. Our movability takes a full form and displays the many hidden natures that are unique to every individual. This hidden but stable form of movement is presented herein as our "mobility code" along with traces of DNA elements, like our biological DNA but influenced or changed by the living environment, geography, and built or mobility environment, our adaptation culture and the ecosystem available to us. When these systems change, our mobility along with its DNA changes to adjust to new conditions but stabilizes and reemerges after a period to show the same individual traits.

### Mobility boundary

Our mobility system has emerged as a major strain on the planet's systems. Ever expanding mobility infrastructures are pushing the planetary boundary to an unsafe zone. The link between the limits of mobility system expansion and the planet's limits is missing in the daily mobility planning process. The mobility boundary concept was introduced by the author (Karim, 2017) to identify the limits of mobility expansion, toward the maximum benefit of human well-being while keeping the strain on the planetary system within a safe zone (Fig. 1.2). Both unchecked expansion and growth and never-ending new 'efficient' and sustainable technologies are equally unsustainable. The boundary concept proposes to abandon our "infinite cycle of repeated growth and failure" ideology built into the broken utility-based 'slash-and-burn' unchecked capitalism system (Williaams and Khanna, 2020) in favour of setting new mobility limits to control demand and limit unchecked megastructure supply practices. The intention is to impose a boundary to push the system planners and decision makers to a low-emission and multimodal ecosystem.

> *"Normality is paved road: It's comfortable to walk, but no flowers grow."*
> —Vincent van Gough

### Shifting normal, shifting mobility

'Normal' dramatically shifted to "the new normal" during the Covid-19 pandemic. But any normal is just another illusion waiting to shift into another short transition. The "shifting normal"[9] (Afroz, 2020) has become the dominant new form of adjusting and readjusting to a constantly changing environment. The shifting mobility concept incorporates resiliency into the building process to prepare the mobility system for constant shifts, create flexibility for human variations, and to adjust mobility form because of natural, technological, cultural, or social changes. Inspired by artistic philosophy and Covid-19 learnings, this book proposes different layers of shifting mobility. Incorporating dominant short trips and reversing the future demand process to downsize mobility facility hardware (i.e., facilities of infrastructures) is the first step in shifting mobility. Shifting mobility inhabits different seasons, different conditions, flexible space design, and moves away from the rigid boundary towards placemaking for human usage, reflects area-built forms, and exhibits the status of different planetary conditions. Shifting mobility service to the digital platform is the next proposed step to developing resiliency by offering shifting options when conditions change. The final layer of shifting mobility is shifting mobility space. Implementation starts with a combination of the elimination of unused space or reusing underutilized spaces, and rightsizing vehicle facility (Price, 2021). Shifting space comes with four major components: shifting uses of mobility gathering

---

[9] The concept "shifting normal" was first invented by artist, dancer, and choreographer Mushtari Afroz in 2020 during the Covid-19 pandemic. As per his definition, "Shifting normal gives us a sense of comfort for a short while, then it disappears before reappearing in a new form."

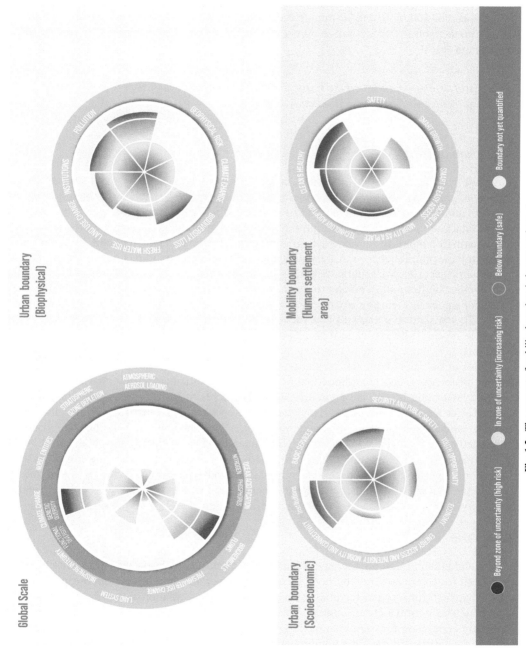

**Fig. 1.2:** The concept of mobility boundary in human settlement areas.

spaces such as multimodal eco-mobility hubs; adding more green space by adopting shift and equitable streets that are resilient toward environmental adaptation; developing human space to shift toward new social conditions; and shifting mobility flow space to adapt with the changing new mobility ecosystem. These concepts are bonded together with the basic elements from the mobility boundary concept of rightsizing facility, proposed in the form of a maximum 30-metre street size, maximum speed of 30 kmph, and 30-minute access to connections by walking. The aim is to build resiliency into the mobility ecosystem so it may survive beyond the anthropogenic[10] (Crutzen, 2000) climate change era.

> *"Establishing a politics on the basis of identity is not only reckless politically, it is also theoretically unfounded: identity is a fiction."*
> —Joan Copjec

### Human resonance

Although we built a large mobility system in the 20th century, our numerous quantitative and qualitative assumptions about humans remain rigid, obscured, vague, and unknown among the practitioners and decision makers who build our cities. If we are truly focusing on rebuilding for people, the fatal flaws in planning and design assumptions about humans must be fixed before building a new low-emission mobility ecosystem. Segmenting and dividing identity and mobility-isms failed to achieve any meaningful change. A fresh new approach is proposed in this book to incorporate all known human aspects that we experience in life. The simple premise of this approach is cities built for women are cities built for all. Women generally have a finer sense of place, security, and safety than men. If a woman feels safe using any mobility system or infrastructure, the system covers everyone in society. To translate this known phenomenon, the human resonance concept proposes visible and invisible layers of human experience. The visible level incorporates three levels of complex human forms: (1) comprehensive variations of human form and performance for all demography; (2) variations of human conditions and status such as age, physical condition, social, cultural, and geographic differences; and (3) unmeasurable variations or anticipated additional changes in the future. Besides visible layers, the approach broadens the realm to include: (1) the preconscious level that creates feelings, emotions, and preconceptions about mobility services, facility, and space; (2) the drives and desires that shape our unconscious mobility behaviours; and (3) connectors of body and mind that make provisions for uncertainty in human behaviour assumptions. Human limits are introduced to avoid the exploitation of this idea, and to self-impose limits when the conscious level is reached on all possible variations, and to stop at the boundary before the idea turns into infinite combinations. This strong foundation generates numerous ideas in this book toward reinventing each mobility mode ecosystem and rethinking mobility planning and facility design.

### Mobility form

Built form and urban design principles and philosophy guide almost every step of the city building process. Built form creates neighbourhood identity. However, the mobility system escaped the link between urban built form and its facilities. This book proposes a new approach, to develop "mobility form" to match built form and area context. This new mobility form will provide clarification on the new mobility ecosystem for each area while providing the strategic direction needed to gradually get through the layers that protect automobility culture. Car(ownership)-free, car-lite, car-less, and less car-dependent areas in the city's form will be gradually replaced with a multimodal ecosystem,

---

[10] The Anthropocene, characterized by global scale anthropogenic forcing since the latter part of the 18th century, is the name of the present geological epoch.

with a backbone of rapid transit in dense areas, frequent transit in the inner suburbs or in mid-sized cities, flexible transit in the outer suburbs or in smaller cities and rideshare or pooled transit in the exurbs or rural areas. This is a major departure from today's directionless street and placemaking process and provides clear guidance on what combination of a multimodal mobility ecosystem is appropriate for each built form, and how to deliver mobility supply instead of building mega streets and parking lots everywhere regardless of area context.

## Mobility in motion

The constantly changing world of mobility needs ever-changing, shifting capacity as things change over time. The vehicle-oriented world borrowed the 'accelerationism' ideology (Boys, 2014) through a 'slash-and-burn' unbridled capitalism that needs an ever-increasing speed of industrial process. Necessity to maintain without a specific purpose became a notion of the modern vehicle mobility system. Hyper speed needs numerous separations between mobility modes, but separation consumes limited precious space. This book proposes to reverse the hyper-speed mobility system down to an "uber slow pace" that matches with the city's lifestyle and quality of life. The concept proposes to reinvent moving space in the slow activity lane, slow lane, and moving lanes to be compatible with slow moving flexible and autonomous freight and transit systems. The remaining moving space would be converted to slow moving micro-mobility, cycling, and micro delivery ecosystems that may operate with or without dedicated shared space. Liquid modernism may or may not survive (LaPierre, n.d.) but humans will move regardless of political ideology. The concept proposes to exit the hyper speed and endless separation concept between the mobility modes.

## Mobility in stillness

The desire for activity moves us from one place to another. Staying defines why we move. Staying in place tells us the purpose of destinations, attractiveness, and reason for repeated trips. Without stillness, mobility has no meaning. We only know the value of moving when we stay still and reflect on our experiences (Iyer, 2014). There is little concept of staying or stopping in the hyper speed world of the vehicle. Without stopping, we never create places. Without places, we have no community. Creating streets with an infinite movement ideology is eroding our forms of community, suppressing our local participation, and ultimately damaging the fabric of our natural everyday peaceful lives (Crary, 2014). Lingering space is as equally important as flow space. This book proposes to reverse the relentless focus on moving and recommends the reinvention of places to linger at every street corner, at intersections, building frontages or stations or in small public realms. One-third of urban mobility space is trapped under unused and underutilized asphalt. Reclaiming these lost human spaces as an everyday practice of city building is one of the key professional practices proposed in this book. Redesigning space for human staying or lingering or enjoyment should be an everyday design habit. In an aging society and when restitching community fabric, these places will bring back the richness of stillness and avoid the darkness and destruction of the selfishness (Ricard, 2016) of the personal vehicle culture that have eroded the most defining feature of the human species – altruism.

## Eco-energy mobility

Energy depletion, the reality of this century, remains an untouchable topic in mobility planning. The illusion of electrification has resulted in rising GHG (greenhouse gases) emissions (Sleire, 2019). Alternative sources of energy are still dirty and only shift the problem from one source to another. The best energy demand management is travel demand measures. A low-emission multimodal mobility ecosystem is the second layer of the most effective energy shift. It still requires some energy but remains out of reach. Mobility energy demand for each stage of planning and design is vital to creating an energy ecosystem. The energy-space continuum and eco-energy hubs concept enables system builders to make alternative energy available in every corner of our public and private edges. These places though still need new urban design and space redesign knowledge, and mobility energy policy techniques can act as a door opener and gatekeeper to the new energy landscape. This fresh new proactive approach addresses the practical issues instead of keeping the "we'll see when it arrives" mindset. There will be very limited energy for any aggressive form of electric personal mobility system in the Anthropocene era. This book's concepts ensure we will survive without requiring excessive energy use to just move short distances in the city.

> *"Every instant the world is being renewed, and we are unaware of its perpetual change."*
>
> – Rumi

### *Mobility as a place – Four major mobility space concepts*

Beneath truly well-designed places are complex economic, social, and cultural revival layers. We can apply progressive design ideas to fix the hardware of our broken mobility spaces, identical to fixing digital software, but the Covid-19 pandemic has already pointed out very clearly our mobility hardware problems – and reduced uses and unnecessary consumption and enabled us to right-size our mobility infrastructures or facilities (Price, 2021). Fortunately, we have been paying attention to the better design of our streets over the last two decades. Human relation with space is embedded in four basic instincts. Human's lack of blueprint creates a desire to interact with other human in public space. This initial impression is built through dialectic process of mental and physical wellbeing. Second relation is building our urban environment including public space in postmodern era that replaced the sensitivity of time of modern era that started in early 20th century. But the knowledge of this relation is sporadic and haphazard. Engineers or planners who oversaw redesigning walkable, bikeable, transit-oriented places were often inspired by progressive ideas, without paying attention to the four distinct layers of mobility facilities as public space. This book introduces four new major mobility space concepts. This third layer would intentionally build our public space for daily life activity. The final layer would be understanding how our emotions, feelings, and human resonance is connected to build style to avoid inequality and alienation from space. The author expects that the final layers will need artistic and cultural convergence once the third layer is accomplished properly. To incorporate the first three layers, human and space relation in the 21st century living space, the author proposes four new concepts of mobility space transportation. The first concept incorporates people's habit of gathering in popular places, referred to as "Multimodal eco-mobility hubs". Instead of centralizing multimodal access at transit stations, the eco-mobility hub concept spreads the mobility hub to every corner of a neighbourhood within a very short walking distance. The hubs would act as a one-stop service spot for all types of mobility modes that would be context-sensitive and align with local mobility cultures. Ineffective traditional travel demand management becomes effective at multimodal eco-mobility hubs. The second concept is invisible spaces. Ironically, many "traffic spaces" given over to vehicles are never used by vehicles. These spaces make up roughly one-third to more than 40% of total mobility space in our cities. This book provides a systematic process through space typology, category, identification, and the reclaiming of these invisible spaces. The third concept is green (mobility) spaces. The concept of creating six major types of green space in mobility facilities is introduced to bring back at least one-third of the space for organic nature that was lost to the 'modern' vehicle. The fourth concept is intentionally creating human spaces. Through a reclaiming and greening process, another one third of spaces would be dedicated for various daily human activities. The objective is to revive lost mobility culture through social interaction, recreation, gathering and lingering activities, and the observing of human by humans. The creation or revival of these new mobility spaces is not a utopian dream, but rather a barebone basic human right to equity, daily life necessities, and the long-term viability of well-designed places.

## Sequencing Mobility DNA

With the discovery of a mobility code that resembles our biological DNA and translating it into a series of new practical concept ideas, this book takes a different approach by incorporating our values and social well-being as the primary focus of building a new multimodal mobility ecosystem. After introducing the broader social, cultural backgrounds of mobility in this introductory chapter, the second chapter starts with the evolution of mobility that shaped our planetary system and our manmade civilization. The chapter starts with the gradual development of mobility from temporary settlements to prototype villages to organized cities. The third chapter briefly describes the mobility data evolution, influence of information, the current flawed process, mobility planning knowledge and models, a proposed new way of mobility demand, and a forecasting process based on new mobility code. A new form of data and its interpretation provides a valuable clue to how to reverse mega mobility structures and replace them with compact, energy and space efficient facilities, and downsize and reclaim our right-to-space in cities. Findings of mobility code along with DNA elements, its nature and pattern are described in Chapter 4 along with a fresh new concept of fundamental safety, land-use, mobility service, and infrastructure scale. Chapter 5 provides the reality of the depletion of fossil fuels and a contradictory counter argument against over reliance on renewable energy without controlling mobility demand. Chapter 6 introduces several new concepts for creating new mobility spaces while identifying invisible spaces and reclaiming our lost public realm for natural everyday life. Redefining mobility-as-a-place, the second-last chapter provides the details of reinvention, redesign, and reuse of the city's spaces using a series of innovative approaches proposed earlier in the book. The final chapter deals with the most difficult issue of creating innovative and creative policies that will survive when environmental and social conditions change. Highlighted secretive but successful policy examples and stages of implementation provide a glimpse into why and how a livable city always contains the most energy and space efficient mobility at its heart.

The bond between humans and space remains at the heart of our social existence. Without the presence of a human, a space cannot communicate its perception. Without perception and feeling the human species would not exist.

One of the key underlying philosophies of all the new concepts in this book is to adapt to change during this existential climate change era. And to emerge with the notion of our mobility mode and its DNA elements, while utilizing the incredible advantages of a very low energy and resource oriented multimodal mobility ecosystem.

## References

Adams, J. (1995). *Risk.* London: Ruthledge, University College London.

Adorno, T.W. and Horkheimer, M. (1979). *Dialectic of Enlightenment.* Tr. Cumming, J. *London: Verso, 1979.* London: Verso.

Afroz, M. (Director). (2020). *Shifting Normal* [Motion Picture].

Ahn, Y. and Yeo, H. (2015). An analytical planning model to estimate the optimal density of charging stations for electric vehicles. *PLoS ONE*, 10(11): 1–26.

Ainsalu, J., Ville Arffman, V., Bellone, M., Ellner, M., Haapamäki, T., Haavisto, N., Josefson, E., Ismailogullari, A., Lee, B., Madland, O., Madžulis, R., Müür, J., Mäkinen, S., Nousiainen, V., Pilli-Sihvola, E., Rutanen, E., Sahala, S., Schønfeldt, B., Smolnicki, P.M., Soe, R., Sääski, J., Szymańska, M., Vaskinn, I. and Åman, M. (2019). *State of the Art of Automated Buses.* MDPI.

Akndi. (2020). *Greening Government Fleets: A Helpful Guide to Understanding.* Ottawa: Natural Resources Canada.

Albert, A. and Gonzalez, M.C. (2017). Using convolutional networks and satellite imagery to identify patterns in urban environments at a large scale. *Proceedings of the 23rd ACM SIGKDD International Conference on Knowledge Discovery and Data Mining*, pp. 1357–1366.

Amadoa, M. and Poggi, F. (2014). Solar energy integration in urban planning: GUUD model. *Energy Procedia*, 50: 277–284.

Anderson, J.M., Kalra, N., Stanley, K.D., Sorensen, P., Samaras, C. and Oluwatola, O.A. (2016). *Autonomous Vehicle Technology: A Guide for Policymakers*. Santa Monica, California: RAND Corporation, RR-443-2-RC.

Anguelovski, A. (2021). *From Green Privilege to Green Gentrification: Environmental Justice vs White Supremacy in the 21st Century American and European City*. Online, California, USA: Shareable.

Appleby, K. (2015). *Five Cities Proving that We Can Quit Fossil Fuels*. Retrieved from City Monitor: https://citymonitor.ai/horizons/five-cities-proving-we-can-quit-fossil-fuels-1444.

Appleyard, D., Gerson, M.S. and Lintell, M. (1981). *Livable Streets*. Berkeley: University of California Press.

Appleyard, D., Lynch, K. and Myer, J.R. (1964). *The View from the Road*. Cambridge: MIT Press.

Araujo, J.A., Barajas, B., Kleinman, M., Wang, X., Bennett, B.J., Gong, K.W., Navab, M., Harkema, J., Sioutas, C., Lusis, A.J. and Nel, A.E.. (2008). Ambient particulate pollutants in the ultrafine range promote early atherosclerosis and systemic oxidative stress. *Circular Research*, 102(5): 589–596.

Ashcroft, R.T. and Bevir, M. (2018). Multiculturalism in contemporary Britain: Policy, law, and theory. *Critical Review of International Social and Political Philosophy*, 21: 1–21.

Automotive World. (2020). *Multimodal Mobility is a Transportation Revolution*. Retrieved from Automotive World: https://www.automotiveworld.com/articles/multimodal-mobility-is-a-transportation-revolution/.

Bae, S., Lee, E. and Han, J. (2020). Multi-period planning of hydrogen supply network for refuelling hydrogen fuel cell vehicles in urban areas. *Sustainability*, 12(4114): 1–23.

Bar-On, Y.M., Phillips, R. and Milo, R. (2018). The biomass distribution on Earth. *Proc. Natl Acad. Sci. USA*, 115: 6506–6511.

Barry, K. (2013). *Wired*. Retrieved from In South Korea, Wireless Charging Powers Electric Buses: https://www.wired.com/2013/08/induction-charged-buses/.

Bauman, Z. (2000). *Liquid Modernity*. New York: Wiley.

Becic, E., Zych, N. and Ivarsson, J. (2018). *Vehicle Automation Report*. Washington, USA: National Transportation Safety Board, HWY18MH010.

Becky, P.Y., Lo, O. and Banister, D. (2016). Decoupling transport from economic growth: Extending the debate to include environmental and social externalities. *Journal of Transport Geography*, 57: 134–144.

Beddoes, Z.M. (2020). Time to make coal history. *The Economist*.

Begault, L. and Khazrik, J. (2019). *Smart Cities: Dreams Capable of Becoming Nightmares*. Retrieved from Amnesty International: https://www.amnesty.org/en/latest/research/2019/06/smart-cities-dreams-capable-of-becoming-nightmares/.

Benjamin, L. and Richards, D. (1981). Electrification is the way to move Canada in the 1980s. *Canadian Public Policy*, 7(81).

Bentham, J. (1789). *An Introduction to the Principles of Morals and Legislation*. London: T. Payne and Son.

Berg, N. (2020). *This AI-powered Parking Garage Rewards You for Not Driving*. Retrieved from Fast Company: https://www.fastcompany.com/90575914/this-ai-powered-parking-garage-rewards-you-for-not-driving/.

Berg, P. (2011). *The Finite Planet: How Resource Scarcity will Affect Our Environment, Economy, and Energy Supply*. Oshawa, Canada: Island Press.

Bhat, C. (2017). *Travel Modeling in An Era of Connected and Automated Transportation Systems: An Investigation in the Dallas-Fort Worth Area*. Austin, USA: Technical Report 122. Center for Transportation Research. The University of Texas at Austin.

Bhat, R.V. and Waghray, K. (2000). *Profile of Street Foods in Asian Countries*. Basel, Karger: World Rev Nutr. Diet.

Billings, C.E. (1980). *Human-centered Aircraft Automation: A Concept and Guidelines*. Moffet Field, CA: NASA Technical Memorandum, NASA Ames Research Center.

Blanchard, P., Lemaire, S., Bancel, N. and Thomas, D. (2014). *Colonial Culture in France Since the Revolution*. Indiana: Indiana University Press.

Bloomberg, J. (2018). *Don't Trust Artificial Intelligence? Time To Open The AI 'Black Box'*. Retrieved from Forbes: https://www.forbes.com/sites/jasonbloomberg/2018/09/16/dont-trust-artificial-intelligence-time-to-open-the-ai-black-box/.

Bojarski, M., Testa, D.D., Dworakowski, D., Firner, B., Flepp, B., Goyal, P., Jackel, L.D., Monfort, M., Muller, U., Zhang, J., Zhang, X., Zhao, J. and Zieba, K. (2016). End-to-end learning for self-driving cars. *Computer Vision and Pattern Recognition*, Cornell University, pp. 1–9.

Bojji, R. (2011). Gravity powered transport systems for rail, road, water, and airport use. *13th International Conference on Automated People*, pp. 22–25. Paris, France: American Society of Civil Engineers.

Borzino, N., Chng, S., Mughal, M.O. and Schubert, R. (2020). Willingness to pay for urban heat island mitigation: A case study of Singapore. *Climate*, 8: 82.

Botsman, R. (2010). *What's Mine Is Yours: The Rise of Collaborative Con-sumption.* Harper Business.

Bourdieu, P. and Wacquant, L.D. (1992). *An Invitation to Reflexive Sociology.* Cambridge, UK: Ploity Press and Blackwell Publishers.

Boys, B. (2014). *Malign Velocities: Accelerationism and Capitalism.* Winchester: Zero Books.

Braess, D., Wakolbinger, A. and Nagurney, T. (2005). On a paradox of traffic planning. *Transportation Science*, 39(4): 446–450.

Branderhorst, G. (2020). *Update to Limits to Growth: Comparing the World3 Model With Empirical Data.* Boston: Harvard University.

Briggs, H. (2020). *Human-made Objects to Outweigh Living Things.* Retrieved from BBC News: https://www.bbc.com/news/science-environment-55239668.

Britton, E. (2000). Carsharing 2000: Sustainable transport's missing link. *Journal of The Commons*, 1–351.

Campanella, T.J. (2017). *Robert Moses and His Racist Parkway, Explained.* Retrieved from Bloomberg Citylab: https://www.bloomberg.com/news/articles/2017-07-09/robert-moses-and-his-racist-parkway-explained.

Canada Energy Regulator. (2020). *Market Snapshot: Canada's Retiring Coal-fired PowerPlants will be Replaced by Renewable and Low-carbon Energy Sources.* Retrieved from Canada Energy Regulator: https://www.cer-rec.gc.ca/en/data-analysis/energy-markets/market-snapshots/2020/market-snapshot-canadas-retiring-coal-fired-power-plants-will-be-replaced-renewable-low-carbon-energy-sources.html.

*Carsharing.org.* (2017). Retrieved from What is carsharing? https://carsharing.org/what-is-car-sharing/.

Carter, C. (2019). *Autonomous Passenger Ferries: Congestion-buster or Hype on the High Seas?* Retrieved from Smart Cities World: https://www.smartcitiesworld.net/special-reports/special-reports/autonomous-passenger-ferries-congestion-buster-or-hype-on-the-high-seas.

Center for Sustainable Systems. (2020). *Geothermal Energy.* Detroit, Michigan: University of Michigan. Retrieved from Geothermal Energy.: http://css.umich.edu/sites/default/files/Geothermal%20Energy_CSS10-10_e2020.pdf.

Certeau, M.D. (1980). *The Practice of Everyday Life.* Paris: Union générale d'éditions.

Certeau, M.D. (1984). *The Practice of Everyday Life.* Berkeley: University of California Press (English).

Charles, A.S., Lambert, H.G. and Balogh, S.B. (2014). EROI of different fuels and the implications for society. *Energy Policy*, 64: 141–152.

Chellapilla, K. (2018). *Rethinking Maps for Self-driving.* Medium.

Christensen, A. and Petrenko, C. (2017). *$CO_2$-Based Synthetic Fuel: Assessment of Potential European Capacity and Environmental Performance.* Brussels: European Climate Foundation and the International Council on Clean Transportation.

Chua, A. (2018). *How America's Identity Politics Went from Inclusion to Division.* Retrieved from The Guardian: https://www.theguardian.com/society/2018/mar/01/how-americas-identity-politics-went-from-inclusion-to-division.

City of Toronto. (2018). *Draft Official Plan Amendment, ConsumersNext Secondary Plan.* Toronto: City of Toronto.

City of Toronto. (2018). *Toronto Green Standard Version 3.* Toronto, Canada: City of Toronto.

City of Toronto. (2020). *Energy Efficiency Report Submission & Modelling Guidelines: For the Toronto Green Standard (TGS) Version 3.* Toronto, Canada: Environment and Energy Division & City Planning Division, City of Toronto.

City of Vancouver. (2019). *EV Charging Infrastructure Requirements for New Residential Buildings Guidance.* Vancouver, Canada: City of Vancouver.

Civitas. (2016). *Cities Towards Mobility 2.0: Connect, Share and Go!* Brussels, Belgium: CIVITAS WIKI consortium.

CMA. (2008). *No Breathing Room National Illness Costs of Air Pollution.* Ottawa: Canadian Medical Association.

Cook, C. (2014). *Transforming the Transportation Industry with Renewable Energy.* Retrieved from Renewable Energy World: https://www.renewableenergyworld.com/2014/09/18/transforming-the-transportation-industry-with-renewable-energy/.

Cooper, D. (2018). *It's Too Early to Write off Hydrogen Vehicles.* Retrieved from Engadget: https://www.engadget.com/2018-05-29-hydrogen-fuel-cell-toyota-mirai-evs.html.

Copjec, J. (2020). Psychoanalysis and consequences (PDF). via www.chiasma-journal.com. *Chiasmus*, 6(1): 189–203.

CPCS and Hatch Associates. (1992). *Commuter Rail Services: Electrification Study.* Toronto: GO Transit.

Crary, J. (2014). *24/7 Late Capitalism and the End of Sleep.* New York: Verso.

Crutzen, P.a. (2000). The anthropocene. *Glob. Chang. News*, 41: 17–18.

Curie, J. and Pierre, C. (1880). Développement, par pression, de l'électricité polaire dans les cristaux hémièdres à faces inclinées. *Comptes Rendus* (in French), 9: 294–295.

Curtis, A. (Director). (2002). *The Century of the Self –Part 1: "Happiness Machines"* [Motion Picture].

Daelen, C.V. and Bruneau, C. (2020). *Capitalism and Patriarchy: Two Systems that Feed off Each Other*. Retrieved from Committee for the Abolition of Illigitimate Debt: https://www.cadtm.org/Capitalism-and-Patriarchy-Two-Systems-that-Feed-off-Each-Other.

Dan, K. (2007). Flight of the pigeon. *Bicycling, Rodale, Inc.*, 48: 60–66.

Dave. (2018). *Car-Sharing vs. Private Vehicle Ownership Costs.* Retrieved from Carsharing US: https://arlingtonva.s3.amazonaws.com/wp-content/uploads/sites/19/2017/03/DES-Carshare-CarShare_vs_PrivateCarOwnership_Cost_Analysis.pdf.

David, H. (2004). *Bicycle: The History.* Yale University Press. ISBN 0-300-10418-9.

Debhia, P. (2019). *The History of Electric Scooters.* Retrieved from LinkedIn: https://www.linkedin.com/pulse/history-electric-scooters-prashant-dedhia-negotiation-ninja-/.

Debord, G. (1957). *Report on the Construction of Situations: Situationist International Anthology.* Berkeley: Bureau of Public Secrets.

Debord, G. (1967). *La société du spectacle (The Society of the Spectacle).* Paris: Buchet-Chastel.

Deluchhi, M.Z. and Jaconson, M.A. (2009). A path to sustainable energy by 2030. *Secitific American*, 58–65.

DeMaio, P. (2009). Bike-sharing: Impacts, models of provision, and future. *Journal of Public Transportation*, 12(4): 41–56.

DeMaio, P.J. (2003). Bikes: Public transportation for the 21st century. *Transportation Quarterly*, 57(1): 9–11.

Dennis, R.M. (1995). Social darwinism, scientific racism, and the metaphysics of race. *The Journal of Negro Education*, 64(3): 243–252.

Dijkema, M.B., Mallant, S.F., Gehring, U., Hurk, K.V., Alssema, M., van Strien, R.T., Fischer, P.H., Nijpels, G., Stehouwer, C.D.A., Hoek, G., Dekker, J.M. and Brunekreef, B. (2011). Long-term exposure to traffic-related air pollution and Type 2 diabetes prevalence in a cross-sectional screening-study in the Netherlands. *Environmental Health*, 10: 76.

DoT, UK. (2019). *Future of Mobility: Urban Strategy.* London: Department of Transport, UK.

Driver, J. (2014). *The History of Utilitarianism.* Retrieved from Stanford Encyclopedia of Philosophy: https://plato.stanford.edu/entries/utilitarianism-history/.

Driving. (2015). *Company Wants to Bring Rickshaws to North America.* Retrieved from Driving: https://driving.ca/auto-news/news/company-wants-to-bring-rickshaws-to-north-america.

Duffy, M.C. (2003). *Electric Railways: 1880–1990. London.* London: The Institution of Engineering and Technology.

Duignan, B. (2019). *Jeremy Bentham: British Philosopher and Economist.* Retrieved from Britannica: https://www.britannica.com/biography/Jeremy-Bentham.

Eden, E. (2017). *Walking While Black: The Racial Disparity in Pedestrian Fatalities.* Retrieved from Planetizen: https://www.planetizen.com/node/91280/walking-while-black-racial-disparity-pedestrian-fatalities.

Elhacham, E., Ben-Uri, L., Grozovski, J., Bar-On, Y.M. and Milo, R. (2020). Global human-made mass exceeds all living biomass. *Nature*, 588: 442–444.

Endsley, M.R. and Kiris, E.O. (1995). The out-of-the-loop performance problem and level of control in automation. *Human Factors. The Journal of the Human Factors and Ergonomics Society*, 2: 27.

Energy Information Administration EIA. (2017). *Study of the Potential Energy Consumption Impacts of Connected and Automated Vehicles.* Washington, D.C. 20585: US Department of Energy.

Energy Innovation. (2015). *Comparing the Costs of Renewable And Conventional Energy Sources.* Retrieved from Energy Innovation: https://energyinnovation.org/2015/02/07/levelized-cost-of-energy/.

Eugster, J.W. (2007). Road and bridge heating using geothermal energy. Overview and examples. *Proceedings European Geothermal Congress* (pp. 1–5). Unterhaching, Germany: European Geothermal Congress.

European Commision. (2020). *Energy Efficiency Indicator.* Retrieved from European Commision: https://ec.europa.eu/transport/themes/energy-efficiency-indicator_en.

Ewing, R., Pendall, R. and Chen, D. (2002). *Measuring Sprawl and Its Impact: Smart Growth America.* Washington, D.C.: Transportation Research Board of the National Academies.

Fishbone, A., Shahan, Z. and Badik, P. (2017). *Electric Vehicle Charging Infrastructure: Guidelines for Cities.* Warsaw, Poland: CleanTechnica.

Fishman, E. (2014). Bikeshare: A review of recent literature. *Transport Reviews*, 92–113.

Forum for the Future. (2010). *Megacities on the Move. Your Guide to the Future of Sustainable Urban Mobility in 2040.* New York: Forum for the Future.

Foucault, M. (1977). *Discipline and Punish: The Birth of the Prison.* New York: Pantheon Books.

François-Lavet, V., Henderson, P., Islam, R., Bellemare, M.G. and Pineau, J. (2018). An introduction to deep reinforcement learning. *Foundations and Trends in Machine Learning*, 11(3-4): 1–102.

Frayer, L. and Cater, F. (2015). *How a Folding Electric Vehicle Went from Car of The Future to 'Obsolete'.* Retrieved from NPR: http://www.npr.org/sections/alltechconsidered/2015/11/05/454693583/how-a-folding-electric-vehicle-went-from-car-of-the-future-to-obsolete.

Freud, S. (1929). *Civilization and Its Discontents.* Vienna: Internationaler Psychoanalytischer Verlag Wien.

Furman, B., Fabian, L., Ellis, S., Muller, P. and Swenson, R. (2014). *Automated Transit Networks (ATN): A Review of the State of the Industry and Prospects for the Future.* San José: Minata Transportation Institute.

Galatoulas, N.F. and Genikomsakis, K.N. (2020). Spatio-temporal trends of e-bike sharing system deployment: A review in Europe, North America and Asia. *Sustainability*, 12: 4611.

Galster, G., Hanson, R., Ratcliffe, M.R., Wolman, H., Coleman, S. and Freihage, J. (2001). Wrestling sprawl to the ground: Defining and measuring an elusive concept. *Housing Policy Debate*, 12(4): 681–717.

Gawron, V.J. (2019). *Automation in Aviation - Definition of Automation.* McLean, VA: The MITRE Corporation.

Gee, M. (2016). *Raise the Roof? Union Station Reno Runs into Problem: New trains won't fit.* Retrieved from The Globe and Mail: https://www.theglobeandmail.com/news/toronto/union-station-shed-renovation-stalled-by-low-arches-and-an-electrified-future/article28448568/.

Geidl, M., Koeppel, G., Favre-Perrod, P., Klöckl, B., Andersson, G. and Fröhlich, K. (2007). The energy hub—A powerful concept for future energy systems. *Third Annual Carnegie Mellon Conference on the Electricity Industry* (pp. 2–10). Pittsburgh: Carnegie Mellon University.

Gerber, D.A. (1999). Caucasians are made and not born: How european immigrants became white people. *Reviews in American History*, 27: 437–443.

Gilcher-Holtey, I. (2014). *A Revolution of Perception? Consequences and Echoes of 1968.* New York: Berghahn Books.

Gilpin, L. (2017). *Can Car-Sharing Culture Help Fuel an Electric Vehicle Revolution?* Retrieved from Insideclimatenews: https://insideclimatenews.org/news/07122017/car-rental-sharing-electric-vehicles-zipcar-evs-uber-lyft-green-commuter.

Global Union. (2020). *Top 10 principles for Ethical Artificial Intelligence.* Nyon, Switzerland: The Future World of Work.

Goel, R. (2021). *Pandemic after One Year.* Mumbai, India: Bicar Institute.

Gomes, L. (2014). *Hidden Obstacles for Google's Self-Driving Cars: Impressive Progress Hides Major Limitations of Google's Quest for Automated Driving.* Cambridge, USA: MIT Technology Review.

Griloa, F., Pinho, P., Aleixo, C., Catita, C., Silva, P., Lopes, N., Freitas, C., Santos-Reis, M., McPhearson, T.M. and Branquinho, C. (2020). Using green to cool the grey: Modelling the cooling effect of green spaces with a high spatial resolution. *Science of the Total Environment*, 1–10.

Grosholz, E. (1991). *Cartesian Method and the Problem of Reduction.* Oxford: Oxford University Press.

Gross, S. (2020). *Why are Fossil Fuels so Hard to Quit?* Retrieved from Brookings Institution: https://www.brookings.edu/essay/why-are-fossil-fuels-so-hard-to-quit/.

GTA Clean Air Council. (2017). *Climate Action for a Healthy, Equitable and Prosperous Toronto.* Toronto: City of Toronto.

Harms, S. and Truffer, B. (1998). *The Emergence of a Nationwide Car Sharing Co-operative in Switzerland: A Case Study for the Project "Strategic Niche Management as a Tool for Transition to a Sustainable Transportation System.* 1998: EAWAG-Eidg. Anstalt für Wasserversorgung und Gewässerschutz.

Haugneland, P., Lorentzen, E., Bu, C. and Hauge, E. (2017). Put a price on carbon to fund EV incentives – Norwegian EV policy success. *EVS30 Symposium* (pp. 1–8). Stuttgart, Germany: Norwegian EV Association.

Haywood, J.B. (2006). Fueling Our Transportation Future. *Scientific American.*

Herkert, J.R. (2001). Future directions in engineering ethics research: microethics, macroethics and the role of professional societies. *Science and Engineering Ethics*, 7(3): 403–414.

Hess, A. and Schubert, I. (2019). Functional perceptions, barriers, and demographics concerning e-cargo bike sharing in Switzerland. *Transportation Research Part D: Transport and Environment*, 71: 153. Retrieved from Science daily: https://www.sciencedaily.com/releases/2019/07/190710121536.htm.

Hoopengardner, R. and Thompson, M. (2012). *FTA Low-Speed Urban Maglev Research Program: Updated Lessons Learned.* Arlington, USA: Federal Transit Administration.

Hordnes, E. (2019). *Race to Electrification – Norway in a Pole Position.* Retrieved from Urban Insight: https://www.swecourbaninsight.com/urban-energy/race-to-electrification--norway-in-pole-position/.

Hughes, B. (Director). (2016). *Genius of the Modern World – Friedrich Nietzsche* [Motion Picture].

Hughes, I. and Huo, R. (2018). *Autonomy-level Classification for Robots in an IIoT World.* Retrieved from 451 Research: https://go.451research.com/MI-Robots-in-IIoT-World.html.

Hull, G.J., Roberts, C. and Hillmansen, S. (2008). Energy Efficiency of a Railway Power Network with Simulation. *International Conference on Energy Technologies and Policy.* Birmingham, UK: University of Birmingham.

IISD. (2015). *The End of Coal: Ontario's Coal Phase-out.* Winnipeg, Canada: International Institute for Sustainable Development.

Institute, R.M. (2019). *Electric Mobility: Best Practices.* Rocky Mountain Institute, Government of India and Smart City.

Intelligent Transport. (2021). *Saudi Arabia to Build Residential Project THE LINE Centred around Walking*. Retrieved from Intelligent Transport: https://www.intelligenttransport.com/transport-news/113973/the-line/.

Islam, A. and Ahiduzzaman, M. (2012). Biomass energy: Sustainable solution for greenhouse gas emission. *American Inst. Phys. Conf. Proc.*, 1441(1): 23–32. American Institute of Physics.

ISO. (2020). *Road Vehicles — Human Performance and State in the Context of Automated Driving – Part 2: Considerations in Designing Experiments to Investigate Transition Processes*. ISO/TR 21959-2: 2020.

Itoh, M., Zhou, H. and Kitazaki, S. (2018). What may happen or what you should do? Effects of knowledge representation regarding necessity of intervention on driver performance under level 2 automated driving. *ICPS'18: Proceedings of the 2018 IEEE Industrial Cyber-Physical Systems* (pp. 621–626). St. Petersburg, Russia: IEEE.

Iyer, P. (2014). *The Art of Stillness: Adventures in Going Nowhere*. New York: Simon & Schuster/TED.

J 2954. (2019). *Wireless Power Transfer for Light-Duty Plug-in/Electric Vehicles and Alignment Methodology*. SAE International.

J3068. (2018). *Electric Vehicle Power Transfer System Using a Three-Phase Capable Coupler*. J3068. SAE International.

J3105. (2020). *Electric Vehicle Power Transfer System Using Conductive Automated Connection Devices*. SAE International.

Jackson, R.J. (2003). The impact of the built environment on health: An emerging field. *American Journal of Public Health*, 93(9): 1382–1384.

Jacobs, J. (1961). *The Death and Life of Great American Cities*. New York: Random House.

Jacobs, J. (1985). *Cities and the Wealth of Nations: Principles of Economic Life*. New York: Random House.

Jayasuriya, D.C. (1994). Street food vending in Asia: Some policy and legal aspects. *Food Control*, 5(4): 222–226. Elsevier.

Jefferies, I. (2019, November 20). Retrieved from Association of American Railroads: https://www.aar.org/article/freight-rail-highly-automated-vehicles/.

Jettanasen, C., Songsukthawan, P. and Ngaopitakkul, A. (2020). Development of micro-mobility based on piezoelectric energy harvesting for smart city applications. *Sustainability*, 1–16.

Jonuschat, H., Stephan, K. and Schelewsky, M. (2015). Understanding multimodal and intermodal mobility. *Sustainable Urban Transport (Transport and Sustainability)*, 7: 149–176. Retrieved from Eltis.: https://www.eltis.org/glossary/multimodality#:~:text=Definition%20E2%80%93%20Multimodality%20(not%20to%20be,public%20transport%20to%20visit%20friends.

Jorna, A. (2012). *Synthetic Fuel Costs*. Stanford, California: Stanford University.

Joshi, N. (2019). *7 Types Of Artificial Intelligence*. Retrieved from Forbes: https://www.forbes.com/sites/cognitiveworld/2019/06/19/7-types-of-artificial-intelligence/#48c88ca9233e.

Junkin, K. (2013). *Regional Rapid Rail: A Vision for the Future*. Toronto: Transport Action, Ontario.

Kalra, N. and Paddock, S.M. (2016). *How Many Miles of Driving Would it Take to Demonstrate Autonomous Vehicle Reliability? Driving to Safety*. Santa Monica, California: RAND Corporation.

Kane, M. (2019). *Chile Launches Latin America's First 100% Electric Bus Corridor*. Retrieved from Inside EVs: https://insideevs.com/news/377241/chile-first-100-electric-bus-corridor/.

KAPSARC. (2016). *Mobility-on-demand: Understanding Energy Impacts and Adoption Potential*. Riyadh: KASARC.

Karim, D.M. (2017). Creating an innovative mobility ecosystem for urban planning areas. pp. 21–47. *In*: Meyer, G.S. (ed.). *Disrupting Mobility: Impacts of Sharing Economy and Innovative Transportation on Cities*. Cham: Springer.

Karim, D.M. and Shallwani, T. (2010). Toward a clean train policy: Diesel versus electric, the Ontario Centre for Engineering and Public Policy. *Ontario Centre for Engineering and Public Policy (OCEPP)*, 3: 18–22.

Khayal, O. (2019). The history of Bajaj rickshaw vehicles. *Global Journal of Engineering Sciences*, 3(2): 1–8.

Klein, N.J. (2017). Millennials and car ownership: Less money, fewer cars. *Transport Policy*, 53(C): 20–29.

Kleinman, M.T. (2000). *The Health Effects of Air Pollution on Children*. Irvine, California: South Coast Air Quality Management District (SCAQMD).

Kour, R. and Charif, A. (2016). Piezoelectric roads: Energy harvesting method using piezoelectric technology. *Innovative Energy & Research*, 5: 132.

Kunstler, J.H. (1994). *Geography of Nowhere: The Rise and Decline of America's Man-made Landscape*. Toronto: Simon & Schuster.

Kwon, D. (2018). Self-taught robots. *Scientific American*, 26–31.

Kwon, H., Ryu, M.H. and Carlsten, C. (2020). Ultrafine particles: Unique physicochemical properties relevant to health and disease. *Experimental & Molecular Medicine*, 52: 318–328.

Lambert, F. (2020). *Uber and Hyundai Unveil New Electric Air Taxi with 60-mile Range*. Retrieved from Electrek: https://electrek.co/2020/01/07/uber-hyundai-electric-air-taxi-evtol/.

LaPierre, S. (n.d.). *One Last Chance to Fix Capitalism*. Retrieved from Harvard Business Review: https://hbr.org/2020/03/one-last-chance-to-fix-capitalism.

Layton, B.E. (2008). A comparison of energy densities of prevalent energy sources in units of houles per cubic meter. *International Journal of Green Energy*, 5: 438–455.

Le Corbusier. (1929). *The City of Tomorrow and its Planning*. London: Dover Publications.

Le Vine, S., Lee-Gosselin, M., Sivakumar, A. and Polak, J. (2014). New approach to predict the market and impacts of round-trip and point-to-point carsharing systems: Case study of London. *Transportation Research Part D*, 32(C): 218–229.

Le Vine, S., Zolfaghari, A. and Polak, J. (2014). *Carsharing: Evolution, Challenges and Opportunities*. London: Centre for Transport Studies, Imperial College London.

Ledsham, T. and Savan, B. (2017). *Building a 21st Century Cycling City: Strategies for Action in Toronto*. Toronto: Metcalf Foundation.

Lee-Shanok, P. (2017). *Ontario Condo Act a Roadblock for Electric Vehicle Owners*. Retrieved from CBC News: https://www.cbc.ca/news/canada/toronto/ontario-hopes-revised-condo-act-ev-friendly-1.4155747.

Lefebvre, H. (1947). *The Critique of Everyday Life*. London: Verso.

Lefebvre, H. (1968). *Le Droit à la Ville*. Paris: Anthropos.

Lefervre, H. (1974). *La Production de l'espace (The Production of Space)*. Paris: Anthropos.

Lessing, H. (2001). What led to the invention of the early bicycle? *Cycle History 11, San Francisco 2001*, 11: 28–36. Retrieved from New Scientist. https://www.newscientist.com/article/mg18524841-900-brimstone-and-bicycles/.

Li, L. and Loo, B.P. (2014). Alternative and transitional energy sources for urban transportation. *Current Sustainable/Renewable Energy Reports*, 1: 19–26.

Li, X. and Strezov, V. (2014). Modelling piezoelectric energy harvesting potential in an educational building. *Energy Conversion and Management*, 85: 435–442.

Li, X., Gorghinpour, C., Sclar, R. and Castellanos, S. (2018). *How to Enable Electric Bus Adoption in Cities Worldwide*. Berlin: World Resources Institute, WRI and German Federal Ministry.

Lima, M. (2015). *The Bicycle in the 21st Century*. Retrieved from the Protocity: http://theprotocity.com/the-bicycle-in-the-21st-century/.

Linklater, A. (2010). Norbert Elias, The Civilizing Process: Sociogenetic and Psychogenetic investigations—An overview and assessment. *History and Theory*, 49(3): 384–411.

Litman, T. (2018). Retrieved from Carsharing: Vehicle Rental Services that Substitute for Private Vehicle Ownership: https://www.vtpi.org/tdm/tdm7.htm.

Little, A. (2015). *The Future of Urban Mobility 2.0: Towards Networked, Multimodal Cities of 2050*. Rome, Italy: International Association of Public Transport (UITP).

Liu, J.a. (2020). Are young Americans carless across the United States? A spatial analysis. *Transportation Research Part D: Transport and Environment*, 78.

Loos, A. (1908). *Ornament and Crime*. Innsbruck: Programs and Manifestos on 20th Century Architechture.

Lu, Z., Happe, R., Cabrall, C., Kyriakidis, M. and de Winter, J. (2016). Human factors of transitions in automated driving: A general framework and literature survey. *Transportation Research Part F*, 43: 183–198.

Lucas, A., Prettico, G., Flammini, M.G., Kotsakis, E., Fulli, G. and Masera, G. (2018). Indicator-based methodology for assessing EV charging infrastructure using exploratory data analysis. *Energies*, 11(1869): 1–18.

Marlow, C. (2018). *How to Stop 'Smart Cities' from Becoming 'Surveillance Cities'*. Retrieved from ACLU: https://www.aclu.org/blog/privacy-technology/surveillance-technologies/how-stop-smart-cities-becoming-surveillance-cities.

MaRS Discovery District. (2016). *Microtransit: An Assessment of Potential to Drive Greenhouse Gas Reductions*. Toronto: MaRS Discovery District and Richmond Sustainability Initiatives.

Marshall, J.D. (2004). *Poststructuralism, Philosophy, Pedagogy*. Dordrecht: Kluwer Academic Publishers.

Martret, O. (2020). *Electric Vehicles – Cleaner, Greener and On-Demand?* Retrieved from Shotl: https://shotl.com/news/electric-vehicles-cleaner-greener-and-on-demand.

Marx, K. (1976). *Capital*, Vol. 1. Harmondsworth: Penguin.

Matuka, R. (2014). *The History of the Electric Car*. Retrieved from Department of Energy, USA.

Mazzetti, M., Perlroth, N. and Bergman, R. (2019). *It Seemed Like a Popular Chat App. It's Secretly a Spy Tool*. Retrieved from New York Times: https://www.nytimes.com/2019/12/22/us/politics/totok-app-uae.html.

McCormack, D.P. (2013). *Refrains for Moving Bodies: Experience and Experiment in Affective Spaces*. Oxford: Due University Press.

McFarlane, C. and Söderström, O. (2017). On alternative smart cities: From a technology-intensive to a knowledge-intensive smart urbanism. *Analysis of Urban Change, Theory, Action*, 21(3-4): 312–328.

McKelvey, T. (2021). *Biden's Unlikely Plan to Use Roads to Fight Racism.* Retrieved from BBC News: https://www.bbc.com/news/world-us-canada-58106414.

McMahon, J. (2019). *9 Shared-Mobility Startups Eager To Disrupt Transportation.* Retrieved from Forbes: https://www.forbes.com/sites/jeffmcmahon/2019/03/06/9-shared-mobility-startups-eager-to-disrupt-transportation/.

McNabb, M. (2019). *DRONEII: Tech Talk – Unraveling 5 Levels of Drone.* Drone Talk.

Meadows, D.H. (1972). *The Limits to Growth.* New York: Universe Books.

Medina-Tapiaa, M. and Robusteb, F. (2018). Exploring paradigm shift impacts in urban mobility: Autonomous vehicles and smart cities. *Transportation Research Procedia*, 33: 203–210.

Melaina, M., Bush, B., Muratori, M., Zuboy, J. and Ellis, S. (2017). *National Hydrogen Scenerios: How Many Stations, Where, and When?* Washington. D.C.: National Renewable Energy Laboratory for the H2USA.

Metrolinx. (2008). *The Big Move: Transforming Transportation in the Greater Toronto and Hamilton Area.* Toronto: Metrolinx.

Millard-Ball, A. (2019, March). The autonomous vehicle parking problem. *Transport Policy*, 75: 99–108.

MIT Media Lab. (2019). *Persuasive Electric Vehicle (PEV).* Retrieved from MIT Media Lab City Science Group: https://www.media.mit.edu/projects/pev/overview/.

Mitchell, W.J., Borroni-Bird, C.E. and Burns, L.D. (2015). *Reinventing the Automobile.* Cambridge, USA: The MIT Press.

Mohorčich, J. (2020). Energy intensity and human mobility after the anthropocene. *Sustainability*, 12: 2376–2389.

Morawska, L., Moore, M.R. and Ristovski, Z.D. (2014). *Health Impacts of Ultrafine Particles: Desktop Literature Review and Analysis.* Canberra: Australian Government Department of the Environment and Heritage.

Movmi. (2018). *Carsharing Market Analysis: Growth and Industry Analysis.* Retrieved from Movmi.net: https://movmi.net/carsharing-market-growth/.

Muheim, P. and Partners. (1996). *Car Sharing Studies: An Investigation.* Dublin, Ireland: Graham Lightfoot.

Müller, V.C. (2020). *Stanford Encyclopedia of Philosophy.* Retrieved from Stanford University: https://plato.stanford.edu/entries/ethics-ai/.

Münzel, K., Boon, W., Frenken, K., Blomme, J. and van der, D. (2019). Explaining carsharing supply across Western European cities. *International Journal of Sustainable Transportation*, 1–12.

NACTO. (2013). *Urban Street Design Guide.* New York: National Association of City Transportation Officials.

Najini, H. and Muthukumaraswamy, S.A. (2017). Piezoelectric energy generation from vehicle traffic with technoeconomic analysis. *Journal of Renewable Energy*, 1–16.

Namazu, M. (2017). *The Evolution of Carsharing: Heterigeneity in Adoption and Impacts.* Vancouver: The University of British Columbia.

Network Rail Infrastructure Limited. (2020). *Network Statement 2020.* London, UK: Network Rail.

Newswire. (2010). *Vancouver First City in the World to Endorse the Fossil Fuel Non-Proliferation Treaty.* Retrieved from Fossil Fuel Non-Proliferation Treaty: https://www.newswire.ca/news-releases/vancouver-first-city-in-the-world-to-endorse-the-fossil-fuel-non-proliferation-treaty-843699223.html.

NHTSA. (2016). *Federal Motor Vehicle Safety Standards: Minimum Sound Requirements for Hybrid and Electric Vehicles.* Washington D.C.: National Highway Traffic Safety Administration, NHTSA.

Nilsson, N. (1982). *Principles of Artificial Intelligence.* Elsevier Inc.

NTSB. (2020). *Tesla Crash Investigation Yields 9 NTSB Safety Recommendations.* National Transportation Safety Board.

Oakil, A.T., Manting, D. and Nijland, H. (2016). Determinants of car ownership among young households in the Netherlands: The role of urbanisation and demographic and economic characteristics. *Journal of Transport Geography*, 51: 229–235.

O'Carroll, T. and Franco, J. (2017). *Why Build a Muslim Registry when You Can Buy It?* Retrieved from Medium: https://medium.com/amnesty-insights/data-brokers-data-analytics-muslim-registries-human-rights-73cd5232ed19.

Ohta, K. (1998). TDM measures toward sustainable mobility. *IATSS Research*, 22(1).

Omi, K. (2018). *Alternative Energy for Transportation.* Retrieved from Issues in Science and Technology: https://issues.org/omi/.

Ongel, A., Loewer, E., Roemer, F., Sethuraman, G. and Chang, F. (2019). Economic assessment of autonomous electric microtransit vehicles. *Sustainability*, 2–18.

Ontario Medical Association. (2005). *The Illness Costs of Air Pollution: 2005–2026 Health and Economic Damage Estimates.* Toronto: OMA.

Orenstein, M. (2020). *COVID-19's Effect on Energy and Emissions – and Implications for the Future.* Retrieved from Canawest Foundation: https://cwf.ca/research/publications/what-now-covid-19s-effect-on-energy-and-emissions-and-implications-for-the-future/.

Padeiro, M.a. (2019). Transit-oriented development and gentrification: A systematic review. *Transport Reviews*, 39(6): 1–22.

Panchal, D.U. (2015). *Two and Three Wheeler Technology*. PHI Learning Pvt. Ltd., ISBN 9788120351431.

Parasuraman, R. (1992). Adaptive function allocation effects on pilot performance. *NASA/FAA Workshop on Artificial Intelligence and Human Factors*. Daytona Beach, Florida, USA.: NASA and FAA.

Parasuraman, R., Sheridan, T.B. and Wickens, C.D. (2000). A model for types and levels of human interaction with automation. *IEEE Transactions on Systems, Man, and Cybernetics-Part A: Systems and Humans*, 30(3): 286–297.

PBS. (2009). *Timeline: History of the Electric Car*. Retrieved from PBS.org: https://www.pbs.org/now/shows/223/electric-car-timeline.html.

Perner, J., Unteutsch, M. and Lövenich, A. (2018). *The Future Cost of Electricity-based Synthetic Fuels*. Berlin: Agora Energiewende.

Pete. (2015). *Electric Cargo Bike Guide*. Retrieved from Electric Bike Report: https://electricbikereport.com/electric-cargo-bike-guide/.

Peteritas, B. (2012). *Seoul's Transit System Serves as a Model for America*. Retrieved from Governing: https://www.governing.com/archive/col-seoul-subway-offers-lesson-in-transportation.html.

Plautz, J. (2020). *The Gas Tax was Already Broken. The Pandemic Could End It*. Retrieved from Smart Cities Drive: https://www.smartcitiesdive.com/news/the-gas-tax-was-already-broken-the-pandemic-could-end-it/587653/.

Polak, S.a. (2015). Introduction to special issue: New directions in shared-mobility research. *Transportation*, 42(3): 407–411.

Pope III, C.A., Burnett, R.T., Thun, M.J., Calle, E.E., Krewski, D., Ito, K. and Thurston, G.D. (2002). Lung cancer, cardiopulmonary mortality, and long-term exposure to fine particulate air pollution. *The Journal of the American Medical Association*, 287(9): 1132–1141.

Porru, M., Serpi, A., Mureddu, M. and Damiano, A. (2020). A multistage design procedure for planning and implementing public charging infrastructures for electric vehicles. *Sustainability*, 2889(12): 1–17.

Potoglou, D.a. (2008). Modelling car ownership in urban areas: A case study of Hamilton Canada. *Journal of Transport Geography*, 16(1): 42–54.

Price, S. (2021). *Rightsizing the Automobile for Local Mobility*. Retrieved from Public Square, a CNU Journal: https://www.cnu.org/publicsquare/2021/10/13/rightsizing-automobile-local-mobility.

Priemus, H. (2007). Dutch spatial planning between substratum and infrastructure networks. 15(5): 667–686: European Planning Study.

Province of Ontario. (2017). *Growth Plan for the Greater Golden Horseshoe*. Toronto: Province of Ontario.

Puchalsky, C.M. (2005). Comparison of emission from light rail transit and bus rapid. *Transportation Research Record*, 1927(1): 31–37.

Qiu, C., Chau, K.T., Ching, T.W. and Liu, C. (2014). Overview of wireless charging technologies for electric vehicles. *Journal of Asian Electric Vehicles*, 12: 1679–1685.

Rajvanshi, A.K. (2002). Electric and improved cycle rickshaw as a sustainable transport system for India. *Current Science*, 83(6): 703–707.

Ram, G., Mouli, C., Duijsen, P.V., Grazian, F., Jamodkar, A., Bauer, P. and Isabella, O. (2020). Sustainable E-Bike charging station that enables AC, DC and wireless charging from solar energy. *Energies*, 13(3549): 1–21.

Reddy, T. (2008). *Synthetic Fuels Handbook: Properties, Process, and Performance*. McGraw-Hill.

Regnier, E. (2007). Oil and energy price volatility. *Energy Economic*, 29(3): 405–427.

Ricard, M. (2016). *Altruism: The Power of Compassion to Change Yourself and the World*. New York: Back Bay Books.

Richard, F. and Cooper, H. (2005). Why electrified rail is superior. *21st Century Science & Technology*, 18: 26–29.

Rickstrom, J. and Klum, M. (2015). *Big World, Small Planet: Abundance within Planetary Boundaries*. New Haven and London: Yale University Press.

Rideamigos. (2018). *What is Transportation Demand Management?* Retrieved from Rideamigos: https://rideamigos.com/transportation-demand-management-tdm/.

Rider, D. (2020). *Toronto Adds Electric Bicycles to Bike-share Fleet — at No Extra Cost to Users*. Retrieved from Toronto Star: https://www.thestar.com/news/city_hall/2020/08/19/toronto-adds-electric-bicycles-to-bike-share-fleet-at-no-extra-cost-to-users.html.

Rieti, J. (2017). *CBC News*. Retrieved from Toronto Discourages Electric car use by Denying on-street Chargers, Driver says: https://www.cbc.ca/news/canada/toronto/electric-vehicles-blocked-1.4368014.

Ritchie, H. (2020). *What Are the Safest and Cleanest Sources of Energy?* Retrieved from Our world in data: https://ourworldindata.org/safest-sources-of-energy.

Rodenbach, J., Mathis, J., Chicco, A., Diana, M. and Nehrk, G. (2017). *Car Sharing in Europe: A Multidimensional Classification and Inventory*. European Union: STARS and AUTON.

Rowling, M. (2019). *Smart Cities' Urged to Look Beyond Rich, White Men*. Retrieved from The Reuters: https://www.reuters.com/article/us-global-technology-cities-idUSKBN1XV24T.

Sadik-Khan, J.a. (2016). *Streetfight: Handbook for an Urban Revolution.* New York: Penguin Random House LLC.

SAE. (2014). *Taxonomy and Definitions for Terms Related to On-road Motor Vehicle Automated Driving Systems.* USA: SAE International.

SAE. (2018). *Taxonomy and Definitions for Terms Related to Shared Mobility and Enabling Technologies.* USA: SAE International.

SAE International. (2014). *Ground Vehicle Standards.* USA: SAE International.

SAE International. (2019). *A Dictionary of Terms for the Dynamics and Handling of Single Track Vehicles (Motorcycles, Scooters, Mopeds, and Bicycles).* Warrendale, PA, USA: J1451_201909. Society of Automotive Engineers.

SAE International. (2019). *J3194 Taxonomy and Classification of Powered Micromobility Vehicles.* Warrendale, PA, USA: Society of Automotive Engineers.

Saunders, K. (2017). *Where's the Hype for Automated Trains? Part 1: History and Background.* Automation.

Sawilla, S. and Oskar, S.a. (2018). *Ipt-technology.* Retrieved from Wireless Opportunity Charging buses in Madrid: https://ipt-technology.com/case-opportunity-charging-madrid/.

SCAQMD. (2000). *Multiple Air Toxics Exposure Study.* San Francisco: South Coast Air Quality Management District.

Schneider, C.G. and Hill, L.B. (2007). *No Escape from Diesel Exhaust: How to Reduce Commuter Exposure.* Boston: Boston: Clean Air Task Force.

Sclar, R., Gorghinpour, C., Castellanos, S. and Li, X. (2018). *Barriers to Adopting Electric Buses.* Berlin: World Resources Institute, WRI and German Federal Ministry.

Scott, A.J. (2014). Beyond the creative city: Cognitive–cultural capitalism and the new urbanism. *Regional Studies,* 48(4): 565–578.

Shaheen, S. and Cohen, A. (2019). *Shared Micromobility Policy Toolkit: Docked and Dockless Bike and Scooter Sharing.* Schmidt Family Foundation.

Shaheen, S., Cohen, A. and Zohdy, I. (2016). *Shared Mobility: Current Practices and Guiding Principles.* Washington D.C.. USA: Federal Highway Administration.

Shared-Use Mobility Center. (2017). *Share-use Mobility Reference Guide.* Chicago, USA: Shared-Use Mobility Center.

Sheldrake, R. (2009). *Morphic Resonance: The Nature of Formative Causation.* Rochester, Vermont: Park Street Press.

Shell, E.R. (2020). The role of air pollution. *Scientific American,* 42–47.

Shepertycky, M. and Li, Q. (2015). Generating electricity during walking with a lower limb-driven energy harvester: Targeting a minimum user effort. *PLoS ONE,* 1–16.

Shladover, S.E. (2016). The truth about "self driving" cars. *Scientific American,* 52–57.

Siemens Mobility. (2015). *Sustainable Urban Infrastructure: Vienna Edition – Role Model for Complete Mobility.*

Sleire, S. (2019). *Norway Greenhouse Gas Emissions Rise Despite Renewable Push.* Retrieved from Bloomberg News: https://www.bnnbloomberg.ca/norway-greenhouse-gas-emissions-rise-despite-renewable-push-1.1267569.

Smith, R.A. (2008). Enabling technologies for demand management: Transport. *Energy Policy,* 36(12): 4444–4448.

Society of Automobile Engineers, SAE. (2018). *Shared Mobility: Taxonomy and Definitions in SAE J3163™.*

Spaen, B. (2019). *This All-Electric Water Taxi Could Revolutionize Green Transportation.* Retrieved from Green Matters: https://www.greenmatters.com/news/2018/06/25/qSvID/water-taxis-transportation.

Sperling, D. and Shaeen, S. (1999). Carsharing: Niche market or new pathway? *ECMT/OECD Workshop on Managing Car Use for Sustainable Urban Travel* (pp. 1–25). Dublin, Ireland: OECD.

Spulber, A., Dennis, E.P. and Wallace, R. (2016). *The Impact of New Mobility Services on the Automotive Industry.* Ann Arbor, Michigan: Cargroup.Org.

Squires, G.D. (2002). *Sprawl: Causes and Consequences and Policy Responses.* Washington: The Urban Institute Press.

Staffell, I., Scamman, D., Abad, A.V., Balcombe, P., Dodds, P.E., Ekins, P., Shah, N. and Ward, K.R. (2019). The role of hydrogen and fuel cells in the global energy system. *Energy & Environmental Science,* 12: 463–491.

Stanford University. (2019). *Leonardo's Vitruvian Man.* Retrieved from Stanford University: http://leonardodavinci. stanford.edu/submissions/clabaugh/history/leonardo.html.

Stangor, C.a. (2010). *Introduction to Psychology – 1st Canadian Edition – 2.2 Psychodynamic Psychology.* Vancouver: Creative Commons. Retrieved from BC Campus.: https://opentextbc.ca/introductiontopsychology/chapter/2-2-psychodynamic-and-behavioural-psychology/.

STAPPA and ALAPCO. (2000). *Cancer Risk from Diesel Particulate: National and Metropolitan Area Estimates for the United States.* San Francisco: State and Territorial Air Pollution Program Administrators and the Association of Local Air Pollution Control Officials.

Steer Davies Gleave. (2009). *GO Transit Lakeshore Express Rail Benefit Case.* Interim Report. Toronto: Metrolinx.

Steffen, W., Richardson, K., Rockström, J., Cornell, S., Fetzer, I., Bennett, E., Bennett, E.M., Biggs, R., Carpenter, S.R., Vrie, W.D., Wit, C.A.D., Folke, C., Gerten, D., Heinke, J., Mace, G.M., Psersson, L.M., Ramanathan, V., Reyers, B. and Sörlin, S. (2015). Planetary boundaries: Guiding human development on a changing planet. *Science*, 15: 1–10.

Steinert, H. (1983). The development of "discipline" according to michel foucault: Discourse analysis vs. social history. *Crime and Social Justice*, 20: 83–98.

Stohler, W. and Giger, P. (1989). *Cost-Benefit Analysis of the Electrification of the Beira Alta Line in Portugal.* London: Institution of Electrical Engineers.

Stone, T. (2017). *Lessons Learned from the History of Car Sharing.* Retrieved from https://tiffanydstone.com: https://tiffanydstone.com/2013/08/23/lessons-learned-from-the-history-of-car-sharing/.

Stone, T. (2018). *Siemens to Demonstrate World's First Autonomous Tram Running in Real Traffic in German City.* Retrieved from traffic technology.com: https://www.traffictechnologytoday.com/news/autonomous-vehicles/siemens-to-demonstrate-worlds-first-autonomous-tram-running-in-real-traffic-in-german-city.html.

Strompen, F., Litman, T. and Bongardt, D. (2012). *Reducing Carbon Emissions through Transport Demand Management Strategies: A Review of International Examples.* Final report. GIZ China, Transport Demand Management in Beijing.

Sturrock, J. (1981). *Structuralism and Since: From Levi Strauss to Derrida.* Oxford: Oxford University Press.

Swenson, R. (2016). The solarevolution: Much more with way less, right now—the disruptive shift to renewables. *Energies*, 9(9): 676.

Takefuji, Y. (2008). And if public transport does not consume more of energy? (PDF). *Le Rail*, 31–33.

Tao, P., Stefansson, H., Harvey, G. and Saevarsdottir, G. (2014). Potential use of geothermal energy sources for the production of Li-ion batteries. *Renewable Energy*, 61.

Tate. (2021). *Situationist International.* Retrieved from Tate: https://www.tate.org.uk/art/art-terms/s/situationist-international.

The Economist. (2017). A world turned upside down. *Renewable Energy*, 18–20.

The Guardian. (2011). *19th-century Cyclists Paved the Way for Modern Motorists' Roads.* Retrieved from The Guardian: https://www.theguardian.com/environment/bike-blog/2011/aug/15/cyclists-paved-way-for-roads.

The Guardian. (2017). *Smaller, Lighter, Greener: Are Micro EVs the Future of City Transport?* Retrieved from The Guardian: https://www.theguardian.com/sustainable-business/2017/may/11/micro-evs-city-transport-suemens-renault-green-air-pollution.

The TEV project. (2017). *Tracked Electric Vehicle System.* Reference technical booklet. Retrieved from The TEV project: http://tevproject.com/.

Tolliday, S.a. (1987). *The Automobile Industry and its Workers: Between Fordism and Flexibility.* New York: St. Martin's Press.

Toole Design Group and Pedestrian and Bicycyle Information Centre. (2012). *Bike Sharing in the United States.* USDOT, Federal Highway Administration.

Transport Canada. (2009). *Bike Sharing Guide.* Ottawa: Transport Canada.

Traube, E.G. (1989). Secrets of success in postmodern society. *Cultural Anthropology*, 4(3): 273–300.

Trencher, G. (2019). Towards the smart city 2.0: Empirical evidence of using smartness as a tool for tackling social challenges. *Technological Forecasting and Social Change*, 89: 80–91.

TUMI. (2019). *Remarkable Women in Transport: Female Change-makers Transforming Mobility.* Bonn: Transformative Urban Mobility Initiative.

TuSimple. (2020). *TuSimple Launches World's First Autonomous Freight Network with UPS, Penske, U.S. Xpress, and McLane Company, Inc.* Retrieved from stockhouse.com: https://stockhouse.com/news/press-releases/2020/07/01/tusimple-launches-world-s-first-autonomous-freight-network-with-ups-penske-u-s.

UITP. (2013). *Press Kit: Metro Automation Facts, Figures, and Trends.* International Association of Public Transport.

UITP. (2014). *Metro Automation Facts, Figures and Trends.* International Association of Public Transport (UITP).

US Bureau of Transportation Statistics. (2020). *Energy Intensity of Passenger Modes.* Retrieved from US Energy Consumption by the Transportation Sector: https://www.bts.gov/content/energy-intensity-passenger-modes.

US Department of Energy. (2018). *Alternative Fuel Vehicles.* Retrieved from US Department of Energy: https://www.energy.gov/public-services/vehicles/alternative-fuel-vehicles#/find/nearest?country=US.

US EPA. (2008). *Heat Island Compendium.* Washington D.C.: Environmental Protection Agency USA.

van de Poel, a.L. (2011). *Ethics, Technology, and Engineering.* Oxford: Wiley-Blackwell.

Venugopal, P., Shekhar, A., Visser, E. and Scheele, N. (2018). Roadway to self-healing highways with integrated wireless electric vehicle charging and sustainable energy harvesting technologies. *Applied Energy*, 212: 1226–1239.

Vynck, G.D. and Wong, N. (2020). *Alphabet's Dream of a Smart City in Toronto is Over.* Retrieved from Bloomberg News: https://www.bloomberg.com/news/articles/2020-05-07/alphabet-s-dream-of-a-smart-city-in-toronto-is-over.

Ward, W. (1967). The sailing ship effect. *Bulletin of Institute of Physics and The Physical*, 18: 169.

*Watch: Toronto's Surge in E-bike Ownership Creates Concerns over Safety.* (2018). Retrieved from Iheartradio: https://www.iheartradio.ca/newstalk-1010/news/watch-toronto-s-surge-in-e-bike-ownership-creates-concerns-over-safety-1.3726810.

WCED. UN. (1987). *Our Common Future.* Oxford: World Commission on Environment and Development, Oxford University Press.

Weichenthal, S., Ryswyk, K., Goldstein, A., Shekarrizfard, M. and Hatzopoulou, M. (2015). Characterizing the spatial distribution of ambient ultrafine particles in Toronto, Canada: A land-use regression model. *Environmental Pollution*, 47(PT A): 1–8.

Weir, L. (2018). *Pina Bousch's Dance Theatre: Tracing the Evolution of Tanz Theatre.* Edinburgh: Edinburgh University Press.

Weißbach, D., Ruprecht, G., Hukeac, A., Czerski, K., Gottlieb, S. and Hussein, A. (2013). Energy intensities, EROIs (energy returned on invested), and energy payback times of electricity generating power plants. *Energy*, 52: 210–221.

Wiener, E.L. and Curry, R.E. (1980). Light deck automation: Promise and problems. *Ergonomics*, 995–1011.

Williaams, J.C. and Khanna, R. (2020). *It's Time to End Slash-and-Burn Capitalism.* Retrieved from Harvard Buisness Review: https://hbr.org/2020/10/its-time-to-end-slash-and-burn-capitalism.

Wilson, K. (2018). *An Overview of SAE International: Standards Activities Related to Charging of Hybrid/Electric Vehicles.* Ground Vehicle Standards. SAE International.

Wilson, K. (2020). *Four Ways Cities Can Repeal the Legacy of Robert Moses.* Retrieved from USAStreetBlog: https://usa.streetsblog.org/2020/10/19/four-ways-cities-can-repeal-the-legacy-of-robert-moses/.

Wilson, L. (2013). Shades of green: Electric cars' carbon emissions around the globe. *Shrink That Footprint*, 1–28.

Wolverton, T. (2016). *Wolverton: Elon Musk's Hyperloop Hype Ignores Practical Problems.* Retrieved from The Mercury News: https://www.mercurynews.com/2013/08/13/wolverton-elon-musks-hyperloop-hype-ignores-practical-problems/.

Xiong, H., Wang, L., Wang, D. and Druta, C. (2011). Piezoelectric energy harvesting from traffic induced deformation of pavements. *International Journal of Pavement Research and Technology*, 5(5): 333–337.

Younan, D., Petkus, A., Widaman, K., Wang, X., Casanova, R., Espeland, M., Gatz, M., Henderson, V.W., Manson, J.E., Rapp, S.R., Sachs, B.C., Serre, M.L., Gaussoin, S.A., Barnard, R., Saldana, S., Vizuete, W., Beavers, D.P., Salinas, J.A., Chui, H.C., Resnick, S.M., Shumaker, S.A., Chen, J. and Chui, H.C. (2020). Particulate matter and episodic memory decline mediated by early neuroanatomic biomarkers of Alzheimer's disease. *Brain*, 143(1): 289–302.

Zhang, W. and Guhathakurta, S. (2016). Parking spaces in the age of shared autonomous vehicles: How much parking will we need and where? *Sustainable Cities and Society*, 19: 34–45.

Zhang, Z., Hoek, G., Chang, L., Chan, T., Guo, C., Chuang, Y.C., Chan, J., Lin, C., Jiang, W.K., Guo, Y., Vermeulen, R., Yeoh, E., Tam, T., Lau, A.K.H., Griffiths, S. and Lao, X.Q. (2018). Particulate matter air pollution, physical activity and systemic inflammation in Taiwanese adults. *Int. J. Hyg. Environ. Health*, 221(1): 41–47.

Zielinski, S. (2006). New mobility: The next generation of sustainable urban transportation. *National Academy of Engineering*, 36(4).

# CHAPTER 2A

# The Invisible Footprint
# of Human Mobility Code

## PART 1

## Evolution of Our Mobility Footprint

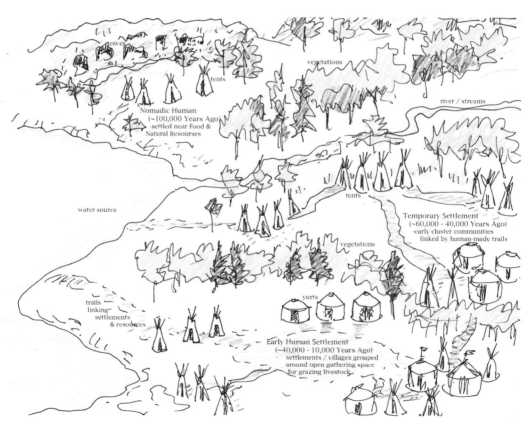

**Fig. 2.0:** An artistic illustration of human mobility and civilization.

> *"I am not interested in how people move, but what moves them."*
> —Pina Bausch (German artist and choreographer)

## Introduction—Why Species Move

Despite the modern image of mobility often linked to economic gains and benefits, mobility in different species started for a greater cause. Mobility started the process of evolution. Moving gave us the greatest tool of survival. Evolution and the gradual development of human mobility shaped our planet, increasing the opportunity to interact, and became one of the most influential driving forces behind developing a new culture. The way we move defines our identity. Mobility gives us a sense of freedom. A child takes their first step in a quest for learning and adapting to the environment. As an adult we move to satisfy our curiosity, finding the sources of our daily needs and discovering new things around us. As life wanes with aging, we keep moving to remain active until almost our last breath. Human life and experiences are deeply rooted in our mobility activities. Our memory develops, consciousness grows, and we build a foundation of knowledge and innovation based on things we pick up on along our way, including mutual interactions with other humans and nature. When we grow very old, we take a few slow steps every day to keep our memory alive. At the end, all that is left with us is memories from our lifelong movements and experiences.

And through our movements, we create our unique mobility blueprint – our mobility DNA, our unique mobility code.

In the modern day we forgot the true purpose of mobility and generally link it to economic activity, sidelining our original instinct for mobility. We are not machines, and our movements are not simply the result of a mechanical process (Kanga and Scott, 2010). Our movements are influenced by several factors that change from one place to another, one demography to another: our social, cultural, and personal or family relations. Despite these established facts, mobility planning in cities has been wrongfully combining individual and group or collective activities based on just a snapshot of a single day of travel data or pooled models, to predict what mobility facility or services we need every day. The current mobility problems in cities are deeply rooted in this wrongful interpretation of our mobility intensions, and in our flawed methods to replicate our urban utilitarian activities.

To rectify the root causes, we need to go back to basics – understanding our hidden human mobility instinct that creates our unique yet invisible mobility DNA.

And examining why we as a species move in the first place would be a good starting point.

> *"I have never felt salvation in nature. I love cities above all."*
> —Michelangelo

## History of Movement

Movement is the defining feature of all living things on earth. Without movement, there is no life on our planet. Both flora and fauna move, albeit differently, to survive (Laumond et al., 2015). Flora or plant life generally stays in the same place but still 'moves' through self-centred motions throughout their life. Fauna or animal life has developed the unique ability to move from one place to another place. Flora, fauna, and other forms of life are collectively now known as 'biota'. The first microorganic single cell life appeared on earth 3.5 billion years ago. But the first 'recognizable' life on earth was discovered in a quiet corner of an ancient community in Charnwood Forest in

Leicestershire, England, and subsequently found with the dramatic discovery at Mistaken Point cliffs on the east coast of Newfoundland, Canada. In the Ediacaran[1] era, recognizable life-like Charnia creatures (Leicester Literary and Philosophical Society, 2007) could barely move when they first appeared on the dark ocean floor 550–570 million years ago. The first meaningful 'moving' animal, the Dickinsonia[2] (Hall, 2018), sparked an evolutionary process around a half a billion years ago. About 542 million years ago when the Cambrian explosion[3] begun, animal life on our planet increased in diversity and size, with ever more complexity, generating an explosion of life (Attenborough, 2010). Moving fauna shaped our planetary ecosystem through mobility that played a central role in changing courses of migration on land and in air and marine systems. First mouths, eyes and legs appeared in the animal world (Duggan, n.d.) but they were still living under water. Looking for food sources, the first land vertebrates – likely the amphibians evolved from fish with brawny fins that inhabited shallow waters – appeared about 375 million years ago (Reuters, 2020). These are the closest ancestors of all reptiles, birds, and mammals alive today, including our current human species. Within 10 million years, the earliest vertebrate, Acanthostega,[4] was capable of 'walking'. The evolutionary modification for movement from fins into limbs is considered a unique adaptation of terrestrial vertebrates (Ashley-Ross et al., 2013). Then with a resounding sound and vibrations the mammal family, including dinosaurs, arrived around 256 million years ago and completely changed the earth's surface like no other evolution period. In terms of movement, our closest cousin, from mammals to lemurs to monkeys arrived between 85–25 million years ago. They used their hands, legs, and an upright walking capability to spark another important step in animal movement. Then Hominidae, such as the Gibbon, our closest bipedal cousin, appeared just before early homo sapiens evolved around 2.5 million years ago. Mobility had an enormous implication on the evolution of life on earth and laid the foundation for the development of modern animals. Each evolutionary step was gradually adding basic body elements to become a species – teeth, mouth, eyes, noses, skin, a backbone, and finally hands, legs, and a sensory system leading to an intelligent, balanced, and stable mobility.

Walking upright as a mode of mobility with a balanced symmetrical body system has become the most defining feature and a crucial initiating event of the evolution of the human species.

The first step to becoming a human species was to move from trees to the ground and gain the symmetrical body system to help us to walk in the upright mode of locomotion found only in human beings and our immediate ancestors. A recent scientific discovery indicates the first human-like creatures, "Sahelanthropus tchadensis" in West-Central Africa (Chad), about 7 million years ago started the upright body movement that is generally associated with walking on two legs, beginning an amazing journey and adding a key ingredient of survival as a species in diverse habitats, including forests and grasslands (Brunet et al., 2002). Elsewhere in East Africa near modern Kenya, "Orrorin tugenensis", locally known as the "original man in the Tugen region", around 6 million years ago continued the evolution of walking with a bipedalism technique (Alexander, 2004), a form of terrestrial locomotion where an organism moves by means of its two rear limbs or legs (Pickford and Senut, 2001). Any physical action by animals or even a modern humanoid robot in the real world requires self-centred movements or exploration movements, or a combination of both (Laumond et al., 2015). The discovery of Lucy, an early hominin, in a remote region of Ethiopia in 1974 provided direct evidence of how humans freed up their hands with an increased brain size

---

[1] Ediacaran Period is an interval of geological time ranging from 635 to 541 million years ago.
[2] Dickinsonia is an extinct genus of basal animal that lived during the late Ediacaran period in what is now Australia, China, India, Russia, and Ukraine.
[3] Cambrian explosion, the unparalleled emergence of organisms between 541 million and approximately 530 million years ago at the beginning of the Cambrian Period.
[4] Acanthostega is an extinct genus of stem-tetrapod, among the first vertebrate animals to have recognizable limbs.

that enabled them to develop efficient tools and collect high-energy foods, while nearly mirroring the walking mobility of a modern human roughly 3.2 million years ago (Johanson and Edey, 1990). Bipedality sets the human apart from apes or other mammals with an accompanied set of behaviour adaptations that become the key evolutionary innovation of humanity's earliest ancestors (Lovejoy, 1988). Humans exert a unique bipedal mobility skill with a two-peaked pattern of force on the ground when walking, and an essential single-peaked pattern when running (Alexander, 2004). This sets us apart from our closest Hominidae cousin.

Upright walking with two-peaked hopping ability enabled humans to move faster and further.

This hallmark of bipedal walking glimmers in the most innovative chapter of human history – shaping the planetary environment primarily though temporary and permanent settlements that became the towns and cities we live in today. Walking enabled us to negotiate with the environment on earth like the ancient humans (Fox, 2016). Through walking, ancient humans drew lines across the planet, expanding our understanding of the environment, and connecting us across the continents in search of human survival.

> *"Walking is a mode of making the world as well as being in it."*
> —Rebecca Solnit, author of *History of Walking*

## Development of Civilization through Human Mobility

Human mobility is one of the primary drivers of civilization and the most inducing factor of human settlement since the beginning of our species on this planet. Like other animals, the nature of human movement influenced the adoption of a human lifestyle in early settlements. Used since the early periods of our evolution, walking as a medium of mobility is as old as human civilization itself and considered our most ancient mode of transportation. Walking is the first thing a baby wants to do and the last habit an older person wants to give up. Every person starts and ends their journey as a pedestrian. The function of walking remains the same in the modern era despite technological advancement, however patterns and the nature of walking have changed over time.

Our desire to walk the shortest possible route using minimum energy remains as the basic principle of walking by humans and other mammal species. Early walking routes used the principle of the "desire line" as a foundation of early human settlements or town planning. The principle was gradually forgotten with the mechanization era during the first (beginning in roughly 1765), and second (beginning in roughly 1870) industrial revolutions, and completely overtaken by the automobile-oriented approach during the third industrial revolution (beginning in the 1970s). And yet the modern human still retains this ancient "desire line" trait by default without even thinking.

The concept was gradually recuperated in the modern planning era by progressive modern thinkers. The "'desire line" even romantically popularized by the New Orleans Tramway which Tennessee Williams made famous in 1947 with the name of his play "A Streetcar Named Desire". In his 1958 book *The Poetics of Space or Desire Path*, French philosopher Gaston Bachelard described the human tendency to carve a path between two points where humans subconsciously desire to walk (Copenhagezine, 2009). In 1967, British artist Richard Long popularized the "desire line" principle through his demonstration now famously known as "A line made by walking" (Long, 1967). Human scale planning and design was the bedrock of all the greatest civilizations on earth. Whether taking advantage of human desire lines or keeping the size of infrastructures on a human scale, the Inca civilization masterminded the philosophy of people-friendly city building. The "shortest path" concept or "desire lines" for pedestrian facilities was developed by the Inca civilization, roughly

800 years before modern civilization started to realize the importance of walking in the city building philosophy. The walkable community become a reality in the early stages of the environmental movement in the 1970s and the idea of desire lines of pedestrian and bicycle movement become a critical element of the modern sustainable mobility network (*The Guardian*, 2018) and human-scale planning (Colville-Andersen, 2013). Even in an automobile-oriented built environment, human desire lines are still vividly visible (Luckert, 2013). The internet of things (IoT) gave birth to the fourth industrial revolution and provided easy access to oceans of real-time and probed data. This new data started to reveal the original pattern of human movement that had persisted over millennia, sparking new ideas to address the need for infrastructure for the shorter walkable trips that represent over 60% of urban mobility.

Human mobility profoundly influenced the evolution of human settlement. Though it is not easy to reconstruct the relationship between mobility and human settlement, a few turning points are more evident (Rabinowitz, 2014), hence, their influence on mobility is assumed to be spread over 10 different eras of homo sapiens. Details of the evolution of mobility are summarized in the relevant chapters of this book.

### First era – Nomadic civilization before human settlement (100,000 years ago)

The first era of mobility influence was the longest period. Homo sapiens were still nomadic after their appearance around 300,000 years ago during the Lower Palaeolithic[5] Age, and with no permanent or temporary settlement found until around 100,000 years ago during the Middle Palaeolithic.[6] Walking distance shaped early human temporary stops or settlement. Humans started to explore for better sources of food and shelter within small regions in Africa. A finite energy budget and low body fat to maintain daily activity influenced ancient nomadic movement. Human tracks on grasslands were the only mobility facilities during this era.

### Second era – Temporary human settlement (100,000–50,000 BC)

The second stage of this evolution, temporary settlement would have seen primitive human 'houses' between roughly 100,000–50,000 years ago. 'Tents' of tree branches were built for temporary stops. Dirt pathways, roughly one to two metres wide, were created by organic human and sporadic animal movements. Dirt paths connected the temporary stops and were used by the different nomadic groups that started to shape temporary human form around 60,000 years ago.

### Third era – Early human settlement (50,000–10,000 BC)

The third stage of mobility evolution (50,000–10,000 years) has distinct human settlement signs. Human settlements for relatively longer periods started to appear including cave settlements with paintings (Brumm et al., 2014), round stone houses, bone huts, and tipi tents (Atlantic, 2015). A compact settlement area within a 20-minute walking distance started to appear as a form of early human temporary settlement size and an approximate half-day walking distance between the early 'villages'. The distance between the communities was 5–10 miles, roughly the daily limit of human walking distance, and would be covered comfortably in pursuit of trade and prototype commercial exchange activities (*Smart Cities World News*, 2019). Multiple pathways, sometimes framed by trees or vegetation, started to appear during the Upper Palaeolithic[7] era. Small reed boats and rafts

---

[5]  The Lower Paleolithic (or Lower Palaeolithic) is the earliest era that spans from the time around 3 million years ago when the first evidence for stone tool production to around 300,000 years ago.

[6]  The Middle Palaeolithic broadly spanned from 300,000 to 30,000 years ago.

[7]  The Upper Paleolithic (or Upper Palaeolithic), known as Late Stone Age, is the third and last subdivision of the Palaeolithic or Old Stone Age and spans between 50,000 and 12,000 years ago (the beginning of the Holocene).

in primitive form were believed to have been used for short distance passenger transport, fishing, and carrying small goods along waterways. Most of the marine mobility activity likely occurred in the southeast islands and Pacific region, and partly in Europe.

## Fourth era – Permanent settlement in the early agriculture era (10,000–7,000 BC)

The fourth period of mobility evolution started with early agricultural periods, roughly 10,000 years ago. As humans gradually settled from their nomadic lifestyle during the early agricultural periods, roughly 10,000 years ago, the use of animals for people and carrying goods, predominantly by horse, elephant, and donkey, provided a faster travel option and heavier carrying capacities. The most common method of mobility was marine mobility since most early settlements were close to water, either on the bank of a river or seashore. Mobility came in various forms: rafts, reed boats, canoes, small kayaks, and primitive boats made from local materials (Jean Vaucher, 2014). The relatively higher capacity of people and goods movement started to change the scale of human settlements when wider dirt roads and systematically built pathways were created over time. However, human settlement, most commonly in round houses, remained compact with daily short walking or boating distances between villages. Connections between neighbouring communities were predominantly narrow pathways. Narrow and shaded streets and alleyways that facilitated walking started to appear in human settlements such as Çatalhöyük, the first proto-city establishment in modern Turkey (Wilson, 2020). Early walkways were as narrow as the width of two people passing or a two-way for loaded animals (Alsayyad, 1991), roughly 1–3.5 m (6–10 feet). Walkways usually ended at prominent destinations or public places, creating a landmark view (known as the vista in the modern era) to identify places and give a sense of community. This mobility network combined with the concept of the vista were the most prominent forms of early human mobility networks.

## Fifth era – Early prototype cities (7,000–2,000 years ago)

The fifth period of evolution started with dramatic changes in organized urban settlements and a burst of mobility technology. The shape and form of cities remained prototype experiments during the early eras. A more organized and skilful city building practice emerged between 5000 BC–2000 BC. Mud brick structures, some even multistorey houses started to appear. A higher density of people demanded a higher mobility capacity. Animals were the common mobility mode on land in the early periods of this era. Marine mobility flourished as the major mobility technology between early human settlements. The people of the Polynesian region became skilled builders of marine mobility, mainly rafts, canoes, and reed boats (SAHO, 2011). The Egyptian reed boat was prominent among other forms of marine mobility (Peña, 2012) that could carry 20 people and over one ton of goods by the same carrier. But one mobility invention changed our cities forever. The invention of the wheel, as a form of mass scale transportation, changed the scale and form of early human settlements once again. Narrow alleyways and narrow streets became the focus of organized yet organic town planning in the early agriculture periods when early empires started to shape human civilization around 7,000–10,000 years ago. Historians are divided on where the wheel was invented in the first place, however, all evidence indicates the Middle East, mainly Mesopotamia, as the birthplace of the earliest form of wheel that gave birth to the Bronze Age. Wheeled transport needed relatively wider urban streets. A network of cobble stone, or flat gravel surface streets roughly 3–6 m (10–20 feet) wide (University of Washington, 2018) was the most visible urban mobility infrastructure (Ellis, 2015) dating back to roughly 5,000 years ago. A linear and organic grid of streets shaped the urban form, especially in areas where elite rulers resided, whereas streets in residential areas for the general people remained on a human scale. A unique example of this era is the Indus Valley Civilization, known as Mohenjo Daro and Harappa and other ancient civilizations in Giza, Babylon, Mexico, and Greece. A well-planned street grid (McIntosh,

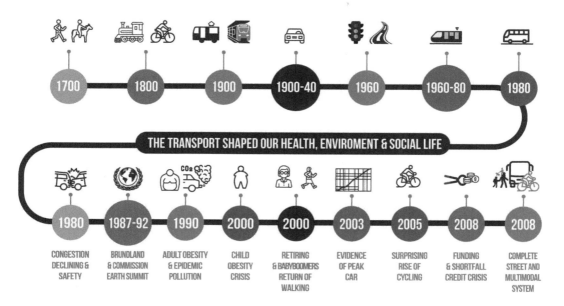

**Fig. 2A.1:** History of human mobility – early era.

2008) and an elaborate drainage system indicates that the occupants of the ancient Indus civilization city of Mohenjo Daro were highly skilled urban mobility network planners with a reverence for the control of water (Roach, 2011). Around 3500 BC, the expansion of agricultural systems pushed mobility innovation into a new era – with early forms of wheel mobility systems (Gambino, 2009) in Mesopotamia, eastern Europe and later the Harappa civilization around 2600 BC (Kenoyer, 2004). Innovation led to a new urban mobility system. A combination of wider main streets and narrow alleyways dividing city blocks emerged as the new network of urban mobility. This new mobility was the foundation of the first common template of town planning, formalized across ancient Europe and Asia by Greek pioneer planner Hippodamus and later Miletus who called urban areas a 'Polis', around 500 BC (Burns, 2005). Hundreds of new 'polis's spread through southern Europe during this golden age of ancient civilizations. Today, the large and organized city is often referred to as a 'Metropolis', a modern interpretation of the ancient town.

## *Sixth era – Ancient empire cities – Roman, Greek, China, India (AD 2,000–AD 500)*

The sixth stage of mobility evolution is seen in ancient empire cities such as Roman, Greek, and Chinese cities that are well organized and established permanent human settlement in around 2,000 BC–AD 500. Most of those cities still exist today, albeit in a different form. A mobility system and a citywide network were also established through systematic knowledge of mobility, and in some cases, data was consciously used to design the system. The introduction of the metal ring and axle system increased the speed of wheel-based vehicles such as human or horse-pulled chariots and paved the way for Roman civilization's wider main street system and intercity highways around 600BC–300 BC that connected cities for military movement and helped build a vast empire around the Mediterranean Sea. Mass mobility in water using the galley,[8] a large warship, around 1,500 BC and the carriageway on land around 1,600 BC appeared in the large cities of major empires (The Altantic, 2015). Mass mobility led to a hierarchy of street systems and organized route systems including waterways. Smaller canals for local connections were built and connected major rivers and intercity routes already established as major seaways. On land, major thoroughfares widened the street width to up to 12.2 m to accommodate two-way carts or chariots. Carts or chariots were generally used on secondary streets measuring 6 m, and loaded animals dominated on tertiary streets with a 4.5 m width. Narrower pedestrian streets, typically 3 m or less, generally connected to residential neighbourhoods (See Table 2A.1). Secondary connectors or residential streets, however, remained at a human scale before the arrival of the horse drawn carriage and then the automobile during the modern era's second and third industrial periods. Mapping emerged as a new visualization tool of mobility planning which also assisted in the maintenance and operation of an organized mobility management system during this era. Travel demand measures were introduced in Roman cities to restrict wheeled carts during peak hours. Pedestrian-only areas were common during major daily trade events in some areas and sometimes in entire central areas during major festivals or local events.

## *Seventh era – Dark mediaeval era and brilliant innovation and creative design in Old Asia and Middle East Asia (AD 500–AD 1400)*

The seventh stage of the evolution of mobility saw many creative mobility networks develop in the Middle East and east Asian cities. After the fall of Roman emperor Romulus Augustulus, around AD 500, western civilization entered a dark era. Over 1,000 years of innovation and creativity vanished from western cities while a golden era of city building began in old Asian cities and in parts of north Africa. The Arabian Peninsula, the far east, and south and southeast Asia became the centres of innovation and human knowledge. Everything from medicine to physics, to chemistry to mathematics, to any branch of science, to philosophy and cultural knowledge peaked during the early mediaeval era across the middle east and north Africa. Mobility knowledge was no exception. One civilization stands out in this era – the Spanish Moor civilization. Southern Spain's Moor city builders first came up with the idea of separating wheeled traffic using flat cobble stone roads and pedestrians on a raised sidewalk. Coverage for the drainage of sewage and the open drainage system for stormwater (BHS, 2009) was first developed systematically to control water flow, avoid health hazards, and collect reusable water for infrastructure maintenance. On the contrary, European cities were mixing sewage and drinking water, where filth used to run through the streets causing frequent outbreaks of cholera until the 19th century (Fry, 2016). The invention of the courtyard

---

[8] Galleys were the warships used by the early Mediterranean naval powers, including the Greeks, Illyrians, Phoenicians, and Romans.

**Table 2A.1:** Evolution of mobility network system in cities.

| General Classification -Common Names | Roman and Greek Cities (Marshall, 2005) | | | Asian-Arabic-Islamic Cities (Alsayyad, 1991) | | | North American Cities (Post Second World War II) (ITE, 2008) | | |
|---|---|---|---|---|---|---|---|---|---|
| | Name of Street Classification | Street Width (m) | Function | Name of Street Classification | Street Width (m) | Function | Name of Street Classification | Street Width (m) and Lanes | Function |
| Main Streets | Major Throughfares | 12 | Two-way wheel cart or chariots. | First Order Connector | 3.25–3.5 | Two-way loaded animal, crosses city centre and connect to city gates. | Major Arterial or Multiway Boulevard | 4 to 6 lanes (36–45 m) | Mainly cars, trucks, parking, mixed/dedicated lane for bus and bicycle, sidewalk for pedestrian. |
| Secondary Streets | Secondary Streets | 6 | One-way wheel cart or chariots. | Second Order Connector | 2.5–3 | One-way goods carrying animal. | Minor Arterial or Avenue | 2 to 4 lanes (27–36 m) | Mainly cars, trucks, parking, mixed lane for bus, bicycle lanes, sidewalk for pedestrian. |
| Tertiary Streets | Tertiary Streets | 5 | Load or passenger carrying animals. | Third Order Connector | 1–2 | Shared street between pedestrian, wheel cart or goods/passenger carrying animals. | Collector or Street | 2/3 lanes (22–27 m) | Mainly cars, trucks, parking lane, mixed lane for bus and bicycle, sidewalk for pedestrian. |
| Local Streets | Narrow Pedestrian Alleyways | < 3 | Pedestrian only. | Cul-de-sac | 0.5–1 | Pedestrian only, connection between courtyards and location open space. | Local | 2 lanes (22–27 m) | Local vehicle uses, shared lane for bicycle and sidewalk for pedestrian. |
| Laneways | | | | | | | Alley or Rare Lane | 1 lane | Local access or deliveries only. |

**Notes:** This is an author's collection from citied sources and other data/measurements from various cities around the world.

system, public square for trade exchange, and options for both local and general mobility users were other shining achievements from the Arabian Peninsula. Very narrow pathways called 'sikkak' were used to connect courtyards to neighbouring homes and local destinations. The systematic use of shared streets or 'mushtaraks' was introduced for multiple modes connecting local neighbourhoods to public squares and key trading, administration, or public centres. Combined with main streets and connecting narrow roads, alleyways, and pathways, these would have been the most walkable cities of the mediaeval periods. While Egyptians started planting trees on main corridors and Chinese cities planted trees during the Tang dynasty (MacDonagh, 2013), using trees to provide shade to mobility facility users became common in the Arabian world during this era. Asian cities developed their own city building practices and many features imitated the philosophy of the Inca's mobility systems (see next section). Human-scale shared urban mobility was adopted in Asian cities ensuing from the approach of ancient middle eastern and European cities. Instead of long straight streets and a perfect grid, a modified offset grid and offset network emerged as the common theme for building a community focused street network in early Asian cities. The concept combined two basic features: (1) no direct or cut through paths within the neighbourhood, mimicking mediaeval Europe and preventing traffic infiltration into residential areas, and (2) main streets were kept as vibrant walkable places with commercial activities leading to central public places, roughly following the Greek design philosophy. Sadly, some of these ancient urban mobility inventions remain unknown to modern traffic engineers.

## *Eighth era –An empire of sustainable mobility (~ 1200–1600 AC)*

The eighth stage of mobility's innovation came from an isolated, quiet corner of South America. This era features one of the most innovative concepts and creative designs ever developed for an entire empire. The brilliant idea to develop a system empire-wide, using only sustainable mobility was the greatest gift to mankind's quest for the low-carbon mobility that modern planners are struggling to achieve in today's climate change era. The rejection of wider streets, straight, boring alignment and the sprawling Roman city approach came from a different continent – the ancient Inca civilization in South America. Their complex network of a hierarchical pathway system, including a well-planned drainage system in the middle of the pathways, was the most impressive example of the first and still the largest active transportation network in human history. The Inca era network of wider urban pathways and narrow mountainous connectors was built over roughly 40,000 km of hierarchical networks, but without an iron and wheel transportation system (O'Brien, 2015). The Inca empire expanded over the Andes mountains with main routes as arterials, with many supporting secondary routes and smaller trails for walking and running. Instead of in straight alignment, their paths or roads tended to follow natural contours, in harmony with nature. The network was frequently connected by bridges, causeways, stairways, and an impressive series of small stations (chaskiwasi) and sometimes larger, more luxurious complexes (tambos) about every 20 km to refresh travellers and spend the night (Cartwright, 2014). Any information or goods were exchanged by runners (chaski) using the main artery, passing on to the next runner at key milestones/resting points. On secondary routes, the shortcut trails information and goods could be delivered within two days, spreading out over roughly 500 kilometres, faster than today's internet system in remote areas. This brilliant innovation sparked a new mobility concept – the context-based approach and the urban street hierarchy system, which gave birth to the key foundation of the livable city building concept that is currently spreading via a new mobility renaissance and taking us toward sustainable and resilient cities.

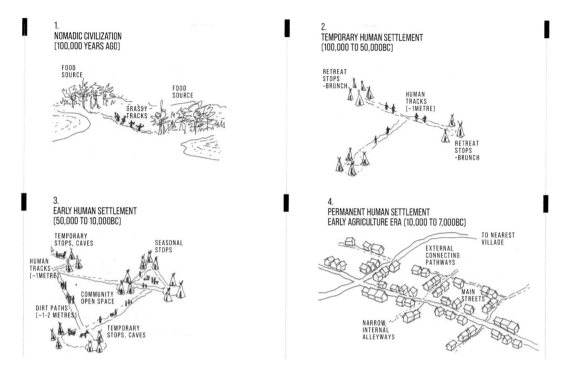

**Fig. 2A.2:** History of human mobility – the middle age era.

## *Ninth era – Third industrial era – The invasion of ideology in city building (20th century)*

Thousands of years of human scale mobility planning and street design were abruptly departed from towards the downward of the unsustainable path and introduced urban sprawl philosophy at the beginning of second industrial revolution. This dramatically turned mobility system toward automobile centric city planning. Historical evidence of urban street design suggests our current wider-than-needed main streets were designed to accommodate horse carriages during the 1920s (Friedman, 2010). Surprisingly, these standards are still in use today in North America despite the disappearance of the horse carriage long ago as a mode of mobility.

Ideology replaced the organic human settlement approach after World War II. The third industrial revolution in the 1960s introduced new urban sprawl ideas, such as strict access by street hierarchy, curvilinear streets, and dead-end networks including the concept of the cul-de-sac. The new network system disconnected local neighbourhood streets from main streets, making walking connections extremely difficult while favouring automobile usage. At the same time main street corridors and intersections were widened to accommodate more vehicles. And a bizarre form of street network with a curvilinear and cul-de-sac pattern with gigantic blocks was introduced with no scientific basis or reasonable grounding in city building. The lack of connectivity and walking facilities encouraged 'induced' vehicle demand, and increased levels of intense congestion and further road widening. Commonly known as "urban renewal", which fuelled suburbanization after the end of World War II, this new vicious cycle of infinite demand for automobile usage planted the seed of a declining quality of life (Eleanor and Lebeaux, 1967) and ultimate degradation of the city's livable conditions (Ammon, 2016). The best-known example is the decline of the City of Detroit during the financial meltdown of 2008. While this network configuration of suburbs and exurbs dominates in the United States, Canada, Australia, and the UK, it was not favoured by European, South American, Asian, especially Chinese cities until the 1990s.

The introduction of globalization in the 1990s and subsequent expansion to producing cheaper products in poorer countries (Jackson, Prosperity without Growth: Foundations for the Economy of Tomorrow, 2009) accelerated the pace of urban renewal. Overengineered wider roads and highways and the big-box retail model further fuelled automobile usage to an extreme level. A sea of parking lots to support big-box establishments along with continuous road widening and highway expansion gradually deteriorated the quality of life in our cities. Roughly half of the space in cities is now covered with street and car parking (KIT, 2015). Parking alone, on and off-street, consumes 15–30% of city space in New York, Paris, Vienna, Boston, and Hong Kong (WSP et al., 2019). More than 40% of the impervious surfaces of wider roads, parking, and automobile infrastructures created the ground work for transportation becoming the largest cause of greenhouse gas (GHG) emissions (EPA, 2017), exceeding any other sector of the economy in the post financial meltdown era (IPCC, 2007). Without aggressive and sustained mitigation policies being implemented, transport emissions could increase at a faster rate than emissions from all other energy end-use sectors by 2050 (Sims et al., 2007). These dire consequences have pushed our backs against the wall. A systematic and paradigm shift has become imminent to address the root cause of our continued highly inefficient and wasteful city building. At the end of the 20th century, our massive system built around automobiles began to take a back seat to the global environmental, social, and cultural crisis. Starting with a revolt from prominent builders, dramatic changes in technology, and a severe financial strain, opposition grew against maintaining the current car-oriented system, in the first decade of the 21st century.

### *Tenth era – Mobility renaissance with revival of sustainable city building (21st century)*

The new millennium started with deep inequality and division along mobility lines. Instead of sustainable development and tackling climate change, the frontline has changed from ideological city building to a people-oriented approach. This history is long. Hence, the next section and evolution of each type of mobility development in this book are dedicated to the root causes of new city building's struggle. A return to short blocks, mixed-use, and building sustainable mobility, including the revival of transit, cycling, walking, and many more progressive ideas, are a few of the cornerstones of the new people-centred city building philosophy. These ideas embrace one of the first city building concepts based around the artistic aesthetics of a city rather than its movements (Sitte, 1889). As first an urban planning theory resource, this book argues the most critical element of city building is not the architectural shape or form of each building, but the inherent creative quality of the whole urban space. The whole is much more than the sum of its parts. Numerous influences of this early theory are still visible today. One of the most famous challenges was Barcelona's "modern super block" – the city blocks and streets of Barcelona as conceived by Ildefonso Cerdá. Although originally influenced by Le Corbusier and modernist influences, the city blocks now include wide open spaces that continue across the street to adjacent blocks. This broke the block down to a human scale. But transforming the whole 'modernist' ideological landscape has emerged as a Mount Everest-like task in the hands of 21st-century planners who inherited the 20th-century landscape without knowing its origin and dark history. As seen in the next sections, the last century's ideological mindset percolates in every layer of 21st-century society, which makes it extremely difficult to identify, let alone address head-on.

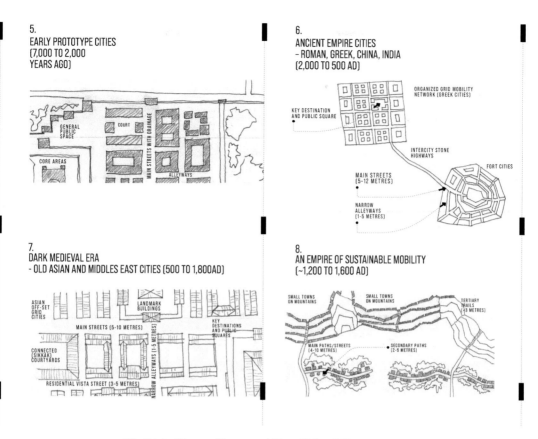

**Fig. 2A.3:** History of human mobility – 20th and 21st century.

# CHAPTER 2A

# The Invisible Footprint of Human Mobility Code

## PART 2

## Ideology of Vehicle Mobility and its Discontents

*"Just as in older periods the automobile is consumed as much for its libidinal value and symbolic overtone as for its practical use value, so today... the computer and internet and their ramifications are already well integrated into utopian political fancies."*

—Fredric Jameson

### Mobility at the Crossroads of Ideology and City Building

In search of the root cause that forced an abrupt departure from sustainable city building and human scale mobility systems, a deeper look will take us to a different origin of the ideology that shaped city building during the industrial periods. Development of civilization and human identity are often linked to three basic foundations: art, culture, and food – three basic human experiences that shaped urban life and experiences across human history. Invisible links between these basic elements of human experience and people's mobility are underestimated and most often ignored. Graffiti for example, one of the purest forms of human art, thrives and survives on the walls of urban streets (Gleaton, 2012) or places (Ross, 2018). The greatest place to display human culture is on our urban streets and public places (Ilan, 2015). Food shaped our cities and consuming food along public streets remains the most visible sign of a vibrant city, particularly in Asia and Africa (Steel, 2013). But these basic human living experiences are often overshadowed by a narrow vision of ideology. The recently developed 'ideological' city building vision was shaped by the history of art and culture toward the beginning of the second and third industrial revolutions.

Development of ideological city building started earlier however, before the pre-industrial era.

> *"Car-dependent suburban sprawl is the most publicly expensive and publicly subsidized form of human habitation per capita in human history."*
> —Brent Toderian

## Early marriage of ideology and city building

Over the progress of human civilization, the cultural perception and line of thought process of western and eastern parts of Eurasia (all of Europe and Asia) and North America were fundamentally different. While eastern intellectuals were inclined toward a spiritual and organic thought process, the western thinkers, particularly in Greek and Roman eras, focused on the linear approach. Europe however gradually blended eastern philosophy into its western approach over the last millennium. The number zero is a perfect example and a product of eastern philosophy, frequently opposed by western thinkers and repeatedly defeated by those who opposed the idea of zero (Seife, 2000). The philosophical clash continues today, especially when zero is used for mobility concepts. When "Vision Zero" (Government Offices of Sweden, 2019) was introduced by Sweden in 1997, it moved the blame on drivers or other mobility systems users to the core responsibility for collisions on the overall system design. By addressing vision zero infrastructure design, vehicle technology, and enforcement, it confused the traffic engineering community. They were baffled. Some even opposed the idea of having zero fatalities or serious injuries in city streets (Marohn, 2019). The concepts of a zero emission vehicle (Project Syndicate, 2019) and a zero carbon economy (Gutstein, 2019) are also facing monumental political and social resistance despite being the path to a carbon negative country, as demonstrated by another eastern culture success – Bhutan (GVI, 2019). History will repeat itself. Ideological resistance to these three 'zero' concepts will be defeated in the long run.

All mobility systems are built around an ideal, and all facilities reflect an ideal human body, size, and shape. The idealization of body image and size is another philosophical thought process which became an ideological norm in ancient western empires. Ancient Greek sculptures of humans reflected the ideal body shape, encouraging the change of the individual toward a "classical, ideal body" figure (Pountney, 2014). In the Dark Ages of mediaeval Europe, the fantasy of the "Greek body ideal" was taken in a completely different direction. In the middle of the 17th century, a German art historian and archaeologist Johann Joachim Winckelmann (Winckelmann, 1764) wrote a book on the history of ancient art and promoted the fantasy of a "pure, marble-white antiquity" – a pure falsehood that the ideal body must be made of white marble, such as the famed Apollo of the Belvedere was the epitome of beauty, despite many hints that the sculpture was not white and often painted in different colours (Bond, 2017). Historians often point to Winckelmann's popular book ultimately producing a grave healthcare concept known as Nazi eugenics – a "national body" created by eliminating biologically threatening genes from the population (Bengtsson, 2018). The concept rejects any natural variation in people's body size and performance. Besides cultural stereotypes, the impact of this ideology unintentionally percolated into every aspect of modern human life, including the designing of mobility systems, and making basic assumptions about people, their body size, and performance. When designing automobile or rail or transit systems, the ideal human size, average walking speed, and many other parameters were based on the "standard reference person", defined as "being between 20–30 years of age, weighing 70 kg, is 170 cm in height, and lives in a climate with an average temperature of 10°C–20°C. He is a 'Caucasian' and is a Western European or North American in habitat and custom" (International Commission on Radiological Protection, 1975). This new "national body" swept through every product, service, and facility design in the modern era.

The deeply discriminatory ideology around the "ideal human" percolated into mobility planning and engineering through a linear and rigid system design and planning approach in the modern era, making variation of body size, shape, and form nearly nonexistent in the mobility system. Students in engineering will graduate without ever knowing the impact of facilities on women, children, seniors, or people with different conditions. The presence of the human mind, its desires, and its unconscious level remain unknown to modern practitioners. For instance, when designing crosswalk speeds for pedestrians, traffic engineers typically use 1.2 m/second as the 'acceptable' parameter to time the signal for automobiles. This assumption generally excludes one-third of senior pedestrians and 90% of pedestrians using an assistive device such as a walker or cane (Asher et al., 2012). Women walk slower due to their higher level of sense for safety and habit of observing details and enjoying the environment while they are walking. Teenagers and senior citizens walk slower, and people in groups follow the group's slowest member (Gahl, 1968). Despite the suggestion of the variation of crosswalk speeds, most traffic signal walking speeds were not reduced (Laplante and Kaiser, 2004) to include senior citizens, women, children, groups, and persons with physical limitations. Similarly, accessing transit stations within an 'acceptable' walking distance[9] often mistakenly uses the 'average' walking capability of a healthy Caucasian male person, and distances are treated as 'Euclidean' distances.[10] For instance, Ontario's provincial policy previously used 500 m (Ontario, 2006) as the acceptable walking distance to transit which typically excludes one-fourth of demography, particularly senior citizens (TCRP, 2003). The policy standard was later increased to 800 m (Ontario, 2020) to satisfy real estate industry demand that included larger areas for high-density development, but excluded nearly half of demography (El-Geneidy et al., 2014) from accessing rapid transit service locations. Worst of all, transit planners repeatedly use 'linear' or "as the crow flies" measurements, despite much evidence suggesting actual "walking shed" or distances are typically longer, excluding more people from transit access (Walker, 2011). Increasing walking distances to transit generally aimed to increase transit coverage but the unintentional consequence excluded more people and led to lower mobility access and larger service gaps, particularly in suburban locations where walking distances and poor quality of facility make walking difficult. Safety assumptions follow a similar ideological mindset. Crash test dummies are generally modelled from the adult healthy male body which has been linked to higher injury rates in collisions among women (Holder, 2019). Despite a "reference women" and "reference child" being developed (Ellis, 1990) three decades ago, astonishingly the 'standard' human as a healthy Caucasian male assumption is still being used for transit, and street and traffic design, despite recent complete streets, transit planning, and other urban mobility practices pointing out its obvious connection to systematic discrimination.

With the combination of a free-market ideology and the rise of consumer culture, everything about the foundation of society's structure changed during the tail end of the first industrial revolution.

The colonial era utilitarian approach remains the epicenter of the modern mobility system for the sprawling city. A few key defining features of the widespread sprawling urban city are long, wide, and linear streets, and endless surface parking lots or structures from the post-WWII era. Making streets long and linear is deeply rooted in the philosophical ideology of Cartesianism 'linear' thinking that typically rejects other forms of street networks and design approaches. The linear grid network was the result of Pythagoras, who reportedly killed his own student Hippasus for discovering the existence of irrational numbers (Huffman, 1993). Irrational numbers provide an indication of the existence of non-linear forms and the possibility of 'infinity'. The infinity idea was

---

[9] Walking distances are typically measured or ascribed as influence buffers or service areas around transit facilities.

[10] The Euclidean distance between two points in Euclidean space is the length of a line segment between the two points.

born in eastern philosophy, with the expression of a qualitative infinity connected either directly to the natural world (Taoism) or to the spiritual foundation of the phenomenal world of change (Hinduism and Buddhism). Rejection of variations in human forms and the adoption of a strictly 'linear' street design approach in mobility planning or design is rooted in Pythagorean philosophy. Driven by professional dogma, and frequently departing from their own standards, modern old-school traffic engineers 'believed' that wide, straight streets were safer (Schlossberg and Amos, 2015), discarding their neighbourhood context and creating streets that encourage speeding and increase the risk of serious traffic injuries. The practice of rigid 'standards' to tackle liability issues distracted many old-school traffic engineers from addressing desperately needed safety needs of 'invisible' mobility users (Marohn, 2021). Despite engineering's claim that "streets are designed as per standards", most streets, intersections, and mobility facilities are frequently found with severe discrepancies with the standards which did not even exist until the end of the 20th century. Safety manuals didn't exist until 2010. Urban street designs were crafted by NACTO in 2013 yet remain 'unacceptable' in the 'traditional' standard community. Typical mobility practices or guidelines for station design, transit design, mass mobility planning, and goods movement don't even exist in many cities today since traditional traffic engineering does not count these places or issues as important elements of the mobility network.

> *"Lack of ornamentation is a sign of spiritual strength."*
> —Adolf Loos

## Era of rigid doctrine – Ornament as crime

The revival of Winckelmann's ideology took a dramatic turn during the impressionist art era of the late 18th century. And city building, including mobility systems, was the first victim.

While Europe was going through an art and cultural renaissance in the middle 18th century, several artists inserted Winckelmann's ideology into art, later shaping the look and form of community. James Abbott McNeill Whistler, an American born artist, started to paint his houses in white colour. Whistler's White House (MacDonald et al., 2008) was a symbolic creation which was later wrongly promoted as a "pure and elite" neighbourhood (Marks, 2015), a crossroads of community divide between the rich and poor. He started to call his house 'Whitehouse', a name which would later cross the Atlantic and brand the presidential residence with the same sense of "pure, marble-white antiquity". Today, the white colour painted "gated community" (Blakely and Snyder, 1997) still mimics his white house appearance while privatizing public space with extremely wide local streets. These planning practices still exist today despite their well-known connection to urban sprawl, racial segregation, isolation, and depressed neighbourhoods (Berkoz and Tepe, 2013). The gated community spread across the world in a similar form. In these neighbourhoods homeowners typically own multiple private cars (Berkoz and Tepe, 2008), an extreme form of vehicle usage in suburban cities.

An ideological vision of city building, by removing the human scale, changed the course of modern city building, particularly at the dawn of fascism and after WWII. And with this ideological desire the multimodal nature of modern urban mobility gradually disappeared in the new 'rationalized' and 'functional' philosophy of the city building world. At the dawn of industrialization, colonizing European nations needed a powerful tool in support of colonial expansion. Utilitarianism was born out of this need. Utilitarianism is generally held to be the view that the morally right action is the action that produces the maximum good. And morally appropriate behaviour will not harm others, but instead will increase 'happiness' or 'utility.' (Driver, 2014). Classical utilitarianism founder Jeremy Bentham (along with John Stuart Mill, and the modern era's Peter Singer) expanded and spread the utilitarianism principles toward building a "functional society". The heart of this functionalism was measured and centred around the ideology of the manufactured "white European male" view (Gerber, 1999) that remains the dominant city building perspective, particularly toward mobility system planning. An Austrian, Adolf Loss, pushed the boundary to its extreme edge, conceptualizing the aesthetic-less and lack of sensuality by removing ornamentation, i.e., diversity and beauty in building structures (Loos, 1910). These principles are embedded beneath every layer of modern society – from legal systems to moral foundations, to capitalism to mass consumerism, to the current era of high-tech culture to the building of mega mobility infrastructures that remove the presence of the human being from every stage of planning and design. The barren, linear, and ugly mega urban streets in our current era are the legacy of Loos's idea implanted into old-school traffic engineering practice.

> *"A roaring motor car which seems to run on machine-gun fire, is more beautiful than the Victory of Samothrace."*
>
> —F.T. Marinetti

### Era of rigid doctrine – Fusing machine and human

Around the time of Adolf Loss, one of the most dominant yet dark and disturbing era was born. One that would define, and which gave birth to the ideological foundation of the vehicle-oriented culture we live in today. Hallmarks of vehicle culture today were born from the ideological movement of the first decade of the 20th century and are now embedded in our planning practice and design foundations of mobility system facility. Obsession with speed is now synonymous with vehicle usage. Making vehicles a part of life, a part of our body advanced the vehicle-oriented form in the 21st century. Today we can't even think about making any trips in the suburbs without using a car, no matter how insanely short a distance the trip. Destroying anything from the past that is standing in the way of mega streets or highway expansion has become the defining professional principle of 'modernist' transportation planning and traffic design. A new obsession with technology, to bypass more practical solutions and treat it as the silver lining solution, is another culture that is now sweeping through the high-tech mysticism surrounding the autonomous vehicle. Ignoring the present problems while looking at delusional future magic solutions has become the dominant citywide mobility planning practice. Today we take these hallmark features of transportation planning and design for granted. However, these defining characteristics have a dark and most troubling past, during the rise of fascism in Europe and at the beginning of the 20th century (Eveleth, 2019).

Originating from fusing art and technology together to reconstruct the future, a futurist manifesto started the most problematic form of art movement that ultimately inspired and aligned with the most notorious and inhuman fascist leader of the 20th century. A strange breed in the avant-garde movement was fascinated with the destructive form of technology and war. Calling himself a 'futurist', poet and artist, Marinetti published *The Futurist Manifesto* (Marinetti, 1909) which ultimately aligned with the Italian fascist culture of Mussolini. A similar idea later spread in Russia. During a car collision, Marinetti felt thrilled instead of traumatized and described it as a "red-hot iron of joy". He described the incident as melding his body and car into a fused entity. He recommended speed, violence, and destruction as a spirit of new technology to reshape human life, and to pave the way to a joyous new noble world (Gerspacher, 2020). He suggests the contempt of women, destroying libraries, museums, and universities, and getting rid of moralism, feminism and anything that created a more equitable society. Winckelmann's ideal body concept again surprisingly resurfaced through the "three women" painting fetishizing machine-like solidity and precision reminiscent of technology (Leger). Even futurists vehemently opposed Winckelmann's neoclassical or neoconservatism ideology. The ideal body as a standard design parameter is one of the basic foundations of all traffic engineering concepts. Everything that's old should be destroyed to pave the way to the ideological and glorified future with a clean slate in the hands of noble man (McKever, 2008). The utopian futurist city, the "New City", emerged as a city building concept. Other forms of the utopian ideological city concept such as Ebenezer Howard's "Garden City" or "the city beautiful" evolved around the movement of machines rather that a social network. The movement also suggested that the ride euphoria of the crowd would take control of mass populations. Euphoric screaming is still a part of traffic complaints today, most of the time overshadowing public meetings.

At the end of WWII, they all perished. But it was too late. Like Winckelmann's neoclassical ideology, futurist's hysteria entered city building through the hands of a few 'modern' town planners, architects, and designers. When we read the militaristic and futuristic history of mega freeways, streets, and gigantic parking lots, we still find vestiges of futurist manifesto in the current daily practices of our vehicle-oriented culture.

Hidden in the today's layers of traditional car-oriented measures we can still find traces of the hallucinations of the high-speed 'futurist' culture. And behind the rhetoric of high-tech mobility's unicorn solutions, Marinetti's shadows are today still clearly visible.

> *"The civilization of the automobile is replacing that of the railroad."*
> —Le Corbusier, the definite principles, and rules of
> conduct for "The Radiant City" doctrine.

### Era of rigid doctrine – Futurist mega mobility

Although current 'modern' city building ideology distances itself from the last two doctrines, it basically embraces a similar ideological mindset and blends those ideas into all aspects and elements of modern mobility systems.

It did not take too long to spread this new concept of utility-based and utopian futurist urban mobility design and planning into city building. One self-trained architect turned Winckelmann's idea into a city building practice that changed the lives of all city residents forever. His name is Charles-Édouard Jeanneret, commonly known as Le Corbusier, a Swiss-French architect, designer, painter, urban planner, writer, and one of the pioneers, who is now called the godfather of "modern architecture". His new town planning is based on four strict and rigid principles: living, working, recreating (in free hours), and circulating. He gave birth to prefabricated housing and 'brutalist' bare bone concrete buildings in square shapes that were practical and mass-produced for working class families, providing a piece of "sky and green" in a "tower in the park". Instead of mixed-use, Le Corbusier proposed the toxic separation of the functions of land-uses (districts for work, entertainment, and recreation) by wide avenues and highways in the cities that brought ultimate dehumanization of city life. Instead of 'agora' or key destinations, his ideas fill the city centre with tall glass towers for business where workers spend their daytime inside the building but it's a no-go place in the evening. Le Corbusier's neighbourhood soon deteriorated rapidly into the "urban ghetto", filled by immigrants, the unfit and homeless shelters, gradually becoming a crime-ridden, socially troubled, and polluted place, while moving the middle-class out with the dream of a single, detached suburban home. Winckelmann's dark, race-separated ideology through "The Athens Charter" (Eric, 2000), an urban planning document based on his Radiant City – ideas and urban studies undertaken by the Congrès International d'Architecture Moderne (CIAM) in 1933 – finally penetrated into every layer of city planning which had taken for granted the ideology of antiquity that continued into the 21st century. Behind Le Corbusier's glorious and glittery world of glamorous life, his ideas inspired the darkest period of urban renewal, overtaking thousands of years of people-centric practice with his top-down, autocratic, fascism-inspired, and siloed approach (Flint, 2014). These ideas ultimately aligned with fascism, and Benito Mussolini's, who met Le Corbusier in 1934 (Brott, 2013). He later aligned himself with Pierre Winter, a doctor who became a leader of the Revolutionary Fascist Party, to publish his urban planning journals *Plans* and *Prelude* (Nechvatal, 2015). Straight, square, repeatedly boring buildings with endless wide streets resembled the three governance philosophies of the time: Autocratic, Fascism, and Bourgeoisie communism. All three regimes would later adopt a similar city building approach when it came to automobile-oriented land development. Le Corbusier's "functional city" turned into the "most dysfunctional" neighbourhood. The 1951 Pruitt–Igoe housing scheme in St Louis, Missouri was built using Le Corbusier ideas and CIAM principles. The neighbourhood then rapidly declined from 10,000 to a leftover population of only 600 and was finally demolished with dynamite on 15 July 1972 at 3.32 p.m., typically declared as the death of 'Modern' architecture (Charles, 1978). Postmodernism rose following this monumental moment, with the idea from Cartesianism of decentralization through multiculturism, derived ideas or culture, and the opening-up of individual autonomy (Jameson, 1991). From this fragmented and isolated postmodernism cultural society, the car would emerge as a colossal symbol of individual autonomy.

Le Corbusier's baleful influence, however, is ever stronger today, in many cases in aggravating urban sprawl. Every city that struggled to provide affordable housing after war devastated urbanization fell into his dark vision of city building. After World War II, several movements helped to fuel ideological city building, keeping the most modern machine – the car – at its heart. Mimicking Cartesianism doctrine, the city builders assumed architecture as a "solitary object" while separating it from one's individual's experience, memories, associations (Voigt, 2021). The first trend was the low-density suburban concept with a central premise evolving around cars and mega streets as the foundation of a new suburban city concept. Inspired by "structured and disperse", the dark city ideology in Europe that aimed at supremacy over race and space (Fuhrmeister et al., 2021), low-density suburbs began to mushroom on the outskirts of every city, starting a "white flight" when most steady jobs and wealthy residents started to move in (Belshaw, 2016). New immigrants, minorities, and low-income earners moved into empty downtown buildings. The new suburban format was connected by mega streets, minimal or no pedestrian facilities, and built large, big-box shopping malls with endless parking spaces as the de facto place for "social interaction". Consumerism became the centre point of everyday life, replacing all possible community contact. Another trend inserted machines for mass production. Walter Gropius, founder of Bauhaus, later joined the 'modernist' movement, and led cities to the concept of good design for all social classes. The world-famous handbook by Ernst Neufert, a Bauhaus protagonist, was produced in 1939. However, two Bauhaus obsessions undermined its reputation: the machine and a focus on mass production. The former gave birth to the car-friendly city, while the latter enabled sub-standard suburban housing. According to prominent urban planner Ali Modarres, "From an aesthetic perspective, the global uniformity of form made Bauhaus outdated in the age of cultural awareness and the celebration of diversity" (Modarres, 2019). Most North American cities would then turn their countries into a suburban nation (Gordon and Shirokoff, 2014), sowing a seed of deeper division between classes in society, the opposite of the reality originally envisioned by the 'modern' ideologists. The rise of front-line puppet soldiers of 20th century antiquity based on Le Corbusier ideology, such as Robert Moses in New York, and Sam Cass in Toronto, would eventually transform all major cities. This version of architectural ideology that we are currently living in is rooted in cheap fossil-fuels. The enormous cost of this "artificial complexity" from an environmental and economic perspective is unbearable (Huston, 2021) and literally obliterated "the art" in the architecture profession to nurture "self-indulgence" and personal fame (Silber, 2007). But the segregated and disperse city built around cars would face grassroots opposing forces in "New Urbanism" and another influencing figure of the organic but scientific city planning approach – Jane Jacobs.

> *"There is racism physically built into some of our highways."*
> —Pete Buttigieg, US transportation secretary

### *Disorder in automobility heaven – The birth of "racist mega streets and highways"*

Remnants of the 20th century dark era ideology did survive in the lifeless streets of the post-modern era, albeit with a difference in form and shape.

City building and urban mobility would soon come to be shaped by a few undercover and misguided city building individuals and old-school thought-oriented professions. Art and culture would be the new 'modernism' banner to hide their dark ideology.

While the planning society finally encountered the "functional city" through new urbanism and later sustainable development during or following the 1970s oil-crisis era, the profession responsible for developing and maintaining the mobility system in cities – transportation engineering – arrived on the street scene with a pre-world war 'linear' approach from the practice of military style road building. The distance between city building and mobility planning professions started to grow, and frequently displayed a public rift created by nascent urban planning policies considered entirely based on private automobile travel (Mancebo, 2008). Implementing Le Corbusier ideology to decimate vibrant streets and divide communities with wide and polluted highways or expressways would lead to widespread suburbanization "characterized by the decentralization of the population and workplaces within conurbations" (Rossi, 1983). Influenced by Le Corbusier's machine-driven vision of a vehicle-oriented city, the traffic engineering practice thought the car should be the cornerstone of normative and standardized mobility planning (LeCorbusier, 1946). A group of automobile manufacturing companies (mainly GM and the American Automobile Association) formed the "National Highway Users Conference" in 1932 lobbying for taxes to build a network of highways to reduce the 62-day cross continent trip to today's 42-hour journey (Highways, 2006). A combination of Le Corbusier's mega highway vision and the perspective of a nationwide highway network was at the heart of the city building ideology presented as Futurama (General Motors pavilion) by Bel Geddes at the 1939 Universal Exhibition in New York (Herman, 2012). This extreme automobility vision later influenced a gigantic wave of motorway development through a colossal highway building proposal – Interstate Highways in 1956 (Weingroff, 1996). This proposal turned into $250 billion of spending for the construction of 41,000 miles (66,000 km) of the Interstate Highway System over a 10-year period and become the largest public works project in American history after WWII. City governments welcomed the new economic formula of highway growth since 90% of funding came from the federal government and 10% from state governments. Dissecting the city core with urban highways and isolated tall buildings inspired by Le Corbusier's ideology would turn into a toxic urban inequality that would change the city in every possible way – from political divisions to racial segregation, to social and urban decay, to the permanent decline of the quality of life (Vox, 2016) experienced by many middle class and poor urban residents. Mimicking the futurist movement, historic and dense city core centres (referred as 'blight' by planners) mostly inhabited by African Americans and poor residents became the prime targets of demolition and making way for the mega highways to white neighbourhoods in the suburbs. Displaced residents would move to the city's periphery in segregated ethnic neighbourhoods, forcing them to use vehicles to survive. Traffic engineers introduced completely baseless and unscientific measures such as level-of-service (Toth, 2012) to facilitate the greatest destruction of the oldest built form in human civilization. Realizing this fictitious measure actually increased congestion and emissions (Bertini, 2006), the State of California had to introduce a state law to ban this harmful practice despite strong opposition from the traffic engineering community[11] (ITE California, 2014). Cultural decay will inevitably bring dark periods, converting to abstractions of our suffering and happiness which then become convenient for corrupt practices (Wawrzyniak, 2018). To hide this utilitarian deception, traditional mobility planning was guarded by a 'micro-ethical' professional engineering approach (Herkert, 2001) that turned into professional dogma to continue the vehicle-focus ideology as the centre of the mobility system. Today, social inequality is clearly visible in the mobility landscape. Indeed, clashes between transit-oriented urban life and automobile-oriented suburban or rural life is a new form of inequality in the 21st century, giving rise to authoritarian leaders or regimes. At the heart of the new urban inequality is the information-based economy where income gaps have widened, intercity disparities have grown, and suburbs have been re-sorted into a wide array based on class and race or ethnicity (Nijmana and Weic, 2020). This highway bonanza and destruction of the historic city core would however face an army of protesters led by Jane Jacobs wanting to overthrow the autocratic behaviour of road authority and the concomitant 'ghetto' type public housing movement.

> "*Utilitarianism is a civilization of production and of use, a civilization of 'things' and not of 'persons,' a civilization in which persons are used in the same way as things are used.*"
>
> —Pope John Paul II

### *Rise of resistance against classical utilitarianism mobility*

The utility approach has misguided mobility practitioners for almost half a century without any resistance. Until the aggressive utilitarianism that separates the human from mega structures at some point started to severely damage communities by proposing the destruction of entire neighbourhoods for the dubious needs of expressways. Despite the need for functionality in modern life, utilitarianism did then and has always faced fierce resistance. Even progressive modern philosophers (Williams, 1973) criticized utilitarianism as a "*distinctive, influential, and controversial ethical view*" (Holyoak, 2018).

Until recently however highway building and road widening by powerful traffic authority would face almost no opposition except the occasional rift with New Urbanism.

While ideology swept through during 1930s fascism, fuelled by the collapse of the stock exchange, a better and scientific understanding of the city from human perspectives started as a fringe approach. Today we call the idea the "Livable city", which started with and evolved around making it easier to access transit, walking, and cycling as a replacement of our machine-oriented ideology and to potentially stop the destructive form of sprawling city development. On the surface this appears to link with visible human-built facility. Underneath, the crucial debate was about our human rights to the city and reclaiming the city as a co-created space (Lefebvre, 1968). Lefebvre's organic approach to city building addressed industrial aggression in city space, the philosophical inquiry aligning with the fundamental inquiry about natural everyday life (Lefebvre, 1947) and how it's being turned into a zone of sheer consumption, a method of capitalism reproducing itself to survive. His inspiring concept started to spread and brought back the basic human activity in everyday life as a foundation of city building. Our natural everyday life is where our mass culture develops (Certeau, 1980) which is deeply connected to space surrounding the city and the way we move through natural or manmade facilities. Opposed to the machine-centred city, the subsequent

---

[11] Western ITE wrote a letter to California Environmental Quality Act (CEQA) regarding SB 743 stating, "In addition, there are certain issues related to this topic where our profession has not reached a consensus… Despite any problems, many transportation engineers believe that roadway capacity/LOS analysis is a highly useful tool in analysing roadway operations that is used in the planning, operation, and design of roadway facilities."

philosophy of human feeling and emotion as the central premise of city building (Debord, 1967) emerged as a new urbanism movement in 1957 (Tate, 2021). During the same period, Lefebvre conceived the basic notion of our right to "social space" (Lefevre, 1974). The concept remains today as the most fundamental origin of the placemaking concept that fiercely opposes and rejects pseudo 1930s 'modernism' ideology. Creating places for exploration and interaction (Pallasmaa, 2014) began to provoke people-oriented city building around active mobility during the 1970s. A subsequent philosophical inquiry into the influence of the human body and psychology (McCormack, 2013) on our unsanctioned and unscripted activities in small urban spaces easily accessible to everyone, the default place for social interactions, became the foundation of the vital understanding of public places and mobility space creation. Despite their pioneering efforts however, a lack of practical process, a dubious implementation framework, and political attachments trapped these brilliant ideas in the dusty corners of the academic shelf.

With this fringe, people-oriented city building philosophy, the traditional city builders and their practices would be seriously questioned, by a prolific street observer who later explained these complex ideas in simple language.

Often criticized as having no professional training in planning or urban design and later self-exiled in Toronto in opposition of the war in Vietnam, Jane Jacobs's organic city building thinking (Jacobs, 1961) would inspire a movement, a generation of 'people-centric' city building replacing the steadfast ideology-focused city building approach of the 1920–1930s. Her keen observations of small human activities in everyday life and how we move without machines became the inspiration of a modern form of city building and placemaking (Jacobs, 1961). Jane furiously opposed and vehemently rejected the corrupted machine-oriented urban vision of Le Corbusier (Sennett, 2006). The four pillars of her city building vision were essentially the revival of the ancient self-organizing and people-centric, intelligent town planning philosophy. Jacob's four key principles for city building were: (1) mixed-use neighbourhoods, with residential, commercial, and industrial buildings; (2) small blocks that promote walking; (3) a mix of old and new buildings that cater to high- and low-rent tenants; and (4) sufficient density to create a critical vital mass. Five decades after her initial book all four pillars were proven correct, even by using big data (Kessler et al., 2016). Her grassroots activity saved the historic Soho district in New York and downtown Spadina Avenue area in Toronto by blocking giant and ugly expressways that planned to rip out the historic hearts of the cities. Her vision coincided with realizing the energy and environmental realities of the limited resources of our planet. During the energy crisis period of the 1970s, cracks began to appear in the severe flaws in the mass production concept of the industrial era and the connected philosophy that was running the show behind the scenes, gradually revealing the unsustainable path of car-oriented cities and its hindrance on future prosperity. Hailed a successful "American dream", the cookie-cutter neighborhood business model now faced bankruptcy in an era of changing demography and social changes (Varinsky, 2017) with energy consumption larger in the rich, motorized, sprawled, diffused, and polycentric city (Le Néchet, 2012). The pollution impact of cars, in terms of GHGs, air, soil, water, and human health were causing immediate and long-term effects on the planet's environment (Green, 2018). A dire warning of energy depletion by the "Club of Rome" in the 1970s and environmental movements in the 1980s would reshape the sustainable development concept through the UN's "Our Common Future" agenda (United Nations, 1987). The largest placemaking in cities was its streets (Appleyard et al., 1964) that connected the whole mobility network (Appleyard et al., 1981) and remain even today a most influential formation of social life in cities. Whether Willam Whyte's space between buildings or Jan Gehl's human scale concept or Allan Jacobs's great streets, all modern progressive city builders are greatly indebted to Jane Jacobs's simple concept of building the city around the sidewalk and daily human activities. In the postmodern transit-oriented city, the complete streets and vision zero movements' aims to eliminate traffic fatalities is a byproduct of these earlier philosophical inquires and intense debates. Known as the "Brundtland Report" (WCED, UN, 1987), the new city building agenda targeted multilateralism and interdependence of nations in the search for a path to sustainable development. With the declaration by the UN for the sustainable city, we unfortunately never looked back to last century's failed experiment in vehicle-oriented sprawl in city building practices. These progressive approaches would however present a new reality to city builders – that induced demand for cars had led to a never-ending cycle of infrastructure overbuilding that carries the seeds of decline.

Today the debate is far from over.

The remnants of Le Corbusier's and Loss's ideology resurfaced in the 21st century in the guise of Jane Jacobs. On their utility attire, they wore shiny buttons of environmental protection and sunglasses of social equity and hung the scarf of high density around transit nodes and corridors.

The mobility system would then mistakenly overshadow other aspects of city building and create new divisions among city neighbourhoods, and a new form of mobility inequality would soon become apparent through social division, class segregation, and urban inequality.

> *"If we understand the mechanism and motives of the group mind, it is now possible to control and regiment the masses according to our will without them knowing it."*
>
> —Edward Bernays

## The Master Narrative of Vehicle Culture Ideology

Despite the flaws in livable city building and the wrong utility approach to sustainable mobility, greater societal efforts toward quality city living needs to overcome three monumental foundations created in the 20th century. The first attempt would be overcoming the vehicle-oriented lifestyle started in the latter part of the 20th century. In addition, an underlying attempt to spread the new city building across the world at the dawn of the millennium would have to ride the horses of the boundless free-market economic theories and illusions of globalization and 'smart' technology that are spreading through mobility colonization. These forces have often systematically invaded our natural everyday life and occasionally violently collide with "Livable City" efforts. Like two opposite cosmic forces from parallel universes facing off against each other, often in a destructive form, repercussions of their influences remain at the heart of our current struggles of city building.

> *"Individualism is what makes cooperation worth living."*
>
> —Henry Ford

### *Irrational desires of mass car culture fantasy*

One of the staunchest blockages comes from a century-old machine-oriented lifestyle. Today's car culture has been identified as part of the mass consumerism that helped erode the quality of life in cities. But it has been hardly a coincidence since a series of events embedded in two world changing ideas that swept through the heart of industrial society. The first phenomenon was "Ford capitalism" or Fordism[12] (Clarke, 2015) and its enormous influence on fast-paced production and the emergence of a 'homogeneous' mass consumption culture in the economies of the 20th and 21st centuries. Henry

---

[12] Fordism is based on the mass production of homogeneous products, using the rigid technology of the production line with dedicated machines and standardized ('Taylorist') work routines which secure increased productivity through economies of scale, the deskilling and homogenization of the labour force, and the intensification of labour.

Ford's streamlined production process was not just a new way of mass car production. It was a new path to massive production as a byproduct of homogeneous consumerism. It was the birthplace of the scale-based economy and mass worker system leading to the mass institutions of a bureaucratic welfare state. It was the beginning of a new political order and the platform of the promise of rising living standards and spiralling productivity, that created a virtuous circle of economic stability and cultural harmony. Rigid form and the mobility monoculture were born in the dreamlands of the suburbs. Every house had two or three cars in the suburbs and every trip was made by car. Eventually wage increases ceased, debt increased, and Fordism ideology faced troubling consequences in the 21st century. The second idea was the accidental identification of the human inner self by another modern philosopher, Sigmond Freud. Once he identified the existence of human's inner irrational desires, psychologists were hired to develop a consumer culture by misusing Freud's discovery. Across the ocean, Freud's nephew Edward Bernays invented the public relations profession in the 1920s and was the first person to exploit Freud's ideas to create consumerism propaganda and manipulate the behaviour of targeted masses. A mass consumerism was born out of satisfying our 'self' to make us happy and feeling the pleasure of holding our desired products. An unconscious behaviour around "exchange values"[13] (Marx, 1867) led to consuming more vehicles, and making the mind-boggling shortest possible trips by car even though its original "use value"[14] was to make long distance trips or carry heavier goods. This new psychological experiment was borrowed from the remnants of the fascism era that just ended in 1945.

Bernays showed American corporations how they could make people want things they didn't need by systematically linking mass-produced goods to their unconscious desires. One of the main architects of the modern techniques of mass-consumer persuasion, using every trick in the book from celebrity endorsement and outrageous PR stunts to eroticizing the motorcar (Curtis, 2002), Bernays was convinced that this was more than just a way of selling consumer goods. It was a new political idea of how to control the masses. By satisfying the inner irrational desires that his uncle had identified, people could be made constantly happy and thus docile.

Following Ford capitalism's mass vehicle production, invading all city planning rules became the norm in the 20th century. The same culture percolates today during the dawn of autonomous vehicle technology. The directionless discussion around building new cities for new AI (artificial intelligence) vehicle technology has hijacked the much-needed progress achieved in mobility systems over the last two decades. The AI vehicle approach simply reflects the same philosophy of building the city around cars, almost a copycat repeat of Edward Bernays articulated psychological warfare planting phony dreams of freedom by owning cars in the 1940s as a propagandist for General Motors.

> *"Utilitarianism has no connection to morality."*
> —Jacques Lacan

### *Mobility feudalism in the shadows of 21st century colonization*

World War II changed the world's power balance. European colonization's brutality and its underlying ideological philosophy were exposed. The vehicle-based culture of car ownership, highway building, and road widening without any positive gain and toxic parking culture became the target of the sustainable mobility movement from the 1970s onward in western countries. And it was losing ground. Realizing its weakened position, new colonization techniques were

---

[13] Exchange value is the "quantitative relation, as the proportion in which values in use of one sort are exchanged for those of another sort".

[14] "Use value" refers to a product's utility in satisfying needs and wants as afforded by its material properties.

developed by repacking the old colonized concept of utilitarian principles that assumed "utility as pleasure" (Bentham, 1789) A new mobility colonization ideology applied the basic old principles of utility: (1) study local culture and identify which of its intimate attachments can be replaced by new consumerism under the banner of multiculturalism; (2) remove local sustainable mobility to make way for cars through a 'futurist' ideology with a utilitarianism approach that promotes a "streets are for cars only" mindset; (3) use the 'orientalism' of homogeneous consumption as a "rational society" (Grosrichard, 1998) while projecting car ownership, shopping, and social media status as an improvement in the standard of living and the only way to get out of poverty; and (4) use *people are completely selfish*" as a utility technique toward the hyper-speed automobility ideology that recurrently produces severe congestion and social problems. These urban mobility ideologies started to gain global ground through "foreign expert" consultants working in emerging and developing nations despite knowing their 'modernism' root was a failed city building idea. Exporting the vehicle-based concept to developing nations in the name of delivering the "American Dream" to make people "happy and rich" was suddenly being promoted by local politicians, the media, and leading influential figures in emerging and developing nations during the 1990s. And it continues today, as leading organizations including international economic forums and infrastructure financing institutions from major superpowers have started promoting and giving predatory loans for unproven mega mobility infrastructures (Hurley et al., 2018) and producing enormous debt that is bankrupting nations (Liang, 2022) with a toxic soup of energy crisis, Covid-19 downturn and other events such as the war in Ukraine. Despite the warning of dire consequences of intrastate debt (Wihtol, 2017), finishing mega mobility infrastructures is often used as a "political asset" for the next election cycle, instead of its actual needs or mobility demand.

Underneath this renewed push for a global political economy, an imperial call for 'enlightened' moral interventions into the 'underdeveloped' way of life became a dominant feature of a new form of 21st century colonization (Shweder, 2001). Using intricately planned new colonization techniques, the city building ideology was exported as "'western-like aspirations" in the 1990s (Scheff et al., 2021) across the new unipolar world following the collapse of the Berlin Wall, and is now clearly visible in south Asian, southeast Asian, China, and across many African nations. Anywhere we go today, we see the common vehicle-colonization symptoms: building divisive and toxic elevated highways that bring systematic social inequality; removing non-motorized mobility from urban streets, making middle and poor residents desire to own cars even though they're unaffordable; invading all public spaces with vehicle lanes and parking; and losing public space, erasing memories of human interaction, cultural activities on streets, and socialization in public spaces. In the absence of natural everyday life, internalized human activities through foreign entertainment channels, video games, and an invasive digital colonization technique (Pinto, 2018) took a ferocious form in many Asian cities, where the vehicle was forcefully inserted as the dominant mode of mobility. It arrived, however, with the notion of the old agenda. The new domestic ideology of "home as heaven" where women feel comfortable only within a private sphere (Wolff, 1988) was the direct result of destructive patriarchal city building practices from the global north. Soon women, children, and seniors would disappear from the vibrant streets of South Asia and the Middle East after they were widened to an inhuman scale for high-speed vehicles. Granting women the freedom to "drive a car" in Saudi Arabia was hailed as victory of "human rights" while active mobility usage and spending time outdoors or the creation of public space remained silent in the realm of this new top-down feminism-friendly culture.

Instead of physical space improvements for people, new tools are being used for mobility colonization. A destructive form of social media is creating a new form of colonization in developing and emerging nations (Gerspacher, 2021), as any aspect of vehicle culture that emerges in western countries spreads to them through social media within a few weeks. Ownership of a new vehicle model is constantly promoted as a social status. The second tool is a well-known geo-psychological process. As part of our 'civilization' process, old public spaces, and non-motorized forms of mobility are ridiculed as part of new mobility colonization (Elias, 1939). The most disappointing examples are in South Asian cities, including the city where the author was born, Dhaka. Its first systematic ethnocultural study was conducted by a British researcher on the local mobility of rickshaws in the 1990s (Gallagher, 1992). The rickshaw was not just a mobility mode, but it penetrated every aspect of daily life, was the origin of local culture and a part of a natural lifestyle for centuries in Dhaka. Keeping an archive of knowledge and the understanding of local culture is one of the basic notions of western civilization (Gerspacher, 2021). And learning local culture and identity while reshaping local consumerism is the bedrock principle of the 21st century's liquid economy. It paved the way for a revival of an older colonial attitude, orientalism, (Said, 1978) but in reverse order. Learning that the rickshaw was at the heart of local culture, it soon become the target of automobility colonization. Within a few years, a sudden move to remove the rickshaw from all major streets in Dhaka was proposed by a team from the World Bank, blaming the slow movement of rickshaws for causing cars to move slowly and the root cause of increased pollution (Hasan and Dávila, 2012). It sounds absurd blaming the rickshaw or non-motorized mobility for the root cause of pollution, but mobility feudalist behaviour created no opposition to the absurd false claim. Similar stories arose in all developing nations. Gradually cycling disappeared from China, and local transit disappeared in Kenya, Manila, and many other cities as 'modern' automobility aggressively took over in the 21st century and was assumed to promote an improvement carrier of the "standard of living".

As vehicle-oriented city building became a toxic force behind the declining quality of life in rapidly urbanizing dense cities, every harm originating from the vehicle was being successfully transferred to developing nations. Building 300-feet wide roads is being promoted as a symbol of progress. Even children's books are filled with car models, creating dreams and formulas for success attached to the car as a lifestyle standard. Happiness comes from road trips. Insulting and demoralizing bicycle, rickshaw, and zippy users as 'backwards' while blocking the path to 'modernism' has emerged as social norm. Public squares, trees, and green spaces were removed for vehicle parking. Insulting street retailers and vendors through city enforcement programs (ORF, 2011) became culturally acceptable. Despite knowing there is very little scientific background to vehicle-oriented city building, the failed western utilitarianism ideology once championed by Adolf Loss and Le Corbusier was transferred to developing nations without a common understanding of the local urban mobility system and its user's behaviour (ORF, 2011). Every university course and academic discourse is now full of vehicle system optimization research, and numerous studies are dedicated to maintaining the imaginary level-of-service of the free-flow roadway. But, when major projects are being built, local practitioners are being ignored. Knowing local professionals have only gained from imported knowledge, which is seen as lower quality, local public agencies only 'trust' foreign experts for city master planning. New transit projects, mega highways and oversized bridges are being built by "foreign expert" designers. And these new city plans again propose more road widening, more elevated highways, more mandatory car parking, and more streamlined processes for vehicle-oriented planning and design even though the last round of master planning failed to gain any real benefits. Traffic speed in Dhaka used to be 11–13 kmph before the first implementation of mega highway plans. It reduced to 5–8 kmph after elevated highways were completed. With induced traffic, overall speed currently stands at 3–5 kmph. Yet these measures have never been used by local or foreign experts. Local authority has adopted a mobility separation culture from the new west, the US, and a mega parking culture from Canada, building footbridges to give maximum speed to cars from Singapore, and building mega malls to ban local neighbourhood stores from China. Foreign experts develop planning visions for these master plans and the Chinese or Japanese will come to build them. Maintenance and operation tasks are done by foreign technicians, creating an infinite and vicious cycle of an increased financial burden for developing nations (Marquis, 2021). Instead of solving mobility problems, these mega projects have become the centre of a corrupted infrastructure process.

A vicious cycle of expensive infrastructures that produced very little or negative economic gain only made developing and emerging nations more debt-prone by dragging their economies down further (Buckley, 2009) while pursuing an elusive "catching up with the west" mindset. While these ideas by foreign consultants were invasive, local decision makers and practitioners are equally responsible for not looking forward and not thinking progressively at all about how to build their own cities from local mobility cultures.

> *"Man minus the Machine is a slave; Man plus the Machine is a freeman."*
> —Henry Ford, 1925

### *Liquid modernity of the creative class*

The promises of new technologies and the sharing economy began pouring in the first two decades of the 21st century, as new mega techno companies started to alter mobility and city landscapes. Borrowing from the reintroduction of the utilitarianism ideology (Bentham, 1789) of contemporary environmental protection policies (Jan, 2018), the magic silver lining solution of using new smart mobility technology became a trademark solution to any city problem in the new liquid economy of the 21st century. Liquid modernity[15] is now emerging, borrowing autocratic flavour of modernity of 20th century in its core and friendlier flavours of identity from post-modernity on its outer shell. Postmodernity's culture of isolating any problem is now being blended utopian solutions of city building. The trend has solidified during and post-pandemic periods. The smart city emerged from the philosophy of magic solutions. Progressive city building ideas turned into new banners and buzzwords without any practical path or feasibility test to achieve the vision and became just a new trend under the smart mobility banner. Soon utopian promise turned into a nightmare (Begault and Khazrik, 2019). The functionalism approach (Loos et al., 1908) to shared mobility in its low-occupancy and convenience format turned itself into a new source of pollution, congestion, and crashes, and increased demand for vehicles (Bliss, 2021). Hollow promises of the smart city became an even bigger (SCL, 2015) and troubling nightmare for over- enthusiastic technology bureaucrats. The list is growing: Masdar City, Songdo, Sidewalk Labs, PlanIT Valley including lengthening list of utopian city like Indonesia's new capital (Normile, 2022), Saudi Arabia's 'futuristic' city The Line (ABC, 2022), Nevada's desert city (CNN, 2021). The defeat of the private "smart city" is now a reality, particularly in the Middle East which has become a poster child for failed smart city or mobility projects. Often a foreign 'consultant' or 'expert' is hired to provide the magic solution. Experts then 'throw' cheap and generic solutions or products at the problem that may have failed previously somewhere else or new technology not tested or properly developed. Ignoring core local issues and culturally, socially, or geographically viable solutions, and the lack of due diligence became a root cause of many failed "smart city" projects. A "Dream city of tomorrow" with very little collaboration on the ground, nonexistent technology, little action plans, or the lack of understanding of basic mobility systems led to the most embarrassing of smart city failures by Sidewalk Labs in Toronto (Vynck and Wong, 2020).

Smart technology hysteria is not a new phenomenon. Intelligent traffic controls during the 1990s, such as traffic management centres, were tried but failed to solve congestion, traffic safety problems, and typically excluded non-vehicle users. For instance, Toronto experienced a rapid

---

[15] The author proposes new social structure in the mid-21st century as "liquid modernity" in the context of fourth industrial era and emergence of artificial intelligence towards the creation of post-human. The post-human has emerged as new 'conformist' culture of replacing every social, cultural, and psychological activity of human with new digital consumerism. This new social structure is replacing post-modern era and gradually emerged as new social and cultural realm in 21st century, specially post Covid-19 pandemic era.

decline in pedestrian safety despite having massive traffic management centres. Yet bizarre new smart plans are popping up (Intelligent Transport, 2021) despite continuous failures. Some smart city projects have become a tool for eavesdropping on citizens and a platform of serious human rights violations (Mazzetti et al., 2019). Smart traffic signals and streetlights, video-based traffic monitoring, and vehicle sensors have created a massive invasion of privacy, threatening freedom of expression, and peaceful protests. Commuter data has targeted ethnic or religious backgrounds (O'Carroll and Franco, 2017), and is widening inequality and discrimination (Marlow, 2018). A growing "black box" syndrome of AI applications in mobility has even found a way to discriminate between pedestrian colours, while ignoring pedestrian or cycling detections, and hiding the limitations of autonomous technology (Bloomberg, 2018).

Almost every overpromised smart city turned into a completely failed idea. But as it turned out, the first generation of the smart city was just a corporate business product for business and political elites that failed to tackle problems with people-oriented agendas or authentically respond to the needs of residents (McFarlane and Söderström, 2017). From the ashes of failed "smart cities", "smart city 2.0" emerged as a decentralized, people-centric approach to tackle social problems, address resident needs, and foster collaborative participation using smart technologies (Trencher, 2019). A few new smart city projects for mobility found initial success, such as CityOS in Barcelona, that addressed privatization issues with open-source data, an analytics platform, and access to data by users. More realistic and detailed plans for new mobility also saw brighter lights at the end of the tunnel. A shared mobility and multimodal programme in Vivaldi-Bremen, and a carsharing programme in Ulm, Germany were vigorously planned, and their tested ideas became more sensible role-models for success. Montreal's multimodal MaaS system integrated public carshare, bikeshare, and transit that inspired other cities. A few trends became the cornerstones of the utopian "smart city": privatization of city services, commercialization of data to sell products, and the breaching of human rights became a new tool of oppression. But the fast and overpromised 'solutionism'[16] ideology (Morozov, 2013) that existed in the high-tech culture did not last long. Slow and steady wins the race.

The application of technologies should match the human spirit, and respect our basic human rights, no matter how smart they are.

Nothing escapes the digital colonization world, where our private life, gender, race, identity have become targets in the homogeneous postmodern era. Despite our differences however, a 'positive' and permissive master narrative is now emerging through the micro desires of our individual identity. Multimodal mobility, pedestrianization, cycling, and micromobility have become a part of the conversation while keeping our core vehicle culture intact.

---

[16] The belief that complex issues can be disassembled into neatly defined technical problems that can be adequately solved through technology.

# Chapter 2B

# Wind of Change

*"A city becomes a world when one loves one of its inhabitants."*
—Lawrence Durrell

The disaster of the ideological city building philosophy and its severe negative downside gave rise to a deeper look into the relationship between humans and cities after WWII. Besides postmodern urbanism from Lefevre to Janes Jacob's surprising entry into city building history, sustainable city development and low-emission mobility particularly have become central premises of livable city building practices in the 1980s. The first pressure on new city building came out of the intense incompatibility between urbanization needs and the continuous failures of the haphazard and unscientific practice of the automobility system. Despite its failures, the system flaws remained invisible due to automobility's abstract but ominous presence almost everywhere in the city. Like the hidden repeated downfall of the materialistic society, the repetitive cycle of failure (Karatani, 1989) in the automobility system is only visible through annual crash data, recurring pollution, repeated congestion, and frequent stumbles during energy volatility. While building a new mobility system, these hidden and seemingly invisible foundations may infect the new mobility ecosystem and generate its own crisis of repeated inequality. New mobility including sustainable forms could fall victim to some of the hallmark features of post-modernism[17] (Lyotard, 1979): multiculturism, postindustrial consumer habit, copied/appropriated and fragmented views of the subject (Nandy et al., 2018). This section touches briefly on mobility upheaval during the post-modernism era that we currently live in.

> *"The operative choice is not between rationality and its opposite, but between decency versus degradation."*
>
> —Robert Wicks

---

[17] In 1979, **Jean-François** Lyotard first introduced the term 'postmodern' which made its way to the philosophical lexicon in his publication, *La Condition Postmoderne* (*The Postmodern Condition: A Report on Knowledge*).

# PART 1

# Struggle for Sustainable Mobility in a Livable City

Cities are expanding at an astonishing rate: London gains nine new residents every hour, double that number is gained in Sao Paulo, and over 70 residents arrive per hour in New Delhi, Kinshasa, and Dhaka (Burdett, 2016). The explosion of 'megacities' (over 10 million in population) is the most striking story of the 21st century. In the 1950s there were only two megacities (Tokyo and New York). Three more were added by the 1980s (Sao Paulo, Osaka, and Mexico City). Today we have 32 megacities, roughly half of them located in Asia (*Economist*, 2017). Something else other than the automobile must be the future mobility solution to maintain the same equity for every resident in cities. As we are entering an era of the most complicated mix of urbanization and climate risk, the systematic change of the failed and crumbing automobility system is inevitable. This subchapter provides a brief glimpse at the continuous struggle for better mobility that aligns with human scale instead of overriding it.

> "*To plan is human, to implement, divine.*"
> —Jerold Kayden, Professor of planning and design,
> Harvard University – Quoted in *Streetfight*
> (Sadik-Khan and Solomonow, 2016)

## *New forms of city building around sustainable mobility*

Facing pressure from urbanization and the repeated failures of vehicle-oriented sprawl, new city building that looked toward high-density and sustainable development began to (re)emerge near the end of the 20th century. Shrinking usable urban land and a serious intrusion into the last remaining green spaces started to settle as a real fear among city builders. Never-ending automobile expansion, an enormous burden on society, started to insert itself into the last remaining living and nature conservation areas, a precedent for unsafe land-use with an irreversible impact on the environment. Under immense pressure, some cities started to depart from ideological vehicle-oriented city building. New urbanism started to appear in city building practices. Among those new city building efforts, three distinct forms evolved around sustainable mobility.

- The first serious attempts emerged in the 1980s with the idea set around building a new transit network as the backbone of new city regeneration projects. The next part of this chapter discusses the success and side effects of those new sustainable mobility-based practices.

- The second concept kept transit-oriented development as the backbone of policies while promoting a new but disturbing social class idea – the creative class. The central promise of the creative class concept was new mobility technology, including in service sectors and other asset-light economic sectors. As these new city ideas started to emerge in new neighbourhoods, the utility approach started invading the core philosophy of new city building.

- The third concept is fictitious smart city urbanism, replicating OEM's aggressive 1940s campaign to forcefully reshape cities via smarter technologies and nonexistent, imaginary future autonomous vehicle technology. As the new shared economy began with the dawn of the new millennium, wrongful applications of shared mobility and the side effect of flawed policies began to appear. New vehicle technology and the high-tech economy is planning to derail another utopian city building effort, sidelining the struggle, opportunity and gains of new mobility and the progress livable city building has achieved in last three decades.

### *A wind of change for better mobility*

After hundreds of years of the same old planning and design practice around vehicles, a meaningful change finally arrived in the 21st century. A few things would align with the change in the air. Under pressure, as urbanization created more pollution, noise and congestion, and repeated failures to cure traffic congestion through the vehicle infrastructure expansion approach, many progressive planners, thinkers, and decision makers took a rebel-like stance to overhaul the failed mobility system. Most noticeable and dramatic changes after the 2008 financial meltdown could be seen in the decay and misery of Detroit, the car capital of the world. Their wide roads, parking and big boxes all collapsed within a few weeks or months. A few bold leaders and practical problem solvers would be called upon by city mayors. The most memorable and audacious step was the appointment of one of the strongest personalities and true advocates for change, who understood the core problem of mobility in cites. After starting in 2007 as commissioner, Janette Sadik-Khan ignited a wildfire in the mobility world by bringing sweeping changes to New York's streets, transit and overall infrastructure planning and design. Her collaborative, innovative and faster but carefully planned approach brought lasting changes, including an extensive bicycle network, pedestrianization, dedicated lanes and systemwide bus/transit improvements. It initiated bikeshare planning and many more innovations that converted unused and underutilized vehicle space for active mobility use (Sadik-Khan and Solomonow, 2016). Her most lasting change was to develop new urban street design and planning guidelines that questioned the flaws and gaps in old fashioned engineering approaches (NACTO, 2013). A series of NACTO guidelines provided tools and techniques to the silent majority to test and experiment proven success somewhere else. Despite bringing much needed change, she was criticized sometimes by those touting Nietzsche's "the last man", but none prevailed. It took time for the rest of the world to digest her achievements. Soon Chicago appointed Gabe Klein, another visionary who started wildly successful bikeshare, formalized the food truck concept into a reality, laid out a vast bicycle network, an initial bus rapid transit network, and vision zero initiatives. Well known in private consulting as exceptional, Jeffrey Tumlin was appointed in San Francisco. Soon many cities appointed innovators: Seattle, Washington D.C., Austin, San Francisco, Maryland, Portland, and many more. To the north, winds of mobility change were less visible in large cities except Montreal. Mostly chief planners attempted to change mobility discussions in Canada: Vancouver's Brent Toderian, Toronto's Jennifer Keesmaat, and Hamilton's Jason Thorne. Keesmaat attempted to change mobility through city policy but faced a constant struggle. Though her policies are now bringing incremental and gradual progress to the city. TTC general manager Andy Byford's changes to Toronto transit were brief but significant. Thorne's #coollittlethings that reinvent through small space changes is the most practical and meaningful approach. Toderian's effort to change mobility pushed Vancouver's sustainable mode share over 50% and was ahead of its time. Montreal as an entire city brought many lasting changes and showed pioneering leadership by bringing in the first bikeshare, first mobility integration platform, and the first eMobility regulations in North

America. This series of successes along with a vast transit and bicycle network, and widespread changes in pedestrian and public squares. Unlike in the US, small Canadian cities progressed well to bring in more meaningful changes such as Peterborough, Kingston, Guelph, Burlington, and Calgary, and most recently shared mobility and on-demand transit experiments were completed in Belleville and Innisfail.

North America however arrived late in the game. Across the world, progress in mobility started much earlier. Latin America now leads the world in the bus, cycling, and pedestrian-friendly environment. Asia set pioneering examples in transit innovation and urban highway removal despite their failures. Jaime Lerner of Curitiba introduced a new model for transit, introducing the world to bus rapid transit. Bogota's mayor Enrique Peñalosa brought surprising and the most lasting innovation in city mobility by introducing the massively popular Ciclovía by banning cars every Sunday, bus rapid transit via TransMilenio, and citywide massive changes in cycling and public space via pedestrianization. A new era of the surprising return of cyclists and pedestrians began in the middle of the first decade of the 21st century. Paola Tapia's leadership brought many changes to Santiago which has already introduced the world's largest and first pedestrian-only network, along with sweeping changes in transit, including time-based transit fares, quality public spaces, and eMobility for city buses. Paula Bisiau introduced vision zero and deployed a massive network of protected bicycle lanes at an affordable cost in Buenos Aires. Latin America is still ahead of the rest of the world in implementing sustainable mobility in a neighbourhood context and human scale. Under the brainwashing of automobility illusion, Asia was very late in the game of mobility change, except for its renowned transit system, especially in southeast and east Asia. The earliest transit and systemwide change happened in the land of the rising sun. Noritsugu Hayakawa, known as the father of the Japanese subway, funded Japan's first subway system along the Ginza Line in 1927. This was beginning of the world's most complex, intricately connected and most heavily used transit system. Japan also reached its railway miracle when it introduced the world's first and fastest bullet train by the hands of Hideo Shima. Seoul's famous subway and overall transit system changes were completed by Kim Gyeng Chul in the mid-2000s (Peteritas, 2012). Another notable Korean pioneer was Seoul's former mayor Lee Myung-bak who brought down a major highway, the Cheonggye Expressway, which he had helped to build as CEO of Hyundai engineering, releasing its toxic impact on the deteriorating quality of life of residents. The project inspired worldwide removal of the unnecessary, destructive, and negative economic drag force of urban highways and freeing-up of lands for the revitalization of the city's prominent landmarks and neighbourhoods. Ong Teng Cheong as a government minister transformed Singapore's transit system in the 1980s which became a model for dense Asian cities. Against all odds Keeree Kanjanapas built Bangkok's iconic sky train transit network. The tenacity and resiliency of these Asian transit systems would show their true success during the Covid-19 pandemic by averting the collapse of transit that happened in rest of the western and middle east world. Besides the public sector, change also percolated in the private sector, particularly with three notable women in mobility. Robin Chase co-founded the first viable car share business and demonstrated the power of new mobility to transfer from car ownership to car usership. Two German young mobility pioneers, Sophia von Berg and Larissa Zeichhardt filled a much-needed gap in the true representation of women in mobility instead of the typical approach of "women as decoration" and brought changes to the German rail maintenance sector (TUMI, 2019) respectively. Sonja Heikkilä pioneered the idea of mobility-as-a-service and turned the concept into a reality in Finland. Compared to the vastness and importance of mobility in cities, these changes are still in their infancy. Deeply rooted vehicle culture will take a longer time for meaningful changes to appear in daily social life worldwide, instead of its limited or spotted success in smaller geography.

## 9.
## THIRD INDUSTRIAL ERA - INVASION OF IDEOLOGY IN CITY BUILDING
## (20TH CENTURY)

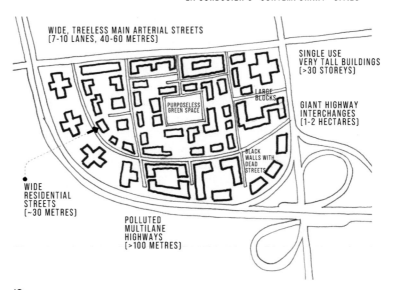

LA CORBUSIER'S "CONTEMPORARY" CITIES

## 10.
## MOBILITY RENAISSANCE & REVIVAL OF SUSTAINABLE CITY
## (21ST CENTURY)

SELF-ORGANIZED CITIES: HUMAN SCALE MOBILITY AND PUBLIC SPACE
(1) VIBRANT CITIES - JANE JACOBS 2) THE TRANSECT - ANDRES DUANY 3) CITIES FOR PEOPLE - JAN GEHL)

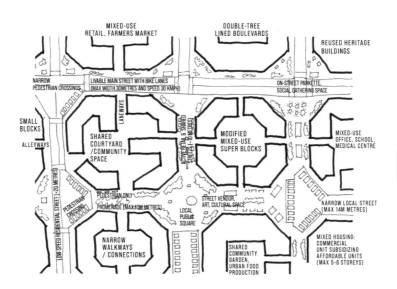

**Fig. 2A.4:** A brief history of revival of people-oriented mobility.

*"If density and diversity give life, the life they breed is disorderly."*
—Jane Jacobs

## A tale of two cities – Montreal vs. Toronto

People-oriented struggles are glaringly visible in two of Canada's largest cities. From the outside they look similar, but they are very different in their qualities of life. One is English speaking, the other French. Influence of the Parisian concept of a beautiful city shaped Montreal, and it is obviously older than Toronto. One might wonder what makes such a difference in city building between two cities that are only a few hundred kilometers apart within the same country, with similar modern cultures and a similar government style. Both hold secrets of the worst and the best of city building practices in North America. The most visible yet remarkable difference is their mobility systems. The maturity of their city building likely came from travelling a long path, along the way experiencing the pains and gains of their different city building approaches.

The first striking difference is in the form of urban density and its intimate influence on mobility. Across the island, Montreal has maintained a gentle density with 3–5 storey buildings with relatively uniform distribution. The uniform gentle density form is influenced by a French socialist style structure. This built form generates higher local trip rates and a larger share of short trips throughout the day. This translates into more walking, cycling, micro mobility needs, and frequent short transit trips. Toronto is the opposite. Most jobs are concentrated in downtown or urban centres that generate longer trips particularly via regional rail systems and highways. Pointed density around transit stations generates very concentrated short trips and aligns with longer travel needs between urban centres that are usually completed by car. In addition, ultra-hyper density in the downtown has recently produced transit overcrowding due to a lack of other multimodal options or facilities for short trips.

The second noticeable difference is in the land-use mix and the diversity of non-residential and community facilities. On every corner of neighbourhoods such as Le Plateau or Villa Marie or Mile End in Montreal, there is a convenient, grocery, medical, and other daily needs store. Daily basic needs can be accessed within a few minutes of walking distance via a neighbourhood's local or main streets. From healthcare to community places, all are located within short walking or cycling distances. Even parks, children's playgrounds, public squares, and small green corners are available on every block, providing easy access for mental health and physical well-being. Toronto built these facilities with the exact opposite philosophy. Mixed-use is very rare and most retail stores are miles away from residential areas except in a few wealthy and walkable neighbourhoods. Community centres, healthcare, and childcare is far and mostly surrounded by car parking lots due to their location isolated from the community. An uneasiness to require specific policy for non-residential usage among decision makers and planners led to inaccessible daily life needs despite the golden opportunity provided over the last two decades of unprecedented growth in Toronto.

Matching human scale is the third most notable difference. Montreal neighbourhood streets, except for new or a few main streets, are roughly 10–12 m wide, roughly on a one to one scale with the height of the buildings. People can easily see, chat, interact with each other on this scale. Neighbourly streets encouraging especially women, children, seniors, and friends to gather and linger are common public spaces in Montreal. Toronto streets are completely out of scale. Even suburban streets are mostly 40 m or wider in a two-storey low-density neighbourhood. Downtown streets are 25–30 m wide while 80% of space is occupied by mostly empty vehicle travel lanes 23 hrs a day. Except for a few small streets (like parts of Queen or Bloor streets), it's extremely rare to see people lingering on the streets. Women, children, and seniors have absolutely disappeared from the street scene. Indeed, in an office quiz conducted by the author asking to name at least one street in North York where people can linger for long periods, the answer came back from all planners that there were none in the four entire suburban centres of Toronto. Mega streets and ugly highways had historically torn apart the communities, an identical ideology once suggested by Le Corbusier or Adolf Loss or Ronald Reiner.

The fourth remarkable difference is the between the cultural conditions of built form and mobility facilities. Montreal boroughs have more intimate connections to the community, diverse groups of people with different backgrounds, and cultural influence on built form and the mobility system. Most houses are directly connected to sidewalks, alleyways, and on-site parking is mostly restricted to on-street parking. This form by default activates the streets, engaging the community through its public spaces and encouraging art and cultural activity between people, built form, and mobility forms. To the contrary, built form is internalized and mostly privatized in Toronto. Despite the higher density, Toronto's built form produces very little, or no community feeling and encourages a bizarre mix of car, transit, walking and cycling, instead of enjoying them as it is. Streets are activated by cars in peak times but are in a disconnected form and deserted during off-peak hours since most daily life activities are internalized.

The fifth easy difference is the existence or absence of art and culture on public mobility spaces and the public's or decision makers' approach to mobility systems. Public spaces in Montreal are gradually getting more artistic with the help of residents, local artists, or activists. The city's in-house capacity develops intimate relationships, creates local cultural influence and a sensible vision of public spaces. Consultant or contractors are only hired after the planning, design, and vision is realized, just to build what has been envisioned by the community. In sharp contrast, Toronto has limited mobility or no mobility master plans, and on the most pressing issues, guiding principles are nearly nonexistent, blindly depends on consultant-led planning projects, has very little in-house skills or capacity, does limited community outreach and engages residents only to showcase and impose their spectacle vision which is the common approach to city building. The presence or art and culture in mobility space are almost nonexistent. Many grade-separated highways or mega streets in urban centres – appear to be from the aftermath of a nuclear war – and dark, gloomy, and unattractive looking neighbourhoods are common outcome of disconnected and isolated mobility planning in Toronto.

The philosophical difference between the two city's approaches provides a great lesson learned for other city builders. Not every neighbourhood in Montreal is the same. Some neighbourhoods look just like Toronto, particularly in the new suburbs of Laval or the Rosemont borough. But better neighbourhoods are gradually and consistently moving toward lovable streets, and mobility design is almost everywhere, in contrast to Toronto where isolated neighbourhood revitalizations are done with gentrification in mind and to showcase projects on social media, leaving most city residents with deep resentments toward the downtown or limited mixed-use wealthy areas.

It would not be exaggerating to say Torontonians live the life of spectacles. Montrealers live the life of the everyday. At least there is a growing understanding of people-oriented planning and an awareness in the remaining boroughs in Montreal and the city is focused on the small activities of the natural activity of people's everyday lives.

> *"Cities are emergent complex adaptive social network systems resulting from the continuous interactions among their inhabitants…"*
>
> —Geoffrey West

### Science of the self-organizing city and its mobility

While ancient movements of humans shaped the development of the early mobility system in settlements, the hidden nature of the human settlement and how it influences mobility remains off topic in philosophical, scientific, and systematic inquiry. Ancient cities used to observe their people, gather to discuss, and without having structure they eventually built the most lovable of cities and beautiful mobility facilities that have now become a target of cultural tourism. This practice of "observed truth" started to decline at the end of the 19th century, particularly during the second and third industrial revolutions.

Scientific evidence to connect the true nature of human mobility and its settlement gained attention recently with the availability of smart data, the dramatic advances in AI in mobility, and the search for alternative sustainable mobility to address the pressure on resources due to rapid urbanization. Besides mobility systems, urban planning and urban design are often considered a vital link between two critical elements of urban science. However, urban planning and design are not considered a topic of scientific inquiry despite human settlements, particularly cities, considered "maybe one of the most complex systems in the universe" (Sarah, 2012). This simple inquiry starts with the self-organizing nature of the human settlement (West, 2017). Recent research has discovered, despite notable differences in appearance and governance, ancient human settlements functioned in much the same way as modern cities. The clustering of humans and space gradually developed into human settlements. These clustered places depend on a complex network of interconnected systems (Bera, 2022). The clustering of human settlements can bring both merits and demerits (Bera et al., 2021). Larger and denser cities are more resource efficient (Bettencourt, 2013). If doubling the population, a city would only need an 85% increase in the street network, saving 15% of the cost with higher density (Bettencourt and West, 2010). But there is a downside. Crime, pollution, congestion, and all bad indicators of growth increase at a rate of 1.15 factor,[18] i.e., an extra 15% in addition to doubling the growth (West, 2017). Unlike traditional traffic engineering theory that often isolates the mobility system from everything else, a series of research has firmly established that the city can only be understood if the interactions between infrastructure, and economic and social components are clearly established through city building practices. This book, therefore, connects seemingly unrelated things to understand the future possibilities of a sensible mobility ecosystem.

Knowledge of the formation and organic structure of cities has become the centre of a new city science. Eventually, every city follows an organic fractal 'tree-like' and chaotic formation as new areas of the city develop, and entire cities experience a unique evolution to becoming a city with its own identity through social interaction and networks. Fractal cities discover the many hidden geometric forms and functions of a seemingly chaotic city (Batty and Longley, 1994). Scale, size, and shape of cities become intricately linked to mobility systems. As the city grows larger, taller buildings appear as a common shape at its centre. Tension between travel costs or distances (traditional mobility model attributes) and renting costs or land-uses generate a patten of employment concentration in city centres and lower densities in the suburbs. The combined density of population and employment falls as the distance from the city centre grows. This is a perfect replication of the sprawl formula that ultimately developed travel demand models to build the city's mobility systems. With the rise of postmodernism's simulacra culture that imitates the operation of real-world processes toward a hyper reality without incorporating actual reality (Baudrillard, 1981), the mobility system planning in cities is reduced to computer simulations that pretend to mimic our travel habits based on assumptions linked to the rigid doctrine of machine-oriented cities. Traditional traffic modelling however entirely focuses on the random understanding of traffic flow (Wilson, 1970) without using the properties of network relations in cities. The appearance of network science[19] (Newman et al., 2005) showed pedestrian densities and connectivity of the street network increase (Helbing et al., 2005) where population, retail, and employment density is higher and evenly distributed, and gradually become disconnected toward the periphery of dense centres (Scellato et al., 2006), i.e., suburban or exurban locations. This background practical

---

[18] Infrastructure relation to population is sublinear with exponent of power law of 0.85. Reversely, bad indicators relation to population is super linear with exponent of power law of 1.15.

[19] As per US NRC, network science is referred to as "the study of network representations of physical, biological, and social phenomena leading to predictive models of these phenomena".

observation, multimodal mobility science, and new knowledge is the basis of "*mobility form*" in this book, to connect the gap between built form and the mistaken assumptions of formless mobility systems.

### Size of the 20-minute city and multimodal mobility

A series of early research ideas inspired the recent sustainable and compact city concept. Some say the 15-minute city, others the 20-minute city, by walking distance. The size roughly equivalent to ancient cities without motorized mobility. In search of the optimal city size, shape, and form, a century-old effort came out with a few "rules of thumb", but it's not a deterministic formula. Ebenezer Howard, through his Garden City ideal, first suggested that the ideal garden city should have a population of some 30,000, which became the model for the British New Towns in the mid-20th century (Howard, 1898). But it turned out to be a guessing game and the ideologically flawed approach of geometry rather than people. A second approach emerged from economics of scale (Alonso, 1971). An economics approach closely linked to the "optimum growth" concept (Mirrlees, 1972) that became the focus of city economics in the 1970s. From the economic perspective of urban size, cities of some 250,000 people appear to generate higher benefit–cost ratios (Batty, 2005). Richardson once suggested there might be a function[20] that could generate the optimal city size analytically (Richardson, 1973) but later abandoned that because of the difficulties of defining such a function. Some efforts to define optimal city size as the maximum total surplus or a city size in which total benefits are equal to total costs came up with the optimal size of a population for a city of 393,000–433,000 people (Yang, 2020). While the city economic perspective provided a greater understanding of city scale and size, these theories were mainly based on automobile commuting within 'optimal' suburbs and downtown and associated parameters (Riley, 1973). The flaw is obviously excluding sustainable mobility from theoretical foundations. Finally, the most reasonable understanding of city size should come from the pedestrian scale in the compact city form (Dantzig and Saaty, 1973). Connecting background research findings of the walkable city, the author established a rule of thumb that the threshold of a sustainable city emerges when it generates at least a 10% of pedestrian mode share (Gordon and Shirokoff, 2014) to total trips at any given hour. Eventually the walking share increases and stabilizes when it reaches half of total trips. The recent 15-minute city suggests a variation of 50,000 to 100,000 as an indicator of a healthy city. Using minimal density for frequent bus and light rail rapid transit,[21] the author derived the optimal 20-minute walking city size would be an 80,000, 120,000, and 200,000 population. Inside the city area, most mobility can be completed by walking, cycling, and micro mobility. Transit would facilitate the relatively longer trips between these 15-minute cities or areas. However, these quantitative approaches should include complex factors in cities. A different equilibrium of urban sizes depends on functions performed, quality of life, industrial diversity, and social conflicts with the uncertainty of error related to urban governance (Camagni et al., 2013). As cities grow larger, these estimates would provide a reasonable optimal administrative size (a city could contain multiple administrative zones or wards) that can be sustainably developed with the smallest footprint on the environment and social conditions.

> "*...twentieth-century science will be remembered for just three things: relativity, quantum mechanics, and chaos.*"
>
> —James Gleick

---

[20] Difference between benefits and costs could predict optimal city size, $S = P^\alpha - \beta P$ where P = population and $\alpha$ and $\beta$ are parameters.

[21] Assuming population and employment density 100, 150, and 250 per hectare. Walking speed 5 km/h, a typical person can walk roughly 20 min, from an area of 8.1 sq. km.

## *A pattern of shifting mobility*

Human movement seems chaotic, yet it's a dynamic beauty. It seems disorderly but when observed carefully it appears as ordered chaos. Traditionally, we typically assume human mobility patterns are heavily influenced by mobility infrastructure, population density and distribution, socioeconomic conditions, and the attendance of citizens, therefore it is natural to expect similar connections.

Cities with a strong hierarchical mobility structure (a dense network, shorter blocks, higher connectivity) display extensive usage of public transport, higher levels of walkability, lower pollutant emissions per capita and better health indicators (Bassolas et al., 2019).

Like a complex city structure, although the human mobility of everyone is unique but also follows some regular collective pattern. One of the earliest human mobility pattern debates erupted between a philosopher, physicist, and planner on how mobility shapes city forms and patterns. Bertrand Russell first noted that mobility technology that went longer distances compelled people to move further away, which erased the gain and was expanding the city size (Mumford, 1934). Zahavi noted people seem to have a constant "time travel budget" (Zahavi, 1979). Italian physicist Marchetti later confirmed the existence of a 'one-hour' travel budget constant (Marchetti, 1994). These discoveries sharply contradicted governments and environmentalists who generally assume infrastructure improvements will lower consumption. However, no evidence was ever found to support that argument. Indeed, it revived the century-old debate in the 1970s. Jevons' paradox discovered the rate of consumption increases as efficiency gain is introduced through newly built or widened highways (Jevons, 1865). Known now as "induced demand", the German mathematician confirmed through his famous mathematics that adding one or more roads to a road network can slow down overall traffic flow (Braess, 1969). A more recent discovery firmly established that removing a redundant road or travel lane improves overall traffic flow (Wang et al., 2012). Despite the Mount Everest-level of evidence, traditional old-school mobility planners continue to ignore the science in travel demand modelling and the master planning process and recommend never-ending expansion of vehicle infrastructure in the name of the mirage of illusive economic progress. However, recent changes in street design focusing on the urban street and the road diet concept avoid excessive road additions or widening to better reflect our limits of mobility.

Human movement is not simply the result of a mechanical process. Our movement to a great extent is influenced by several factors that vary from place to place and from population to population (Kanga and Scott, 2010). Despite the appearance of random mobility behaviours our mobility patterns are more regular than we assume. A few patterns were established through a scientific and evidence-based approach that contradicted traditional travel demand modelling assumptions: (1) Using smart phone tracked data, research has uncovered that people tend to spend most of their time at a few geographic "anchor points" or common locations (Aasa et al., 2008); (2) Behavioural research established that the potential cause of identified common patterns in daily routine is due to community affiliations and people's social network (Eagle, 2009); (3) The regularity of temporal and spatial individual daily travel patterns was observed to follow simple reproducible patterns in terms of travelling similar distances, using common routes and nodes, and a significant probability of returning to a few highly frequented locations (González et al., 2008); (4) In addition, there is significant regularity in urban mobility at different hours, days, and weeks (Sevtsuk and Ratti, 2010). There are differences in activity patterns between different areas of the city which can partially be attributed to differences in demographics, establishments, and the built environment; (5) Using the concept of motifs from network theory, research studies found only 17 unique networks are present in daily mobility and they follow simple rules. These networks, called here motifs, are sufficient to capture up to 90% of the population in surveys and mobile phone datasets for different countries. Each individual exhibits a characteristic motif, which seems to be stabilized over several months (Schneider et al., 2013); and (6) Evidence of day-to-day variability in activity time-use patterns was found, specifically a time-use pattern on weekdays is substantially different from those on weekends (Zhong et al., 2008). The excitement inherent in the new mobility pattern approach is not just on what factors affect travel decisions but more on how these factors have shed light on the underlying complexities involved in human travel. If mixed land-use options and short trip facilities or services are available, these basic mobility patterns have significantly altered supplied mobility networks down to compact sizes, thus avoiding a gargantuan impact on social life and the environment in urban areas.

> *"The concepts of the 20th century emerged from an era in which humanity saw itself as separated from the web of life."*
>
> —Kate Raworth

### Shift in lifestyle in the postmodern era

Changes in the post-modern era and the digital age have had a dramatic impact on our travel habits. Unfortunately, they have had little or no impact on the mysterious travel demand and traditional mobility master planning process. Working from home during or post Covid-19 became a norm. On-demand services, including for passengers and goods, are changing mobility demand. In the era of the liquid economy, traditional master mobility plans and models that mostly exclude these major changes of lifestyle will become obsolete. Working from home was not a new option. It has been there for a couple of centuries without us taking the option seriously (*The Economist*, 2020). The hybrid work style of part home-based and part office-based presence had already been implemented before the Covid-19 pandemic era (Williams, 2021). Whether we travel or not, regional rail tracks, highways or streets, parking lots or on-street spaces must be maintained, and excessively sized and mega mobility infrastructures following the 20th century lifestyle have already become an enormous waste and huge financial burden on cities. This lifestyle is also creating more isolation and disconnected lives particularly in suburban locations where most urban residents live. The liquid economy is taking full advantage of deteriorating mental health and promoting unnecessary products to fill the gap. But unlimited consumption never fills the gap of a basic human desire to live in a place that has community connections. Connected neighbourhoods, active mobility, high quality public spaces, and social interactions are not fancy items anymore. These basic, fundamental changes are needed for our survival in the 21st century's liquid economy if we want to address our mental and physical health.

Like the piper of Hamelin, people-oriented city practices are the cure for the car infestation of our cities. If we deny their progress, the lure of the 'magic' pipers will lead us again down the wrong path using the mirage of new mobility and more technology illusions.

### Planetary and mobility economics

The winds of the 'change' story will remain untold if it never forces the truth behind the marriage between the toxic couple: the economics of the third industrial era and the critical elements of urban mobility. Mobility economics shaped the pre- and postmodern era like no other part of society.

At the beginning of the colonial era, ideological philosophy started to infiltrate almost every aspect of the first industrial revolution. The most influential economic theory of the "classical free market" was born in the fertile brain of the Scottish economist, philosopher, and author – Adam Smith. He argued that man should be as equally important as money. Although he is regarded as "The Father of Economics" or "The Father of Capitalism", his theory planted the seed of class division between society's elite and the industrial worker (Weingast, 2017) with the concept of minimum wage and controlling the life of general workers by "invisible hands". He is widely thought to have advocated for unbridled greed and selfishness in the name of allowing the invisible hand of the market to work its magic (Rasmussen, 2016). For the first time in human history, his economic theory linked growth with building infrastructure, especially mega highways, wrapped into one package which would be paid for by the user (Smith, 1776). While the US created a vast network of highways across America, none of them were paid for by users and their crumbling infrastructures represent a failure of Adams' economic theory in the era of environmental constraints (Boarnet, 1995). He was the first economist to propose exploiting our by-birth lack (lack of blueprint). He promoted celebrating the wild side of every human to become a 'whole' human by fulfilling the lack with endless products. Everyone can flourish if we are independently greedy. His capitalism created a structural hole that exists everywhere and is creating the compulsion of a crisis and the repetition of a vicious cycle of failure (Karatani, 1989). The first visible hole was inequality. Every time an innovation comes along, old technology becomes obsolete and creates a new crisis. In the 1880s, rail powered by steam engines become the force behind the British empire. Everywhere the British would colonize, rail tracks were built. First to carry out the exploited product locally then to create more surplus for the abstract capitalist system. A new "innovation fix" was proposed by Ford to fix the "new hole" of capitalism at the end of the 19th century. The car emerged as the new way to buy unnecessary product, filling every activity of our life to become a 'whole' human by filling our lack. As a negative force the car repressed many things in society specifically during the 1970's energy crisis era. The new "spatial fix" of capitalism proposed to ship jobs and factories to cheap labour locations in developing nations. Marine transportation become the new carrier of global capitalism, giving birth to a new social structure of post modernity and created enormous surplus and of course a new crisis of nationalism. The new crisis was unemployment in rich nations and the beginning of severe inequality in the 1980s when Reaganism tried to fix it with a "temporal fix" (Reagan, 1983), i.e., financing the future. Enormous highways and mega streets become the new allies of the temporal fix and became a carrier of the merging of space and time to secure the future. But the concept of unpaid highways and 'free' parking created its own vicious hole. In the 1990s an economic stumble led to another new fix. The 'credit' fix of the 1980s, that started after the collapse of "Bretton Woods"[22] (Amadeo, 2022), and lasted less than two decades when it finally crashed in 2008. Risk management through derivatives would bet on "at risk" people (such as the black community, and poor, ethnic migrants) to promote the troubled vehicle-oriented suburban formula of selling multiple cars to the same family. The neoclassical economy created its deepest loophole. And the 21st century "social fix" through emergence "liquid modernity" has become the new tool to invade our identity, gender, race, and every aspect of our social life, particularly through social media as a tool of neo-colonialism. The electric car, transit-oriented urban revitalization, and keeping the car as the core of new multimodal mobility has become a digital mobility ally. Autonomous vehicle hysteria soon came to derail the decoupling of the car and economic growth efforts, during the first two decades of the 21st century. In an era of growing environmental problems, resource scarcity, and financial constraints, the decoupling of growth and vehicle usage (Gray et al., 2006) has become a central focus of economic policy, particularly post-2015, facing the impending climate crisis (Zeller, 2015). In the Covid-19 era, we have seen a new 'digital' colonization emerge at a hyper accelerated speed to 'fix' the pre-Covid era by taking advantage of isolated labour working from home. But after accelerating the new liquid economy for only a few months, a new crisis cycle created a highly volatile society and fragile economic conditions, including the highest level of inequality in human history.

Parallel to the unbridled capitalism crisis and the collapse of utopian communism ideology, a more sombre economic model did emerge in the 1990s. True multimodal mobility that avoided consuming excessive resources was intimately linked to fringe ideas but hopefully formed the

---

[22] The Bretton Woods agreement of 1944 established a new international monetary system. It replaced the gold standard with the US dollar as the global currency.

new economy that would fundamentally transform a never-ending surplus and its vicious cycle of crises. "Prosperity without growth" was one of a series of new economic principles that provided evidence that growth does not increase human well-being and as a function of investment should be a commitment to the future and contribute to human development objectives (Jackson, 2009). The Stern review proposed to fix the 'rate-of-return' of infrastructure (Stern, 2006) that was robbing our environmental assets. Instead of a high return such as 6–10% for new infrastructure capital recovery, Stern proposed to reduce it to less than 1.5% to account for the potential of future generations and its survival. This would avoid the repeated dependance of the "Keynesian infrastructure growth theory" which turned out to be a triumphant failure for cities. The new 3P (Planet, People, Profit) approach proposed to fix the financing of transit projects. Micro financing to grow small scale "social business" was proposed by Dr. Yunus (Yunus, 2011) to avoid capital accumulation for the sake of surplus and to recycle reasonable profits to social well-being and avoid destroying everything in the future while ignoring our present. If the emergence of the shared economy and shared mobility is properly regulated, the beginning of the "asset-light business model" would be able to create the "circular economy" concept (Lovins et al., 2018) that limits demand and endless environmentally unfriendly consumption. In 2017, "doughnut economics" (Raworth, 2017) was proposed, and partially implemented in the Netherlands (Naught, 2021). This new economic approach expected to create a practical way to implement a circular economy by reducing our environmental footprint. This book borrows some of these new economic approaches to develop a new low-emission mobility system that would survive in the post-Anthropocene era.

We should not forget the lesson learned from this cycle of relations between mobility and the economy. Mobility infrastructure in cities is an indispensable example of technological success, as well as a hinderance.

*"When we are tired, we are attacked by ideas we conquered long ago."*
—Friedrich Nietzsche

# PART 2

# The Invisible People of Mobility

## The Forgotten People in Mobility Planning and Design

There is no space for 'differences' inside the 200-year-old industrial society. It was and still is built on the premise of homogeneity, an innovation both capitalism and in many ways communism and socialism ideologically embraced. To repress the ever-growing source of social inequality, the essence of 'difference' in our society has given us a platform to flourish if it consumes global 'multicultural' consumer products within their own culture and customized context. Percolating every aspect of daily life has become the central premise of neo-digital colonization (Martin, 2002) or more precisely high-tech feudalism.

These postmodern narratives never entered our mobility systems despite our society moving on from feudalism to self-interested 'modernism' to 'decentralization' narratives of decolonization after World War II. There are few traces of gender, age differences, different physical conditions, or cultural footprints into mobility facilities (NACTO, 2017). Traffic signals are male. Theories of traffic speed are manly. Straight mega streets are patriarchal. Operations of transit vehicles and the space around transit stations feels like male space. Anyone practising mobility planning, design, and implementation will always feel the presence of a mysterious 'typical' person – an able-bodied, healthy, white Caucasian male.

To be clear there were some changes. Mostly outside of mobility practitioners. But with hidden narratives. Those changes remain fringe topics to add a flavour of 'alternative' mobility options rather than transforming the foundation of the vehicle culture. The choice of words reveals it very clearly. Despite the highest level of intelligence and enormous capabilities, in the beginning and the end periods of our life we are fragile and weak. It's the same for all species on our planet, but particularly for humans. Often referred to as "vulnerable users", we should first acknowledge our "vulnerable understanding" of different demography, cultural, and stages of human life. The vulnerable users' concept was commonly used to address the special needs of 'special' demographics (e.g., seniors, children, people with physical limitations). However, the perception of 'vulnerable' originates from comparing them to a standard or stronger counterpart – the middle-aged healthy white male. The concept also 'boxed-in' these demographics as a special case and treated their requirements as "additional needs". Humans live in stages and there is no alternative but to accept our stages of life and build environments to accommodate the different stages of life of different types of people.

*"One is not born, but rather becomes, a woman."*
—Simone de Beauvoir

### *Imagine there are no women[23]*

The event occurred at Union station in Toronto. A female tourist in her sixties was asking for directions to a male staff in a tourist booth. In response, the male guide replied, "Please walk north for 10 minutes and turn east to find your destination". The women asked, "Which way is north". The man replied, "Well, when you go out you will see Scotiabank tower, walk toward it for 10 minutes and then turn…". This classic question by the women is not unique. Women perceive our world in different ways than men. Men usually follow utility direction (such as north, south, east, or west) however, women find a place by comparing it to the location of a landmark.

Our world has different types of people who do things in different ways. It is not supposed to be a problem. But when standardized or stereotypical ideology forces everyone to think only one way, problems appear.

From the first known women Lucy to the dancing girls of ancient Harappa, to post-modern's decolonized feminine struggle, women have led society toward a progressive, tolerant, and knowledge-based inclusive society since the first human walked on the planet. Our liberation toward the general adoption of low-carbon mobility in the late 19th century to the modern-day success of mixed-use developments is being silently led by women. And yet despite women making up more than half of the planet's population, and that they are always around us, along with others, city systems including mobility system planning and design often discount the true, hidden, complex and nonlinear existence of women. While men and women evolved in nature in a similar timeframe, the "unconscious discourse" of women is predominantly excluded by "conscious men". A few extraordinary natural senses also set women apart from men and other demography.

The mobility system suffers the same providence.

The dominance of males in mobility is probably one of the reasons for ignoring or misunderstanding the needs of women in the mobility system. However, simply blaming the male is not going to solve a desperately needed reset and complex overhaul of the mobility system that provides equitable mobility access to women. The problem may be deeply connected to social stereotypes, cultural 'acceptable' norms or simply the philosophical thought process that guides our society behind the scenes. And until we understand and develop a truly gender-balanced mobility system, no 'smart-city' will be smart enough despite the deployment of the most sophisticated technologies.

Truths are, however, uncomfortable and take a long time to be established.

Over the course of human history, a crowd of extraordinary women and their unthinkable sacrifices have touched human hearts and provided visible signs to comprehend the nature of the coming age and open the door to possible solutions. Like Lucy, some women took audacious steps out of declining areas toward an unknown path, a remarkable decision that saved the human species during prehistoric resource depletion. Around 4500 BC, a stone figure known as "dancing girl" provoked intense debate and evidence of a progressive and equitable civilization (Hirst, 2019). Egypt gave us not just an astonishing civilization but a few exceptional women that planted the seeds of the imagination of the modern human. Known for her physical beauty in a man's world, Cleopatra was renowned for her scientific skills, multilanguage skills, sharp practical knowledge of equal society, wise leadership abilities, and for being one of the greatest thinkers of all time. Hypatia, often downgraded to a history footnote, was known as the last great philosopher of Alexandria. Her invention the 'astrolabe' sparked the greatest interest in marine mobility with guidelines for everyone on the seas to explore and discover every corner of the planet. These historical intellectual achievements, however, remain forgotten in the modern era.

---

[23] This series of section title is inspired by Joan Copjec's and Jacques Lacan's idea that women do not exist. Only our lack (i.e., −1) exists as the one and only human species identity in the real world.

There were a few attempts to fix the problem, mostly by women and in western counties. But they got lost in the "glittery talk" of the feminist, women-friendly cities, inclusive city banner. Starting from 1792 with the Rights of Women (Wollstonecraft and Lync, 1792) to the 1848 in-church protests to the 1920s right to vote, the first wave of women mostly focused on the portrayal of women as caregivers and on predominantly Caucasian women's issues. This classical view of feminism shaped many modern-day attempts to build neighbourhoods, space, and mobility around the caregiver function. Except for those fighting for women's education rights such as Begum Rokeya in Bangladesh or Raden Ajeng Kartini in Indonesia, women remained mostly invisible in the non-western world. Women's adoption of cycling as a major mode of transportation remains as one of the most inspiring mobility transformations led by women. Although psychoanalysis provided a deeper understanding and the root causes of women's exclusion from mobility, populist feminism frequently rejected the deeper links to systematic oppression. The second wave came with monumental insights from Simone de Beauvoir (Beauvoir, 1949) which were later ignited during the 1960s, aligning with the greater civil rights movement and focused on systematic oppression, equal pay, and women's role in society. Three forms of feminism came from the second wave: mainstream focused on institutional reforms; cultural identification of women having a different essence from men; and a radical version that wanted to reshape and complete overhaul the system. The symbolic act of Rosa Parks claiming a front seat on a public transit vehicle remains a defining moment of the human rights movement. The third wave in the 1990s paid more attention to racial disparities (Crenshaw, 1996) and reclaiming women's place in society. Cultural feminism become the dominant movement following gender performativity (Butler, 1990). This stream often suffers from a typical populist approach to solving women's issues without addressing the structurally repressed root causes (Copjec, 2014) and vulnerabilities to exploitation by the consumer culture. Adoption of walkable, bikeable, and transit-friendly cities by women became a symbol of the city building process in the 1990s, particularly in European cities. The fourth or current wave started in the digital era with the #MeToo movement and revealed a fragmented version of women's rights and a variety of voices clashing with each other. But within a fringe group, this period started to spread the repressed topic of the exclusion of women from the city building process, particularly their nonexistence in mobility systems. While South Asia or the Middle East adopted more commercial versions of corporate feminism, fragmented western Europe, Latin America, and parts of North America avoided the commercialization approach of women in the unbridled capitalism which remains mostly patriarchal still today.

The simple premise of introducing this complex issue is based on millennium-old lessons learned. The history of civilization has repeatedly proven that the decline of an empire or states always displays a common syndrome – when women are treated badly the society shows signs of spiraling downward, a decline that leads to ultimate system collapse. We can try to save ourselves from a sixth extinction using gigantic infrastructures or with technology unicorns or we can simply let go of the current male dominated city building and mobility system. The latter has a proven successful record. The former option has never been proven as the right path to building society.

Supplanting the dream of women's rightful place in society, we can feel Hypatia's tears in every corner of the street where women remain invisible despite their progress elsewhere over the last 2000 years.

> *"The path to a man's heart is through his stomach, but there are women who know a shorter way."*
>
> —Jacques Tati

### *Do women exist in mobility systems – An extraordinary exclusion*

Over time, some bold city building ideas were born to make the invisible into a visible entity. Very few or almost none account for women. While other bold and progressive theories for city design, such as "8–80 cities" are theoretically valid, the practical path to real accomplishment leads to nowhere. Children under eight are supposed to play and have very little opportunity to interact in the city planning process. Seniors have provided their greatest service over an entire lifetime and would generally like to live a worry-free life after 80. While both groups should be included in the planning and design process of the existing or future mobility system, only women can understand to a great extent the needs of the 8- or the 80-year demography and can provide meaningful solutions to complex demography-related mobility problems. There are many ideas for a more walkable city but very few point out the needs of pedestrians. There are bicycle urbanism cities, but women are largely excluded through vehicle-like infrastructure design. There are transit-oriented cities, but women face uncomfortable rides inside transit and outside of stations deprived of landscape or other features that would help women feel safer. Whether a radiant city or garden city, or smart growth or green city, or smart city, women still today do not exist anywhere in the city building process.

Indeed, the discussion on the very notion of the inclusion of women in city or mobility planning is immediately placed under the guillotine. Threatened with harsh treatment in the workplace, public engagement or other processes in city building are those who ever dare to raise the issues. Issues of women in mobility are surprisingly frequently silenced by not only by men but occasionally by women to avoid an uncomfortable discussion in a landscape dominated by men. Often, talking about women in mobility only leads to fixing "bad spots" with 'patches'. This is a recent trend but mostly soon leads to a dead-end, as did the other human rights problems in history. It's time to provide a permanent solution not just by women but also by men. From the author's point of view, this section could be perceived as a confession of a patriarchal traffic engineer on an unconscious discourse of women's invisibility in mobility. Like a hacker knows how to make a better system when knowledge is applied toward greater benefits, (progressive) male mobility planners or designers know where and how the hidden components were inserted that created the concealed discrimination intentionally or unintentionally. They are pointing the spotlight on the right place to fix the problem. To understand this complex topic, we must look back on our history, on psychological insights, and to clues from art and culture that would provide evidence of how and why we see women suffering from gender stereotypes in mobility systems despite the advancement of laws, norms, and acceptance in the postmodern era. The author proposes altering the basic elements of the mobility system to include all types of different people as the default approach to find the way to true and permanent mobility system change for the benefit of all people in society. This section of this chapter, and Chapter 4 provide the details behind these approaches.

> *"We are guilty of many errors and many faults, but our worst crime is abandoning the children, neglecting the fountain of life."*
>
> —Gabriela Mistral

### *Imagine there are no children*

After the discovery of a dinosaur fossil by a four-year-old girl, a female BBC interviewer asked her how she found the rare dinosaur bone. The kid replied it was at her eye level. This was a natural answer for a child.

The child's world is different from that of the adult. Due to their physical size, and different perceptions and cognitive abilities.

Cities used to be playful places for children. Neighbours used to keep an eye on playing kids as a form of social security. Jane Jacobs' famous sidewalk observation tells the story of playful cities that existed for thousands of years before the 20th century when cars took over our public spaces.

Removing all traces of children's places and real-life education from the street is still embarrassingly visible through the banning of children's activity on streets. Children now play games inside, and the normal development of their brain is slowing as most activity is confined to indoors and they have no safe access to outdoor spaces to play (McCarthy, 2020). To make way for cars, we've made playing in the street illegal. We've allowed sport utility vehicles (SUVs) to flourish without correcting the greater (50% higher) risk of pedestrian fatalities, particularly of head injuries to children (Desapriya et al., 2010). We now place criminal charges on parents for collisions when their child is hurt on the street (Iannelli, 2021), instead of charging the system designers for outdated large and straight mega roads that make crossing difficult, create greater traffic volumes, and poor visibility, low-light conditions are other road-related characteristics associated with increased child pedestrian collisions (Wazana et al., 1997). These brutal omissions from utilitarian 'micro' ethics came back to haunt us during the Covid-19 pandemic in the form of having no places for children to go while parents were working from home. But the revolt started much earlier.

The rapid decline of active mobility uses and the rise of pedestrian/cyclist fatalities, particularly among children, have now become a global epidemic. Traffic crashes are the leading cause of death for children under 20 years in both high-, middle- or low-income countries (Peden et al., 2008). The death of 830,000 children every year has become another systematic but invisible black hole in our society. Even parents argue in support of these gruesome collisions if it's not their children (Nikitas et al., 2019). Dangerous driving by parents and the deteriorating safety zones around schools are the leading cause of childhood deaths (Rothman et al., 2017). At least 10 high crash zones have been identified around school zones in Toronto, all of them located outside of downtown. Although parents drive their children to school in fear of a lack of safety, studies indicate walking to school reduces overall traffic crashes around school zones. In Canada, 55 fatalities occurred since 2009 (for ages less than 14) (Transport Canada, 2013), costing $1.7 billion in 2013 alone (Transport Canada, 2007). Despite police and politicians often blaming "distracted pedestrians", no evidence was found against either children or adults as a pedestrian-caused fatality (Mwakalonge et al., 2015).

Several myths persist behind deteriorating safety and high vehicle usage when it relates to children. Drivers expect children will behave as a "mature person" when they are using the streets. Children's ability to perceive is however different. Children have a limited understanding of 'danger', are easily distracted, and confused by sudden changes, and most importantly, they have limited peripheral vision which restricts their ability to judge the speed and distance of moving vehicles. Residential areas, community centres, children's areas and school zone planning and design, therefore, needs to pay special attention to society's most precious citizens. Children up to early teenagers lack the perceptual judgment and motor skills to safely cross a busy road in daily life (O'Neal et al., 2018). Children on bicycles (10 to 12 years old) take more time to cross, particularly girls, increasing the risk on the streets not designed for this demography (Plumert et al., 2007). Until the age of 14, children do not have the fully developed judgement to understand safety risk (Lewis, 2017). It's not a coincidence that traffic crashes have become the leading cause of mortality among children under fourteen.

Successes from east Asian and European countries, however, have proven that by increasing active mobility to children's destinations, and child-oriented streets and mobility routes to school, zero children's deaths are an achievable target in a relatively short period of time. And the international Safe Routes to School movement has become a safety movement during the last decade. No children died in Norway in 2015 (The Local, 2015) even though the country has the highest rates of walking and cycling to school. Norway deployed safety laws and very strict enforcement in addition to child-friendly street design and vehicle safety. South Korea eliminated 97% (as of 2021) of child deaths with stringent policies such as banning cars around school areas (Sung and Rios, 2015) and successful political will as a result of very strong advocacy (Jaehoon, 2014) work from organized parent groups. Both the United Kingdom and Scotland have made significant progress on sustainable school travel with mandatory funding requirements backed by binding legislation. By adopting vision zero policies in school zone areas, school travel has become a centerpiece of success in Japan, Sweden, and the Netherlands. Amsterdam and most recently Paris restricted vehicles from entire city blocks around schools and other children's destinations. The strategic location of schools, safety programmes, and the community hub ideas were implemented in Hamilton. Although the approach was different between pioneers, they have a common theme: the loss of human life in traffic crashes is preventable and can be treated as a curable disease with a special focus on creating children-friendly street design principles and planning practices.

### *Imagine there are no aging people*

The most visible failure of our vehicle-oriented culture is the failure of planning or design for when we grow old. Almost every aspect of our vehicle-focused ideology creates both hidden and visible problems for our senior citizens. An increasingly aged population in rural areas is common in developing nations, as opposed to the observed trend of the younger population moving to urban areas (OECD, 2019). We travel less after we retire, gradually seniors have limited access to mobility services and many have activity impairments (Bezirgani and Lachapelle, 2018). The impact of traffic pollution is greater among seniors. Bad air damages the brain. The likelihood of developing Alzheimer's Disease is twice and 1.5 times more likely from increased exposure to nitrogen dioxide and particulate matter 2.5 (Shell, 2020). The absence of the aging demography in mobility systems is most clearly visible in crash data. The aging population takes a greater hit when there is an incident or collision or an unexpected situation. Speed is the central premise of the vehicle-oriented culture. A senior's body loses the capacity by half compared to a 24-year-old person's, to absorb the sheer impact of high-speed collisions (Leaf and Preusser, 1999). Figure 2B.1 illustrates how high-speed crashes have a devastating impact on the aging population, revealing the ignorance of this population in traffic planning and design. Aging reduces our walking speed, and we take a roughly 34% longer time than a middle-aged person (Asher et al., 2012). As we grow older, every year we see one foot less of typical sight distance while driving after the age of fifty-five (Smiley, 2004). Insurance companies have suggested driving only in daylight hours after 55 due to the impact of age on the body (G of C, 2019). Our reaction time gets slower. Turning at an intersection takes a senior twice the time of a middle-aged person. Safety records indicate as we age our ability to see well reduces when we are moving quickly due to headlights. Also, the ability of the pupil opening to adjust in proportion to the available light deteriorates considerably with aging. The eye gate becomes smaller and smaller even in the daytime, but the critical feature is the inability to open at twilight and in darkness to let in whatever little light might be available, particularly past the age of 60 (FHWA, 2001). Reduced visibility reduces senior pedestrians' ability to see motor vehicles and avoid crashes (Lutkevich et al., 2012) in addition to a heightened risk due to the lower reaction time and travel speeds of both the aged driver and pedestrian. Despite known performance differences between young and old demography, street illumination is rarely considered to be adjusted or increased for the aging population, particularly near retirement areas.

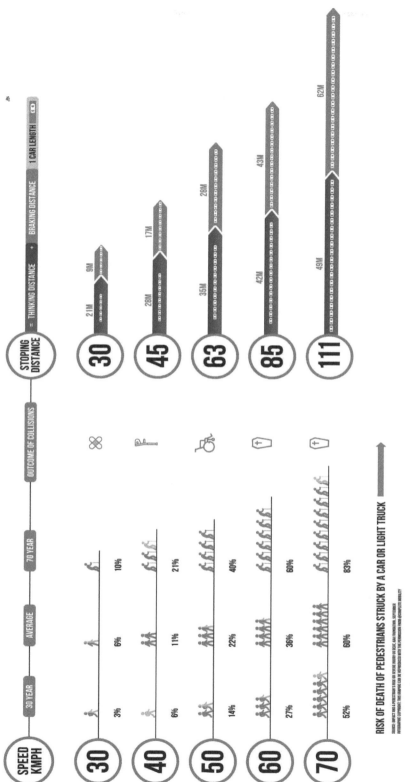

**Fig. 2B.1:** Impact of speed on different ages.

> *"History, despite its wrenching pain, cannot be unlived, but if faced with courage,*
> *need not be lived again."*
>
> —Dr. Maya Angelo

### Imagine there are no people with physical difficulty

Like other demographic groups, mobility systems are visibly uncomfortable for people with physical limitations. People with physical limitations are expected to increase 17% in Canada, partly due to gains in injuries from traffic collisions or incidents. Most cities in North America have enacted accessibility laws to forcefully impose rules to include the disabled population. In Toronto, the local transit authority was finally forced to provide accessible buses and subways in 2017. Regional transit only completed accessibility requirements in 2019. Both resulted from fear of a class action lawsuit, not because of lack of awareness in mobility practices. The installation of tactile surfaces to indicate a safe path on the sidewalk or intersection scanners are still ongoing. The absence of pedestrian ramps is common in developing nations. Obstacles in the middle of the sidewalk or extending the raised median over pedestrian crossings are common in modern cities. Even today parking layby or on-street parking has no accessible ramp, forcing people in wheelchairs to continue into a live traffic lane to access a ramp at intersections. These are not isolated errors, rather notions of industry-wide omissions. While most items are being corrected over the last decade, there is still no comprehensive approach to how to include these demographics before developing design practices or building mobility facilities.

### Imagine there are no culture

The non-existence of culture in mobility systems remains an untouchable topic today. Most of our streets look the same with no cultural traces of community living. All parking lots or structures today look alike but replaced century old community historic public squares or used spaces that used to be gathering places or farmer's markets at town centres. Many small or medium sized cities in Canada are removing their unused parking lots and restoring old public squares to revive vibrant cultural places that used to connect communities. The local business community reclaiming the boulevard or streetscape has become a new movement in the last decade. But restored old glory sometimes comes at the cost of gentrifying original residents out of revitalized areas. For instance, Denmark's famous Superkillen, restored a public park to reflect local ethnic residents, starting with benevolent placemaking objectives, but turned into "place marketing", driving out its original ethnic residents to make way for wealthy Caucasian residents. A similar story is told about almost every revitalized street in Canada or the US. The presence of cultural or community history can be done while preserving the original residents if planning principles and creative design approaches are developed carefully.

> *"Everything that has been written by men about women should be viewed with*
> *suspicion, because they are both judge and party."*
>
> —Poulain de la Barre

# PART 3
# Shifting Mobility with an Indifference to Differences

Endless inclusive talks and a flurry of social media buzz have not solved any mobility problems. In the real world, we need a practical and implementable approach. This is a monumental task, nonetheless inspired by three ingenious grounds: the fundamental human psychological proposition that there is no "whole of being", i.e., a human can never fully achieve enlightenment or wholeness by filling their lacks with commodities or external superficial items or elements (Lacan, 1964); psychoanalysis projection that avoids segmenting humans into classes (Copjec, 2014); and the philosophical ground of creating a system that works for all people regardless of their differences (Menon, 2015). Based on these comprehensive foundations, this book proposes a new approach to "human resonance" to understand the needs of every segment of society but develop a unified approach to solutions instead of adding 'patch' work layers to a broken system base. Figure 2B.1 illustrates an example of a unified approach rather than segmented solutions for each part of demography or identity or cultural background. The approach initially identifies all potential social, environmental, and economical aspects of mobility. Later this section addresses two more mobility cultures issues. The first issue is a hidden culture that is now sweeping through the mobility world to keep the vehicle at its core when new autonomous and connected vehicles arrive in the future. Instead, this book proposes to create a true multimodal oriented approach that keeps different forms of transit in different built form and context. The second issue is providing a sense of what it means to reduce cars and replace them with multimodal mobility options. This broader set of systematic identification of issues leads to a specific planning and design concept. Details of the concept are described in Chapter 4.

## *A city that feels all people and cultural differences*

The visible ignorance of invisible people in mobility leads to a simple solution to the complex problem – what are the fundamentals for mobility planning and design that work for every human.

The book proposes three simple principles to address this millennium-old ignorance.

1. Cities designed for women, by women are cities for all people.
2. Fundamental but gradual redesign of mobility spaces to create safer and lovable cities.
3. The inclusion of "human resonance" to incorporate all decision elements or parameters based the true nature and pattern all people's mobility.

### Foundations of mobility transformation

This section briefly summarizes some basic principles reflecting the learnings from the evolution of city building and how mobility systems have shaped us over thousands of years. These principles reveal the mechanism of the hidden true mobility code and how to develop practical approaches to a local culture of multimodal mobility that embraces a local and sustainable ecosystem.

### Inclusion of differences

One of the basic principles of the human species is we are born without a blueprint. This drives us to live in a communal set-up and remains the central force of building relations between each other. We are also born with a 'non-relation' psychological status, the driving force of creativity. The other referred to herein is building relations with other people, spaces, and associations, and mobility is the simple mechanism toward these 'relational' drives. Our relations, however, are temporary but fundamental in the way we deal with our lacking. This remains the underlying reason for our natural human right to urban or natural spaces. The quality of places and city building gives us a short window to get rid of boredom and maintain our mental or physical health conditions.

### Inclusion of a sense of differences

Our lack cannot be filled with just materialistic commodities to achieve the "whole of being". Consumer culture, religion, and many external forces however have invaded the premises and promised us 'enlightenment'. But nothing has worked. A few of our differences were rarely included in our approach to building cities. For instance, men are mainly about the present, follow a horizontal timeline, and dwell within a domain of the finite and a visual field of the conscious world. On the contrary, women can feel the past and recognize an absence due to a more dominant unconscious presence. Women follow a vertical time and are driven by the search for the infinite (Colette, 2006). Women generally develop intellectual capability earlier than men, making them generally equipped to handle complex situations with more relatively simple thinking than men. On a different level, children and senior's activities are different than middle aged men's and they perceive things through the inner unconsciousness of human psychology. These elements require sophisticated efforts to bring out our emotions, feelings, and perceptions when city facilities or services are being developed. Inclusivity, access, and safety are dynamically produced through space (Beebeejaun, 2016), completing the opposite idea of alienating mega mobility infrastructure due to its inhuman scale. Without women, children, and seniors, our cities would be unpleasant, and uninhabitable.

### The human mobility code

When we move, we spend energy. And it's different for different people. A human needs a certain amount of food every day to stay alive. Metabolism within the human body is a common mechanism that links energy expenditure, biochemical interactions, and controls our daily activity rates. The metabolic rate determines the distance an animal can travel (McMorrough, 2015). Our common activity is reflected in our daily movements and the movement pattern shows how and where we move. On an average, metabolism rate and body mass are lower for women compared to men (West, 2017). When any animal moves, the distance it covers is linked to its metabolic rate. For instance, migrant species have higher rates than non-migrant species. It is no wonder women make more shorter distance trips than men (White, 1977). The same is true for children and seniors. Short distances are often underestimated and sometimes intentionally ignored in mobility planning and design. Gender bias is notable in winter maintenance priorities, for instance. People are three times more likely to be injured while walking, predominantly women, than driving and the cost of injury exceeds the cost of snow clearance. To remove systematic gender bias, Stockholm flipped snow clearance priority by cleaning walkways and bike paths near transit stops or schools first, followed by local roads and finally highways. Recognizing the short trips of the majority of people's mobility pattern (Yapp, 2021), Stockholm recently adopted the 'one-minute' city, moving toward a hyperlocal approach.

## Human safety

Similarly biological difference often ignored, creating a disadvantage in mobility for women, children, seniors, and people with physical limitations. It remains a mystery women's apparent ability to store fat more efficiently than men, despite eating proportionally fewer calories (Blaak, 2001). A low resting metabolic rate has been identified as a possible cause for the increased body fat of women (Buchholz et al., 2001). A softer body is linked to a higher rate of crashes among women. Women are nearly 47% more likely to be seriously injured (Bose et al., 2011) to 73% more likely to be seriously or fatally injured in frontal collisions (Forman et al., 2019) after controlling for the car's model and year, and the passenger's or driver's age, height, weight, BMI, and proximity to the steering wheel. Women are 17% more likely to die (Kahane, 2013) due to high-speed design principles. While comparing driving between males and females, the national Canadian collision statistics compiled by Transport Canada repeatedly show a female driver displayed half of the crash rates compared to a male driver when other factors are normalized. This trend repeats itself in all cities and countries around the world, confirming a natural and definitive pattern of women's extraordinary sense of safety. Reaction times are slower among women and seniors, but they have proven safer techniques in safety performance. Seniors share of pedestrian fatalities has surpassed 70% in Toronto and elsewhere. Children face the highest causality rates due to vehicle impact of any other age groups due to the lack of safety assessment capacity of under 10-year-old. Safety disparity in different genders is still unknown, however, a few safety procedures do put women or children in a disadvantaged position compared to men (Hux, 2019). Crash test dummies are typically modeled on an average man for vehicle safety tests (Holder, 2019). Crash test dummies and other driving experiences include less than 5% of specimens, the excuse given that there are no manufacturers available for different-sized bodies. Highways and streets are intentionally designed for higher speeds, often more than 70 kmph, increasing the risk for women or the obese or overweight population (Zhu et al., 2010). Health policies and vehicle regulations must focus on effective safety designs specifically tailored toward the female population for equity in injury reduction (Forman, et al., 2019). These facts indicate the need for a change in fundamental system design elements. For instance, posted speeds in urban areas should be reduced to typical 30kmph urban conditions and traffic signals or devices adjusted from 70 kmph to 30 kmph.

## Environmental inclusion

Despite being more environmentally motivated (e.g., willing to make compromises that benefit the environment) and less skeptical about the importance of environmental issues (OECD, 2019), women face a disproportionate exposure to pollution. Women's participation is double in green and renewable resources compared to traditional jobs (OECD, 2018). Traffic pollution and other negative impacts are more pronounced for women than for men (Dijkema et al., 2011). Women suffer more from residential particulate matter (OECD, 2019) generated from vehicles. Women are generally capable of detecting faint sound level sources, are more sensitive to noise exposure and perform significantly better at a lower sound frequency (less than 65 dBA) than men (Abbasi et al., 2022). Increasing age causes people to experience hearing loss of high frequencies and this reduces the individual's sensitivity to mid-high frequencies (Abbasi et al., 2015). Positive links between average road noise exposure and health problems (Björk et al., 2006) were found among females (hypertension), and sleep deprived persons, was more stressful among the unemployed, and created concentration problems for persons with financial problems. The effect of sound on frequencies causes reductions in sleep quality among women (Röösli et al., 2014), which has distinct long-term health consequences. Noise activates the central nervous system which accelerates the response to some stressors (Paunović et al., 2009), and noise pollution is linked to heart disease and high blood pressure (Kempen et al., 2002). In general, residents living in noisy areas were found to have a 2.25 times higher risk per 5 dBA increments in the noise levels, and noise levels greater than 60 dBA are associated with coronary artery disease in adults (Gilani and Mir, 2021). Despite seven million people dying every year, including one million due to noise pollution, the environmental threshold was never adjusted for different people other than the 'mysterious' average person.

## Leaders of sustainable mobility

Mobility choices are strongly associated with age and gender. Women are more adaptable to sustainable mobility than men. Women generally use more public transit and less private vehicles (9% less) than men (OECD, 2019). When women drive a car, they are less likely to carpool than males, but they prefer to carpool with two passengers over one (Monchambert, 2020). Women make a more trip chaining pattern of travel behaviour than men. Women walk more and use the sidewalk more often than men. Northern and western Europe have seen more cycling usage among women. In Toronto, a dramatic change in mobility shift toward transit, walking, cycling, and carshare in the downtown area has been led by women after mixed-use was implemented in the last two decades. Despite changed behaviours, space allocation is biased toward cars (roughly 70–80% of downtown is still occupied by vehicles). This book proposes to change roughly two-thirds of that space to human and green space to address space discrimination and different demography needs.

## Adaptation to change

Females are more resourceful than males and have a greater sense of discovery. This nature is reflected in technology adaptation. Women are more adaptable to change, and take initiatives toward new systems, technology, innovation, and creative thinking. Technology adoption is much slower among men, and they typically resist change, particularly in mobility sectors. On the contrary, women and younger generations find easy ways to adapt to societal changes. The refusal to improve mobility access for invisible people remains as one of the enduring rigid mobility practices among men that bring back vehicle-oriented cities whenever there is an opportunity to restrict meaningful multimodal mobility options.

## Connection to space

The inclination for better spaces and livable environments among women, children, and seniors is not a secret anymore. Instead of the imaginary orientation of coordinates, women identify places with an associated landmark. Many cities are now changing street directions to include landmarks, expected walking distances, and trip time in way finding signs. Women are three times more likely to suffer from depression and mental illness than men, followed by seniors and children. Interaction in public space is a well-known remedy for depression. Following these patterns, only a handful of cities addressed the connection between space and health. Indeed, pedestrian promenades and boulevards were invented in Paris, reflecting millennium-old city building practices in the ancient Middle East or Latin American public space culture (Lawrence, 1988). Tree-lined boulevards of the 19th and 20th centuries were derived from ten different formats of use of trees in European cities. However, the need for public and open spaces, accessible within a 15-min walking distance, is rarely considered in mobility planning programs. This book proposes invisible space, green (mobility) and human space to reverse and reclaim unused or underutilized vehicle spaces, bring back space for human interactions, and rebuild the community connections that remain at the heart of humans even today.

> *"[a playful city is] Getting children off their devices and making cities more playful."*
>
> —The Irish Times

## *Playful mobility*

Better urban design, playful places design, child friendly streets, careful school zone planning, innovative school travel plans and most importantly, safer street designs and effective awareness campaigns can prevent the unnecessary deaths of children. NACTO recently started a new practice of Kids placemaking on streets (NACTO, 2020). Speed limited 20 mile/hour zones reduced by 70% child pedestrian fatalities in the UK (Webster and Mackie, 1996). Participating schools and real kids turning intersections into murals became a new social and educational tool around the world (Baldwin, 2022). The playful street concept is spreading (Playful city, 2016) across western Europe and Latin America to avoid the thoughtless loss of life of children on the city streets. This idea needs to combine with curb extensions combined with a corner micro garden and treed buffer seating area to attract children to nearby street play areas daily and permanently maintain the space when the programme is completed.

This is not a complete list of mobility changes for different demographics. But this would be considered a good starting point on the long path to a livable mobility evolution.

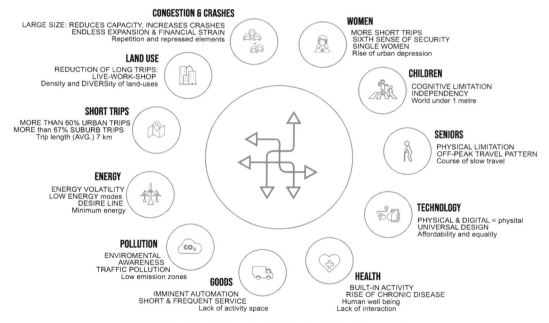

**Fig. 2B.2:** Indifferent elements of different mobility microecosystems.

> *"The desire of which the individual is the consequence begins to shape and mark his whole destiny."*
>
> —Jacques Lacan

## Competing Visions of Cities

If we are going to be able to build livable and low-emission cities, it's time to think deeply on how new city building ideas or new vehicle or mobility technologies will change our cities. Should we encourage its most beneficial usage and features or continue with the most efficient and low carbon form of mobility that has been proven successful in recent years. Or is it a combination of both?

A century-old debate of building cities for people or cars is coming back under a new banner and is now often the centre of debate between progressive city builders and technology inventors. The latter half of the 20th century was dominated by this debate and the vehicle-oriented approach won the battle for better or for worse for the inhabitants of cities. Now facing declining vehicle ownership, urbanization and being forced to acknowledge or adopt a different business model, automobile manufacturing is bringing back Le Corbusier's "Tower in the park" with a mega roads vision under the driverless banner. An oversold autonomous vehicle strategy from "smart mobility" groups started to steer the sustainable mobility discussion while sugar-coating the benefits of driverless vehicles and adding hollow 'buzz-words' to align with sustainable mobility modes since it has proven and achieved remarkable success in improving quality of life in cities. Without a true vision for a people-oriented city and a resilient mobility approach, these recent trends mimic the same failed philosophy once again, mirroring similar efforts by the automobile industry in the early part of the last century.

### *Cars-as-a-backbone*

Through the rise of the autonomous vehicle industry, Le Corbusier's nightmare still haunts us in a new form. It has a new face. The vision of autonomous vehicles is often repeated and intermingled with the so called "smart city" movement. Subtext of the new mobility vision around the autonomous vehicle is often exposed as the old and failed car-oriented vision for cities (West, 2017). A dedicated autonomous vehicle travel lane is often ballyhooed as a critical element of autonomous vehicle success, disguising current or future technology's weakness to operate in the busy and complex city environment (Alessandrini et al., 2015). But the "adding a lane" strategy is not new. It has been used, more precisely misused, every time by members of the traffic engineering society when a highway or road widening is presented as the miracle solution to a 'congestion' problem. There are benefits of a dedicated lane for high-occupancy vehicle or a bus lane when exiting travel lanes are repurposed instead of widening the streets. Shared transit, bikeshare and carshare were thrown into the equation, but no design changes for people are proposed for streets or highways with those ideas in mind. Private vehicle manufacturing companies are promoting a shifting role of public space for private activities (Sumar et al., 2014) identical to the OEM efforts that in the 1930s resulted in a major takeover of public space for private cars in cites. There is little understanding of how shared autonomous vehicles will impact city mobility problems, when it is well established that small or medium sized autonomous vehicles and zero-occupancy will increase congestion due to induced demand (Harb et al., 2018). The shared vehicle requires major changes in space and street design, especially curb lanes and boulevards, and on-street parking operations. None of these facility changes are envisioned as part of the autonomous vision. Even alternative energy plans for autonomous vehicles often lack a comprehensive recharging or refuelling plan. The most disturbing trend is suggesting to bypass better mobility systems and safer street design until 2075 (Shladover, 2016) when true autonomous (level 4 or 5) vehicles will be feasible, thus squandering all the opportunities – and then finding full automation will never come – and denying human mobility rights for the next five decades. Any type of increased vehicle usage, regardless of private, shared, or autonomous, will have a similar negative impact, including increased congestion, urban sprawl, air pollution, and GHG emissions.

Are there any better and sustainable alternatives?

## *Transit-as-a-backbone*

The transit-oriented city is frequently lauded as the best alternative solution. There is no doubt public transit provides low-cost, energy-efficient, better environmental and pollution outcomes while addressing socially equitable travel options (Banister, 2011). Policymakers are now recognizing the benefits of mode shift from vehicle to transit will address climate change in addition to equity and environmental gains. At the same time, building a successful transit city requires local technical knowledge and culture. Very few cities have achieved building equal access to transit like vehicle access. Tokyo is the most successful, followed by Paris, London, Zurich, Barcelona, and many European cities. Most of the attempts at a transit-oriented city face monumental challenges due to their fixed schedule and routes, lower population density, longer travel times, existing sprawling land-use that results in lower ridership (Liao et al., 2020). Ironically and most unfortunately, an unintended consequence is gentrification, creating further inequality between rich and poor within the same city. A most common practice that leads to transit's struggle is focusing on only a few corridors or nodes and ignoring short trip options when riders come out of transit systems and try to reach their destinations by walking, cycling, or micromobility. Not all trips, notably short trips (less than 5 km), are suitable for transit usage.

The flaw in transit-oriented development points to a new direction or solution.

## *Multimodal mobility-as-a-backbone*

Taking advantage of transit efficiency and filling the gaps with active, flexible transit, high-occupant shared mobility, and micromobility is gradually gaining ground as practical, affordable, resilient, and equitable city mobility. Multimodal mode integration was an obscure concept, often applied to multi-vehicle terminals or currently being wrongly used as a hollow promise by smart city enthusiasts. True integration of all modes is giving proportional importance and facility for short trip needs as a starting point, then adding longer trip mobility modes with easier access (Litman, 2017). Truly transformative technology such as mobility-as-a-service has a tremendous advantage to offer multiple mobility modes through a common platform, payment, and travel plans (Matyas, 2020). But we need to get over the imaginary competition between cars and transit, or cars versus cycling, allocate public space for people or really-high-occupancy transit, and rebalance mobility networks toward short-trip users. Multimodal street design and truly equitable transit planning should be the starting point (Global Designing Cities, 2019). Small cities and rural areas could avoid vehicle usage by introducing flexible transit for citywide ecosystem or intercity trips, active and micro-mobility for shorter trips, and shared vehicle services for seniors, medical needs, and others who have no access or ability to own a vehicle. Medium-sized cities could redesign, keeping buses and flexible transit as their backbone while combining limited use of shared and autonomous vehicles where it is essential, active, and micro-mobility modes exist. Larger cities will require high-capacity transit, while filling remote or accessible areas with flexible transit, adding shared autonomous mobility only where it's essential, and expanding the citywide network for active and micromobility.

## Unimodal to Multimodal – Gradual and Slow Escape from Cars

While city builders are recently focusing intensely on reducing private vehicle use in cities, there is very little detail behind what else will fill cars' big shoes. Despite applying all possible travel demand measures to avoid making trips, there will still be a substantial demand to move in cities for various reasons. The big question is what the future mobility mix will be. Many multimodal concepts were proposed over time to find the illusive mobility mix, many policies were written, numerous actions were explored for vehicle reduction. Most did not see the light of day except in a few European cities. Core failures are easy to spot: most plans come with very little detail, a

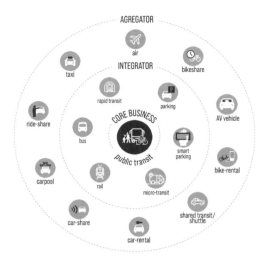

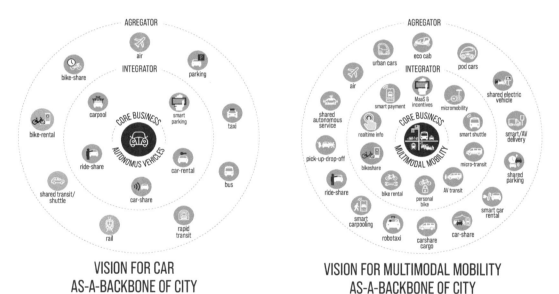

**Fig. 2B.3:** Competing visions of future mobility.

vague timeframe, isolating modes by not fitting them into an ecosystem where they complement each other. And most importantly, a reasonable quantity of multimodal systems needs to be in place to achieve the illusive target. For instance, Transform TO's plan aims to achieve 75% active and sustainable mobility in Toronto, but real alternative plans and policies for enticing city residents or visitors to sustainable mobility are nearly non-existence. There is no need for a forceful mode shift. People gradually move toward easier, affordable, and efficient services if available.

Practical solutions to quantify the replacement of private vehicles are difficult. Using simple but actual vehicle replacement rates of multimodal mobility services, the author estimated it will take another 50–60 years to replace all private vehicle trips in Toronto, for instance, if sufficient comfortable, easier, and affordable alternatives, facilities, and services are provided to city inhabitants. Figure 2B.4 illustrates a feasible and practical approach that starts with a reasonable

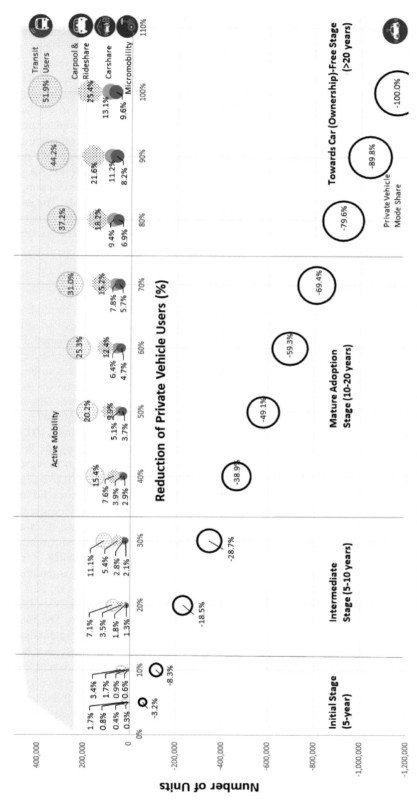

**Fig. 2B.4:** Slow and effective plan for gradual replacement of private vehicle mobility in Toronto.

replacement rate that eventually achieves the target in four stages. The fourth stage may not be practical to achieve but part of it could eventually see no vehicle ownership is necessary. Big question marks remain for active mobility since walking, cycling, and other active forms of mobility are highly sensitive to safety and appropriate infrastructures are required to achieve major transformations of mobility systems. Many North Americans want it but are not ready to sacrifice current vehicle infrastructure to push it to the extreme end. Nevertheless, this approach brings back the many illusive goals or plans, with the check and balance of transformation, in the face of the reality of the 'on-the-ground' truth of vehicle reduction in the future. Gradual replacement scales and staged implementations need to be built into a city's capital plan, projects, construction, financing, and taxation processes. Not easy to do overnight, but very reasonable to do over time. Amsterdam, Copenhagen, and many other cities that are targeting the car-free vision did not go after drastic changes. Parking for instance was replaced at only a 3% rate per year in Amsterdam. A city takes time to build, and sometimes even needs a century to achieve its eventual goals. The next few sections and remaining chapters provide every detail of mobility ecosystem change that needs careful planning to implement sufficient supply systems for each mobility mode, and the associated integration to build a peaceful ecosystem to coexist with each other.

## Summary

The chapter provides an elaborate version of human mobility history and evolution throughout human civilization to introduce a broader understanding of the role of mobility in cities. No other elements of the human species can influence like human mobility. Human mobility shaped and moulded our species, living spaces, and civilizations. All defining features of our culture, societal foundations, and harmony with natural connections are born in a city's third spaces. The mobility system is a city's largest and most visible third space. Nothing, however, stays the same for long time in the third space. The constantly shifting pattern of human mobility was misunderstood and replaced by rigid ideology in the early part of the 20th century. Knowledge, skills, competency, and creative processes were lost after carefully building cities for people for more than 10,000 years. Larger societal changes and the very existence of humans came under fire during the third industrial era. From art to culture to social foundation to human identify, everything was reshaped, remoulded, and drastically altered within a few decades of the early 20th century. Almost overnight the basic living elements of cities were ripped apart and forcefully invaded by the powerful and most destructive consumer product in human history. A rigid doctrine, darker political ideology, and professional dogma replaced humans with a machine vision that brought endless suffering, division, and inequality to urban residents. While the vehicle-oriented approach created the most profound and destructive reallocation of land and open space in cities, it also deteriorated quality of life drastically in the name of mythical freedom, a utopian dream of the 'full' human, and manipulation of a human's wild desire to change every element of our daily life. The most significant part of our demography remains invisible under the mythical vehicle-oriented regime. There is very little trace of women, children, seniors, the disabled, of our culture in the mobility system. Despite a postmodernism transfer from a destructive modernism society in the 1980s, the fundamentals of the mobility system remain utility-centric modern era mindset, continue to be applied to a new form of colonization, and have deeply divided our community along a vehicle-oriented fault line. Ideological drivers simply forget that a fault line will generate an earthquake. So, resistance grew over time from new urbanism and a livable city concept was born toward the end of the 20th century. Mass transit and multimodal mobility ecosystems made inroads with small area successes. A few inspiring and visionary leaders joined the force to overturn the 20th century's ideological foundation of a vehicle-oriented regime. But the struggle is long and painful. Economic changes are now linked to underlying flaws of unbridled capitalism. Feudalistic approach in our current of the liquid digital modernism era and contemporary identity politics are reshaping everything in our society. Mobility is not immune to these destructive forces. As we are weaving through fundamental economic, societal, and cultural storms in the climate crisis era, innovative, creative, and practical concepts and approaches are necessary to replace the old machine-oriented mobility regime. This book identifies those ideological links, identifies systematically repressed elements and visible hidden flaws, and proposes new concepts to make the multimodal ecosystem a potentially new possibility for better mobility access for all types of people regardless of their differences in body shape or size, cultural, or societal background. These are not utopian dreams. There are no alternatives left for us but to transform the fundamental mobility system toward low-emission, low-energy, and small-scale facility in the upcoming post Anthropocene era.

# References

Aasa, A., Jarv, O., Saluveer, E., Silm, S. and Ahas, R. (2008). Methodology of determination of the anchor points based on passive mobile positioning database. *Social Positioning Method*, 17(1): 3–27.

Abbasi, Darvishi, E., Rodrigues, M.A. and Sayehmiri, K. (2022). Gender differences in cognitive performance and psychophysiological responses during noise exposure and different workloads. *Applied Acoustics*, 189(28).

Abbasi, M., Esmaielpour, M.M., Akbarzadeh, A., Zakerian, S.A. and Ebrahimi, M.H. (2015). Investigation of the effects of wind turbine noise annoyance on the sleep disturbance among workers of Manjil wind farm. *Journal of Health and Safety at Work*, 5(3): 51–62.

ABC. (2022). *Saudi Arabia has Unveiled Plans for a Mirrored Skyscraper Eco-city, but the Project is not Without Controversy*. Retrieved from ABC News: https://www.abc.net.au/news/2022-07-30/saudi-arabia-neom-eco-city-the-line-designs/101281532.

Adams, J. (1995). *Risk*. London: Ruthledge, University College.

Ahas, R., Silm, S., Järv, O., Saluveer, E. and Tiru, M. (2010). Using mobile positioning data to model locations meaningful to users of mobile phones. Journal of Urban Technology, 17(1): 3–27.

Ahn, Y. and Yeo, H. (2015). An Analytical planning model to estimate the optimal density of charging stations for electric vehicles. *PLoS ONE*, 1–26.

Ahn, Y. and Yeo, H. (2015). An analytical planning model to estimate the optimal density of charging stations for electric vehicles. *PLoS ONE*, 10(11): 1–16.

Ainsalu, J., Ville Arffman, V., Bellone, M., Ellner, M., Haapamäki, T., Haavisto, N., Josefson, E., Ismailogullari, A., Lee, B., Madland, O., Madžulis, R., Müür, J., Mäkinen, S., Nousiainen, V., Pilli-Sihvola, E., Rutanen, E., Sahala, S., Schønfeldt, B., Smolnicki, P.M., Soe, R., Sääski, J., Szymańska, M., Vaskinn, I. and Åman, M. (2019). *State of the Art of Automated Buses*. MDPI.

Akndi. (2020). *Greening Government Fleets: A Helpful Guide to Understanding*. Ottawa: Natural Resources Canada.

Albert, A. and Gonzalez, M.C. (2017). Using convolutional networks and satellite imagery to identify patterns in urban environments at a large scale. *Proceedings of the 23rd ACM SIGKDD International Conference on Knowledge Discovery and Data Mining*, pp. 1357–1366.

Alessandrini, A., Campagna, A., Site, P.D., Filippi, F. and Persia, L. (2015). Automated vehicles and the rethinking of mobility and cities. *SIDT Scientific Seminar, Centre for Transport and Logistics (CTL) – Sapienza University of Rome*, 5: 145–160. Rome: Transportation Research Procedia.

Alexander, R.M. (2004). Bipedal animals, and their differences from humans. *Journal of Anatomy*, 204(5): 321–330.

Alonso, W. (1971). The economics of urban size. *Papers and Proceedings of the Regional Science Association*, 26: 67–83.

Alsayyad, N. (1991). *Cities and Caliphs: On the Genesis of Arab Muslim Urbanism*. Cambridge University: Greenwood Press.

Amadeo, K. (2022). *Bretton Woods System and 1944 Agreement*. Retrieved from The Balance: https://www.thebalance.com/bretton-woods-system-and-1944-agreement-3306133.

Amadoa, M. and Poggi, F. (2014). Solar energy integration in urban planning: GUUD model. *Energy Procedia*, 50: 277–284.

Ammon, F.R. (2016). *Bulldozer: Demolition and Clearance of the Postwar Landscape*. Bloomsbury: Yale University Press.

Anderson, J.M., Kalra, N., Stanley, K.D., Sorensen, P., Samaras, C. and Oluwatola, O.A. (2016). *Autonomous Vehicle Technology: A Guide for Policymakers*. Santa Monica, California: RAND Coportation, RR-443-2-RC.

Appleby, K. (2015). *Five Cities Proving that We Can Quit Fossil Fuels*. Retrieved from City Monitor: https://citymonitor.ai/horizons/five-cities-proving-we-can-quit-fossil-fuels-1444.

Appleyard, D., Gerson, M.S. and Lintell, M. (1981). *Livable Streets*. Berkeley: University of California Press.

Appleyard, D., Lynch, K. and Myer, J.R. (1964). *The View from the Road*. Cambridge: MIT Press.

Araujo, J.A., Barajas, B., Kleinman, M., Wang, X., Bennett, B.J., Gong, K.W., Navab, M., Harkema, J., Sioutas, C., Lusis, A.J. and Nel, A.E. (2008). Ambient particulate pollutants in the ultrafine range promote early atherosclerosis and systemic oxidative stress. *Circular Research*, 102(5): 589–596.

Asher, L., Aresu, M., Falaschetti, E. and Mindell, J. (2012). Most older pedestrians are unable to cross the road in time: A cross-sectional study. *Age and Ageing*, 41(5): 690–694.

Ashley-Ross, M.A., Hsieh, S.T., Gibb, A.C. and Blob, R.W. (2013). Vertebrate land invasions—Past, present, and future: an introduction to the symposium. *Integrative and Comparative Biology*, 53(2): 192–196.

Atlantic, T. (Director). (2015). *Housing Through the Centuries* [Motion Picture].

Attenborough, D. (Director). (2010). *First Life –BBC Documentary* [Motion Picture].

Bae, S., Lee, E. and Han, J. (2020). Multi-period planning of hydrogen supply network for refuelling hydrogen fuel cell vehicles in urban areas. *Sustainability*, 12(4114): 1–23.

Baldwin, E. (2022). *10 Actions to Improve Streets for Children.* Retrieved from Arc daily News: https://www.archdaily.com/945350/10-actions-to-improve-streets-for-children.

Banister, D. (2011). Cities, mobility, and climate change. *Journal of Transport Geography*, 19: 1538–1546.

Barry, K. (2013). *Wired.* Retrieved from In South Korea, Wireless Charging Powers Electric Buses: https://www.wired.com/2013/08/induction-charged-buses/.

Bassolas, A., Barbosa-Filho, H., Dickinson, B., Dotiwalla, H., Eastham, P., Gallotti, R., Ghoshal, G., Gipson, B., Hazarie, S.A., Kautz, H., Kucuktunc, O., Lieber, A., Sadilek, A. and Ramasco, J.J. (2019). Hierarchical organization of urban mobility and its connection with city livability. *Nature Communications*, 10: 4817.

Batty, M. (2005). Optimal cities, ideal cities. *Environment and Planning B: Planning and Design*, 42: 571–573.

Batty, M. and Longley, P.A. (1994). *Fractal Cities: A Geometry of Form and Function.* San Diego: Academic Press.

Baudrillard, J. (1981). *Simulacra and Simulation.* Paris: Éditions Galilée.

Beauvoir, D.S. (1949). *Le Deuxième Sexe (The Second Sex).* Paris: Gallimard.

Becic, E., Zych, N. and Ivarsson, J. (2018). *Vehicle Automation Report.* Washington, USA: National Transportation Safety Board, HWY18MH010.

Becky, Loo, P.Y. and Banister, D. (2016). Decoupling transport from economic growth: Extending the debate to include environmental and social externalities. *Journal of Transport Geography*, 57: 134–144.

Beddoes, Z.M. (2020). Time to make coal history. *The Economist.*

Beebeejaun, Y. (2016). Gender, urban space, and the right to everyday life. *Journal of Urban Affairs*, 39(3): 323–334.

Begault, L. and Khazrik, J. (2019). *Smart Cities: Dreams Capable of Becoming Nightmares.* Retrieved from Amnesty International: https://www.amnesty.org/en/latest/research/2019/06/smart-cities-dreams-capable-of-becoming-nightmares/.

Belshaw, J.D. (2016). *Canadian History: Post-Confederation.* Vancouver: BC campus. Retrieved from BC Camps.: https://opentextbc.ca/postconfederation/chapter/9-13-cities-and-suburbs/.

Bengtsson, S. (2018). The nation's body: Disability and deviance in the writings of Adolf Hitler. *Disability & Society*, 33(3): 416–432.

Benjamin, L. and Richards, D. (1981). Electrification is the way to move Canada in the 1980s. *Canadian Public Policy*, 7(81).

Bentham, J. (1789). *An Introduction to the Principles of Morals and Legislation.* London: T. Payne and Son.

Bera, A. (2022). Space: From the Beginning to Today. *University of Illinois (Urbana-Champaign), USA.* Dhaka, Bangladesh: Brac University.

Bera, A.K., Ivliev, S. and Lillo, F. (2021). *Financial Econometrics and Empirical Market Microstructure.* Geneva: Springer International Switzerland.

Berg, N. (2020). *This AI-powered Parking Garage Rewards You for Not Driving.* Retrieved from Fast Company: https://www.fastcompany.com/90575914/this-ai-powered-parking-garage-rewards-you-for-not-driving.

Berg, P. (2011). *The Finite Planet: How Resource Scarcity will Affect Our Environment, Economy and Energy Supply.* Oshawa, Canada: Island Press.

Berkoz, L. and Tepe, E. (2008). Gated residential areas in Istanbul: Private cars versus public transport systems. *University of Liverpool* (pp. 27–31). Liverpool: ERSA Congress.

Berkoz, L. and Tepe, E. (2013). The impacts of the gated residential areas on the urban sprawl of Istanbul. *Academic Research International. Part-I: Natural and Applied Sciences*, 4(3): 1–17.

Bertini, R.L. (2006). You Are the Traffic Jam: Examination of Congestion Measures. *Transportation Research Board 85th Annual Meeting* (p. 17). Washington D.C.: Transportation Research Board.

Bettencourt, L.M. (2013). The Origins of Scaling in Cities. *Science*, 340: 1438.

Bettencourt, L. and West, G. (2010). A unified theory of urban living. *Nature*, 467: 912–913.

Bezirgani, A. and Lachapelle, U. (2018). Does access to transport options increase travel in older age? Analyzing travel for discretionary and non-discretionary purposes in aging Canadians. *Transportation Research Board 97th Annual Meeting* (p. 17). Washington D.C.: Transportation Research Board.

Bhat, C. (2017). *Travel Modeling in an Era of Connected and Automated Transportation Systems: An Investigation in the Dallas-Fort Worth Area.* Austin, USA: Technical Report 122. Center for Transportation Research. The University of Texas at Austin.

Bhat, R.V. and Waghray, K. (2000). *Profile of Street Foods in Asian Countries.* Basel, Karger: World Rev Nutr. Diet.

BHS. (2009). *15 Things You Did Not Know About the Moors of Spain.* Retrieved from Black History Studies: https://blackhistorystudies.com/resources/15-facts-on-the-moors-in-spain/.

Billings, C.E. (1980). *Human-centered Aircraft Automation: A Concept and Guidelines.* Moffet Field, CA: NASA Technical Memorandum, NASA Ames Research Center.

Björk, J., Ardö, J., Stroh, E., Lövkvist, S., Ostergren, P. and Albin, M. (2006). Road traffic noise in Southern Sweden and its relation to annoyance, disturbance of daily activities, and health. *Scandinavian Journal of Work, Environment & Health,* 32(5): 392–401.

Blaak, E. (2001). Gender differences in fat metabolism. *Curr. Opin. Clin. Nutr. Metab. Care,* 4(6): 499–502.

Blakely, E.J. and Snyder, M.G. (1997). *Divided We Fall: Gated and Walled Communities in the United States. Architecture of Fear.* New York: Princeton Architectural Press.

Bliss, L. (2021). *That Uber or Lyft Trip May Be Worse for the Planet Than Driving Yourself.* Retrieved from Bloomberg City Lab: https://www.bloomberg.com/news/articles/2021-09-30/adding-up-ride-hailing-s-hidden-environmental-costs.

Bloomberg, J. (2018). *Don't Trust Artificial Intelligence? Time to Open the AI 'Black Box'.* Retrieved from Forbes: https://www.forbes.com/sites/jasonbloomberg/2018/09/16/dont-trust-artificial-intelligence-time-to-open-the-ai-black-box/.

Boarnet, M.G. (1995). New highways & economic growth: Rethinking the link. *Access,* 7: 11–15.

Bojarski, M., Testa, D.D., Dworakowski, D., Firner, B., Flepp, B., Goyal, P., . . . Zieba, K. (2016). End-to-End learning for self-driving cars. *Computer Vision and Pattern Recognition,* Cornell University, pp. 1–9.

Bojji, R. (2011). Gravity powered transport systems for rail, road, water, and airport use. *13th International Conference on Automated People* (pp. 22–25). Paris, France: American Society of Civil Engineers.

Bond, S. (2017). *Whitewashing Ancient Statues: Whiteness, Racism and Color in The Ancient World.* Retrieved from Forbes: https://www.forbes.com/sites/drsarahbond/2017/04/27/whitewashing-ancient-statues-whiteness-racism-and-color-in-the-ancient-world/#4f98a5587.

Borzino, N., Chng, S., Mughal, M.O. and Schubert, R. (2020). Willingness to pay for urban heat island mitigation: A case study of Singapore. *Climate,* 8: 82.

Bose, D., Segui-Gomez, M. and Crandall, J.R. (2011). Vulnerability of female drivers involved in motor vehicle crashes: An analysis of US population at risk. *American Journal of Public Health,* 101(12): 2368–2373.

Botsman, R. (2010). *What's Mine Is Yours: The Rise of Collaborative Consumption.* Harper Business.

Bourdieu, P. and Wacquant, L.D. (1992). *An Invitation to Reflexive Sociology.* Cambridge, UK: Ploity Press and Blackwell Publishers.

Braess, D. (1969). Über ein Paradoxon aus der Verkehrsplanung [On a Paradox of Traffic Planning]. *Unternehmensforschung* (in German), 12: 258–268.

Britton, E. (2000). Carsharing 2000: Sustainable transport's missing link. *Journal of the Commons,* 1–351.

Brott, S. (2013). Architecture et Revolution: Le Corbusier and the Fascist Revolution. *Thresholds,* 41: 146–157.

Brumm, A., Ramli, M., Dosseto, T. and van den Bergh, G.D. (2014). Pleistocene cave art from Sulawesi, Indonesia. *Human Evolution, Rock Art (Archeology),* 17–223.

Brunet, M., Guy, F., Pilbeam, D., Mackaye, H., Likius, A., Ahounta, D., Beauvilain, A., Blondel, C. Bocherens, H., Boisserie, J., De Bonis, L.D., Coppens, Y., Dejax, J., Denys, C., Duringer, P., Eisenmann, V., Fanone, G., Fronty, P., Geraads, D., Lehmann, T., Lihoreau, F., Louchart, A., Mahamat, A., Merceron, G., Mouchelin, G. Otero, O., Campomanes, P.P., Leon, M.P.D., Rage, J., Sapanet, M., Schuster, M., Sudre, J., Tassy, P., Valentin, X., Vignaud, P., Viriot, L., Zazzo, A. and Zollikofer, C. (2002). A new hominid from the upper miocene of chad, Central Africa. *Nature,* 418(6894): 145–151.

Buchholz, A.C., Rafii, M., and Pencharz, P.B. (2001). Is resting metabolic rate different between men and women? *British Journal of Nutrition,* 86(6): 641–646.

Buckley, R.P. (2009). The bankruptcy of nations: an idea whose time has come. *The International Lawyer,* 1189–1216.

Burdett, R. (2016). *Inequality and Urban Growth.* Retrieved from OECD Forum: https://www.oecd.org/social/inequality-urban-growth.htm.

Burns, R. (2005). *Damascus: A History.* London: Routledge.

Butler, J. (1990). *Gender Trouble: Feminism and the Subversion of Identity.* New York: Routledge.

Camagni, R., Capello, R. and Caragliu, A. (2013). One or infinite optimal city sizes? In search of an equilibrium size for cities. *Annals of Regional Science,* 51(2): 309–341.

Canada Energy Regulator. (2020). *Market Snapshot: Canada's Retiring Coal-fired Power Plants will be Replaced by Renewable and Low-carbon Energy Sources.* Retrieved from Canada Energy Regulator: https://www.cer-rec.

gc.ca/en/data-analysis/energy-markets/market-snapshots/2020/market-snapshot-canadas-retiring-coal-fired-power-plants-will-be-replaced-renewable-low-carbon-energy-sources.html.

*Carsharing.org*. (2017). Retrieved from what is carsharing? https://carsharing.org/what-is-car-sharing/.

Carter, C. (2019). *Autonomous Passenger Ferries: Congestion-buster or Hype on the High Seas?* Retrieved from Smart Cities World: https://www.smartcitiesworld.net/special-reports/special-reports/autonomous-passenger-ferries-congestion-buster-or-hype-on-the-high-seas.

Cartwright, M. (2014). *The Inca Road System*. Retrieved from Ancient History: https://www.ancient.eu/article/757/the-inca-road-system/.

Center for Sustainable Systems. (2020). *Geothermal Energy*. Detroit, Michigan: University of Michigan. Retrieved from Geothermal Energy.: http://css.umich.edu/sites/default/files/Geothermal%20Energy_CSS10-10_e2020.pdf.

Certeau, M.D. (1980). *The Practice of Everyday Life*. Paris: Union générale d'éditions.

Charles, A., Lambert, H.G. and Balogh, S.B. (2014). EROI of different fuels and the implications for society. *Energy Policy*, 64: 141–152.

Charles, J. (1978). The language of post-modern architecture. Balding and Mansell Ltd. *Journal of Aesthetics and Art Criticism*, 37(2): 239–240.

Chellapilla, K. (2018). *Rethinking Maps for Self-Driving*. Medium.

Christensen, A. and Petrenko, C. (2017). *CO2-based Synthetic Fuel: Assessment of Potential European Capacity and Environmental Performance*. Brussels: European Climate Foundation and the International Council on Clean Transportation.

City of Toronto. (2018). *Toronto Green Standard Version 3*. Toronto, Canada: City of Toronto.

City of Toronto. (2020). *Energy Efficiency Report Submission & Modelling Guidelines: For the Toronto Green Standard (TGS) Version 3*. Toronto, Canada: Environment and Energy Division & City Planning Division, City of Toronto.

City of Vancouver. (2019). *EV Charging Infrastructure Requirements for New Residential Buildings Guidance*. Vancouver, Canada: City of Vancouver.

Civitas. (2016). *Cities towards Mobility 2.0: Connect, Share and Go!* Brussels, Belgium: CIVITAS WIKI consortium.

Clarke, S. (2015). *The Crisis of Fordism and the Crisis of Capitalism*. University of Warwick, UK.

CMA. (2008). *No Breathing Room National Illness Costs of Air Pollution*. Ottawa: Canadian Medical Association.

CNN. (2021). *Plans for $400-billion New City in the American Desert Unveiled*. Retrieved from CNN News: https://www.cnn.com/style/article/telosa-marc-lore-blake-ingels-new-city/index.html.

Colette, S. (2006). *What Lacan Said about Women*. New York: Other Press, ISBN 9781590511701.

Colville-Andersen, M. (2013). *The Choreography of an Urban Intersection—Part One: On Bicycles & Behavior*. Retrieved from The Copenhagenize: http://www.copenhagenize.com/2013/06/the-choreography-of-urban-intersection_14.html.

Cook, C. (2014). *Transforming the Transportation Industry with Renewable Energy*. Retrieved from Renewable Energy World: https://www.renewableenergyworld.com/2014/09/18/transforming-the-transportation-industry-with-renewable-energy/#gref.

Cooper, D. (2018). *It's too Early to Write off Hydrogen Vehicles*. Retrieved from Engadget: https://www.engadget.com/2018-05-29-hydrogen-fuel-cell-toyota-mirai-evs.html.

Copenhagezine. (2009). *Subconscious Democracy and Desire*. Retrieved from Copenhagezine: http://www.copenhagenize.com/2009/04/subconscious-democracy-and-desire.html.

Copjec, J. (2014, March 2). The Inheritance of Potentiality: An Interview with Joan Copjec. (O.E. Journals, Interviewer).

CPCS and Hatch Associates. (1992). *Commuter Rail Services: Electrification Study*. Toronto: GO Transit.

Crenshaw, K. (1996). *Critical Race Theory: The Key Writings that Formed the Movement*. New York: The New Press.

Curie, J. and Pierre, C. (1880). Développement, par pression, de l'électricité polaire dans les cristaux hémièdres à faces inclinées. *Comptes Rendus* (in French), 9: 294–295.

Curtis, A. (Director). (2002). *The Century of the Self –Part 1: "Happiness Machines"* [Motion Picture].

Dan, K. (2007). Flight of the pigeon. *Bicycling, Rodale, Inc.*, 48: 60–66.

Dantzig, G.B. and Saaty, T.I. (1973). *Compact City: A Plan for a Liveable Urban Environment*. San Francisco: W.H. Freeman and Company.

Dave. (2018). *Car-Sharing vs. Private Vehicle Ownership Costs*. Retrieved from Carsharing US: https://arlingtonva.s3.amazonaws.com/wp-content/uploads/sites/19/2017/03/DES-Carshare_CarShare_vs_PrivateCarOwnership_Cost_Analysis.pdf.

David, H. (2014). *Bicycle: The History*. Yale University Press. ISBN 0-300-10418-9.

Debhia, P. (2019). *The History of Electric Scooters*. Retrieved from LinkedIn: https://www.linkedin.com/pulse/history-electric-scooters-prashant-dedhia-negotiation-ninja-/.

Debord, G. (1967). *La société du spectacle (The Society of the Spectacle)*. Paris: Buchet-Chastel.

Deluchhi, M.A. and Jaconson, M.Z. (2009). A path to sustainable energy by 2030. *Scientific American*, 58–65.

DeMaio, P. (2009). Bike-sharing: Impacts, models of provision, and future. *Journal of Public Transportation*, 12(4): 41–56.

DeMaio, P.J. (2003). Smart bikes: Public transportation for the 21st century. *Transportation Quarterly*, 57(1): 9–11.

Desapriya, E., Subzwari, S., Sasges, D., Basic, A., Alidina, A., Turcotte, K. and Pike, I. (2010). Do light truck vehicles (LTV) impose greater risk of pedestrian injury than passenger cars? A meta-analysis and systematic review. *Traffic Inj. Prev.*, 11: 48–56.

Dijkema, M.B., Mallant, S.F., Gehring, U., Hurk, K.V., Alssema, M., van Strien, R.T., Fischer, P.H., Nijpels, G., Stehouwer, C.D.A. Hoek, G., Dekker, J.M. and Brunekreef, B. (2011). Long-term exposure to traffic-related air pollution and Type 2 diabetes prevalence in a cross-sectional screening-study in the Netherlands. *Environmental Health*, 10: 76.

Driver, J. (2014). *The History of Utilitarianism*. Retrieved from Stanford Encyclopedia of Philosophy: https://plato.stanford.edu/entries/utilitarianism-history/.

Driving. (2015). *Company Wants to Bring Rickshaws to North America*. Retrieved from Driving: https://driving.ca/auto-news/news/company-wants-to-bring-rickshaws-to-north-america.

Duffy, M.C. (2003). *Electric Railways: 1880–1990*. London: The Institution of Engineering and Technology.

Duggan, G. (n.d.). *Meet the Weird, Wacky and Wonderful Creatures that Lived in Cambrian Seas over 500 Million Years Ago*. Retrieved from CBC News: https://www.cbc.ca/natureofthings/features/meet-the-weird-wacky-and-wonderful-creatures-that-lived-in-cambrian-seas-ov.

Duignan, B. (2019). *Jeremy Bentham: British Philosopher and Economist*. Retrieved from Britannica: https://www.britannica.com/biography/Jeremy-Bentham.

Eagle, N.P. (2009). Eigenbehaviors: Identifying Structure in Routine. *Behavior Ecology Sociobiology*, 63: 1057–1066.

Economist, T. (Director). (2017). *Urbanisation and the Rise of the Megacity* [Motion Picture].

Edmondson, A.C. (2011). *Strategies for Learning from Failure*. Retrieved from Harvard Business Review: https://hbr.org/2011/04/strategies-for-learning-from-failure.

Eleanor, P.W. and Lebeaux, C.N. (1967). On the destruction of poor neighborhoods by urban renewal. *Social Problems*, 15(1): 3–8.

El-Geneidy, A., Grimsrud, M., Wasfi, R.P., Tétreault, T. and Surprenant-Legault, J. (2014). New evidence on walking distances to transit stops: Identifying redundancies and gaps using variable service areas. *Transportation*, 41: 193–210.

Elias, N. (1939). *Über den Prozeß der Zivilisation (The Civilizing Process)*. Basel: Haus Zum Falken.

Ellis, C. (2015). *History of Cities and City Planning*. Retrieved from Art Net: http://www.art.net/~hopkins/Don/simcity/manual/history.html#:~:text=The%20building%20of%20cities%20has,in%20their%20layout%20and%20functioning.&text=Religious%20elements%20have%20been%20crucial%20throughout%20urban%20history.

Ellis, K.J. (1990). Reference man and woman more fully characterized. *Biological Trace Element Research*, 26: 385–400.

Endsley, M.R. and Kiris, E.O. (1995). The out-of-the-loop performance problem and level of control in automation. *The Journal of the Human Factors and Ergonomics Society*, 2: 27.

Energy Information Administration EIA. (2017). *Study of the Potential Energy Consumption Impacts of Connected and Automated Vehicles*. Washington, D.C. 20585: US Department of Energy.

Energy Innovation. (2015). *Comparing the Costs of Renewable and Conventional Energy Sources*. Retrieved from Energy Innovation: https://energyinnovation.org/2015/02/07/levelized-cost-of-energy/.

EPA. (2017). *Sources of Greenhouse Gas Emissions*. Retrieved from Environmental Protection Agency: https://www.epa.gov/ghgemissions/sources-greenhouse-gas-emissions.

Eric, P.M. (2000). *The CIAM Discourse on Urbanism, 1928–1960*. Cambridge: The MIT Press.

Eugster, J.W. (2007). Road and bridge heating using geothermal energy. overview and examples. *Proceedings European Geothermal Congress* (pp. 1–5). Unterhaching, Germany: European Geothermal Congress.

European Commision. (2020). *Energy Efficiency Indicator*. Retrieved from European Commision: https://ec.europa.eu/transport/themes/energy-efficiency-indicator_en.

Eveleth, R. (2019). *When Futurism Led to Fascism—and Why It Could Happen Again*. Retrieved from Wired: https://www.wired.com/story/italy-futurist-movement-techno-utopians/.

FHWA. (2001). *Guidelines and Recommendations to Accommodate Older Driver and Pedestrians*. Washington D.C.: FHWA-RD-01-051.

Fishbone, A., Shahan, Z. and Badik, P. (2017). *Electric Vehicle Charging Infrastructure: Guidelines for Cities*. Wassaw, Poland: CleanTechnica.

Fishman, E. (2014). Bikeshare: A review of recent literature. *Transport Reviews*, 92–113.

Flint, A. (2014). *Modern Man: The Life of Le Corbusier, Architect of Tomorrow. New Harvest.* Stafford: New Harvest. Retrieved from https://www.citylab.com/design/2014/11/the-hazardous-business-of-celebrating-le-corbusier/382584/.

Forman, J., Poplin, G.S., Shaw, C.G., McMurry, T.L., Schmidt, K., Ash, J. and Sunnevang, C. (2019). Automobile injury trends in the contemporary fleet: Belted occupants in frontal collisions. *Traffic Injury Prevention*, 20(6): 607–612.

Foucault, M. (1977). *Discipline and Punish: The Birth of the Prison.* New York: Pantheon Books.

Fox, D.J. (Director). (2016). *Forest, Field, Sky: Art out of Nature –BBC Documentary* [Motion Picture].

François-Lavet, V., Henderson, P., Islam, R., Bellemare, M.G. and Pineau, J. (2018). An introduction to deep reinforcement learning. *Foundations and Trends in Machine Learning*, 11(3-4): 1–102.

Frayer, L. and Cater, F. (2015). *How a Folding Electric Vehicle Went from Car of The Future to 'Obsolete'.* Retrieved from NPR: http://www.npr.org/sections/alltechconsidered/2015/11/05/454693583/how-a-folding-electric-vehicle-went-from-car-of-the-future-to-obsolete.

Friedman, A. (2010). *A Symposium of Sustainability. World Town Planning Day Event.* Whitby: Ontario Professional Planners Institute and the Oak Ridges District.

Fry, H. (Director). (2016). *The Joy of Data* [Motion Picture].

Fuhrmeister, C., Heß, R. and Platzer, M. (2021). *Racism in Architecture.* Retrieved from Networks. H-net: https://networks.h-net.org/node/73374/announcements/6848445/racism-architecture#_ftn4.

Furman, B., Fabian, L., Ellis, S., Muller, P. and Swenson, R. (2014). *Automated Transit Networks (ATN): A Review of the State of the Industry and Prospects for the Future.* San José: Minata Transportation Institute.

G of C. (2019). *Canada's Aging Population.* Retrieved from Government of Canada: https://www.ic.gc.ca/eic/site/Oca-bc.nsf/eng/ca02099.html.

Gahl, J. (1968). People on foot. *Arkitekten*, 435.

Galatoulas, N.F. (2020). Spatio-temporal trends of e-bike sharing system deployment: A review in Europe, North America and Asia. *Sustainability*, 12: 4611.

Gallagher, R. (1992). *The Rickshaws of Bangladesh.* Dhaka: University Press, Dhaka.

Gambino, M. (2009). *A Salute to the Wheel.* Retrieved from Smithsonian Magazine: https://www.smithsonianmag.com/science-nature/a-salute-to-the-wheel-31805121/.

Gawron, V.J. (2019). *Automation in Aviation–Definition of Automation.* McLean, VA: The MITRE Corporation.

Gee, M. (2016). *Raise the Roof? Union Station Reno Runs into Problem: New Trains Won't Fit.* Retrieved from the Globe and Mail: https://www.theglobeandmail.com/news/toronto/union-station-shed-renovation-stalled-by-low-arches-and-an-electrified-future/article28448568/.

Geidl, M., Koeppel, G., Favre-Perrod, P., Klöckl, B., Andersson, G. and Fröhlich, K. (2007). The energy hub—a powerful concept for future energy systems. *Third Annual Carnegie Mellon Conference on the Electricity Industry* (pp. 2–10). Pittsburgh: Carnegie Mellon University.

Gerber, D.A. (1999). Caucasians are made and not born: How European immigrants became white people. *Reviews in American History*, 27: 437–443.

Gerspacher, A. (2020). *Historic Avant-garde: Futurism.* Retrieved from YouTube: https://www.youtube.com/watch?v=zpTcp7gIhso.

Gerspacher, A. (2021). *Postcolonial.* New York, USA: Bicar Institute.

Gilani, T.A. and Mir, M.S. (2021). Association of road traffic noise exposure and prevalence of coronary artery disease: A cross-sectional study in North India. *Environmental Science and Pollution Research*, 28: 53458–53477.

Gilpin, L. (2017). *Can Car-Sharing Culture Help Fuel an Electric Vehicle Revolution?* Retrieved from Insidecliemate: https://insideclimatenews.org/news/07122017/car-rental-sharing-electric-vehicles-zipcar-evs-uber-lyft-green-commuter.

Gleaton, K.M. (2012). *Power to the People: Street Art as an Agency for Change.* Masters Thesis. Minnesota: University of Minnesota Digital Conservancy.

Global Designing Cities. (2019). *Multimodal Streets Serve More People.* Retrieved from Global Designing Cities: https://globaldesigningcities.org/publication/global-street-design-guide/defining-streets/multimodal-streets-serve-people/.

Global Union. (2020). *Top 10 Principles for Ethical Artificial Intelligence.* Nyon, Switzerland: The Future World of Work.

Gomes, L. (2014). *Hidden Obstacles for Google's Self-Driving Cars: Impressive Progress Hides Major Limitations of Google's Quest for Automated Driving.* Cambridge, USA: MIT Technology Review.

González, M.C., Hidalgo, C.A. and Barabási, A. (2008). Understanding individual human mobility patterns. *Nature*, 453: 779–782.

Gordon, L.A. and Shirokoff, I. (2014). *Suburban Nation? Population Growth in Canadian Suburbs, 2006–2011. Working Paper #1*. Ottawa: Council for Canadian Urbanism.

Government Offices of Sweden. (2019). *Renewed Commitment to Vision Zero Intensified Efforts for Transport Safety in Sweden*. Retrieved from Government Offices of Sweden: https://www.government.se/4a800b/contentassets/b38a99b2571e4116b81d6a5eb2aea71e/trafiksakerhet_160927_webny.pdf.

Gray, D., Anable, J., Illingworth, L. and Graham, W. (2006). *Decoupling the Link between Economic Growth, Transport Growth and Carbon Emissions in Scotland*. Aberdeen: The Centre for Transport Policy: The Robert Gordon University.

Green, J. (2018). *Effects of Car Pollutants on the Environment*. Retrieved from Sciencing: https://sciencing.com/effects-car-pollutants-environment-23581.html,

Griloa, F., Pinho, P., Aleixo, C., Catita, C., Silva, P., Lopes, N., Freitas, C., Santos-Reis, M., Timon McPhearsond, T., and Branquinho, C. (2020). Using green to cool the grey: Modelling the cooling effect of green spaces with a high spatial resolution. *Science of the Total Environment*, 1–10.

Grosrichard, A. (1998). *Sultan's Court: European Fantasies of the East*. Geneva: Verso.

Gross, S. (2020). *Why are fossil fuels so hard to quit?* Retrieved from Brookings Institution: https://www.brookings.edu/essay/why-are-fossil-fuels-so-hard-to-quit/.

GTA Clean Air Council. (2017). *Climate Action for a Healthy, Equitable, and Prosperous Toronto*. Toronto: City of Toronto.

Gutstein, D. (2019). *What's the Difference between a Low-Carbon and Zero-Carbon Future? Survival*. Retrieved from the tyee: https://thetyee.ca/Opinion/2019/04/02/Low-Zero-Carbon-Future-Survival/.

GVI. (2019). *Bhutan is the Only Carbon Negative Country in the World*. Retrieved from GVI: https://www.gvi.co.uk/blog/bhutan-carbon-negative-country-world/.

Hall, S. (2018). *Say Hello to Dickinsonia, the Animal Kingdom's Newest (and Oldest) Member*. Retrieved from Scientic American: https://www.scientificamerican.com/article/say-hello-to-dickinsonia-the-animal-kingdoms-newest-and-oldest-member/.

Harb, M., Xiao, Y., Circella, G., Mokhtarian, P.L. and Walker, J.L. (2018). Projecting travelers into a world of self-driving vehicles: Estimating travel behavior implications via a naturalistic experiment. *Transportation*, 45: 1671–1685.

Harms, S. and Truffer, B. (1998). *The Emergence of a Nationwide Carsharing Co-operative in Switzerland: A Case Study for the Project "Strategic Niche Management as a Tool for Transition to a Sustainable Transportation System*. 1998: EAWAG-Eidg. Anstalt fur Wasserversorgung und Gewasserschutz.

Hasan, M.U. and Dávila, J.D. (2012). The politics of (im)mobility: Rickshaw bans in Dhaka, Bangladesh. *32nd International Geographical Congress* (pp. 1–23). Cologne: University of Cologne.

Haugneland, P., Lorentzen, E., Bu, C. and Hauge, E. (2017). Put a price on carbon to fund EV incentives – Norwegian EV policy success. *EVS30 Symposium* (pp. 1–8). Stuttgart, Germany: Norwegian EV Association.

Haywood, J.B. (2006). Fueling our transportation future. *Scientific American*.

Helbing, D., Buzna, L., Johansson, A. and Werner, T. (2005). Self-organized pedestrian crowd dynamics: Experiments, simulations, and design solutions. *Transportation Science*, 39(1): 1–24.

Herkert, J.R. (2001). Future directions in engineering ethics research: Microethics, macroethics, and the role of professional societies. *Science and Engineering Ethics*, 7(3): 403–414.

Herman, A. (2012). *Freedom's Forge: How American Business Produced Victory in World War II*. New York: Random House.

Hess, A. and Schubert, I. (2019). Functional perceptions, barriers, and demographics concerning e-cargo bike sharing in Switzerland. *Transportation Research Part D: Transport and Environment*, 71: 153. Retrieved from Science daily: https://www.sciencedaily.com/releases/2019/07/190710121536.htm.

Highways. (2006). *Historical Milestones: Celebrating 75 Years of Advocacy*. Washington D.C.: Highways.org.

Hirst, K.K. (2019). *Ancient Dancing Girl of Mohenjo-Daro*. Retrieved from ThoughtCo: https://www.thoughtco.com/the-dancing-girl-of-mohenjo-daro-171329.

Holder, S. (2019). *Clue to the Reason for Women's Pervasive Car-Safety Problem*. Retrieved from Bloomberg City Lab: https://www.bloomberg.com/news/articles/2019-07-18/why-women-are-likelier-to-be-hurt-in-a-car-crash.

Holyoak, K.J. (2018). Beyond sacrificial harm: A two-dimensional model of utilitarian psychology. *Psychological Review*, 125(2): 131–164.

Hoopengardner, R. and Thompson, M. (2012). *FTA Low-Speed Urban Maglev Research Program: Updated Lessons Learned*. Arlington, USA: Federal Transit Administration, USA.

Hordnes, E. (2019). *Race to Electrification – Norway in a Pole Position*. Retrieved from Urban Insight: https://www.swecourbaninsight.com/urban-energy/race-to-electrification--norway-in-pole-position/.

Howard, E. (1898). *To-morrow: A Peaceful Path to Real Reform*. London: Routledge.

Huffman, C.A. (1993). *Philolaus of Croton: Pythagorean and Presocratic*. Cambridge: Cambridge University Press.

Hughes, I. and Huo, R. (2018). *Autonomy-level Classification for Robots in an IIoT World*. Retrieved from 451 Research: https://go.451research.com/MI-Robots-in-IIoT-World.html.

Hull, G.J., Roberts, C. and Hillmansen, S. (2008). Energy Efficiency of a Railway Power Network with Simulation. *International Conference on Energy Technologies and Policy*. Birmingham, UK: University of Birmingham.

Hurley, J., Morris, S. and Portelance, G. (2018). *China's Belt and Road Initiative may Bankrupt 8 Nations while Financing Infrastructure*. Retrieved from the Print: https://theprint.in/opinion/chinas-belt-and-road-initiative-bankrupt-nations-financing-infrastructure/39561/.

Huston, M. (2021). *Architecture and the Environmental Impact of Artificial Complexity*. Retrieved from Common Edge: https://commonedge.org/architecture-and-the-environmental-impact-of-artificial-complexity/.

Hux, P.D. (2019). *The Influence of Gender in Motor Vehicle Fatalities*. Retrieved from Allen and Allen: https://www.allenandallen.com/the-influence-of-gender-in-motor-vehicle-fatalities/.

Iannelli, V. (2021). *When is An Accident a Crime and when Should Parents Be Charged?* Retrieved from Very Well Family: https://www.verywellfamily.com/charging-parents-kids-accident-3969696.

IISD. (2015). *The End of Coal: Ontario's Coal Phase-out*. Winnipeg, Canada: International Institute for Sustainable Development.

Ilan, J. (2015). *Understanding Street Culture: Poverty, Crime, Youth and Cool*. London: Palgrave MacMillan ISBN: 9781137028587.

Institute, R.M. (2019). *Electric Mobility: Best Practices*. Rocky Mountain Institute, Government of India and Smart City.

Intelligent Transport. (2021). *Saudi Arabia to Build Residential Project THE LINE Centred around Walking*. Retrieved from Intelligent Transport: https://www.intelligenttransport.com/transport-news/113973/the-line/.

International Commission on Radiological Protection. (1975). *Report of the Task Group on Reference Man*. New York: Committee 2 of the International Commission on Radiological Protection.

IPCC. (2007). *Summary for Policymakers, in: Climate Change 2007: The Physical Science Basis. EXIT Contribution of Working Group I to the Fourth Assessment Report of the Intergovernmental Panel on Climate Change*. Cambridge and New York: Cambridge University Press.

Islam, A. and Ahiduzzaman, M. (2012). Biomass energy: Sustainable solution for greenhouse gas emission. *American Inst. Phys. Conf. Proc.*, 1441(1): 23–32. American Institute of Physics.

ISO. (2020). *Road vehicles—Human Performance and State in the Context of Automated Driving—Part 2: Considerations in Designing Experiments to Investigate Transition Processes*. ISO/TR 21959-2: 2020.

ITE. (2008). *Designing Walkable Urban Thoroughfares: A Context Sensitive Approach*. Washington D.C.: Institute of Transportation Engineers.

ITE California. (2014). *The Implementation of California SB 743: Revisions to Transportation Analyses Conducted for CEQA*. San Diego: ITE California SB 743 Task Force.

Itoh, M., Zhou, H. and Kitazaki, S. (2018). What may happen or what you should do? Effects of knowledge representation regarding necessity of intervention on driver performance under level 2 automated driving. *ICPS'18: Proceedings of the 2018 IEEE Industrial Cyber-Physical Systems* (pp. 621–626). Saint Petersburg, Russia: IEEE.

J2954. (2019). *Wireless Power Transfer for Light-Duty Plug-in/Electric Vehicles and Alignment Methodology*. SAE International.

J3068. (2018). *Electric Vehicle Power Transfer System using a Three-Phase Capable Coupler*. SAE International.

J3105. (2020). *Electric Vehicle Power Transfer System using Conductive Automated Connection Device*. SAE International.

Jackson, T. (2009). *Prosperity without Growth: Foundations for the Economy of Tomorrow*. London: Routledge.

Jacobs, J. (1961). *The Death and Life of Great American Cities*. New York: Random House.

Jacos, J. (2004). *Dark Age Ahead*. New York: Random House.

Jaehoon, S. (2014). *Korea's 95% Reduction in Child Traffic Fatalities: Reduction in Child Traffic Fatalities: Policies and Achievements*. Seoul: Korea Transport Institute. Retrieved from Koti.: https://www.koti.re.kr/component/file/ND_fileDownload.do?q_fileSn=4948&q_fileId=20140423_0004948_00150840.

Jameson, F. (1991). *Postmodernism, or, the Cultural Logic of Late Capitalism*. Durham: Duke University Press.

Jan, W. (2018). The utilitarian stigma of environmental protection. *Journal of Philosophy*, 3(1): 89–110.

Jayasuriya, D.C. (1994). Street food vending in Asia: Some policy and legal aspects. *Food Control, Elsevier*, 5(4): 222–226.

Jean Vaucher, J. (2014). *History of Ships–Prehistoric Craft*. Retrieved from University of Montreal: http://www.iro.umontreal.ca/~vaucher/History/Prehistoric_Craft/.

Jefferies, I. (2019, November 20). Retrieved from Association of American Railroads. https://www.aar.org/article/freight-rail-highly-automated-vehicles/.

Jettanasen, C., Songsukthawan, P. and Ngaopitakkul, A. (2020). Development of micro-mobility based on piezoelectric energy harvesting for smart city applications. *Sustainability*, 1–16.

Jevons, W. (1865). *The Coal Question*. London: Macmillan & Co.

Johanson, D. and Edey, M. (1990). *Lucy: The Beginnings of Humankind*. New York City: Wayne & Schuster.

Jorna, A. (2012). *Synthetic Fuel Costs*. Stanford, California: Stanford University.

Joshi, N. (2019). *7 Types of Artificial Intelligence*. Retrieved from Forbes: https://www.forbes.com/sites/cognitiveworld/2019/06/19/7-types-of-artificial-intelligence/.

Junkin, K. (2013). *Regional Rapid Rail: A Vision for the Future*. Toronto: Transport Action, Ontario.

Kahane, C.J. (2013). *Injury Vulnerability and Effectiveness of Occupant Protection Technologies for Older Occupants and Women*. Washington, D.C.: NHTSA. DOT HS 811 766.

Kalra, N. and Paddock, S.M. (2016). *How Many Miles of Driving Would it Take to Demonstrate Autonomous Vehicle Reliability? Driving to Safety*. Santa Monica, California: RAND Corporation.

Kane, M. (2019). *Chile Launches Latin America's First 100% Electric Bus Corridor*. Retrieved from Inside EVs: https://insideevs.com/news/377241/chile-first-100-electric-bus-corridor/.

Kanga, H. and Scott, D.M. (2010). Exploring day-to-day variability in time use for household members. *Transportation Research Part A: Policy and Practice*, 44(8): 609–619.

KAPSARC. (2016). *Mobility-on-demand: Understanding Energy Impacts and Adoption Potential*. Riyadh: KASARC.

Karatani, K. (1989). *History and Repetition*. New York: Columbia University Press.

Karim, D.M. and Shallwani, T. (2010). Toward a clean train policy: Diesel versus electric, the Ontario centre for engineering and public policy. *Ontario Centre for Engineering and Public Policy (OCEPP)*, 3: 18–22.

Kempen, E.E., Kruize, H., Boshuizen, H.C., Ameling, C.B., Staatsen, B.A. and de Hollander, A.E. (2002). The association between noise exposure and blood pressure and ischemic heart disease: A meta-analysis. *Environ. Health Perspect.*, 110(3): 307–317.

Kenoyer, J.M. (2004). Wheeled vehicles of the indus valley civilization of Pakistan and India. *Mainz am Rhein, Verlagg Philipp von Zabem*, 87–106.

Kessler, F.B., Staiano, J., Larcher, R., Sebe, N., Quercia, D. and Lepri, B. (2016). The death and life of great italian cities: A mobile phone data perspective. *26th International ACM Conference on World Wide Web (WWW)*. Montreal: International ACM.

Khayal, O. (2019). The history of Bajaj rickshaw vehicles. *Global Journal of Engineering Sciences*, 3(2): 1–8.

KIT. (2015). *Det pågår en kamp om gatorna. Och bilen är redan förloraren*. Stockholm: KIT.

Kleinman, M.T. (2000). *The Health Effects of Air Pollution on Children*. Irvine, California: South Coast Air Quality Management District (SCAQMD).

Kour, R. and Charif, A. (2016). Piezoelectric roads: Energy harvesting method using piezoelectric technology. *Innovative Energy & Research*, 5(1).

Kwon, D. (2018). Self-taught robots. *Scientific American*, 26–31.

Kwon, H., Ryu, M.H. and Carlsten, C. (2020). Ultrafine particles: Unique physicochemical properties relevant to health and disease. *Experimental & Molecular Medicine*, 52: 318–328.

Lacan, J. (1964). *The Four Fundamental Concepts of Psychoanalysis*. New York: W.W. Norton and Company.

Lambert, F. (2020). *Uber and Hyundai Unveil New Electric Air Taxi with 60-mile Range*. Retrieved from Electrek: https://electrek.co/2020/01/07/uber-hyundai-electric-air-taxi-evtol/.

Laplante, J.N. and Kaiser, T.P. (2004). The continuing evolution of pedestrian walking speed assumptions. *ITE Journal*, 32–40.

Laumond, J., Mansard, N. and Lasserre, J.B. (2015). Optimization as motion selection principle in robot action. *Communications of the ACM*, 58(5): 64–74.

Lawrence, H.W. (1988). Origins of the tree-lined boulevard. *Geographical Review*, 78(4): 355–374.

Layton, B.E. (2008). A comparison of energy densities of prevalent energy sources in units of houles per cubic meter. *International Journal of Green Energy*, 5: 438–455.

Le Corbusier. (1946). *Manière de penser l'urbanisme* (édition 1946). Paris: Gonthier.

Le Néchet, F. (2012). Urban spatial structure, daily mobility and energy consumption: A study of 34 European cities. *European Journal of Geography*, 580(23).

Le Vine, S., Lee-Gosselin, M., Sivakumar, A. and Polak, J. (2014). New approach to predict the market and impacts of round-trip and point-to-point carsharing systems: Case study of London. *Transportation Research, Part D*, 32: 218–229.

Le Vine, S., Zolfaghari, A. and Polak, J. (2014). *Carsharing: Evolution, Challenges and Opportunities*. London: Centre for Transport Studies, Imperial College London.

Leaf, W.A. and Preusser, D.F. (1999). *Literature Review on Vehicle Travel Speeds and Pedestrian Injuries*. Washington D.C.: US Department of Transportation.

Ledsham, T. and Savan, B. (2017). *Building a 21st Century Cycling City: Strategies for Action in Toronto.* Toronto: Metcalf Foundation.

Lee-Shanok, P. (2017). *Ontario Condo Act a Roadblock for Electric Vehicle Owners.* Retrieved from CBC News: https://www.cbc.ca/news/canada/toronto/ontario-hopes-revised-condo-act-ev-friendly-1.4155747.

Lefebvre, H. (1947). *The Critique of Everyday Life.* London: Verso.

Lefebvre, H. (1968). *Le Droit à la Ville.* Paris: Anthropos.

Lefevre, H. (1974). *La Production de l'espace (The Production of Space).* Paris: Anthropos.

Leger, F. (n.d.). Three women. *Oil Canvas.* Museum of Modern Art (MoMA), New York.

Leicester Literary and Philosophical Society. (2007). Leicester's fossil celebrity: Charnia and the evolution of early life. *Annual Saturday Seminar* (pp. 1–2). Leicester: University of Leicester.

Lessing, H. (2001). What led to the invention of the early bicycle? *Cycle History 11, San Francisco*, 11: 28–36. Retrieved from New Scientist. https://www.newscientist.com/article/mg18524841-900-brimstone-and-bicycles/.

Lewis, R. (2017). *Why Children Struggle to Cross Busy Streets Safely.* Retrieved from Iowa Now: https://now.uiowa.edu/2017/04/why-children-struggle-cross-busy-streets-safely.

Li, L. and Loo, B.P. (2014). Alternative and transitional energy sources for urban transportation. *Current Sustainable/Renewable Energy Reports*, 1: 19–26.

Li, X. and Strezov, V. (2014). Modelling piezoelectric energy harvesting potential in an educational building. *Energy Conversion and Management*, 85: 435–442.

Li, X., Gorghinpour, C., Sclar, R. and Castellanos, S. (2018). *How to Enable Electric Bus Adoption in Cities Worldwide.* Berlin: World Resources Institute, WRI and German Federal Ministry.

Liang, A. (2022). *Non-essential Petrol Sales Halted for Two Weeks in Sri Lanka.* Retrieved from BBC News: https://www.bbc.com/news/business-61961821.

Liao, Y., Gil, J., Pereira, R.H., Yeh, S. and Verendel, V. (2020). Disparities in travel times between car and transit: Spatiotemporal patterns in cities. *Nature*, 10: 4056.

Lima, M. (2015). *The Bicycle in the 21st Century.* Retrieved from Theprotocity: http://theprotocity.com/the-bicycle-in-the-21st-century/.

Litman, T. (2017). *The Future of Mobility in Cities—Multimodal and Integrated.* Retrieved from Planetizen: https://www.planetizen.com/news/2017/10/95204-future-mobility-cities-multimodal-and-integrated.

Litman, T. (2018). Retrieved from Carsharing: Vehicle Rental Services that Substitute for Private Vehicle Ownership: https://www.vtpi.org/tdm/tdm7.htm.

Little, A. (2015). *The Future of Urban Mobility 2.0: Towards Networked, Multimodal Cities of 2050.* Rome, Italy: International Association of Public Transport (UITP).

Long, R. (1967). *A Line Made by Walking.* Retrieved from https://www.tate.org.uk/art/artworks/long-a-line-made-by-walking-ar00142.

Loos, A. (1908). *Ornament and Crime.* Innsbruck: Programs and manifestos on 20th-century architecture.

Loos, A. (1910). *Ornement et Crime.* Vienna: Les Cahiers d'aujourd'hui.

Lovejoy, C.O. (1988). Evolution of human walking. *Scientific American*, 259(5): 82–89.

Lovins, H., Wallis, S., Wijkman, A. and Fullerton, J. (2018). *A Finer Future: Creating an Economy in Service to Life.* Gabriola Island, BC.: New Society Publishers.

Lu, Z., Happe, R., Cabrall, C.D., Kyriakidis, M. and de Winter, J. (2016). Human factors of transitions in automated driving: A general framework and literature survey. *Transportation Research, Part F*, 43: 183–198.

Lucas, A., Prettico, G., Flammini, M.G., Kotsakis, E., Fulli, G. and Masera, M. (2018). Indicator-based methodology for assessing EV charging infrastructure using exploratory data analysis. *Energies*, 11(1869): 1–18.

Luckert, E. (2013). Drawings we have lived: Mapping desire lines in edmonton. *Constellations*, 4(1).

Lutkevich, P., McLean, D. and Cheung, J. (2012). *Light Handbook.* Washington D.C.: FHWA.

Lyotard, J. (1979). *Postmodern Condition: A Report on Knowledge.* Minneapolis: Univ of Minnesota Press.

MacDonagh, L.P. (2013). *The History of Street Trees: "This will be easy!".* Retrieved from Deeproot: https://www.deeproot.com/blog/blog-entries/the-history-of-street-trees-this-will-be-easy.

MacDonald, M.F., de Montfort, P. and Thorp, N. (2008). *The Correspondence of James McNeill Whistler.* October 14, 2003. Retrieved 15 July 2013. Retrieved from University of Glasgow: https://www.whistler.arts.gla.ac.uk/correspondence/.

Mancebo, F. (2008). Coping with urban sprawl: Toward a sustainable peri-urbanization, giving way to residential path. *Les Annales de la Recherche Urbaine, PUCA*, 51–57.

Marchetti, C. (1994). Anthropological invariants in travel behavior. *Technological Forecasting and Social Change*, 47(1): 75–88.

Marinetti, F.T. (1909). *The Futurist Manifesto.* Retrieved from Bactra: http://bactra.org/T4PM/futurist-manifesto.html.

Marks, T. (2015). *The Street of Wonderful Possibilities: Whistler, Wilde and Sargent in Tite Street by Devon Cox, Review: 'Richly Anecdotal'*. Retrieved from University of Glasgow: Whistler.arts.gla.ac.uk.

Marlow, C. (2018). *How to Stop 'Smart Cities' From Becoming 'Surveillance Cities'*. Retrieved from ACLU: https://www.aclu.org/blog/privacy-technology/surveillance-technologies/how-stop-smart-cities-becoming-surveillance-cities.

Marohn, C. (2019). *Four Ways Traffic Engineers Thwart Public Will*. Retrieved from Strong Towns: https://www.strongtowns.org/journal/2019/9/16/four-ways-traffic-engineers-thwart-public-will.

Marohn, C.L. (2021). *Confessions of a Recovering Engineer*. Hoboken: Wiley. Retrieved from Strong Towns: https://www.strongtowns.org/journal/2010/11/22/confessions-of-a-recovering-engineer.html.

Marquis, E. (2021). *Highway to Nowhere Drives Entire Country Deep into Debt*. Retrieved from Jalopnik: https://jalopnik.com/highway-to-nowhere-drives-entire-country-deep-into-debt-1847204969.

MaRS Discovery District. (2016). *Microtransit: An Assessment of Potential to Drive Greenhouse Gas Reductions*. Toronto: MaRS Discovery District and Richmond Sustainability Initiatives.

Marshall, S. (2005). *Streets and Patterns*. London: Routledge, Taylor and Francis.

Martin, R. (2002). *Financialization of Daily Life*. Philadelphia, Pennsylvania: Temple University Press.

Martret, O. (2020). *Electric Vehicles – Cleaner, Greener and On-Demand?* Retrieved from Shotl: https://shotl.com/news/electric-vehicles-cleaner-greener-and-on-demand.

Marx, K. (1867). *Capital I, (MECW 35)*. London: Lawrence and Wishart.

Matuka, R. (2014). *The History of the Electric Car*. Retrieved from Department of Energy, USA.

Matyas, M. (2020). Opportunities and barriers to multimodal cities: Lessons learned from in-depth interviews about attitudes towards mobility as a service. *European Transport Research Review*, 12(7): 1–11.

Mazzetti, M., Perlroth, N. and Bergman, R. (2019). *It Seemed Like a Popular Chat App. It's Secretly a Spy Tool*. Retrieved from New York Times: https://www.nytimes.com/2019/12/22/us/politics/totok-app-uae.html.

McCarthy, C. (2020). *6 Reasons Children Need to Play Outside*. Retrieved from Harvard Health Blog: https://www.health.harvard.edu/blog/6-reasons-children-need-to-play-outside-2018052213880.

McCormack, D. (2013). *Refrains for Moving Bodies: Experience and Experiment in Affective Spaces*. Oxford: Duke University Press.

McFarlane, C. and Söderström, O. (2017). On alternative smart cities: From a technology-intensive to a knowledge-intensive smart urbanism. *Analysis of Urban Change, Theory, Action*, 21(3-4): 312–328.

McIntosh, J. (2008). *The Ancient Indus Valley: New Perspectives*. ABC-CLIO.

McKever, R. (2008). 'More beautiful than the Victory of Samothrace': Sculpting a Futurist Classicism. *Jornades Internacionals L'Actualitat del Clàssic*, 45–78. Retrieved from NewYorker.: https://www.newyorker.com/culture/goings-on/futurism-now.

McMahon, J. (2019). *9 Shared-Mobility Startups Eager to Disrupt Transportation*. Retrieved from Forbes: https://www.forbes.com/sites/jeffmcmahon/2019/03/06/9-shared-mobility-startups-eager-to-disrupt-transportation/.

McMorrough, D.W. (2015). *Evaluating the Drivers of Metabolic Rate and Movement in Homeotherms*. London: Imperial College London.

McNabb, M. (2019). *DRONEII: Tech Talk – Unraveling 5 Levels of Drones*. Drone Talk.

Medina-Tapiaa, M. and Robusteb, F. (2018). Exploring paradigm shift impacts in urban mobility: Autonomous vehicles and smart cities. *Transportation Research Procedia*, 33: 203–210.

Melaina, M., Bush, B., Muratori, M., Zuboy, J. and Ellis, S. (2017). *National Hydrogen Scenerios: How Many Stations, Where, and When?* Washington, D.C.: National Renewable Energy Laboratory for the H2USA.

Menon, M. (2015). *Indifference to Difference: On Queer Universalism*. Minneapolis: University of Minnesota Press.

Metrolinx. (2008). *The Big Move: Transforming Transportation in the Greater Toronto and Hamilton Area*. Toronto: Metrolinx.

Millard-Ball, A. (March 2019). The autonomous vehicle parking problem. *Transport Policy*, 75: 99–108.

Mirrlees, J.A. (1972). The optimum town. *The Swedish Journal of Economics*, 74(1): 114–135.

MIT Media Lab. (2019). *Persuasive Electric Vehicle (PEV)*. Retrieved from MIT Media Lab City Science Group: https://www.media.mit.edu/projects/pev/overview/.

Mitchell, W.J., Borroni-Bird, C.E. and Burns, L.D. (2015). *Reinventing the Automobile*. Cambridge, USA: The MIT Press.

Modarres, A. (2019). *100 Years of Bauhaus. Has the Bauhaus Ruined Our Cities? Glimpses of An Old Debate*. Retrieved from Bauhaus 100: https://www.bauhaus100.com/magazine/discover-the-bauhaus/has-the-bauhaus-ruined-our-cities/.

Mohorčich, J. (2020). Energy intensity and human mobility after the anthropocene. *Sustainability*, 12: 2376–2389.

Monchambert, G. (2020). Why do (or don't) people carpool for long distance trips? A discrete choice experiment in France. *Transportation Research Part A: Policy and Practice*, 132: 911–931.

Morawska, L., Moore, M.R. and Ristovski, Z.D. (2014). *Health Impacts of Ultrafine Particles: Desktop Literature Review and Analysis.* Canberra: Australian Government Department of the Environment and Heritage.

Morozov, E. (2013). *To Save Everything, Click Here: Technology, Solutionism, and the Urge to Fix Problems that Don't Exist.* Bristol: Allen Lane.

Movmi. (2018). *Carsharing Market Analysis: Growth and Industry Analysis.* Retrieved from Movmi.net: https://movmi.net/carsharing-market-growth/.

Muheim, P. and Partners. (1996). *Car Sharing Studies: An Investigation.* Dublin, Ireland: Graham Lightfoot.

Müller, V.C. (2020). *Stanford Encyclopedia of Philosophy.* Retrieved from Stanford University: https://plato.stanford.edu/entries/ethics-ai/.

Mumford, L. (1934). *Technics and Civilization.* San Diego: Harcourt, Brace and Company.

Münzel, K., Boon, W., Frenken, K. and van der Blomme, J.D. (2019). Explaining carsharing supply across Western European cities. *International Journal of Sustainable Transportation,* 1–12.

Mwakalonge, J., Siuhi, S. and White, J. (2015). Distracted walking: Examining the extent to pedestrian safety problems. *Journal Traffic Transp. Eng.,* 2: 327–337.

NACTO. (2013). *Urban Street Design Guide.* New York: National Association of City Transportation Officials.

NACTO. (2017). *Designing for All Ages & Abilities.* New York: National Association of City Transportation Officials. Retrieved from National Association of City Transportation Officials.: https://nacto.org/publication/urban-bikeway-design-guide/designing-ages-abilities-new/.

NACTO. (2020). *Designing Streets for Kids.* New York: NACTO.

Najini, H. and Muthukumaraswamy, S.A. (2017). Piezoelectric energy generation from vehicle traffic with technoeconomic analysis. *Journal of Renewable Energy,* 1–16.

Namazu, M. (2017). *The Evolution of Carsharing: Heterigeneity in Adoption and Impacts.* Vancourver: The University of British Columbia.

Nandy, U.K., Nandy, S. and Nandy, A. (2018). A Perceptive Journey through Postmodernism. *Journal of Civil Engineering and Environmental Sciences,* 4(1): 020–023.

Naught, C. (2021). *Amsterdam is Embracing a Radical New Economic Theory to Help Save the Environment. Could It Also Replace Capitalism?* Retrieved from Time: https://time.com/5930093/amsterdam-doughnut-economics/.

Nechvatal, J. (2015). *Revisiting Le Corbusier as a Fascist.* Retrieved from Hyperallergic: https://hyperallergic.com/221158/revisiting-le-corbusier-as-a-fascist/.

Network Rail Infrastructure Limited. (2020). *Network Statement 2020.* London, UK: Network Rail.

Newman, M., Barabasi, A.L. and Watts, D.J. (2005). *The Structure and Dynamics of Networks.* Princeton: Princeton Univ. Press.

Newswire. (2010). *Vancouver First City in the World to Endorse the Fossil Fuel Non-Proliferation Treaty.* Retrieved from Fossil Fuel Non-Proliferation Treaty: https://www.newswire.ca/news-releases/vancouver-first-city-in-the-world-to-endorse-the-fossil-fuel-non-proliferation-treaty-843699223.html.

NHTSA. (2016). *Federal Motor Vehicle Safety Standards: Minimum Sound Requirements for Hybrid and Electric Vehicles.* Washington D.C.: National Highway Traffic Safety Administration, NHTSA.

Nijmana, J. and Weic, Y.D. (2020). Urban inequalities in the 21st century economy. *Applied Geography,* 117: 102188.

Nikitas, A., Wang, J.Y. and Knamiller, C. (2019). Exploring parental perceptions about school travel and walking school buses: A thematic analysis approach. *Transportation Research Part A: Policy and Practice,* 124: 468–487.

Nilsson, N.J. (1982). *Principles of Artificial Intelligence.* Elsevier Inc.

Normile, D. (2022). *Indonesia's Utopian New Capital May Not be as Green as it Looks.* Retrieved from Science: https://www.science.org/content/article/indonesia-s-utopian-new-capital-may-not-be-green-it-looks.

NTSB. (2020). *Tesla Crash Investigation Yields 9 NTSB Safety Recommendations.* National Transportation Safety Board.

O'Brien, J. (2015). *Inca Road: The Ancient Highway that Created An Empire.* Retrieved from BBC News, Washington: https://www.bbc.com/news/magazine-33291373.

O'Carroll, T. and Franco, J. (2017). *Why Build a Muslim Registry when You Can Buy It?* Retrieved from Medium: https://medium.com/amnesty-insights/data-brokers-data-analytics-muslim-registries-human-rights-73cd5232ed19.

OECD. (2018). *Dream Jobs? Teenagers' Career Aspirations and the Future of Work.* Paris: OECD.

OECD. (2019). *Gender and Environmental Statistics: Exploring Available Data and Developing New Evidence.* Paris: OECD.

Ohta, K. (1998). TDM measures toward sustainable mobility. *IATSS Research,* 22(1).

Omi, K. (2018). *Alternative Energy for Transportation.* Retrieved from Issues in Science and Technology: https://issues.org/omi/.

O'Neal, E.E., Jiang, Y., Franzen, J.L., Rahimian, P., Yon, J.P., Kearney, J.K. and Plumert, J.M. (2018). Changes in perception–action turning over long time scales: how children and adults perceive and act on dynamic affordances when crossing roads. *Journal of Experimental Psychology: Human Perception and Performance*, 44(1): 18–26. Retrieved from Science Daily.: https://www.sciencedaily.com/releases/2017/04/170420090208.htm.

Ongel, A., Loewer, E., Roemer, F., Sethuraman, G. and Chang, F. (2019). Economic assessment of autonomous electric microtransit vehicles. *Sustainability*, 2–18.

Ontario Medical Association. (2005). *The Illness Costs of Air Pollution: 2005–2026 Health and Economic Damage Estimates.* Toronto: OMA.

Ontario, P.o. (2006). *A Place to Grow: Growth Plan for the Greater Golden Horseshoe.* Toronto: Province of Ontario.

Ontario, P.o. (2020). *A Place to Grow: Growth Plan for the Greater Golden Horseshoe.* Toronto: Province of Ontario.

Orenstein, M. (2020). *COVID-19's Effect on Energy and Emissions – and Implications for the Future.* Retrieved from Canawest Foundation: https://cwf.ca/research/publications/what-now-covid-19s-effect-on-energy-and-emissions-and-implications-for-the-future/.

ORF. (2011). *Integrated Transport Policy: A Vision which Doesn't Work Today – How to Make It a Reality.* Retrieved from Observer Research Foundation: https://www.orfonline.org/research/integrated-transport-policy-a-vision-which-doesnt-work-today-how-to-make-it-a-reality/.

ORF. (2011). *Integrated Transport Policy: A Vision which Doesn't Work Today – How to Make It a Reality (Part II).* Retrieved from Observer Research Foundation: https://www.orfonline.org/research/integrated-transport-policy-a-vision-which-doesnt-work-today-how-to-make-it-a-reality-part-ii/.

Pallasmaa, J. (2014). Space, place, and atmosphere. emotion and peripheral perception in architectural experience. *Lebenswelt: Aesthetics and Philosophy of Experience*, 230–245.

Panchal, D.U. (2015). *Two and Three Wheeler Technology.* PHI Learning Pvt. Ltd., ISBN 9788120351431.

Parasuraman, R. (1992). Adaptive function allocation effects on pilot performance. *NASA/FAA Workshop on Artificial Intelligence and Human Factors.* Daytona Beach, Florida, USA: NASA and FAA.

Parasuraman, R., Sheridan, T.B. and Wickens, C.D. (2000). A model for types and levels of human interaction with automation. *IEEE Transactions on Systems, Man, and Cybernetics-Part A: Systems and Humans*, 30(3): 286–297.

Paunović, K., Jakovljević, B. and Belojević, G. (2009). Predictors of noise annoyance in noisy and quiet urban streets. *Sci. Total Environ,*, 407(12): 3707–3711.

PBS. (2009). *Timeline: History of the Electric Car.* Retrieved from PBS.Org: https://www.pbs.org/now/shows/223/electric-car-timeline.html.

Peden, M., Oyegbite, K., Ozanne-Smith, J. and Hyder, A.A. (2008). *World Report on Child Injury Prevention.* Geneva (Switzerland): World Health Organization.

Peña, A. (2012). *Evolution Water Transport: From Ancient History to the Megaships of Today.* Retrieved from Calayan Educational Foundation Inc.: https://www.slideshare.net/annalyngp/evolution-of-water-transport.

Perner, J., Unteutsch, M. and Lövenich, A. (2018). *The Future Cost of Electricity-Based Synthetic Fuels.* Berlin: Agora Energiewende.

Pete. (2015). *Electric Cargo Bike Guide.* Retrieved from Electric Bike Report: https://electricbikereport.com/electric-cargo-bike-guide/.

Peteritas, B. (2012). *Seoul's Transit System Serves as a Model for America.* Retrieved from Governing: https://www.governing.com/archive/col-seoul-subway-offers-lesson-in-transportation.html.

Pickford, M. and Senut, B. (2001). 'Millennium Ancestor', a 6-million-year-old bipedal hominid from Kenya –Recent discoveries push back human origins by 1.5 million years. *South African Journal of Science*, 97(1-2): 22.

Pinto, R.A. (2018). Digital sovereignty or digital colonialism. *International Journal of Human Rights*, 27: 1–4. Retrieved from https://sur.conectas.org/en/digital-sovereignty-or-digital-colonialism/.

Playful city. (2016). *Playful Street.* Retrieved from Playful city: https://www.aplayfulcity.com/project-1.

Plumert, J.M., Kearney, J.K. and Cremer, J.F. (2007). Children's road crossing: A window into perceptual-motor development. *Curr. Dir. Psychol. Sci.*, 16(5): 255–258.

Pope III, C.A., Burnett, R.T., Thun, M.J., Calle, E.E., Krewski, D., Ito, K. and Thurston, G.D. (2002). Lung cancer, cardiopulmonary mortality, and long-term exposure to fine particulate air pollution. *Journal of the American Medical Association*, 287(9): 1132–1141.

Porru, M., Serpi, A., Mureddu, M. and Damiano, A. (2020). A multistage design procedure for planning and implementing public charging infrastructures for electric vehicles. *Sustainability*, 2889(12): 1–17.

Pountney, M. (2014). *The Ideal Human Form as Manufactured in Ancient Times as it is Today, as Shown in The Body Beautiful Exhibition at Bendigo Art Gallery.* Retrieved from Herald Sun: https://www.heraldsun.com.au/entertainment/arts/the-ideal-human-form-as-manufactured-in-ancient-times-as-it-is-today-as-shown-in-the-body-beautiful-exhibition-at-bendigo-art-gallery/news-story/f54a725285265e5877c2aa90a5fe98f5.

Priemus, H. (2007). *Dutch Spatial Planning between Substratum and Infrastructure Networks*, 15(5): 667–686. European Planning Study.

Project Syndicate. (2019). *A Zero-carbon Eeconomy is Within Reach – but We Must Act Quickly*. Retrieved from European CEO: https://www.europeanceo.com/world-view/a-zero-carbon-economy-is-within-reach-but-we-must-act-quickly/.

Puchalsky, C.M. (2005). Comparison of emissions from light rail and bus rapid transit. *Transportation Research Record*, 1927(1): 31–37.

Qiu, C., Chau, K.T., Ching, T.W. and Liu, C. (2014). Overview of wireless charging technologies for electric vehicles. *Journal of Asian Electric Vehicles*, 12: 1679–1685.

Rabinowitz, A. (2014). It's about time: Historical periodization and Linked Ancient World Data. *Institute for the Study of the Ancient World (ISAW)*.

Rajvanshi, A.K. (2002). Electric and improved cycle rickshaw as a sustainable transport system for India. *Current Science*, 83(6): 703–707.

Ram, G., Mouli, C., Duijsen, P.V., Grazian, F., Jamodkar, A., Bauer, P. and Isabella, O. (2020). Sustainable e-bike charging station that enables AC, DC, and wireless charging from solar energy. *Energies*, 13(3549): 1–21.

Rasmussen, D.C. (2016). *The Problem with Inequality, According to Adam Smith. Business*. Retrieved from the Atlantic: https://www.theatlantic.com/business/archive/2016/06/the-problem-with-inequality-according-to-adam-smith/486071/.

Raworth, K. (2017). *Doughnut Economics: Seven Ways to Think Like a 21st-century Economist*. London: Random House.

Reagan, R. (1983). *A Nation at Risk*. Washington D.C.: United States Government.

Reddy, T. (2008). *Synthetic Fuels Handbook: Properties, Process, and Performance*. McGraw-Hill.

Regnier, E. (2007). Oil and energy price volatility. *Energy Economic*, 29(3): 405–427.

Reuters, T. (2020). *Scientists Find Oldest Fossil of a Land Animal*. Retrieved from CBC News: https://www.cbc.ca/news/technology/oldest-land-animal-1.5592917.

Richard, F. and Cooper, H. (2005). Why electrified rail is superior. *21st Century Science & Technology*, 18: 26–29.

Richardson, H.W. (1973). *The Economics of Urban Size*. Farnborough, Hants, UK: Saxon House, Lexington Books.

Rickstrom, J. and Klum, M. (2015). *Big World, Small Planet: Abundance within Planetary Boundaries*. New Haven and London: Yale University Press.

Rideamigos. (2018). *What is Transportation Demand Management?* Retrieved from Rideamigos: https://rideamigos.com/transportation-demand-management-tdm/.

Rider, D. (2020). *Toronto Adds Electric Bicycles to Bike-share Fleet — At No Extra Cost to Users*. Retrieved from Toronto Star: https://www.thestar.com/news/city_hall/2020/08/19/toronto-adds-electric-bicycles-to-bike-share-fleet-at-no-extra-cost-to-users.html.

Rieti, J. (2017). *CBC News*. Retrieved from Toronto discourages electric car use by denying on-street chargers, driver says: https://www.cbc.ca/news/canada/toronto/electric-vehicles-blocked-1.4368014.

Riley, J.G. (1973). Gammaville: An optimal town. *Journal of Economic Theory*, 6: 471–482.

Ritchie, H. (2020). *What are the Safest and Cleanest Sources of Energy?* Retrieved from Our world in data: https://ourworldindata.org/safest-sources-of-energy.

Roach, J. (2011). *Mohenjo Daro 101: "Faceless" Indus Valley City Puzzles Archaeologists*. Retrieved from National Geographic: https://www.nationalgeographic.com/history/archaeology/mohenjo-daro/.

Rodenbach, J., Mathis, J., Chicco, A., Diana, M. and Nehrk, G. (2017). *Car Sharing in Europe: A Multidimensional Classification and Inventory*. European Union: STARS and AUTON.

Röösli, M., Mohler, E., Frei, P. and Vienneau, D. (2014). Noise-related sleep disturbances: Does gender matter? *Noise and Health*, 16(71): 197–204.

Ross, I.J. (2018). *Reframing Urban Street Culture: Towards a Dynamic and Heuristic Process Model*, 15: 7–13: City, Culture and Society.

Rossi, A. (1983). *La décentralisation urbaine en Suisse*. Lausanne: Presses Polytechniques Romandes.

Rothman, L., Building, R., Howard, A., Macarthur, C. and Macpherson, A. (2017). The school environment and student car drop-off at elementary schools. *Travel Behaviour and Society*, 9: 50–57.

Sadik-Khan, J. and Solomonow, S. (2016). *Streetfight: Handbook for an Urban Revolution*. New York: Penguin Random House LLC.

SAE. (2014). *Taxonomy and Definitions for Terms Related to On-road Motor Vehicle Automated Driving Systems*. USA: SAE International.

SAE International. (2014). *Ground Vehicle Standards*. USA: SAE International.

SAE. (2018). *Taxonomy and Definitions for Terms Related to Shared Mobility and Enabling Technologies*. USA: SAE International.

SAE International. (2019). *A Dictionary of Terms for the Dynamics and Handling of Single Track Vehicles (Motorcycles, Scooters, Mopeds, and Bicycles)*. Warrendale, PA, USA: J1451_201909. Society of Automotive Engineers.

SAE International. (2019). *J3194 –Taxonomy and Classification of Powered Micromobility Vehicles.* Warrendale, PA, USA: Society of Automotive Engineers.

SAHO. (2011.). *Transport on water.* Retrieved from South African History Online.: https://www.sahistory.org.za/article/transport-water.

Said, E.W. (1978). *Orientalism.* New York: Vintage.

Sarah, F. (2012). Jane Jacobs: Is There Good Science behind Urban Planning? *Scientific American.*

Saunders, K. (2017). *Where's the Hype for Automated Trains? Part 1: History and Background.* Automation.

Sawilla, Schütt and Oskar. (2018). *Ipt-technology.* Retrieved from Wireless Opportunity Charging buses in Madrid: https://ipt-technology.com/case-opportunity-charging-madrid/.

SCAQMD. (2000). *Multiple Air Toxics Exposure Study.* San Francisco: South Coast Air Quality Management District.

Scellato, S., Cardillo, A., Latora, V. and Porta, S. (2006). The backbone of a city. *Eur. Phys. J. B.*, 50: 221–225.

Scheff, T.J., Berezin, M. and Stearns, P.N. (2021). *Civilizing Process.* Retrieved from Science Direct: https://www.sciencedirect.com/topics/computer-science/civilizing-process.

Schlossberg, M. and Amos, D. (2015). *Retrofitting Sprawl: Addressing Seventy Years of Failed Urban Form: Chapter 9: Rethinking Residential On-street Parking.* Athens: University of Georgia Press.

Schneider, C.G. and Hill, L.B. (2007). *No Escape from Diesel Exhaust: How to Reduce Commuter Exposure.* Boston: Clean Air Task Force.

Schneider, C.M., Belik, V., Couronné, T., Smoreda, Z. and González, M.C. (2013). Unravelling daily human mobility motifs. *The Royal Society Interface*, 10(84).

SCL. (2015). *The Promise and Perils of Smart Cities.* Retrieved from Tech Law for Everyone: https://www.scl.org/articles/3385-the-promise-and-perils-of-smart-cities.

Sclar, R., Gorghinpour, C., Castellanos, S. and Li, X. (2018). *Barriers to Adopting Electric Buses.* Berlin: World Resources Institute, WRI and German Federal Ministry.

Scott, A.J. (2014). Beyond the creative city: Cognitive–cultural capitalism and the new urbanism. *Regional Studies*, 48(4): 565–578.

Seife, C. (2000). *Zero: The Biography of a Dangerous Idea.* New York: Penguin Books.

Sennett, R. (2006). *The Open City.* Retrieved from Urban Age: https://urbanage.lsecities.net/essays/the-open-city.

Sevtsuk, A. and Ratti, C. (2010). Does urban mobility have a daily routine? Learning from the aggregate data of mobile networks. *Journal of Urban Technology*, 17(1): 41–60.

Shaheen, S. and Cohen, A. (2019). *Shared Micromobility Policy Toolkit: Docked and Dockless Bike and Scooter Sharing.* Schmidt Family Foundation.

Shaheen, S., Cohen, A. and Zohdy, I. (2016). *Shared Mobility: Current Practices and Guiding Principles.* Washington D.C., USA: Federal Highway Administration.

Shared-Use Mobility Center. (2017). *Shared-use Mobility Reference Guide.* Chicago, USA: Shared-Use Mobility Center.

Sheldrake, R. (2009). *Morphic Resonance: The Nature of Formative Causation.* Rochester, Vermont: Park Street Press.

Shell, E.R. (2020). The role of air pollution. *Scientific American*, 42–47.

Shepertycky, M. and Li, Q. (2015). Generating electricity during walking with a lower limb-driven energy harvester: targeting a minimum user effort. *Plos ONE*, 1–16.

Shladover, S.E. (2016). The truth about "self driving" cars. *Scientific American*, 52–57.

Shweder, R.A. (2001). *International Encyclopedia of the Social & Behavioral Sciences.* New York: Elsevier Ltd.

Siemens Mobility. (2015). *Sustainable Urban Infrastructure: Vienna Edition – Role Model for Complete Mobility.*

Silber, J. (2007). *Architecture of the Absurd: How "Genius" Disfigured a Practical Art.* New York: Quantuck Lane Press.

Sims, R., Schaeffer, R., Creutzig, F., Cruz-Núñez, X., D'Agosto, M., Dimitriu, D., Meza, D., Fulton, M.J., Kobayashi, L., Lah, S., Mckinnon, O., Newman, A., Ouyang, P., Schauer, M., Sperling, J.J.-D. and Tiwari, G. (2007). *Transport in: Climate Change 2014: Mitigation of Climate Change. Contribution of Working Group III to the Fifth Assessment Report of the Intergovernmental Panel on Climate Change.* Cambridge and New York: Cambridge University Press.

Sitte, C. (1889). *City Planning According to Artistic Principles.* New York: Kahle/Austin Foundation.

Smart Cities World News. (2019). *Bike and edestrian Analytics Tool Launched.* Retrieved from Smart Cities World News: https://www.smartcitiesworld.net/news/news/bike-and-pedestrian-analytics-tool-launched-3750.

Smiley, A. (2004). Adaptive strategies of older drivers. *Transportation in An Ageing Society: A Decade of Experience* ( 27: 36–43). Washington D.C.: Transportation Research Board.

Smith, A. (1776). *The Wealth of Nations on the Infrastructure Section,* Book V, Part III. London: W. Strahan and T. Cadell.

Smith, R.A. (2008). Enabling technologies for demand management: Transport. *Energy Policy*, 36(12): 4444–4448.

Society of Automobile Engineers, SAE. (2018). *Shared Mobility: Taxonomy and Definitions in SAE J3163™.*

Spaen, B. (2019). *This All-Electric Water Taxi Could Revolutionize Green Transportation.* Retrieved from Green Matters: https://www.greenmatters.com/news/2018/06/25/qSvID/water-taxis-transportation.

Sperling, D. and Shaeen, S. (1999). Carsharing: Niche market or new pathway? *ECMT/OECD Workshop on Managing Car Use forSsustainable Urban Travel* (pp. 1–25). Dublin, Ireland: OECD.

Spulber, A., Dennis, E.P. and Wallace, R. (2016). *The Impact of New Mobility Services on the Automotive Industry.* Ann Arbor, Michigan: Cargroup.Org.

Staffell, I., Scamman, D., Abad, A.V., Balcombe, P., Dodds, P.E., Ekins, P., Shah, N. and Ward, K.R. (2019). The role of hydrogen and fuel cells in the global energy system. *Energy & Environmental Science*, 12(463-491).

STAPPA and ALAPCO. (2000). *Cancer Risk from Diesel Particulate: National and Metropolitan Area Estimates for the United States.* San Francisco: State and Territorial Air Pollution Program Administrators and the Association of Local Air Pollution Control Officials.

Steel, C. (2013). *Hungry City: How Food Shapes Our Lives.* London: Vintage Books.

Steer Davies Gleave. (2009). *GO Transit Lakeshore Express Rail Benefit Case, Interim Report.* Toronto: Metrolinx.

Steffen, W., Richardson, K., Rockström, J., Cornell, S., Fetzer, I., Bennett, E., Bennett, E.M., Biggs, R., Carpenter, S.R., Vrie, W.D., Wit, C.A.D., Folke, C., Gerten, D., Heinke, J., Mace, G.M., Psersson, L.M., Ramanathan, V., Reyers, B. and Sörlin, S. (2015). Planetary boundaries: Guiding human development on a changing planet. *Science*, 15: 1–10.

Steinert, H. (1983). The development of "discipline" according to michel foucault: Discourse analysis vs. social history. *Crime and Social Justice*, 20: 83–98.

Stern, N. (2006). *The Economics of Climate Change: The Stern Review.* Cambridge: Cambridge University Press.

Stohler, W. and Giger, P. (1989). *Cost-Benefit Analysis of the Electrification of the Beira Alta Line in Portugal.* London: Institution of Electrical Engineers.

Stone, T. (2017). *Lessons Learned from the History of Car Sharing.* Retrieved from https://tiffanydstone.com: https://tiffanydstone.com/2013/08/23/lessons-learned-from-the-history-of-car-sharing/.

Stone, T. (2018). *Siemens to Demonstrate World's First Autonomous Tram Running in Real Traffic in German City.* Retrieved from traffictechnology.com: https://www.traffictechnologytoday.com/news/autonomous-vehicles/siemens-to-demonstrate-worlds-first-autonomous-tram-running-in-real-traffic-in-german-city.html.

Strompen, F., Litman, T. and Bongardt, D. (2012). *Reducing Carbon Emissions through Transport Demand Management Strategies: A Review of International Examples, Final Report.* Beijing: GIZ China.

Sumar, F., Mallon, S., Landgarden, S. and Schaer, J. (2014). *Who Really Owns Public Spaces?* Retrieved from Bloomberg News: https://www.bloomberg.com/news/articles/2014-06-30/who-really-owns-public-spaces.

Sung, N.M. and Rios, M. (2015). *Want Dramatic Road Safety Results? Look to South Korea.* Retrieved from The World Bank: https://blogs.worldbank.org/transport/want-dramatic-road-safety-results-look-south-korea.

Swenson, R. (2016). The Solar evolution: Much More with Way Less, Right Now—The Disruptive Shift to Renewables. *Energies*, 9(9): 676.

Takefuji, Y. (2008). And if public transport does not consume more energy? *Le Rail*, 31–33.

Tao, P., Stefansson, H. and Saevarsdottir, G. (2014). Potential use of geothermal energy sources for the production of Li-ion batteries. *Renewable Energy*, 61.

Tate. (2021). *Situationist International.* Retrieved from Tate: https://www.tate.org.uk/art/art-terms/s/situationist-international.

TCRP. (2003). *Transit Capacity and Quality of Service Manual*, Chapter 3, Appendix A. Washington D.C.: Transit Cooperative Research Program (TCRP), Report 165.

The Altantic. (2015). *An Animated History of Transportation.* Retrieved from The Altantic: https://www.theatlantic.com/video/index/397865/animated-history-transportation/.

The Economist. (2017). A world turned upside down. *Renewable Energy*, 18–20.

The Economist. (2020). *Home-working had its Advantages, Even in the 18th Century.* Retrieved from The Economist: https://www.economist.com/christmas-specials/2020/12/16/home-working-had-its-advantages-even-in-the-18th-century.

The Guardian. (2011). *19th Century Cyclists Paved the Way for Modern Motorists' Roads.* Retrieved from The Guardian: https://www.theguardian.com/environment/bike-blog/2011/aug/15/cyclists-paved-way-for-roads.

The Guardian. (2017). *Smaller, Lighter, Greener: Are Micro EVs the Future of CityTtransport?* Retrieved from The Guardian: https://www.theguardian.com/sustainable-business/2017/may/11/micro-evs-city-transport-suemens-renault-green-air-pollution.

The Guardian. (2018). *Desire Paths: The Illicit Trails that Defy the Urban Planners.* Retrieved from The Guardian: https://www.theguardian.com/cities/2018/oct/05/desire-paths-the-illicit-trails-that-defy-the-urban-planners.

The Local. (2015). *No Norway Kids Have Died in Traffic This Year.* Retrieved from The Local Norway: https://www.thelocal.no/20151204/no-norway-kids-have-died-in-traffic-this-year/.

The TEV Project. (2017). *Tracked Electric Vehicle System*. Reference technical booklet. Retrieved from The TEV project: http://tevproject.com/.

Toole Design Group and Pedestrian and Bicycyle Information Centre. (2012). *Bike Sharing in the United States.* USDOT, Federal Highway Administration.

Toth, G. (2012). *Levels of Service and Travel Projections: The Wrong Tools for Planning Our Streets?* Retrieved from Project of Public Spaces: https://www.pps.org/article/levels-of-service-and-travel-projections-the-wrong-tools-for-planning-our-streets.

Transport Canada. (2007). *Social Cost of Collisions*. Ottawa: Transport Canada.

Transport Canada. (2009). *Bike Sharing Guide*. Ottawa: Transport Canada.

Transport Canada. (2013). *Canadian Motor Vehicle Traffic Collision Statistics*. Ottawa: Transport Canada.

Trencher, G. (2019). Towards the smart city 2.0: Empirical evidence of using smartness as a tool for tackling social challenges. *Technological Forecasting and Social Change*, 89: 80–91.

TUMI. (2019). *Remarkable Women in Transport: Female Change-makers Transforming Mobility*. Bonn: Transformative Urban Mobility Initiative.

TuSimple. (2020). *TuSimple Launches World's First Autonomous Freight Network with UPS, Penske, U.S. Xpress, and McLane Company, Inc.* Retrieved from stockhouse.com: https://stockhouse.com/news/press-releases/2020/07/01/tusimple-launches-world-s-first-autonomous-freight-network-with-ups-penske-u-s.

UITP. (2013). *Press Kit: Metro Automation Facts, Figures, and Trends*. International Association of Public Transport.

UITP. (2014). *Metro Automation Facts, Figures, and Trends*. International Association of Public Transport (UITP).

United Nations. (1987). *World Commission on Environment and Development: Our Common Future*. Oxford: UN.

University of Washington. (2018). *Seattle Center City: Alley Infrastructure Inventory and Occupancy Study*. Seattle: University of Washington.

US Bureau of Transportation Statistics. (2020). *Energy Intensity of Passenger Modes*. Retrieved from U.S. Energy Consumption by the Transportation Sector: https://www.bts.gov/content/energy-intensity-passenger-modes.

US Department of Energy. (2018). *Alternative Fuel Vehicles*. Retrieved from US Department of Energy: https://www.energy.gov/public-services/vehicles/alternative-fuel-vehicles#/find/nearest?country=US.

US Environmental Protection Agency. (2008). *Heat Island Compendium*. US EPA.

Varinsky, D. (2017). *An American Cultural Revolution is Killing Cookie-cutter Homes — Here's What Homebuilders are Selling Instead*. Retrieved from Business Insider: https://www.businessinsider.com/the-dream-of-owning-a-cookie-cutter-home-is-dying-heres-where-people-are-moving-instead-2017-2.

Venugopal, P., Shekhar, A., Visser, E. and Scheele, N. (2018). Roadway to self-healing highways with integrated wireless electric vehicle charging and sustainable energy harvesting technologies. *Applied Energy*, 212: 1226–1239.

Voigt, K. (2021). Corporeality of architecture experience. *Dimensions of Architectural Knowledge*, 1: 139–147.

Vox. (2016). *How Highways Wrecked American Cities*. Retrieved from Vox: https://www.youtube.com/watch?v=odF4GSX1y3c.

Vynck, G.D. and Wong, N. (2020). *Alphabet's Dream of a Smart City in Toronto is Over*. Retrieved from Bloomberg News: https://www.bloomberg.com/news/articles/2020-05-07/alphabet-s-dream-of-a-smart-city-in-toronto-is-over.

Walker, J. (2011). *Basics: Walking Distance to Transit*. Retrieved from Human Transit: https://humantransit.org/2011/04/basics-walking-distance-to-transit.html.

Wang, P., Hunter, T., Bayen, A.M., Schechtner, K. and González, M.C. (2012). Understanding road usage patterns in urban areas. *Nature*, 2: 1001.

*Watch: Toronto's Surge in E-bike Ownership Creates Concerns over Safety*. (2018). Retrieved from Iheartradio: https://www.iheartradio.ca/newstalk-1010/news/watch-toronto-s-surge-in-e-bike-ownership-creates-concerns-over-safety-1.3726810.

Wawrzyniak, J. (2018). The utilitarian stigma of environmental protection. *Conatus*, 3(1): 89–110.

Wazana, A., Krueger, P., Raina, P. and Chambers, L. (1997). A review of risk factors for child pedestrian injuries: Are they modifiable? *Injury Prevention, BMJ Journals*, 3: 295–304.

WCED, UN. (1987). *Our Common Future*. Oxford: Oxford University Press.

Webster, D.C. and Mackie, A.M. (1996). *Review of Traffic Calming Schemes in 20 mph Zones*. London: TRL Report.

Weichenthal, S., Ryswyk, K., Goldstein, A., Shekarrizfard, M. and Hatzopoulou, M. (2015). Characterizing the spatial distribution of ambient ultrafine particles in Toronto, Canada: A land-use regression model. *Environmental Pollution*, 47(PT A): 1–8.

Weingast, R.B. (2017). *Adam Smith's Theory of Violence and the Political-Economics of Development*. Retrieved from SSRN: https://ssrn.com/abstract=2881042.

Weingroff, R.F. (1996). Federal-aid highway act of 1956, creating the interstate system. *Public Roads. Federal Highway Administration*, 60(1).

Weir, L. (2018). *Pina Bousch's Dance Theatre: Tracing the Evolution of Tanz Theatre.* Edonburgh: Edinburgh University Press.

Weißbach, D., Ruprecht, G., Hukeac, A., Czerski, K., Gottlieb, S. and Hussein, A. (2013). Energy intensities, EROIs (energy returned on invested), and energy payback times of electricity generating power plants. *Energy,* 52: 210–221.

West, G. (2017). *Scale.* New York: Penguin.

White, M. (1977). A model of residential location choice and commuting by men and women workers. *Journal of Regional Science,* 17: 41–52.

Wiener, E.L. and Curry, R.E. (1980). Light deck automation: Promise and problems. *Ergonomics,* 995–1011.

Wihtol, R. (2017). *Beware the Infrastructure Debt Trap.* Retrieved from The Interpreter: https://www.lowyinstitute.org/the-interpreter/beware-infrastructure-debt-trap-0.

Williams, B. (1973). *Utilitarianism: For and Against.* Cambridge: Cambridge University Press, pp. 96–118.

Williams, C. (2021). *The Fight over the Hybrid Future of Work.* Retrieved from The Economist: https://www.economist.com/the-world-ahead/2021/11/08/the-fight-over-the-hybrid-future-of-work.

Wilson, A. (1970). *Entropy in Urban and Regional Modelling.* London: Pion Press.

Wilson, B. (2020). *Metropolis: A History of the City, Humankind's Greatest Invention.* New York: Doubleday Books.

Wilson, K. (2018). *An Overview of SAE International: Standards Activities Related to Charging of Hybrid/Electric Vehicles.* Ground Vehicle Standards, SAE International.

Wilson, L. (2013). Shades of Green: Electric Cars' Carbon Emissions around the Globe. *Shrink That Footprint,* pp. 1–28.

Winckelmann, J.J. (1764). *History of the Art of Antiquity.* Santa Monica: Getty Research Institute (Translation in 2016).

Wolff, J. (1988). *The Culture of Separate Spheres: The Role of Culture in Nineteenth-century Public and Private Life.* Manchester: Manchester University Press.

Wollstonecraft, M. and Lync, D. (1792). *Vindication of the Rights of Women.* London: Penguin Random House (English).

Wolverton, T. (2016). *Wolverton: Elon Musk's Hyperloop Hype Ignores Practical Problems.* Retrieved from the Mercury News: https://www.mercurynews.com/2013/08/13/wolverton-elon-musks-hyperloop-hype-ignores-practical-problems/.

World Commission on Environment and Development. (1987). *Our Common Future.* Oxford: Oxford Univeristy Press.

WSP, Farrells and P.B. (2019). *Making Better Places: Autonomous Vehicles.* London: WSP, Farrells and Parsons Brinckerhoff.

Xiong, H., Wang, L., Linbing, D., Wang, D. and Druta, C. (2011). Piezoelectric energy harvesting from traffic- induced deformation of pavements. *International Journal of Pavement Research and Technology,* 5(5): 333–337.

Yang, Z. (2020). Development of optimal city size theory: A critical view. *J. of Resources and Ecology,* 11(1): 100–110.

Yapp, R. (2021). *The One-minute City: How Stockholm is Going 'Hyperlocal'.* Retrieved from The Local: https://www.thelocal.se/20211012/one-minute-city-how-stockholm-going-hyperlocal-invest-stockholm-tlccu/.

Yunus, M. (2011). *Building Social Business: The New Kind of Capitalism that Serves Humanity's Most Pressing Needs.* New York: PublicAffairs.

Zahavi, Y. (1979). *The "UMOT" Project.* Washington, D.C.: US Department or Transport.

Zeller, T. (2015). *In Historic Turn, CO2 Emissions Flatline in 2014, Even as Global Economy Grows.* Retrieved from Forbes: https://www.forbes.com/sites/tomzeller/2015/03/13/in-historic-turn-co2-emissions-flatline-in-2014-evan-as-global-economy-grows.

Zhang, W. and Guhathakurta, S. (2016). Parking spaces in the age of shared autonomous vehicles: How much parking will we need and where? *Sustainable Cities and Society,* 19: 34–45.

Zhong, M., Hunt, J.D. and Lu, X. (2008). Studying differences of household weekday and weekend activities—A duration perspective. *Transportation Research Record,* 2054: 28–36.

Zhu, S., Kim, J., Ma, X., Shih, A., Laud, P.W., Pintar, F., Shen, W., Heymsfield, S.B. and Allison, D. (2010). BMI and risk of serious upper body injury following motor vehicle crashes: Concordance of real-world and computer-simulated observations. *PLoS Med.,* 7(3): e1000250.

Zielinski, S. (2006). New mobility: The next generation of sustainable urban transportation. *National Academy of Engineering,* 36(4).

# Section II

# Understanding Our
# New Mobility Code

# CHAPTER 3
# Sensing Mobility DNA

**Fig. 3.0:** An artistic illustration of sensing our daily mobility behaviours and pattern.

> *"An analytic interpretation is not made in order for it to be understood. It is made in order to make waves."*
>
> —Jacques Lacan

## Introduction—Data Problems, Mobility Problems

When we have problems or things are not performing as well as they should, an ancient philosophy tells us to look in the mirror. Metaphorically, looking in the mirror means finding the problem first with us or within our own system. The root cause may be within the basic philosophy, or how the system was built or inside the fundamental elements of systems. If the foundation of the system was built on faulty assumptions or the ground situation has changed over time, the problems will appear in every part of the system.

For mobility, the system starts with data.

Mobility systems in cities are built on current and future infrastructure plans. Capital works implement or maintain the plans based on current or future demand. And the demand generally comes from travel demand models, master plans, or specific needs studies. The future mobility demand is deeply ingrained in municipal finance, such as development charges, cost recovery fees, setting rates, fiscal impact analysis and short- and long-range financial planning. All studies rely on data, mostly static or snapshot data from a particular day, period, peak time, or 'desired' locations. That's a fundamental conundrum since the nature of mobility is not static. It's dynamic. It changes every day or every hour or every season, with our mobility habit built into those changing situations. When a dynamic system is built based on a static snapshot, the system will over or under perform outside the snapshot scenario. The system becomes rigid and outdated.

Mobility data is often collected for a certain day or time or asks questions through a predesigned survey. Almost every developing nation has carried out a national travel survey, a major source of mobility data. Other data, such as traffic counts, speeds, operational performance, are done at a 'desired' spot. The data is used to forecast future travel demand based on past trend or demand generation rates or proportions. An entire city's mobility depends on a static snapshot, without investigating whether the philosophy of data collection or information built into a monumental system was appropriate in the first place.

### *Data from faded trip memories*

In GPS (global positioning system), we trust.

One of most common and largest sources of mobility data comes from predesigned surveys. Most of the travel survey is designed to get the answers we want, not answers on how we move in cities every day. People try their best to answer on their mobility habit from memory, but the simple problem is shorter trips are extremely hard to remember, if not next to impossible. We mostly remember long-distance trips, like taking regional trains or subway trips, and longer car trips to work or shopping or recreation. So, we recollect whatever comes to mind first. No one can remember the numerous short trips we take every day unless they are being tracked and data stored somewhere. The under-reporting of short trips in travel surveys (Stopher et al., 2007) led us to believe those trips do not exist or are insignificant. Travel demand models use the overestimated longer trips to design our mobility systems. Longer trips intimately linked wider streets, more highways, more frequent trains, and sprawled neighbourhoods. We build daily needs places far away from home and with less connectivity since you can always drive more and more. Longer commutes require more energy, resources, and ever-expanding mobility infrastructure. Shorter trips require relatively cheaper, higher capacity and efficient infrastructures such as sidewalks, pathways, trails, bike lanes and multimodal hubs. Compact and mixed-use plans build daily needs within the neighbourhood and more connections between neighbourhoods. The dominance of long trips reporting generates a higher demand for long-distance infrastructures, ignoring the needs of most of our under-reported shorter trips.

### *Data from digital memories*

We will never understand movement without silence. Silence comes in a measurable form when we stay somewhere, continuing our primary activity by staying at home with family, going outside for daily needs, or being at work. How long we stay at places depends on the type of land-use. How far we must travel to access these locations largely depends on good or bad land-use planning. And if our 'stay' ranges within a few hundred metres, though short, silence would be detectable using big data and advanced analytics techniques.

Data on travel patterns and travel demand are an important input into traffic models used today for mobility planning. Traditionally, a travel demand model uses census data, travel surveys, and traffic counts. Problems arise due to limited sample data that are expensive to collect and update annually. Figure 3.1 illustrates the different form and data shape emerging from new real-time and smart data sources. For instance, cellular network data is a large-scale data source with promise to obtain a better understanding of human mobility. To infer travel demand, it starts by extracting trips from cellular network data. To find out which types of trips can be extracted, a small-scale cellular network dataset can be collected from few mobile phones, together with GPS tracks collected on the same device. Using a large-scale dataset of cellular network data, the travel demand inferred from the cellular 'network' data is compared to the municipality's existing urban travel demand model as well as public transit tap-ins or time spent at activity locations. Some studies produced the results that had been long suspected, the severe underestimation of short trips. About 50% of which are short trips of 1–2 km (Breyer et al., 2020). The author's attempt to introduce big data in mobility planning shows more than 80% of trips in the Don Mills and Eglinton area of Toronto stayed within just an 8-by-8 km zone (City of Toronto, 2016). Traditional travel surveys predict the opposite trend. Sharp and contradictory results between an individual's memory and smart mobility from traced or probed data is pointing in embarrassing directions: Did we build our entire city and major auto-oriented mobility system based on wrong data, flawed assumptions, and incorrect forecasting models? We have one last chance to address the fundamental issues of data and models head-on now that we face the existential crisis of climate emergency and resource depletion issues fuelled by sprawled, auto-oriented and lifeless suburban neighbourhoods.

> *"Data is the new currency of our age."*
> —Dr. Hannah Fry

## Evolution of City and Mobility Data

To find the root cause of mobility problems, we need to dig deep into the beautiful underground world of data. Data, the word itself, came from the Latin 'datum' – "that which is given". Precisely, raw data that tells us how we move or what stories are hidden when we do not move. Data acts as the bridge between the visual and the hidden world of human mobility. What we see visually as urban noise in movement could be our self-organized mobility pattern. Like other subjects, the process of capturing, collecting, storing, transferring, and making sense of useful information, that is human mobility is not a straight-forward path. From data to wisdom, it follows a simple four-step process: data, information, knowledge, and wisdom (Fry, 2016). When properly processed,

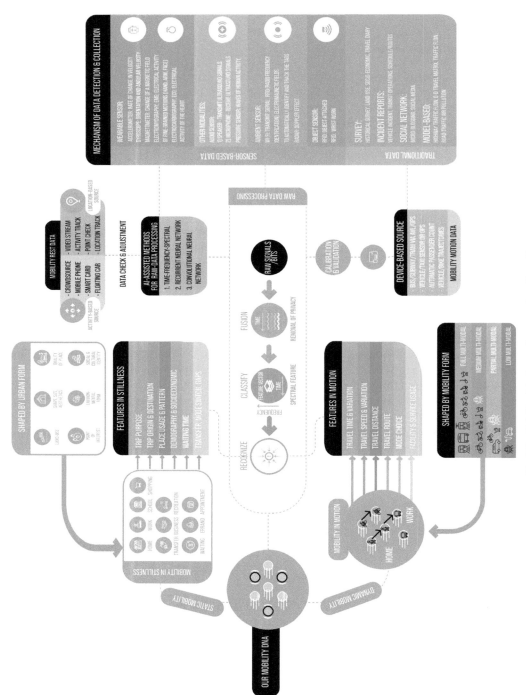

**Fig. 3.1:** Mobility data forms, shapes, and configurations.

cleaned, and analysed, data provides meaningful information. If information is visualized within the local context, it generates knowledge about our mobility pattern. Using built environment context, information gives us a sense of urban activities (Senseable City Lab, 2015). A collection of knowledge ultimately develops our wisdom of how to build a city and its mobility systems that align with the city's social, cultural, and environmental values and objectives. The mobility world often skips the last three steps and leaves behind very little understanding of the stories hidden in the raw data. However, this weakness is linked to a lack of suitable data sources. The core of this incompatibility and travel demand prediction difficulty is using a static and outdated and one-time snapshot data of human movement to understand the most complex and dynamic phenomena of our species. Tracking human activities was not possible until recently. Making sense of such a complex phenomenon, using an outdated snapshot approach, was the wrong starting point to improving the mobility system in cities.

The history of data and information is as fascinating as human evolution itself. And the captivating world of data and information has run parallel to the mobility system for nearly a century in the modern era (Fig. 3.2). Today we cannot separate data, mobility, and technology. But in earlier human civilizations the presence of data was subtle and hidden behind human observations. This section is not a summary of data or information history. It is simply an attempt to connect the evolution of urban data and mobility in similar contexts. Understanding the changes in data and information would lead to changes in mobility demand and system improvements in the real world.

### City and data in ancient times

Thirst for knowledge led to some of the earliest efforts to collect data in ancient cities. Uganda's Ishango Bone discovered in 1960, shows humans stored and analysed data as tally sticks as early as 18000 BCE. Sumerians developed the earliest known city data systems via writing and numbers, Cuneiform, to develop an inventory of food, storage, and anticipation of supply and demand needs around 3500 BC (Barjamovic et al., 2019). Egyptians developed agriculture data collection to keep track of vast field planting and irrigation systems using pictogram writing systems. Mass data storage in the form of the abacus and a library appeared in Babylon around 2400 BCE. The Library of Alexandria was perhaps the largest collection of data in the ancient world around 300 BC–AD 48, before it was destroyed by invading Romans. The Antikythera mechanism of ancient Greece is considered as the first "analogue computer" and was designed for astrological purposes and to track the cycle of Olympic Games in AD 100–AD 200. These attempts of ancient data, or a record keeping habit helped to build their city; astronomical survey was used for street alignment; geometry was used for the city's key infrastructures and periphery; the size of streets came from practical and functional needs of daily human life and commerce activities; and utilities such as drainage along the road was laid out based on gravity and elevation data. These organic observations of human and trade activity were common ingredients of mobility system planning in ancient cities until the end of the Roman era. There is evidence that data was used for controlling and managing traffic too. To avoid congestion at the central crossing point of Rome, wheeled traffic was banned during the Julius Caesar era, and carts had limited entry during the emperor Hadrian era, based on trade traffic peak time observations. The main driving force of the vast road network was invasion and keeping vital supply chain between Roman occupied cities. Roman road density network data was assumed to uncover a link between infrastructure and economic activity (Dalgaard et al., 2018). However, the faulty assumption between physical mobility infrastructures and the economy fell apart at the end of Roman era, leaving a wide misperception of the infrastructure myth that still exists in the 21st century.

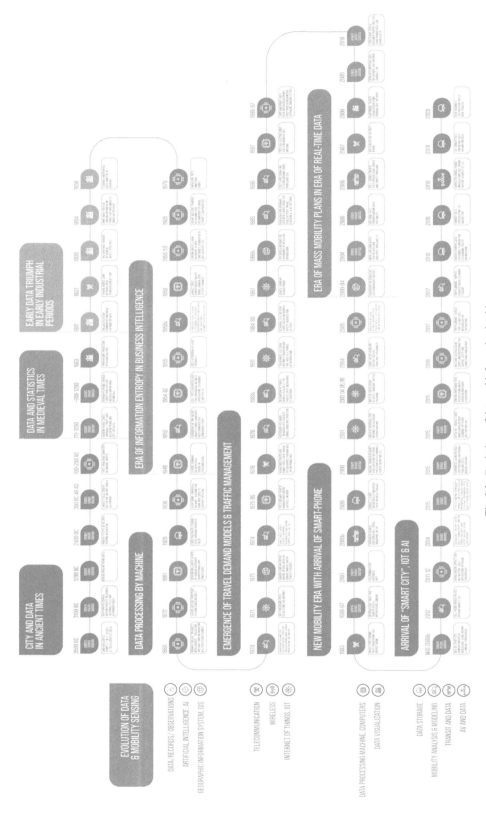

**Fig. 3.2:** Evolutions of data and information in cities.

## Data and statistics in mediaeval times

The emergence of statistics to analyse data to convert into information is an iconic achievement of the mediaeval era. But the era started with a few bright spots during the darkest periods of human history. The Moors in Spain and Arabs in the Middle East used information to develop vast knowledge in mathematics, astronomy, chemistry, physics, geography, philosophy, and health science. Highly skilled Moors from 17 universities used detailed trade and space knowledge to build the first organized and highly efficient urban mobility network systems, unthinkable feats during the dark ages in western Europe (BHS, 2009). Data gathered from people and mobility activity led to well-paved narrow roads for wheeled mobility, raised sidewalks for pedestrians, and public squares for open street vendors and commercial purpose. Street illumination with lamps for 10 miles at key locations helped to continue city life at night. A few centuries later, the Moor's mobility facility design might have inspired Leonardo Da Vinci to suggest separating wheeled and pedestrian traffic in crowded and busy Italian cities. On the other side of the Middle East, intense city life observations and a prolific trading data culture in Arabian cities helped to develop small paths known as 'sikkak', connecting neighbouring homes, community, and public spaces. And the 'mushtarak', a shared street for multiple modes was invented. Based on entering traffic observations, European cities prohibited parking and introduced the one-way street in the 17th century. After the Renaissance, western Europe entered a new era of statistics. Some prominent examples were an early system for the plague by John Graunt, and a series of inventions in human scale city planning ideas in Amsterdam, Italy, and Spain.

## Data triumph in early industrial periods

Life in cities was changing fast during the early days of the industrial era. Very few people had basic ideas of what was going on except some pioneers of data. At the beginning of the 18th century, a Scottish engineer William Playfair started to gather data and graphically represent it in meaningful information (Sack, 2020). Whether a pie chart, Excel graphics, or modern infographics, William paved the way for innovation in the quantitative presentation of data and information using graphs and charts by following Joseph Priestley's early prototypes. Soon after, the Morse code was invented using the telegraph system, becoming one of the most significant data transmissions in communication history and the earliest example of data sharing to alter physical needs for mobility. These events inspired many pioneers, notably John Snow's famous street map linking cholera to a single water pump, and Florence Nightingale's efforts to reduce war causalities using data and statistics. These concepts and discoveries opened the door to the machine assisted data and information era at the end of 19th century.

The early attempts of census, density, and other basic city building data led to mass mobility ideas during the same era. Starting with city census, the most common source of data in ancient and mediaeval civilization was to keep track of community resources supplied by excess food produced during the early agricultural era. One of the most comprehensive census databases of human civilization was catalogued by historian Tertius Chandler for populations over 20,000 from AD 800 to AD 1850 (Chandler, 1987), later by Modelski for urban settlements from 3500 BC to 1000 BC in three different eras (Modelski, 2003), and post 1950s by the UN (Desa, 2014) following a quest suggested by renowned urban historian Lewis Mumford. Based on these works, over 6,000 years of global urbanization are now established using the knowledge of how cities were located geographically and how environment influenced the setup of local and regional systems (Reba et al., 2016). Today we take land-use and census for granted. Yet these pioneering data and information initiatives led to modern land-use practice and process. They are the raw material of current or future city mobility transportation demand assessment and infrastructure supply to match urban growth needs.

### Data processing by machine (pre-WWII)

This era would generally be seen as laying the foundation of the post-WWII computer and digital information age. Several inventions fuelled machine assisted data and information processing systems. Realizing the enormous manual labour needs of a US census system, Herman Hollarith developed a machine-readable punch card system at the end of 19th century (Somersethhouse, 2015). Storing data in magnetic fields was proposed by Fritz Phleumer. Data sharing took a dramatic turn in the NPL (National Physical Laboratory) facility in the UK. Instead of sending big chunks of data, Alan Turing proposed sending "packages of data" in his "universal machine" concept during WWII. Data gathered by military defence operations and the building of wide and high-speed roads was developed during both world wars. Machine readable technology helped to develop highway plans and paved the way for the 'blueprint' of mass and wide road construction. The military approach of high-speed highways later conceived the mega master plan of interstate highway system in the US, and the city highway system in western Europe and Singapore. Still today, city planners struggle to reverse the "high-speed street philosophy" that dissected city neighbourhoods into pieces.

### Era of information entropy in business intelligence (post world war to pre-software era 1980s)

A new era begins with the invention of early computer prototypes, and with a strange theory that swept through modern-day data science and information technology. In his theory of communication, Claude Shannon introduced the idea of data communication using three simple elements: a source of data, a communication channel, and a receiver (Shannon, 1948). He proposed to break data down into basic binary digits: 0 and 1, and to break down all types of information into a "bit packet", replicating Alan Turing's "data package" concept. Weight will be given to each packet and its corresponding probability, the basic elements of information entropy. Shannon's source coding tells ways to encode, compress, and transmit messages from a data source. His noisy-channel coding theorem represents entropy as an absolute mathematical limit on how well data from the source can be compressed without loss onto a perfectly noiseless channel. Without his theory, we would not be able to watch YouTube, transmit jpeg data or share data through various internet mediums. Artificial intelligence (AI) soon arrived with a series of prototypes (Marr, 2015): the first AI programme; Minsky and McCarthy's effort to spread AI as new science; face recognition software; and the first industrial software Unimation, that would change the automation process of the automobile industry, particularly in Japan and other far east countries. AI and faster computers enabled vast amounts of data storage, called a "data centre", which led to the idea of the intelligent traffic control system and traffic management centres. Following Shannon's theory, the first mainframe computers emerged in the UK and the US that enabled city planners to develop a few of todays' trademark traffic systems: the first citywide master plan using the so called trip-based 'four-step' travel demand model in Chicago, and the first computerized traffic signal system and the freeway traffic management concept (MTO, 2007) in Toronto. However, these applications were done solely in quest of technology applications, with very little scientific method and few considerations about human travel instinct or behavioural patterns. A fundamental flaw appeared soon. Vast inaccuracy was observed in the trip-based travel demand model which mimicked Newton's gravity formula, without considering why people generate trips, their socioeconomic background, or other factors that influence our travel decisions.

> *"The traditional responses to tackling congestion, like building new roads or widening existing ones are no longer proving effective."*
> —Harold Goddijn, TomTom CEO, and cofounder

## Emergence of activity-based travel demand models & traffic management system on the internet and GIS era (1970s to 2000s)

Great debate erupted over how mobility in cities should be planned and designed during the 1970s rapid urbanization and cultural revolution era. One specific technology would change the city building and mobility world forever. Mobility, about moving from one place to another location, is a spatial characteristic that became almost a synonym for geographic information systems (GIS). In the mid-1960s, with the prospect of handling and analysing spatial data digitally, the idea gave birth to a new spatial science – GIS and remote sensing (Li and Brimicombe, 2012). Remarkable progress began with landmark prototype initiatives, such as the first mapping software SYMAP by Harvard Graduate School in 1964, that mapped existing land uses and analysed land capability for forestry, agriculture, wildlife, and recreation for the Canada Land Inventory (Tomlinson, 1984), and the first digital maps of street blocks and census tracts by the US Bureau of Census in 1971. The birth of the internet and the fast 3G network in around the dawn of millennium opened a floodgate of opportunity to integrate data, spatial information systems, and engage people and organizations (Brimicombe and Li, 2009) into the city planning process. With the development of its third-generation network (3G) in the 2000s that would enable high-speed data transmission for both voice and data communication at 144 Kpbs and later up to 8 Mbps, mobile GIS converged wireless mobile technologies and GIS into real-time technology. Mobile GIS has embedded in many Location–Based Services (LBS) applications via smart phones, giving a gold mine of data and applications to mobility planning: portable individual mobility service; data and services without necessarily requiring a fixed location or wired connection; real-time connectivity and updates; supporting mobile internet access; and multimedia applications.

Equipped with new technology and vast travel data, several prominent geographers, scientists, and researchers pointed out a deep flaw in the gravity-based travel demand approach (see next section for discussion on travel demand models). A few cornerstones of the new mobility debate were the inclusion of demand generated by various daily life activities and participation by Swedish geographer Hagerstrand; the travel choice theory to expand mobility demand for multiple modes in North Carolina; Mafadden and Ben-Akiva's famous discrete choice model to refine multimodal options (Tajaddini et al., 2020); and, the emergence of the first citywide pedestrian and cycling demand and master plans using manual and internet-based data (Turner et al., 1997). Despite all efforts, the deeply flawed static data for the national travel survey and gravity model remained part of mobility planning in all cities around the world until the second decade of the 21st century. This inflicted the deep wound in mobility planning, creating expensive and wasteful car-oriented infrastructures that still haunt a new generation of city planners who fundamentally disagree with heavy finances and resources dedicated toward moving cars instead of transit in cities.

## New mobility era with arrival of smart phone (2007–2015)

The smart phone is sometimes viewed as revolutionary technology, but what it created was freedom. While the first prototype idea of the smart phone was proposed in 1993, called 'Simon', it was not until 2007 when Apple released its first practical version of a usable iPhone that it shocked the industry. Around the same time, Internet 2.0 came with the social media explosion. Wikipedia was created in 2001 giving out vast amounts of free crowdsourced information to the public. Google produced the cloud system which theoretically has the capacity of unlimited data storage. The idea of crowdsourcing for mobility, urban activity, and environmental data collection became a common application using early IoT applications (Waag Society, 2014). Several data visualization and 3D tools as a 'software-as-a-service' were also invented around the same time (Laney, 2001). These series of inventions and technological advancements brought disruption in the mobility world, sometimes in dramatic ways. Several private companies started new businesses for traffic and urban mobility data services: probed data by INRIX, Airsage, TomTom, and Streetlight, and crowdsourced data by Wage, Moovit, Bikemaps, Fitbit, and many more. The systematic and consistent city database was developed by World Bank and UITP (Marie, 2001), and other non-profit mobility organizations to broaden our global-scale understanding of why some cities managed sustainable mobility to reduce vehicle usage while improving equity and quality of life, and why some others were going in the wrong direction. The most dramatic changes however were in public transit service. Public transit tested and successfully implemented real-time scheduling and vehicle arrival display in London, Seoul, Singapore, and some US cities, and automated vehicle location services that made transit dramatically more user-friendly and increased travel demand, particularly in Southeast Asia. A vast amount of detailed travel and location specific data gave birth to microsimulation modelling for specific locations, intersections and stations, and the idea of agent-based travel demand for shared and new mobility technology that attempted to repair the flaws in traditional travel demand models.

### *Arrival of real-time, IoT, and AI (second decade of 21st century)*

The arrival of real-time with mass artificial intelligent tools dramatically changed the mobility landscape. While the industrial robot was replacing human jobs in automobile and other manufacturing, applications of robot or machine self-learning and easy access to AI applications was not available until the last decade. AI was making headlines: Sony's mass produced AIBO; Deep Blue defeated Kasparov; the speech recognition concept produced Apple's Siri; Google's Brain identified a cat from a YouTube video; and IBM's Watson won Jeopardy. AI made real inroads in the mobility sector with machine learning or software like Tensorflow, and deep learning applications for data processing and analysis techniques such as the convolutional neural network, CNN in 2016. Some hardware makers, such as Nvidia, enabled high-speed computing and meaningful applications for autonomous driving. With the arrival of IoT, the smart city concept also gained popularity although core concepts and applications in cities remain vague. AI driven vast amounts of real-time data processing produced cell phone and crowdsource data applications for mobility demand and operation assessment. A few startups took it to the next level: Waycare developed AI driven incident and safety prediction in highways (Waycare, 2019); Geotab produced real-time data without the need for storage (Geotab, 2020), hence, tackling privacy issues directly; MotionTag produced the most sophisticated personal track data capability (MotionTag, 2016) which helped to develop the mobility DNA concept in this book; Google introduced multimodal travel information and shared mobility options in its online maps; Streetlight produced multimodal data to model walking, cycling, vehicle, trucks (Streetlight Data, 2017); and Moovit produced a precise transit modelling capacity using crowdsourced and AI integrated data and schedules from transit agencies (Moovit, 2020). A series of concepts and tools turned into practical initiatives and produced change in mobility data usage and policy development. Mobility data sharing gradually became a complex field without proper protocol in place. The first baby step was inevitably data standards and specifications for new data.

Recently, a few data specifications, which is prescribed as a policy of the application programming interfaces (APIs), were adopted to develop common ground for data capture, storage, and sharing between private service providers and public agencies (Clewlow, 2019). The first attempt was to standardize the most used format for specifying public transit schedules through General Transit Feed Specification (GTFS) for real-time transit data (Zervass, 2014) by a Google and Trimet joint project in 2006. The multimodal user was secondly attempted by Sidewalk Lab's Toronto Transit Explorer (ToTX). With the wild success of the GTFS idea in transit, General Bikeshare Feed Specification (GBFS) was officially adopted for docked bikeshare system availability in real-time by the North American Bike Share Association in November 2015 (Motivate, 2016). The third attempt was Mobility Data Specification (MDS) to share data with cities from mobility operators through "provided API" (LADOT, 2018), and cities could communicate back to operators through an "Agency API". The fourth attempt was the connected and autonomous vehicle interface specification by HERE in Europe (Kent, 2015) and the PEGASUS business-to-business data sharing and test assessment program for highly automated vehicles (HAV) in Germany (PEGASUS, 2020), which is similar to ITS America data exchange and Davi (Data for Automated Vehicle Integration) for AV data exchange needs and the Auto-ISAC cybersecurity risk program. The fifth attempt was initiated by a series of private or non-government initiatives such as developing the global referencing of streets and pick-up-drop-off data via the Taxi and TNC activity system (World Bank's Open Transport Partnership); an open-source "digital street" system (SharedStreets, 2019); a smart curb operation and monitoring system by Coord (Smyyth, 2019); and fleet-specific data by Swiftly, Replica, and Remix for real-time travel demand modelling. Finally, the impact of all mobility ecosystems of multimodal travel on standards and the ongoing development of standards was introduced by a multimodal and accessible travel (MAT) programme (Schweiger et al., 2019) which was inspired by an initiative of the City of Seattle (City of Seattle, 2017) to create a neutral trusted data platform for multimodal on-demand mobility that would house data from new mobility service providers, sensors, and other data sources, automate data analytics, and enable predictive analytics.

Private efforts to integrate multimodal data predominantly focused on the next vehicle system for transit, except TransitScreen, which successfully integrated several mobility modes showing availability, distance to facility, schedule, and multimodal score for each neighbourhood. A recent partnership between TransitScreen and OpenMobilityData is promising to develop open transportation data for all mobility modes (TransitScreen, 2019).

These attempts, however, are being explored in a relatively isolated manner. The SAE mobility data consortium, a multi-stakeholder collaboration between private and public partners, is developing best practices with guidance on responsible data licensing practices in the rapidly changing mobility space (SAE, 2019). Another general mobility data system, Data as a Service (DaaS), is currently being explored as medium for rapid exchange of real-time conditions and mobility service information between providers, customers, and the supporting infrastructure (Hand, 2016). DaaS requires a seamless data exchange with a variety of partners and stakeholders, privacy and security protections, the capacity to analyse data from a variety of resources, and the ability to integrate this insight into a data-driven decision-making process for both system managers and elected politicians. DaaS may cover fleet, trip, parking, storage, maintenance, and incident data (T4America, 2018). Managing the complex flow of ever-changing new mobility technology is difficult task. Secure third-party data platforms driven by AI solutions (Lempert, 2019) are likely a very cost-efficient path forward to process data feeds from multiple operators with economies of scale, and to allow cities to efficiently harness mobility data for important policy and planning decisions (Clewlow and Stiles, 2020). While private mobility providers are the key to implement new mobility systems in cities, access to mobility infrastructures will remain in the hands of public agencies. A new private-public collaboration through real-time mobility data sharing is the most beneficial path forward for future mobility systems in cities.

Among all these rapid developments in advanced mobility planning, a few pressing issues emerged. In general, city planners or politicians are not hands-on using highly complicated data. It needs easier language to transfer the raw information into knowledge that can be used for policy development, implementation plans, or steps for actions. Data visualization becomes the focus of mobility data as some pioneers married science, data, and art to inspire mobility visualizations. Hans Rosling developed Trendalyzer software (later acquired by Google) as art for the Gapminder Foundation (Rosling et al., 2018). Data visualization becomes a professional field (McCandless, 2012) with efforts that inspired mobility data visualization frameworks that combined GIS and computer graphics, and brought almost obscure and massive real-time data into an easily processable information format that assisted policy makers in identifying issues and ways to solve them through policy and mobility services or programmes (Sobral et al., 2019). Traffic management centres use the data driven ITS (Intelligent Transport System) that combines computer vision, data visualization, multisource data management, and machine learning (Zhang et al., 2011). The mobility data visualization framework was established in three layers: (1) data preprocessing, (2) visual transformation, and (3) visual mapping (Chen et al., 2015) making mobility data visualization as common as Google Maps. During the current pandemic Apple released their "Apple Mobility Trend", Google produced "Community Mobility" and Facebook opened the door through their "Good Mobility Dashboard". Doubt remains, how new mobility data will address the numerous misperceptions of our own mobility pattern, collective nature of city mobility, and sensible mobility policy making without an overall mobility planning framework.

### *Data beyond fourth dimension*

Advancement of data and information in the recent decade achieved a status that no one could have imagined even at the beginning of this century. But a few phenomena and limitations are exposing the current method of information sharing with big question mark. Explaining the human mind and how it works remains unexplained. The theory of "information fields" with extra dimensions providing additional layers of information is now being explored as a possible explanation of how the human mind could rapidly pass on information to each other like ants do without complicated technology. Do humans develop a habit such as their mobility pattern through quantum and sub-quantum levels of consciousness that reside in a field surrounding the brain in another dimension? (Meijer and Geesink, 2018). If true, information contained in personal and interactions through crowdsourcing would be game-changing phenomena in the data and information world. For now, the nature of personal mobility, as explained in the Mobility DNA concept earlier, is typically viewed as 'noise' uncertainty and remains an unexplored subject beyond typical movement tracking. Even simple consistency in capturing, storing, privacy protection, and sharing of personal data standard is still hotly debated and a common reasonable approach is under development. Urban sensing, where things are happening in cities, emerged as another greater application of the so-called "smart city" concept but remains in infancy. Wireless sensor driven technology was able to penetrate a few 'intelligences' such as utility consumption, electronic tagging, contamination control, and disaster monitoring, but is facing the challenges of vast sensor needs, processing, and storing of data (Tirri, 2006) that becomes a burden on a city's financial resources. Urban movement including air quality from traffic sources, however, was implemented with partial success in Europe and Southeast Asia (Sag and Blaschke, 2014). Yet no general-purpose architecture of urban sensing has emerged empowering all stakeholders in a city to partake in data collection and data-driven decision making (Flanigan and Lynch, 2018). The most notable failure of a smart city attempt was 'Masdar' (Miller, 2016), a ghost tech town in the Abu Dhabi desert that used electric cars and guided transit to create a zero-emission city and became a local planning nightmare. If data and information is better understood through quantum mechanism, the way animals interact without vast infrastructure needs, we would see major changes in the mobility system particularly with some promising applications with better virtual reality.

> *"A 10 percent increase in capacity, for instance, meant a 10 percent increase in vehicle miles, on average."*
>
> —Matthew Turner and Gilles Duranton, author of
> *Fundamental Law of Road Congestion*

# The Rise and Fall of the Mobility Demand and Supply Machine

It is not an exaggeration if someone claims that a mysterious model shapes everything in urban mobility. This mysterious and obscure model is commonly known among traffic planners as the "travel demand forecasting model". For more than half a century an attempt to understand how individuals schedule their activities and travel has been an intense focus among transportation planners to improve urban mobility and accessibility, predominantly for automobile modes. Most pre-WWII era highways and roads were built without proper guidelines, with little understanding of citywide mobility demand, and often directed by political or local demand. It may sound inexplicable, but historical evidence of urban street design suggests that many road planning and design assumptions were based on the standards for horse carriages used during the 1920s (Friedman, 2010), and some Roman road building basics are still practiced by British and North American road pavement engineers (Pavement Interactive, 2014). Many of these outdated assumptions remain hidden in current road design manuals and guidelines. Albeit some updates were introduced recently to modify those outdated assumptions. The approach to mobility planning changed after WWII, with the housing boom and massive interstate highway expansion. Then a gold rush of transportation demand forecasting for citywide master plans started a vicious cycle of "predict and provide", the predicting of future travel demands and providing of massive infrastructure programmes, predominantly to accommodate automobiles in cities. Computer models utilized basic land-use, growth projections, static travel survey data, and travel attributes to develop regional demand models. Forecasts of these models are now built into every stage of city building – from infrastructure plans to development charges and requirements, to general taxation or fees, property taxes, and everything else linked to city's operations and maintenance.

Many attempts have been made to formulate personal, group, and collective travel demand and then predict scale and variations in infrastructure supply for regions, cities, towns, and villages. None came close to predicting and replicating this most complex human activity. The travel demand model and infrastructure evolved very little in the 20th century, whereas rapid developments in data science, big data or real-time data, and the new arrival of AI are exposing the deeply flawed travel demand and infrastructure supply system. Figure 3.3 illustrates the new innovative mobility planning process that would replace traditional data and master plans' process.

## *Early travel demand models*

One of the earliest attempts in the 1950s to use newly developed mainframe computers to predict human mobility was replicating Newton's gravity model for predicting travel demand between two locations, cities, or regions. It was known as the 'trip-based' four-step model. Instead of the mass of the object, the population of cities and commercial scale were used for generating travel demand between two locations. The closest destinations would produce more travel demand. The model considered individual trips as the unit of analysis, broken down into four sequential steps: (1) trip generation: generating demand for a specific city, region or area; (2) trip distribution: distributing the generated demand to possible destinations using a simple proportion method; (3) mode choice: assigning the demand for different travel modes like cars, transit, walking, and cycling; (the first three steps are considered demand); and, (4) trip assignment: assigning the distributed demand for each mode to real street or transit lines or routes. The last step is used to estimate transportation infrastructure supply. Looking at trip demand for each street or transit or route, planners figured out how many travel lanes would be needed, and what type of transit technology or frequency would be satisfactory. These infrastructures' sizes would then be inserted into 'long-range' infrastructure plans, and the capital works department would search for funding, develop the implementation timeline, and implement the construction schedule. But a fundamental flaw started to appear with the trip-

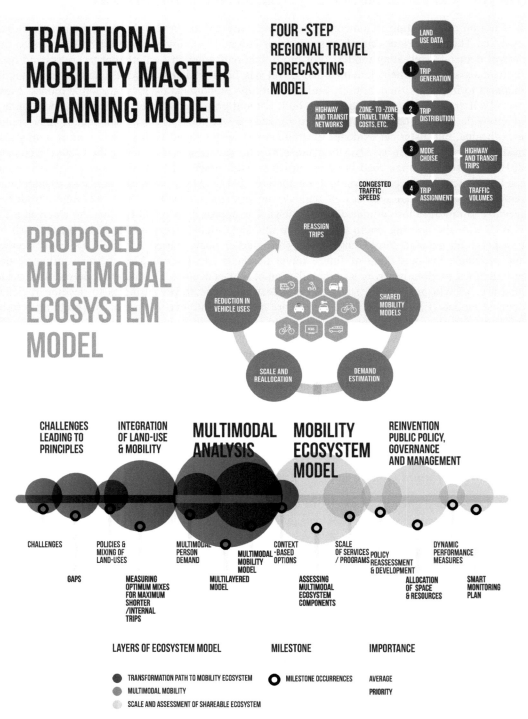

**Fig. 3.3:** Mobility master plans and forecasting models: Traditional and new approaches.

based model (Chu et al., 2012). The gravity model is good for an object like a planet, but not good to psychologically influence phenomena like human travel. It ignores the basic fact that travel demand comes from various activities. Location and time variation of demand was ignored. The influence of the group travel or built environment was absent from the mobility scene. But it was too late. By the 1960s almost every city had literally embraced the flawed travel demand model as the "orthodox model" for large-scale infrastructure. The 'bible' model remains immune to any scrutiny. When transport planning turned into a global infrastructure programme in the 1970s (Jovicic, 2001), all city planning process, technical tools, policy practices, infrastructure implementation, and funding allocation process were consumed by the traditional trip-based model, hiding its fundamental error. The lack of data and ways to refine trip-based disaggregate models were known, but city planners built a psychological barrier to never challenge the flawed demand forecasting system.

## *Activity-based demand models*

A few researchers took a fresh-look mobility demand approach resolving flaws with the trip-based model in the early 1970s and 1980s. The basic premise of the new activity-based travel demand approach is travel is a demand derived from the desire for human activities that are distributed over space and time. This new idea was first proposed by a Swedish sociologist in his famous time-geography theory that suggests travelling to certain destinations, at certain times of the day and by certain travel modes resulted from the participation in the demand activity (Hagerstrand, 1970). North Carolina planner Chapin proposed a similar concept, that people travel to carry out activities as an individual and each person could travel in a different pattern within the same household as per their daily needs and intentions of activities. They are subject to several detailed person-level and household-level travel attributes, a broader set of performance metrics, and the explicit representation of realistic constraints of time and space as it happens in real life (Chapin, 1974). Instead of aggregate zone-level features in trip-based models, activity-based models work at a disaggregate person-level.

Based on these two pioneers' works, a series of travel demand models were proposed in the next three-decades. Albeit there are some variations among the activity-based modes, these models share some commonality with the traditional 4-step models: (1) activities are generated; (2) destinations for the activities are identified; (3) travel modes are determined; and, (4) the specific network facilities or routes used for each trip are predicted (McNally, 2000). Variation among activity-based models created at least four families of models (Barthélemy and Toint, 2013) from the 1990s until the current decade.

## *Discrete choice models*

The first attempt was the discrete choice model. Originally proposed by a transportation economist, it assumes that the daily activity-travel pattern was characterized by the primary activity, primary tour type, and the number and purpose of secondary tours (Ben-Akiva and Lerman, 1985). People choose to travel in one of four discrete times, discrete "traffic zones"[1] or areas, and the discrete choice of travel modes. The theory was based on consumer choice known as random utility maximization and assumes that a consumer with a finite set of brands picks the brand that gives them the maximum amount of utility (Guadagni and Little, 1983). The discrete choice model included trip chain[2] phenomena in limited fashion but suffered from inadequate context of space and time dimensions of travel activity. The Portland model later expanded the concept for multiple tours and

---

[1] A traffic analysis zone or transportation analysis zone (TAZ) is the unit of geography like a census block, typically under 3,000 population, most used in conventional transportation planning models.
[2] A trip chain is a scheduling of activities in time and space, made by linking together work and non-work trips or two or more non-work trips.

trip chaining activity details, at-home based, or on-tour activities (Bowman, 1998). Both concepts were fairly limited to commuter trips, which was later expended to non-work trips (Bhat, 1997). Major drawbacks of these models were that they require an extremely large choice set to capture a sufficient fraction of feasible mobility patterns. All travel decisions are not fully rational in the real world, nor was latent behaviour in making decisions considered in random maximization models. Some mathematical programming technique was attempted (Gan and Recker, 2008) but lack of tracing of decision processes' formulation made it very complex.

### Hazard duration models

The introduction of probability in making trips was the basis of hazard-based models. It models the length of time a traveller spent at home before making another trip (Mannering et al., 1994). For instance, a person is not going to make a work trip until he or she finds a job. Extension of the models included shopping activity matching shop open hours (Bhat, 1996). This approach corrected a few flaws but still faces caveats. Data for length of stay between trips was not available before Google introduced their real-time travel diary in 2014, and this data is restricted due to privacy issues. Matching open hours for travel projections was somewhat applicable to predictable 'big-box' stores, but extremely difficult to predict for short and frequent trips made in urban mixed-use areas. Only digital tracked personal travel could fix the problem but it remains in its infancy.

### Structural equation models

The foundation of this approach is that knowledge of the causal mechanisms of an individual's activity participation behaviour could influence travel demand forecasting. Using simultaneous exogenous and endogenous variables,[3] causal relations among activity engagement and travel patterns could predict travel demand more precisely (Cheng et al., 2017). This concept opened the door for including latent influences on travel and socioeconomic factors to influence travel demand. The first attempt was to jointly model time allocation for activity and travel (Kitamura et al., 1992). This approach was later expanded by linking socio-demographics to activity participation and travel behavior (Lu and Pas, 1999). Working from home and shopping close to home (Gould and Golob, 1997) and the inclusion of a 'time-budget' (Golob, 2000) were significant improvements in overcoming previous model weaknesses. Despite significant improvements the task of model development is still daunting due to data sample size, overall model fit, and other technical issues (Hoe, 2008). The utilization of static, outdated national travel data for independent variables also added a forecasting discrepancy with real world travel activity.

### Rule-based simulation models

The marriage between macro simulation for larger area travel demand and microsimulation for specific location infrastructure detail was a significant change to simulation models. The approach deploys the first three stages (generation, distribution, and modal choice) similar to that of the traditional four-stage model, but the last stage, traffic assignment, utilizes dynamic traffic assignment procedures[4] (Barthélemy and Toint, 2013) whose adoption has been made easier by the development of powerful open source agent-based simulation systems such as MatSim developed in Israel (Horni

---

[3] An exogenous variable is one whose value is determined outside the model and is imposed on the model. An endogenous variable is a variable whose value is determined by the model.

[4] Travel forecasting models represent the static regional travel analysis capability, whereas microscopic traffic simulation models are superior for dynamic corridor-level travel analysis. Dynamic traffic assignment (DTA) models fill in the gap by enabling dynamic traffic to be modeled at a range of scales from the corridor level to the regional with expanded and unique functional capabilities enabled by the DTA methodology (Chiu, 2011).

et al., 2016). Two main groups of models are built into simulation models (Jovicic, 2001): activity schedule building models that construct an activity schedule from scratch and switching models that alter the predefined schedule because of proposed policy changes or infrastructure changes. Testing alternative scenarios for infrastructure planning or environmental assessment are possible outcomes of a new simulation approach.

Despite three decades of substantial improvements, activity-based model's abilities in reflecting behavioural realism are still limited. Several remedies were suggested. Possible solutions include increasing the accuracy of the primary data, improved integrity of models across days of the week, and tackling the uncertainty via integrating demand and supply (Tajaddini et al., 2020).

> *"However, when asked about evidence to support their belief, they (experienced traffic engineers) could not point to any."*
> —Dr. Ezra Hauer, professor emeritus of University of Toronto

## Frequent Derailment of the Forecasting Machine

On the surface travel demand, forecasting process looks logical, scientific, and systematic. But underneath a complexity arises in each layer. Despite all sophisticated theories and highly complex computer models, most models barely address the complex phenomena of mobility behaviour in real life and its true nature in cities. Flaws in results were often blamed on the "reliable black-box" computer. Other than personal folklore, a proper answer was rarely explored. By the 1980s, model limitations and flaws were showing a disturbing trend. The more roads were built, the more people would drive. Then the process started again from square one and revised the model again, which generated more infrastructure demand. The inability of regional travel demand models to mimic travel conditions accurately is now well known (Pulugurtha et al., 2019). Activity-based models are more sophisticated. However, a complex mobility pattern and associated assumptions are often too simplified and flawed in primary outdated data are rarely acknowledged when actual models are built for citywide master plans.

Financial and economic risks of highly inaccurate demand forecasting are typically ignored by city planners and downplayed by politicians. This leaves an enormous, life-long tax burden for the public, particularly low-income city residents, due to overbuilt but underutilized infrastructures. Accountability for making flawed infrastructure projections is nonexistent. Any uncovering of travel demand forecast flaws is vehemently opposed by traffic planners, mostly because of psychological barriers. Despite rejections, the following flaws are still embedded in modern travel forecasting and mobility master planning process.

### *High cost of flawed models*

Due to its fundamental flaws, the demand forecasting model often derails large infrastructure plans and is too often used as a platform for scandalous projections and political controversy. Modelling projections are often manipulated for political gain. The Scarborough subway plan in Toronto was promoted instead of the previous LRT plan by inflating ridership projections from 9,500 to 14,000 riders in the morning peak-hour without major changes in growth projections. The consequences of the flawed infrastructures were severe: the wrong transit technology cost an extra $2 billion for taxpayers. A local development group later sued the city for additional subway development surcharges and settled for $6 million in damages; and the city's forecasting team saw major turnover due to the flawed transit ridership projections (Munro, 2016). Toronto built the Sheppard subway line in the 1990s without sufficient ridership levels, which is costing taxpayers today $10-per-ride. It immediately became a white elephant, boring a hole in the transit agency's budget year after year

(Pagliaro, 2015). A recent proposal for the removal of a short section of the Gardiner expressway in Toronto was overturned, based on flawed travel time increases and inaccurate congestion projections, soon spiralling the cost of the 60-year-old highway's rehabilitation by $1 billion (Rider, 2020). While reviewing massive $54 billion large infrastructure projects, highly inaccurate forecasting was identified using projected and actual demand, but after the project was built. More than two-thirds of the city's rail projects were overestimated by 106%, and roughly 50% of the road projects were projected by ±20% to 25% of projects by ±40% of the difference between actual and forecasted traffic (Flyvbjerg et al., 2005). Despite major discrepancies between the computer models and the actual data, no transparency process was setup, nor was it asked to take responsibility for wrong travel demand results. Infrastructure decisions based on misleading forecasts lead to a misallocation of funds and underperforming projects (Flyvbjerg and Skamris, 1997), and this habit of unscientific, often undemocratic process remains a major source of overall mobility inefficiency in cities.

## Belief-based modelling

A lack of scientific knowledge among travel demand professionals often pointed to fundamental problems and key sources of error. The basic understanding of the science behind forecast modelling, the limitations of the data or modelling processes, and the correct interpretations of results are often not incorporated when an infrastructure supply list is given to decision makers. Embarrassing lack of openness, not understanding basic science, and the skipping of evaluations of alternatives by modellers while developing models were identified as core issues in modelling blunders (Parthasarathi and Levinson, 2010). Instead of scientific process and evidence, a 'belief' system among traffic planners often lead to erroneous modelling results or the misinterpretation of future demand results. Until today, no ethical consequence was ever incorporated despite widespread modelling inaccuracies.

## Ignoring mobility DNA

Besides modellers' poor knowledge, fundamental travel behaviour shifts due to technology advancement in mobility, internet use, and societal changes and these are not reflected in forecasting models. Despite claims to the understanding of human travel in theory, many true natures of human mobility remain unknown or ignored by forecasting professionals. Many modellers don't even know their own personal mobility habit, how many modes they use, how long they travel, what is their travel budget, nor what is their percentage of short trips. Recent research using real-time smart or historic probed data is showing that our understanding of basic laws of human mobility is limited (González et al., 2008). If personal or group travel behaviour remains unknown or misunderstood, it is not surprising that long-range regional demand forecasting will generate inaccurate results.

## Flawed primary data

If primary data is flawed, the results from travel demand data should be questionable. The raw ingredient of travel demand models, survey data asks participants to 'remember' their daily travel diary, interrupting people at busy locations or online to report 'trips' or conduct mail-in surveys (TTS, 2016). Most of these questionnaire or survey methods are outdated and suffer from a biased response (Griffiths et al., 2010). Large survey data may overcome some weaknesses but is prohibitively expensive. Age, language, social and economic conditions also create bias in survey data. One of the most notable sources of data inaccuracy is participants reporting longer trips and ignoring their shorter and frequent trips. Besides natural human bias, it is nearly impossible to remember short and frequent trips. The most disturbing issue is that surveys and models never define what a 'trip' is. If one walks to the station or the parking lot to access their car or transit, is this counted as a 'trip'? If we are going for lunch mid-day while working, is that considered a 'trip'?

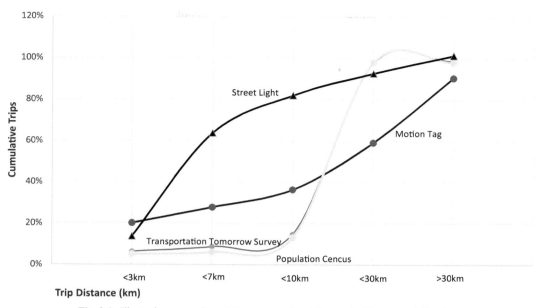

**Fig. 3.4:** Illustrative comparison static survey and real-time probed human mobility data.

If a parent drops their kid at school, is that a 'trip'? If we perform multiple activities within a short period (e.g., work, shopping, dining, meeting friends), how many trips are coded in the model? These seemingly fundamental questions have received very little answer from mobility modelling professionals. As discussed, and illustrated in the previous chapter, we get a very different answer when we systematically define, properly synthesize the data with the help of AI, and dig very deep into real-time tracked human mobility data. Ever though there has been an option of more reliable data available for the last two decades, the ideological mindset that fuels our mega mobility perverted projects remains at the heart of our deeply flawed approach. When the author introduced a new source of probed historical data (such as StreetLight) and real-time mobility traced data (such as MotionTag), the results were astonishingly the opposite. Although the definitions of trips are slightly different, the results show most of our trips are of short or medium distance (Fig. 3.4). Historic real-time probed data for trip distance shows completely reverse distribution. Real-time data shows at least three times higher trip length for 3 km, 5 km, and 7 km compared to census or travel survey data. This sharply contrasts with the trip distribution data collected through traditional travel survey and census data collection processes.

## *Induced demand*

Improving transportation facilities attracts more users, until appropriate pricing and congestion appear as a sign of saturation. "Induced trips" are a combination of latent demand (making new trips because of lower travel costs), modal shifts from other mobility modes, diverted trips from congested or longer routes, and destination shifts due to a change in the traveller's destinations or origins (Cervero, 2001). This phenomenon is generally known as induced traffic which occurs in a short timeframe, and induced demand which is longer phenomena that repeats in consistent pattern when increased traffic becomes a norm (Lee et al., 1999). If demand increases for sustainable mobility, which consumes less space, resources, energy, and costs per person, it would be a manageable mobility facility and desired city planning outcome for sustainable city growth (Litman, 2020). If vehicle demand increases due to road capacity expansion, it experiences increased congestion after a few years and roads need to be widened again. This scenario is unsustainable and eventually blocks city growth (Noland and Cowart, 2000). There is no doubt that increasing vehicle demand consumes more space, energy, resources, funding, and is polluted, the most undesirable outcome for cities. And undoubtedly that more roads do not mean less traffic and less congestion. It has never happened and not a single city has ever reported that their congestion has been eliminated after 75 years of road building. Despite mounting evidence, neither transportation policies nor travel demand models address the induced demand phenomena head on.

> *"Models had predicted that traffic would back up to Sacramento."*
> —Jeffrey Tumlin, after Loma Prieta earthquake did not generate such
> Armageddon congestion in San Francisco

### Real-world paradox

Once infrastructure is built and produces a negative outcome, there is another folklore in traffic engineering that believes it can never be removed. But true events tell a different story. When a few high-level overbuilt infrastructures were demolished intentionally or during natural events, it revealed a deeply flawed travel demand model issue in the public eye during the last two decades. Once city planners and residents started to point out flawed highways like the polluted Cheonggye Expressway in Seoul, the collapse of the West Side Highway in New York, or the Loma Prieta earthquake that brought all the city's highways to a standstill in San Francisco, it become apparent that burying a city's precious river system, running high-speed polluted highways along waterfronts, or dissecting a city's historic or populated districts with highways were bad ideas. Strangely no traffic congestion nightmare ever materialized as predicted by travel demand forecasting models, and traffic behaviour was adjusted after just a few weeks (Goodwin, 1977). This traffic behaviour was not a surprise, rather a known phenomenon called the "Braess Paradox" (Braess et al., 2005).[5] The simple premise of the paradox is people always chose the shortest path, i.e., shortest travel time using wider roads or highways which then become congested over time. If this congested link is removed from a city's network, travel time for everyone in the city will improve. But the removal of the "most precious" is like touching a bible. The car culture's fear keeps the paradox fact out of mobility plans even though it was repeated everywhere.

### Paradox of ignoring public transit

The second paradox in mobility was ignored like the Braess Paradox. Downs-Thomson Paradox was identified as a second systematic issue with travel demand modelling between two competing mobility modes. So, when highway expansion or road widening is proposed, it hurts the public transit systems as well as overall mobility system performance (Zhang et al., 2014). Like induced demand for traffic, there is little evidence that potential lack of demand of public transit extensions will reduce traffic congestion (Duranton and Turner, 2009). Toronto's most underutilized Sheppard subway line is a burning example. Transit expansion replacing roadway widening, however, paves the way for sustainable city growth which comes with additional demand. While new activity-based travel demand models now incorporate transit planning, none of the models seriously explore the serious negative effects on transit systems because of citywide massive road widening recommendations.

Scientists has been warning travel demand professionals for over a century to include these real-world travel phenomena in travel demand forecasting models. Until today, not a single traffic model has even been considered to include these real-world results into computer models.

---

[5] Original article was published in 1968 in German Language.

## Past trends are not the future

One of the common methods of developing models is making future assumptions based on past or present data or trends. Past trends are based on past mobility programmes and policies. Future policies are supposed to address fault in past policy and improve future mobility conditions. Unfortunately, past trends and objectives to improve mobility contradict each other, and the consequences of such paradoxes are typically ignored in the attempts to predict the future (Robinson, 1988). These contradictory origins and outcomes are not considered seriously when modellers 'calibrate' current conditions to verify assumptions to predict the future. Calibration is usually performed to correlate the reading (an instrument) with those in 'standard' order. Travel demand usually calibrates with the current year, which is different from five or ten years ago. When conditions change, the calibration is meaningless. For instance, if the current work-from-home trend during the Covid-19 pandemic continues, albeit at a reduced scale, travel demand models will never 'calibrate' the model for current conditions. This will lead to major errors in future projects.

## Rigidity of timeframe

Transportation technology has been changing faster than any other technology in the last decade. Most travel demand models assume base conditions will remain the same during long construction periods of expansive road projects. Transportation projects are expensive, complex, require extraordinary funding efforts, and take time to build due to property acquisition, design challenges, and planning complications. And once they finally get built, mobility technology may have moved on. The St. Lawrence Seaway is a good example. Hailed as one of the largest-scale and most expensive projects on the planet, the project took nearly 70 years from proposal to finally getting built in 1959. In that time the automobile had become the major mode of transportation, making the project redundant. The Masdar smart city based on guided personalized transit soon became obsolete when the autonomous vehicle became technically feasible. Figure 3.5 illustrates the life span of common mobility or city plans while comparing regular mobility infrastructure lifespan. Rail and transit facility lifespans are twice or three times longer than low and inefficient automobile infrastructures. Active mobility and street life are much longer due to less wear and tear from highly efficient usage. Travel demand rarely comprehends the complexity of mobility technology and its impact on travel behaviour change.

## Changes in demography, socioeconomics and mobility technology

Complex socioeconomics deeply affect travel demand outcomes. Most travel surveys neither include new mobility such as shared mobility, nor changes in smartphone technology that has dramatically altered travel patterns and demand, nor do they reflect demographic changes (Parthasarathi and Levinson, 2010). One embarrassing example is the province of Ontario's province wide travel survey database that eventually realized a demographic shift, low response rate, and the impact of land-based phone technology in 2016. The TTS's new digital crowdsource approach to the travel survey, however, will take another decade to fix the major flaws in the travel data. Meanwhile mobility service providers and modellers will continue to use a flawed database to develop models and recommend infrastructure for next 20 or 30 years. Flaws in data and delays in responding to changes will be deeply problematic for future generations.

## Lack of resiliency

Most travel demand models do not incorporate alternative scenarios that may arise in the future. Whether it's a mandate, or natural or technological disruption, predictions for a changed future are often ignored. The Covid-19 pandemic shows how work-from-home created the "empty street"

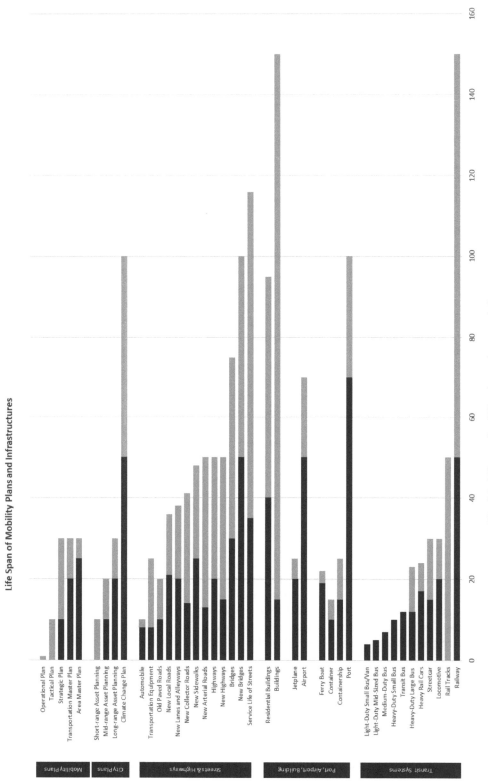

**Fig. 3.5:** Lifespan of mobility plans and common infrastructures.

syndrome, while the most popular modes of walking and cycling infrastructures were not even included in the models. Natural disaster can occur more frequently and may bring the mobility system to a standstill. No model generally incorporates any resilient alternative scenarios to predict what happens when suggested infrastructure fails or becomes obsolete.

> *"Everything should be made as simple as possible, but not simpler."*
> —Albert Einstein

## Predicting Human Mobility

Human life is one of the most chaotic things in nature. It is extremely difficult to predict human nature. When we move, our pattern mimics highly dynamic movement like the weather. A slight change in underlying assumptions could alter a few details, leading to major changes in future predictions.

Predicting the future is also an extremely difficult task. In human history, there are no single future predictions that became identically true. There is no magic, nor exact scientific basis for future predictions. Above all, nothing stays same in the long run. Long-range predictions, very common in travel demand forecasting, are simply an illusion and a fallacy created by a highly mechanized industrial ideology (Sousa, 2020).

What would make predictions more reliable, with minimal error? Only short-term predictions with relatively higher accuracy are possible albeit they still suffer some error. There are ways to minimize the error. Small 'arcs' of projections can help understand how things look on a small scale, replicating the bigger picture, and real-time and constant feedback for short-range projections would be meaningful and worth building a practical model to predict them. The city system however runs on a longer timeframe. Instead of rigid future projections, the long-range forecast is only possible for a very high-level understanding while exploring multiple or alternative potential scenarios. This approach avoids building larger or expanded facilities based on flawed 'mono-forecasting' projections. Once facilities are built, there is no point of return if that projection was wrong, or the facility was built for wrong conditions that will never happen in the future.

Everything else will suffer from severe bias. A city cannot be built on systematic bias.

> *"Cities are fast-moving things. The conventional wisdom even of the immediate past is not a good guide even to the immediate future."*
> —*The Economist*, 2000.

### *Paradigm shift in the mobility ecosystem model*

A few of the major drawbacks of the traditional approach to quantitative model process need complete overall. First, key city building vision is often overlooked in complex algorithms and translating city vision into the model building process was poor or nonexistent. Second, one of the major weaknesses of traditional travel demand models is focusing too much on reading trends in current data to project the future. Generating future mobility trips is generally estimated without any attachment to different urban forms. Models generally develop a mobility choice matrix, known as mode share, for an entire city. Models do not change the mobility matrix for future possible alternative scenarios, nor do they account for a different built environment in different parts of the city. Third, very little constraint of the proposed infrastructures was inserted into the modelling system. Constraints inform the model not to exceed the "safe boundary" of planet, or urban or mobility systems. Boundless capacity expansion of the recommended infrastructure without limits was not usually part of model scenario assessment. Fourth, the outcome of mobility improvements for gains in quality-of-life, a genuine indicator of prosperity, was completely missed in the traditional approach.

To reverse these major pitfalls, a simple 3T (test, trace, treat) approach is proposed here that has become a hallmark formula for success during the current Covid-19 pandemic. Replicating similar philosophy, the proposed approach first lays out an overall path that follows Mobility DNA to transformation to a future ecosystem that maximizes the social, environmental, and economic well-being of users. Without testing the influence of these fundamentals there is no way forward. The second stage establishes the 'tracing' link between the seven policy variables of land-use and mobility options, while formulating the multimodal demand forecasting and infrastructure needs assessment process. The development of basic principles including limiting boundaries or constraints, and interdependency between the six fundamental elements is tested at this stage to eliminate or reduce the potential negative impact of a future mobility network. Finally, the demand and supply scale of future mobility is developed with innovative policy and implementation strategies that improves quality of life. The 'treatment' should be a combination of multimodal mode ecosystems which is customized for each land-use type to avoid a 'one-mode-for-all', i.e., car-only formula. Figure 3.6 shows the layers of the mobility ecosystem planning model and development process.

> *"You are not stuck in traffic. You are traffic."*
> —An outdoor billboard poster by TomTom

### Phase 1 – Test: A big bang of the Human Mobility Code

The evolution of data and computer models proved that complex models do not solve our problems. Simple mobility needs and facilities were lost in complex algorithms. Basics were forgotten in black-box models. 'Paralysis-by-analysis', a term coined by visionary leader Janette Sadik-Khan, refers to unnecessary complexities inflicted by traditional transportation models to achieve a simple mobility system that aligns with people's behaviour. To fix our mobility problems, we must start with city building basics. Learning from past shortcomings and recent opportunities, this section proposes a comprehensive launch pad for travel demand and supply assessment approach based on basic city building blocks and innovative concepts[6] (Karim, 2017) while considering real world limitations and constraints.

The mobility system may have a different component for each neighbourhood, but it should start with understanding the basic features of mobility DNA that shape every aspect of the future system.

### Phase 1a: Understanding current conditions

The first fix is learning where the starting point is, often referred to in modelling as the 'base' or current conditions, and where the model results will be ending, the product "mobility supply". "The end is where we start from", poetic guidance from T.S. Eliot, gives us a clue to how to understand 'now'. We always live in the current, the 'now'. To 'calibrate' current, we need to start with a basic mobility pattern from individuals while linking group and collective behaviour. The second fix is incorporating the mistakes that generated our enormous and expansive infrastructure while ignoring facilities for sustainable mobility. As suggested in the previous chapter, summarizing individual

---

[6] This approach is built on a preliminary process proposed by the author as part of a planning conference at MIT Media lab and later published book, *Disrupting Mobility*.

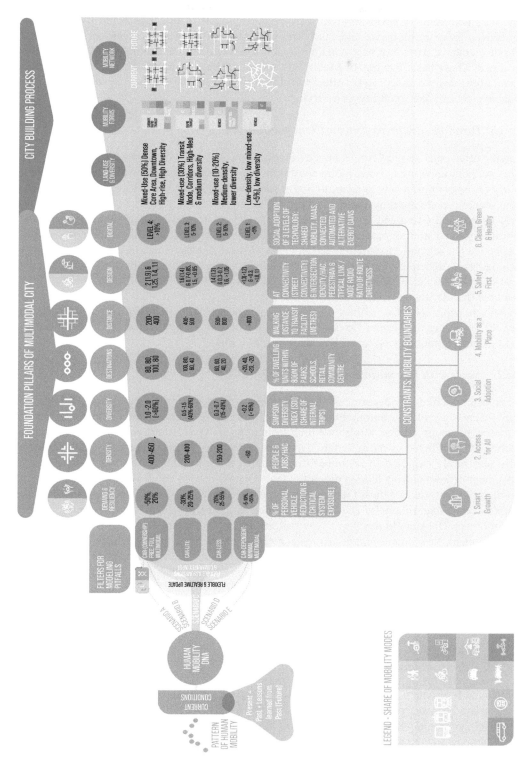

**Fig. 3.6:** Comprehensive framework of multimodal mobility ecosystem planning model.

mobility in scientific ways led us to group behaviour. And the basic constants are not going to change. We make roughly seven to eight trips every day. Half of our trips come from walking, no matter what primary mode we take, and it remains stubbornly constant across all cities. Using these basic elements, current or base conditions should be verified (i.e., calibrated) instead of using current trend. These basic features of Mobility DNA will be the end use of the model result, since at the end of the day we are going to 'offer' mobility service that every individual needs to move in cities using a system like 'mobility-as-a-service'.

## Phase 1b: Develop scenarios and resilient method

Forecasting often ends up predicting a bunch of mobility demand and converting it into supply, i.e., facilities, without knowing to what future conditions these number are attached. It can be difficult to modify transportation assets to adapt to unforeseen changes in the environment. The science of strategic scenario planning only emerged in the last few years (Leney et al., 2004) and is still not properly understood (Ringland, 2002). Instead of typical or stereotypical "alternative scenarios" in mobility master planning process, a four-step process for future scenario planning has proven more effective (Leney and Mackinnon, 2002): (1) worldwide changes in conditions and prosperity, (2) national level objectives, (3) global responsibility and a caring community for all citizens, and (4) local stewardship. Scenarios should be developed with the community, while clearly identifying key features that define the future mobility 'end', and keep an option open for the worst or best possible future conditions. One of best successes was New Zealand having a strategic resilient plan (Parker, 2020) during the current Covid-19 pandemic that took proactive and strategic actions for the fast recovery of mobility systems (Hughes and Healy, 2014).

## Phase 1c: Start with key mobility idea – Mobility DNA

All previous urban mobility demand and supply assessment process was modelled around specific mobility technology, such as automobiles in the 20th century, and human and urban environments were forced to adapt around those mobility technologies. Over time, we built an imaginary automobile DNA inflicted by the automobile industry and aiding ideology. The true nature of human mobility was rarely explored in meaningful ways toward a city building purpose. The previous chapter elaborated details of a hidden mobility DNA. Once the 'base' model is calibrated using true human mobility features, we must focus on what could influence those mobility DNA features, the input for future demand models. The theory provided in the earlier chapter shows clear evidence that our mobility DNA could develop a new pattern if there is a change in external factors or the built environment. New unique and fundamental mobility characteristics would be developed after a few weeks or months after we settle into the environment. This is the stage where we develop those possible parameter changes based on the alternative scenarios developed earlier. For instance, the pandemic reduced the overall number of trips due to work-from-home changes or goods delivered at home. But within a few months a stable pattern in DNA emerged, displaying slightly higher trip rates per person, for instance, but still lower than regular trip rates. The composition of multiple modes used by same person changed when supply changes and stabilized after a few months.

## Phase 1d: Filtering data and assumption pitfalls

When demand forecasting goes wrong, it is often blamed on the 'computer'. When results produce ever increasing infrastructure demand for vehicles repeatedly, we suffer from "the computer just produced it" syndrome. As we know, a computer does not produce results on its own. We teach them with given parameters. In the AI world, we 'train' with data where error is already built in. The model just produces the intention of the modellers. The intentions are simply intrinsic assumptions, current knowledge, and assumed predictions of human behaviour (Parthasarathi, 2010). To avert these mistakes, two rigorous filter systems should be screened before building a demand forecasting model: (1) Developing flexibility to feed the model with constantly changing feedback and real-time data. Traditional models use roughly 10-year-old data or older data. Data formats, standards, and consistent updates should be in place to accomplish this goal; and (2) Assumptions including associated model parameters should have a flexible setup that can incorporate changing multiple scenarios developed by a city's vision, intensive feedback from the community, and a neutral review body review panel to provide guidance and direction for developing or changing conditions in demand forecasting models.

> *"The traffic model is the slave, not the master."*
> —Burgess Steven

## *Phase 2 − Trace: Fundamentals of modelling for mobility ecosystem planning*

This is a crucial stage of reestablishing the basic building of city planning and design elements while formulating the quantitative impact of the critical factors that change human mobility behaviours toward active or micro-mobility usage supported by transit and sustainable shared mobility services. "Smart Growth" policies pertaining to the built-environment variables and mobility access are strongly associated with mobility demand and its key indicators. These key indicators include but are not limited to the number of trips staying within the neighbourhood using very low carbon mobility modes, better health, affordability, and well-being (Yevdokimov and Mao, 2004), access to jobs or daily needs destinations, and the reduction of energy usage and long-distance and vehicle use (Ewing and Cervero, 2010) including Vehicle Kilometres Travelled (VKT) and determinants of sustainable mobility (such as the Smart Growth Index (SGI) Model) (Criterion Planners/Engineers Inc., 2002). VKT is strongly correlated to measures of easy access to destinations and street network design variables. To bind these major influencing movers and shakers of good mobility design, the approach proposes a three-layer innovative mobility ecosystem model: (1) Creating "mobility form" to match the built form that by default reduces vehicles usage; (2) Seven layers of key city building policy variables; and (3) Six layers of mobility boundary constraints that keep the checks and balances of the future mobility system within the safe zone and avoids building pressures on the planetary system.

### *Phase 2a: Mobility form to match the built form*

Despite past efforts toward transit-oriented by most cities, or car-free by a few cities, the reality turned out different. City policy and plans need a more realistic and gradual approach to address high vehicle usage. Each area or neighbourhood in cities built with a different urban form. Downtown areas have generally less car usage and some streets can be car-free. Downtown shoulder or inner suburbs typically have more transit focused mobility. Outer centres have pockets of high density that rely on key transit services, but the rest of the area may depend on vehicles in the short term. Exurbs, or rural areas, generally experience more car uses. To address vehicles usage reduction systematically while increasing more sustainable mobility options, the approach proposes to customize a city's areas or neighbourhoods with practical targets to reduce vehicle usage: (1) 'Car(ownership)-free' is only possible to some extent in dense core areas; (2) 'Car-lite' areas see slightly less aggressive vehicle mode sharing while the majority of trips are completed by non-automobile modes; (3) 'Car-less' area features would provide limited facility expansion within a city's affordable budget; and (4) 'Car-dominated' areas would be on the outer fringe where non-urban highways are located. Mobility DNA in each area will be modified toward a city's growth plan while minimizing expensive infrastructure or the typical road widening approach.

## Phase 2b: Seven layers of mobility foundations

The proposed approach links to city building key variables and mobility behaviour reflects the primary components of multimodal-oriented development (MOD). The basic foundation of this approach incorporates transit-oriented development (FTA, 2002) that originally proposed three Ds (Design, Diversity, Density) as key policy variables (Cervero and Kockelman, 1997). Two additional Ds (Distance and Destinations) were added later (De Witte et al., 2013) to reflect the distance to transit and variety of destinations that make a vibrant public transit city (Agarwal et al., 2018). Transportation planners later added the sixth D: Demand management (Ogra and Ndebele, 2014) to control mobility demand before building facilities. This section revises the sixth D to include "demand resiliency" to identify a mobility system to withstand unforeseen future changes. The author introduced the last, seventh D in the series – 'Digital' access to incorporate shared mobility, new technology, and future mobility changes like MaaS (Karim, 2017). However, the previously proposed method by the author has now significantly modified to incorporate the defining features of human mobility DNA, like dominant short trips that can be carried out using active transportation, micro-mobility and reflect the true mobility DNA features in new public space creation and design, future mobility policies, and incorporate additional resiliency into mobility planning process.

The policy variable (P) is a function of seven city building fundamentals, denoted here as the 7Ds. The 7Ds are: 'density' – residents plus employees divided by land area; 'diversity' – the jobs-population ratio; 'design' – a combination of sidewalk completeness, route directness, and street network density; 'destination' – regional accessibility; 'distance' – the distance to the nearest transit or eco-mobility stations or stops; 'digital access' – information and telecommunication technologies (Cohen and Kietzmann, 2014) for shared/on-demand services; and, 'demand and resiliency' – controlling all types of mobility trip demand and adding a resiliency lens to planning process.

The modified 7Ds policy variables are:

### Demand and resiliency

Effective transportation demand management actions shift the demand from the single occupant automobile toward more sustainable modes. Mandatory policy targets to reduce single occupant personal vehicle[7] (City of Toronto, 2018) use and car ownership should be part of every future project scenario to shift the demand to sustainable modes. The ability to develop natural resiliency in the overall mobility network from a system perspective should be reflected in capital works, service management, operation and maintenance while identifying the importance of city assets during natural and manmade disruptions. Identifying priorities, recovery processes and resources (Weilant et al., 2019) dedicated to restoring the important mobility system should be part of future attention to maximum usage of critical infrastructure before recommending new or infrastructure expansion.

### Density

Density ensures that there is a critical mass of transit and active mobility demand generated by residents and employees within an area, facilitating frequent transit service (elasticity[8] −0.04 for

---

[7] The author formulated the mandatory single occupant vehicle reduction policy for new development as a systematic demand management control under low-emission transportation section.

[8] Elasticity of demand is an important variation on the concept of demand. Demand can be classified as elastic, inelastic, or unitary. An elastic demand is one in which the change in quantity demanded due to a change in price is large. An inelastic demand is one in which the change in quantity demanded due to a change in price is small.

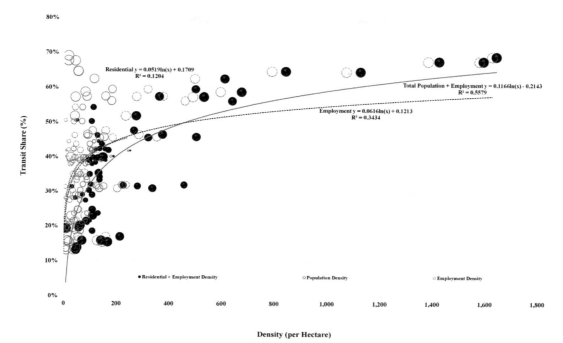

**Fig. 3.7:** Land-use density impacts on transit mode share.

VKT decrease and +0.07 for transit ridership increase as per (Ewing and Cervero, 2010)) and higher quality facilities. Typically, cities establish a density target around a "Mobility Hub", i.e., transit station, density suggestions based on a radius of 800 m, comfortable walking distance from transit facilities (Metrolinx, 2011). Density target generally identifies a threshold for transit supportive density such as 150– 300+ people and jobs per hectare for areas served by express regional rail, 200–400 people and jobs per hectare for areas served by frequent light rail, and 50–150 people and jobs for frequent bus/streetcar service. Rental and more diverse residential housing in apartment or high-rise mixed-use form generates at least 20% more sustainable mobility trips compared to low-density single detached housing (City of Toronto, 2015). These targets intend to achieve target transit ridership to accommodate major demand of long-distance trips generated by the growth (Fig. 3.7). Beyond mobility hub areas, access to transit remains a challenge and achieving density targets is difficult. Recognizing this gap the author introduced new multiple layers, such as several types of a secondary and tertiary "eco-mobility hub"[9] (City of Toronto, 2018) that would cover areas beyond the typical 500 or 800 m, and ultimately reach the evenly distributed density target instead of 'pointed' density around a mobility hub.

## *Diversity*

A mix of land-uses that provides easy access to daily needs within the neighbourhood or area. Land-use diversity encourages and increases transit usage, creates more shorter trips for active or micro-mobility, and minimizes the need to travel longer for different purposes (elasticity −0.09 for VKT decrease and +0.12 for transit ridership increase as per (Ewing and Cervero, 2010)). Daily needs and amenities in a city should be easily accessible, converting the need for longer travel to

---

[9] To promote shared mobility and alternative modes of travel to reduce single-occupant automobile trips, "Eco-Mobility Hubs" will establish one-stop service points for multimodal systems including bikeshare, rideshare, and carshare facilities at identified locations.

Fig. 3.8: Land-use diversity impacts on mobility demand.

shorter distance. Typically, diversity of land-use is measured through the Simpson Index (Province of Ontario, 2017), calculated for a specific geographic area by comparing the amount of land in each land-use category to the amount of land occupied by all land uses. The share of internal trips because of increased land-use diversity is a key parameter (NCRHP, 2016) altering mobility behaviour. The author's developed process the appropriate share of right mixed land-use policies against shared internal trips in several city centres of the City of Toronto (Karim, 2017). The higher the mixed-use, the higher the internal trips (Fig. 3.8). It creates more balanced two directional trip demand and avoids the "tidal wave", a typical suburban traffic rushes toward downtown or the employment districts during peak periods. Office trips go in opposite directions to residential demand. Schools in the same neighbourhood avoid morning rush hour congestion. Care homes, seniors or retirement places are low peak demand generators, reducing the peak periods demand to the off-peak periods. Recreation or community centres within neighbourhoods avoid cross-neighbourhood congestion during afternoon peak hours. The benefits of diverse and mixed-use development solve major mobility problems without building expensive infrastructures.

## Destinations

Transit service could carry people to key destinations for daily needs including work purposes. Closer destinations increase shorter trips, creating walkable and bikeable places at key city destinations, centres and around transit service points. An increasing variety of land-uses and higher number of destinations are key variables that define destinations (Province of Ontario, 2017). For instance, the percentage of dwelling units in selected areas that are within walking distance (generally 800 m) of a park, a school, shopping, and community centre opportunities are good indicators of a high destination community that generates a higher rate of walking, cycling and micro-mobility trips.

## Distance

Distance to available alternative mobility modes is a critical element of future mobility demand and a defining feature of the mobility supply system. Providing a shorter distance to mobility facilities generates the highest demand for transit (elasticity −0.05 for VKT decrease and +0.29 for transit ridership increase as per (Ewing and Cervero, 2010)), shared and sustainable mobility modes. Distance is sometimes hidden in neighbourhood design or visible through better mobility facility design. First is network wide design with features that reduce the distance and could be measured using connectivity measures. Connectivity measures such as the connectivity index in

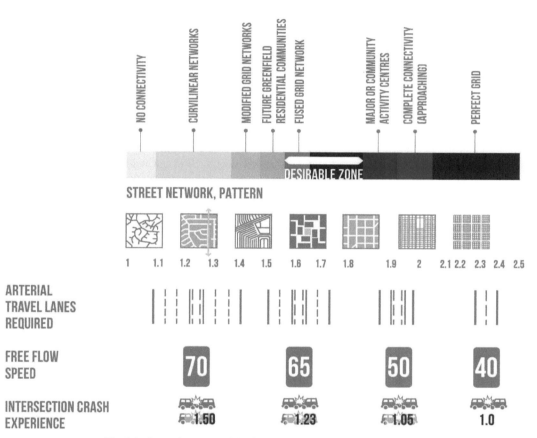

**Fig. 3.9:** Increasing connectivity for better neighbourhood layout design.

terms of link-to-node ratio[10] (i.e., shorter blocks and availability of crossings) are one of the critical conditions of creating shorter walking distances to mobility nodes (Province of Ontario, 2017). As illustrated in Fig. 3.9, increasing connectivity through neighbourhood network layout reduces the size of infrastructures, lowers speed on streets, and improves safety crash rates for all users. Second is removing barriers or adding connections to provide transit that is frequently available within a short walking distance (e.g., 500–800 m) representing roughly 10-min walking distance (Province of Ontario, 2020), and greater service coverage to transit routes for majority of the population and workplaces. Finally, reducing route deviation for pedestrian or cycling or micro-mobility users can be achieved by providing additional walkway or cycling connections to the active mobility network

---

[10] Link-node ratio measures the ratio of road segments (links) to intersections (nodes). A higher number means that travelers have increased route choices, allowing more direct connections for access between any two locations. According to this index, a simple box of streets would score a 1.0. A four-square grid of streets would score a 1.33, while a nine-square grid of streets would score a 1.5. Dead-end streets would reduce the index value. While there is no accepted standard for link-node ratio, some studies recommend that a score of 1.4 is needed to support a walkable community.

and usually measured through various key indicators such as circuity (Levinson et al., 2015) and walking permeability index (Soltani and Allan, 2005).

## *Design*

Design remains the most hidden but critical and influential element of mobility behaviour. Levels of design are complex and constitute in several layers: (1) modified grid or fused grid neighbourhood layout design generally a more active mobility and transit friendly design which determines the urban built form and a greater positive mobility outcome; (2) designing streets or public spaces with equal spaces for all multimodal modes is the most visible change that adds a second layer of mobility behaviour change; and (3) mobility system and network design combining hardware and the software of mobility services that target group or customized individual mobility behaviour through multimodal service. Neighbourhood design that captures basic urban structural elements such as shorter blocks, higher intersection and street density (elasticity is +0.23 for increasing transit ridership as per (Ewing and Cervero, 2010)), and grid-like street patterns for higher connectivity (elasticity is +0.21 for increasing transit ridership as per (Ewing and Cervero, 2010)) are key determinants of transit, walking and cycling friendly design. Without walking and cycling, transit service points are less accessible. For instance, density of intersections (Province of Ontario, 2017) encourage walking and cycling, particularly when infrastructure and associated facilities are provided. The complete street philosophy, when combined with green and human space concepts, and kept in manageable street size while reclaiming unused vehicle space that is converted into public space through placemaking (placemaking design increased profits by 25% and ridership gained by 20% as per (Cervero, 2013)), visualizes the hidden neighbourhood design and increases comfort and safety of non-automobile users. Mobility system design ensures pedestrian, cycling, and micro-mobility has the highest order of access to city destinations or transit services. For instance, pedestrian route directness ensures additional link or path connections (more direct routes result in 18% more pedestrian trips as per (CMHC, 2008)) are added to the typical street network to reduce distances for pedestrians, cyclists, or micromobility users. Similarly, higher network coverage is a critical design element for new shared mobility. Availability translates to higher network coverage for carshare (Carlier, 2016), bikeshare (Kabra et al., 2019) or micromobility, and generally increases the system usage per vehicle or device. Network design and easy access are of the key ingredients of future shared and autonomous mobility.

## *Digital*

Access to multimodal mobility information makes it easier for users to locate, book, pay for, and make travel as seamlessly and conveniently as possible. Transfers between modes or between transit routes become easy, easing the complexity of switching modes at different parts of the journey by different modes. Multimodal access and real-time information at transit service points is a key element of digital mobility. The approach incorporates several key innovative concepts to make multimodal mobility digitally accessible. The Mobilityscore (Transitscreen, 2018) tool is one of the best multi-modal digital access measures recently introduced in the US. Besides ride hailing options (such as Uber or Lyft), a few shared mobility options (such as bikeshare, high occupancy rideshare or shuttle, and shared micromobility, i.e., shared scooters) could be available to city residents. From a user perspective, there are three levels of mobility technology and access depending on demographic trends and social adoption rates of new technology: (1) High-occupant shared mobility in the short-term, (2) Four levels of Mobility-as-a-Service or MaaS to access multimodal mobility modes (see Chapter 12 for detail), and (3) Access to connected, automated, and alternative energy mobility modes in the long term.

## *Phase 2c: Six layers of constraints: Resiliency through mobility boundaries*

Physical constraints to future demand and supply introduces reasonable limits to growth or expansion plans. There is a misperception that moving car-oriented to low-emission mobility would solve the problem. Without limits, sustainable mobility will eventually become unsustainable. Our planet is finite, so are urban areas or open spaces, or the resources required by mobility systems. Aligning with the "planetary boundary" concept to keep earth's precious system with safe zone, the author introduced the "Mobility boundary" concept (Karim, 2017) to keep the future mobility network within the safe urban zone. For other urban or natural ecosystems, urban boundary (Hoornweg et al., 2016) and planetary boundary (Steffen et al., 2015) restrictions would act as the limiting boundary of system growth to avoid pressure on planetary capacity. Identifying future aspects of the symbiotic relationship between six fundamental interactive elements in a mobility ecosystem, the proposed innovative mobility planning model envisions a novel urban morphology, shapes a new experience of urban space, and turns unexplored assets into an ecosystem of vibrant, sustainable innovation. The next chapter describes detail of mobility boundary concept that was modified from author's original work (Karim, 2017).

> *"Models are informative but not concrete. Everything together tells us a story."*
> —Muge Cevik, University of St. Andrews

## *Phase 3: Treatment: Multimodal mobility supply*

In the traditional approach to mobility planning, this stage takes a completely wrong turn. Using long-distance trips from flawed data, traditional models project an enormous scale of infrastructure for vehicles, trucks, and long-distance transit routes regardless of sensitive land-use and built form, a misinterpretation of Keynesian economic theory to boost consumption by building more infrastructure during an economic downturn. This "aggregate demand" from 20th century ideas to create large and aggregate infrastructure does not fit well with individual mobility needs in the 21st century.

We need a more realistic mobility supply philosophy that matches our individual and collective needs.

Through the filters of demand management and resilient scenarios, stage two would shed unnecessary and excess mobility demand, and generate basic and fundamental mobility needs for the future mobility ecosystem. Using this reduced mobility demand and smaller scale of facility needs, the last stage of citywide mobility master plans would provide more realistic, affordable, and lean mobility supply systems for future generations and avoid additional strain on limited planetary resources. The right side of Fig. 3.6 illustrates the proposed new multimodal network and mobility forms combination that reduces vehicle usage systematically instead of a patching fix after the network is built.

However, a few innovative thoughts are necessary to accomplish this balancing act. Three creative approaches may achieve that target.

## *Multimodal land-use*

The first stage would be a reality check of proposed or planned land-use, of whether the future land-use combination would generate sufficient trips that are of short distance, stay within neighbourhoods, produce enough jobs, and create equitable and affordable housing for all city residents. A combination of different types of low-peak land-use generators, higher shares of mixed-use, higher but 'gentle' density with appropriately higher density at large transit nodes, are magic land-use and mobility combination solutions. However, "market demand" for a single residential type, particularly at transit nodes, is a monumental challenge. The development industry needs incentives. Land-use incentives such as little or no density limit for non-residential uses, a density bonus for community uses, and parking relief for ancillary retail or commercial usage was recently used in Toronto's new secondary plan for the Dufferin Avenue corridor (City of Toronto, 2015).

To achieve the best mobility performance, the following land-use modifications are necessary with appropriate land-use incentives:

- Increasing the mandatory percentage of non-residential usage from lower-density and diversity to a minimum 5% to 20% for medium density for intensification corridors, to a moderate (30%) for suburban centres, to the highest 50% share in downtown or central business and mixed-use areas.

- Encouraging more low-peak generator residential uses such as institutional, schools, senior or student focused housing, recreational and community centres with density bonusing incentives.

- Encouraging more "complete community" development or self-sustained development complexes that incorporate all types of commercial or retail opportunity with shared, little or no parking incentives.

- Mandatory requirements for more complete street and active mobility connections within or outside neighbourhood connections, but with narrower public right-of-way and wider setbacks to reduce excessive land requirements for developers that are often dedicated to wide and polluted streets.

This list is long, but the intention is to provide more tools to modify and achieve appropriate land-use that by default reduce vehicle usage instead of building more and wider streets and parking spaces.

### *Missing mobility form*

Often initial mobility mode share or mobility choice assumptions (that generate future demand and distribution of trips) remain unchanged once land-use is modified. Future alternative scenarios for land-use and mobility need to be adjusted during this stage. The traditional approach to mobility supply often disregards or is insensitive to future land-use changes and recommends a series of new streets or widening regardless of land-use. The additional land, resources and process required for new streets or widening become a planning burden and often derail land-use objectives or a city's overall vision.

### *Multimodal mobility network*

This stage lays out the future mobility network for neighbourhoods. Detailed implementation, design philosophy, and policies are described in the next chapters, as well as the last two chapters of this book. A few fundamental principles are proposed here to develop the future mobility network framework for each part or neighbourhood of the city. And they should match the human mobility code and mobility principles, or constraints laid out earlier.

## Summary

The urban mobility system depends on data, mysterious models, and numerous assumptions. The lack of real human mobility data was holding back the progress of systemwide mobility improvements. This chapter explains the importance and evolution of data in the mobility world. It identifies hidden black-box assumptions, often flawed, that create mobility models and ultimately decide entire construction, service, operation, and maintenance of urban mobility systems. Flaws in static data and rigid assumptions lead to more and more expansive infrastructures. To reverse the trend, the chapter proposes the use of big data, innovative mobility planning models and true multimodal assessment process. Mobility form was proposed to match built form. Organic and improvised methods of mobility demand and supply approach were proposed for different natures of city neighbourhoods, instead of the unimodal vehicle mode and its expansion. To spread mobility access to all residents, the neighbourhood mobility hub model and the quantification of facility supply was proposed. The hope is a new approach will imitate true-nature short trips generated by humans. Affordable mobility not only follows our true nature of mobility DNA but also replaces the never-ending expansion of expensive infrastructure geared towards imaginary dominance of long trips assumed by the flawed traditional mobility models and brings back a sound scientific approach in mobility planning, supply, implementation, and funding process.

# References

Adams, J. (1995). *Risk.* London: Ruthledge, University College London.
Agarwal, O.P., Kumar, A. and Zimmerman, S. (2018). *Public Transit in Emerging Paradigms in Urban Mobility.* eBook: Elsevier.
Ahmed, T., Boris, N., Oreshkin, N. and Coates, M. (2007). *Machine Learning Approaches to Network Anomaly Detection.* Montreal: McGill University.
Ahn, Y. and Yeo, H. (2015). An analytical planning model to estimate the optimal density of charging stations for electric vehicles. *PLoS ONE*, 10(11): 1–26.
Akndi. (2020). *Greening Government Fleets: A Helpful Guide to Understanding.* Ottawa: Natural Resources Canada.
Albert, A., Kaur, J. and Gonzalez, M.C. (2017). Using convolutional networks and satellite imagery to identify patterns in urban environments at a large scale. *Proceedings of the 23rd ACM SIGKDD International Conference on Knowledge Discovery and Data Mining*, pp. 1357–1366. Halifax: ACM.
Alexander, L.P. and González, M. (2015). Assessing the impact of real-time ridesharing on urban traffic using mobile phone data. *Proc. UrbComp*, 1–9.
Aljalbout, E., Golkov, V., Siddiqui, Y., Strobel, M. and Cremers, D. (2018). Clustering with deep learning: Taxonomy and new methods. *Computer Science, Machine Learning*, 1–12.
Amadoa, M. and Poggi, F. (2014). Solar energy integration in urban planning: GUUD model. *Energy Procedia*, 50: 277–284.
Anagnostopoulos, T., Anagnostopoulos, C. and Hadjiefthymiades, S. (2011). Mobility prediction based on machine learning. *2011 IEEE 12th International Conference on Mobile Data Management*, pp. 27–30. IEEE.
Anderson, J. (2018). *Curbside-management-improving-cities-with-curb-data.* Retrieved from Coord: https://www.coord.com/blog/curbside-management-improving-cities-with-curb-data.
Anderson, J.M., Kalra, N., Stanley, K.D., Sorensen, P., Samaras, C. and Oluwatola, O.A. (2016). *Autonomous Vehicle Technology: A Guide for Policymakers.* Santa Monica, California: RAND Coportation, RR-443-2-RC.
Angel Swing. (2015). *About Angel Swing.* Retrieved from Angel Swing: https://www.angelswing.io/.
Appleby, K. (2015). *Five Cities Proving that we can Quit Fossil Fuels.* Retrieved from City Monitor: https://citymonitor.ai/horizons/five-cities-proving-we-can-quit-fossil-fuels-1444.
Apte, J.S., Messier, K.P., Gani, S., Brauer, M., Kirchstetter, T.W., Lunden, M.M., Marshall, J.D., Portier, C.J., Vermeulen, R.C.H. and Hamburg, S.P. (2017). High-resolution air pollution mapping with Google street view cars: Exploiting big data. *Environ. Sci. Technol.*, 51(12): 6999–7008.
Araujo, J.A., Barajas, B., Kleinman, M., Wang, X., Bennett, B.J., Gong, K.W., Navab, M., Harkema, J., Sioutas, C., Lusis, A.J. and Nel, A.E. (2008). Ambient particulate pollutants in the ultrafine range promote early atherosclerosis and systemic oxidative stress. *Circular Research*, 102(5): 589–596.
Asakura, Y. and Hatob, E. (2004). Tracking survey for individual travel behaviour using mobile communication instrument. *Transportation Research Part C: Emerging Technologies*, 12(4): 273–291.
Asensio, O.I., Mi, X. and Dharur, S. (2020). Using machine learning techniques to aid environment policy analysis: A teaching case regarding big data and electric vehicle charging infrastructure. *Case Studies in the Environment*, 4(1): 961302.
Ashbrook, D. and Starner, T. (2002). Learning significant locations and predicting user movement with GPS. *Proceedings Sixth International Symposium on Wearable Computers*, pp. 101–108. Seattle: IEEE.
Ashley, S. (2008). Driving forward: Crashless cars. *Scientific American*, 86–94.
Avineri, E. (2007). *Artificial Intelligence in Transportation: Information for Application.* Number E-C113: Transportation Research Circular: Number E-C113, TRB.
Awad, E., Dsouza, S., Kim, R., Schulz, J., Henrich, J., Shariff, A., Bonnefon, J. and Rahwan, I. (2018). The moral machine experiment. *Nature*, 563: 59–64.

Aydin, O.F., Gokasar, I. and Kalan, O. (2020). Matching algorithm for improving ride-sharing by incorporating route splits and social factors. *PloS ONE*, 1–13.

Bae, S., Lee, E. and Han, J. (2020). Multi-period Planning of hydrogen supply network for refuelling hydrogen fuel cell vehicles in urban areas. *Sustainability*, 12(4114): 1–23.

Barjamovic, G., Chaney, T., Cosar, K. and Hortacsu, A. (2019). Trade, merchants, and the lost cities of the Bronze Age. *The Quarterly Journal of Economics*, 1455–1503.

Barry, K. (2013). *Wired*. Retrieved from In South Korea, Wireless Charging Powers Electric Buses: https://www.wired.com/2013/08/induction-charged-buses/.

Barthélemy, J. and Toint, P.L. (2013). *A Simple and Flexible Activity-based Simulation for Belgium*. Bruxelles: Universite de Namur.

Becic, E., Zych, N. and Ivarsson, J. (2018). *Vehicle Automation Report*. Washington, USA: National Transportation Safety Board, HWY18MH010.

Becky, P.Y., Lo, O. and Banister, D. (2016). Decoupling transport from economic growth: Extending the debate to include environmental and social externalities. *Journal of Transport Geography*, 57: 134–144.

Beddoes, Z.M. (2020). Time to make coal history. *The Economist*.

Bello, P. and Bringsjord, S. (2013). On how to build a moral machine. *Topoi*, 32(2): 1–25.

Ben-Akiva, M. and Lerman, S.R. (1985). *Discrete Choice Analysis: Theory and Application to Travel Demand*. Cambridge: The MIT Press.

Benjamin, L. and Richards, D. (1981). Electrification is the way to move Canada in the 1980s. *Canadian Public Policy*, 7(81).

Berg, N. (2020). *This AI-powered Parking Garage Rewards You for Not Driving*. Retrieved from Fast Company: https://www.fastcompany.com/90575914/this-ai-powered-parking-garage-rewards-you-for-not-driving.

Berg, P. (2011). *The Finite Planet: How Resource Scarcity Will Affect ur Environment, Economy, and Energy Supply*. Oshawa, Canada: Island Press.

Bernhardt, K.L. (National Research Council, TRB). (2007). Agent-based modeling in transportation. Artificial Intelligence in transportation: Information for application. *Transportation Research Circular E-C113, Artificial Intelligence and Advanced Computing Applications Committee*, 72–80.

Bhat, C. (2017). *Travel Modeling in an Era of Connected and Automated Transportation Systems: An Investigation in the Dallas-Fort Worth Area*. Austin, USA: Technical Report 122. Center for Transportation Research. The University of Texas at Austin.

Bhat, R. (1996). A hazard-based duration model of shopping activity with non-parametric baseline specification and non-parametric control for unobserved heterogeneity. *Transportation Research Part B*, 30: 189–208.

Bhat, R. (1997). Work travel mode choice and number of non-work commute stops. *Transportation Research Part B*, 31: 41–54.

Bhat, R.V. and Waghray, K. (2000). *Profile of Street Foods in Asian Countries*. Basel, Karger: World Rev. Nutr. Diet.

BHS. (2009). *15 Things You Did Not Know about the Moors of Spain*. Retrieved from Black History Studies: https://blackhistorystudies.com/resources/15-facts-on-the-moors-in-spain/.

Billings, C.E. (1980). *Human-centered Aircraft Automation: A Concept and Guidelines*. Moffet Field, CA: NASA Technical Memorandum, NASA Ames Research Center.

Blumenstock, J. and Cadamuro, C.R. (2015). Predicting poverty and wealth from mobile phone metadata. *Science*, 350(6264): 1073–1076.

Bohte, W. and Maat, K. (2008). Deriving and validating trip destinations and modes for multi-day GPS-based travel surveys: A large-scale application in the Netherlands. *Transportation Research Part C Emerging Technologies*, 17(3): 285–297.

Bojarski, M., Testa, D.D., Dworakowski, D., Firner, B., Flepp, B., Goyal, P., Jackel, L.D., Monfort, M., Muller, U., Zhang, J., Zhang, X., Zhao, J. and Zieba, K. (2016). End-to-end Learning for Self-Driving Cars. *Computer Vision and Pattern Recognition*, Cornell University, pp. 1–9.

Bojji, R. (2011). Gravity powered transport systems for rail, road, water, and airport use. *13th International Conference on Automated People* (pp. 22–25). Paris, France: American Society of Civil Engineers.

Borzino, N., Chang, S., Mughal, M.O. and Schubert, R. (2020). Willingness to pay for urban heat island mitigation: A case study of Singapore. *Climate*, 8: 82.

Botsman, R. (2010). *What's Mine is Yours: The Rise of Collaborative Consumption*. Harper Business.

Boulos, M.N., Resch, B., Crowley, D.N., Breslin, J.G., Sohn, G., Burtner, R., Pike, W.A., Jezierski, E. and Chuang, K.S. (2011). Crowdsourcing, citizen sensing, and sensor web technologies for public and environmental health surveillance and crisis management: Trends, OGC standards and application examples. *International Journal of Health Geographics*, 10: 67.

Bourdieu, P. and Wacquant, L.D. (1992). *An Invitation to Reflexive Sociology*. Cambridge, UK: Polity Press and Blackwell Publishers.

Bowman, J. (1998). *The Day Activity Schedule Approach to Travel Demand.* Cambridge: MIT.

Braess, D., Nagurney, A. and Wakolbinger, T. (2005). On a paradox of traffic planning. *Transportation Science*, 39(4): 446–450.

Breyer, N., Rydergren, C. and Gundlega°rd, D. (2020). Comparative analysis of travel patterns from cellular network data and an urban travel demand model. *Journal of Advanced Transportation*, 1–17.

Brimicombe, A.J. and Li, C. (2009). *Location-based Services and Geo-information Engineering.* Chichester, UK: Wiley.

Britton, E. (2000). Carsharing 2000: Sustainable transport's missing link. *Journal of the Commons*, 1–351.

Bukhsh, Z.A., Saeed, A. and Stipanovic, I. (2018). A machine learning approach for maintenance prediction of railway assets. *Proceedings of 7th Transport Research Arena TRA* (pp. 1–10). Vienna: TRA.

Buranyi, S. (2017). *Rise of the Racist Robots – How AI is Learning All Our Worst Impulses.* Retrieved from The Guardian: https://www.theguardian.com/inequality/2017/aug/08/rise-of-the-racist-robots-how-ai-is-learning-all-our-worst-impulses.

Cadwalladr, C. and Graham-Harrison, E. (2018). *Revealed: 50 million Facebook Profiles Harvested for Cambridge Analytica in Major Data Breach.* Retrieved from The Guardian: https://www.theguardian.com/news/2018/mar/17/cambridge-analytica-facebook-influence-us-election.

Calabrese, F., Colonna, M., Lovisolo, P., Parata, D. and Ratti, C.R. (2011). Real time urban monitoring using cell phones: A case study in Rome. *IEEE Trans Intell. Transp. Syst.*, 12(1): 141–151.

Canada Energy Regulator. (2020). *Market Snapshot: Canada's Retiring Coal-fired Power Plants will be Replaced by Renewable and Low-carbon Energy Sources.* Retrieved from Canada Energy Regulator: https://www.cer-rec.gc.ca/en/data-analysis/energy-markets/market-snapshots/2020/market-snapshot-canadas-retiring-coal-fired-power-plants-will-be-replaced-renewable-low-carbon-energy-sources.html.

Carlier, A. (2016). *Optimal Design of a One-way Carsharing System Including Electric Vehicles.* Paris: Université Pierre et Marie Curie.

*Carsharing.Org.* (2017). Retrieved from What is carsharing?: https://carsharing.org/what-is-car-sharing/.

Carter, C. (2019). *Autonomous Passenger Ferries: Congestion-buster or Hype on the High Seas?* Retrieved from Smart Cities World: https://www.smartcitiesworld.net/special-reports/special-reports/autonomous-passenger-ferries-congestion-buster-or-hype-on-the-high-seas.

Center for Sustainable Systems. (2020). *Geothermal Energy.* Detroit, Michigan: University of Michigan. Retrieved from Geothermal Energy.: http://css.umich.edu/sites/default/files/Geothermal%20Energy_CSS10-10_e2020.pdf.

Cervero, R. (2001). *Induced Demand: An Urban and Metropolitan Perspective.* Berkeley: EPA, FHWA, USDOT and Eno Transportation Foundation.

Cervero, R. (2013). *Urban Planning & Sustainable Mobility.* Retrieved from Asia-Pacific Economic Cooperation: https://aperc.or.jp/file/2013/3/21/S2-1-2_Prof._Robert_Cervero.pdf.

Cervero, R. and Kockelman, K. (1997). Travel demand and the 3Ds: Density, diversity, and design. *Transportation Research Part D: Transport and Environment*, 2(3): 1999–219.

Chandler, T. (1987). *Four Thousand Years of Urban Growth: A Historical Census.* Lewiston: The Edwin Mellen Press.

Chapin, S. (1974). *Human Activity Patterns in the City: Things People Do in Time and Space.* New York: Wiley.

Charles, A.S., Lambert, H.G. and Balogh, S.B. (2014). EROI of different fuels and the implications for society. *Energy Policy*, 64: 141–152.

Chellapilla, K. (2018). *Rethinking Maps for Self-Driving.* Medium.

Chen, C., Ma, J., Susilo, Y., Liu, Y. and Wang, M. (2016). The promises of big data and small data for travel behavior (aka human mobility) analysis. *Transp. Res. Part C Emerg. Technol.*, 68: 285–299.

Chen, C., Zhang, D., Castro, P.S., Li, N., Sun, L., Li, S. and Wang, Z. (2013). iBOAT: Isolation-based online anomalous trajectory detection. *IEEE Transactions on Intelligent Transportation Systems*, 14(2): 806–818.

Chen, K., Zhang, L., Yao, L., Guo, B., Yu, Z. and Liu, Y. (2018). Deep learning for sensor-based human activity recognition: overview, challenges, and opportunities. *Journal of the Association for Computing Machinery ACM*, 37(4): 1–40.

Chen, W., Guo, F. and Wang, F.Y. (2015). A survey of traffic data visualization. *IEEE Trans. Intell. Transp. Syst.*, 16: 2970–2984.

Cheng, L., Chen, X., Yang, S., Wu, J. and Yang, M. (2017). Structural equation models to analyze activity participation, trip generation, and mode choice of low-income commuters. *Transportation Letters*, 1–9.

Chiu, Y., Bottom, J., Mahut, M., Paz, A., Balakrishna, R., Waller, T. and Hicks, J. (2011). Dynamic Traffic Assignment - A Primer. Transportation Research Board of the National Academies, Washington, D.C.

Christensen, A. and Petrenko, C. (2017). *CO₂-Based Synthetic Fuel: Assessment of Potential European Capacity and Environmental Performance.* Brussels: European Climate Foundation and the International Council on Clean Transportation.

Christofides, N. (1976). *Worst-case Analysis of a New Heuristic for the Travelling Salesman Problem.* Pittsburgh: Graduate School of Industrial Administration, CMU.

Chu, Z., Cheng, L. and Chen, H. (2012). A review of activity-based travel demand modeling. *The Twelfth COTA International Conference of Transportation Professionals* (pp. 48–59). Beijing, China: American Society of Cilvil Engineers.

Cipresso, P., Giglioli, I.A., Raya, M.A. and Riva, G. (2018). The past, present, and future of virtual and augmented reality research: A network and cluster analysis of the literature. *Front. Psychol.*, 9: 1–20.

Cision. (2018). *Maxar Technologies' Digital Globe and Ecopia Tech Corporation Produce First High-precision U.S. Building Footprints Dataset Created with Machine Learning.* Retrieved from Newswire: https://www.newswire.ca/news-releases/maxar-technologies-digitalglobe-and-ecopia-tech-corporation-produce-first-high-precision-us-building-footprints-dataset-created-with-machine-learning-696526241.html.

City of Seattle. (2017). *New Mobility Playbook.* City of Seattle: Seattle Department of Transportation.

City of Toronto. (2015). *Dufferin Street Secondary Plan: By-law No. 1351–2015.* Toronto: City of Toronto.

City of Toronto. (2015). *Sheppard East Corridor: Transportation Review.* Toronto: City of Toronto.

City of Toronto. (2016). *Don Mills Crossing Transportation Phase 1 Report.* Toronto: City of Toronto.

City of Toronto. (2016). *Keele Finch Plus Transportation Study: Overview of Existing Conditions.* Toronto: City of Toronto.

City of Toronto. (2018). *Draft Official Plan Amendment, Consumers Next Secondary Plan.* Toronto: City of Toronto.

City of Toronto. (2018). *Laird in Focus – Mobility Report.* Toronto: City of Toronto.

City of Toronto. (2018). *Toronto Green Standard Version 3.* Toronto, Canada: City of Toronto.

City of Toronto. (2019). *The Future of King Street: Results of the Transit Pilot.* Toronto: City of Toronto.

City of Toronto. (2020). *Energy Efficiency Report Submission & Modelling Guidelines: For the Toronto Green Standard (TGS) Version 3.* Toronto, Canada: Environment and Energy Division & City Planning Division, City of Toronto.

City of Toronto and UTTRI. (2019). *The Transportation Impacts of Vehicle-for-Hire in the City of Toronto.* Toronto: City of Toronto and University of Toronto Transportation Research Institute.

City of Vancouver. (2019). *EV Charging Infrastructure Requirements for New Residential Buildings Guidance.* Vancouver, Canada: City of Vancouver.

Civitas. (2016). *Cities Towards Mobility 2.0: Connect, Share and Go!* Brussels, Belgium: CIVITAS WIKI consortium.

Clewlow, R. (2019). *A Practical Guide To Mobility Data Sharing.* Retrieved from Forbes: https://www.forbes.com/sites/reginaclewlow/2019/08/28/a-practical-guide-to-mobility-data-sharing/.

Clewlow, R. and Stiles, R. (2020). *A Complete Solution to Manage Shared Mobility.* San Francisco: Populus. Retrieved from Populus.Ai.: https://www.populus.ai/solutions/mobility-manager.

Clickworker. (2018). *Crowdsourcing from its Beginnings to the Present.* Retrieved from Clickworker: https://www.clickworker.com/2018/04/04/evolution-of-crowdsourcing/.

CMA. (2008). *No Breathing Room National Illness Costs of Air Pollution.* Ottawa: Canadian Medical Association.

CMHC. (2008). *Giving Pedestrians an Edge—Using Street Layout to Influence Transportation Choice.* Ottawa: Canada Mortgage and Housing Corporation.

Cohen, B. and Kietzmann, J. (2014). Ride on! Mobility business models for the sharing economy. *SAGE Publications*, 27(3): 279–296.

Cook, C. (2014). *Transforming the Transportation Industry with Renewable Energy.* Retrieved from Renewable Energy World: https://www.renewableenergyworld.com/2014/09/18/transforming-the-transportation-industry-with-renewable-energy/.

Cooper, D. (2018). *It's Too Early to Write off Hydrogen Vehicles.* Retrieved from Engadget: https://www.engadget.com/2018-05-29-hydrogen-fuel-cell-toyota-mirai-evs.html.

CPCS and Hatch Associates. (1992). *Commuter Rail Services: Electrification Study.* Toronto: GO Transit.

Criterion Planners/Engineers Inc. (2002). *Smart Growth Index: A Sketch Tool for Community Planning, Version 2.0.* Washington D.C.: Environmental Protection Agency.

Curie, J. and Pierre, C. (1880). Développement, par pression, de l'électricité polaire dans les cristaux hémièdres à faces inclinées. *Comptes Rendus* (in French), 9: 294–295.

Dalal, M.K. and Zaveri, M.A. (2011). Automatic text classification: A technical review. *International Journal of Computer Applications*, 28(2): 1–4.

Dalgaard, C., Kaarsen, N.I., Olsson, O. and Selaya, P. (2018). Roman roads to prosperity: Persistence and non-persistence of public goods provision. *C.E.P.R. Discussion Papers*.

Dan, K. (2007). Flight of the pigeon. *Bicycling, Rodale, Inc.*, 48: 60–66.

Dave. (2018). *Car-Sharing vs. Private Vehicle Ownership Costs.* Retrieved from Carsharing US: https://arlingtonva. s3.amazonaws.com/wp-content/uploads/sites/19/2017/03/DES-Carshare-CarShare_vs_PrivateCarOwnership_ Cost_Analysis.pdf.

David, H. (2004). *Bicycle: The History.* Yale University Press. ISBN 0-300-10418-9.

de Bruin, T., Verbert, K. and Babuška, R. (2017). Railway track circuit fault diagnosis using recurrent neural networks. *IEEE Transactions on Neural Networks and Learning Systems,* 28(3): 523–533.

De Witte, A., Hollevoet, J., Dobruszkes, F., Hubert, M. and Macharis, C. (2013). Linking modal choice to mobility: A comprehensive review. *Transp. Research Part A Policy and Practice,* 49: 329–341.

Debhia, P. (2019). *The History of Electric Scooters.* Retrieved from LinkedIn: https://www.linkedin.com/pulse/ history-electric-scooters-prashant-dedhia-negotiation-ninja-/.

Deluchhi, M.Z. and Jaconson, M.A. (2009). A path to sustainable energy by 2030. *Scientific American,* 58–65.

DeMaio, P. (2009). Bike-sharing: Impacts, models of provision, and future. *Journal of Public Transportation,* 12(4): 41–56.

DeMaio, P.J. (2003). Smart bikes: Public transportation for the 21st century. *Transportation Quarterly,* 57(1): 9–11.

Desa, U.N. (2014). *World Urbanization Prospects, the 2014 Revision.* New York: United Nations.

Descant, S. (2019). *Next-Gen Scooter Tech Could Help Address City Pain Points.* Retrieved from GvTech: https:// www.govtech.com/fs/Next-Gen-Scooter-Tech-Could-Help-Address-City-Pain-Points.html.

DiPietro, R. and Hager, G.D. (2020). Deep learning: RNNs and LSTM. pp. 503–519. *In*: Zhou, D.R.S.K. (ed.). *Handbook of Medical Image Computing and Computer Assisted Intervention.* London: The Elsevier and MICCAI Society Book Series.

Diversity, A.I. (2019). *A Think Tank for Inclusive Artificial Intelligence.* Retrieved from Diversity AI: http://diversity. ai/#firstpage.

Dong, X., Li, R., He, H., Zhou, W., Xue, Z. and Wu, H. (2015). Secure sensitive data sharing on a big data platform. *IEEE,* 20(1): 72–80.

Downs, A. (1962). The law of peak-hour expressway congestion. *Traffic Quarterly,* 16(3): 393–409.

Driving. (2015). *Company Wants to Bring Rickshaws to North America.* Retrieved from Driving: https://driving.ca/ auto-news/news/company-wants-to-bring-rickshaws-to-north-america.

Duffy, M.C. (2003). *Electric Railways: 1880–1990.* London: The Institution of Engineering and Technology.

Duives, D.C., Wang, G. and Kim, J. (2019). Forecasting pedestrian movements using recurrent neural networks: An application of crowd monitoring data. *Sensors (Basel),* 19(2): 382.

Duranton, G. and Turner, M.A. (2009). *The Fundamental Law of Road Congestion: Evidence from US Cities.* Cambridge: National Bureau of Economic Research.

EDF. (2019). *Why New Technology is Critical for Tackling Air Pollution around the Globe.* Retrieved from Environmental Defense Fund: https://www.edf.org/airqualitymaps.

Endsley, M.R. and Kiris, E.O. (1995). The out-of-the-loop performance problem and level of control in automation. *The Journal of the Human Factors and Ergonomics Society,* 2: 27.

Energy Information Administration EIA. (2017). *Study of the Potential Energy Consumption Impacts of Connected and Automated Vehicles.* Washington, D.C. 20585: US Department of Energy.

Energy Innovation. (2015). *Comparing the Costs of Renewable and Conventional Energy Sources.* Retrieved from Energy Innovation: https://energyinnovation.org/2015/02/07/levelized-cost-of-energy/.

Eugster, J.W. (2007). Road and bridge heating using geothermal energy overview and examples. *Proceedings European Geothermal Congress* (pp. 1–5). Unterhaching, Germany: European Geothermal Congress.

European Commission. (2020). *Energy Efficiency Indicator.* Retrieved from European Commission: https://ec.europa. eu/transport/themes/energy-efficiency-indicator_en.

Ewing, R. and Cervero, R. (2010). Travel and the built environment. *Journal of the American Planning Association,* 265–294.

Fishbone, A., Shahan, Z. and Badik, P. (2017). *Electric Vehicle Charging Infrastructure: Guidelines for Cities.* Warsaw, Poland: CleanTechnica.

Fishman, E. (2014). Bikeshare: A review of recent literature. *Transport Reviews,* 92–113.

Flanigan, J.K. and Lynch, J.P. (2018). Community engagement using urban sensing: technology development and deployment studies. pp. 92–110. *In*: Smith, I.A. (ed.). *Advanced Computing Strategies for Engineering.* New York: Springer, Cham.

Flannery, L. (2020). *Studying AI's Potential to Optimize Public Transit Systems.* Retrieved from Planetizen: https:// www.planetizen.com/news/2020/10/111035-studying-ais-potential-optimize-public-transit-systems.

Flyvbjerg, B.K. and Skamris, M. (1997). Inaccuracy of traffic forecasts and cost estimates on large transport projects. *Transport Policy,* 4(3): 141–146.

Flyvbjerg, B., Skamris, M.K. and Buhl, S. (2005). Inaccuracy in traffic forecasts. *Transport Reviews,* 26(1): 1–24.

Fraley, C. and Raftery, A.E. (2002). Model-based clustering, discriminant analysis, and density estimation. *J. Am. Stat. Assoc.*, 97: 611–632.

François-Lavet, V., Henderson, P., Islam, R., Bellemare, M.G. and Pineau, J. (2018). An introduction to deep reinforcement learning. *Foundations and Trends in Machine Learning*, 11(3-4): 1–102.

Frayer, L. and Cater, F. (2015). *How a Folding Electric Vehicle Went from Car of The Future to 'Obsolete'*. Retrieved from NPR: http://www.npr.org/sections/alltechconsidered/2015/11/05/454693583/how-a-folding-electric-vehicle-went-from-car-of-the-future-to-obsolete.

Friedman, A. (2010). *A Symposium of Sustainability. World Town Planning Day Event.* Whitby: Ontario Professional Planners Institute and the Oak Ridges District.

Fry, H. (Director). (2016). *The Joy of Data* [Motion Picture].

FTA. (2002). *Transit-oriented Development and Joint Development in the United States: A Literature Review.* Washington D.C.: Transit Cooperative Research Program, FTA.

Furman, B.a. (2014). *Automated Transit Networks (ATN): A Review of the State of the Industry and Prospects for the Future.* San José: Minata Transportation Institute.

Galatoulas, N.F. (2020). Spatio-temporal trends of e-bike sharing system deployment: A review in Europe, North America, and Asia. *Sustainability*, 12: 4611.

Gambs, S. and Killijian, M. (2011). Towards temporal mobility markov chains. *1st International Workshop on Dynamicity Collocated with OPODIS 2011* (pp. 1–2). Toulouse, France: OPODIS.

Gambs, S., Killijian, M. and del Cortez, M.N. (2010). Show me how you move and i will tell you who you are. *Proceedings of the 3rd ACM SIGSPATIAL International Workshop on Security and Privacy in GIS and LBS* (pp. 103–126). San Jose, California: ACM.

Gan, L.P. and Recker, W. (2008). A mathematical programming formulation of the household activity rescheduling problem. *Transportation Research Part B Methodological*, 42(6): 571–606.

Gately, C., Hutyra, L. and Wing, I. (2015). Cities, traffic, and $CO_2$: A multidecadal assessment of trends, drivers, and scaling relationships. *PNAS*, 112(16): 4999–5004.

Gawron, V.J. (2019). *Automation in Aviation –Definition of Automation.* McLean, VA: The MITRE Corporation.

Gee, M. (2016). *Raise the Roof? Union Station Reno Runs into Problem: New Trains won't Fit.* Retrieved from The Globe and Mail: https://www.theglobeandmail.com/news/toronto/union-station-shed-renovation-stalled-by-low-arches-and-an-electrified-future/article28448568/.

Geidl, M., Koeppel, G., Favre-Perod, P., Klöckl, B., Andersson, G. and Fröhlich, K. (2007). The energy hub – A powerful concept for future energy systems. *Third Annual Carnegie Mellon Conference on the Electricity Industry* (pp. 2–10). Pittsburgh: Carnegie Mellon University.

Geotab. (2020). *fleet-management-solutions/driver-safety-reports*. Retrieved from Geotab: https://www.geotab.com/fleet-management-solutions/driver-safety-reports/.

Gil, G. (2015). Building multimodal urban network model using OpenStreetMap data for analysis of sustainable accessibility. *In*: Arsanjani, a.A.J.J. (ed.). *OpenStreetMap in GIScience: Experiences, Research, Applications.* Springer Verlag Heidelberg Berlin.

Gilpin, L. (2017). *Can Car-Sharing Culture Help Fuel an Electric Vehicle Revolution?* Retrieved from Inside climate: https://insideclimatenews.org/news/07122017/car-rental-sharing-electric-vehicles-zipcar-evs-uber-lyft-green-commuter.

Global Union. (2020). *Top 10 Principles for Ethical Artificial Intelligence.* Nyon, Switzerland: The Future World of Work.

Golob, T.F. (2000). A simultaneous model of household activity participation and trip chain generation. *Transportation Research Part B: Methodological*, 34: 355–376.

Gomes, L. (2014). *Hidden Obstacles for Google's Self-Driving Cars: Impressive Progress Hides Major Limitations of Google's Quest for Automated Driving.* Cambridge, USA: MIT Technology Review.

González, M.C., Hidalgo, C.A. and Barabási, A. (2008). Understanding individual human mobility patterns. *Nature*, 453: 779–782.

Goodchild, A., Ivanov, B., McCormack, E., Moudon, A., Scully, J., Leon, J.M. and Valderrama, G.G. (2018). *Are Cities' Delivery Spaces in the Right Places? Mapping Truck Load/Unload Locations.* Seattle: ISTE Ltd., and John Wiley & Sons, Inc.

Goodfellow, I., Bengio, Y. and Courville, A. (2016). *Deep Learning.* Cambridge, Massachusetts, and London, England: The MIT Press.

Goodwin, P. (1977). Habit and hysteresis in mode choice. *Urban Studies*, 14: 95–98.

Gordon, L.A. and Shirokoff, I. (2014). *Suburban Nation? Population Growth in Canadian Suburbs, 2006–2011. Working Paper #1.* Ottawa: Council for Canadian Urbanism.

Gould, J. and Golob, T.F. (1997). Shopping without travel or travel without shopping: An investigation of electronic home shopping. *Transport Reviews*, 17: 355–376.

Griffiths, R., Richardson, A.J. and Lee-Gosselin, M.E. (2010). *Travel Survey Methods.* Transportation in the New Millennium, TRB.

Gross, S. (2020). *Why are Fossil Fuels so Hard to Quit?* Retrieved from Brookings Institution: https://www.brookings.edu/essay/why-are-fossil-fuels-so-hard-to-quit/.

GTA Clean Air Council. (2017). *Climate Action for a Healthy, Equitable and Prosperous Toronto.* Toronto: City of Toronto.

Guadagni, P.M. and Little, J.D. (1983). A logit model of brand choice calibrated on scanner data. *Marketing Science*, 2(3): 203–238.

Hagerstrand, T. (1970). What about people in regional science. *Papers and Proceedings of the Regional Science Association*, 24: 7–24. Stockholm: European Congress of the Regional Science Association.

Hand, A.Z. (2016). *Urban Mobility in Digital Age.* Los Angeles: LADOT.

Harms, S. and Truffer, B. (1998). *The Emergence of a Nationwide Carsharing Co-operative in Switzerland: A Case Study for the Project "StrategicNiche Management as a Tool for Transition to a Sustainable Transportation System.* 1998: EAWAG-Eidg. Anstalt fur Wasserversorgung und Gewasserschutz.

Haugneland, P., Lorentzen, E., Bu, C. and Hauge, E. (2017). Put a price on carbon to fund EV incentives – Norwegian EV policy success. *EVS30 Symposium* (pp. 1–8). Stuttgart, Germany: Norwegian EV Association.

Haywood, J.B. (2006). Fueling our transportation future. *Scientific American*.

Hess, A. and Schubert, I. (2019). Functional perceptions, barriers, and demographics concerning e-cargo bike sharing in Switzerland. *Transportation Research Part D: Transport and Environment*, 71: 153. Retrieved from Science daily: https://www.sciencedaily.com/releases/2019/07/190710121536.htm.

Hinton, G.E. (2006). *To Recognize Shapes, First Learn to Generate Images.* Toronto: Technical Report UTML TR 2006-003, University of Toronto.

Hoe, S.L. (2008). Issues and procedures in adopting structural equation modeling technique. *Journal of Applied Quantitative Methods*, 3(1): 76–83.

Hoopengardner, R. and Thompson, M. (2012). *FTA Low-Speed Urban Maglev Research Program: Updated Lessons Learned.* Arlington, USA: Federal Transit Administration.

Hoornweg, D., Hosseini, M., Kennedy, C. and Behdadi, A. (2016). An urban approach to planetary boundaries. *Royal Swedish Academy of Sciences*, 45(5): 567–580.

Hordnes, E. (2019). *Race to Electrification – Norway in a Pole Position.* Retrieved from Urban Insight: https://www.swecourbaninsight.com/urban-energy-race-to-electrification--norway-in-pole-position/.

Horni, A., Nagel, K. and Axhausen, K.W. (2016). *The Multi-agent Transport Simulation MATSim.* London: Ubiquity Press.

Huang, L.Q., Li, Q. and Yue, Y. (2010). Activity identification from GPS trajectories using spatial temporal POIs' attractiveness. *Proceedings of the 2nd ACM SIGSPATIAL International Workshop on Location Based Social Networks*, pp. 27–30. New York: ACM.

Huang, Y., Sun, M. and Sui, Y. (2020). *How Digital Contact Tracing Slowed Covid-19 in East Asia.* Retrieved from Harvard Business Review: https://hbr.org/2020/04/how-digital-contact-tracing-slowed-covid-19-in-east-asia.

Hughes, I. and Huo, R. (2018). *Autonomy-level Classification for Robots in an IIoT World.* Retrieved from 451 Research: https://go.451research.com/MI-Robots-in-IIoT-World.html.

Hughes, J.F. and Healy, K. (2014). *Measuring the Resilience of Transport Infrastructure.* Aukland: NZ Transport Agency Research Report 546.

Hull, G.J., Roberts, C. and Hillmansen, S. (2008). Energy efficiency of a railway power network with simulation. *International Conference on Energy Technologies and Policy.* Birmingham, United Kingdom: University of Birmingham.

Hussein, M. and Sayed, T. (2018). Validation of an agent-based microscopic pedestrian simulation model at the pedestrian walkway of brooklyn bridge. *Transportation Research Board*, 2672(35): 33–45.

IEEE-USA. (2017). *Position Statement, Artificial Intelligence Research, Development, and Regulation.* Washington D.C.: IEEE-USA.

Iemgroup. (2020). *How the Covid-19 Pandemic Affected Parking Behaviour.* Retrieved from Iemgroup: https://www.iemgroup.com/en-au/2020/07/01/how-the-covid-19-pandemic-affected-parking-behaviour/.

IISD. (2015). *The End of Coal: Ontario's Coal Phase-out.* Winnipeg, Canada: International Institute for Sustainable Development.

Ingram, M. (2020). *Google Silences and then Fires a Black Artificial-intelligence Expert.* Retrieved from Columbia Journalism Review: https://www.cjr.org/the_media_today/google-researcher.php.

Institute, R.M. (2019). *Electric Mobility: Best Practices.* Rocky Mountain Institute, Government of India and Smart City.

Iovan, C., Olteanu-Raimond, A.-M., Couronné, T. and Smoreda, Z. (2013). Moving and calling: Mobile phone data quality measurements and spatiotemporal uncertainty in human mobility studies. *Geogr. Inform. Sci. Heart Europe Lect. Notes Geoinform Cartogr.*, 247–265.

Iqbal, M.S., Choudhury, C.F., Wang, P. and Gonzalez, M. (2014). Development of origin-destination matrices using mobile phone call data. *Transp. Res. Part C*, 40: 63–74.

Islam A.S. and Ahiduzzaman, M. (2012). Biomass energy: Sustainable solution for greenhouse gas emission. *American Inst. Phys. Conf. Proc.*, 1441(1): 23–32. American Institute of Physics.

ISO. (2020). *Road Vehicles — Human Performance and State in the Context of Automated Driving – Part 2: Considerations in Designing Experiments to Investigate Transition Processes.* ISO/TR 21959-2: 2020.

Itoh, M., Zhou, H. and Kitazaki, S. (2018). What may happen or what you should do? Effects of knowledge representation regarding necessity of intervention on driver performance under level 2 automated driving. *ICPS'18: Proceedings of the 2018 IEEE Industrial Cyber-Physical Systems* (pp. 621–626). Saint Petersburg, Russia: IEEE.

Jameson L. Toole, Colak, S., Sturta, B., Alexander, L.P., Evsukoff, A. and González, M.C. (2015). The path most traveled: Travel demand estimation using big data resources. *Transportation Research Part C: Emerging Technologies*, 58(B): 162–177.

J2954. (2019). *Wireless Power Transfer for Light-Duty Plug-in/Electric Vehicles and Alignment Methodology.* SAE International.

J3068. (2018). *Electric Vehicle Power Transfer System Using a Three-Phase Capable Coupler.* J3068. SAE International.

J3105. (2020). *Electric Vehicle Power Transfer System Using Conductive Automated Connection Devices.* SAE International.

Jayasuriya, D.C. (1994). Street food vending in Asia: Some policy and legal aspects. *Food Control, Elsevier*, 5(4): 222–226.

Jefferies, I. (2019, November 20). Retrieved from Association of American Railroads: https://www.aar.org/article/freight-rail-highly-automated-vehicles/.

Jettanasen, C., Songsukthawan, P. and Ngaopitakkul, A. (2020). Development of micro-mobility based on Piezoelectric energy harvesting for smart city applications. *Sustainability*, 1–16.

Jorna, A. (2012). *Synthetic Fuel Costs.* Stanford, California: Stanford University.

Joshi, C. (2019). *Automating Consultation Analysis.* Retrieved from Data science for public good: https://datasciencecampus.ons.gov.uk/projects/automating-consultation-analysis/.

Joshi, N. (2019). *7 Types of Artificial Intelligence.* Retrieved from Forbes: https://www.forbes.com/sites/cognitiveworld/2019/06/19/7-types-of-artificial-intelligence/#48c88ca9233e.

Jovicic, G. (2001). *Activity Based Travel Demand Modeling – A Literature Study.* Copenhagen: Danmarks Transport Forskning.

Junkin, K. (2013). *Regional Rapid Rail: A Vision for the Future.* Toronto: Transport Action, Ontario.

Kabra, A., Belavina, E. and Girotra, K. (2019). Bike-share systems: Accessibility and availability. *Management Science.* Chicago Booth Research Paper No. 15-04, 1–59.

Kalra, N. and Paddock, S.M. (2016). *How Many Miles of Driving Would it Take to Demonstrate Autonomous Vehicle Reliability? Driving to Safety.* Santa Monica, California: RAND Corporation.

Kamyab, M., Remias, S., Najmi, E., Rabinia, S. and Waddell, J.M. (2020). Machine learning approach to forecast work zone mobility using probe vehicle data. *Journal of Transportation Research Board*, 2674(9): 157–167.

Kane, M. (2019). *Chile Launches Latin America's First 100% Electric Bus Corridor.* Retrieved from Inside EVs: https://insideevs.com/news/377241/chile-first-100-electric-bus-corridor/.

KAPSARC. (2016). *Mobility-on-demand: Understanding Energy Impacts and Adoption Potential.* Riyadh: KASARC.

Karim, D.M. (2017). Creating an innovative mobility ecosystem for urban planning areas. pp. 21–47. *In*: Meyer, G. and Shaheen, S. (eds.). *Disrupting Mobility: Impacts of Sharing Economy and Innovative Transportation on Cities.* Cham: Springer.

Karim, D.M. and Schewel, L. (2017). *Multimodal Planning Beyond Toronto's Urban Core.* Online Webinar: Streetlight Data.

Karim, D.M. and Shallwani, T. (2010). Toward a clean train policy: Diesel versus electric. *Ontario Centre for Engineering and Public Policy (OCEPP)*, 3: 18–22.

Kemmeter, F.D. (2019). *How Artificial Intelligence will Revolutionize Mobility.* Retrieved from MediaRail: https://mediarail.wordpress.com/how-artificial-intelligence-will-revolutionize-mobility/.

Kent, L. (2015). *HERE Shares How Automated Cars Can 'Heal' Maps on the Fly.* Retrieved from Here 360: https://360.here.com/2015/06/23/here-sensor-data-ingestion/.

Khaghani, F. (2020). *A Deep Learning Approach to Predict Accident Occurrence Based on Traffic Dynamics.* Virginia Polytechnic Institute and State University.

Khayal, O. (2019). The history of Bajaj rickshaw vehicles. *Global Journal of Engineering Sciences*, 3(2): 1–8.

Kincade, K. (2019). *Machine Learning Algorithms Help Predict Traffic Headaches*. Retrieved from Berkeley Lab Computing Science: https://cs.lbl.gov/news-media/news/2019/machine-learning-algorithms-help-predict-traffic-headaches/.

Kitamura, R., Robinson, J.P., Golob, T.F., Bradley, M.A., Leonard, J. and Hoorn, T. (1992). A comparative analysis of time use data in the Netherlands and California. *Proceedings of the 20th PTRC Summer Annual Meeting: Transportation Planning Methods* (pp. 127–138). London: PRTC.

Kleinman, M.T. (2000). *The Health Effects of Air Pollution on Children*. Irvine, California: South Coast Air Quality Management District (SCAQMD).

Kour, R. and Charif, A. (2016). Piezoelectric roads: Energy harvesting method using piezoelectric technology. *Innovative Energy & Research*, 5(1).

Krumm, J. (2009). A survey of computational location privacy. *Personal and Ubiquitous Computing*, 13: 391–399.

Kulkarni, V. and Garbinato, B. (2017). Generating synthetic mobility traffic using RNNs. *Proceedings of the 1st Workshop on Artificial Intelligence and Deep Learning for Geographic Knowledge Discovery* (pp. 1–4). Los Angeles: ACM.

Kwon, D. (2018). Self-taught robots. *Scientific American*, 26–31.

Kwon, H., Ryu, M.H. and Carlsten, C. (2020). Ultrafine particles: Unique physicochemical properties relevant to health and disease. *Experimental & Molecular Medicine*, 52: 318–328.

LADOT. (2018). *Mobility Data Specification*. Los Angeles: Los Angeles DOT.

Lambert, F. (2020). *Uber and Hyundai Unveil New Electric Air Taxi with 60-mile Range*. Retrieved from Electrek: https://electrek.co/2020/01/07/uber-hyundai-electric-air-taxi-evtol/.

Laney, D. (2001). *3D Data Management: Controlling Data Volume, Velocity and Variety*. Stamford: META Group Research Note, 6.

Lara, O.D. and Labrador, M.A. (2013). A survey on human activity recognition using wearable sensors. *IEEE Communications Surveys & Tutorials*, 15(3): 1192–1209.

Layton, B.E. (2008). A comparison of energy densities of prevalent energy sources in units of houles per cubic meter. *International Journal of Green Energy*, 5: 438–455.

Le Vine, S., Lee-Gosselin, M., Sivakumar, A. and Polak, J. (2014). New approach to predict the market and impacts of round-trip and point-to-point carsharing systems: Case study of London. *Transportation Research Part D*, 32(C): 218–229.

Le Vine, S., Zolfaghari, A. and Polak, J. (2014). *Carsharing: Evolution, Challenges and Opportunities*. London: Centre for Transport Studies, Imperial College London.

Leao, S., Long, K.L. and Krezel, A. (2014). Community mapping of exposure to traffic noise with mobile phones. *Environmental Monitoring and Assessment*, 186(10): 6193–6206.

LeCun, Y. and Bengio, Y. (1995). Convolutional networks for images, speech, and time-series. pp. 255–258. *In*: Arbib, A.A. (ed.). *The Handbook of Brain Theory and Neural Networks*. Cambridge: MIT Press.

Ledsham, T. and Savan, B. (2017). *Building a 21st Century Cycling City: Strategies for Action in Toronto*. Toronto: Metcalf Foundation.

Lee, D.B., Klein, L.A. and Camus, G. (1999). Concepts of induced demand: Induced traffic and induced demand. *Journal of the Transportation Research Board*, 1659(1): 68–75.

Lee, J.-K. and Hou, J.C. (2006). Modeling steady-state and transient behaviors of user mobility: Formulation, analysis, and application. *Proceedings of the 7th ACM International Symposium on Mobile Ad hoc Networking and Computing*, pp. 85–96. Florence: ACM.

Lee-Shanok, P. (2017). *Ontario Condo Act a Roadblock for Electric Vehicle Owners*. Retrieved from CBC News: https://www.cbc.ca/news/canada/toronto/ontario-hopes-revised-condo-act-ev-friendly-1.4155747.

Lempert, R. (2019). *Shared Mobility Data Sharing: Opportunities for Private-public Partnerships*. Vancouver: TransLink New Mobility Lab.

Leney, T. and Mackinnon, I. (2002). *Scenarios for Three Transport Industries*. London: QCA.

Leney, T., Coles, M., Grollman, P. and Vilu, R. (2004). *Scenarios Toolkit*. Luxembourg: Office for Official Publications of the European Communities.

Lessing, H. (2001). What led to the invention of the early bicycle? *Cycle History 11, San Francisco 2001*, 11: 28–36.Retrieved from New Scientist: https://www.newscientist.com/article/mg18524841-900-brimstone-and-bicycles/.

Levinson, D., Giacomin, J. and David, M. (2015). Road network circuity in metropolitan areas. *Environment and Planning B*, 42(6): 1040–1053.

Li, L. and Loo, B.P. (2014). Alternative and transitional energy sources for urban transportation. *Current Sustainable/Renewable Energy Reports*, 1: 19–26.

Li, X. and Strezov, V. (2014). Modelling piezoelectric energy harvesting potential in an educational building. *Energy Conversion and Management*, 85: 435–442.

Li, X., Gorghinpour, C., Sclar, R. and Castellanos, S. (2018). *How to Enable Electric Bus Adoption in Cities Worldwide.* Berlin: World Resources Institute, WRI and German Federal Ministry.

Li, Y. and Brimicombe, J. (2012). Chapter 9: Mobile geographic information systems. pp. 230–253. *In:* Chen, R. (ed.). *Ubiquitous Positioning and Mobile Location-based Services in Smart Phones.* Igi Global.

Liang, X. and Wang, G. (2017). A convolutional neural network for transportation mode detection based on smartphone platform. *14th International Conference on Mobile Ad Hoc and Sensor Systems (MASS)* (pp. 338–342). Orlando: IEEE.

Lima, M. (2015). *The Bicycle in the 21st Century.* Retrieved from Theprotocity: http://theprotocity.com/the-bicycle-in-the-21st-century/.

Litman, T. (2018). Retrieved from Carsharing: Vehicle Rental Services that Substitute for Private Vehicle Ownership: https://www.vtpi.org/tdm/tdm7.htm.

Litman, T. (2020). *Generated Traffic: Implications for Transport Planning.* Victoria: Victoria Transport Policy Institute.

Little, A. (2015). *The Future of Urban Mobility 2.0: Towards Networked, Multimodal Cities of 2050.* Rome, Italy: International Association of Public Transport (UITP).

Lorenzo, G.D., Sbodio, M., Calabrese, F., Berlingerio, M., Pinelli, F. and Nair, R. (2016). All aboard: Visual exploration of cellphone mobility data to optimise public transport. *IEEE Trans. Vis. Comput. Graph,* 22(2): 1036–1050.

Love Clean Streets. (2018). *Love Clean Streets.* Retrieved from http://www.lovecleanstreets.org/.

Lu, X. and Pas, I. (1999). Socio-demographics, activity participation, and travel behavior. *Transportation Research Part A,* 33: 1–18.

Lu, Z., Happe, R., Cabrall, C.D., Kyriakidis, M. and Winter, J.C. (2016). Human factors of transitions in automated driving: A general framework and literature survey. *Transportation Research Part F,* 43: 183–198.

Lucas, A., Prettico, G., Flammini, M.G., Kotsakis, E., Fulli, G. and Masera, M. (2018). Indicator-based methodology for assessing EV charging infrastructure using exploratory data analysis. *Energies,* 11(1869): 1–18.

Ma, J., Yuan, F., Joshi, C., Li, H. and Bauer, T. (2012). A new framework for development of time-varying O–D matrices based on cellular phone data. *4th TRB Innovations in Travel Modeling (ITM) Conference* (pp. 1–8). Tampa: TRB.

Ma, Y., Lee, E.W. and Yuen, R.K. (2016). An artificial intelligence-based approach for simulating pedestrian movement. *IEEE Transactions on Intelligent Transportation Systems,* 17(11): 1–12.

Mannering, F., Murakami, E. and Kim, S.G. (1994). Temporal stability of travelers' activity choice and home stay duration: Some empirical evidence. *Transportation,* 21: 371–392.

Marie, R.S. (2001). *Millennium Cities Database for Sustainable Transport, Analysis, and Recommendations.* Brussels: International Association of Public Transport.

Marouf, M., Pollard, E. and Nashashibi, F. (2014). Automatic parking and platooning for electric vehicles redistribution in a car-sharing application. *IOSR Journal of Electrical and Electronics Engineering,* 10(1): 94–102.

Marr, B. (2015). *A Brief History of Big Data Everyone Should Rad.* Retrieved from World Economic Forum: https://www.weforum.org/agenda/2015/02/a-brief-history-of-big-data-everyone-should-read/.

MaRS Discovery District. (2016). *Microtransit: An Assessment of Potential to Drive Greenhouse Gas Reductions.* Toronto: MaRS Discovery District and Richmond Sustainability Initiatives.

Martret, O. (2020). *Electric Vehicles – Cleaner, Greener and... On-Demand?* Retrieved from Shotl: https://shotl.com/news/electric-vehicles-cleaner-greener-and-on-demand.

Matuka, R. (2014). *The History of the Electric Car.* Retrieved from Department of Energy, USA.

McCandless, D. (2012). *Information is Beautiful.* UK: Collins.

McMahon, J. (2019). *9 Shared-Mobility Startups Eager to Disrupt Transportation.* Retrieved from Forbes: https://www.forbes.com/sites/jeffmcmahon/2019/03/06/9-shared-mobility-startups-eager-to-disrupt-transportation/#79ca1bf5177e.

McNabb, M. (2019). *DRONEII: Tech Talk – Unraveling 5 Levels of Drones.* Drone Talk.

McNally, M. (2000). The four-step model. *Handb. Transp. Model,* 1: 35–41.

Medina-Tapiaa, M. and Robusteb, F. (2018). Exploring paradigm shift impacts in urban mobility: Autonomous vehicles and smart cities. *Transportation Research Procedia,* 33: 203–210.

Meijer, D.K. and Geesink, H.J. (2018). Life and consciousness are guided by a semi-harmonic EM background field. *NeuroQuantology,* 17(4): 37–44.

Meireles, M. and Ribeiro, P.J. (2020). Digital platform/mobile app to boost cycling for the promotion of sustainable mobility in mid-sized starter cycling cities. *Sustainability,* 12(2064): 1–27.

Melaina, M., Bush, B., Muratori, M., Zuboy, J. and Ellis, S. (2017). *National Hydrogen: How Many Stations, Where, and When?* Washington D.C.: National Renewable Energy Laboratory for the H2USA.

Metrolinx. (2008). *The Big Move: Transforming Transportation in the Greater Toronto and Hamilton Area.* Toronto: Metrolinx.

Metrolinx. (2011). *Mobility Hub Guidelines for the Greater Toronto and Hamilton Area.* Toronto: Metrolinx.

Millard-Ball, A. (2019, March). The autonomous vehicle parking problem. 75: 99–108.

Millennium Ecosystem Assessment Board. (2005). *Ecosystems and Human Well-being: A Framework for Assessment.* New York: Island Press.

Miller, M. (2016). *A Rare Tour of Masdar, The Failed Smart City in The Arabian Desert.* Retrieved from Fast Company: https://www.fastcompany.com/90587491/shop-these-after-christmas-sales-for-up-to-50-off.

Milo, R., Shen-Orr, S., Itzkovitz, S., Kashtan, N., Chklovskii, D. and Alon, U. (2002). Network motifs: Simple building blocks of complex networks. *Science,* 298(5594): 824–827.

Minerva, R., Biru, A. and Rotondi, D. (2015). *Towards a Definition of the Internet of Things (IoT).* San Francisco: IEEE.

MIT Media Lab. (2019). *Persuasive Electric Vehicle (PEV).* Retrieved from MIT Media Lab City Science Group: https://www.media.mit.edu/projects/pev/overview/.

Mitchell, W.J., Borroni-Bird, C.E. and Burns, L.D. (201). *Reinventing the Automobile.* Cambridge, USA: The MIT Press.

Modelski, G. (2003). *World Cities: 3000 to 2000.* FAROS 2000.

Mohorčich, J. (2020). Energy intensity and human mobility after the anthropocene. *Sustainability,* 12: 2376–2389.

Moovit. (2020). *Transit Station Report: Improve and Optimize Station Use.* Retrieved from Moovit: https://moovit.com/maas-solutions/urban-mobility-analytics/.

Morawska, L., Moore, M.R. and Ristovski, Z.D. (2014). *Health Impacts of Ultrafine Particles: Desktop Literature Review and Analysis.* Canberra: Australian Government Department of the Environment and Heritage.

MotionTag. (2016). *Intermodal Insights into People's Travel Behaviours.* Retrieved from MotionTag: https://motion-tag.com/transport-analytics/traveler-system-insights/.

Motivate. (2016). *General Bikeshare Feed Specification.* Retrieved from Mobility Lab: https://docs.google.com/presentation/d/1YwkATrCmikTBYsoP9tvzAnzISgTEmbHjSVvh6woJ7Cs/edit#slide=id.g11142e806a_0_2.

Movmi. (2018). *Carsharing Market Analysis: Growth and Industry Analysis.* Retrieved from Movmi.net: https://movmi.net/carsharing-market-growth/.

MTO. (2007). *Advanced Traffic Management Systems – Book 19, Ontario Traffic Manual.* Toronto: Ministry of Transportation, Ontario.

Muheim, P. and Partners. (1996). *Car Sharing Studies: An Investigation.* Dublin, Ireland: Graham Lightfoot.

Müller, V.C. (2020). *Stanford Encyclopedia of Philosophy.* Retrieved from Stanford University: https://plato.stanford.edu/entries/ethics-ai/.

Munro, S. (2016). *Scarborough Subway Ridership and Development Charges.* Retrieved from Steve Munro: Transit and Politics: https://stevemunro.ca/2016/06/08/scarborough-subway-ridership-and-development-charges/.

Münzel, K., Boon, W., Frenken, K. and van der Blomme, J.D. (2019). Explaining carsharing supply across Western European cities. *International Journal of Sustainable Transportation,* 1–12.

Najini, H. and Muthukumaraswamy, S.A. (2017). Piezoelectric energy generation from vehicle traffic with technoeconomic analysis. *Journal of Renewable Energy,* 1–16.

Namazu, M. (2017). *The Evolution of Carsharing: Heterogeneity in Adoption and Impacts.* Vancouver: The University of British Columbia.

Nasrollahi, M., Bolourian, N. and Hammad, A. (2019). Concrete surface defect detection using deep neural network based on LiDAR scanning. *7th International Construction Conference Jointly with the Construction Research Congress.* Laval, QC: CSCE.

NCRHP. (2016). *Enhancing Internal Trip Capture Estimation for Mixed-Use Developments.* Washington D.C.: Transportation Research Board. Report 684.

Network Rail Infrastructure Limited. (2020). *Network Statement 2020.* London, UK: Network Rail.

Newswire. (2010). *Vancouver First City in the World to Endorse the Fossil Fuel Non-Proliferation Treaty.* Retrieved from Fossil Fuel Non-Proliferation Treaty: https://www.newswire.ca/news-releases/vancouver-first-city-in-the-world-to-endorse-the-fossil-fuel-non-proliferation-treaty-843699223.html.

Ng, G. (2019). *Find Bike Parking in Toronto with BikeSpace, a City-Funded Crowdsourced App.* Retrieved from iPhone Canada: https://www.iphoneincanada.ca/app-store/bike-parking-toronto-bikespace.

NHTSA. (2016). *Federal Motor Vehicle Safety Standards: Minimum Sound Requirements for Hybrid and Electric Vehicles.* Washington D.C.: National Highway Traffic Safety Administration, NHTSA.

Nilsson, N.J. (1982). *Principles of Artificial Intelligence.* Elsevier Inc.

Noble, A.U. (2018). *Algorithms of Oppression: How Search Engines Reinforce Racism.* New York: New York University Press.

Noland, R. and Cowart, W. (2000). Analysis of metropolitan highway capacity and the growth in vehicle miles of travel. *79th Annual Meeting of the Transportation Research Board.* Washington D.C.: Transportation Research Board.

NTSB. (2020). *Tesla Crash Investigation Yields 9 NTSB Safety Recommendations.* National Transportation Safety Board.

OECD. (2019). *Recommendation of the Council on Artificial Intelligence.* Retrieved from OECD: https://legalinstruments.oecd.org/en/instruments/OECD-LEGAL-0449.

Ogra, A. and Ndebele, R. (2014). The role of 6Ds: Density, diversity, design, destination, distance, and demand management in transit oriented development (TOD). *Neo-International Conference on Habitable Environments* (pp. 539–546). India: CreateSpace Independent Publishing Platform.

Ohta, K. (1998). TDM measures toward sustainable mobility. *IATSS Research*, 22(1).

Omi, K. (2018). *Alternative Energy for Transportation.* Retrieved from Issues in Science and Technology: https://issues.org/omi/.

Ongel, A., Loewer, E., Roemer, F., Sethuraman, G. and Chang, F. (2019). Economic assessment of autonomous electric microtransit vehicles. *Sustainability*, 2–18.

Ontario Medical Association. (2005). *The Illness Costs of Air Pollution: 2005–2026 Health and Economic Damage Estimates.* Toronto: OMA.

Orenstein, M. (2020). *COVID-19's Effect on Energy and Emissions – and Implications for the Future.* Retrieved from Canawest Foundation: https://cwf.ca/research/publications/what-now-covid-19s-effect-on-energy-and-emissions-and-implications-for-the-future/.

Pagliaro, J. (2015). *Chief Planner Says Rushed Scarborough Subway Analysis was 'Problematic'.* Retrieved from The Toronto Star: https://www.thestar.com/news/city_hall/2015/07/17/chief-planner-says-rushed-scarborough-subway-analysis-was-problematic.html.

Panchal, D.U. (2015). *Two and Three Wheeler Technology.* PHI Learning Pvt. Ltd., ISBN 9788120351431.

Parasuraman, R. (1992). Adaptive function allocation effects on pilot performance. *NASA/FAA Workshop on Artificial Intelligence and Human Factors.* Daytona Beach, Florida, USA: NASA and FAA.

Parasuraman, R., Sheridan, T.B. and Wickens, C.D. (2000). A model for types and levels of human interaction with automation. *IEEE Transactions on Systems, Man, and Cybernetics–Part A: Systems and Humans*, 30(3): 286–297.

Parker, R.W. (2020). *Lessons from New Zealand's COVID-19 Success.* Retrieved from The Regulatory Review: https://www.theregreview.org/2020/06/09/parker-lessons-new-zealand-covid-19-success/.

Parkunload. (2019). *Dynamic Parking Conditions.* Retrieved from Parkunload: https://www.parkunload.com/en_us/product/.

Parkunload. (2019). *Improving City Logistics.* Retrieved from Parkunload: https://www.parkunload.com/en_us/solutions/smart-loading-zone/.

Parthasarathi, P. and Levinson, D. (2010). Post-construction evaluation of traffic forecast accuracy. *Transport Policy*, 17(6): 428–443.

Pavement Interactive. (2014). *Pavement History.* Retrieved from Pavement Interactive: https://pavementinteractive.org/reference-desk/pavement-types-and-history/pavement-history/.

PBS. (2009). *Timeline: History of the Electric Car.* Retrieved from PBS.Org: https://www.pbs.org/now/shows/223/electric-car-timeline.html.

PEGASUS. (2020). *PEGASUS Method: An Overview.* Berlin: Federal Ministry for Economic Affairs and Energy, Germany.

Perner, J., Unteutsch, M. and Lövenich, A. (2018). *The Future Cost of Electricity-based Synthetic Fuels.* Berlin: Agora Energiewende.

Pete. (2015). *Electric Cargo Bike Guide.* Retrieved from Electric Bike Report: https://electricbikereport.com/electric-cargo-bike-guide/.

Pope III, C.A., Burnett, R.T., Thun, M.J., Calle, E.E., Krewski, D., Ito, K. and Thurston, G.D. (2002). Lung cancer, cardiopulmonary mortality, and long-term exposure to fine particulate air pollution. *The Journal of the American Medical Association*, 287(9): 1132–1141.

Porru, M., Serpi, A., Mureddu, M. and Damiano, A. (2020). A multistage design procedure for planning and implementing public charging infrastructures for electric vehicles. *Sustainability*, 2889(12): 1–17.

Portela, J.N. and Alencar, M.S. (2008). Cellular coverage map as a voronoi diagram. *Journal of Communication and Information Systems*, 23(1): 22–31.

Priemus, H. (2007). *Dutch Spatial Planning between Substratum and Infrastructure Networks*, 15(5): 667–686: European Planning Study.

Primault, V., Boutet, A., Mokhtar, S.B. and Brunie, L. (2019). The long road to computational location privacy: A survey. *IEEE Communications Surveys & Tutorials*, 21(3): 2772–2793.

Province of Ontario. (2017). *Performance Indicators.* Toronto: Province of Ontario.

Province of Ontario. (2020). *A Place to Grow: Growth Plan for the Greater Golden Horseshoe.* Toronto: Province of Ontario.

Prytz, R. (2014). *Machine Learning Methods for Vehicle Predictive Maintenance Using Off-board and On-board Data.* Lund: Halmstad University.

Puchalsky, C.M. (2005). Comparison of emission from light rail and bus rapid transit. *Transportation Research Record*, 1927(1): 31–37.

Pulugurtha, S.S., Duvvuri, S.V., Jain, R.N. and Venigalla, M. (2019). How accurate is the regional travel demand model in mimicking real-world travel times? *Urban, Planning and Transport Research*, 7(1): 53–73.

Qiu, C., Chau, K.T., Ching, T.W. and Liu, C. (2014). Overview of wireless charging technologies for electric vehicles. *Journal of Asian Electric Vehicles*, 12: 1679–1685.

Rajvanshi, A.K. (2002). Electric and improved cycle rickshaw as a sustainable transport system for India. *Current Science*, 83(6): 703–707.

Ram, G., Mouli, C., Duijsen, P.V., Grazian, F., Jamodkar, A., Bauer, P. and Isabella, O. (2020). Sustainable e-bike charging station that enables AC, DC, and wireless charging from solar energy. *Energies*, 13(3549): 1–21.

Reba, M., Reitsma, F. and Seto, K.C. (2016). Spatializing 6,000 years of global urbanization from 3700 BC to AD 2000. *Nature: Scientific Data*, 3: 160034.

Reddy, T. (2008). *Synthetic Fuels Handbook: Properties, Process, and Performance.* McGraw-Hill.

Regnier, E. (2007). Oil and energy price volatility. *Energy Economic*, 29(3): 405–427.

Reyad, P. (2016). *Application of Computer Vision Techniques in Safety Diagnosis and Evaluation of Safety Treatments.* Vancouver: University of British Columbia.

Richard, F. and Cooper, H. (2005). Freeman, Richard, and Hal Cooper. "Why Electrified Rail is Superior". *21st Century Science & Technology*, 18: 26–29.

Rickstrom, J. and Klum, M. (2015). *Big World, Small Planet: Abundance within Planetary Boundaries.* New Haven and London: Yale University Press.

Rideamigos. (2018). *What is Transportation Demand Management?* Retrieved from Rideamigos: https://rideamigos.com/transportation-demand-management-tdm/.

Rider, D. (2020). *How the Gardiner Expressway Hogs the Road during Budget Talks.* Retrieved from The Toronto Star: https://www.thestar.com/news/city_hall/2020/02/10/how-the-gardiner-expressway-hogs-the-road-during-budget-talks.html.

Rider, D. (2020). *Toronto Adds Electric Bicycles to Bike-share Fleet — at No Extra Cost to Users.* Retrieved from Toronto Star: https://www.thestar.com/news/city_hall/2020/08/19/toronto-adds-electric-bicycles-to-bike-share-fleet-at-no-extra-cost-to-users.html.

Rieti, J. (2017). *CBC News.* Retrieved from Toronto discourages electric car use by denying on-street chargers, driver says: https://www.cbc.ca/news/canada/toronto/electric-vehicles-blocked-1.4368014.

Ringland, G. (2002). *Scenarios in Public Policy.* Chichester: John Wiley.

Ritchie, H. (2020). *What are the Safest and Cleanest Sources of Energy?* Retrieved from Our world in data: https://ourworldindata.org/safest-sources-of-energy.

Robinson, J. (1988). Unlearning and backcasting: Rethinking some of the questions we ask about the future. *Technological Forecasting and Social Change*, 33: 325–338.

Rodenbach, J., Mathis, J., Chicco, A., Diana, M. and Nehrk, G. (2017). *Car Sharing in Europe: A Multidimensional Classification and Inventory.* European Union: STARS and AUTON.

Rosling, H., Rosling, O. and Rosling, A.R. (2018). *Factfulness: Ten Reasons We're Wrong about the World – and Why Things are Better Than You Think.* New York: Flatiron Books.

Sack, H. (2020). *William Playfair and the Beginnings of Infographics.* Retrieved from SciHi Blog: http://scihi.org/william-playfair-and-the-beginnings-of-infographics/.

SAE. (2014). *Taxonomy and Definitions for Terms Related to On-road Motor Vehicle Automated Driving Systems.* USA: SAE International.

SAE. (2018). *Taxonomy and Definitions for Terms Related to Shared Mobility and Enabling Technologies.* USA: SAE International.

SAE. (2019). *SAE International® Brings Together Public and Private Partners to Address Mobility Data-Sharing Principles.* Retrieved from SAE International: https://www.sae.org/news/press-room/2019/05/sae-international-brings-together-public-and-private-partners-to-address-mobility-data-sharing-principles.

SAE International. (2014). *Ground Vehicle Standards.* USA: SAE International.

SAE International. (2019). *A Dictionary of Terms for the Dynamics and Handling of Single Track Vehicles (Motorcycles, Scooters, Mopeds, and Bicycles).* Warrendale, PA, USA: Society of Automotive Engineers, J1451_201909.

SAE International. (2019). *J3194 – Taxonomy and Classification of Powered Micromobility Vehicles.* Warrendale, PA, USA: Society of Automotive Engineers.

Safran, M. and Chea, D. (2017). Real-time recommendation algorithms for crowdsourcing systems. *Applied Computing and Informatics*, 13(1): 47–56.

Sag, G. and Blaschke, T. (2014). Integrated urban sensing in the twenty-first century. p. 440. *In*: Weng, Q. (rd.). *Global Urban Monitoring and Assessment through Earth Observation*. Boca Raton: Taylor and Francis.

Santi, P., Resta, G., Szell, M., Sobolevsky, S., Strogatz, S.H. and Ratti, C. (2014). Quantifying the benefits of vehicle pooling with shareability networks. *PNAS*, 111(37): 13290–13294.

Sarker, I.H., Hoque, M.M., Uddin, M.K. and Alsanoosy, T. (2020). Mobile data science and intelligent apps: Concepts, AI-based modeling and research directions. *Mobile Networks and Applications*, 1–19.

Sarwar, B., Karypis, G., Konstan, J. and Reidl, J. (2001). Item-based collaborative filtering recommendation algorithms. *10th International Conference on World Wide Web* (pp. 285–295). Hong Kong: Google Scholar.

Saunders, K. (2017). *Where's the Hype for Automated Trains? Part 1: History and Background*. Automation.

Saunier, N., Ismail, K. and Sayed, T. (2009). Automated pedestrian safety analysis using video data in the context of scramble phase intersections. *Annual Conference of the Transportation Association of Canada* (pp. 1–18). Vancouver: TAC.

Sawilla, Schütt and Oskar. (2018). *Ipt-technology*. Retrieved from Wireless Opportunity Charging buses in Madrid: https://ipt-technology.com/case-opportunity-charging-madrid/.

SCAQMD. (2000). *Multiple Air Toxics Exposure Study*. San Francisco: South Coast Air Quality Management District.

Schlaich, J., Otterstatter, T. and Friedrich, G. (2010). Generating trajectories from mobile phone data. *89th Annual Meeting of the Transportation Research Board*, 339: 1–18. Washington D.C.: TRB.

Schneider, C.G. and Hill, L.B. (2007). *No Escape from Diesel Exhaust: How to Reduce Commuter Exposure*. Boston: Clean Air Task Force.

Schneider, C.M., Beli, V., Couronné, T., Smoreda, Z. and González, M.C. (2013). Unravelling daily human mobility motifs. *The Royal Society Interface*, 10(84).

Schweiger, C., O'Reilly, K., Chang, A., Guan, A., Okunieff, P., Neelakantan, R., Gopalakrishna, D., Les Brown, L., and Peck, C. (2019). *Forward-looking Assessment White Paper*. Washington D.C.: FHWA-JPO-18-744.

Sclar, R., Gorghinpour, C., Castellanos, S. and Li, X. (2018). *Barriers to Adopting Electric Buses*. Berlin: World Resources Institute, WRI and German Federal Ministry.

Scott, A.J. (2014). Beyond the creative city: Cognitive–cultural capitalism and the new urbanism. *Regional Studies*, 48(4): 565–578.

Senseable City Lab. (2015). *Urban Imagination and Social Innovation through Design & Science*. Retrieved from Senseable City Lab: https://senseable.mit.edu/.

Senseable City Lab. (2019). *How Much Urban Area Can we Monitor by Putting Sensors on Taxis?* Retrieved from Urban Sensing, MIT: http://senseable.mit.edu/urban-sensing/.

Shaheen, S. and Cohen, A. (2019). *Shared Micromobility Policy Toolkit: Docked and Dockless Bike and Scooter Sharing*. Schmidt Family Foundation.

Shaheen, S., Cohen, A. and Zohdy, I. (2016). *Shared Mobility: Current Practices and Guiding Principles*. Washington D.C. USA: Federal Highway Administration.

Shannon, C.E. (1948). A mathematical theory of communication. *Bell System Technical Journal*, 27(3): 379–423.

SharedStreets. (2019). *SharedStreets is a Shared Language for the World's Streets*. Retrieved from SharedStreets: https://sharedstreets.io/.

Shared-Use Mobility Center. (2017). *Shared-use Mobility Reference Guide*. Chicago, USA: Shared-Use Mobility Center.

Sheldrake, R. (2009). *Morphic Resonance: The Nature of Formative Causation*. Rochester, Vermont: Park Street Press.

Shepertycky, M. and Li, Q. (2015). Generating electricity during walking with a lower limb-driven energy harvester: Targeting a minimum user effort. *PLoS ONE*, 1–16.

Shi, L., Chi, G., Liu, X. and Liu, Y.H. (2015). Human mobility patterns in different communities: A mobile phone data based social network approach. *Ann. GIS*, 21(1): 15–26.

Shladover, S.E. (2016). The truth about "Self Driving" cars. *Scientific American*, 52–57.

Siemens Mobility. (2015). *Sustainable Urban Infrastructure: Vienna Edition – Role Model for Complete Mobility*.

SingaporeEDB. (2019). *Urban Mobility*. Singapore: SingaporeEDB.

Smart Growth. (2017). *What is Gentle Density and Why Do We Need It?* Retrieved from Smart Growth: https://www.smartergrowth.ca/what-gentle-density-and-why-do-we-need-it.

Smith, R.A. (2008). Enabling technologies for demand management: Transport. *Energy Policy*, 36(12): 4444–4448.

Smyyth, S. (2019). *Open Curbs: The First Open Data, Multi-City Platform to Unlock Curbs*. Retrieved from Coord: https://www.coord.com/blog/open-curbs-the-first-open-data-multi-city-platform-to-unlock-curbs.

Sobral, T., Galvão, T. and Borges, J. (2019). Visualization of urban mobility data from intelligent transportation systems. *Sensors* (Basel), 19(2): 332.

Society of Automobile Engineers, SAE. (2018). *Shared Mobility: Taxonomy and Definitions in SAE J3163™.*

Soltani, A. and Allan, A. (2005). A computer methodology for evaluating urban areas for walking, cycling and transit suitability: Four case studies from suburban Adelaide, Australia. *Computers in Urban Planning and Urban Management*, 1–16.

Somersethhouse. (2015). *The Evolution of Data.* Retrieved from Big Bang Data, Somersethhouse: http://bigbangdata.somersethouse.org.uk/the-evolution-of-data/.

Sousa, R. (2020). The always present. *Beginnings and Endings.* Toronto, Ontario, Canada: Charanam Conversations.

Spaen, B. (2019). *This All-Electric Water Taxi Could Revolutionize Green Transportation.* Retrieved from Green Matters: https://www.greenmatters.com/news/2018/06/25/qSvID/water-taxis-transportation.

Sperling, D. and Shaeen, S. (1999). Carsharing: Niche market or new pathway? *ECMT/OECD Workshop on Managing Car Use for Sustainable Urban Travel* (pp. 1–25). Dublin, Ireland: OECD.

Spinsanti, L., Celli, F. and Renso, C. (2010). Where you stop is who you are: Understanding people's activities by places visited. *Proceedings of the Workshop on Behavior Monitoring and Interpretation* (pp. 1–15). Kuala Lumpur: BMI.

Spulber, A., Dennis, E.P. and Wallace, R. (2016). *The Impact of New Mobility Services on the Automotive Industry.* Ann Arbor, Michigan: Cargroup.Org.

STAPPA and ALAPCO. (2000). *Cancer Risk from Diesel Particulate: National and Metropolitan Area Estimates for the United States.* San Francisco: State and Territorial Air Pollution Program Administrators and the Association of Local Air Pollution Control Officials.

Steer Davies Gleave. (2009). *GO Transit Lakeshore Express Rail Benefit Case, Interim Report.* Toronto: Metrolinx.

Stohler, W. and Giger, P. (1989). *Cost-benefit Analysis of the Electrification of the Beira Alta Line in Portugal.* London: Institution of Electrical Engineers.

Stone, T. (2017). *Lessons Learned from the History of Car Sharing.* Retrieved from tiffanydstone.com: https://tiffanydstone.com/2013/08/23/lessons-learned-from-the-history-of-car-sharing/.

Stone, T. (2018). *Siemens to Demonstrate World's First Autonomous Tram Running in Real Traffic in German City.* Retrieved from traffictechnology.com: https://www.traffictechnologytoday.com/news/autonomous-vehicles/siemens-to-demonstrate-worlds-first-autonomous-tram-running-in-real-traffic-in-german-city.html.

Stopher, P., FitzGerald, C. and Xu, M. (2007). Assessing the accuracy of the Sydney household travel survey with GPS. *Transportation*, 6: 723–741.

Streetlight Data. (2017). *The World in Motion on Your Desktop — Our Data Makes IPossible.* Retrieved from Streetlight Data: https://www.streetlightdata.com/our-data/.

Strompen, F., Litman, T. and Bongardt, D. (2012). *Reducing Carbon Emissions through Transport Demand Management Strategies: A Review of International Examples, Final Report.* GIZ China, Transport Demand Management in Beijing.

Sütfeld, L.R., Gast, R., König, P. and Pipa, G. (2017). Using virtual reality to assess ethical decisions in road traffic scenarios: Applicability of value-of-life-based models and influences of time pressure. *Front. Behav. Neurosci.*, 11: 122.

Sutton, R.S. and Barto, A.G. (2018). *Reinforcement Learning: An Introduction.* Cambridge: The MIT Press.

Sweet, M., Harrison, C., Bullivant, B. and Kanaroglou, P. (2015). *Congested Days in Toronto.* Toronto: McMaster University and City of Toronto.

Swenson, R. (2016). The solar evolution: Much more with way less, right now—The disruptive shift to renewables. *Energies*, 9(9): 676.

T4America. (2018). *Data – Shared Micromobility Playbook.* Retrieved from Transportation4America: https://playbook.t4america.org/data/.

Tachet, R., Sagarra, O., Santi, P., Resta, G., Szell, M., Strogatz, S.H. and Ratti, C. (2017). Scaling law of urban ride sharing. *Scientific Reports*, 7: 42868.

Tajaddini, A., Rose, G. and Kockelman, K.M. (2020). *Recent Progress in Activity-based Travel Demand Modeling: Rising Data and Applicability.* San Francisco: IntechOpen.

Takefuji, Y. (2008). And if public transport does not consume more energy? (PDF). *Le Rail*, 31–33.

Tao, P., Stefansson, H. and Saevarsdottir, G. (2010). Potential use of geothermal energy sources for the production of Li-ion batteries. *Renewable Energy*, 61.

The Economist. (2017). A world turned upside down. *Renewable Energy*, pp. 18–20.

The Guardian. (2011). *19th Century Cyclists Paved the Way for Modern Motorists' Roads.* Retrieved from The Guardian: https://www.theguardian.com/environment/bike-blog/2011/aug/15/cyclists-paved-way-for-roads.

The Guardian. (2017). *Smaller, Lighter, Greener: Are Micro EVs the Future of City Transport?* Retrieved from The Guardian: https://www.theguardian.com/sustainable-business/2017/may/11/micro-evs-city-transport-suemens-renault-green-air-pollution.

The TEV project. (2017). *Tracked Electric Vehicle System. Reference Technical Booklet.* Retrieved from The TEV project: http://tevproject.com/.

Tirri, H. (2006). Challenges of urban sensing. pp. 5–15. *In*: Fürnkranz, T.S.J. (ed.). *Lecture Notes in Computer Science.* Berlin, Heidelberg: Springer.

Tomlinson, R.F. (1984). Geographic information systems: A new frontier. *The Operational Geographer*, 5: 31–35.

Toole Design Group and Pedestrian and Bicycle Information Centre. (2012). *Bike Sharing in the United States.* USDOT, Federal Highway Administration.

Transitscreen. (2018). *Introducing Mobility score.* Retrieved from Transitscreen: https://transitscreen.com/products/mobilityscore.

TransitScreen. (2019). *TransitScreen and MobilityData Launch OpenMobilityData, Building the "OpenStreetMap for Transportation".* Retrieved from PNRewswire: https://www.prnewswire.com/news-releases/transitscreen-and-mobilitydata-launch-openmobilitydata-building-the-openstreetmap-for-transportation-300776016.html.

Transport Canada. (2009). *Bike Sharing Guide.* Ottawa: Transport Canada.

TTS. (2016). *Transportation Tomorrow Survey.* Retrieved from Data Management group: http://dmg.utoronto.ca/transportation-tomorrow-survey/tts-introduction.

Turner, S., Hottenstein, A. and Shunk, G. (1997). *Bicycle and Pedestrian Travel Demand Forecasting: Literature Review.* College Station: Federal Highway Administration and Texas DOT.

TuSimple. (2020). *TuSimple Launches World's First Autonomous Freight Network with UPS, Penske, U.S. Xpress, and McLane Company, Inc.* Retrieved from stockhouse.com: https://stockhouse.com/news/press-releases/2020/07/01/tusimple-launches-world-s-first-autonomous-freight-network-with-ups-penske-u-s.

UITP. (2013). *Press Kit: Metro Automation Facts, Figures, and Trends.* International Association of Public Transport.

UITP. (2014). *Metro Automation Facts, Figures, and Trends.* International Association of Public Transport (UITP).

US Bureau of Transportation Statistics. (2020). *Energy Intensity of Passenger Modes.* Retrieved from U.S. Energy Consumption by the Transportation Sector: https://www.bts.gov/content/energy-intensity-passenger-modes.

US Department of Energy. (2018). *Alternative Fuel Vehicles.* Retrieved from US Department of Energy: https://www.energy.gov/public-services/vehicles/alternative-fuel-vehicles#/find/nearest?country=US.

US Environmental Protection Agency. (2008). *Heat Island Compendium.* US EPA.

Venugopal, P., Shekhar, A., Visser, E. and Scheele, N. (2018). Roadway to self-healing highways with integrated wireless electric vehicle charging and sustainable energy harvesting technologies. *Applied Energy*, 212: 1226–1239.

Vulog. (2018). *AI-powered Fleet Operations Suite.* Retrieved from Vulog: https://www.vulog.com/fleet-operations-suite/.

Vulog. (2018). *The Leading Tech Provider for Carsharing Services.* Retrieved from Vulog: https://www.vulog.com/carsharing-solution/.

Vulog. (2019). *AI-Powered Fleet Operations Suite.* Retrieved from Vulog: https://www.vulog.com/fleet-operations-suite/.

Waag Society. (2014). *Eindrapportage Smart Citizen Kit Amsterdam Meten is Weten?* Amsterdam: Waag Society – Institute for Art Science and Technology.

Wang, H., Calabrese, F., DiLorenzo, G. and Ratti, C. (2010). Transportation mode inference from anonymized and aggregated mobile phone call detail records. *Proceedings of 13th International IEEE Conference on ITS* (pp. 318–323). Funchal, Portugal: IEEE.

Wang, M. (2014). *Understanding Activity Location Choice with Mobile Phone Data.* Seattle: Civil and Environmental Engineering (PhD). Seattle: University of Washington.

Wang, M. and Chen, C. (2012). Attitudes, mode-switching behavior, and the built environment: A longitudinal study in the Puget Sound Region. *Transp. Res., Part A*, 46: 1594–1607.

Wang, P., Hunter, T., Bayen, A.M., Schechtner, K. and González, M.C. (2012). Understanding road usage patterns in urban areas. *Scientific Reports*, 2: 1001.

*Watch: Toronto's Surge in E-bikeOwnership Creates Concerns over Safety.* (2018). Retrieved from Iheartradio: https://www.iheartradio.ca/newstalk-1010/news/watch-toronto-s-surge-in-e-bike-ownership-creates-concerns-over-safety-1.3726810.

Waycare. (2018). *Proactive Response.* Retrieved from Waycare: https://waycaretech.com/solutions/#proactive-response.

Waycare. (2019). *Pairing ITS Infrastructure with CV Data for Insights into Traffic Safety Events.* Retrieved from Waycare: https://waycaretech.com/case_studies/its-cv-data/.

Weichenthal, S., Ryswyk, K., Goldstein, A., Shekarrizfard, M. and Hatzopoulou, M. (2015). Characterizing the spatial distribution of ambient ultrafine particles in Toronto, Canada: A land-use regression model. *Environmental Pollution*, 47(PT A): 1–8.

Weilant, S., Strong, A. and Miller, B.M. (2019). *Incorporating Resilience into Transportation Planning and Assessment*. Washington D.C.: Transportation Research Board.

Weir, L. (2018). *Pina Bousch's Dance Theatre: Tracing the Evolution of Tanz Theatre*. Edinburgh: Edinburgh University Press.

Weißbach, D., Ruprecht, G., Hukeac, A., Czerski, K., Gottlieb, S. and Hussein, A. (2013). Energy intensities, EROIs (energy returned on invested), and energy payback times of electricity generating power plants. *Energy*, 52: 210–221.

Welch, G. and Bishop, G. (2006). *An Introduction to the Kalman Filter*. Chapel Hill: TR 95-041, University of North Carolina.

Wiener, E.L. and Curry, R.E. (1980). Light deck automation: Promise and problems. *Ergonomics*, 995–1011.

Wilson, K. (2018). *An Overview of SAE International: Standards Activities Related to Charging of Hybrid/Electric Vehicles*. Ground Vehicle Standards. SAE International.

Wilson, L. (2013). Shades of Green: Electric Cars' Carbon Emissions around the Globe. *Shrink That Footprint*, pp. 1–28.

Wolverton, T. (2016). *Wolverton: Elon Musk's Hyperloop Hype Ignores Practical Problems*. Retrieved from The Mercury News: https://www.mercurynews.com/2013/08/13/wolverton-elon-musks-hyperloop-hype-ignores-practical-problems/.

World Commission on Environment and Development. (1987). *Our Common Future*. Oxford: Oxford University Press.

Wu, L., Yang, B. and Jing, P. (2016). Travel mode detection based on GPS raw data collected by smartphones: A systematic review of the existing methodologies. *Information*, 7(4): 67.

Wu, N. (2010). Artificial intelligence solutions for urban land dynamics: A review. *Journal of Planning Literature*, 24(3): 246–265.

Xie, K., Deng, K. and Zhou, X. (2009). From trajectories to activities: A spatio-temporal join approach. *Proceedings of the 2009 International Workshop on Location Based Social Networks* (pp. 25–32). New York: ACM.

Xiong, H., Wang, L., Linbing, D., Wang, C. and Druta. (2011). Piezoelectric energy harvesting from traffic induced deformation of pavements. *International Journal of Pavement Research and Technology*, 5(5): 333–337.

Ye, Y., Zheng, Y., Chen, Y., Feng, J. and Xie, X. (2009). Mining individual life pattern based on location history. *Tenth International Conference on Mobile Data Management: Systems, Services, and Middleware* (pp. 1–10). Taipei: IEEE.

Yevdokimov, Y. and Mao, H. (2004). A systems approach to measuring sustainability of transportation. *Proceedings of the International Conference on Transportation Systems Planning and Operation* (pp. 519–528). Chennai: Allied Publishers Pvt. Ltd.

Zalakeviciute, R., Buenaño, A., Sannino, D. and Rybarczyk, Y. (2018). Urban air pollution mapping and traffic intensity: Active transport application. *IntechOpen*, 99–110.

Zangenehpour, S. (2015). *A Video-based Methodology for Extracting Microscopic Data and Evaluating Safety Countermeasures at Intersections Using Surrogate Safety Indicators*. Montreal: Department of Civil Engineering and Applied Mechanics, McGill University.

Zervass, Q. (2014). *The Definitive Guide to GTFS*. Adelaide, Australia: TransitFeeds.

Zhang, F., Yang, H. and Liu, W. (2014). The Downs–Thomson Paradox with responsive transit service. *Transportation Research Part A Policy and Practice*, 70: 244–263.

Zhang, J., Wang, F.Y., Wang, K., Lin, W.H., Xu, X. and Chen, C.D. (2011). Data-driven intelligent transportation systems. *IEEE Trans. Intell. Transp. Syst.*, 12: 1624–1639.

Zhang, P. (2010). *Advanced Industrial Control Technology*. Nanyang: William Andrew.

Zhang, W. and Guhathakurta, S. (2016). Parking spaces in the age of shared autonomous vehicles: How much parking will we need and where? *Sustainable Cities and Society*, 19: 34–45.

Zhang, X. and Chen, M. (2019). Quantifying the impact of weather events on travel time and reliability. *Journal of Advanced Transportation*, 1–9.

Zhang, Z., He, Q., Gao, J. and Nic, M. (2018). A deep learning approach for detecting traffic accidents from social media data. *Transportation Research Part C: Emerging Technologies*, 86: 580–596.

Zheng, Y. (2015). Trajectory data mining: An overview. *ACM Transactions on Intelligent Systems and Technology*, 6(3): 1–41.

Zhou, C., Frankowski, D., Finnerty, P.J., Shekhar, S. and Terveen, L.G. (2004). Discovering personal gazetteers: An interactive clustering approach. *12th ACM International Workshop on Geographic Information Systems, ACM-GIS* (pp. 1–8). Washington, D.C.: ACM.

Zielinski, S. (2006). New mobility: The next generation of sustainable urban transportation. *National Academy of Engineering*, 36(4).

# CHAPTER 4A

# Our Hidden Mobility Code

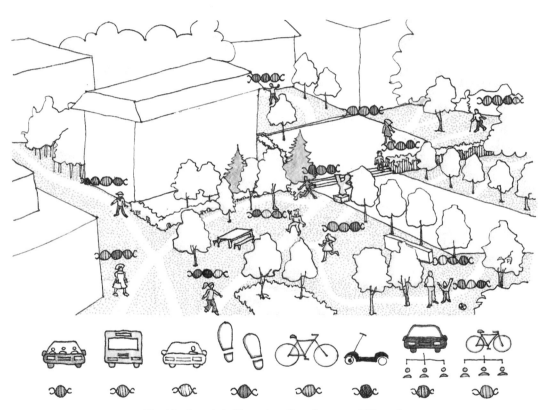

**Fig. 4.0:** An artistic illustration of new human mobility code.

*"The only thing I did all the time was watching people... I don't know anything more important."*

—Pina Bausch, In Hoghe, 1980

## Introduction—Ontology of Human Mobility

Tension between our individual presence as a human and our collective form as a mortal in society remains at the heart of 'modern' society's struggles with ideological political division. Mobility systems unfortunately, face the same destiny. Separating individualism from collective existence often colludes to create its own Utopia in the 20th century. Illusive freedom and its unbridled enjoyment remain at the heart of all modern catastrophes. During the modern era, automobility is promoted as the highest choice of individual freedom which is typically assumed as part of the fundamental foundation of capitalism. On the contrary, public transit is most often viewed as a communal mode of transportation (particularly in eastern Europe and Asia) and often rejected as restrictive to individual freedom. The rigidity and restrictive boundaries of each side faced their downfall, in 1989 with the fall of communism, and in 2008 with the fall of unbridled capitalism. Both sides' human existence formed a dialectical relation that embraced parts of two opposing worlds. A dialectical movement between the two sides of human mobility is one of the philosophical foundations of the multimodal mobility solutions proposed in this two-part book series.

Comprehensive views, concepts, and fundamental research lay out the unique patterns of the human mobility code. The code defines the unique traits of individual behaviour. A human develops a tendency to utilize multiple mobility modes, akin to the hallmark of the human who can use multiple things for different purposes. 'Freedom' is not a choice but a necessity that we cannot live without (Žižek, 1997). That necessity is an everyday habit that develops into a unique collective behaviour of human movement. This book proposes a series of new concepts on how to understand these codes, transform the mobility system framework, and customize mobility supply services with the multiple portability options that will lead to naturally avoiding automobility, and to discarding the utility approach of our unimodal ideology.

Contrary to the belief of the superiority of the human species, a human is by nature ontologically incomplete. Humans' attempts to address the ontological lack (Jameson, 2002) have resulted in bursts of creativity while living together in a society. Human life has evolved around the third space, between our first living space and second working or learning space. The entire mobility system occupies the largest portion of the third space in cities. Human interaction in the third space, including mobility spaces, develops a natural everyday city life. Our mobility performance is intricately linked to our sensorial reactions and interactions with public space, particularly with mobility spaces in cities. This book develops a new way of looking at mobility systems, by developing human-oriented multimodal mobility planning and by designing third spaces that facilitate human interaction through our collective use of our public mobility spaces. Combining multimodal mobility options that serve customized services and are redeveloped through a new concept of redesigning and reshaping the public mobility space is the heart, brain, and senses of the multimodal mobility ecosystems in this two-part book series.

As our lives become more technology-oriented and the hybrid work lifestyle becomes more prominent, the distance between our first space and second space will become blurred. We will spend more time in non-work or school or institutional places. We will spend more time in the third space. Spending more time inside our homes in isolated and depressed bedroom communities or exurban places will create an enormous physiological and mental health burden on humans. Having seen the consequences of working from home without quality spaces during the Covid-19 pandemic, the quality of the third space will gradually become the heart of city life, distancing itself from the assumption that it is just a feature of the wealthy in society. The demand and pattern of mobility is already gradually evolving around the third space, particularly along the edges of moving lanes and boulevards. Current rigid, linear, monolithic, and aesthetically unpleasant automobility spaces will gradually become redundant and a burden on society due to their over-sizing, inefficiency, and incompatibility with our current or upcoming city life. This book in response proposes an interconnected world of mobility life and vibrant human interactions in the third space. A new way to look at the repressed elements that remain invisible despite their visible presence. The approach focuses on identifying, reclaiming, and redesigning through practical and feasible practices, policies, and cultural condition shifts. The shifting nature of the mobility space will make the transformed places the most resilient part of city life, as we face the greatest ecological challenge of the human species in the 21st century.

## *Poetics of human mobility space*

Humans' relationship with space is as old as our species itself. Compared to other species, humans are born with some defining hallmarks – an exceptionally high degree of sociality, cooperation, and communal care (Nelson, 2022). Because of our lack of a blueprint compared to other animals, we tend to live in a communal space. The urgency of communal living created the original human settlement, early prototype civilizations and gradually developed manmade cities or metropolitan areas that we live in today. One of largest and most visible signs of communal living in cities are public spaces.

Culture is the identity of the human species. Civilizations are born out of culture. And culture was born, matured, and thrived in the transition places of human settlements. Transition places are the "third spaces". Entire mobility systems including other third spaces such open spaces and public spaces are part of common public space which shapes our cultural and social form through human interactions and behaviours. Human activity, performance, and interactions create invisible waves and vibrations that pass through public space (McCormack, 2013), like the magnetic field of solar waves that touch or pass through our planet. These cultural "magnetic fields" are closely linked to the quality of a public space. Streets, public squares, open spaces are intimately linked to our perception and emotions. Human feelings about space were born when we built our first settlement but existed pre-settlement. Like the millions of neutrons that pass through the earth every second and interact with matter outside of our visible field, we know the feeling towards space exists even though it remains invisible. We feel jubilant, vibrant, happy, sad, or depressed because of the way a space is designed and created (Debord, 1957). Yet the relationship between our body, mind, and medium that connects the two worlds remains disconnected from the built environment, mostly divorced from the mobility system and its placemaking process.

The multimodal mobility ecosystem is intricately linked to the quality of a public space. A mobility system without vehicle ownership or with sustainable low-emission personal mobility devices needs to engage, spend time, wait, and interact with public mobility spaces. Vehicle users rarely get out of their outer shell and rarely need to interact with the public space to complete their journey. This gave birth to the attitude of aesthetically unpleasing and poorly designed public space that followed the ideological approach of the avant-garde movement and a few misguided professionals who followed a 'beauty-less' and functional approach to placemaking. The conditions for multiple mobility users are the opposite and are a very human experience with a close relationship with urban space. But without understanding and solving mobility space quality, there will be no success in reaching sustainable mobility goals.

To counter our basic mobility space planning failures and poor design principles, this book reestablishes our ancient connection to space by using new and fresh perspectives, and concepts, and reintroduces the golden principles of quality space creation. The first step is fixing the misunderstanding of who is the user and how the human is perceived wrongly in the traditional planning process. The human resonance concept is proposed to introduce a variety of human needs and behaviours, and translate them into planning, design, and implementation elements. A new "poetics of space" is introduced to reorganize and reallocate the city's largest transition space – their mobility system. The concept proposes a new framework of traditional or 'third' space, and reestablishes social, cultural, and environmental elements into mobility space creation. The concept is simplified to reallocating mobility spaces for green space, human space, and interaction space and multimodal hubs to rewire all types of daily life activities in everyday urban life. The dialectical relation between the practice of daily life and a comprehensive mobility system view is reestablished through a series of practical changes that achieve a quality of space where humans always thrive.

**Fig. 4A.1:** Poetics of human mobility space.

*"Society had become obsessed with images and appearances at the expense of experiences and observable truth."*

—Guy Debord

## From utilitarian to human mobility code

To solve any problem, we must ask the right question. Before the industrial era, the question was simple. Cities were built based on where and how people walked, on the natural language of human movement. The occasional use of animals, carts, or other mobility modes was built into the movement of natural daily life. When facilities got crowded, we added new access to increase the connectivity. Unnecessary peak demand was avoided by prohibiting mass movement during rush hours.

Besides the modernism ideology of utility of movement creating large and rigid mobility systems, the postmodern era brought the hyper-real conditions by manipulating hyper individualism. The cultural realm of capitalism expansion found its way into new postmodernism human behaviour and infiltrated into mobility planning. The simulacra movement swept through with a 1980s postmodernism upheaval and representation of the real where the essence of the real is missing (Baudrillard, 1981). Instead of understanding the different kinds of mobility modes, and multimodal needs, mobility planning became a victim of simulacra culture, one of the defining features of the current hyper-reality of postmodern society. Travel demand models in the 1980s became the basis of an extremely narrow point-of-view of unimodal system planning in cities. One of the central premises of the mobility planning process is selecting alternative mobility modes available in certain conditions or locations (Ben-Akiva, 1985), commonly known as discrete choice.[1] When there is a barrier to sustainable modes and available facilities are in poor conditions (Masoumi, 2019), peoples' "discrete choice" of different mobility modes by default selects automobility as it serves the utilitarian purpose of relatively long-distance trips. For instance, work, education, and shopping are typical examples of the utility motive of mobility, although short-trip phenomena were recognized earlier (Akiva and Atherton, 1977) but only in non-work-related movement. Long-distance trips mimicked the spectacle of mobility, Simulation models for travel demand were solely built for an automobility system where short trips are discarded and deemed insignificant and typically seen to not contribute toward city building. This is, however, a "discretely discriminatory" method that defines human moves for no other purpose, but utility, and alternative modes are generally nonexistent. Utilitarian mobility unimodal choice (Pratt, 1970) is a mere reflection of a linear colonization philosophy that assumes we have no other purpose in life other than being functional.

In our daily lives, however, we ritually perform small and routine tasks. The human sense is full of small sensations. Our life is really nothing but these sensations. These sensations are partially functional but mostly emotional and full of perceived images of our environment. Mobility is the largest part of these daily rituals. We work. We learn. We buy things from shops. These are typically treated as "utility reasons of mobility" but we move for more than just those shallow reasons. There are many more trips made by humans simply to survive as a species. More importantly, we move because of our 'unconscious' nature to see other people, and a desire for interaction, to create social bonding, and to live in a community to avoid isolation. Short and frequent trips define a human, and they should be of the utmost importance over forced long trips that are only possible if one acquires a machine or can pay for an expensive long trip. The short trip, as a human movement, is diverse, uses multiple means to travel and aligns with the easier and less energy intensive form of human mobility. This book reveals this wonderful world of natural human movement through a human mobility code series that discloses the multimodal nature of our movement in cities. The rest of the chapter proposes a few central concepts that bring back the process of asking the right questions with a creative new approach to human mobility in cities.

> "*The earth will be a heaven in the 21st century in comparison with what it is now.*"
> —Madame Blavatsky

### *Philosophy of shifting mobility*

The rigidity of the vehicle-oriented world and its inability to adapt to changing social, cultural, environmental, and particularly alternative energy resources have created a repeating and compulsive crisis that is strangling cities in the climate change era of the 21st century. Automobility's rigidity resembles the philosophical ideological system[2] (Kant, 1781) where knowledge already exists, hence there's no need to create new knowledge, and we need to just access it. For three centuries it's haunted us and been misrepresented by creating a rigid boundary of knowledge and developing professional practices and dogma such as building cities around machines while neglecting the residents' living conditions in the built environment. To counter this rigidity and create low-carbon

---

[1] Discrete choice models are used to explain or predict a choice from a set of two or more discrete (i.e., distinct, and separable; mutually exclusive) alternatives.
[2] Kant's "antinomies of reason".

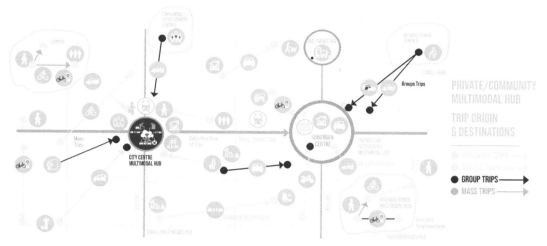

**Fig. 4A.2:** Human mobility trips, nodes, and network.

mobility, a near infinite number of alternatives is being promoted by livable city proponents. But each of the mobility-isms gradually falls victim to the underlying modernism or post-modernism ideology of the fragmented society and identity that creates divisions and brings back the very scenario it originally opposed (i.e., the removal of vehicles from city life).

Learning a new mobility ecosystem and developing cities to adapt with changing conditions would start at the very root of knowledge development, the creation and interpretation of our societal conditions. A successful mobility system is closely linked to fundamental human living and touches every aspect of the human or natural or social environment. While technical society often adopts the Cartesian philosophy of separating items from one another, there is always an opposing philosophy that embraces something else through an inclusive philosophy of reasoning and associated decision-making process. This is an ancient human skill, usually applied through a "Dialectical Approach" (Evans, 2001). In ancient times, dialectics technique,[3] first introduced by Plato (Badiou, 2012), gave birth to a rational but rigid approach to viewing the world. To address a human's existence, the irrational side does not fit well in the rational world. So, a modified dialectical approach was later popularized by Socrates to bring together the opposite sides of philosophy to generate an argument about the public decision-making process. The back-and-forth debate between opposing sides produces a kind of linear progression or evolution in philosophical views or positions (Maybee, 2020). This remains a foundation of knowledge creation and an origin of democracy. To the contrary, a mass population's consensus on ideological style can give birth to an authoritarian system. To fix the flaws of the ancient form of policy debate the dialectical approach was reinvented in the 17th century by Hagel in introducing that "opposing sides" are of different definitions of consciousness of the object (Hagel, 1977). Instead of selecting the 'right' path, it encourages us to go through a struggle in search of the right path. Of course, it may end in a different situation when it takes too long a period and the time for the 'right' path no longer exists. To address this Hagelian loophole, and in search of contradiction within materialist capitalism, Marx-Engels modified Hagel's approach to emphasize the importance of the real world and the presence of contradiction within it (Jordan, 1967). These processes gradually focus on developing absolute knowledge toward a final synthesis. In the real world however, everything is relative and the existence of absolute knowledge changes over time, with environment or societal conditions. Both Hagel and Freud rejected a rationalistic

---

[3] 'Dialectics' is a term used to describe a method of philosophical argument that involves some sort of contradictory process between opposing sides.

approach to the modern era with their simple logic that human nature remains ontologically irrational and repeatedly rejects the rigid rational world. Inspired by Nietzsche's and Marx's theory of the human born with lack that fundamentally contradicted Darwinian philosophy, postmodern era leading philosopher Jacques Marie Émile Lacan developed his own version of the dialectic process ((Lacan, Le Séminaire. Livre VIII. Le transfert, 1960–61) to create knowledge or understanding of things, developing policy in relative form comparing relative conditions and situations. This brilliant approach tried to bypass creating an 'Avatar' ideology of achieving absolute knowledge, often claimed by ultra-neo-liberalism as to becoming a better human[4] (González-Campo et al., 2011). This book's author adopted this philosophical path to avoid the new mobility ecosystem becoming a new platform of inequality, as happened to the accelerating high-tech liquid capitalism of the Covid-19 pandemic era.

The real world faces constant change. Our knowledge, systems, and society move to a new equilibrium with shifting changes. The constantly shifting 'normal' of city space and society regularly adapts to changing conditions in the third space. The city's third space remains the most dynamic and constantly shifting reflection of our changes in society. The author proposes a "shifting mobility" approach to adapt to the constantly changing conditions of the third space where the entire mobility system is located. It may sound frustrating, the thought of rebuilding the next round of shifting mobility combinations after just finishing a new one. But shifting conditions create a hole in even the best knowledge and system created with good intentions. Those holes need to be fixed by adapting them to a new human condition. With fast changing environment and resources, a human has no alternative but to adapt to a new condition as it changes. The same is true for a mobility ecosystem. The future is not going to be the autonomous vehicle no matter what the magical solutions proposed by its innovators. Despite good intentions, any new system can turn itself into the victim of an "ideological fantasy"[5] that remains hidden beneath the layers of the society and political reality we live in. New systems such as the multimodal ecosystem proposed in this book need "ideological disidentification" (Sharpe, 2008) to avoid intentional or unintentional bias, i.e., our default vehicle-oriented ideology that is so often now overshadowing the thoughts and process of emerging multimodal mobility systems. A new dialectic approach for the 21st century would ultimately reject the flawed neo-liberal multicultural ideology foundation as the tool of late capitalism that is now giving birth to a new form of nationalism and extremism (Žižek, 2012). Realizing the flaws of unbridled capitalism's attempt to invade all aspects of our lives, the living philosopher Žižek has developed a new reality and dialectic approach in the 21st century in pursuit of a desperate hope for something radically new. His approach identifies the ideology, disassociates itself from it from a distance, and finally, reconstructs a new approach that will avoid past ideological attachments to avoid biases.

In the post tech-feudalism era, a new form of materialism such as the new autonomous vehicle is not going to cure humanity's ecological ills. While developing a new ecosystem of mobility options, both parts of the book adopt the shifting conditions of our knowledge, reasoning, and concepts through the Lacanian dialectic philosophy to avoid the rigidity and inequality traditionally built into vehicle-oriented or pseudo-scientific approaches to a transit-oriented system. Most of the multimodal theory development process in this chapter and the real-world examples in the rest of the book are based on disassociating from underlying ideology to make way for new knowledge and reasoning, and the philosophical grounds of a multimodal mobility ecosystem that incorporates the possibility of city building based on our organic human mobility code.

---

[4] By adopting some spiritual objectives (such as achieving Nirvana though meditation), we purify ourselves and become a 'better' human while ignoring present problems or issues or suffering through life to achieve Nirvana.

[5] As per philosopher Žižek, no political regime can sustain the political consensus upon which it depends. He referred the ideologically positioned as 'traitors' or "enemies of the people".

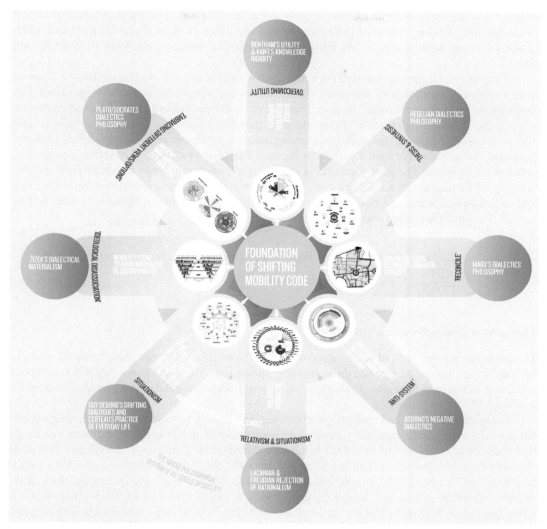

**Fig. 4A.3:** Philosophy of shifting mobility through disassociation of ideology and reestablishing connection to human.

> *"I don't care. People here have to find their own way, negotiate for themselves, use their own brains."*
> —Hans Monderman (Dutch traffic engineer and inventor of shared streets)

## In Search of a Blueprint of Human Mobility Code

The human soul and mind appear to work in a phantom world, at least from the perspective of the visible outside world. "The outward things" are however, short-lived illusions. To understand the depths of our hidden world, the unwithered, abstract, and innermost patterns of human behaviour, untangle the true light at the end of the unknown tunnel. By judging the world with only tangible eyes, the mobility world has created never-ending hard infrastructure expansion to satisfy our automobility needs. It was a short-lived illusion, and it never solved the real human mobility needs that remained invisible from its first appearance onward. Our personal inner world develops its own abstract movements that remain mostly invisible to the 'tangible' world of mobility. Our movements' dynamics and blueprint ride on a different medium. And that medium is chosen from the hidden patterns of a nonphysical form of "mobility code", akin to our biological DNA but different in many ways.

In any attempt to discover something new, a casual streamlined approach is ineffective. It comes from a culture of curiosity and inquisitive habits that look at simple things from a new perspective. Japanese mobility inventions for instance, come from a culture widespread in their everyday life and society. A simplistic modern 'water-ink' style painting created by Sesshū Tōyō took roughly 500 years to reappear in a different form among western European artists such as Paul Cezanne. Similarly, the modern-day transit system in Japan is the most extensive, efficient, and convenient in the mobility world. The author's working and living experience in Japan influenced and initiated thinking of finding the true mobility code beyond the classic utility-oriented approach and (mis) understandings of human mobility. This section describes the process, methodology and the next section describes the overall high-level findings.

> *"You can't connect the dots looking forward; you can only connect them looking backward."*
>
> —Steve Jobs

### The source code: Data and processing

The existence of the idea of a blueprint of human mobility came after more than 25 years of lifelong observation, the practice of cultivating innovation, digging deeper beyond schoolbook texts, and developing the habit of attempting to connect seemly unrelated things that appear on the surface.

The search for a true and realistic pattern of human mobility remains an enigma among our city builders. To bypass actual mobility pattern and understand its needs, mobility planners repeatedly relied on static data or rigid travel survey questionnaires that could never reveal our true daily mobility activities. Recent technology however, unlocked the prospect of tracing our daily natural activities. This is not new, but most of the recent research has focused on vehicle trips, particularly in North America. A human's natural tendency to use multiple modes in an urban environment is often ignored or lacks attention due to limitations on data. The author collaborated with mobility technology companies and data providers to overcome those limitations. The following section describes the process, high-level methodology and some of the key findings uncovered during mobility code research conducted by the author. The author collaborated with tracked data provider MotionTag for personal research, and mass mobility data provider StreetLight for professional experiences. Tracked mobility data includes seven European cities (Berlin, Bern, Hamburg, Munich, Muenster, Vilnius, and Zurich), one Japanese city (Osaka) and the author's own personal mobility data in North America. StreetLight data includes several Canadian cities including Toronto.[6]

### Developing a framework

Despite over half-a-century of mobility demand modelling and system building, there are a few fundamentals that remain unanswered. And the basic assumptions for these mobility models are built on shaky foundations. True mobility pattern and its needs was not even known until recently, before tracking technologies became available in the middle of this century's second decade. This book proposes to focus on the very fundamentals of human nature and its foundational components

---

[6] The findings in this book are repeated from publicly available studies and findings completed by the author. The references of these studies are provided throughout the book.

to explore a new beginning. The initial concept is briefly described in this section; however, it will take more than just one attempt to uncover such a monumental task.

## Fundamental problem – What is a trip?

Despite numerous mobility demand models developed by almost every city around the world, none clearly identifies what exactly is an actual trip. Human trips are not an industrial product that starts and finishes within specific rules. Many of our trips are in chains, contain numerous pauses, and stop-or- transfer between modes or activities. Typically, the survey that all demand models depend on never tells participants what trip they should report. The same problem exists now with digital data. To stop avoiding this vagueness and void, this book defines more than a five-minute trip duration as a trip. If a user changes mobility modes, a transfer point is detected, and the trip is separated at access point or as a local short trip.

## Natural trip making and scale of demand

One of the fundamental assumptions of all mobility models or estimate processes is the number of trips made by each person on an average day. Although trip making varies on different days or in different seasons, a constant number of trips over a long time is relatively constant. Having a clear definition of a trip and tracking nearly all trips made by each person via tracking devices, avoids making random assumptions and common errors when discarding short trips in traditional and the absolute method of travel demand surveys. An automated travel diary (MotionTag, 2022) with an appropriate processing and geo-sanitization technique to remove privacy information is emerging as the true representative of our mobility pattern.

## Multimodal mode

The tracked data for this research contains a multiple mobility instead of unimodal approach to traditional travel demand models, and their deeply flawed assumptions despite detailed technical models developed in the past 60 years. The data provider uses machine learning techniques, and mode detection using an accelerometer, and develops a range of trip characteristics that define each mode. These methods are not full-proof, but they are highly accurate compared to the traditional survey-based method that depends on one-day snapshots and faded trip-making memories.

## Characteristics of trips

Unlike the traditional survey, trip characteristics such as speed, duration, origin, destination, and acceleration are tracked and proceed to use for machine learning algorithms. Traditional models make numerous assumptions and always focus on the utility aspects of trip making. We make trips for functional and recreational purposes or simply going out without any purpose or objective. Tracked data can capture all the hidden attributes of a trip far more accurately than typically reported trip characteristics.

| Concept of Mobility Code and its DNA Elements |
|---|
| Framework of Human mobility blueprint (Refer to Fig. 4A.4) |
| P = Purpose of trip |
| IP = Indeterminate of chain trips purpose |
| p () = Probability of choosing trip attributes |
| D = Trips distance |
| M = Modal choice for destination, day, service availability |
| S = Speed of travel time for destination, day, service availability |
| i = Types of mobility services and infrastructures quality |
| For instance, |
| $p_2(d)$, $p_2(m_2)$, $p_2(s_2)$, $p_2(i_2)$, $p_2(ms_2)$ |
| = Probability of choosing specific mobility modes ($m_j$) for a distance (d) for specific day, service availability ($MS_i$), speed ($S_i$), infrastructures services (i) |

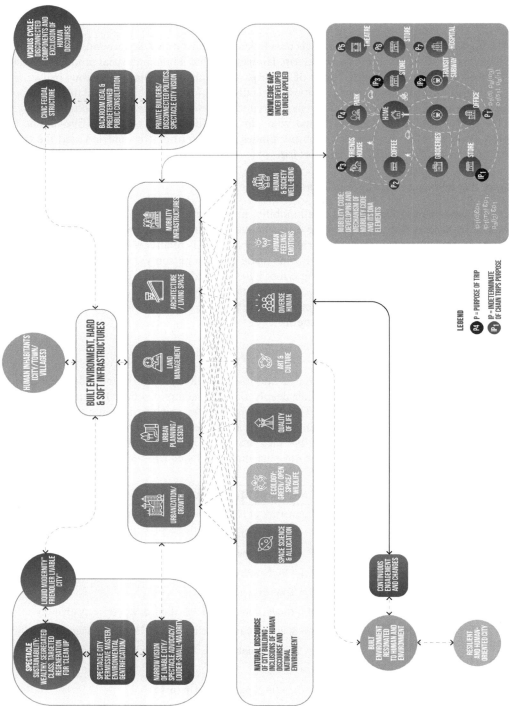

**Fig. 4A.4:** Framework of a human mobility blueprint.

*"I am not interested in how people move, but what moves them."*
—Pina Bausch (German artist and choreographer)

## The Hidden and Beautiful World of Human Mobility Code

Human mobility is a critical element of our daily activities. Whether we move inside our home, within the neighbourhood, or for work or other purposes, or simply physically move for different activities, we create a daily habit. A daily habit is repetitive. It repeats after short, medium, or long intervals. All signature features of our unique mobility code and its DNA elements come from our habits (Weir, 2018). Maybe in the form of the notion of habitus[7] (Bourdieu and Wacquant, 1992). Mobility code is the unique personal traces of an individual's movement history. The hallmark blueprint of mobility code and its DNA elements are also imprinted (Sheldrake, 2009). Historical deposits of collective memory are reflected in our mental, corporeal, temporal, and spatial schemata, and are shaped by our perception, reaction, causation, and prior or continuous learning process. It is reminiscent of our personal desire to explore things around us, or it traces our activities for daily needs and builds on the series of superimposed layers of influence, predominantly cultural, social, physical, and natural environments that surround our daily living.

Despite modern or postmodern efforts to understand human mobility, it remains a mystery. The simple reason is human mobility is viewed through a vehicle window. This book attempts to uncover the preliminary and basic understanding of true human mobility, but not under the influence of machines or utilitarian ideology. However, it's a monumental task. This chapter will reveal some of the fundamental principles, findings, and formulations of new theories and approaches. The remaining chapters will present detailed findings. In the future, detailed analysis and findings will be published gradually by the author when the research is completed.

This section describes a series of new mobility findings from the author's personal research and practical experience from real-life projects.

### Multimodal mobility code

Using multiple tools for different purposes is rooted in human DNA. The same is true for mobility. It is our natural habit to use multimodal mobility options, if service is available, affordable, comfortable, and access is quick and easy.

All users in the database have shown repeated use of the same combination of multiple modes. None were unimodal. At least two mobility modes (an extreme example is the car and walking) were used by everyone in the database. The most common multimodal users regularly use at least three or four mobility modes. Those who combine five modes are less frequent but not rare. Occasionally, some users switch mobility modes but over time (roughly six months) their behaviour stabilizes. Unlike

**Multimodal Mobility Code**

Total multimodal person trip,

$$T_{i,j}$$

$$= Wc + V_{i,j}
\begin{array}{ccl}
C_{i,j} & \in & \textit{short distance} \\
& \in & \textit{medium to long distance} \\
PT_{i,j} & \in & \textit{medium to long distance} \\
PT(od)_{i,j} & \in & \textit{Medium to shorter distance} \\
+ \quad TR_{i,j} & \in & \textit{Very long distance} \\
MM_{i,j} & \in & \textit{shorter distance}
\end{array}$$

where

$T_{i,j}$ = Total person trips
Wc = Walking trips (constant)
$C_{i,j}$ = Total cycling trips
$PT_{i,j}$ = Total public transit person trips
$PT(od)_{i,j}$ = Total on-demand transit trips
$TR_{i,j}$ = Total train trips
$MM_{i,j}$ = Total micromobility trips

[7] "Notion of habitus: A concept he defines as a set of historical relations deposited within individual bodies in the form of mental and corporeal schemata of perception, appreciation, and action. Bourdieu has further described habitus as a kind of embodied history."

folklore among vehicle-oriented practitioners, not a single person used a single mode (i.e., car-only), meaning a unimodal person really does not exist. It's practically impossible to use a car for all possible trips and conditions. Using the Mobility Markov Chain method (Gambs et al., 2011), a clear mobility pattern of the individual emerged. Each person has a unique combination of multiple modes, their distance, travel time, and speed are unique to that individual. No single person displays identical or a similar mobility pattern. Every person's mobility pattern is statistically significant, indicating a unique mobility footprint is not accidental. This unique discovery is called in this book "human mobility code" with distinct elements of DNA that constitute every individual's mobility code. The characteristics of each DNA element that constitutes mobility code is described in the upcoming sections.

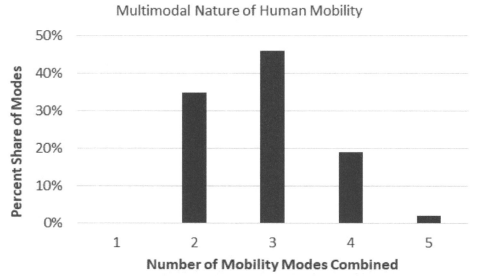

**Fig. 4A.5:** Combination of mobility modes used by each person.

### *No matter what, our daily trips are constant*

We move every day for various reasons or sometimes without reason. Our total number of trips constitutes our total moving activity. Totals trips generated by each person are also the fundamental assumption of mobility demand estimation and the basis of travel demand models. Unlike the traditional flawed phone or paper-based travel survey, the research database shows we make nearly six to eight trips every day during post- and pre-Covid-19 pandemic periods, respectively. Larger city residents have more destinations to choose from, hence, the number of trips is slightly higher, roughly 6.5–7.5 total trips per day. Smaller city residents make roughly six trips per day. During the Covid-19 full lockdown, trips/day/person reduced to 3.5 to four. Very similar findings were observed in other pandemic studies that reported daily trips reduced by half. These findings are also very similar to another research conducted during the Covid-19 pandemic (Molloy et al., 2021). When combined in a city or a group, the total trips per day by each person becomes nearly a constant. The number of trips varies over different demography but overall, on an average we make the same number of trips every day, weekly, and monthly.

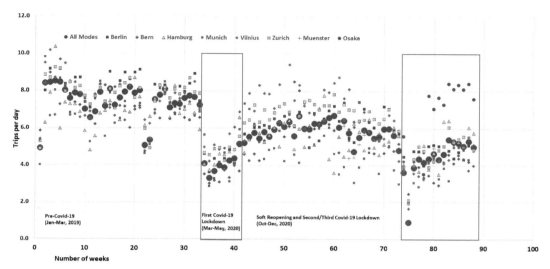

**Fig. 4A.6:** Daily total trips per person for all eight cities.

## Non-walking modes are interchangeable

Earlier, the findings of the mobility code confirmed every person uses at least two or more common mobility modes every day. Trip generation characteristics and shifting modes, however, have their own unique DNA elements.

Two distinct "mobility mode couples" have a unique collective pattern. The first mobility mode couple is vehicles and public transit. Both vehicles and public transit are direct competitors for medium to long-distance trips. The shift between these modes is common depending on convenience, affordability, faster travel needs, and seasonal influence. These two modes roughly constitute one-third of the total daily trips. The second mobility mode couple is conditional between bicycles and public transit. During the Covid-19 pandemic, this new 'complementary' mobility mode couple emerged as a common shift between modes. Roughly one-fourth of medium or relatively shorter distance public transit trips were replaced by bicycles due to the fear of infection. There are 'dependent' mobility mode couples too. The dependent modes are usually walking, bicycling, and

| **Mobility Couple** |
|---|
| 1a. Total multimodal person trip, |
| $V_{i,j} \overset{0.5}{\Leftrightarrow} PT_{i,j} \quad \in \quad$ *medium to long distance* |
| $C_{i,j} \overset{\Delta d}{\Leftrightarrow} PT_{i,j} \quad \in \quad$ *shorter distance* |
| where: |
| 0.5 = Half of trips |
| $\Delta d$ = Smaller segment interchangeable |
| 1b. Dependent couple trips, |
| Public transit couple |
| $PT_n = \sum PT_{i,j} + \sum PT(od)_{i,j} + \sum C_{i,j} + \sum W_{i,j} + \sum MM_{i,j}$ |
| Vehicle couple |
| $V_n = \sum V_{i,j} + \sum W_{i,j}$ |
| where: |
| $PT_n$ = Total public transit trips including access trips |
| $V_n$ = Total vehicle trips |

micromobility. The common access modes to relatively longer distance trips such as vehicles and public transit. Despite a common but mistaken rivalry, vehicles and walking are strange bedfellows (see next section). There are also 'romantic' mobility mode couples. Public transit and trains are a mobility transfer couple who are forever in love due to their interdependence. Walking and public transit are the most common romantic mobility mode couple that cannot exist without one another. Finally, there are two "mobility singles". The first is walking, described earlier as the core DNA element of our mobility code. The second mobility single is rail transit, which is the candidate for very long-distance suburban trips and constitutes less than 10% (roughly 5–7%) of total trips. These two mobility modes are rarely interchangeable because of their unique very short and very long-distance characteristics. Like other DNA elements of our mobility code, shifting modes or connecting modes are unique behaviours among urban people, a unique mode shift that is nonexistent in the traditional travel demand process.

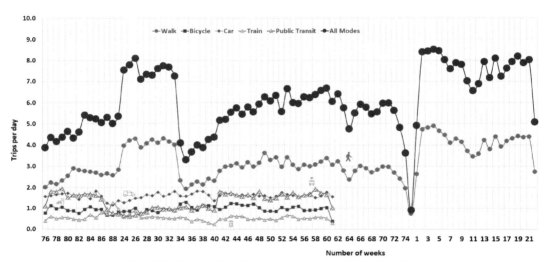

**Fig. 4A7:** Daily total multimodal trips per person for all eight cities.

## *Walking is the fundamental building block of human mobility identity*

Walking is the most fundamental of the building blocks of human mobility. While this fact was commonly known to modern city builders, it has played very little or no role in mobility system planning, design, and building. The results from eight cities, from 210 individual's data, displayed a remarkable stability of walking habits every day. The variation in walking mode share of everyone's total trips stay below 10% (except for a few individuals due to data deficiency).

Monthly walking mode share varies (see Equation 1b) from minimum 17% to maximum 81% (the weekly variation was 18–94%). The majority of personal walking mode share falls within a range from 33% to

---

**The Walking Code and its DNA Elements**

**1a**: The walking constant, $W_c$,

$$T_{i,j} = W_c + MM_{i,j}$$

where:

$T_{i,j}$ = Total number of trips generated by each person between origin i and destination j,

$W_c$ = Total number of walking trips generated by each person between origin i and destination j.

**1b**: The walking variation,

$$\Delta(W_{i,j}) \xrightarrow{\square} \in$$

where:

$W_{i,j}$ = Personal walking mode share

$\in$ = insignificant variation ($\in < 10\%$) of changes in $W_{i,j}$

71%. This is a remarkable walking characteristic which defies the common planning myth that only a few people walk extensively, but only if they live in dense and mix-use areas. The relation between population density and personal walking mode share was not statistically significant, indicating people walk regardless of where they live or whatever the built form. It should be noted that the lengths of walking or other trips are heavily influenced by built form, density, and mixed land-use, but the frequency of trips is independent of the built environment. The walking mode share remains nearly constant (see Equation 1a), displaying the remarkable walking code of each human. Personal walking mode share remains nearly constant for each human while mode share for other modes varies dramatically over weekly, monthly, or yearly time periods depending on their availability, the season, local conditions, and other factors that influence mobility habits.

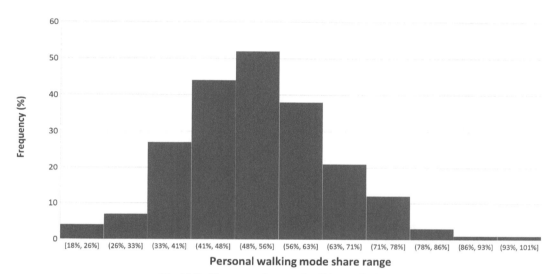

**Fig. 4A.8:** Histogram of personal walking mode share.

## *Half of the city walks*

While an individual shows a remarkable personal walking code, our collective nature shows a surprisingly constant pattern. From the histogram of the personal walking mode, the properties of a walking code emerge. In every city, the walking code remains the same. There are two distinct properties or DNA elements of the walking code.

The first DNA element shows as a community, or group, or city, half of our total trips (in terms of number of trips or frequency of trips) come from walking (Fig. 4A.9). Some people make a large share of walking trips. Some do the opposite. The variation of group walking mode share is however only 2–4%, a surprisingly narrow range given the large amount of weekly data in the research database. If all city data is combined, variation collapses to only 1%. This finding has monumental implications on travel demand models and is based on

| **DNA Elements of Walking Code** |
| --- |
| **2a**: The walking constant, $W_c$, |
| $W_c = C_i$ |
| where: |
| $W_c$ = Walking constant, |
| $C_K$ = Fixed constant number. |
| **2b**: The non-influencing nature of walking contact, |
| $C_K$     *no subject to 7Ds* |
| where: |
| $7Ds_j$ = Seven layers of mobility influence –Demand, Density, Diversity, Distance, Design, Digital, Destinations |

large and mega mobility structures. Contrary to traditional deeply flawed walking mode share data, this finding indicates that at any given period roughly half of the trips are walking trips, which simply and clearly translates to half of mobility facility, planning, and budget should be dedicated to walking infrastructure. Currently most cities spend less than 5% of their budget (City of Toronto, 2012) on walking. The majority budget proportion is spent on mega vehicle infrastructure, based on the flawed assumption behind the significant amounts of long-distance trips' myth. City budget allocation is not based on any scientific findings.

The second DNA element shows that no seasonal, geographic, built form, or any other disruption was able to change the ever-constant group or citywide walking mode share. While other mobility modes' pattern or share changes when conditions change (see next section), the walking share remains constantly half (50%) no matter what the changes in condition. For instance, Covid-19 brought drastic changes in travel patterns. All mobility indicators have shown drastic changes. While the number of walking trips reduced to half, the walking share of total trips stubbornly remained 50%. These findings solidify the first findings, that walking is the most fundamental and strongest indicator of any individual or citywide characteristic no matter who we are or where we live.

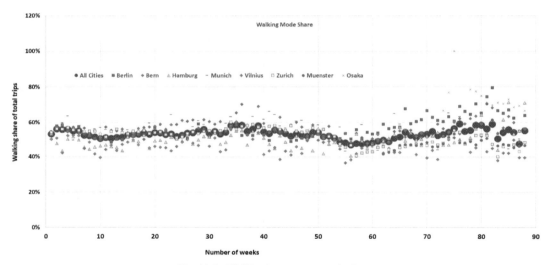

**Fig. 4A.9:** Walking is a constant mode share.

## There is no driving-only human

There is a myth in the extreme car culture that we can make 100% of our trips by car. Many vehicle owners assume they are fused to their machine, and they don't need to walk anywhere. Evidence from real world mobility data shows a remarkably different perspective. Even extreme vehicle users display roughly 20% of their trips completed by walking (Fig. 4A.10). This is just walking to/ from parking spaces to destinations. These walking trips are relatively longer than car access trips. Car users do leave their vehicle at home and go for a walk, occasionally just walking without any attachment to their vehicle. This is in complete opposition to the claim often mythicized by traditional traffic engineers that car drivers rarely walk. This claim has profound implications on mobility infrastructures. Even if a city claims to be vehicle-oriented, they still need to dedicate at least 20% of their mobility budget to walking facilities, even when assuming other multiple modes do not exist. Walking facilities are often disconnected, in poor condition and unsafe due to extremely low funding based on the traditional folklore that vehicle users do not walk at all.

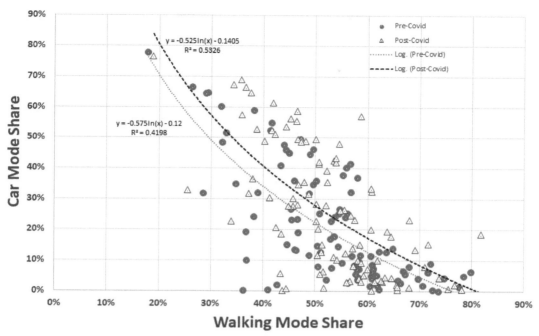

**Fig. 4A.10:** Strange bed fellows between a vehicle and walking.

## *Driving evaporates when we are conditioned for sustainable mobility*

When we build transit, walking, or cycling facility, or adopt shared mobility services, driving alone gradually evaporates. As indicated in the previous section, for instance, people walk more when driving mode share gradually reduces (Fig. 4A.10). All other multimodal modes require walking, cycling, or micromobility to connect the trips to complete a journey. Similarly, people walk relatively more frequently when they use public transit (Fig. 4A.11). However, unlike a myth among transit-oriented practitioners, the relation between public transit and walking is not as strong as claimed. Public transit is not the single reason for walking. Most transit-related walking is access trips, in addition to other forms of access trip modes (cycling, local transit, micromobility, shared mobility). But people walk for multiple reasons, not just when they use public transit. Walking has the greatest volume of access trips as well as independent trips among all the mobility modes.

## *Dynamic and shifting mobility code*

Our mobility habit changes over time with surrounding social, cultural, economic, and other conditions. Tracked data used in this research included Covid-19 pandemic conditions although it was not intentional. During the data preparation stage, pre- and post-mobility data provided a unique window to compare the shifting nature of human mobility besides typical non-disruption mobility behaviour changes. The complete lockdown dramatically changed people's travel behaviour overnight. Total daily trips were halved. However, when the lockdown was lifted, total daily trips only went back to 75% of the typical pre-pandemic periods and remained stable. When additional data from the four lockdowns was analysed, it become clear that people automatically adjusted each time when the pandemic lockdown was announced. After some time, on an average of roughly six months, our mobility habit settles and finds a new equilibrium. There is, however, one exception in the sea of shifting mobility. As described earlier, the walking mode share remained constant at

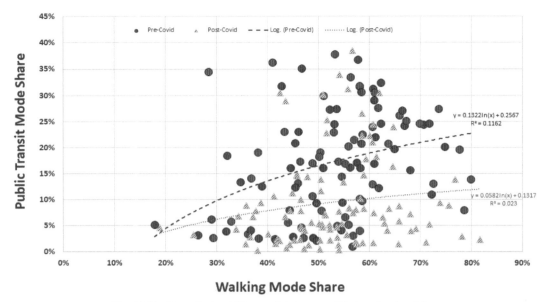

**Fig. 4A.11:**  Dependent mobility couple between public transit and walking.

roughly 50% through all the drastic changes in mobility behaviour during the full lockdowns. These results provide a unique understanding of how human mobility behaviours change, what happens during a disruption, and when our new travel pattern re-emerges and returns to our individual unique code. Traditional travel demand models typically ignore the shifting nature of human mobility and are completely clueless to the details behind travel behaviour changes.

## *Natural pattern of human trips*

Although travel attributes, such as distance, speed, travel time, are typically used in travel demand models as a basic assumption, the nature of these attributes' details are typically unknown, or ignored. Traditionally, speed studies are conducted at certain spots instead of considering every individual's movement speed. Similarly, trip distances are asked using rough origin and destination estimations. And these rough methods are acceptable for typical facility design purposes. However, as a matter of fact, people move on weekdays or weekends, or on non-workdays or on vacation in different fashions. Tracked data reveals more interesting mobility DNA elements. At the individual level, people display the unique characteristic of covering similar distances and speeds during typical daily trips. On weekdays, people move a shorter distance at a higher speed. Weekend, vacation, or recreational trips are much longer and at a relatively lower speed. There is surprising a very small but notable increase in trip frequency between 20–45 km, an indication of recreational hiking, cycling, or intercity tours (Fig. 4A.12.1). Distances covered while walking are nearly identical for all eight cities (Fig. 4A.12.2). At the collective level, an even more stable and repeated behaviour pattern emerges. For instance, most urban trips are remarkably short (Table 4A.1) except for long-distance train trips. When average or median speed is compared between mobility modes, vehicles and public transit emerge again as direct competitors (Fig. 4A.12.3). European streets are relatively narrow and rarely have dedicated spaces for public transit. Yet their average distance and speed profiles are nearly identical due to transit priority at critical service points such as intersections, loading spaces, and priority part-time lanes instead of entirely dedicated lanes. The complementary nature between vehicles and transit debunks the long-standing myth among transit-oriented practitioners that only transit can solve mobility problems. It can, but for only less than 30% of urban trips. Even better transit systems in Europe were able to capture only half of vehicle trips. We must deal with short trips by providing dense, interconnected, and safe facilities for short trips. The sheer importance of short trips often fails to understand its importance in the transit-oriented ideological mindset.

**Table 4A.1:** Illustration of collective trip pattern.

| Mobility Modes | Percent of Trips Less than 10 km | Percent of Trips Less than 15 km | Average Speed (km/h) | Median Speed (km/h) |
|---|---|---|---|---|
| Walking | 71% | 85% | 4.6 | 5 |
| Cycling | 56% | 65% | 15.6 | 16 |
| Public Transit | 22% | 27% | 28.7 | 25 |
| Car | 38% | 47% | 35.1 | 29 |
| Train | 17% | 20% | 77.6 | 61 |
| All Modes | 46% | 55% | 16.6 | 31 |

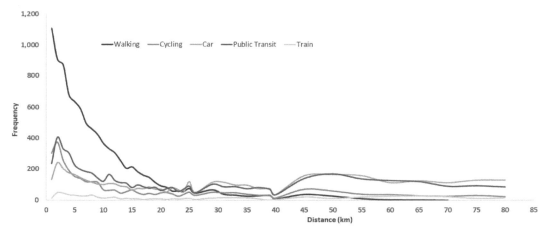

**Fig. 4A.12-1:** Distribution of trip distances for all major mobility modes.

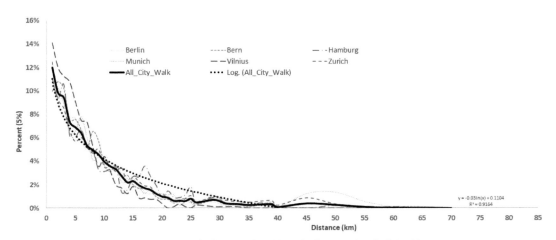

**Fig. 4A.12-2:** Distribution of walking trip distances for all eight cities.

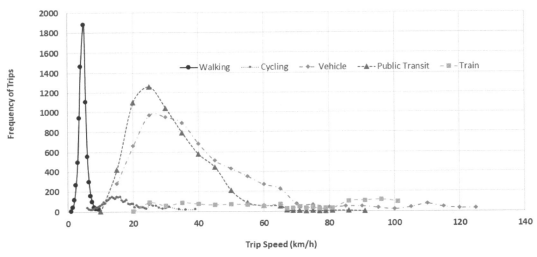

**Fig. 4A.12-3:** Distribution of trip speed for all multimodal modes.

## Beautiful world of short mobility

No other feature of human mobility contains as deep an ideological mindset as our trip distance profile. Depending on our desire, we travel a certain distance. As revealed earlier, urban trips are full of short trips. So, it remains a mind-boggling puzzle why and how we ended up with our interconnected and mega mobility infrastructures mostly dedicated to long-distance trips. The answer is found in a simple trip distance distribution profile that describes what percentage of our trips are short, medium, or long. As indicated in Chapter 3, a traditional travel survey invariably asks the wrong questions about the travel diary and mobility experiences. It does not define what a trip is. The survey, whether it's by landline, mobile phone, online or paper-based, asks people to report their trip, distance, origin, and destination, even though their short or medium trips are the most frequent but nearly impossible to remember. And the surveyors know about this unreliability of human memory. Yet every survey still asks deeply flawed questions. Naturally almost everyone reports mostly long-distance and 'important' trips (i.e., typical work or long-distance trips). As indicated in Fig. 4A.9, a census or travel survey (such as Ontario's Transportation Tomorrow Survey) shows nearly the nonexistence of short trips and a sudden jump in trip frequency after 10 km. This is extremely illogical, physically impossible, and deeply unscientific. Yet this deeply flawed travel data collected is often fiercely defended by 'top' mobility experts, wrongly and knowingly claiming their "travel information is reliable" (Miller, 2017). Despite the availability of more reliable travel data, mobility systems including travel demand models use deeply flawed questionnaire or paper or telephone-based memory-dependent surveys. Simple example of sharp discrepancy is travel demand data is illustrated in Fig. 4A.13. When the author invited a new source of probed historical data (such as StreetLight), the sharp contrast and unreliability of travel demand particularly for short trips became glaringly visible. Probed real-time smart data showed nearly 60% of vehicle trips stay within compact neighbourhood area (roughly 8 by 8 km area). Adding short trips by transit and activity mobility, total short trips less than 10 km was roughly 75% of total trips. Traditional travel demand only predicted less 35–40% within the same geographic area. This difference has catastrophic consequences on mobility supply planning and implementation. Short trips obviously do not require mega vehicle infrastructures, or expensive transit or rail projects. They require medium trip distance-oriented transit (such as light or bus rapid transit), on-demand transit for shorter trip distances, and numerous walking, cycling, micromobility, or other short trip facilities. Compared to mega mobility, short and medium trip mobility solutions are a city's core mobility needs, but unfortunately short or medium trip mobility facilities are not a good political tool to get votes, not an attractive show-off of government works, and unquestionably not a feasible proposition for the mega loans or funding from financial institutions that usually end in a corrupted project, particularly in developing countries.

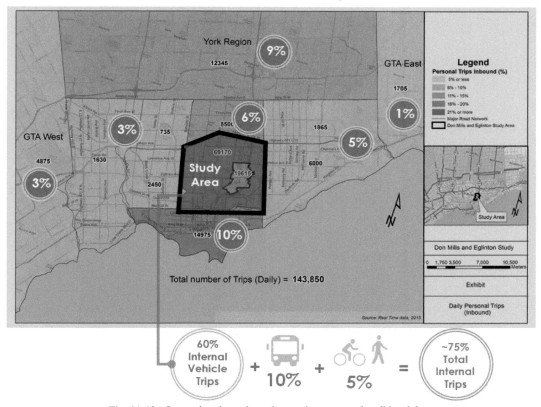

**Fig. 4A.13:** Comparing short trips volume using smart and traditional data.

## *Mobility in stays*

No mobility planning ever looks at our staying time in between our movements, trips, or activities. This practice of ignoring a natural daily life activity is what created the most destructive process of designing mobility spaces without stops. And yet, planners have been warned numerous times not to ignore this fundamental natural human activity. Staying is, however, more complicated. Not all stays are the same. The most common is staying between movements or trips. People stay in between movements for short periods of time. These are usually for food, recreation, short meetings, appointments, work or other errands. These stays however are only a pause between our series of short trips. After a certain time, people move again. The second type of stay is longer. Longer stays outside of the home between trips that are usually work or school related, or another type that requires a longer time to finish. Longer stays outside the home often have the potential for a return trip in the reverse direction. Some trips may not reverse but continue to the next work location or activity outside the home. The third type of stay is usually a longer, overnight stay at home, and is usually a two-way trip. The of mobility in stay has profound impact on placemaking approach. Based on these findings, a series of poetic of space concepts are introduced in this chapter.

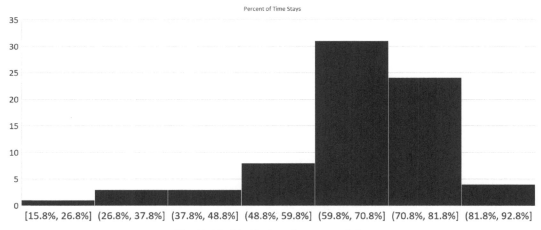

**Fig. 4A.14:** Distribution of our stay periods.

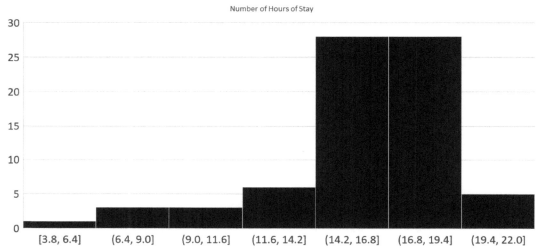

**Fig. 4A.15:** Distribution of short duration stay periods (except home, work, or other long stays).

# CHAPTER 4B
# A Shifting Multimodal Mobility Ecosystem Framework

*"The mind is like an iceberg. It floats with one-seventh of its bulk above water."*
—Sigmund Freud

## The Broader Framework of a Shifting Multimodal Mobility Ecosystem

Mode code provides a profound understanding and insights to develop a new foundation of mobility planning and design. Most of the findings are truly looking at fine-tuned mobility activity that practically removes most of the ideological links to 'function-only' and a deeply cartesian colonialist mindset. But it's not enough to remove systematic bias, repressed elements embedded in culture and social inequality built from socioeconomic conditions. We can never be separated from our surroundings, but we can be aware of systematic flaws and address them head-on. Inspired by the mobility code findings, this section proposes the broader framework of a shifting mobility. Broader principles are a human resonance concept to incorporate our differences, a mobility boundary to avoid the unsafe planetary zone, mobility emergency to prepare and adapt for client emergencies, and shifting the normal concept for right-sizing infrastructure including safety and infrastructure supply and the implementation framework. These broader principles are applied for each new and creative approach to solve complex mobility planning and design principles in the rest of the book.

### *A human resonance concept*

Most mobility system planning, and design process is based on the ideal body and its performance. This approach mimics the ancient tradition of reasoning, rationality, and idealizing an unreal human, particularly in art, culture, and social norms. In the modern era the "representative human" in traditional anthropometry[8] was borrowed from the colonial period's ideology of the "Caucasian European male" to firmly establish that all products, spaces, and facilities are designed around this hardline utilitarian approach. During the cultural changes in the 1970s and the current techno feudalism era (Varoufakis, 2020) of social media we're manipulating the same ideology under a new banner of gender, race, age, and other social and cultural variations. This segmentation of humans has created new social inequalities despite its good intention of diversity.

This book proposes a detour from the rigid paradigm of planning and design and explores a fresh new approach to an old quandary. Typical mistakes in engineering approaches are focused on

---

[8] Anthropometry is the study of human body measurement that characterizes human body with linear distances between anatomical landmarks or circumferences at predefined locations.

biased, utility-based, and linear practices of picking one number or a single dimension for all facility design, typically known as the 'one-size-fits-all' mindset. A new human design approach proposes to include the existence of different aspects of human psychology (Freud, 1901) and include the differences among humans due to different ages, socioeconomic, cultural, and social conditions. Different aspects can be explained by different angles and viewpoints. The approach intentionally incorporates into the typical planning and design processes of city building. The premise is simple – a city is nothing but people. With the over 37 trillion cells of our body starting from only two cells (Bianconi et al., 2013), the complex variations of the human body (Kachlík et al., 2020), different layers of the mind (Cherry, 2020) and the interaction between them is the basis of this refreshing new concept. The human is the only species born with both conscious and unconscious layers. Our built environment, particularly mobility systems, rarely includes unconscious layers or conditions in its building process. The human resonance concept incorporates both layers of human existence in a meaningful and practical way to avoid the most common form of exclusion and improve equity through the mobility system building process. This section describes the human resonance concept in two layers of human status and how it influences planning and design process. To understand it at ground level, street crossing (walking speed and crossing distance) examples will be used as practical examples to illustrate the effectiveness of this new concept.

- **Visible and Conscious Level:** Our most conscious level would see the physical human in a variation of forms and ranges in behaviours. The first layer of this new understanding comes from recognizing the complex variations of humans from different backgrounds. On a conscious level, we see humans in certain shapes, sizes, and forms. This new imaginary human for planning and design would begin by recognizing variation in human form (Azouz, 2005) and develop ranges of values used for mobility facility and services. Instead of specific size or shape of mobility facility or infrastructure, the variation would allow for the modification of the mobility system's elements, parameters, and assumptions. This step is a vast improvement over the standard reference person that only accounts for the standard person as a single parameter of design and excludes most people in our society using the facility. This change avoids "the mechanical human" approach usually practiced or perceived in the scientific research process. For instance, humans cross a street with a walking speed from 1.0 m/s to 1.2 m/s due to variation of human demography. A default speed of 1.2 m/s is typically used for the "average standard person" which excludes everyone else other than the healthy Caucasian male. The second layer would come from adding human body conditions, ages, and variations in age-related mental stages from social, cultural, and geographic perspectives. This would exclude the possibility of discounting human conditions such as adding a ramp for wheelchairs after the facility is built. Instead, this layer would be the doorway to including "indifferent to our differences" (Menon, 2015) when it is designed in the first place, avoiding a flawed and expensive approach of adding "additional features", and subdividing mobility systems for women, seniors, children, and people with physical limitations. For instance, walking speed reduced to 0.9 m/s for senior males and 0.8 m/s for senior females. Crossing distance and timing designed for younger and healthy person would exclude almost all seniors. The final layer is adding an 'unmeasurable' variation to ensure other unknown variations are included in city facility or services planning and design. Despite all our attempts, additional variation in design parameters may still rise in the future due to changes in geography, society, or technological improvements. Those additional ranges in planning and design elements will allow for unknown future variation. For instance, parents with children or persons with physical limitations or mental conditions may not be able to cross in time. A lower walking speed may help but there is a limit to picking a lower speed. In this case, the crossing distance needs to be reduced by new geometric design parameters (such as a tight radius, or curb extension).

- **Invisible and Intangible Level:** As a human, psychoanalysis has established our unconscious mind as a collection of thoughts, memories, urges and feelings that are beyond human consciousness (Freud, 1955). A human uses subconscious and unconscious levels (Sousa, 2011) to display consciousness, and understand or recognize another human, develop memories and knowledge, and recognize environments. Intangible elements in daily practice are the most difficult tasks but vital to avoid unintentional inequality. The approach proposes the three layers of mechanism to develop mobility ecosystem consist of facility, spaces, and services for inhabitants. The first layer incorporates our preconscious level[9] (Sugarman and Kanner, 2002), linking our feelings, emotions, and preconceptions. The central premise from which most engineering assumptions came is the colonial utility myth that the human is the rational species. The adoption of this ancient Greek reasoning and ideology inserted a fatal flaw in city planning and in the traditional engineering design process that produced a modern, dysfunctional mobility system built around vehicles. As a matter of fact, humans form their reasoning based on irrational and incomplete information (Smith, 2019). These irrational elements can be indirectly measured or added through qualitative elements as a design feature. A simple example is how our emotions and perception affect how and what we see (Zadra and Clore, 2011) in places or streets, and making the decision to linger or not is entirely based on the perceived safety of that specific street design. For instance, children or persons with mental illness cross at a very low walking speed such as 0.7 m/s. In some instances, this speed can be used as a design parameter, especially for signal timing or crossing facilities for local streets, internal intersection, and transit facilities. Another solution would be using social, cultural, and natural elements through green and human space concepts to reinvigorate our lack and reconnect community through innovative space creation ideas. These ideas eliminate the number of crossing locations by partially or fully closing streets and reducing crossing distances by geometric design. The second layers would be the drivers and desires of the mind. Desire is a function that all humans experience (Lacan, 1973). The existence of several independent unconscious behavioural guidance systems (perceptual, evaluative, and motivational) is now well known (Bargh and Morsella, 2008). Our desire is reflected in mobility behaviours and shapes our activity in spaces. For instance, our unconscious desire to find the shortest path as a pedestrian, our repeated pattern in cycling in public spaces or intersections or finding the hotspot of places to meet with friends and family are determined mainly by our desire to combine drive with becoming part of the collective community. Several new forms of desire analysis, and multimodal eco-mobility hubs to link our desired paths and hotspots are a few cornerstone ideas in this book that reinvent our stationary and moving places. These concepts are described later in this chapter and throughout the entire book for various mobility mode ecosystems. Using these tools, a network approach to active mobility facilities would find the shortest and safest path to reducing the number of crossings or avoid a crossing at all. The final layer is the provision of uncertainty in human experience. Connections processed between our body and mind are currently known but remain an unknown mechanism. As presented in this chapter, the unique pattern of individual mobility is displayed, and referred to here as mobility code and its DNA elements. But how our body receives the signal from our unconscious mind to repeat an individual, group, or collective pattern is a process of connecting physical traits (like genes) to our mind. This process ultimately forms things in human nature through the long path of evolution. Evolutionary biologists proposed the existence of the field through resonance process (Sheldrake, 1995). Field theory in physics attempted to integrate a realistic description of causality into truly complex hierarchical structures (Ellis, 2005), however, it remains unknown. The presence of this connection to uncertainty excludes it from the city planning and system design process. However, we must make provisions for this uncertainty in mobility mode development, in mobility service planning, and in designing facilities to make sure we understand that a child can run out from a sidewalk or crosswalk due to their lack of safety perceptions, or a senior can stop or slow down due to health complications in a pedestrian

---

[9] The contents of the conscious mind include all the things that we are actively aware of.

crossing. For instance, many European cities particularly in the UK and New Zealand use a simple rule or maximum 10 sec pedestrian crossing rule. Using the time and lowest speed described earlier (for children), the maximum crossing distance would be reduced to just a two narrow lane width in one direction. This means four travel lane city streets are the maximum size of street that can be reasonably safe for all human beings. This includes the possibility of six-lane or wide streets if they're being widened for transit or active mobility facility. Adding these uncertainty ranges as a preventive measure would counteract human-oriented systems or automated machines from running over the person crossing the street and avoid it assuming that they are 'invading' moving spaces. Instead, a reasonable approach would be removing the hard barriers or replacing them with soft separations between the modes.

- **Limits to Humans:** Once a consciousness level is reached about a potential framework that will expand the current rigid status to real humans with all possible and known variations, it would be time to impose self-limits, to avoid infinite variations and the exploitation of the human resonance concept. Though it is practically impossible to list all micro level variations among billions of humans, the mobility community should explore all known variations to avoid grossly excluding most of the population. Once those layers and ranges are identified through the six layers of human resonance concept for planning and design variations that cover all human segments and layers of our minds, it will be time to impose mobility size limits before our wild desires for freedom start to harm collective society benefits. Infinite combinations would also increase costs and complicate the process without meaningful gains.

*"Variability is the law of life."*
—Sir William Osler

## Climate emergency

From Greta Thunberg to Al Gore, the internet and social media is flooded with fluffy, empty talk that rarely explains how our system can achieve resiliency during the client emergency. What is the real meaning of 'emergency'? How many systems are already under pressure or passed "the tipping point"? A lack of clear understanding has led in recent years to the development of "feel good" climate emergency plans by many cities without any concrete action plans. The narrow understanding of climate emergency (Lenton et al., 2019) has created confusion about effective action plans that focus on ineffective mobility issues. These plans typically exclude key urban mobility resiliency actions, directly contributing to an ongoing environmental imbalance and guiding everyone in illusive directions that change very little in the long-term. Some plans did get it right. Some were off-track. For instance, Vancouver's climate emergency plan for 2050 (City of Vancouver, 2020) focuses on highly effective mobility issues such as two-thirds of trips by active mobility and transit, while surpassing 53% sustainable mode share (City of Vancouver, 2018) by 2018, demolishing a waterfront highway viaduct (City of Vancouver, 2015), eliminating minimum parking standards (Chan, 2020), introducing citywide parking permit fees (Howell, 2021), and implementing mandatory travel demand measures (City of Vancouver, 2018), successful electrification plans (City of Vancouver, 2019), remote work options, and many more mobility actions. To the contrary, the City of Toronto's plan (City of Toronto, 2019) has little detail or no directions on how to achieve 75% sustainable mode share (City of Toronto, 2017). The city continues to expand their waterfront highway despite the former chief planner's recommendation to demolish it (Pagliaro and Rider, 2018) and has a much weaker mandate for electrification and travel demand measures or parking requirements. As these two cities in the same country taking on climate change issues with completely different approaches show, it provides a clear picture that mobility resiliency cannot be achieved through hollow plans.

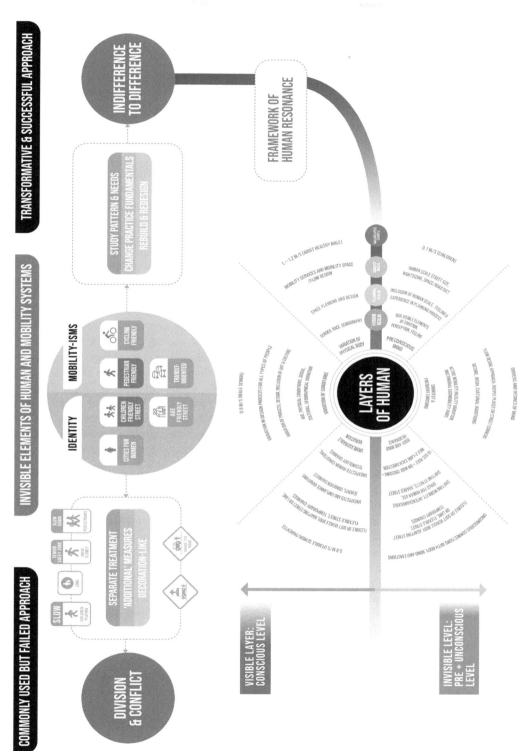

**Fig. 4B.1:** Framework of human resonance concept.

*First Step – What is a climate emergency*: While a planetary boundary established nine critical elements of system status with benchmarks, the Intergovernmental Panel on Climate Change (IPCC) introduced the idea of the tipping point[11] (IPCC, 2018) two decades ago to avoid our false sense of security around a smooth change in climate systems. The "tipping point" threshold of our large-scale planetary system (Lenton et al., 2008) establishes the urgency of climate-related policy discussion to accelerate action plans. IPCC

---

**The Emergency Math[10]**

**1a**: IPCC definition of "Climate Emergency, E",

$$E = R * U = (p * D) * (\tau/T)$$

where:

R = Risk is defined by insurers as probability (p).

$CS_d$ = Carshare demand for each services options j,

**1b**: Amount and types of risk for mobility infrastructure/facility segment is exposed,

$$R_m = C * V * T$$

where:

$R_m$ = Risk of each mobility facility segment

C = the total monetary loss that might occur if the event happens

V = the probability that the amount C will be lost if the hazard occurs

T = probability that the hazard will occur in a given year.

---

reported recently that three critical elements of earth's systems, extreme weather, rise in sea-levels and loss of biodiversity, are already at or have surpassed the tipping point, creating an irreversible and unavoidable impact on the planet (Berardelli, 2021). Mobility emissions are contributing nearing 40%, making it the largest (second largest globally) emission source that needs to change soon because of the climate emergency that could be adopted through mobility resiliency plans.

The climate emergency (E) is defined as the product of risk and urgency. Risk is defined by insurers as probability multiplied by damage. Urgency is defined in emergency situations as reaction time to an alert divided by the intervention time left to avoid a bad outcome. An emergency refers to the conditions where both risk and urgency are high. If reaction time is longer than the intervention time left ($\tau/T > 1$), the situation cannot be reversed. The IPCC and other studies predict the intervention time left to prevent tipping could already have shrunk toward zero and the reaction time to achieve net zero emissions is 30 years at best. This timeframe is the first and the most critical step to set the stage for the maximum implementation timeframe of mobility resiliency plans.

*Second Step – What is mobility resiliency?* Urban transportation systems are vulnerable to congestion, accidents, weather, special events, and other costly delays. Whereas typical policy responses prioritize reduction of delays under normal conditions to improve the efficiency of urban road systems, analytic support for investments that improve resilience (defined as system recovery from additional disruptions) is still scarce. The risks to critical infrastructure from hazards are increasing globally. These hazards can include natural, technological, social, and political hazards, each of which can occur with a varying degree of predictability.

The complex layers of the transportation system make the tasks of resilience planning more difficult than other infrastructure systems. Multimodal passengers or freight systems, multifaceted impacts on society and multilevel design, operation, and management make it difficult to find weaknesses in a transportation system before it faces a sudden disruption, in many cases an entire system collapse. A robust transport system requires learning how to absorb temporary shocks and implement long-term rebounds for operational and functional continuity from an unexpected disruption.

Resilience planning and design, however, a new field of understanding underlies a system robustness, or weakness, under future possible scenarios of disruption from system shocks. It is not full proofing the system, rather it's preparing a framework that will be able to face a situation without major surprises. Since this knowledge is relatively new, confusion exists on how and what

---

[10] This definition was adopted form emergency math article (Lenton et al., 2019).

[11] The term "tipping point" commonly refers to a critical threshold at which a tiny perturbation can qualitatively alter the state or development of a system.

can be done to create system resilience. Often traditional risk analysis is assumed as resilient in systems. Resilience, however, is not stable against risk. Rather, it identifies that the components of a system may be vulnerable and provides a framework for procedures for a speedy recovery when unstable conditions appear, during or after a disruption.

In general, resilience is the ability of households, communities, and nations to absorb and recover from shocks, while positively adapting and transforming their structures and means for living in the face of long-term stresses, change, and uncertainty (Mitchell, 2013). A resilient transportation system is one which could:

(i) anticipate and absorb potential disruptions from social, physical, and environmental perspectives;

(ii) develop adaptive means to accommodate changes within or around the multilayered and multimodal system; and,

(iii) establish preparation, operational and speedy response behaviours aimed at either building the capacity to withstand the disruption or recovering as quickly as possible after an impact.

The influencing factors common to general layers of resilience are to: (i) anticipate; (ii) absorb; (iii) adapt; (iv) recover.

Based on guiding principles and components of resilience, resilience engineering was recently developed to implement resiliency into key transportation systems. Practical resilience engineering must consider how organizations and systems function in totality. Four basic abilities should be considered to give an overview of how an organization or system functions: how it responds, how it monitors, how it learns, and how it anticipates. Urban mobility that comprises resiliency should incorporate these four capabilities and suggest how it can be established and managed and how mobility systems should be managed during disruptions.

### Systemwide mobility network resiliency

From an overall system resilience understanding, the resiliency often contradicts system stability or the general sustainability of the transportation system.

The resilience system can be unstable (Meadows, 2008). A strong resilient transportation system prepares for short or long-duration disruptions to restore unstable situations. Stable transportation systems, such as smooth vehicle traffic flow, may appear stable until a disruption completely breaks its backbone, leading to a collapse and an inability to restore itself. An alternative network, such as transit or an active mobility network, may provide a quicker recovery option to rebound and restore the basic system.

Similarly, sustainable mobility is often referred to as a diverse system, to provide alternatives to vehicle usage in cities. While a sustainable system requires less space and energy, it is equally vulnerable to future disruptions. The recent rise in rideshare or on-demand systems diverting transit, walking, and cycling trips is the best example. Without tackling infinite demand, unsustainable increases in sustainable infrastructures will lead to similar financial and resource pressure on the broader mobility system. Resiliency is not a substitute for sustainable development, but a necessary component.

The concept of resilience is difficult to see or feel. Constant adaptability between transportation system components through various interactions with social, cultural, or physical environment can be viewed through the lens of transportation resiliency. We live in Complex Adaptive Systems (Levin, 1998), in which a perfect understanding of the individual parts does not automatically convey a perfect understanding of the whole system's behaviour. It is assumed that a Complex Adaptive System has the following characteristics:

- Sustained diversity and individuality of components;
- Localized interactions among those components; and,
- An autonomous process that selects from among those components, based on the results of local interactions, a subset of replication or enhancement.

In brief, a whole-system viewpoint will not provide a "crystal ball" look into the future and enable us to predict these types of disruptions. But instead, it will provide a better framework (Martinson, 2017) to understand why these changes are effective and how we can frame our policies and practices to recognize these new contexts.

## System resilience indicators for transportation

As a result of this invisibility of resilience in transportation networks, measuring and monitoring programmes have been developed and studied to provide metrics that would help indicate the health of a resilient system. Often the phrase "what matters, gets measured" or "what is measured, gets managed" is used. System indicators have been suggested for resiliency to provide something to manage and advance a more resilient system. These indicators are from guidelines published by the OECD for the analysis of a resilient system (OECD, 2014) and illustrated in Fig. 4B.2:

- System resilience indicators (outcome indicators) look at the resilience of the main components of the system over time, including how the overall well-being of people and the system is affected when shocks occur. For example, how political capital is affected by an actual earthquake, or how social capital is affected by a new or escalating conflict. These indicators should be complemented by negative resilience indicators.
- Negative resilience indicators look at whether people are using strategies to boost resilience that may have negative impacts on other areas of the system, e.g., turning to crime to deal with unemployment; or negative impacts on certain vulnerable people, such as by reducing the number of meals eaten a day or taking children out of school.
- Process indicators ensure that the resilience roadmap is being used in policy making and programming.
- Output indicators show the results of implementing different parts of the resilience roadmap.
- Proxy impact indicators help show the results of resilience programming. These must be used with caution but can be necessary when other more nuanced measures (such as system resilience indicators) are difficult to create, or difficult to communicate to a specific target audience.

Possible metrics that could be used to monitor the resiliency of a transportation system are shown in the exhibit below. The scope of the system that you are concerned with will determine the

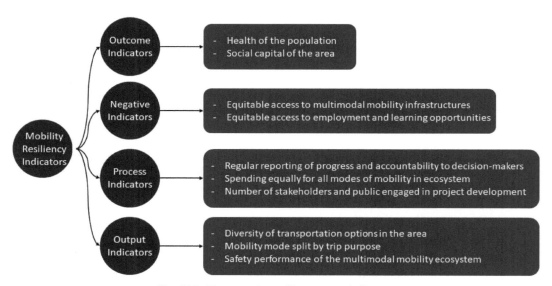

**Fig. 4B.2:** Transportation resilience system indicators.

headings or parts of the system that are evaluated. Then, these various parts of the system and the associated well-being can be mapped. The monitoring of the various parts is necessary to determine how the system is performing over time.

### Basic elements of transportation network assessment

Various researchers (Mostashari et al., 2013) defined two resilience metrics and proposed a modelling framework for assessing the resiliency of regional road networks. Two basic metrics of assessment are travel time between network nodes and environmental resilience due to delays. The first metric, travel time, is used to measure the impact of disruptions to travel time between network nodes. The second metric is environmental resiliency that is used to capture the increase in environmental impact due to delays. The researchers used multiple performance and level of service metrics, taking into consideration the impact of recovery and adaptation time. They defined four ways that resiliency can be integrated into a system including a reduction in vulnerability, an increase in adaptive capacity, agile response, and effective recovery. The resilience measurement process for regional networks is called the Networked Infrastructure Resilience Assessment (NIRA) as illustrated in Fig. 4B.3.

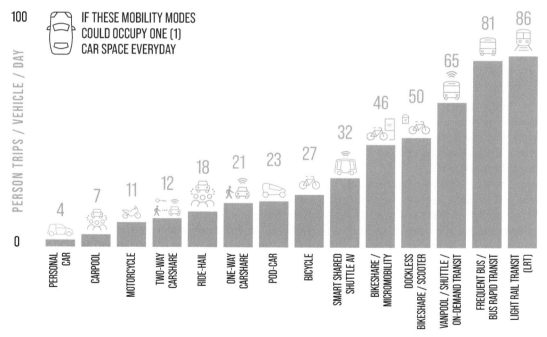

**Fig. 4B.3:** Basic elements of assessing the transportation network resilience.

### Measuring resilience

This section touches briefly on two basic approaches to a resiliency measuring system developed for disruptive events and potentially applicable to measuring mobility resilience.

*Conceptual Framework – Community Resilience*: Scientists and researchers in various disciplines (Bruneau et al., 2003) have been proposing both a conceptual framework and quantitative measures to define the resilience of communities during a disruptive event and its impact on the transportation network. One of the common approaches is to define resilience in terms of the four Rs that are listed and defined in the bullets below.

- Robustness: "The inherent strength or resistance in any system to withstand a given level of stress or demand without degradation or loss of functionality."
- Redundancy: "Ability of a system to satisfy the functional requirements using alternate options, choices, and substitutions in the event of disruption, degradation, or loss of functionality."
- Resourcefulness: "The ability to identify problems, establish priorities, and mobilize resources and services in emergencies to restore the system performance."
- Rapidity: "The speed with which losses are overcome and safety, serviceability, and stability are re-achieved."

*TOSE Approach*: The four Rs approach was later integrated into the conceptual framework to provide four dimensions of community resilience including Technical, Organizational, Social, and Economic (TOSE).

- Technical: "This dimension refers to the physical properties of the system or its components to resist the loss in functionality when a disruptive event occurs. It also includes physical components that add redundancy to the system."
- Organizational: "This dimension refers to the capacity of institutions or organizations to manage the physical components of the system and improve disaster related organizational performance and problem solving."
- Social: "This dimension is formed by measures concerned with lessening the negative consequences due to loss of critical services following a disaster upon a community."
- Economic: "This dimension is related to capacity to reduce both direct and indirect disaster-induced economic losses."

In the resilience framework, resilience of a community is measured by the difference between the ability of community's infrastructure to provide services prior to the occurrence and expected ability of infrastructures to perform after an environmental, technical, or abrupt incident. Each of these dimensions can be used to quantify measures of resilience for various types of physical and organizational systems.

Community seismic resilience is "the ability of social units (e.g., organizations, communities) to mitigate hazards, contain the effects of disasters when they occur, and carry out recovery activities in ways that minimize social disruption and mitigate the effects of future earthquakes." They conceptualized the broader definition of resilience in terms of system performance, which states, "resilience can be understood as the ability of the system to reduce the chances of a shock, to absorb a shock if it occurs (abrupt reduction of performance), and to recover quickly after a shock (reestablish normal performance)." This concept can be represented in the "resilience triangle concept", as shown in Fig. 4B.4, representing the loss of network functionality from damage and disruption. The triangle's

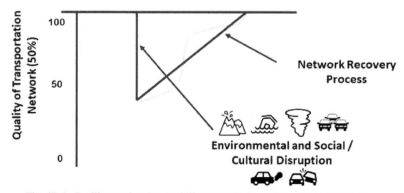

**Fig. 4B.4:** Resilience triangle – Mobility network disruption and recovery process.

depth represents the severity of the system's performance loss, and the length of the triangle shows the time needed for recovery. The area within the resilience triangle relates directly to the resiliency with smaller areas indicating greater resilience. Actions, behaviours, and properties of social units, organizations and networks all contribute to reducing the area of the resilience triangle.

## *Shifting normal – A resilient travel demand management approach*

Instead of accommodating travel demand in unsustainable or sustainable ways, reducing travel demand by not making trips or shifting them toward non-peak periods has become the focus of the recent mobility policy targets of many city governments. Travel demand measures avoid building the unnecessary or redundant mobility infrastructures or services that may not be needed when a condition changes. For instance, work-from-home measures during the Covid-19 pandemic caused the largest reduction in travel demand ever experienced, in almost every country.

The basic framework of travel demand measures remains, however, a source of confusion among mobility planners. This confusion often giving a wrong impression to decision makers and politicians about their effectiveness and the scale of their impact. This section proposes a brief description of a comprehensive travel demand framework that captures broader travel demand issues and identifies the critical components to providing a clear path to the end goal of reducing mobility demand.

1. *'Normal' – Conventional approach*: The traditional city building approach toward a mobility system is the typical response of expanding infrastructures. Whether adding additional travel lanes or adding expensive transit or rail services, traditional building assumes travel demand will grow infinitely and there is no way to manage mobility demand (Ohta, 1998). This is the typical approach of our consumer-focused philosophy that assumes resources are infinite or technology can always overcome resource limitations to continue ever-expanding demand in the future. The approach, however, rarely considers the tremendous pressure we exert on the planet's boundary, pushing it to an unsafe zone. Social, cultural, or environmental conditions remain external forces and are excluded from the system building process. With system unsafe zone disasters repeating at regular time intervals (Karatani, 2011), this vicious cycle of increased costs and risks will ultimately become unsustainable. And when disaster strikes from repressing its hidden flaws, the mobility system will collapse within a short period of time (Fig. 4B.5). While it can temporarily go back to 'normal', the system flaws will however lead to another collapse, generating a never-ending cycle of failures.

2. *"Shifting Normal" – Resilient approach*: Instead of going back to illusive 'normal' conditions, the shifting normal approach identifies a practical and reasonable way to avoid generating demand at source. With reduced demand only requiring selected and limited sustainable mobility facility or services improvement, and due to its low-carbon footprint and low-cost nature, the shifting normal approach is sustainable, in longer periods, and builds its own resilient capacity to finish against shifting conditions. Three fundamental travel demand strategies to reduce emissions from the transportation sector, collectively known as the 'Avoid-Shift-Improve' approach (Strompen et al., 2012), are gradually being commonly accepted due to the prospect that future road improvements cannot satisfy unlimited traffic growth (Fig. 4B.5). By combining multimodal ecosystems including new and shared mobility services through a mobility-as-a-service integrator platform, the shifting normal approach to reducing mobility would use these three fundamental approaches. Obviously, this approach would need a new mobility government set-up. It would need a new demand management body for developing demand control measures. It would need to create incentive programmes and introduce true pricing policies for mobility services by removing wasteful subsidies. The digital platform including IoT (the Internet of Thing) is already playing a critical role after the Covid-19 pandemic in various hybrid work and daily necessity activities. And finally, deployment

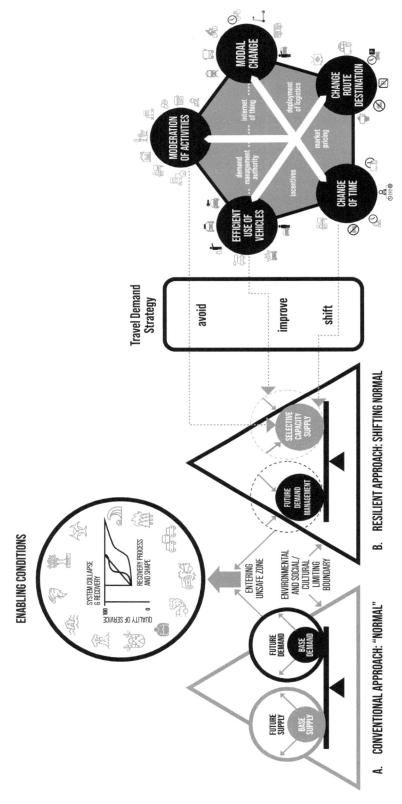

**Fig. 4B.5:** Traditional travel demand and limited capacity concept.

resources and various logistical systems need to come together to implement the travel demand measures.

This approach is closely linked to planetary system components, particularly the mobility boundary approach (see next section) developed by the author of this book.

## *Identifying safe boundary for a multimodal ecosystem*

The new mobility ecosystem focusing on "shifting mobility" will need to assess, measure, and integrate every possible element of a new supply system and connect the system components on a planetary scale. To develop this new mobility boundary, the approach incorporates several pioneering and recent concepts in approaches to mobility system and city building. The conceptual mobility ecosystem framework was built on the premise that physical space constraints and economic and resource constraints will increasingly set the "safe operating limits" of a city's carrying capacity, i.e., in recognition of the basic philosophy and science of "planetary boundary" (Steffen et al., 2015). It also recognizes that our precious and limited resources need careful consideration (Berg, 2011) before we consume all resources and leave very little for future generations.

Identifying future aspects of the symbiotic relationship between the six fundamental interactive elements in a mobility ecosystem, the proposed shifting mobility approach (see Fig. 4B.3) envisions a novel urban morphology, shapes a new experience of urban space, and turns unexplored assets into an ecosystem of vibrant, sustainable innovation. The concept is built on six fundamental elements (and associated planning policies) of the mobility ecosystem: (1) healthy environment, low-carbon footprint, and clean energy; (2) smart growth principles using multimodal ecosystem; (3) sociability and livability by enhancing social capital and innovation; (4) smart and easy access to all types of mobility services; (5) sustainable safety by reducing crash risk and severity; and (6) very low impact and resilient infrastructures that prioritizes sustainable and shared uses.

## *Elements of mobility boundary*

Elements of six mobility boundaries are generally intended to be included in the official plan with policy targets including key indicators (policy priority and targets are illustrated in Fig. 4B.3). These elements including policies will address fundamental constraints to identify the limits or boundaries of mobility system growth and improve human well-being[12] (Millennium Ecosystem Assessment Board, 2005). Associated planning policies depend on the following elements:

*Healthy environment, low-carbon footprint, and clean energy*: These constraints are pollution thresholds for mobility sources imposed by regulatory policy or local, regional, or nationwide acceptable limits, carbon emission targets set by city and global climate change thresholds for transportation, and low-carbon energy sources for mobility systems set out by local or nationwide green energy policies.

*Smart Growth*: Smart growth principles linking the right mobility mix by limiting the "pointed density" around transit stations that hurts urban growth (Gordon and Shirokoff, 2014) while incorporating the missing-middle such as mid-rise housing options for car-lite mobility along rapid transit routes. Expanding the "gentle density" (Smart Growth, 2017) concept[13] for car-less mobility form and transition to lower density areas will address the current formula relying too much on the density of the transit node only. These principles and constraints are based on environmental outcomes and are generally excluded from city growth policies. For instance, total on-road $CO_2$

---

[12] Human well-being has multiple constituents, including basic material for a good life, freedom and choice, health, good social relations, and security.

[13] Gentle density is attached, ground-oriented housing that's denser than a detached house, but with a similar scale and character such as duplexes, semi-detached homes, rowhouses, or even stacked townhouses.

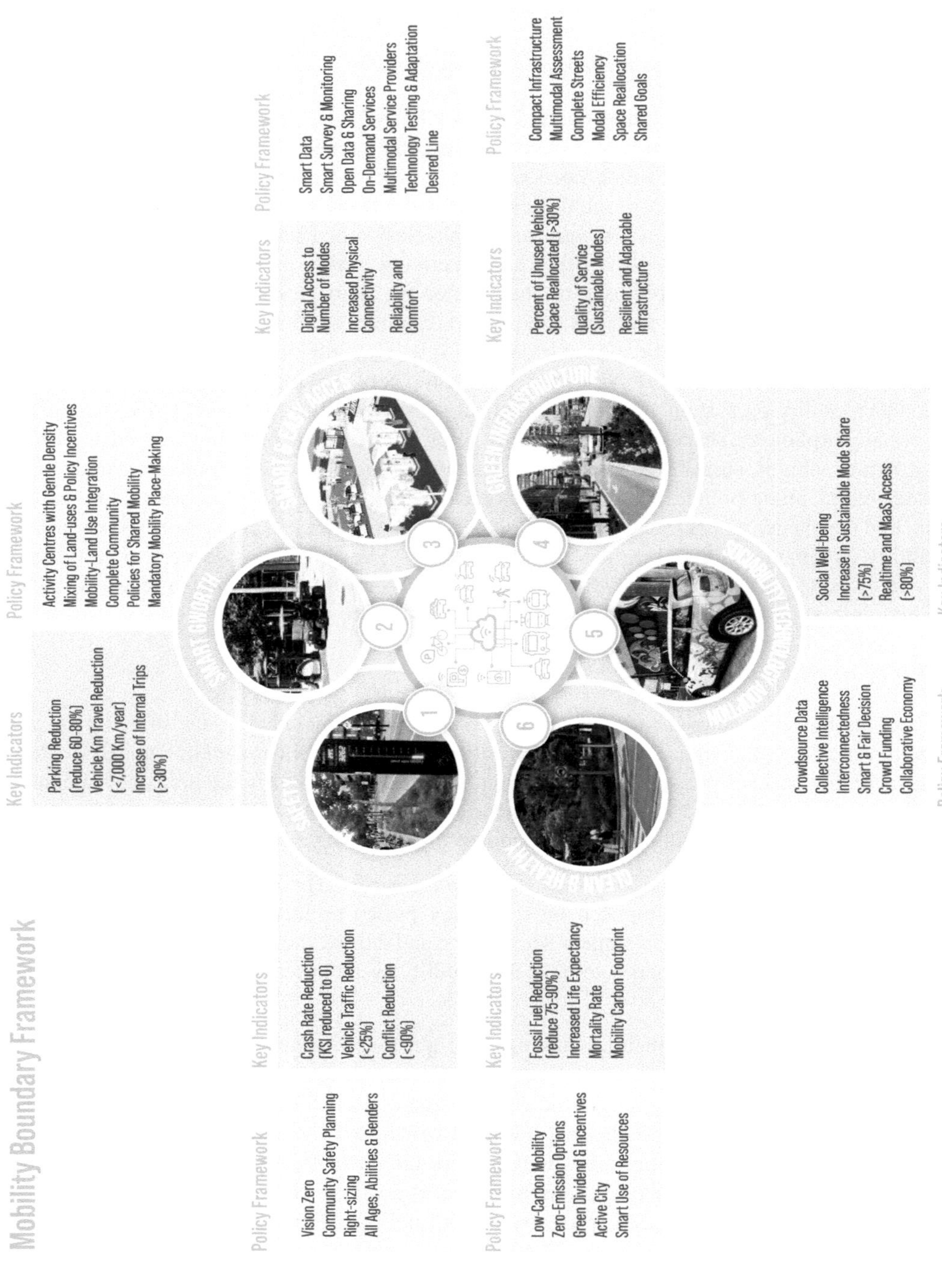

**Mobility Boundary Framework**

**Policy Framework**

**Key Indicators**

Parking Reduction
(reduce 60-90%)
Vehicle Km Travel Reduction
(<7000 Km/year)
Increase of Internal Trips
(>30%)

**Policy Framework**

Activity Centres with Gentle Density
Mixing of Land-uses & Policy Incentives
Mobility-Land Use Integration
Complete Community
Policies for Shared Mobility
Mandatory Mobility Place-Making

**Policy Framework**

**Key Indicators**

Smart Data
Smart Survey & Monitoring
Open Data & Sharing
On-Demand Services
Multimodal Service Providers
Technology Testing & Adaptation
Desired Line

Digital Access to
Number of Modes
Increased Physical
Connectivity
Reliability and
Comfort

**Policy Framework**

**Key Indicators**

Compact Infrastructure
Multimodal Assessment
Complete Streets
Modal Efficiency
Space Reallocation
Shared Goals

Percent of Unused Vehicle
Space Reallocated (>30%)
Quality of Service
(Sustainable Modes)
Resilient and Adaptable
Infrastructure

**Policy Framework**

**Key Indicators**

Social Well-being
Increase in Sustainable Mode Share
(>75%)
Realtime and MaaS Access
(>80%)

Crowdsource Data
Collective Intelligence
Interconnectedness
Smart & Fair Decision
Crowd Funding
Collaborative Economy

**Policy Framework**

**Key Indicators**

Fossil Fuel Reduction
(reduce 75-90%)
Increased Life Expectancy
Mortality Rate
Mobility Carbon Footprint

Low-Carbon Mobility
Zero-Emission Options
Green Dividend & Incentives
Active City
Smart Use of Resources

**Policy Framework**

**Key Indicators**

Crash Rate Reduction
(KSI reduced to 0)
Vehicle Traffic Reduction
(<25%)
Conflict Reduction
(-90%)

Vision Zero
Community Safety Planning
Right-sizing
All Ages, Abilities & Genders

**Fig. 4B.6:** The concept of mobility boundary.

increases rapidly with a population density below 1,650 persons per square kilometre, while per capita emissions decline as density rises (1,650–3,500 persons/sq, km) and emissions begin to rise again as density exceeds 4,000 persons/sq km (Gately, 2015). Optimum density limits and mobility forms to systematically reduce vehicle usage while evaluating emission outcomes.

*Sociability and technology adoption*: Equity for all mobility users raises the most serious social issues, however, they are rarely included as a meaningful planning element in mobility ecosystem development. Network coverage of any new shared, active mobility and transit modes must cover a city's priority neighbourhoods and make facilities available within an acceptable walking distance. Digital mobility should be accessible through various kiosk, vending machine forms, and media and avoid options for only expensive data plan holders. Instead of just stereotypical public consultation, citizen participation, and crowdsource platforms should be part of continuous mobility data collection for continuous and meaningful citizen participation. Social well-being could be achieved by avoiding the polluted highways and streets in a city's low-income or ethnic majority neighbourhoods or avoiding building the dark and ugly parking structures that are now being proposed for autonomous vehicles. These limits set the boundary, develop fast technology adoption in deprived areas, and ensure equitable mobility to everyone.

*Smart and easy access*: All types of mobility services and facility should be equally distributed. Active mobility and reliable mobility network coverage should provide easy access for all citizens, while limiting excessive concentration of higher mobility access to gentrified neighbourhoods only. Excessive access for new mobility in rich neighbourhoods becomes a social equity issue. City policy targets could reverse these trends by requiring the same access to new and affordable modes for deprived neighbourhoods.

*Safety first principles*: Vehicle traffic volume needs to be under a certain threshold to avoid increasing crash risk and severity, particularly for senior citizens, women, children, and other sensitive mobility users. Increasing activity mobility flow reduces risk for all mobility users. Public transit remains one of the safest modes. Sustainable safety principles also impose limits on street size (maximum four lanes on busy streets and three lanes for residential areas) to reduce street-crossing distances. Avoiding high traffic concentration like big-box malls also reduces the risk, particularly for senior citizens' neighbourhood areas.

> *"The current approach, which favours automobiles and punishes only drivers for crashes, is clearly not working."*
>
> —Jennifer Homendy, NTSB Chair

## Safety DNA

Mobility safety plays a central role in increasing active transportation, transit, and shared mobility mode use. However, traffic collisions are traditionally framed as individual and mechanical failures and are treated through 'reactive' engineering practices rather than a 'proactive' structural process.

The Vision Zero movement has swept through almost every city in the last decade. It is a road safety planning approach, that originally emerged in the Netherlands and later in Scandinavian and East Asian countries, where collisions are treated as a preventable disease. The simple premise of "Vision Zero" is to eliminate facility and severe injury from urban streets and highways.

Despite the rise of Vision Zero, the original Dutch or Swedish safety principle lost its way outside of northern Europe. Like Complete Streets, Vision Zero is trapped inside a "band aid" solution mentality that drags safety problems out without systematically addressing them with practical solutions. The evolution of Vision Zero is going through stages of denial and acceptance.

So where did it go wrong and why did European or some east Asian nations succeed? The answer lies in safety culture.

## Framework of Vision Zero

The lack of a general framework, proven safety measures, and associated action plans created a mountain of confusion among road safety practitioners when the Vision Zero concept arrived in North America in the early 2010s. Confusion led to adding Vision Zero as an 'additional' item within the transportation system that had originally created the underlying safety problem. This book proposes a systematic framework for the Vision Zero planning system to better understand the evolutionary stages of safety, develop safety principles, and a process of identifying root causes, and implement action plans via a mobility equity approach.

## Fundamental principles of framework

Three fundamental principles are proposed to guide the process, keep track of the Vision Zero programme and implementation, and prevent it from common pitfalls. The three key guiding fundamentals are:

1. *Safety for everyone*: One of the common failures of Vision Zero is segmenting priority areas while adopting mobility-isms. Priority areas today are children, seniors, vulnerable users, and mobility users of vehicle modes or types. These are the correct priorities, but mobility systems are built for everyone. Segmenting issues and applying band-aid actions has led to separate treatments of each group, 'additional' measures that led to low-impact or no-impact on overall safety outcomes. This created a 'decoration-like' mindset for each group. This also put one issue against another, leading to conflict, division, and opposition against each other. A woman is not a decoration. Children are not ornaments. Seniors are not just numbers. Instead, this book proposes we adopt a "human resonance" concept to identify priority issues, study their needs, determine impacts, change their planning process, adopt or modify design parameters, and redesign using new parameters. This will lead to the creation of facilities or a system that's indifferent regardless of different (Menon, 2015) people, users, or modes.

2. *Change planning and design parameters*: Once all types of demography, users, modes including social, cultural, and human well-being outcomes are identified, it's time to change the planning process and redesign steps or parameters that are typically used by engineers, planners, and system designers. All layers of a human resonance concept should be part of design including variations of size, space, and human conditions that arise from various physical and mental conditions. Ultimately, these changes need to be reflected in professional practice, standards, policies, and ethical guidelines.

3. *Checking limiting boundaries*: Despite good intentions and progressive ideas, our facilities become oversized and overdesigned. Infrastructure DNA (see next section) should take cues from the mobility boundary concept and check that all types of limitations are met, and facility size is kept under the maximum size to avoid detrimental impacts on various demography.

## Keys stages and evolution of Vision Zero

Gradual and persistent transformation is the best and most successful element of the Vision Zero programme. Changing safety culture is not easy due to the existence of mega infrastructures and underlying systems that are built on hidden ideological principles. This section proposes a comprehensive approach and options for Vision Zero programme implementation. Three key principles described earlier need to be put to the test in roughly 10 different stages or layers, starting from less effective, to low, to medium, to high impact safety components.

1. *Awareness*: The first stage of the evolution of Vision Zero was increasing 'awareness', wearing brighter clothing, waving traffic flags, and fixing human behaviour. It was an old approach that found a new place under the banner of "victim blaming" instead of acknowledging the existence of design flaws. Obviously, it did nothing and failed to achieve any safety targets. These attitudes or actions should be identified as negative visions. In real safety education it's crucial to teach everyone when a system has changed toward everyone, not by altering something, blaming, and forcing us to adopt it.

2. *Signs and markings*: The second stage started with fixing signs, pavement markings, and speed limit changes without changing the hardware of street design. It failed again in the face of towering human loss particularly when adopted sporadically and with a fragmented approach. When an entire neighbourhood's speed is reduced, it is relatively more effective but not sufficient when the city's street sizes, and mega scale remains the same.

3. *Enforcement*: Then the third stage arrived with the "band aid" solutions, i.e., sending police, and sporadic red light and speed cameras. These are useful measures only when applied to an entire city but eventually reduced their need through the permanent repairing of design, planning and operational flaws.

4. *Spatial analysis and crash-prone fixes*: Sporadic actions toward severely risky locations with patchwork fixes has had very low impact. In contrast finding 'hotspots' and fixing them temporarily, but preferably permanently, produces higher impacts. But it too eventually will fail if the programme remains only in selected neighbourhoods.

5. *Downsizing facility*: It's a monumental task, but simply applying a narrower pavement, narrower lane width, and hatching/blocking excess spaces is a powerful temporary tool that does not need major funding to get it done in a short period of time. It must, however, be adopted citywide. Corridor specific fixes will not lead to major risk reduction.

6. *Citywide temporary changes*: Initial funding may not be available but citywide temporary changes can fix design flaws with temporary bollards and pavement markings. This stage also fixes a few crash-prone streets or locations through real design changes and takes advantage of continuous fixes through redevelopment, road resurfacing, or reconstruction projects. While this is close to an effective approach, with limited intervention it will fail to achieve its overall target.

7. *Priority neighbourhood-wide approach*: At this stage instead of changing designs for selected corridors or locations, the city has enough funding to fix temporarily or permanently every corner, intersection, street, and mobility services points for an entire neighbourhood. Permanent fixes for entire neighbourhoods will also provide a lesson learning opportunity to avoid mistakes in the next neighbourhood safety fix.

8. *Vehicle restriction*: Despite all fixes, vehicle volume itself is a safety threat. Vehicle-restriction is necessary and mandatory for a permanent safety fix. It can start with closing streets in the summertime, closing redundant streets permanently, and making them active-mobility-only, closing parts of streets or lanes, and finally closing the most popular and vulnerable user risk-prone streets from vehicles permanently. This approach needs careful maintenance, services, and emergency operations review, and to provide priority vehicle access when needed.

9. *Physical design changes*: Removing all design flaws is the ultimate fix. Redesigning and downgrading facility to a human scale is the most impactful of all changes but needs time to achieve. But if policy is adopted, a city can take advantage of yearly construction, development projects, renovations, and minor street fixes, and combine all changes while the city goes through a 20-year cycle.

10. *Combining physical design, vehicle restriction and a citywide approach*: Only a few cities eventually arrived at the true Vision Zero approach: removing the true cause of safety failure, i.e., reducing vehicles and eliminating all design flaws and installing components that are safer

by design, street by street, and fixing safety problems citywide. Pontevedra is a unique example in Spain. The city achieved the illusive zero death toll on their streets from 2011 to 2018 after banning or reducing vehicles and parking in key locations (Burgen, 2018), establishing a car-free zone, calming traffic with reduced speeds to 10–30 kmph, and changing street designs to reflect the speed reduction. Making the most of city areas for active mobility won Pontevedra a "Road Safety Award" (ETSC, 2020). The same is true for Norway's, South Korea's, and Japan's countrywide safety success.

# EFFECTIVENESS OF SAFETY COUNTERMEASURES

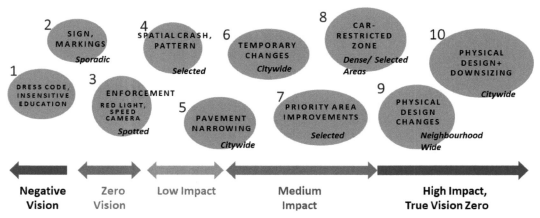

**Fig. 4B.7:** Effectiveness and stages of the Vision Zero programme and implementation.

*"There is more to life than increasing its speed."*
—Mahatma Gandhi

### Removal of design flaws – Dangerous by design

Repeated compulsion of failure is built into the structure of most systems that mainly focus on only one solution to fix all problems. The vehicle-oriented system has the same repetitive compulsion of failure due to repressed (Karatani, 2011) design flaws in the mobility system like to the faults of unbridled capitalism. Repeated traffic safety failures every year or every cycle mimic the exact pattern of the fundamental contradiction of unbridled capitalism. These elements are already known, and often referred to as "dangerous by design". Before implementing a vision, these inherent design flaws should be identified, policy should be developed for their removal, and finally redesign and space repurpose principles should be applied.

The most fundamental design flaw is the road widening argument that traditional traffic engineers often claim makes streets safer. No evidence has ever pointed to wider roads as safer. Collisions are often attributed to bad drivers. There are bad drivers. But not all of them are. Reality paints a different picture. As illustrated in Fig. 4B.8, the more the number of lanes there are, the less safe the streets are. Even when a collision rate is used to normalize the effect of traffic volume, the collision rate increases with the higher number of travel lanes. This simple comparison and its analytics are rarely investigated through safety practices.

There are at least 10 design flaws that are more fatal than other plan components (Fig. 4B.9). Details are provided in Chapter 6 of this book. The 10 organization flaws are:

1. Additional travel lanes, increasing crossing distances, increase pedestrian risks.
2. Wider lanes increase speeds and contribute to higher crash rates.

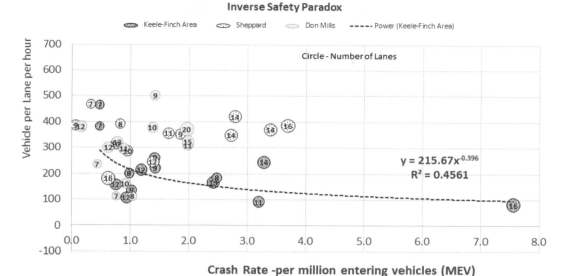

**Fig. 4B.8:** The deteriorating safety performance of the "adding a lane" ideology.

3. Additional 1-metre-wide lanes and additional lanes cause at least a 6% increase in pedestrian crash rates.

4. Dual left-turn lanes increase the number of conflicts with vehicle, cyclists, and pedestrians at crossing locations that ultimately increase collision risks for all users.

5. Frequent driveways increase pedestrian and turning vehicle crash rates.

6. Two-way continuous left-turn lanes with frequent driveways increase turning, cycling, and pedestrian risks.

7. Poor signal design, particularly in high-speed designs over 70 km/h, inherently cause dilemmas during traffic light changes. Aggressive and destructive conditions are unnecessary at intersections which should have been designed for not more than 30 km/h due to complex turning movements and interactions between different users.

8. A wide corner radius is a well-known pedestrian risk and cause of high-speed turning crashes.

9. Right-turn islands also increase speeds and cause high-speed turning crashes among pedestrians.

10. All types of flared, wide, and long right-turn lanes are commonly used in urban areas, wrongly borrowing highway or expressway design principles. However, these design elements encourage high-speed right-turns that are particularly deadly for cyclists, children, and seniors.

There are fundamental reasons why these design flaws lead to catastrophic safety failure. Vision research scientists have revealed the success of measuring minuscule eye movements, generally known as "fixational eye movements" including micro saccades, that may lead to the understanding of the hidden brain mechanisms of human attention while performing a complex task (Susana and Stephen, 2007). During the last four decades, experimental scientists (Moore, 1968) have been warning traffic engineers that drivers can make only a very limited series of responses at complex intersections controlled by traditional traffic control devices. To highlight the foregoing, traffic engineers in collaboration with multidisciplinary expertise could plan and design a system to limit the rate of intake of visual and other forms of information, within the capacity of the user's decision-making limitations. Traffic control devices should not however put the driver in a situation where information is presented simultaneously in different directions. This may simply bring new dangers.

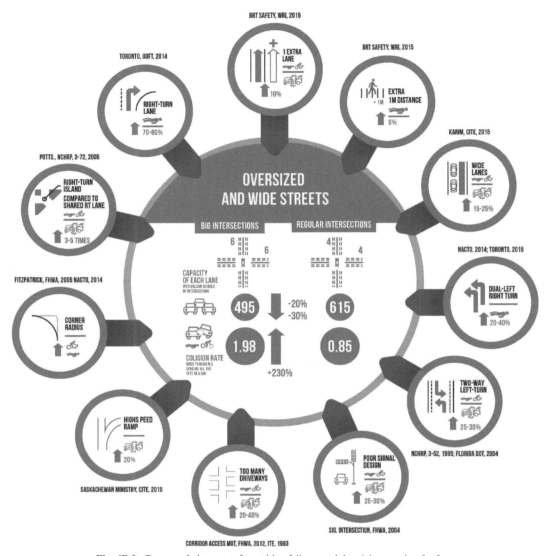

**Fig. 4B.9:** Repressed elements of repetitive failures and the vicious cycle of safety.

Removing the elements of "dangerous by design" will reduce necessary conflicts and stress induced on mobility users and improve overall safety for all users.

### *Adding safer by design*

Once obvious design flaws are eliminated, there are additional proven safety countermeasures that increase safety for all users. Details are provided in both US federal (FHWA, 2017) and urban street design guidelines (NACTO, 2013). These new design concepts assist practitioners in developing priority and permanent street design changes and in establishing safety targets in several stages. Identifying design elements that are safer by design is the last step and high-impact action plans that will accomplish the goal of 'zero' within acceptable timeframes. Instead of fixing safety problems, the process identifies how to redesign and remove the oversized elements of mobility infrastructure that cause recurring collisions. It also brings together safety issues from different demographics, and geographic and social perspectives to ensure equity for all mobility users in all areas of the city.

## Practical approach to implementation

The final step of this proposed systemic framework is to develop action plans that address identified issues through the process of reclaiming and reusing the mobility spaces to improve the overall quality of life of all inhabitants. This process is developed to assist practitioners in avoiding pitfalls, making budget-conscious decisions, and producing maximum benefits by addressing the most critical elements and causes of safety issues in our mobility ecosystems. Some examples of Vision Zero packages are:

1.  *Quick wins approach*: Low-cost and short-term packages include pavement markings for narrowing lanes or delineating excessively wide lanes by hatching, while blocking with bollards the excess spaces that typically cause all types of crash incidences. If applied to neighbourhoods, these quick wins would lead to dramatic changes in crash risks.

2.  *Low-cost temporary vehicle restriction approach*: In addition to temporary and short-term measures, quick and temporary vehicle restrictions are the best combination. These restrictions could be seasonal, include partial street closures, full closures during summers, and neighbourhood traffic diversions or permanent closures of redundant streets segments. They are low-cost safety measures that dramatically reduce traffic volumes in high-risk areas or locations.

3.  *Permanent and strategic approach*: Once full funding for Vision Zero is available in longer-term or capital works or the redevelopment process or combining all possible transportation activities, converting temporary changes to permanent design changes are the ultimate of Vision Zero packages.

In the end, there is one common visible notion of the safest streets. The presence of women in different activities provides a clear sign of safety. On safe streets children move or play without fear. And on the same streets, a senior or person with physical limitations crosses safely.

## Infrastructure DNA

Facilities that are built around a human mobility pattern are a city's ultimate mobility environment. A city's financial and physical health depend on it. Most cities are trapped under an infrastructure burden without having assessed whether we needed a complex network of mobility infrastructure to begin with. Once a complex system (Siegenfeld and Bar-Yam, 2020) is built with its hidden flaws, repetitive failure is imminent and unavoidable (Karatani, 2011). The topic of "scaling down mobility infrastructure" to a human scale remains taboo among city builders. Although the scale of facility in everyday items commonly shapes the daily work of urban planners, urban designers, and transportation engineers/planners, the scaling down and cutting down of unnecessarily fatty infrastructure remains largely overlooked. Overbuilt infrastructures are expansive, unused during off-peak periods, set the stage for serious safety problems particularly off-peak periods, break down frequently and most importantly, create social inequality and exclusion by denying the right to access to sustainable transportation modes. When the concept is applied to redundant mobility infrastructure (ICAU, 2014), or spaces are properly identified in a systematic manner, the system develops its own resiliency to withstand unforeseen events, natural or manmade catastrophes and prevent financial meltdown.

Oversized mobility infrastructures are particularly troubling for developing nations where resource depletion and an energy crisis can bring down an entire country. Building oversized infrastructure without understanding its consequences is especially true for African, South Asian, and Latin American countries where more than half of the people do not own a car. These countries copy and paste many ideas from the western nations believing they will bring prosperity. Without official guidance, many of the policy makers, foreign investors or consultants who often get involved in local projects come without awareness of local context and apply western

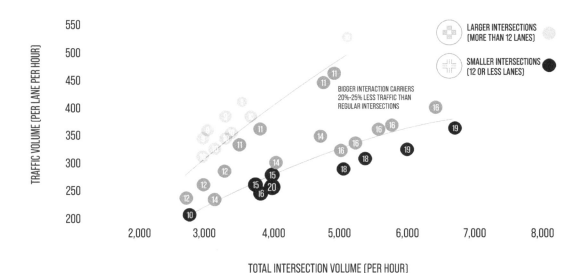

**Fig. 4B.10:** Diminishing capacity returns of "adding a lane" to get more capacity.

context without highlighting the negative impacts of overbuilt and utilitarian western philosophy (North American) that has already created numerous negative impacts through mega streets and highways.

Downgrading mobility infrastructures should be the focus on four major areas to limit enormous resource, energy, and financial strains to survive the low-energy Anthropocene era. As mobility system planners never identified the key aspects and a framework of scaling approach to mobility facilities, this section lists the four major components of mega mobility problems and their corresponding scaling down strategies.

*Limiting lanes – The wider the street, the less we get*: There is a myth among mobility planners that adding infinite amounts of travel lanes will solve congestion problems in cities. Adding lanes to get more capacity is the most widely used practice in traditional traffic engineering without considering the consequences. And it's rooted in capitalism's "upcoming crisis" culture of intimidating users about a future crisis, i.e., constantly making up a nonexistent "congestion disaster". Like capitalism's 'boom-and-bust' never-ending cycle, the crisis of road widening bursts returns after only a few years due to the induced capacity phenomena. And a new crisis is presented by traffic engineers recommending right after another round of widening is completed even though the same approach just failed miserably. The original proposal of getting "more capacity" never materialized. As lanes are added, wide streets experience more delays due to delay caused by traffic control devices and it takes longer for pedestrians to cross the street (Fig. 4B.10). Conflicts arise between the modes, between vehicles going straight or turning. Eventually every lane in a wide street loses its capacity as more lanes are added. This sounds insane but traffic engineering has evolved into a situation that defies all logic. For instance, if we need two litres of milk, the shopkeeper will likely give us two one-litre bottles. But if we need 6 litres, the shopkeeper will give us six 800ml bottles instead of one litre of milk, but we'll pay the 6-litre price. The price paid gets worse when we need more and more. If we need 10 litres, the shopkeeper will give us ten 600 ml bottles of milk, but we'll still pay for the full 10-litre bottles. This sounds insane from the buyer's perspective, but this is exactly what is happening with road widening. Each lane has capacity for roughly 900–1,000 vehicles (i.e., capacity per lane per hour) when the street size is just two lanes. Unit capacity of each lane reduces to 700 when lanes are added to make it a five-lane street. As it is made wider through the lane-adding approach to get more capacity, unit capacity further reduces to 500 or less. This lane-adding practice needs a complete overhaul because it is nothing but a self-destructing strategy for society and every city's budget.

*Limiting of street size*: The ultimate consequences of adding lanes and making mega streets are rarely discussed by the traditional traffic engineering community. But the end results are a widely known scientific phenomenon. Large systems eventually suffer diminishing returns and interject increasing uncertainty. In economics, this is well known as the "law of diminishing returns", i.e., the decrease in marginal (incremental) output of a production process as the amount of a single factor of production is incrementally increased (Pichère, 2015). Humans are not good at interacting with a large and complex system. Human's capacity to handle complex manmade environments should be more carefully explored but is generally ignored in mobility system planning and design. Neuroscientists have pointed out that humans may have approached the hard limit of their ability to process multilayered and complex information (Fox, 2011). Wide streets and complex intersections surpass human capacity to operate in the system safely. Based on these largely known but mostly ignored scientific facts this book proposes to limit street size to 30 mt through the "equitable street code" introduced in the next section. Similarly, more than three-lanes in each direction for an expressway or highway should be scrutinized under the lens of resiliency and resource capacity constraints. Once limits on streets or mobility infrastructures are imposed, mobility planners and engineers will then bring creative planning and design approaches, many of them introduced in space and storage concepts later in this chapter.

Besides dynamic infrastructure size and its limits, the storage problems of vehicles or other mobility modes need to be explored with similar scaling down approaches. This section touches on this briefly but elaborates on parking and storage solutions later in this chapter.

*Limiting parking demand*: Currently most cities assume all persons will eventually own a vehicle and hence mandatory minimum parking spaces are imposed through parking bylaws. This unprecedented and unnecessary practice eventually converted more than half of city lands into barren and empty parking spaces. As vehicle ownership is going down and pay-as-you-go mobility services are growing at an unprecedented rate, cities are gradually abandoning the minimum parking requirement that has no scientific (Shoup, 1999) and practical basis and has become a financial and societal burden (Litman, 2022). Japan and later Singapore introduced the most practical approach to parking, requiring paying appropriately high amounts for parking spaces. Free parking in all locations should be abolished and very restrictive parking except for essential services should be part of all parking policies in urban areas.

*Limiting station footprints*: Similar parking problems but on a gigantic scale exist at or around rapid transit stations. Instead of providing last- and first-mile access, North American and many Middle Eastern and some east Asian cities assume all transit riders are vehicle owners and provide unthinkable free parking spaces in large amounts around transit stations. Instead of higher density mixed-use living spaces, most regional or metro transit stations are lost in a sea of parking spaces. This rampant vehicular transit practice was created by traditional vehicle-oriented transit practitioners. As cities are growing at astonishing paces, lands around the station have become too expansive and park-n-ride practice spaces are being converted into dense mixed-use areas (Bureau of Transportation, 2015). As suggested in Part 2 of this book, only minimal storage for multimodal and high-occupancy vehicles and bus bays should be part of a station footprint. This would dramatically reduce the resources needed for operating and maintaining a transit station.

## The Hidden Framework of Shifting Multimodal Mobility

Providing more choices for the daily activity of humans when we travel remains an unknown to most modern mobility planners. Random assumptions or a fragmented multimodal approach mostly based on a digital platform created the path of repeated failures. Once knowledge is developed and implemented, the multimodal mobility ecosystem provides the greatest flexibility, resiliency, affordability, and adaptability against the constantly shifting environmental, social, and cultural conditions that we live in the 21st century.

A few hidden structures, patterns, and the nature of multimodal mobility often complicate the possibility of becoming a reality when misinterpretation is common among the city builders. The complexity of multiple modes, their local permutation and the combination and seamless connection between the modes remain too complex an ecosystem in cities. This complexity is perceived as a primary barrier to true multimodal mobility. The dynamic behaviours of a multimodal ecosystem add a second layer challenge to exploring its potential at full strength. Dynamic changes between the modes and the constant shifting to a new ecosystem when conditions change shapes the internal framework of multimodal mobility. This shifting pattern emerges from human's travel behaviour changes and habitual patterns in reaction to shifting conditions of surrounding social, cultural, physical, and services changes. Finally, multimodal mobility can only create an ecosystem when its mutual dependence between multiple modes is developed through a natural ecosystem network. Known as "network effect", it distinctly separates itself from unimodal and utility-based automobility systems. When a full, natural network is implemented, the multimodal mobility ecosystem shows its true resiliency compared to extremely vulnerable automobility systems.

This section reveals a few fundamental characteristics of a multimodal system before developing citywide mobility plans, supplying planning, and implementation strategies. Individual vs. collective choice of mobility remains the primary foundation of the multimodal ecosystem. The success of a new ecosystems depends on creating a multimodal-oriented approach that gradually replaces the transit- or auto-oriented flaws that created system vulnerability. A dynamic shift between mobility modes is explained to replace our current flawed approach in mode share practices that harbours a systematic tendency of repeated failures. Finally, a mew mobility form is proposed to bind all the hidden layers of multimodal ecosystems.

### *Personal vs. mass mobility*

An intense clash between individualism and collective commune become a hallmark 20th century ideological conflict, philosophical rupture, and source of societal and political divide. Capitalism needed an individualism fantasy to hide its repressed elements of repetition and predictable cycles of failure. Collective believers walked to the other extreme, believing in a utopian and holistic society, ignoring individual existence and basic human rights. Despite the fall of the Berlin Wall and the demise of collectivism in 1989, the prediction of "the end of history" never materialized (Fukuyama, 1992) in the surreal world of neoliberal democracy and it eventually brought a new world order that essentially split democracy and capitalism (Žižek, 2009), and gave birth to current feudalist capitalism and the liquid economy that often uses collectivism as cultural capital. Mobility systems were drowned in extreme individualism through Fordism and the car was promoted as the freedom tool for each person's personal success. Transit was mostly ignored in western liberal democracies due to its perceived linked to collectivism. In fact, humans have a unique, developed dialectic relationship that captures both worlds and part of both naturally exists within each human. This complex relation is often ignored and was lost in the ideological debates of the last century.

Earlier in this chapter plenty of evidence was provided that every human has their own unique mobility identity, and at the same time they develop a collective mobility pattern. There is in between a form that is often referred to as a group or family form that is neither individual nor collective. Incorporating all three sides into the mobility system could simply avoid all ideological debate and create an ecosystem that captures all aspects of our social structure. Utilizing the findings of mobility code, both sides of the same individual are explained in this section, as well as the hidden links between them.

1. *Individual mobility*: As an individual we develop our unique mobility code through various work, institutional or other individual activities. When a couple moves in together, they still display the behaviours of individuals. While repetitive, daily activity and common destinations can serve individual needs, many personal needs (such as grocery, recreational, seasonal, occasional) are difficult to serve by traditional fixed transit. Increasingly, shared personal mobility options

such as bikeshare, carshare, scooter rental, or delivery options can increase the 'shareability' of vehicles or devices to avoid the negative impact of ownership-based mobility systems. If access, coverage, and affordability factors are addressed through the mobility planning process, individual needs can be satisfied without the need of the 'freedom' of owning a vehicle.

2. *Group or family or proximity mobility*: Between individual and collection mobility, group, or family needs are commonly ignored in typical mobility planning. As a human we tend to travel with family, with our favourite friends, or professionals or to recreational activities as a group. Neither vehicle nor transit systems are ideal for such group travel. On-demand transit, high-occupancy rideshare, on-demand large, shared vehicle systems could conveniently replace the vehicle-oriented trips often assumed as a default for group trips. Group discounts, connecting trips, advanced booking, and other digital mobility options would be able to serve the needs of groups or families.

3. *Collective mobility*: The collective form often works best when a workplace is centred around downtown, with common destinations and a mass amount of people travel in peak times. Traditional transit performs perfectly under these scenarios only if, and it's a big if, access to transit is solved intelligently. For small or medium cities, some form of group shared mobility could still work as a collective mobility system. Adding on-demand to a recipe of traditional fixed transit or creating flexibility to picking up individuals with a flexible route system can solve collective mobility demands. Rigidity in traditional transit needs to change through new digital platforms while paying close attention to equity and affordability.

**Fig. 4B.11:** Multimodal collective and individual characteristics of human mobility.

*"Everything comes to us that belongs to us if we create the capacity to receive it."*
—Rabindranath Tagore

### Multimodal-oriented city

Building a city with a different mobility system has become an ideological battle during the last three decades. We know vehicle-oriented city building has never worked for increasingly urbanized cities. The transit-oriented approach that originated in the 1980s focused on keeping the vehicle-oriented paradigm while adding sparse transit facilities here and there. As a matter of fact, only one-fourth of all urban trips are medium-long or long trips. So, transit can compete with and reducing one-fourth of vehicle trips, assuming we somehow magically solve last- and first-mile access. This transit-oriented approach however failed because it didn't deal with our massive vehicle-usage, predominantly for outrageously short distance trips. More than 60% of urban trips are short distance (8 km or less). Short trips' share increases when a city size gets smaller, such as up to 72% of trips in Guelph (DMG, 2016). Traditional transit was never a good option for short trips. Our changing lifestyle and remote working options are reducing longer trips and slowly increasing the share of shorter trips. Since our intention is to make trips vary, we need an array of solutions to practically address the dominant demands of short trips. Personal and shared active mobility, micromobility, shared and flexible forms of on-demand transit, ridesharing and goods movement is the simple 'combo' package for most urban mobility needs. These options would automatically address access problems to traditional transit and make transit truly the backbone of the broader mobility ecosystem.

Obvious confusion arises from a misunderstanding of a multimodal ecosystem. Any combination of modes around vehicles is the same as automobility. But combinations around only traditional transit work for one-fourth of trips. The combination of multiple modes needs a natural adaptable ecosystem, so as a result local culture and geographic conditions can address the predominant use of vehicles almost everywhere in the city when transit and multimodal are included in the broader ecosystem. However, internal structures unknown to decision makers, lead to confusing shapes, form, and applications within multimodal mobility systems. This book avoids the general characterization of multimodal mobility and develops seven distinct characteristics of a multimodal system to transform cities' currently flawed and troubled automobility conditions.

- *The face of a true multimodal trip*: Multimodal mobility typically means using two or more modes to complete a single trip. However, this book considers using a private car as a single occupant and getting out from parking to walk to the door as a pedestrian as unimodal, not multimodal. A true multimodal trip uses two or more mobility modes and is facilitated by smooth transfers between the modal systems. These multimodal trips could be around traditional or on-demand transit but mostly they are non-transit trips using a combination of mobility modes.

- *Local mobility culture*: Social, political, and geographical conditions develop into their own unique mobility habits. To avoid alienating local culture by forcefully imposing a new mobility system, this book proposes to understand local mobility pattern first through data, cultural attachment, land-use, and built form context. A similar concept is applied to adopt new mobility modes in different forms and scales for various neighbourhoods in different parts of the city. This avoids or minimizes gentrification impact, with a forceful enforcement approach that adopts a more gradual and sensible approach to introducing new low-emission modes and slowly removing automobility facilities and services.

- *Local mobility form*: Ignoring land-use and the mobility ecosystem was the most visible and embarrassing gap in the automobility approach. Local land-use and built form generates different types of mobility demand in different parts of the city. To initially transform an automobility system, a sensible and gradual step-by-step approach is herein proposed through a new concept of 'mobility form'. The approach attempts to rescale the new mobility ecosystem depending on the type, scale, and form of local systems. Eventually every area will go through the next steps of evolution, and ultimately achieve car(ownership)-freedom and a sensible use of vehicle formats.

- *Facility ecosystem*: The automobility system was developed assuming a unilateral approach and ignoring the combination of elements that normally exist in all aspects of city building. This book proposes to develop facilities for all mobility modes that are connected and dependent on each other. An ecosystem could be built around a mobility backbone system (e.g., traditional, or on-demand transit) and/or a mutually dependent system that facilitates alternate modes at the same location or streets. This will ensure different modes are available for different purposes or to switch modes depending on the trip's purpose or needs.

- *Multimodal eco-hubs*: Human systems tend to aggregate in certain locations in the neighbourhood or within the facility. These social behaviours need to be incorporated into the mobility ecosystem. This is in complete contrast to the automobility system which assumes individualism as the ultimate human although it is non-existent. Our collective nature is unconsciously linked to flocking or gathering at popular locations and becoming a fundamental foundation of the "eco-mobility hubs" concept developed and implemented by the author in a real area planning process for various neighbourhoods in Canadian cities. This chapter and Chapter 6 elaborate on the concept and implementation details.

- *Shifting and reclaiming facility options*: The multimodal ecosystem changes its elements as part of continuous and natural changes to social, technology, or environmental conditions. Automobility is built on fixed and rigid facility and cannot be modified for other modes or

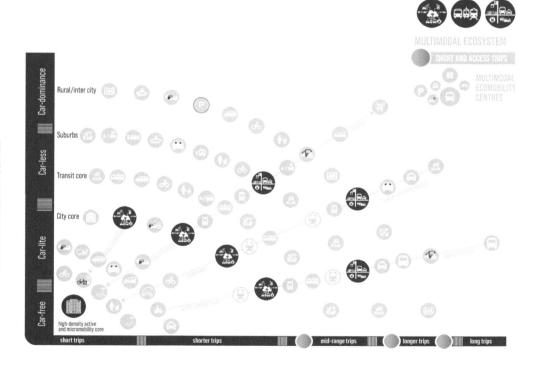

**Fig. 4B.12:** Multimodal-oriented city linking mobility and built form (Diagonal line graphic).

changed conditions. Multimodal spaces are used by multiple mobility users, particularly during transfers, but remain typically invisible until multiple uses are activated. This book refers to mobility's "third space" –the invisible spaces predominantly unused, underutilized, or abandoned in the space-hungry vehicle-oriented mobility system. Once reclaimed, the shifting nature of multimodal mobility would be able to reuse roughly 30–40% of these invisible spaces. To ensure shifting opportunities between modal facilities, the book proposes a unique process of identifying unused, underutilized space for reuse, and provides details of a redesign approach and implementation.

- *Human compatible form and scale*: Automobility is designed for a metal box covered entity system. This philosophy is incompatible with multimodal users. All multimodal users use the mobility system as a human or operate without rigid metal or another form of protection. Throughout this book each multimodal system has been carefully designed to remove hardscaped form and create softscapes using urban mobility design. The approach adopts creating streets, mobility spaces, and services to multiply human proportions and variations per human needs. The human resonance concept elaborates on the details of human scale and form, in this chapter and in both volumes of the book.

### A new multimodal ecosystem framework

The misperception about how a human combines multiple things to accomplish a goal remains at the heart of the flawed current unimodal mobility system. Traditionally, planners take a random target of a specific mode share and modify a few percentages here and there without any sound logic or objectives. Typical mobility master plans develop initial, interim, and ultimate mobility facility and infrastructures based on only a shallow and deeply flawed understanding of human mobility. This process does not align with reality, and natural human behaviour, and faces a real struggle in the face of social, environmental, and other constraints.

Akin to the natural ecosystem, internal structures of the multimodal ecosystem are complex and remain unexplored territory. Although it looks simple on the surface, any ecosystem organically develops a complex internal mechanism through repeated motif and common patterns. Multimodal mobility follows a similar process. This section proposes an internal multimodal ecosystem framework based on personal traced data, successful experiments, and the implementation of several area plans in Canada. True human mobility behaviour displays at least three more layers of complexity in the multimodal nature of our mobility habit:

- *Modal merge*: When a weakness in the traditional modal share approach created a separation between multiple mobility modes, the concept of modal merge[14] emerged in the Netherlands and other countries (Raad Voor Verkeer en Waterstaat, 2001) to mitigate the fragmented approach to multimodal systems. The author used the modal merge concept to develop an advanced "multimodal ecosystem" concept that incorporates three layers of multimodal characters (see Fig. 4B.13). This new framework also incorporates new mobility modes and its sensible inclusion in the local ecosystem. These layers are: (1) natural mode combinations under different built-form and land-use context, (2) seamless transfer between multiple modes while adding information and digital integration, and (3) merging multimodal facilities at eco-mobility hubs, a neighbourhood mobility hub that provides multiple travel options within 3–5-minute walking distances.
- *Modal interdependence*: Unlike the unimodal automobility system, the multimodal system is intricately dependent on other modes to complete a single trip. While people choose certain modes over others for social, economic, and convenience reasons, combinations of modes work as complementary to each other depending on safety, availability of modes, service quality,

---

[14] A combined, transparent whole of transport services with excellent transfer facilities between all kinds of modalities, including cars.

weather, and many other non-utility reasons. The same person can use a combination of multiple modes at different times, in different seasons, for different purposes, and in different personal or geographic situations. Although many combinations of modal interdependency may exist, we typically flock around three common types: (1) *Central dependency*: Rapid transit and frequent transit stations or stops usually display common modal interdependencies. While multimodal spectacle around large stations is accepted as normal, bus stops or shuttle service locations rarely facilitate multimodal access in North American or the Middle Eastern or south Asian cities. All types of traditional, on-demand, or paratransit transit could act a central node of multimodal interdependency. (2) *Mutual dependency*: Besides transit dependent multimodality, many mobility modes are natural allies in surviving as combination modes. Rideshare and carshare users commonly depend on cycling and walking combinations, particularly in medium or small cities where transit service is not frequent. The same is true for cargo bikes that work as a complement to cycling and walking with dependent users who typically avoid expensive transit passes or vehicle sharing. (3) *Conditional dependency*: This form of mobility mode interdependency is the most common. Permutations of combinations are endless in urban areas. Even extreme car users change their habit in different cities or countries and conditionally depend on rail or cycling or other non-habitual modes while travelling. Nightlife users often rely on rideshares, but typically may use other combinations in everyday life.

- *Diversion of modes*: Once we select a combination of modes under certain conditions, it's not static. It's dynamic and changes over time. While we typically depend on or develop an everyday habit of a certain combination of mobility modes, we initially adopt a certain combination based on perceived affordability, convenience, and personal preferences. Over time, we gradually tweak the combination of mobility modes depending on rewards, packages, and other criteria that match our personal or family or group needs. However, mobility remains dynamic for various reasons. New modes, technology, natural or manmade disasters or disruptions, conditional changes, conveniences, and attractiveness continue to change our mobility habits. These three forms of mobility ecosystem changes usually lead to "mode diversion". Naturally we 'divert' one mode to another mode. If conditions change, we change our mobility combo. New combinations are formed within 3–6 months when changes occur. This book utilizes the "diversion rate" concept using data from other cities and different new mobility technology to create an 'ecosystem' mobility mode combo to estimate demand, plan for a new framework, determine scale of supply and implementation stages of the multimodal mobility ecosystem. The last section describes different ways to develop a shifting approach to a multimodal ecosystem.

## *Multimodal mobility form*

Whether they are transit stations or streets or service points, mobility facilities look similar. Linear, rigid, continuous, unpleasant, and absent of any beauty or aesthetics or ornamentation are the defining features of nearly all automobility systems in our cities. Mobility facilities have no relation to the surrounding built environment, built form and design context. This is a major disconnection from society and culture, a human-created alienation from its own users.

This book develops the comprehensive principle of mobility systems. The concept of mobility form encapsulates a context-sensitive relation with its surroundings and society. A context-sensitive approach is not new. New street classification was based on a context-sensitive attempt to capture the surrounding built form, but it failed to broaden its horizons beyond linear street systems. This concept lays out a multimodal mobility ecosystem and its network for each type of neighbourhood to capture the local mobility culture, and pattern of land-use that generates different types of multimodal mobility demand, social adaptation, and nature of human mobility code. A few fundamental principles from the findings of the human mobility code and its DNA are the foundation of mobility form. Two silent features of the concept are an abolition hierarchy concept that dominates the mobility system and a rigid boundary between different forms. Instead of the

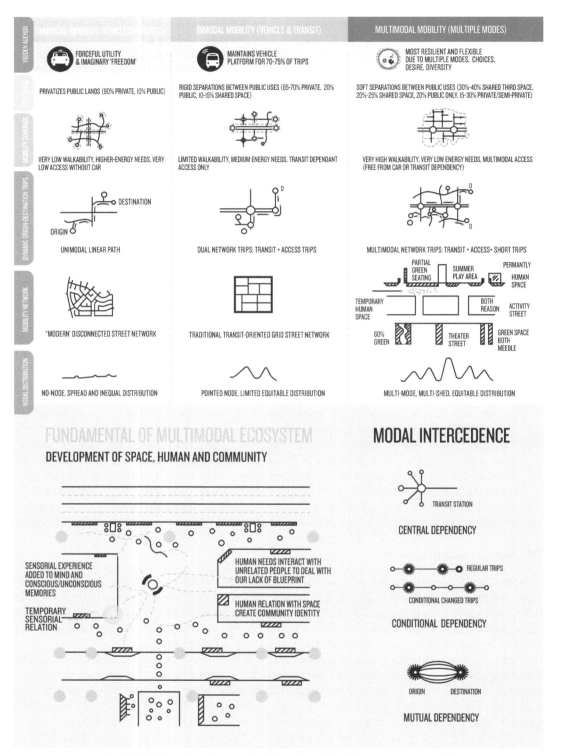

**Fig. 4B.13:** Internal mechanism of multimodal mobility (Modal merge, network).

traditional method of mode hierarchy that creates tension between the modes, this concept captures the nature of the human habit of using multiple combinations of modes in different contexts or built forms. Eventually all neighbourhoods in the city will expect to adopt multimodal mobility albeit on a different scale, in different combinations, and in a local ecosystem context. The second feature is avoiding a sharp boundary, mimicking the 'transition' concept in urban design between two adjacent built forms. The boundary between these forms is fluid on its border areas. Mobility demand, supply, and implementation strategies are then built on mobility forms that recognize the scale of the gradual and slow reduction of vehicle usage following the urban form, density and built environment.

Detailed implementation, design philosophy, and policies are described in the next few chapters, as well as the last two chapters of this book. Key mobility network principles for each mobility form area are:

1. *Complete multimodal form: Car free areas*

   Dense urban centres, downtowns, and urban centres are primary areas where full multimodal mobility could be feasible without owning a vehicle. A series of connected and seamless multimodal mobility services should be available to replace vehicle ownership mobility forms. No street widening or capacity expansion should be proposed in full multimodal form. A maximum of two shared slow lanes would be allowed as flow space. Adding new but narrow and active mobility links should be the priority. Except for local streets, all streets should have protected bicycle and separated micromobility lanes, wider pedestrian boulevards, enhanced transit facilities, and shared mobility services including amenities. Human and green spaces should occupy more than three-fourths of mobility space. No private parking spaces will be required in this form. Dense and closely spaced, all types of eco-mobility hubs should replace the single point transit-node mobility hub concept. Mixed-use centres and evenly distributed eco-mobility hubs will spread the density equally to all parts of centres or downtowns and keep options open to extending the growth boundary without damaging local neighbourhood identity. Instead of parking, private development contributions with the highest-level of development incentives would focus on creating storage space for future or new multimodal mobility modes, improved or new facilities and new placemaking that creates new green and human space around every eco-mobility hub and major intersection.

2. *Saturated multimodal form: Car (ownership) free areas*

   Transit corridors, downtown shoulder areas, dense neighbourhoods, rental dense and suburban centres, particularly intensification and secondary planning areas are primary candidates for saturated multimodal form. Flow space would be a maximum of four with only two travel lanes. The rest of the mobility spaces are dedicated to human and green mobility spaces. Street improvements will be allowed to only add active mobility or transit lanes, keeping the total width under 30 mt, and avoiding any major widening of existing mobility corridors in intensification areas or secondary plan areas. New street and active mobility connections should be the priority with all major and residential streets installing protected bike lanes, wide boulevards and comfortable transit, and shared mobility activity spaces, services, and amenities. Only limited parking for shared high-occupancy vehicles will be allowed, while making development contributions with the second highest level of development incentives toward closely spaced medium density eco-mobility hubs, active mobility, and amenities including creating new green and human spaces at key locations.

3. *Gentle multimodal form: Car-lite areas*

   Mid-rise corridors, frequent-bus services areas and suburban, dense residential or employment complexes are primary candidates for gentle multimodal form. Dedicated transit lanes and active and micromobility mobility flow space within a maximum of five-lane mobility flow. Street improvements will be allowed for only dedicated active mobility or transit lanes and avoid any major widening for private vehicle travel lanes. Off-street active mobility connections should be the priority with all main streets and collector streets installing buffered bike lanes, wider boulevards, and standard transit and shared mobility facilities, services, and amenities. Only limited off-street parking for private and shared vehicles will be allowed. Development contributions will be made with the third highest level of development incentives going toward neighbourhood eco-mobility hubs, active mobility, and amenities including creating new green and human spaces at key intersections and neighbourhood centres.

4. *Partial multimodal from: Car-less areas*

   Townhouse and midrise areas are primary candidates of car-less partial multimodal form. Limited mobility expansions would be allowed up to a maximum of two-lanes, slow and travel lanes in each direction, off-street urban bike boulevards and standard buffered sidewalks for all main and major neighbourhood streets. With moderate development incentives and higher contributions from mid-rise development limits, parking space for private and shared vehicles would be allowed if key eco-mobility hubs, placemaking, and other sustainable mobility facilities are built by new developments.

5. *Minimal multimodal: Reduced vehicle areas*

   Some pockets of city neighbourhoods will experience lower gentle density like low-density built form but will limit supply of new single detached housing options. Parking, both private and shared will be allowed, if reasonable development contributions and facilities are provided for connected active mobility corridors if residents choose to leave their cars at home. Streets would be up to four-lanes maximum with basic bicycle and pedestrian facilities on major corridors.

Even with all these new innovative concepts and creative ideas, there will still be a need for additional help. Master mobility planning for citywide solutions is one of the most complex processes of human civilization. New technology and artificial intelligence opportunities knocking at our door can gradually reduce our remaining vehicle usage if they improve human well-being and avoid being new platforms for inequality. The next few chapters in Part 2 provide details of supplementary help from new technology while keeping the key principles proposed in this chapter.

## *Shifting multimodal ecosystem*

Our shifting planetary conditions can no longer afford a rigid mobility system. Dynamism was the central feature of mobility which was overturned in the last century by utilitarian objectives and rigid infrastructure ideology. But the mobility ecosystem is the fastest changing world compared to any other city building components.

Three shifting mobility subcomponents are proposed throughout this chapter and the rest of the book. They are shifting mobility, shifting streets, and shifting normal ideas for resiliency. One of the key features of a multimodal system is that it changes continuously over time. Instead of mode share, new ecosystem demand, supply estimations, and implementation process depend on identifying a shifting mobility culture that emerges over time when mobility modes, services, land-use, or built form changes. These simple premises are usually left out in the traditional planning approach while selecting travel choices. The first layer is finding strategic objects and turning them into quantitative ways to estimate interchangeable mode merge.

1. *Initial multimodal ecosystem*: Existing mode share comes from a traditional survey of asking travelers to remember their travel diary. But this method is deeply flawed since it only counts the frequency of trips. When time and distance are considered, mode share looks very different for each person. Three layers of mode share comprise our true multimodal mode share.

2. *Interim multimodal ecosystem*: A city changes slowly, so do our mobility choices. Once new facility is installed or new mobility modes became more mature, we change our habit. Rate changes from other cities or past behaviours will provide clues to our interim behaviour.

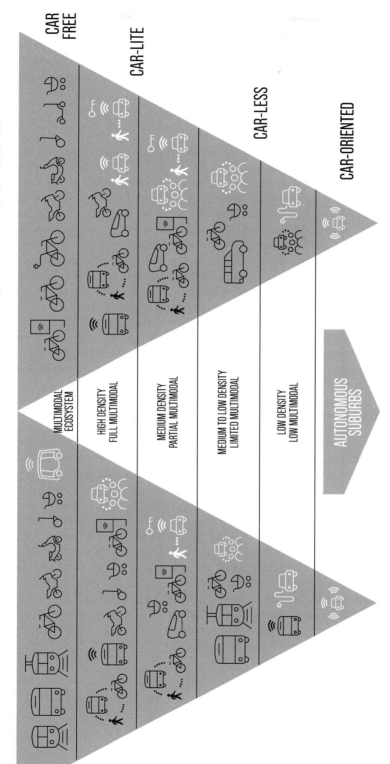

**Fig. 4B.14:** Multimodal mobility ecosystem characteristics of human mobility.

3.  *Ultimate multimodal ecosystem*: The final stage of modal combination estimation mainly comes from community and city vision interventions. Mobility changes can happen but only if they creep into the sensitive zone of mobility limits, and states or cities target drastic measures toward low-emission, low-energy, and low-resource oriented sustainable modes. This is built into the city's vision, community objections and finding a balance between the objectives of mobility boundary.

## Multimodal demand and city building process

A complete mobility ecosystem depends on the diversity of mobility options, and variation in smart land-use policies. To establish the link between smart growth polices and mobility ecosystem elements, the ecosystem model integrates five layers of policy variables: (1) The appropriate share and right mix of land-use policies were tested against shared internal trips by several activity centres in the city. (2) Through iteration and testing in the second stage, internal trips in planning areas were estimated against the optimum share of nonresidential and intensity of diverse land-use. (3) Modal shares of all fundamental modes were produced for all land-uses and directions of travel within or outside the city. Context-sensitive and reliable targets were adopted using limiting boundaries of density and sustainable modal combination and a citywide internal trips scale (Fig. 4B.15). (4) Person trips, multimodal trips, and parking space demand for each mode of mobility were estimated to realize the scale and number of connections for each area. Existing multimodal trips, the combination mode share of transit station users, and trips generated by other developments immediately next to planning areas were added to the total future multimodal trips. (5) Multimodal trips were reassigned into the "shareable mobility service" mode to generate the scale of demand for all available or potential future shared mobility systems within the planning areas.

## Linking transit and density

The appropriate density varies with the area and overall context. In-depth analysis using Toronto data (within 500 m of subway stations) reveals benefits of density diminish beyond a "density sweet spot". While the minimum subway density threshold is usually 100 population and employment per hectare, the optimum transit share (i.e., 40–50% transit) is achieved when density is around 200–450 people. The downtown core, with a density exceeding 450, leads to a marginal increase in transit mode share (Fig. 4B.16). While employment is the key ingredient of maximum transit usage, the appropriate share of diverse land-use (25–40%) is critical to providing access to daily needs. The reason behind low-performing subway stations (around 58%) are vehicle focused retail or employment usage, poor physical and digital connectivity, or a lack of real-time information and pointed density around rapid transit stations. Optimum limits of density also determine emission outcomes. Total on-road $CO_2$ increases rapidly with population density below 1,650 persons/sq km while per capita emissions decline as density rises (1,650–3,500 persons/sq km) and emissions begin to rise again as density exceeds 4,000 persons/sq km. These boundaries set the limits of mode split, appropriate density, and the extent of diversity of land-use that maximizes self-contained trips.

**Fig. 4B.15:** Changing the equation of transportation demand and supply to land-use.

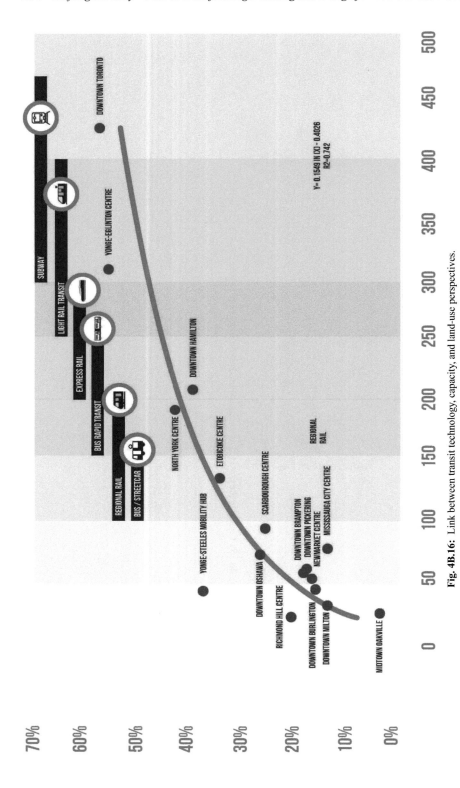

**Fig. 4B.16:** Link between transit technology, capacity, and land-use perspectives.

# CHAPTER 4C

# Ecosystem of Shifting Mobility Space

*"Those who say it can't be done are usually interrupted by others doing it."*
—James Baldwin

## Poetics of Space: Human and Mobility Space DNAs

Human's relationship with space is as old as is our species. Compared to other species, humans are born with some defining hallmarks—exceptionally high degrees of sociality, cooperation, and communal care (Nelson, 2022). Because of our lack of a natural blueprint compared to other animals however, we tend to live in communal spaces. The urgency of communal living created the original human settlements, the earliest prototype for civilization from which humans gradually developed the cities and metropolitan areas that we live in today. One of largest and most visible signs of communal living in cities is public spaces.

Culture is the identity of the human species. Civilizations are born out of culture. And culture was born, matured, and thrived in the open spaces and public spaces of human settlements. Public space shaped cultural forms. Human activity, performance, and interactions created invisible waves and vibrations that pass through public space (McCormack, 2013). It is like the magnetic field of solar waves that touches or passes through our planet. These cultural 'magnets' are closely linked to the quality of a public space. Streets, public squares, and open spaces are intimately linked to our perception and emotions. Human feelings about space were born when we built our first settlement but were with us since pre-settlement. Like the millions of neutrons that pass through the earth every second and interact with matter outside of our visible field, we know it exists even though it is invisible. We feel jubilant, vibrant, happy, sad, or depressed because of the way a space is designed and created (Debord, 1957). Yet relations between our body, mind, and the medium that connect the two worlds remains disconnected from the built environment, mostly divorced from the mobility system and its placemaking process.

The concepts and practical processes in this book deliberately add those missing links and elements into the mobility system.

Through daily life activities, we experience space in cities (Certeau, 1984). Humans go through roughly three layers of "sedimentary deposits" of space during their daily mobility routine. Taking an impression of space into our conscious and unconscious layers of body and mind interactions. Daily mobility activity is the most important mechanism of creating a unique bond between space and humans.

- *First impression*: Moving from one place to another place we create first impressions of space in our body and mind. When we arrive at a destination (or trip origin location), we develop daily relations with the space. If we are inside a metallic box like when in vehicles, these impressions are temporary and fragmented. Walking or slow-moving mobility modes do the opposite as we can 'see' spaces in more detail, create personal memories, and develop temporary bonds with spaces. However, short stays in certain locations do create general relations with that space.

- *Second impression*: Mobility is a repetitive experience. Repetition creates the second layer of space impression in our mind and body. If the place has its own identify, we will build a new bond with the space. If the space has no identity such as ugly wide streets or parking spaces, we never create any meaningful bond with the space. Well-designed human scale spaces do exactly the opposite. The repetition of mobility activity for a few months (roughly 3–6 months) settles the second space impression and we develop a long-lasting bond within our body and mind. This sedimentation of space in our corporal and cerebral experiences creates our perception about space and life in cities.

- *Third impression*: Once we stay in certain places for longer periods in the city, we create the third layer of space impression. This impression comes from seeing acquaintances every day, performing daily activities at work, learning, shopping, or recreational activities, and gradually developing a relation with the community. Community and space start to settle in our body and mind if city space is designed and oriented toward a human scale. Space designed with a utility purpose never creates that community bond, particularly in typical suburban places or dense high-rise areas where ground spaces remain deserted. The best example is when we visit or tour other places. When we go to cities with better space designs, our body and mind does not register the difference. It's when we come back that our long-term space perception of utility approach rejects those experience and registers their spaces as a 'spectacle' that cannot be achieved where we live.

This process of creating a special bond between humans and space is not an easy task. This book takes a different approach to humans and mobility space. Utility takes a back seat. The front face is human, and human psychology is the heart of this new approach. Our feelings are attached to the places and streets we like. Our everyday life is full of small activities. Our body reactions and interactions evolve and mature through the space we live in. These hidden layers of human mind, space, and environment are blended into many non-utility sources. These new concepts and ideas re-establish our ancient and natural relation between mobility space and the practice of daily activities overriding the last century's ideological narratives.

### Mobility space code

Despite their entire mobility system being a city's largest and most visible third space, mobility is barely heard of in the broader framework of city space and its relation to other diverse and variations of space in cities. Before building mega mobility structures, we must ask how and why we should recover the vast amounts of public lands that were dedicated to private usage and automobility storage. This book starts with the basic relations of all types of space located outside of living, working, learning, or other institutional spaces.

1. *First and second space*: While we spend our downtime in the first space, such as home, and most working or daily activity time in the second space, such as the office or in an enclosed building, these are not "active and interactive spaces" that a human needs to spend a specific amount of time in. The idea of making bigger homes in isolated suburbia is deeply rooted in a gender-biased city building ideology from the third industrial era. As we are gradually moving toward liquid modernization from the postmodern era, we are spending more time in the first

space. The lack of public space and an uninviting mobility system is creating a timebomb of health issues that we've only seen a glimpse of during the Covid-19 pandemic. The Dutch are used to working from home and realize the sheer importance of the third space for the minimum human interaction. As we leave our workforce for increasing freelance work (18% of Canadians 65+ and expected to grow to 30% in the next decade), we will spend more time in the first place and the need for quality space within a very short walking distance should be at the heart of city building principles in the 21st century and it could be achieved through a well-designed mobility space.

2. *Third space*: Besides first and second spaces, we spend most of our activity time in the third space. Our life revolves around the third space or transition spaces. These transition or liminal spaces are corridors to the past and future. The third space, however, is mostly located outdoors unlike liminal space that can be both indoor and outdoor. In the face of the vehicle invasion, public spaces for everyday life disappeared. People-centric organic city building collapsed within a few decades of the early 20th century with the authoritarian approach of separating land uses. Our natural human rights to a third space (Lefebvre, 1947) disappeared with the rigid ideological approach of spending public funding to create private space for vehicles. The loss of the transition or liminal space (Gennep, 2011) that used to harbour the secrets of city living and maintained our physical and mental well-being (Teodorescu and Calin, 2015) was placed under the guillotine during the modernism era led by the avant-garde fascist-inspired artistic movement. Machine-oriented city visions tactfully removed all types of "third spaces" through automobility systems. During crisis periods, "space repression" reappeared, particularly in the pandemic era. Through zoning regulations in the name of 'misuse' of lands and to protect the 'values' of suburban private properties (Oldenburg, 1999), the space between inside (home or first space) and outside (work or second space), often referred to as the "third space", started to disappear as machine-oriented 'modernism' devoured our everyday gathering places.

One might wonder what the components of the third space are. There is an intense debate over the characteristics of the third space in cities. Traditional third space, however, excludes another form of everyday space - public space and mobility places. To clear up this confusion before explaining the place of mobility system in urban space, third spaces are loosely characterized as:

1. *Indoor third space*: Tradition mostly considers café, restaurant, retail, and recreational spaces as typical third space. This view generally ignores other outdoor third spaces in cities. These places are vital for human interactions and social bonding, and a symbol of community identity and local cultures. But there are more third spaces in the city.

2. *Outdoor areas*: Outdoor areas such as parks, open spaces, bodies of water, urban forests, are mostly natural environments that we occasionally spend our out of home time in. But these spaces are mostly inaccessible and located far away from typical residential living areas in cities.

3. *In-between spaces*: In-between space became the heart of the 1980s public space movement following monumental work by Lefebvre, followed by many more pioneers such as William Whyte, Jan Gehl and, of course, the great Jane Jacobs. In-between space has become the dominant public space concept which includes: (1) Space between buildings and life in small spaces; (2) Space between indoor and outdoor spaces such as building frontages (excluding setback); and (3) Great public squares.

4. *Entire mobility system*: In between the rest of third spaces, the mobility system is the most continuous, extremely complex, easily accessible, and truly vibrant, cultural, and social bonding space in the city. Unfortunately, "the city" is now built on the vehicle-focused strategies of governments, corporations, and other institutional bodies (Certeau, 1984) which literally ignore the human tactical movement of everyday life connected by our mobility systems. In the end,

these mistakes are opportunities to rebuild the mobility space with true mobility code in mind.

Despite mobility space being the largest form of third space in cities, mobility planners forgot to think of mobility systems as an ecosystem of spaces. From the public to politicians to artists to every layer of citizen, perceive mobility space is nothing but vehicle 'flow' space. Nothing stops in the mobility space. In rapidly accelerating liquid modernization, the impact of flow is increasing like never before with completely impractical ideas of technology such hyperloops, air mobility, or automated moving space ideologies. It's time to take a U-turn from these traditional narrow mobility space ideologies and reintroduce a new way to understand our ancient and greatest public spaces in cities. The next few sections describe these mobility spaces in detail, but overall, the big components of mobility spaces are:

### The Space Equation

**1a**: Total urban space,
$$TUS_n^1 = H_j^i \cup W_j^i \cup TS_j^i$$
where:

TUS = Total urban space of n types of spaces in city,

H = Living place like home,

W = Working or learning or production space,

TS = Third space from i number types to j types of form.

**1b**: Total third space TS,
$$TS_j^i = ID_j^i \cup OS_j^i \cup IB_j^i \cup MS_j^i$$
where:

ID = Indoor third spaces,

OS = Open spaces,

IB = In-between spaces,

MS = Entire mobility space in city.

**1c**: Total mobility space MS,
$$MS_j^i = HS_j^i \cup G_m S_j^i \cup IS_j^i \cup SF_j^i$$
where:

HS = Human spaces,

$G_m$S = Green (mobility) spaces,

IS = Interaction spaces,

SF = Shared flow spaces.

1. *Human spaces*: Mobility systems are the most lingering time for city residents. In no other spaces in civilization does the human species spend so much time. But modern human mobility spaces are nonexistent. Typical human spaces are mobility squares (particularly space in front of transit stations), street corners, stationary human spaces such as seating or resting areas, playing and recreational areas, and wide boulevards and promenades.

2. *Green (mobility) spaces*: This is another form of invisible mobility space. In the era of climate change, this book proposes at least five types of mobility parks where multimodal storage and waiting areas (see eco-mobility spaces) could be integrated into green mobility spaces.

3. *Interaction spaces*: Usually the smallest but most active spaces in mobility systems, these include setback areas, edges of boulevards, portions of the curb lane, and frontages of indoor third spaces.

4. *Eco-mobility multimodal hubs*: At the intersection of human and green mobility spaces, the book proposes to create a unique and equitable multimodal mobility access location. These spaces are mobility services stops, stations, waiting areas, drop-off areas, and temporary storage areas.

5. *Mobility's third spaces*: At the intersection of the first three mobility spaces, we have mobility's third spaces. These places are around eco-mobility hubs where people neither need access to any mobility services nor functionally use mobility systems. These are the lingering spaces on street edges, small corners, and building frontage areas. These spaces are the largest part of invisible spaces, a new concept introduced and expanded on in this book in detail.

6. *Shared moving spaces*: The book also proposes to get rid of private flow space and replace it with only shared mobility flow space. Common shared flow spaces are bicycle lanes, micromobility lanes, pedestrian ways such as sidewalks (located within the boulevard), dedicated or shared transit lanes, and finally slow lanes for shared vehicle flow.

This is not a synthesis or deterministic categorization of urban space. This work is intended to broaden the current narrow view of vehicle-only space as urban mobility spaces. As we evolve to

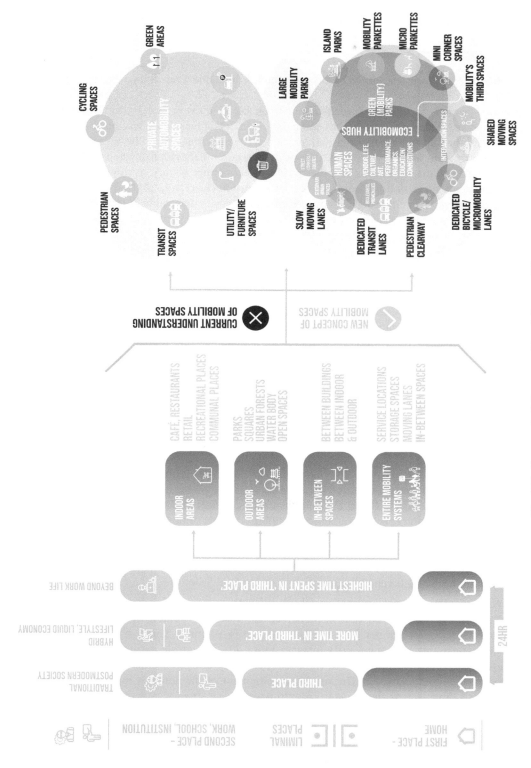

**Fig. 4C.1:** Framework of city space and its relation to mobility space.

new lifestyles, a new economy and new environmental conditions, the line between mobility spaces and other third spaces may become blurry. And that's the truly organic way to build the city as Jane Jacobs once dreamed about but rarely saw in real life on a broader city scale.

## Invisible (public) space

So where are these third spaces? Why do they remain invisible even though these spaces exist literally in front of our eyes?

When a system is built on ideological dogma or unable to reinvent itself with changes in society and culture, every system tends to harbor some dark elements. Over time these repressed elements repeat themselves through breakdown, failure, and frequent waste. With the repression of these elements by members of the system controllers, authorization behaviour develops into hiding the faults with a patchwork approach. Whether political, economic, history, or literary forms, these repressed elements recur in a period of a cycle of repetition (Karatani, 2011). The most common reaction is these repressed elements must be hidden and not easily detectable. It is the exact opposite. They are literally in front of us, used every day, and exist everywhere. And just because they're everywhere, they manage to make themselves invisible since things considered 'normal' are viewed as invisible. It is like our monetary system, like when money becomes a repressed item during economic downturns and people rush to the bank to secure their money, the very system is dragging itself down.

The mobility system is deeply ingrained in global economics and suffers the consequences of the capitalism system. Many urban spaces, particularly third spaces, are gradually given to vehicles and considered "essential spaces needed for vehicles" to attain economic achievement. In reality, a large portion of these remain completely unused, abandoned, and wasted. Many other 'active' spaces are heavily underutilized such as curb lanes or the third lanes of six-lane streets.

The book refers to these spaces as "invisible spaces" that used to be for our common human interaction, cultural, and society's breathing places. As streets are widened to more than two lanes, street edges or islands and linear public spaces disappear. As turning lanes and on-street or off-street parking spaces are expanded for vehicles, the remaining third spaces vanish from city life.

Ironically, the spaces given to vehicles remain a waste of space, unused, underutilized, and practically invisible in our life today.

- *Stationary invisible spaces*: Roughly one-third of 'stationary' mobility space remains invisible under the constant hyper speed of the mobility system. Street corners or islands, gathering spaces on the edge of the street, building frontages adjacent to boulevards, wide promenades, and common meeting spaces around major mobility points or nodes are common examples of mobility's invisible third spaces. They are now occupied by right-turn or 'death' islands, traffic utility spaces or 'dead' medians, "turning radius" that are rarely or never used by large vehicles, 'dead' edges of curb lanes due to unnecessary travel lane widths, asphalt boulevard parking and many more rarely used vehicles spaces.

- *Moving invisible spaces*: Another one-third of linear space remains heavily underutilized or practically abandoned even if it is perceived as 'essential' vehicle space. Although traffic engineers used capacity per lane per hour to justify so many lanes, it is extremely rarely applied on existing streets to verify whether those 50–70-year-old assumptions are still valid or irrelevant. Heavily underutilized right turns or rarely utilized second lanes of dual turning lanes are common examples. During the development of the author's multiple master plans for various cities across the Greater Toronto Area, every street was investigated using urban street geometric configurations that repeatedly showed the same symptoms of wasted vehicle space. Figure 4.C2 is an illustration of wasted space and the consequences of extraordinary wide streets in the suburban area of North York along the Sheppard Avenue corridor. Roughly, 20–25% of moving spaces are never used by vehicles due to unnecessarily wide lanes or unused flared lanes. Despite typical "wider is safer" traffic engineering, the real-world data shows that adding unnecessary travel lanes reduces overall capacity of each lane and increases collision risk due to the excessive speed and aggressive driving that wide streets encourage during off-peak time periods. Ironically, intersections remain utilized less than half of the time even though the intersection was widened to accommodate peak-hour traffic. This illustration shows how completely contradictory evidence is given to the public and politicians to justify building excessive mega streets, even though the evidence is never checked or verified for its deteriorating performance, enormous safety risk and huge waste of public funding without any positive return to society.

Aggressive vehicle space does more than create mobility problems, it has monumental consequences on the urban quality of life. With the disappearance of everyday space, our local culture collapsed. Instead, a "proscenium arch" was created within four walls for cultural display, mainly in Europe during the early colonial expansion era when utilitarianism was rising to make everything 'functional'. Organic human culture was replaced with commercial "cultural products", from shopping malls to entertainment streamlining systems.

One of the primary focuses of this book is to rediscover those invisible spaces underneath our transparent ground. Techniques have been proposed from real life efforts to using special x-ray eyes to detect these invisible spaces, to reclaim invisible street spaces in Canada and other places, and to make those places visible again. Numerous types of invisible spaces are categorized and classified by shape, size, and pattern in Chapter 6. Once reclaimed, the possibilities are endless. But new progressive ideas such as Complete Streets suffered the same fate without the building of proper concepts and principles of how to rescue these spaces. The following sections provide a glimpse of those possibilities and fundamental principles toward grand space reclaiming goals.

Once visible, it will be easy to reclaim, redesign, and repurpose space for everyday human uses. The intention is to bring back our lost third space life and street culture that remains the pinnacle and most visible symbol of human civilization.

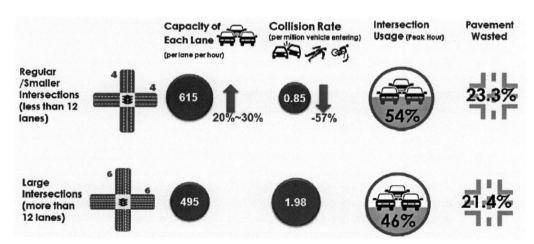

**Fig. 4C.2:** An illustration of wasted vehicle space and its consequences.

*"In an age of speed, I began to think, nothing could be more invigorating than going slow. In an age of distraction, nothing can feel more luxurious than paying attention. And in an age of constant movement, nothing is more urgent than sitting still."*

—Pico Iyer, *The Art of Stillness*

## *Equitable street code*

Street spaces remain the largest portion of mobility space in cities. Yet equitable principles have remained out of planning and design process for the last eight decades. The livable street concept of the 1980s and Complete Streets started to reverse vehicle-only street design. Unfortunately, the livable street came with very little basic principles (Dumbaugh, 2005) and most of them were built in wealthy or privileged neighborhoods in the city. Complete Streets came with the big promise to incorporate all users into street planning and design. Though resisted by old school traffic engineering practitioners and politicians alike, the complete street concept started to show its incompleteness and turned into a new way of "road widening" disguised under the glossy banners of transit and bicycle lanes when it swept North America. Ignoring symbolic and social spaces resulted in an 'incompleteness' that is now systematically reproducing urban spatial and social inequalities through environmental gentrification (Zavestoski and Agyeman, 2015) among the neoliberal foundations of the "progressive street design" cultural realm.

The underlying cause of the failure of the progressive street design concept was starting principles, values and ethics that prevented it from becoming a new platform for fixing inequitable streets. A lack of basic principles brought back old vehicle-oriented ideology in a new form. Like the emerging postmodernist achievement of completeness without changing lifestyle and consumption habits but accessing 'external' means of meditation to fix problems in life and achieve nirvana, the 'complete' street literally fell into a fragmented culture of mimicking the same old ideology without fixing the real issues on the ground. In this process, active transportation, transit, and other human-friendly features become ornaments to hide the underlying vehicle-centred design that has never worked for the people inside the vehicle. With no limiting boundary, and very little consideration of resources, expensive design, and maintenance became the underlying cause of an excessively wide "complete street".

But there is simple way to reverse these practices. There are three basic principles to create a check-and-balance environment and approach before the street planning process begins:

*Rule-of-third*: To address very basic issues, this book proposes to start a new rule and borrow a page from the mobility boundary concept, a second page from the human resonance concept, a third page from the resiliency perspective, a fourth page from space allocation science, and a final page from an equitable lens. When these principles are applied correctly, a new equation of street planning and design emerges. The formula is simple. Three basic components of urban street space should be equally divided between human space, green (mobility space). and shared flow

> **The New Equation of Street**
>
> Total street space,
> $$SS_n^i = \frac{1}{3}HS_j^i + \frac{1}{3}G_mS_j^i + \frac{1}{3}SFS_j^i$$
> where:
>
> n = 1 types of street classification to n is total number of streets in cities.
>
> i = types of space in each mobility space to j types of street urban design form.

space. One third of total street space should be dedicated to human space and associated interaction space. This space is dedicated to the social, cultural, and daily life of human activity. Another one-third would be dedicated to green (mobility) spaces that can share space with pedestrian amenities, storage for active or micromobility, or other less intrusive mobility activities. Finally, the remaining one-third should be dedicated to shared flow or moving space such as shared slow lanes or dedicated transit lanes. This equation reverses the old school vehicle-oriented paradigm where typically 70–90% of space is taken away from the community and dedicate to vehicles whether they are using them every hour or not. Equitable distribution of space ensures every activity and community need is given equal attention where moving mobility modes are minor objectives, instead of relentlessly moving vehicles.

*Rule of 30*: Road widening has become an untreatable cancer in traffic engineering. To prevent spreading the cancerous infection, strict boundary should be imposed to avoid catastrophic resources and financial failure under the energy and resource constraint era that we are moving toward. Like the rule-of-third, this concept is simple:

- First, limit any street width to maximum 30 m. Without imposing width restrictions, any progressive street planning concept and creative design approach will turn into an ideological expansion of oversized mobility facility. Based on a purely dedicated 3-metre linear space for different usage on street, the typical travel lane, bicycle lane, multi-use lane or sidewalk are typically 3 m wide. This also helps to restrict moving flow to a maximum of three travel lanes for a 30-metre street and two travel lanes for a 20-metre street. The concept facilitates the way to the rule-of-third formula, guaranteeing the remaining two-thirds are equitably distributed to green and human spaces.

- Second, in all urban street redesigns the speed limit should be 30 km/h. When people collide with vehicles this speed does not cause fatalities to humans even if there is a mistake (NCCHPP, 2014). This should be achieved through the physical redesign of streets instead of the ideological neoliberal fetishism of speed limit reduction using signs and banners that fails to reduce or eliminate aggressive speeding in typical urban streets. This is based on the simple scientific logic that traditional traffic planners mostly ignored the fact that the average operating speed in all urban areas rarely exceeds 30 km/h[15] (Cardelino, 1995) and all major cities average speeds range from 10 (Trigg, 2015) to 15 km/h[16] (Mao et al., 2002). Despite high-tech illusive claims, these average speeds are in just typical urban areas, not gridlocked cities (Geotab, 2018). Since no city ever exceeded a 30 km/h speed range, despite its endless highways or road widening infrastructure bonanza, it is meaningless to design a street for 70 km/h, a typically assumed design speed for urban streets. Many cities like New York, Paris, and parts of Toronto have adopted 30 km/h speed limits without an apocalypse, and life goes on in those cities.

- Finally, limiting the city's boundary or administrative zone size (Keeble, 1961) to 30 minutes cycling distance and 30 min walking (15 min each way) to keep neighbourhood sizes at a human scale. The 30-minute city policy concept is not new (Marchetti, 1994) however street sizes and networks were never aligned with the concept. Limiting street size and increasing connectivity, particularly in dense active mobility networks, would avoid the need for mega streets.

*Affordable and resilient streets*: Both old school engineering and politicians are stuck in the 1930s Keynesian era of highway and road expansion. In an era of resource and financial severity, the increasing cost and most dominant forms of climate change impact are the highways and road expansions that have become a budgetary nightmare for most cities (Frontier Group, 2020). Meanwhile the funding of regular maintenance and operations has become a yearly budgetary headache. Just resurfacing an existing lane in a major urban area costs $1.5 USD million per mile, reconstruction costs $7.6 USD million, and reconstruction while widening a lane exceeds $11.5 USD million per lane per mile (FHWA, 2019). These are not resilient streets no matter how wide the sidewalk is or how protected bike lanes are. Resilience comes from low-cost street elements such as green streets (Im, 2019) and human space elements that require minimal maintenance and operation costs.

## Green (mobility) space

Typical green spaces such as parks and open areas are mostly inaccessible, located far from living areas and centralized. Hidden in isolated locations, these typical city parks remain mostly unused, disconnected, and unloved by city residents due to the lack continuous connectivity, poor design, and surroundings of heavy traffic corridors or asphalt parking spaces. The utilitarian approach of

---

[15] Average speed of major and minor materials is roughly 28–32 km/h and local streets speed around 25 km/h.
[16] Average speed is 10 km/h in Austin, Texas, 11 km/h in Los Angeles, London, New York, Haerbin, and Pittsburgh, Pennsylvania, and 15 km/h in Beijing, Guangzhou, Tianjin, China, Cincinnati, Ohio and 16 km/h in Wuhan, China.

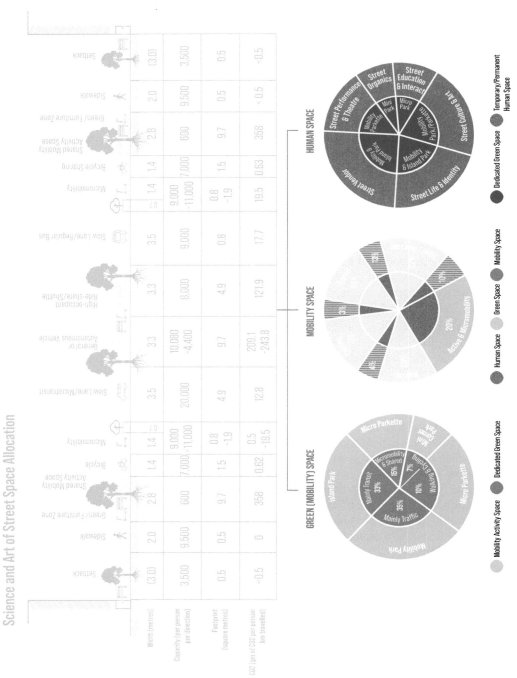

**Fig. 4C.3:** Framework of equitable street.

pushing green spaces into distant parks and forests did not work well for living areas with treeless and lifeless streets. Humans have a deeper connection with green space. And the only way to make green space frequently accessible is recreating that lost space in the most common and continuous mobility corridors in our cities. Older images of city streets and corners show people flocking around those green spaces. To make the way 'hazard' free and for high-speed vehicle flow, traffic planners and engineers gradually removed all the green spaces from entire mobility systems without knowing the devastating social, cultural, and most importantly environmental consequences of this practice. Frequent and flash flooding, heat islands, and intolerable heat from impervious mobility systems are now central to the initial impacts of climate changes.

In the 'modern' era, street and mobility facilities often exclude "green mobility" space to keep the "flow of traffic". This trend has reversed in the last couple of decades, and many planners, politicians, and the public have come together to bring green space (Im, 2019), water features, and wildlife back to city mobility systems. Even a large and dense city like New York, or Paris, or Seoul, or Melbourne is now trying to bring natural green space back into their mobility corridors or stations or stops in addition to typical open spaces or parks. They have taken down their monstrous-sized invisible vehicle spaces, underutilized highways, as well as redesigned small vehicle spaces for mini or micro green space. Learning from these examples and the author's systematic concept of green mobility space creation in Canada and Asia, this book develops at least five types of green (mobility) spaces (details of space shape, redesign and rebuilding strategies and techniques are provided in Chapter 6):

1. *Large mobility parks*: Large invisible spaces are the most striking example of how such enormous spaces can remain hidden and invisible to the public or the practitioner's view. These spaces are elevated structures that have no use anymore, elevated, or at-grade interchange ramps, recovered space after 'normalizing' ramps, abandoned parking or loading spaces, underutilized car parks, transit park-n-rides, and parking structures that are typically empty on higher floors. Many Asian cities typically have very

   > **The Green (mobility) Spaces**
   >
   > Total green space,
   >
   > $$G_m S \frac{1}{5} = \frac{1}{3} MS_j^i$$
   >
   > where:
   >
   > 1 to 5 = Represent 5 types of mobility parks or green spaces reclaimed from invisible vehicle spaces

   little or no green spaces, yet they build gigantic mobility structures that are unaffordable to their own residents. Part of these can be converted into considerably large mobility parks. However, some reclaimed spaces are larger than soccer fields. On those reclaiming spaces affordable houses can be built since public agencies are typically cash-strapped and have very little land to build public housing for struggling residents. Careful usage reviews and critical views of these enormous spaces can easily reveal the facts and increase the prospect of reclaiming them into green spaces. Typical costs are minimal except structure demolition costs.

2. *Island parks*: The middle of all mega streets in cities are usually abandoned and buried beneath utilities, fences, and other traffic control devices. Similarly, spaces adjacent to dedicated transit lanes or spaces in between subsequent stations are abandoned and filled with concrete and asphalt to avoid using them for public uses. The space between two left-turn lanes or concrete medians to support traffic signal poles is another form of dead island space. These dead and ugly spaces make streets aesthetically unpleasant and riskier due to poor design. These spaces can be reclaimed and converted into island mobility parking that incorporates a new form of public realm. But they need careful planning, particularly frequent crossings, maintenance, and sensible operations to become everyday public space.

3. *Mobility parkettes*: Most of our urban streets were built in the post-World War II era when road alignment and intersection shape was not practised or developed scientifically. Traffic planners randomly created bizarrely shaped and sized street alignments that are now considered collision-prone and unfriendly to pedestrians or bicycle users. When realigned and reshaped

properly using urban street design tools, these spaces can be converted into small parks or parkettes, increasing the volume of frequently accessible parks in cities. A similar idea can be applied to dead vehicle spaces. Hundreds of dead or abandoned islands or corner spaces, irregular shaped intersections, or large unused on-street spaces can be reclaimed and converted into green space. These spaces require careful design to avoid hazard elements or shapes. They also require careful planting and a maintenance strategy, including special operational techniques to make them easily accessible from adjacent sidewalks, and the installations of new connections in neighbourhoods.

4. *Micro parkettes*: Many urban streets and small on-street or car parks are built on the wrong assumptions. Extra wide lanes, flared corners, deserted building entrances or corner areas assume vehicles will access these spaces while maintaining a high turning speed. A high turning speed is an inherently faulty assumption. No vehicles turn at more than 20 km/h, large vehicles turn at less than 10 km/h, and trailers turn at a speed of 5 km/h. Despite these facts, these spaces were made unnecessarily wide, for a 50 km/h or higher turning speed. These consequences were never considered while creating these most frequent and most invisible mobility spaces. Small green gardens, flower beds, urban agricultural spaces with seasonal produce could be one of the multiple reuses of these small but frequent mobility spaces if reclaimed and redesigned appropriately.

5. *Mini green spaces*: These spaces are the most frequent but most often ignored by even progressive urban planners. It's impossible to list the numerous types of unused vehicle space uses. But the most common ideas are eliminating the generous corner radius, restricting parking areas to near intersections (the spaces are never used by vehicles and could have curb extensions installed), ground floor setbacks (with an upper floor balcony overhang), making building corners a chamfered shape, and eliminating the most notorious boulevard parking for retail owners and numerous unused utility areas, and many more. These areas could be reclaimed in every redevelopment and street redesign process while collaborating with building owners or local business associations to regreen and reuse the spaces.

Greening the most easily accessible spaces, mobility links or places, is almost an equitable approach since streets run basically everywhere in cities. The ideas herein however go beyond typical green (City of Portland, 2005) and low-impact street concepts (City of Toronto, 2021). Redesigning all unused, underutilized, invisible mobility, and other 'third spaces' in cities will need to find a way to incorporate daily human life and environmental activities whether they have monetary value or not. We already know it will bring huge environmental value. The Covid-19 pandemic and subsequent hybrid work-lifestyles are providing enormous returns on green space initiatives. These benefits will multiply when resource-intensive vehicle spaces become a real burden to society, since maintaining green spaces is extraordinarily cheap and can be done by volunteers and citizens, and urban and social programmes.

> "*A walk expresses space and freedom and knowledge of it can live in the imagination of anyone.*"
>
> —Richard Long

## Human space

The second layer is designing and planning cities with a human and environmental spirit, usually undefined and an intangible field in planning practice even though the human species is intricately related to our everyday urban life. Often mixed with humanity, our spirit is larger than human rights. The organic nature of the human species is often linked to "ordered chaos" which is viewed with great uncertainty among hardware fixated mobility professionals. Human activities bring a space alive. An artistic performance in a public space has an invisible ability to mutate a seemingly mere space into a swirling vortex of human landscape and urban beauty, an ultimate display of the shared space.

Akin to green mobility spaces, human space creations atop mobility facility depend on reclaiming trapped vehicle spaces. But once reclaimed many spaces are simply covered with fresh concrete to make an extra wide sidewalk that serves no special purpose for people who want to linger for long periods. Humans need more than concrete or asphalt surfaces even after reclaiming them properly. We conduct our everyday life with various activities in the mobility space. Those activities were gradually replaced with only one function – moving cars as fast as possible. Fast cars, however, drove life off the streets in cities. Activities require the specific space configurations that are commonly ignored in the mobility planning process. The human space has specific sizes, shapes, and qualities to hold people longer in mobility spaces. This book reintroduces the possibility of bringing back our ancient, pre-automobile mobility life, and lays out at least six typologies (in reality, it's likely many more) to include in the mobility planning and design process that would purposely rebuild mobility spaces focusing on human needs of everyday life (see details of space shapes, redesigns, and rebuilding strategies and techniques in Chapter 6):

1. *Street economic spaces*: Commercial activity in the mobility space is the earliest form of economy for any civilization. Retail and financial vendors used to occupy a linear series of shops along wide promenades and island areas of streets. Square-shaped spaces were full of economic activities and usually happened on large street corners, in squares, near stations or old farmer's markets.

> **The Human Spaces**
>
> Total human space,
>
> $$HS\,\frac{1}{6} = \frac{1}{3}MS_j^i$$
>
> where:
>
> 1 to 6 = Represent 6 types of human spaces reclaimed from invisible vehicle spaces

Many activities were daily, some time-specific or weekend-only and the rest were seasonal activities. Large mobility parks and island parks can be properly designed to bring back many cities' most enjoyable aspects of economic life.

2. *Street identity and life*: Street life revolves around small lingering spaces across mobility systems. Most of them can be regenerated into mobility parkettes. Play areas, senior gathering spots, tree-shaded seating in curb extensions are some of the simple examples of street life. The careful redesign of boulevard edges and street edges (the curb lane) are the secret to regenerating everyday life. In these places, people remember all the small things, the sensorial resonance, and small events that shape daily urban life.

3. *Street art and cultural spaces*: Among all artistic and cultural inventions, there are no other places as important as mobility places. Displays of art in mobility and mini parkettes are common memories for almost every human. We find our culture through various small activities on streets or in station areas. Most of these types of places are in small circular shapes that need to be surrounded by green space and suitable furniture or equipment that facilitates these activities.

4. *Street performance and theatre*: Street theatre, open theatre, and common small corridors or laneway networks should be used to work as the city's great performance places. Street performances require much longer rectangular shapes for large events. Flexible streets with movable bollards are popular design examples. However, theatre or performances need 360-degree view locations and could be in station squares or in closed streets dedicated to pedestrian and performance purpose alternatives. Too frequently side streets segment length less than 100/200 m long are the most popular form of street reallocation strategies that many small cities in North America are taking advantage of due to reduced traffic volumes during the Covid-19 pandemic.

5. *Street organics and wildlife*: Urban agriculture, local produce, and micro forests are prominent examples of vibrant and organic mobility places until the 19th century. Long rectangle-shaped, in-boulevard or setback, and square-spaced planter beds are common examples of the recent trend of organic spaces in mobility systems spreading across Europe and Asia. The introduction of local vegetation brings wildlife back to our doorsteps. Extended curbs and island parks are the best example of mobility's organic spaces. Water retention features combined with the revival of old waterways or creeks are another new common configuration along the edges of curb lanes.

6. *Street education, political, and neighbourhood connecting spaces*: Public space is the most easily accessible, frequent connection, and open space answer for society's problems. As we build disconnected and isolated suburbs, we gradually forget the foundation of our society. Frequent gathering in circular spaces with seating or spaces around a podium should be common configurations of informal information or debate exchange activities on street corners. Small open square spaces or appropriate rectangular shapes in island parks are other common examples that can facilitate these activities. If curb space is designed with flexibility, temporarily closing the slow lane or small streets in warmer seasons is another alternative. During political debates or protests, streets can be closed without "road closure preparation" if designed and planned properly.

### Shared flow space

Making trips without a destination is meaningless. Yes, most of our streets are designed to never stop anywhere along the way until we reach home or our workplace or institution. Flow spaces are typically known as travel lanes and currently most of those lanes are dedicated to private vehicle lanes. In the last decade, transit and bicycle lanes have started to appear in a few isolated streets. Those non-vehicle lanes typically end abruptly and have no network connectivity. Indeed, the allocation of flow space remains far from scientific and rarely follows any logical framework. Adding travel lanes is typically the result of a 'hyperreal' simulacra culture where even the slightest delay and lower than 'optimal' speed shown in traffic simulation models results in a euphoric practice of adding new travel lanes even though it is now proven to cause higher risk, lower capacity per lane, and an enormously expensive burden on society outside of 15-min peak-hour simulation periods.

This section proposes a logical framework of flow space allocation for multiple mobility modes and an ecosystem of flow space based on mobility performance, social equality, efficiency, and environmental outcome. These principles became a major mobility planning approach during the Covid-19 pandemic and in the last decade saw declining vehicle volumes on city streets. The focus of this flow space approach (Vuchic,

---

**Mobility Flow Code[17]**

1a. Individual mobility sharing.

$$Total\ user = r * n * p$$

$$n = n_s * n_h$$

where:

r = Usage rate = Number of users per vehicle per hour

p = number of passengers per vehicle

$n_s$ = Number of vehicles per station

$n_h$ = Number of stations per hub

1b. Passenger capacity,

$$Passenger\ capacity,\ Q = f * n * p$$

$$Line\ capacity = \left(\frac{3600}{S + D_w + W}\right) * p * n * LF$$

where:

N = Number of vehicles per transit/mobility unit

p = Number of passengers per vehicle

LF = Load factor

W = Layover waiting

$D_w$ = Maximum peak station swell

S = Minimum train/vehicle control separation

---

[17] Basic formulation is derived from Vuchic, 2005.

2005) is based on shared flow space for multimodal mobility modes, the combination of modes that can share the same lane, or the conditions for dedicated lanes. The first principle is giving priority to its higher people carrying capacity per travel lane or line capacity of different mobility modes (NACTO, 2017). The second principle is space efficient mobility modes, whether they are stationary or moving conditions (Karim, 2019). The third principle is environmental performance, particularly life-cycle emissions of multiple modes (ITF, 2022). The fourth principle is the sharing ability of new mobility modes that have higher vehicle occupancy (Karim, 2017). The fifth principle is the shifting flow space concept, where the principle is to switch the underutilized flow space or lanes from motorized mobility lanes to shared and transit lanes based on condition changes that occur at different times of the day, on weekends, seasonally, or other temporary conditions. The final principle is an equitable approach for priority users and mobility modes. The details of this principle are laid out in the "Sharing Rides" chapter in Volume two of this set of books.

The framework of shared flow space is laid out in Fig. 4C.4. This nomograph provides a clear solution to when and what mode becomes a priority based on its contributions to equitable mobility access. This is like the current approach to selecting dedicated transit lanes. However, the current approach mostly focuses on non-automobile modes as a last priority instead of considering the actual performance of different mobility modes.

Five types of flow space have been selected as candidates for a shared slow-space framework:

1. *Mixed vehicle lane*: The framework provides clear evidence that the current practice of travel lanes for single occupant private vehicles is unsustainable and impractical from a resource perspective. Private vehicle lanes should be phased out gradually where shared vehicle, active/micromobility, and transit combined would exceed one-fourth share of total person trips on any streets. It may remain a mixed vehicle flow lane (capacity per lane per hour 1,000–2,800 with mixed traffic and frequent buses (NACTO, 2017) during off-peak hours while imposing peak-hour congestion charges to discourage private vehicle usage except for essential services. However, when shared mobility modes surpass half of the total person trips, the mixed vehicle lane should be phased out permanently.

2. *Shared flow lanes or slow lanes*: Two stages of a slow mixed lane are viable candidates. The first scenario is when the designed speed is very low (under 30 km/h), mixed with active, micromobility, shared mobility, and low-frequency or on-demand transit that can share a single lane in each direction. This is particularly applicable for residential streets. The second scenario is removing a private vehicle lane from four-lane main streets and replacing it with shared flow lanes only for shared mobility modes – or mixed or dedicated lanes shared with slow travelling vehicles.

3. *Dedicated lanes*: Two types of dedicated lanes should be a priority over the last two categories of flow space. The priority is active and micromobility users replacing the vehicle curb lane or parking lane. Depending on the conflict potential ratio between bicycles and micromobility modes, this lane can be split between separated bicycle and micromobility lanes, particularly during peak hours. If conflict is low during off-peaks, unidirectional wide lanes could be utilized by both modes. The second priority is permanent full- or part-time dedicated transit lanes. If transit service is low (30 minutes or a higher frequency of on-demand service), part-time, peak-hour transit lanes should be a priority, replacing private vehicle lanes. If rapid transit or higher-frequency (less than 30 min) on-demand transit becomes the major share of total person trips, permanent transit lanes would stay, alongside permanent active and micromobility lanes.

4. *Dynamic and flexible lanes*: A time-based approach is practical and feasible during transition times before temporarily or permanently removing private vehicle lanes in cities. Dynamic mobility flow space allocation has become an emerging approach (Valença et al., 2021) to the precious road space often blocked by nearly empty private vehicle lanes. The first approach to switching flow space between different mobility modes, was mainly shared high-occupant

autonomous vehicles, transit, and active mobility (Berghauser, 2019), however the idea failed to gain traction (such as with the Sidewalk Lab project in Toronto) and is impractical and proved biased toward autonomous vehicle form. The modified approach is proposed here to switch only between transit and mixed shared or slow lanes during peak and non-peak hours. The second approach was relatively successful in the architecture realm, known as space syntax (Hillier, 1996) which could be applicable to mobility systems. This option focuses on adjacent land-use patterns and associated activities to anticipate multimodal mobility demand. However, a prototype of a modular and reconfigurable paving system for a dynamic street (Ratti, 2018) proved data hungry, expensive, and too immature a technology to use in real street conditions. A more practical approach would be focusing on only the vehicle curb lane (ITE, 2021) and switching between the moving slow lane and storage/activity time for shared high-occupancy modes depending on their peak usage. During peak hours the curb lane becomes the flow lane for shared modes, and in off-peak periods it is used for activity space for all types of storage, delivery, and other essential services for adjacent lands.

5. *Pedestrian flow space*: Without any doubt, pedestrian flow or clear space should be the most comfortable with a wider safety buffer that includes amenities. And it should be the first space to start street design. The only situation where it would be shared is if the street is designed as a "shared street". If wider space is available, a pod delivery flow space could be installed parallel to the sidewalk with safe flow between the facilities. Vendors or retail pop-ups can be in the extended curb extension space with direct access to the pod delivery flow lane. Facility width, associated amenities, and width of safety buffer depend on the adjacent land-use, the scale of demand and other multimodal services, particularly transit systems. Details of pedestrian flow space and redesign principles are provided in Part 2 of this book in the "Active Mobility" chapter.

The last two dynamic approaches still require data, spatial analysis tools, understanding dynamic local conditions, and priority user selection. This method may be practical until dynamic street condition technology becomes automated using crowdsourcing or another cheaper monitoring

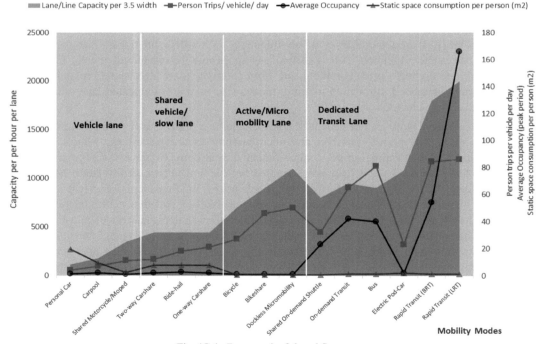

**Fig. 4C.4:** Framework of shared flow space.

system as it matures and is practically accessible to city staff. The proposed method, however, practically abandons the current practice of wrong assumptions and approaches managing congestion solely based on delays for private vehicles.

> *"Even in the internet age, revolts still take place on the street. The street is a public space, and it belongs to urban residents."*
>
> —Willi Dorner

## Storage Space Management for Multimodal Mobility

If there is a place that clearly demonstrates the monstrosity of the space invasion by automobiles on a human scale, it is the landscape of endless seas of parking spaces that stay empty most of the time. These empty spaces come with the hidden and invisible destruction of urban quality of life. The sheer amount of land consumed by private vehicle parking spaces gradually destroys the lungs of city life. With public spaces disappearing, we are slowly "eating the alive" with private vehicle parking spaces (Goodyear, 2014).

Private vehicle users receive a huge financial subsidy through 'free' parking in all cities across North America. There are eight parking spaces for every car in North America, and 95% are free. Installing and maintaining a parking space costs roughly $50,000 in parking structures or underground areas, more than the price of a new car. Most city-required minimum parking space regulations have no scientific basis. Searching for parking spaces is the root cause of roughly one-fourth of traffic congestion in peak hours. These bizarre and deeply inequitable policies are being copied all over the world and are one of root causes of severe financial strain on local businesses and government capital and operating budgets.

Instead of the parking management of automobiles, this book proposes to develop new knowledge from space allocation science, particularly for storage systems for new multimodal mobility systems that require only small spaces for their temporary service or storage time. The low-emission multimodal mobility ecosystem and space science proposed in earlier sections will have profound implications on eliminating a city's white elephant in the form of parking and will enable inhabitants to truly live without a car. The first approach is developing a space science by simply comparing the space required when each mobility mode comes to a rest. The second approach is creating a new urban land management system for managing city space, from identifying underutilized and unused invisible parking or a practical and gradual replacement of vehicle spaces in problematic areas where it reduces human well-being. In Part Two of this book, details of parking's impact for each multimodal mode and redesign and reuse strategies are elaborated on to continue this new space science.

It won't be an easy transformation, as everyone—from Nobel prize winners to celebrities to scientists, to environmentally conscious employees or citizens—loves their parking space. The reallocation of public space as well as parking for more efficient modes is facing steep challenges from traditional inefficient system entities (IDTP, 2011). To protect the last precious remaining urban green spaces, intensifying the remaining developable urban lands (Government of Ontario, 2019) and replacing surface parking spaces with infill developments (Listokin et al., 2007) have emerged as leading city building strategies in the last decade.

### *From parking to science of space planning*

Space allocation was never considered a science, nor was it developed as a practice. Most planning professions, engineering practices, and cites focus on a developing folklore-based approach to vehicle parking. But unscientific and baseless practices creating more problems are gradually being replaced with logical and practical approaches toward multimodal ecosystems.

Two major traditional parking approaches remain convoluted:

- *Storage hubs form*: The first problem with dedicated parking for each land-use is that it creates multiple parking spaces for the same private vehicle users, in addition to their own space at home. This can be replaced with multimodal eco-mobility hubs both in private and public form (see the last section). Instead of dedicated spaces, shared mobility service space will replace private vehicle spaces. This reduces the ownership of parking space by landowners who are replaced with a separate space management authority who operates and maintains the hubs and collects revenue.

- *Shared multimodal storage space*: To develop shared land and multimodal storage space programmes, a comprehensive understating of space allocation science is the first step toward a new multimodal space management system. We need a clear understanding of the different mobility space footprint modes as illustrated in Fig. 4C.5. Of course, this approach needs mixed-use development and smart growth to start replacing inefficient low-density and vehicle-dependent city building policies. Both low-density and dense urban area examples are illustrated, contrasting the land-uses of traditional and mixed-use land mobility storage spaces. The space equation provides the detail of space needed for multimodal mobility modes. Besides a small space footprint advantage, a shared multimodal ecosystem has another clear advantage as the same storage space will be used 10–20 times more per day than a typical private vehicle space. Public agencies need to create new policy and multimodal storage mobility byelaws to replace our unscientific and highly inefficient private vehicle parking system.

This creative space management and new revenue stream approach opens a huge window of opportunity. It provides equitable mobility access to those who cannot afford to own or operate a vehicle. New opportunities for new revenue streams for cities and private properties using excess capacity will offer more choices and connections to public transit services (SUMC, 2015), and gradually and naturally reduce private vehicle parking demand while decreasing traffic congestion intensity. And, once established, a multimodal storage system can free-up vast amounts of precious urban land for living and green spaces in addition to allocating up to 20–30% of land (Doctoroff, 2015) for the new multimodal and shared mobility ecosystem.

### Space management

The supply of parking, an intersection between mobility and land-use, depends entirely on mandatory minimum parking requirements that fail to account for the complex relationship between parking supply and demand, and the importance of space in urban life. These complex relations have evolved with many forms that now require urgent attention. Started during the last decade with the search for new land for growing urban populations, these efforts have failed so far to significantly alter the urban landscape due to limited scope. This section identifies the current issues of different forms of parking and proposes a new space management concept instead of parking management.

1. *Abolishing mandatory parking requirements*: The first vehicle form started with surface parking in the 1970s when municipalities started with a modern land feudalism policy, requiring mandatory parking for every land-use. Minimum parking requirements in cities are a likely cause of increased driving among residents and employees, and a higher cost of housing (Litman, 2011). Although municipalities regularly update their parking requirements to reflect high-density uses, the impact on human quality of life and market-based pricing on parking demand is largely unknown. Most cities have started to abandon minimum parking requirements in the last decade, realizing vast amounts of parking spaces can be reused for living space. Most of the parking byelaws were replaced with maximum parking areas and park-n-rides around stations or transit corridors or downtown areas. However, these are relatively small

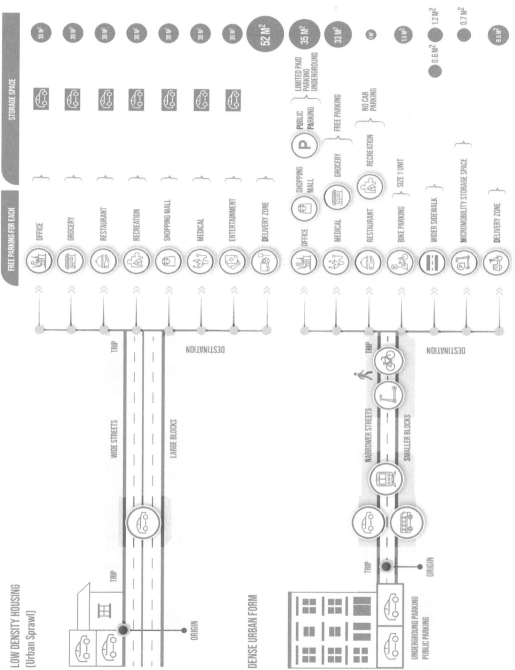

**Fig. 4C.5:** Science of space planning and multimodal storage space.

lands, therefore, this book proposes to apply a new "multimodal eco-mobility hub" (see last sections) to further eliminate or drastically reduce or minimize parking depending on the scale of hub that would enable cities to apply a parking replacement approach to every corner of every neighbourhood.

2. *Reclaiming and reusing surface parking*: The first form of private vehicle parking appears in its most destructive form – surface parking. Clustered surface parking creates heat islands (Rosenzweig et al., 2006), vast impervious surfaces causing polluted stormwater runoff (Greenstein et al., 2004) and frequent basement or local flooding (USGS, 2003). Parking consumes significant energy and creates significant GHG emissions (up to 12%), and at least 24% of other emissions (Chester et al., 2010). To replace these monumental parking spaces, there is a series of strategies needed: (1) Set up programmes to reduce or eliminate parking for transit; (2) Further reduce parking with a different form of multimodal hub, matching land uses and urban form; (3) Replace parking with shared high-occupancy vehicle mobility; (4) Reduce further parking for active and micromobility; and (5) Create a mobility concept to reclaim underutilized parking space and replace it with living space or green space (80%), and use the rest for multimodal eco-mobility hubs and low-emission mobility storage spaces with proper urban mobility design.

3. *Minimizing underground*: To address the visual distraction of surface parking space and its vast space consumption, planners proposed to move entire parking spaces underground. And yet it created more problems while making land development enormously expansive. Vast amounts of underground parking remain half empty whereas on-street parking is operating at close to capacity in Toronto's major urban centers. This indicates a shift in land-use and changing demographics that prefers easily accessible parking spaces. Underground parking is infested with an array of urban problems. Frequent crimes are experienced in urban areas particularly against women and seniors. Climate change has elevated groundwater levels and it is seeping through deep underground parking structures. Most underground parking spaces cost $50,000~$80,000 in North America, making affordable housing nearly impossible. They also disrupt underground river flow. Entrance areas on the surface consume large spaces, are hostile to pedestrians, and create additional safety risks for all users. Other environmental impacts or emissions remain akin to surface parking. As illustrated in Fig. 4C.6, a maximum of a one-storey underground should be the limit of underground parking if needed, for very intense land-uses only. These spaces should, however, only accommodate shared mobility such as carshare, car rental, shared private active mobility, or micromobility.

4. *Creating mobility parks*: Creating mobility parks from all reclaimed vehicle and abandoned spaces is one of the new space management concepts introduced in the last section and elaborated on in a detailed planning and design approach and strategies in Chapter 6 of this Part 1. It needs a new urban mobility design profession, an extension of current urban design programmes in cities. It also needs new urban public space management programmes, new revenue streams, and a management body for the reused spaces and services, and new maintenance and operations programmes to carefully repurpose these spaces safely and in a sustainable way.

5. *Environmental measures*: Many cities are now developing strategies, policies, and programmes to counter the negative impacts of parking. Urban forestry, lighter permeable surfaces, living roofs, green infrastructure, and green parking spaces are a few examples. However, these programmes try to maintain the same amount of parking instead of replacing or eliminating parking spaces. Despite their downside, if these programmes are applied to reclaimed mobility park spaces, they can regenerate them into usable, greener, and human spaces for urban residents.

**Fig. 4C.6:** Multimodal mobility storage systems.

## Eco-mobility Hub: A Multimodal Hub for Social Mobility Ecosystem

The mobility system in the 20th century acted as a primary source of social segregation and a common form of urban inequality. Access to the mobility system or nodes are concentrated in dense and downtown areas, aggravating social sentiment against dense urban places by suburban residents. Transit-oriented planning promised to address social inequality in the 21st century by constructing new transit systems in suburban areas and connecting to employment centres downtown. However, this approach with underlying flaws created new transit gentrification with better access only around transit stations, leaving behind vast amounts of land and people without these new sustainable mobility options.

The author developed a unique and equitable neighbourhood mobility hub concept to address the social problems created by the deeply flawed vehicle-oriented approach and the wrong application of transit-oriented formula. The concept is a one-stop multimodal mobility access point equally distributed within 3–5 minutes walking distance. But it requires attention to the details of all the missteps created by the two extreme spectrums of vehicle-oriented and transit-oriented city building approaches. This section provides a theoretical foundation and framework for new "social hubs" (Donnelly, 2016) whereas Chapter 6 of this Part 1 provides master planning process, demand, new space creation and system implementation details.

### *Creation of social multimodal hubs*

As humans, we tend to flock together in popular places. Some places are more popular due to their attractiveness or presence of key landmarks, key destinations, or they're simply places to hang out for social interactions. The healthiest and most livable places, particularly old or ancient communities before cars, are full of these everyday spaces (Burden, 2021). The availability of mass and multimodal mobility could make these spaces vital places for social interaction in the community as well as de facto waiting areas for mobility services. Most of these places are located on street corners and curbsides and are covered by tree shadows. Mixed land-use nodes in different form could be used as a frame for these multimodal mobility nodes. The rest of them are found in public squares, markets, open public places, or parks. The remaining potential locations are narrow alleyways, courtyards, and building corners. These "social hubs" are the heart and mind of the community. In almost everything we do in daily life, using these small places relieves urban stress, creates social life, and facilitates cultural displays, continuous green corridors and links, wildlife spots, water management facilities, and general economic sources for cities.

The invasion of cars changed everything. Street corners were replaced with the bizarre concept of right-turn islands or right-turn lanes. Street curb spaces were filled with treeless, lifeless on-street parking. All public squares were filled with car parking. Street markets and open-air bazaars were replaced with megamalls with endless parking. Alleyways become dark and gloomy access points for cars to our backyards. Over the last 70 years, the existence of social life and everyday phenomena was deliberately taken out of the public realm through the traditional vehicle-oriented mobility planning process. Mobility services tend to ignore the needs of these social spaces for every life and sidelines the importance of our natural tendency for social gatherings around mobility spaces.

### *Foundation of eco-mobility hubs*

*Formal definition*: What are multimodal eco-mobility hubs? A formal definition was provided by the author during the early stages of concept development (Karim, 2017) as part of an innovative mobility master planning process (Karim, 2017).

Eco-mobility, or multimodal one-stop service points are intended for all users by redesigning public and private parking spaces, finding first-and-last-mile solutions, and focusing on short trip needs and multimodal trip behaviours, enhancing transit service access, and assessing infrastructure to reflect the true nature of human travel.

Eco-mobility hubs are designated for the facilitation of the use of emerging technologies, including scooter sharing, bike sharing, bicycle parking, car sharing, and ride sharing or on-demand or regular transit service points. These hubs are intended to have bikeshare racks, car share vehicles, and comfortable ride share waiting areas in addition to transit and active mobility amenities. The design of eco-mobility hubs can take on various forms depending on the context they are being built within – the hubs can be public stations, on-street, integrated into bus stops, or on private edges around building frontages.

The concept is a major departure from various other forms of mobility concepts that have come out of traditional mobility hub concepts. The "mobility hub" concept (Metrolinx, 2011) started to recognize the importance of hubs around rail or rapid transit stations in Ontario. However, giving importance to one place over the rest of the places in cities is a deeply flawed land-use principle and has become a recipe for the creation of new social inequality through placemaking. After the publishing of the author's initial concept, several more versatile concepts were adopted by cities around the world. For instance, the City of Austin uses the transit mobility hub for all types of transit service points – including multimodal services and amenities (Holland et al., 2018). The City of Bremen in Germany first developed a prototype concept of their own multimodal hub (SUMC, 2017) and it was later spread through selected city neighbourhoods, but in limited form that does not provide citywide coverage. Canadian Urbanism proposed a similar social auto hubs concept for creating socials hubs for autonomous shared vehicles (Donnelly, 2016). This concept however mainly considers autonomous vehicles and excludes multimodal mobility options. More recently, Sweden has proposed peoples' meeting places by replacing on-street parking facilities (Fleming, 2021). However, these concepts did not provide any theoretical foundations, hub forms, basic structures, and integration with the master planning process, policy development, and the implementation process. This book covers all the critical elements addressing these theoretical, practical, and policy gaps.

## *Role and identity of hubs*

Our tendency to gather in urban spaces, particularly mobility locations has become very clear as we move toward more dense urbanization. A few basic principles are:

- *Last-mile, First-mile, Last-metre*: These hubs offer multiple mobility options for people traveling to transit stations/stops, making transit a more accessible and appealing option, and potentially reducing the number of single occupancy vehicle trips and parking spaces needed to complete first- and last-mile trips.
- *Integration*: The flexibility in design and location of these mobility hubs allows for their integration with the existing transit system, working in a supportive capacity for multimodal journeys and integrated with other modes into one-stop services locations.
- *Short trips*: Eco-mobility hubs are ideal for the completion of short trips without using vehicles or even transit trips that require changes between their origin and destination. Shorter trips, generally less than 5 km in length and more than half of total daily trips in Toronto, are typically an ideal length for walking, cycling, or innovative or shared options such as bikeshare, micromobility, or shared mobility.
- *Resiliency*: Eco-mobility hubs could provide several convenient and more resilient alternatives to the single occupancy private vehicles while reducing fossil-fuel consumption and greenhouse gas emissions, with low-emission options and measurable health and safety benefits.

### *Developing an eco-hub framework*

The mobility hub concept for transit-only has been around for the last 15 years. However, none of the planning or transit agencies clearly formulated a scientific and practical framework of transit-only mobility hubs except high-level network concepts in Japan and station area planning in a few western European countries. The inclusion of station access and multimodal facilities is unclear. This section details a few fundamental tools to develop a comprehensive framework for the eco-hub concept.

The framework is based on five principal components. These basic components are: (1) basic access issues; (2) forms of hubs; (3) basic elements of hub planning; (4) evolution and implementation process and steps; and (5) scaling multimodal facilities for different forms. Additional planning rationale, demand estimation and design process are described in Chapter 6. Chapter 7 provides policy and implementation details.

#### *1) Theoretical framework of eco-mobility hubs*

When accessing a mobility hub, access to the hub consists of two access components. The first issue is distance decay. For every short trip mode (such as walking, cycling, micromobility or on-demand transit), trip distance decays drastically from origin toward destination (see distance decay equation for different modes). This book defines multimodal access-shed instead of just walkshed. Secondly, distance decay is heavily influenced by types of mobility services at the centre of the hub (Fig. 4C.7). Traditionally, this would be types of transit services. People walk or bike further for rapid

| **Theory of Human Flocking** |
| --- |
| Eco-hub trip intensity, |
| $$EH_i = Trips \big/ Area$$ |
| where: |
| i = Number of eco-hubs (EH) |

transit services, which gradually reduces with low frequency services. This is not a full picture, particularly for multimodal services that could increase attractiveness of a hub even without transit services. To fix this problem, different scales, sizes, and types of eco-hubs are proposed in the next section. Finally, the types of destinations for eco-hubs depends on land-use attractions if it is not a transit hub. It also needs "network effect" to develop a dense network of eco-hub locations and be a successful solution for equitable mobility access.

#### *2) Form of hubs*

One of the defining features, and weaknesses of previous mobility hub concepts is their lack of urban context and corresponding form that would match surrounding urban form. Urban social mobility hotspot places generally emerge around large, concentrated areas such as major transit stations, leisure centres, and areas of major economic activity (Bassolas et al., 2019). Mobility forms and multimodal hub forms depend on adjacent land-uses, the type of neighbourhoods and local context (Fig. 4C.8). For instance diverse land-use and more evenly distributed populations (like Paris) have a higher concentration of hubs in almost every part of the city's neighbourhoods. Usually hubs are clustered and dense, at or around city centres. In contrast, sprawling cities (like Los Angeles and Sydney) have scatted hotspots across the city. In-between cities (like Bangkok and Santiago) have evenly scattered hotspots. These variations and their diversity indicate the need for an eco-hub form that would evolve around the adjacent neighbourhoods' characters.

This section proposes different forms of eco-mobility hubs depending on mobility services, locations, and mobility network conditions.

1. *Transit interchanges*: A station-style eco-hub is combining all eco-mobility options into existing or future stations and surrounding streets. These larger hubs are suitable in the suburban context but can be adapted on a smaller scale for urban centres or remodelling public parking lots.

    a. *Transit stations*: The multimodal options of eco-mobility hubs can be built as part of existing local and regional transit stations.

    b. *Public multimodal storage hubs*: Public surface or structured lots can be repurposed or retrofitted with bikeshare stations or bicycle racks, shared vehicles, rideshare, or shared

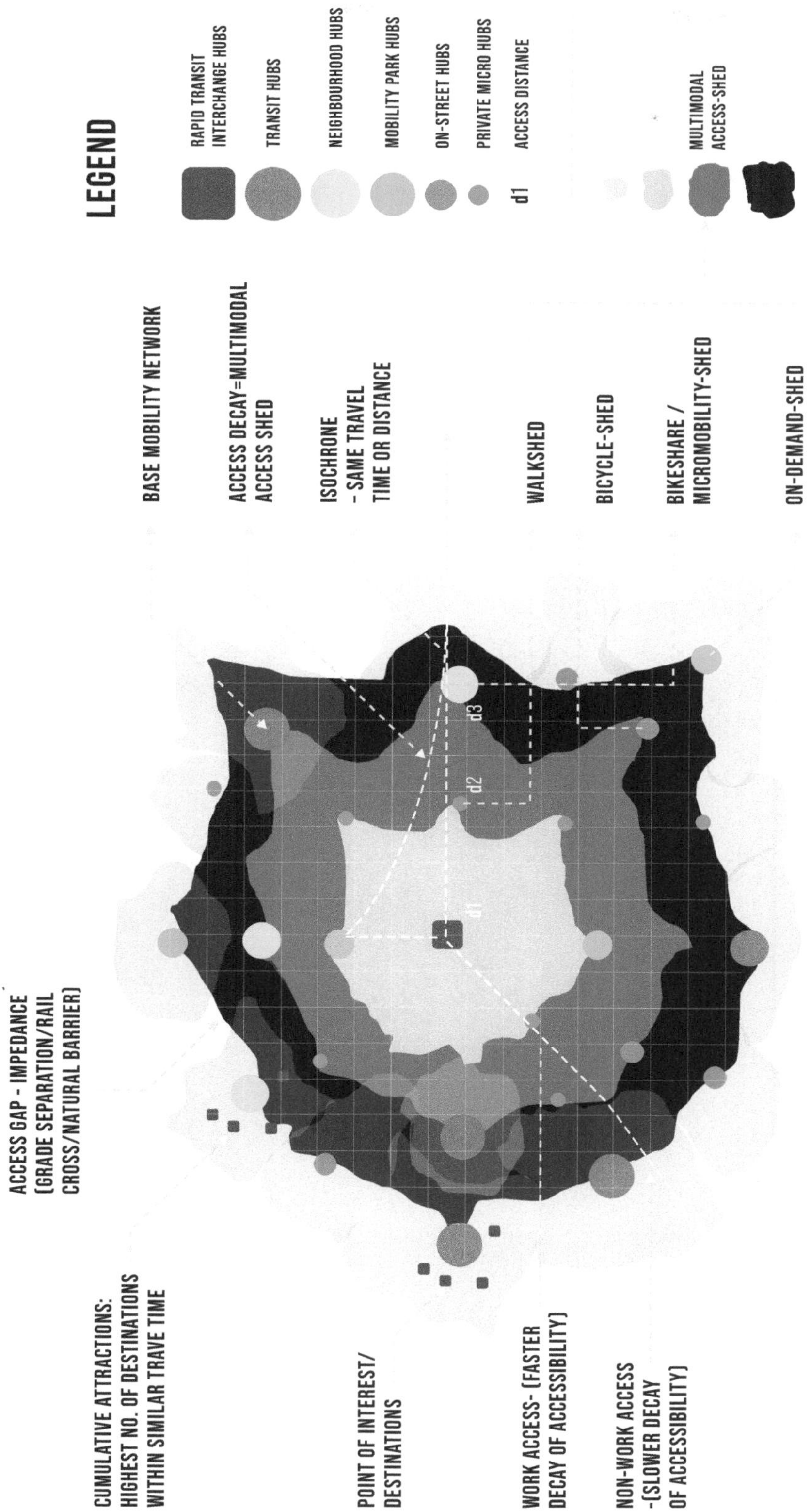

## LEGEND

RAPID TRANSIT INTERCHANGE HUBS

TRANSIT HUBS

NEIGHBOURHOOD HUBS

MOBILITY PARK HUBS

ON-STREET HUBS

PRIVATE MICRO HUBS

d1  ACCESS DISTANCE

MULTIMODAL ACCESS-SHED

BASE MOBILITY NETWORK

ACCESS DECAY=MULTIMODAL ACCESS SHED

ISOCHRONE – SAME TRAVEL TIME OR DISTANCE

WALKSHED

BICYCLE-SHED

BIKESHARE / MICROMOBILITY-SHED

ON-DEMAND-SHED

ACCESS GAP - IMPEDANCE (GRADE SEPARATION/RAIL CROSS/NATURAL BARRIER)

CUMULATIVE ATTRACTIONS: HIGHEST NO. OF DESTINATIONS WITHIN SIMILAR TRAVE TIME

POINT OF INTEREST/ DESTINATIONS

WORK ACCESS- (FASTER DECAY OF ACCESSIBILITY)

NON-WORK ACCESS -(SLOWER DECAY OF ACCESSIBILITY)

**Fig. 4C.7:** Theoretical foundation of multimodal ecomobility hub concept.

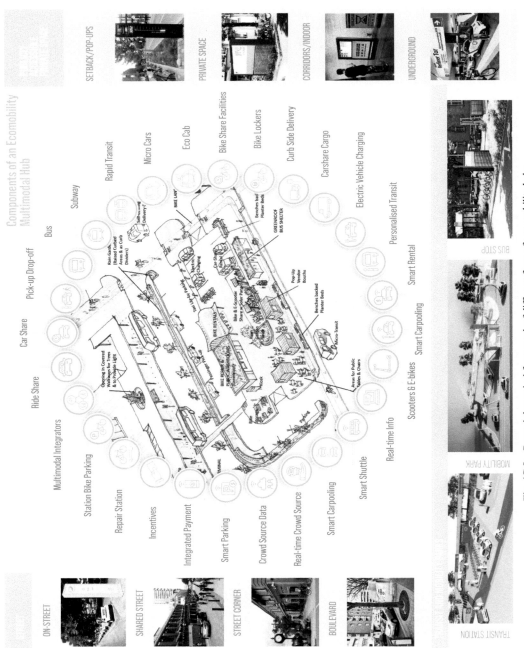

**Fig. 4C.8:** General theoretical framework of different form of eco-mobility hubs.

transit drop-off facilities, and other sustainable mobility user amenities to create new indoor and weather protected eco-mobility hubs.

    c. *Mobility parks*: Like the POPS (Privately Owned Public Spaces) concept, small scale mobility hubs could be integrated into mobility parks to blend into the landscape or city parkette programmes. These hubs are mostly non-vehicular modes such as bicycle, micromobility, or personal mobility devices.

2. *Transit stops/service points*: Eco-mobility hubs can be integrated next to bus or LRT stops where most of the first- and last-mile journeys cannot be conveniently completed on foot. Easy access will fill the gap in the connecting modes to high frequency and rapid transit services. Multiple modes and facilities can be placed strategically in or next to weather-protected transit bus shelters and space can be shared with micro-transit or connected/automated shared transit services.

3. *Neighbourhood gateway and mobility park hubs*: Intersecting main street corners are active and vibrant places where sensible design could bring easy access to multimodal modes while enhancing the public realm with enhanced landscapes and comfortable boulevard experiences. These could act as transfer points between two transit routes or connecting points between transit and connecting modes while taking advantage of street retail and commercial activities at mixed-use nodes. A combination of on-street, intersection corners, setbacks and private corner spaces, facilities and spaces for shared mobility, and conventional sustainable modes could be integrated while creating a vibrant neighbourhood gateway in urban cores, suburban centres, or intensification corridors.

4. *On-street linear hubs*: Smaller-scale linear hubs at continuous intervals can be located on-street while redesigning the extended green curb space to facilitate carshare or bikeshare or bike corrals in lay-bys or extended corners of sidewalks. On-street mobility hubs are generally more suited to a dense urban, downtown, suburban centre context.

5. *Private edges with public access – micro hubs*: Private property and land developers can integrate eco-mobility hubs into new or existing land-uses. The hubs could be used as means to address mobility and parking demand for new developments as well as retrofitting or sharing existing facilities and spaces with broader area users. Private eco-mobility hubs, particularly within parking structures or underground locations are not ideal, as they are inaccessible to many. Private eco-mobility hubs would still be redesigned for exclusive use of building residents or visitors, and will be integrated into redesigned private driveways, frontage spaces, parking garages or structures.

    a. *At-grade facilities:* Buildings with frontage spaces can retrofit them to accommodate eco-mobility options, which could be publicly accessible private spaces.

    b. *Parking garage/structures:* Large residential and commercial developments with higher densities of people or employees can provide public access to eco-mobility hubs within their parking spaces or structures as an essential building amenity as well as for community benefit.

    c. *Corridors/indoor:* Large complex or campus hubs are intimately connected by pathways or weather protected corridors. Hubs would be located every 5-minute walking distance along the pathway corridors.

    d. *Underground facility:* Although not desirable, many underground transit connections to major centres or buildings or underground pathways or retail corridors could be connected via a well-designed wayfinding system to all eco-hub locations.

### Basic elements of eco-mobility hubs

Once the typology of the eco-hub form emerges from surrounding context, the basic elements of eco-hubs would take a natural next step toward planning and designing eco-mobility space at various mobility service points. The basic elements of the multimodal ecosystem are illustrated

Fig. 4C.8 (inside circle) and major characteristics listed in Fig. 4C.10 (the first six columns). The basic criteria of all eco-hubs are similar, but scale and design form will drastically differ.

- *Hub coverage area*: Like transit coverage, eco-hub coverage range or influence area varies drastically depending on transit, on-demand, active and shared mobility service concentrations. This area defines the source of the total population that would generate trips as clusters for multimodal eco-hubs depending on transit or non-transit locations. Unlike traditional mobility hub, eco-hubs have multimodal access-shed instead just walkshed. Unlike transit coverage, multimodal access-shed can overlap between two adjacent hubs. Smaller hubs have walkshed, but additional access shed increase mobility access, increasing mobility equity.

- *Hub zone area*: Unlike coverage area, zone is used purely for mobility access purpose and supply area planning and design purposes. Depending on mobility service, attractions, and trip generation character, an eco-hub core zone area would vary from a 10–3-min walking distance, or smaller cycling and micromobility access shed.

- *Number of access points*: Multiple access points are vital to the survival and success of an eco-hub. Larger hubs need at least four or more access points to the hub. Medium hubs require two to three access points. Each mobility mode may have exclusive or shared access of eco hub.

- *Number of activity lanes*: A larger hub would require multiple slow and active mobility lanes to avoid crowding at access points. Only a private or small eco-hub could operate with one access point.

### Developing eco-hub network and basic process

Once basic principles, elements, and forms are established, the eco-hub process will enter a two-step planning process. The first is developing a dense network of eco-hubs to create a "network effect". This includes area-wide dense multimodality including transit and non-transit locations. Details are provided in Chapter 6. The second is short and long-range planning with land-use redevelopment process. The basic steps are:

- *Evolution of local mobility culture*: Without development in an area, mobility culture could evolve over time if services are available at different levels. The existing culture may not be cycling friendly, but the availability of bikeshare, for instance, changes people's behaviour. But we learned from mobility that these changes are temporary. Over time, mature, altered mobility behaviour emerges from a shift in the nature of the multiple mode combination.

- *Evolution of local mobility culture*: With development, comes land-use changes and mobility culture changes. It follows the same basic pattern without development. But the scale of usage and maturity will be different as interim and ultimate development will increase the population and employment density.

- *Mobility merging and diversion*: Besides typical changes, technology, demography, or other reasons may cause mode switch. Some people adopt more modes and become multimodal. Some people may switch modes to divert to their choice of preferred modes. Eventually equilibrium is reached but it's temporary.

- *Network of eco-hub*: Ultimately, we need to develop dense networks of eco-hubs to make it a successful access formula. Figure 4C.9 illustrates the evolution from an existing fragmented mobility hub approach to developing a new network and eventually changing the form and scale of hubs to match local conditions.

### Scaling multimodal eco-mobility hubs

Once we know the typology and basic elements of the eco-mobility hub, it would be possible to estimate what type of multimodal ecosystem could be eligible for each eco-hub. Figure 4C.10

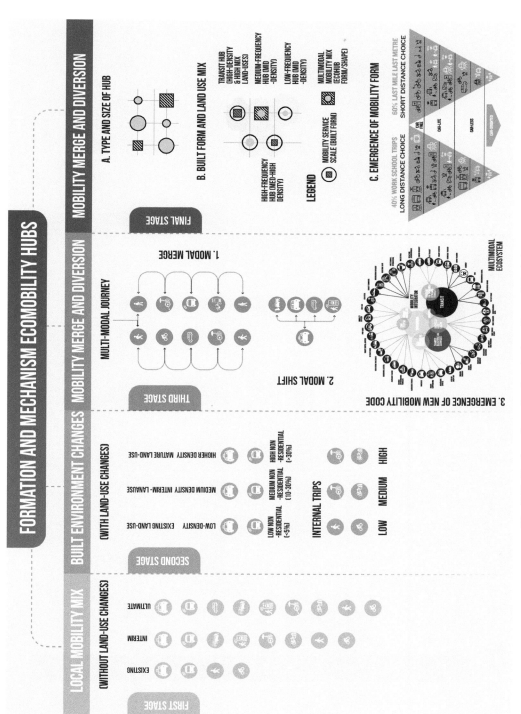

**Fig. 4C.9:** The formation and and mechanism oif ecomobility hub concept.

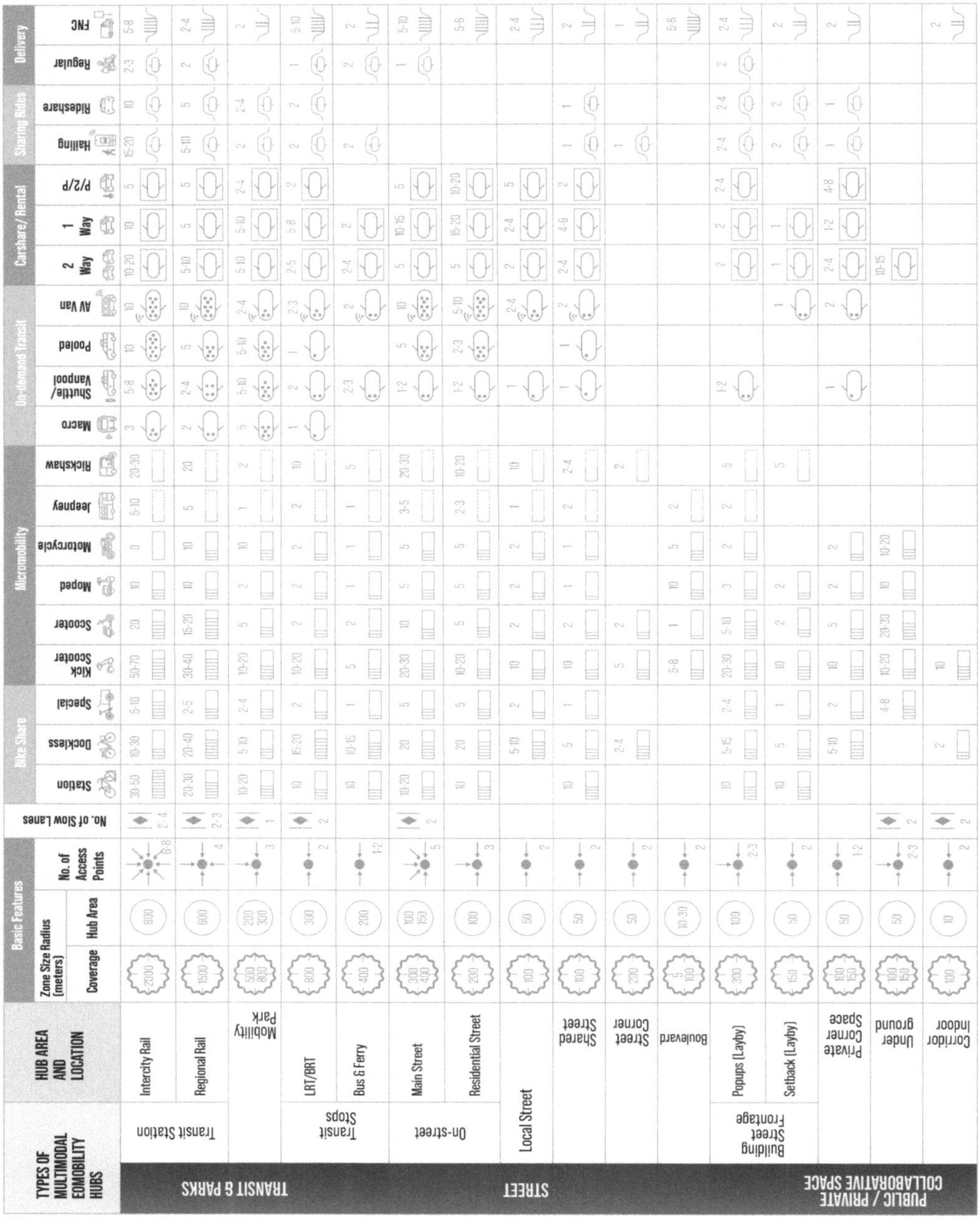

**Fig. 4C.10:** Basic elements and scaling of multimodal ecomobility hubs.

illustrates how potential scale and multimodal mobility facility could be ideal candidates for each eco-mobility hub depending on their corresponding mobility form, built form, mobility services, and locations.

Creating mobility form and corresponding mobility choice with appropriate modal sharing is a successful formula for a multimodal ecosystem provided at each eco-hub. Choice comes from access. Each access point needs to be connected to a network of multimodal services around a hub to avoid users walking tirelessly in large hubs. Multimodal eco-mobility hub network effect is the appropriate remedy for age-old mobility's first-last mile access problem. In addition, setting a timeframe for each mobility form target is critical. For instance, shared mobility may not be available today but bikeshare could be introduced by a city or via a third party, or a carshare network could deployed with a private-public collaboration. Instead of a fluffy policy about autonomous vehicles, actual changes in spaces, or demand reduction, should be planned before they arrive.

## Summary

Human movement is a defining feature of homo sapiens. Natural human movement is the first taste of true freedom. The ontology of human movement is small trips between numerous activities in daily life. Our movement shapes almost all aspects of human civilization. And in our movement, we build an intimate relationship with space, creating lifelong bonds with our environment. This intimate relationship is the fundamental platform of community living. Among all urban space, mobility systems are the largest, continuous, and most vibrant third spaces in cities. Despite its sheer importance in city building, we know very little about our own mobility code. This chapter illustrates a series of new discoveries to understand our hidden mobility code and its DNA components. Most of the findings sharply contradict the traditional assumptions and behaviours of human movement. Every person produces roughly six to seven trips daily, almost twice the trips assumed in traditional travel demand models. Where are those extra trips coming from? The surprising answer is walking and other short trips that are traditionally discounted in mobility system planning. Collectively, people in every city walk half of the total trips they produce every day, stubbornly, in every city, under every condition, in every time. And this walking constant is free of built environment influence. Other modes' pattern shows completely the opposite and a constantly shifting pattern. Every person uses multiple mode combinations in a unique way. Each person's mobility footprint is remarkably similar in that it acts like a unique code. This is remarkably akin to our biological DNA, the unique identifier of a person. Mode switches are common, particularly between the complementary nature of the car and transit competing for the same trip distance segment. When conditions change, our mobility code changes. But it settles after three to six months. There is no unimodal person. Every person uses multiple modes. Even extreme car users' profile consists of 20% of walking trips. Merging multiple modes to complete a journey is a common daily habit. People's modes on the weekend are different from weekdays. Weekday trips are at a faster speed and over a shorter distance. Weekend trips are the opposite. When we don't move, we create the potential for the next movement. Roughly two-thirds of the time we stay still at work, at school, or at home. The Covid-19 pandemic increased this time span. These findings should have a profound impact on mobility system planning, design, implementation, and funding formula. Inspired by these findings, this book develops a series of new concepts to transform the urban mobility ecosystem. A series of multimodal ecosystems is proposed to alter our deeply flawed master planning process and fundamental assumption of travel demand models. Broader principles are introduced to understand using human resonance to improve equity and avoid exclusion. The mobility boundary concept links planetary boundaries to key limits to avoid entering the unsafe zone. The resiliency concept proposes to prepare for impending climate change and adapt with changing conditions. The limit of safe infrastructure identifies the threshold point of harmful effects of mega mobility expansions.

A series of poetics of space is introduced to reclaim, re-use and repurpose unused and invisible vehicle space. New space management, allocation, and government framework are introduced to overturn the completely unscientific and huge waste of land is currently dedicated to empty parking lots. To address equality and improve mobility access, the new multimodal mobility hub concept is introduced to transform the wrong application of transit-oriented development. These are not Utopian dreams, rather practically verified, tested for feasibility, and successfully implemented across many North American and European cities.

# References

Adams, J. (1995). *Risk.* London: Ruthledge, University College.

Ahn, Y. and Yeo, H. (2015). An analytical planning model to estimate the optimal density of charging stations for electric vehicles. *PLoS ONE*, 10(11): 1–26.

Ainsalu, J.V. and Arffman, M.B.-S. (2019). *State of the Art of Automated Buses.* MDPI.

Akiva, B. and Atherton, T.J. (1977). Methodology for short-range travel deamand prediction: Analysis of carpoooling incentives. *Journal of Transport Economics and Policy*, 11(3): 224–261.

Akndi. (2020). *Greening Government Fleets: A Helpful Guide to Understanding.* Ottawa: Natural Resources Canada.

Albert, A. and Gonzalez, M.C. (2017). Using convolutional networks and satellite imagery to identify patterns in urban environments at a large scale. *Proceedings of the 23rd ACM SIGKDD International Conference on Knowledge Discovery and Data Mining*, (pp. 1357–1366).

Alessandrini, A., Campagna, A., Site, P.D., Filippi, F. and Persia, L. (2015). Automated vehicles and the rethinking of mobility and cities. *SIDT Scientific Seminar, Centre for Transport and Logistics (CTL) – Sapienza University of Rome*, 5: 145–160. Rome: Transportation Research Procedia.

Amadoa, M. and Poggi, F. (2014). Solar energy integration in urban planning: GUUD model. *Energy Procedia*, 50: 277–284.

Anderson, J.M., Kalra, N., Stanley, K.D., Sorensen, P., Samaras, C. and Oluwatola, O.A. (2016). *Autonomous Vehicle Technology: A Guide for Policymakers.* Santa Monica, California: RAND Coportation, RR-443-2-RC.

Appleby, K. (2015). *Five Cities Proving that we can Quit Fossil Fuels.* Retrieved from City Monitor: https://citymonitor.ai/horizons/five-cities-proving-we-can-quit-fossil-fuels-1444.

Araujo, J.A., Barajas, B., Kleinman, M., Wang, X., Bennett, B.J., Gong, K.W., Navab, M., Harkema, J., Sioutas, C., Lusis, A.J. and Nel, A.E. (2008). Ambient particulate pollutants in the ultrafine range promote early atherosclerosis and systemic oxidative stress. *Circular Research*, 102(5): 589–596.

Azouz, Z.B., Shu, C., Lepage, R. and Rioux, M. (2005). Extracting main modes of human body shape variation from 3-D anthropometric data. *Fifth International Conference on 3D Digital Imaging and Modeling, (3DIM'05)* (pp. 335–342). Ottawa: National Research Council Canada.

Badiou, A. (2012). *Plato's Republic.* New York: John Wiley & Sons.

Bae, S., Lee, E. and Han, J. (2020). Multi-period planning of hydrogen supply network for refuelling hydrogen fuel cell vehicles in urban areas. *Sustainability*, 12(4114): 1–23.

Banister, D. (2011). Cities, mobility and climate change. *Journal of Transport Geography*, 19: 1538–1546.

Bargh, J.A. and Morsella, E. (2008). The unconscious mind. *Perspect. Psychol. Sci.*, 3(1): 73–79.

Barry, K. (2013). *Wired.* Retrieved from In South Korea, Wireless Charging Powers Electric Buses: https://www.wired.com/2013/08/induction-charged-buses/.

Bassolas, A., Barbosa-Filho, H., Dickinson, B., Dotiwalla, X., Eastham, P., Gallotti, R., Ghoshal, G., Gipson, B., Hazarie, S.A., Kautz, H., Kucuktunc, O., Lieber, A., Sadilek, A. and Ramasco, J.J. (2019). Hierarchical organization of urban mobility and its connection with city livability. *Nature Communications*, 10: 4817.

Baudrillard, J. (1981). *Simulacra and Simulation.* Paris: Éditions Galilée.

Becic, E., Zych, N. and Ivarsson, J. (2018). *Vehicle Automation Report.* Washington, USA: National Transportation Safety Board, HWY18MH010.

Becky, P.Y., Lo, O. and Banister, D. (2016). Decoupling transport from economic growth: Extending the debate to include environmental and social externalities. *Journal of Transport Geography*, 57: 134–144.

Beddoes, Z.M. (2020). Time to make coal history. *The Economist*.

Ben-Akiva, M. and Lerman, S.R. (1985). *Discrete Choice Analysis: Theory and Application to Travel Demand.* Cambridge: The MIT Press.

Benjamin, L. and Richards, D. (1981). Electrification is the way to move Canada in the 1980s. *Canadian Public Policy*, 7(81).

Berardelli, J. (2021). *Climate Tipping Points May Have Been Reached Already, Experts Say*. Retrieved from CBS News: https://www.cbsnews.com/news/climate-change-tipping-points-amazon-rainforest-antarctic-ice-gulf-stream/.

Berg, N. (2020). *This AI-powered Parking Garage Rewards You for Not Driving*. Retrieved from Fast Company: https://www.fastcompany.com/90575914/this-ai-powered-parking-garage-rewards-you-for-not-driving#:~:text=With%20a%20new%20test%20program,in%20to%20work%20at%20all.

Berg, P. (2011). *The Finite Planet: How Resource Scarcity will Affect Our Environment, Economy and Energy Supply*. Oshawa, Canada: Island Press.

Berghauser, P.M., Stavroulaki, G. and Marcus, L. (2019). Development of urban types based on network centrality, built density, and their impact on pedestrian movement. *Environment and Planning B: Urban Analytics and City Science*, 46(8): 1549–1564.

Bhat, C. (2017). *Travel Modeling in an Era of Connected and Automated Transportation Systems: An Investigation in the Dallas-Fort Worth Area*. Austin, USA: Technical Report 122. Center for Transportation Research. The University of Texas at Austin.

Bhat, R.V. and Waghray, K. (2000). *Profile of Street Foods in Asian Countries*. Basel, Karger: World Rev Nutr. Diet.

Bianconi, E., Piovesan, A., Facchin, F., Beraudi, A., Casadei, R., Frabetti, F., Vitale, L., Pelleri, M.C., Tassani, S., Piva, F., Perez-Amodio, S., Strippoli, P. and Canaider, S. (2013). An estimation of the number of cells in the human body. *Ann. Hum. Biol.*, 40: 463–471.

Billings, C.E. (1980). *Human-centered Aircraft Automation: A Concept and Guidelines*. Moffet Field, CA: NASA Technical Memorandum, NASA Ames Research Center.

Bohte, W. and Maat, K. (2008). Deriving and validating trip destinations and modes for multi-day GPS-based travel surveys: A large-scale application in the Netherlands. *Transportation Research Part C Emerging Technologies*, 17(3): 285–297.

Bojarski, M., Testa, D.D., Dworakowski, D., Firner, B., Flepp, B., Goyal, P., Jackel, L.D., Monfort, M., Muller, U., Zhang, J., Zhang, X., Zhao, J. and Zieba, K. (2016). End-to-end learning for self-driving cars. *Computer Vision and Pattern Recognition,* Cornell University, pp. 1–9.

Bojji, R. (2011). Gravity powered transport systems for rail, road, water, and airport use. *13th International Conference on Automated People* (pp. 22–25). Paris, France: American Society of Civil Engineers.

Borzino, N., Chng, S., Mughal, M.O. and Schubert, R. (2020). Willingness to pay for urban heat island mitigation: A case study of Singapore. *Climate*, 8: 82.

Botsman, R. (2010). *What's Mine Is Yours: The Rise of Collaborative Consumption*. Harper Business.

Bourdieu, P. and Wacquant, L.D. (1992). *An Invitation to Reflexive Sociology*. Cambridge, UK: Polity Press and Blackwell Publishers.

Britton, E. (2000). Carsharing 2000: Sustainable transport's missing link. *Journal of The Commons*, 1–351.

Bruneau, M., Chang, S.E., Eguchi, R.T., Lee, G.C., O'Rourke, T.D., Reinhorn, A.M., Shinozuka, M., Tierney, K., Wallace, W.A. and Winterfeldt, D.V. (2003). A framework to quantitatively assess and enhance the seismic resilience of communities. *Earthq. Spectra*, 19: 733–752.

Burden, D. (2021). *Building the Healthy City: Inciting the Healthy Choice*. Retrieved from Healthy City Design: https://healthycitydesign2019.salus.global/uploads/media/conference_lecture_presentation/0001/20/2459bb881e47ab6c074662a39832376707619a43.pdf.

Bureau of Transportation. (2015). *Mixed-use Center and Corridors Livability and Parking Analysis Final Report*. Portland: City of Portland.

Burgen, S. (2018). *For Me, This is Paradise: Life in the Spanish City that Banned Cars*. Retrieved from the Guardian: https://www.theguardian.com/cities/2018/sep/18/paradise-life-spanish-city-banned-cars-pontevedra.

Canada Energy Regulator. (2020). *Market Snapshot: Canada's Retiring Coal-fired Power Plants Will Be Replaced by Renewable and Low-carbon Energy Sources*. Retrieved from Canada Energy Regulator: https://www.cer-rec.gc.ca/en/data-analysis/energy-markets/market-snapshots/2020/market-snapshot-canadas-retiring-coal-fired-power-plants-will-be-replaced-renewable-low-carbon-energy-sources.html.

Cardelino, C. (1995). Daily variability of motor vehicle emissions derived from traffic counter data. *Journal of the Air & Waste Management Association*, 48(7): 637–645.

*Carsharing.Org*. (2017). Retrieved from What is carsharing?: https://carsharing.org/what-is-car-sharing/.

Carter, C. (2019). *Autonomous Passenger Ferries: Congestion-buster or Hype on the High Seas?* Retrieved from Smart Cities World: https://www.smartcitiesworld.net/special-reports/special-reports/autonomous-passenger-ferries-congestion-buster-or-hype-on-the-high-seas.

Center for Sustainable Systems. (2020). *Geothermal Energy*. Detroit, Michigan: University of Michigan. Retrieved from Geothermal Energy.: http://css.umich.edu/sites/default/files/Geothermal%20Energy_CSS10-10_e2020.pdf.

Certeau, M.D. (1984). *The Practice of Everyday Life*. Berkeley: University of California Press (English).

Chan, K. (2020). *Vancouver City Council Approves Study on Eliminating Minimum Parking Standards*. Retrieved from Daily Hive: https://dailyhive.com/vancouver/vancouver-city-council-approves-study-on-eliminating-minimum-parking-standards.

Charles, A.S., Lambert, H.G. and Balogh, S.B. (2014). EROI of different fuels and the implications for society. *Energy Policy*, 64: 141–152.

Chellapilla, K. (2018). *Rethinking Maps for Self-Driving*. Medium.

Cherry, K. (2020). *The Preconscious, Conscious, and Unconscious Minds*. Retrieved from Very Well Mind: https://www.verywellmind.com/the-conscious-and-unconscious-mind-2795946.

Chester, M., Horvath, A. and Madanat, S. (2010). Parking infrastructure: Energy, emissions, and automobile life-cycle environmental accounting. *Environmental Research Letters*, 5(3): 034001.

Christensen, A. and Petrenko, C. (2017). *$CO_2$-Based Synthetic Fuel: Assessment of Potential European Capacity and Environmental Performance*. Brussels: European Climate Foundation and the International Council on Clean Transportation.

City of Portland. (2005). *NE Siskiyou Green Street Project*. Portland: City of Portland.

City of Toronto. (2012). *Road to Health: Improving Walking and Cycling in Toronto*. Toronto: City of Toronto.

City of Toronto. (2017). *2050 Pathway to a Low-Carbon Toronto*. Toronto: City of Toronto.

City of Toronto. (2018). *Toronto Green Standard Version 3*. Toronto, Canada: City of Toronto.

City of Toronto. (2019). *Declaring a Climate Emergency and Accelerating Toronto's Climate Action Plan*. Toronto: City of Toronto.

City of Toronto. (2020). *Energy Efficiency Report Submission & Modelling Guidelines: For the Toronto Green Standard (TGS) Version 3*. Toronto, Canada: Environment and Energy Division & City Planning Division, City of Toronto.

City of Toronto. (2021). *Green Streets Project Selection Process*. Toronto: City of Toronto.

City of Vancouver. (2015). *Northeast False Creek Plan*. Vancouver: City of Vancouver.

City of Vancouver. (2018). *2018 Vancouver Panel Survey*. Vancouver: City of Vancouver. Retrieved from Vancouver is Awesome.: https://www.vancouverisawesome.com/courier-archive/news/vancouverites-set-new-record-in-walking-biking-and-transit-use-3098224.

City of Vancouver. (2018). *Transportation Demand Management for Developments in Vancouver – Schedule B*. Vancouver: City of Vancouver.

City of Vancouver. (2019). *EV Charging Infrastructure Requirements for New Residential Buildings Guidance*. Vancouver, Canada: City of Vancouver.

City of Vancouver. (2020). *Climate Emergency Action Plan*. Vancouver: City of Vancouver.

Civitas. (2016). *Cities Towards Mobility 2.0: Connect, Share and Go!* Brussels, Belgium: CIVITAS WIKI consortium.

CMA. (2008). *No Breathing Room National Illness Costs of Air Pollution*. Ottawa: Canadian Medical Association.

Colorado DOT and FHWA. (2017). *Resilient Colorado*. Denver: Colorado Department of Transportation and Federal Highway Administration.

Cook, C. (2014). *Transforming the Transportation Industry with Renewable Energy*. Retrieved from Renewable Energy World: https://www.renewableenergyworld.com/2014/09/18/transforming-the-transportation-industry-with-renewable-energy/#gref.

Cooper, D. (2018). *It's Too Early to Write off Hydrogen Vehicles*. Retrieved from Engadget: https://www.engadget.com/2018-05-29-hydrogen-fuel-cell-toyota-mirai-evs.html.

CPCS and Hatch Associates. (1992). *Commuter Rail Services: Electrification Study*. Toronto: GO Transit.

Curie, J. and Pierre, C. (1880). Développement, par pression, de l'électricité polaire dans les cristaux hémièdres à faces inclinées. *Comptes Rendus* (in French), 9: 294–295.

Dan, K. (2007). Flight of the pigeon. *Bicycling, Rodale, Inc.*, 48: 60–66.

Dave. (2018). *Car-Sharing vs. Private Vehicle Ownership Costs*. Retrieved from Carsharing US: https://arlingtonva.s3.amazonaws.com/wp-content/uploads/sites/19/2017/03/DES-Carshare-CarShare_vs_PrivateCarOwnership_Cost_Analysis.pdf.

David, H. (2004). *Bicycle: The History*. Yale University Press. ISBN 0-300-10418-9.

Debhia, P. (2019). *The History of Electric Scooters*. Retrieved from LinkedIn: https://www.linkedin.com/pulse/history-electric-scooters-prashant-dedhia-negotiation-ninja-/.

Debord, G. (1957). *Report on the Construction of Situations: Situationist International Anthology*. Berkeley: Bureau of Public Secrets.

Deluchhi, M.A. and Jaconson, M.Z. (2009). A path to sustainable energy by 2030. *Scientific American*, 58–65.

DeMaio, P. (2009). Bike-sharing: Impacts, models of provision, and future. *Journal of Public Transportation*, 12(4): 41–56.

DeMaio, P.J. (2003). Smart bikes: Public transportation for the 21st century. *Transportation Quarterly*, 57(1): 9–11.

DMG. (2016). *Travel Demand Management*. Guelph: University of Toronto.

Doctoroff, D. (2015). Panel Discussion: Disrupting Mobility. *Disrupting Mobility*. Boston: MIT Media Lab and Univerisity of California, Berkeley.

Donnelly, B. (2016). *Social Hubs for Auto-autos*. Retrieved from A CNU Journal: https://www.cnu.org/publicsquare/2016/12/08/social-hubs-auto-autos.

Driving. (2015). *Company Wants to Bring Rickshaws to North America*. Retrieved from Driving: https://driving.ca/auto-news/news/company-wants-to-bring-rickshaws-to-north-america.

Duffy, M.C. (2003). *Electric Railways: 1880–1990*. London: The Institution of Engineering and Technology.

Dumbaugh, E. (2005). Safe streets, livable streets. *Journal of the American Planning Association*, 71(3): 283–300.

Ellis, G.F. (2005). Physics, complexity, and causality. *Nature*, 435: 743.

Endsley, M.R. and Kiris, E.O. (1995). The out-of-the-loop performance problem and level of control in automation. *Human Factors The Journal of the Human Factors and Ergonomics Society*, 2: 27.

Energy Information Administration. (2017). *Study of the Potential Energy Consumption Impacts of Connected and Automated Vehicles*. Washington, D.C.: US Department of Energy.

Energy Innovation. (2015). *Comparing the Costs of Renewable and Conventional Energy Sources*. Retrieved from Energy Innovation: https://energyinnovation.org/2015/02/07/levelized-cost-of-energy/.

ETSC. (2020). *Pontevedra, Spain, Wins the First EU Urban Road Safety Award*. Retrieved from European Transport Safety Council: https://etsc.eu/pontevedra-spain-wins-the-first-eu-urban-road-safety-award/.

Eugster, J.W. (2007). Road and bridge heating using geothermal energy. overview and examples. *Proceedings European Geothermal Congress* (pp. 1–5). Unterhaching, Germany: European Geothermal Congress.

European Commision. (2020). *Energy Efficiency Indicator*. Retrieved from European Commision: https://ec.europa.eu/transport/themes/energy-efficiency-indicator_en.

Evans, M. (2001). Understanding policy networks: Towards a dialectical approach. *Political Studies*, 49: 542–550.

FHWA. (2017). *Proven Safety Countermeasures*. Retrieved from Federal Highway Administration: https://safety.fhwa.dot.gov/provencountermeasures/.

FHWA. (2019). *Status of the Nation's Highways, Bridges, and Transit: Conditions & Performance: Appendix A*. Washington D.C.: Policy and Government Afaairs, Federal Highway Administration.

Fishbone, A., Shahan, Z. and Badik, P. (2017). *Electric Vehicle Charging Infrastructure: Guidelines for Cities*. Wassaw, Poland: CleanTechnica.

Fishman, E. (2014). Bikeshare: A review of recent literature. *Transport Reviews*, 92–113.

Fleming, S. (2021). *Sweden Says goodbye to Parking Spaces, Hello to Meeting Places*. Retrieved from World Economic Forum: https://www.weforum.org/agenda/2021/02/sweden-local-parking-community.

Fox, D. (2011). The limits of intelligence. Scientific American, July. *Scientific American*, 37–43.

François-Lavet, V., Henderson, P., Islam, R., Bellemare, M.G. and Pineau, J. (2018). An introduction to deep reinforcement learning. *Foundations and Trends in Machine Learning*, 11(3-4): 1–102.

Frayer, L. and Cater, F. (2015). *How A Folding Electric Vehicle Went from Car of The Future to 'Obsolete'*. Retrieved from NPR: http://www.npr.org/sections/alltechconsidered/2015/11/05/454693583/how-a-folding-electric-vehicle-went-from-car-of-the-future-to-obsolete.

Freud, S. (1901). *Psychopathology of Everyday Life (Zur Psychopathologie des Alltagslebens)*. Berlin: Fischer Taschenbuch Verlag.

Freud, S. (1955). *The Unconscious XIV* (2nd Edn.). London: Hogarth Press.

Frontier Group. (2020). *America's Highway Spending Binge Goes On And On And On*. Retrieved from Frontier Group: https://frontiergroup.org/blogs/blog/fg/americas-highway-spending-binge-goes-and-and.

Fukuyama, F. (1992). *The End of History and the Last Man*. New York: Free Press.

Furman, B., Fabian, L., Ellis, S., Muller, P. and Swenson, R. (2014). *Automated Transit Networks (ATN): A Review of the State of the Industry and Prospects for the Future*. San José: Minata Transportation Institute.

Galatoulas, N.F., Genikomsakis, K.N. and Loakimidis, C.S. (2020). Spatio-temporal trends of E-bike sharing system deployment: A review in Europe, North America, and Asia. *Sustainability*, 12: 4611.

Gambs, S., Killijian, M. and Cortez, M.N. (2011). Towards temporal mobility markov chains. *1st International Workshop on Dynamicity Collocated with OPODIS* (pp. 1–2). Toulouse, France: OPODIS.

Gately, C., Hutyra, L. and Wing, I. (2015). Cities, traffic, and CO2: A multidecadal assessment of trends, drivers, and scaling relationships. *PNAS*, 112(16): 4999–5004.

Gawron, V.J. (2019). *Automation in Aviation – Definition of Automation*. McLean, VA: The MITRE Corporation.

Gee, M. (2016). *Raise the Roof? Union Station Reno Runs into Problem: New Trains Won't Fit*. Retrieved from The Globe and Mail: https://www.theglobeandmail.com/news/toronto/union-station-shed-renovation-stalled-by-low-arches-and-an-electrified-future/article28448568/.

Geidl, M., Koeppel, G., Favre-Perrod, P., Klöckl, B., Andersson, G. and Fröhlich, K. (2007). The energy hub – A powerful concept for future energy systems. *Third Annual Carnegie Mellon Conference on the Electricity Industry* (pp. 2–10). Pittsburgh: Carnegie Mellon University.

Gennep, V.A. (2011). *The Rites of Passage.* Chicago: University of Chicago Press.

Geotab. (2018). *Gridlocked Cities: Traffic Patterns Revealed across 20 Major U.S. Cities.* Retrieved from Geotab: https://www.geotab.com/press-release/traffic-congestion-patterns/.

Gilpin, L. (2017). *Can Car-Sharing Culture Help Fuel an Electric Vehicle Revolution?* Retrieved from Insideclimate: https://insideclimatenews.org/news/07122017/car-rental-sharing-electric-vehicles-zipcar-evs-uber-lyft-green-commuter.

Global Designing Cities. (2019). *Multimodal Streets Serve More People.* Retrieved from Global Designing Cities: https://globaldesigningcities.org/publication/global-street-design-guide/defining-streets/multimodal-streets-serve-people/.

Global Union. (2020). *Top 10 Principles for Ethical Artifical Intelligence.* Nyon, Switzerland: The Future World of Work.

Gomes, L. (2014). *Hidden Obstacles for Google's Self-Driving Cars: Impressive Progress Hides Major Limitations of Google's Quest for Automated Driving.* Cambridge, USA: MIT Technology Review.

González-Campo, C.H., Solarte, M.G. and Vargas, G.M. (2011). Avatar(A'): Contracting Lacan's theory and 3D virtual worlds—A case study in second life. *Psicología desde el caribe*, 30(2): 309–324.

Goodyear, S. (2014). *How Parking Spaces are Eating Our Cities Alive.* Retrieved from CityLab Transportation: https://www.bloomberg.com/news/articles/2014-07-14/how-parking-spaces-are-eating-our-cities-alive.

Gordon, L.A. and Shirokoff, I. (2014). *Suburban Nation? Population Growth in Canadian Suburbs, 2006–2011. Working Paper #1.* Ottawa: Council for Canadian Urbanism.

Government of Ontario. (2019). *Places to Grow Act.* Toronto: Government of Ontario.

Greenstein, D., Tiefenthaler, L. and Bay, S. (2004). Toxicity of parking lot runoff after application of simulated rainfall. *Archives of Environmental Contamination and Toxicology*, 47(2): 199–206.

Griloa, F.a.-R. (2020). Using green to cool the grey: Modelling the cooling effect of green spaces with a high spatial resolution. *Science of the Total Environment*, 1–10.

Gross, S. (2020). *Why are Fossil Fuels so Hard to Quit?* Retrieved from Brookings Institution: https://www.brookings.edu/essay/why-are-fossil-fuels-so-hard-to-quit/#:~:text=We%20understand%20today%20that%20humanity's,climate%20of%20our%20entire%20planet.

GTA Clean Air Council. (2017). *Climate Action for a Healthy, Equitable and Prosperous Toronto.* Toronto: City of Toronto.

Hagel, G.W. (1977). *Hegel's Phenomenology of Spirit. Translated by A. V. Miller.* Oxford: Oxford University Press.

Harb, M., Xiao, Y., Circella, G., Mokhtarian, P.L. and Walker, J.L. (2018). Projecting travelers into a world of self-driving vehicles: Estimating travel behavior implications via a naturalistic experiment. *Transportation*, 45: 1671–1685.

Harms, S. and Truffer, B. (1998). *The Emergence of a Nationwide Carsharing Co-operative in Switzerland: A Case Study for the Project StrategicNiche Management as a Tool for Transition to a Sustainable Transportation System.* 1998: EAWAG-Eidg. Anstalt für Wasserversorgung und Gewasserschutz.

Haugneland, P., Lorentzen, E., Bu, C. and Hauge, E. (2017). Put a price on carbon to fund EV incentives – Norwegian EV policy success. *EVS30 Symposium* (pp. 1–8). Stuttgart, Germany: Norwegian EV Association.

Haywood, J.B. (2006). Fueling our transportation future. *Scientific American.*

Hess, A. and Schubert, I. (2019). Functional perceptions, barriers, and demographics concerning e-cargo bike sharing in Switzerland. *Transportation Research Part D: Transport and Environment*, 71: 153. Retrieved from Science daily: https://www.sciencedaily.com/releases/2019/07/190710121536.htm.

Hillier, B. (1996). *Space is the Machine: A Configurational Theory of Architecture.* London: Press Syndicate of the University of Cambridge.

Holland, H., House, H. and Rucks, G. (2018). *Reimagining the Urban Form: Austin's Community Mobility Hub.* Austin: Rocky Mountain Institute.

Hoopengardner, R. and Thompson, M. (2012). *FTA Low-Speed Urban Maglev Research Program: Updated Lessons Learned.* Arlington, USA: US Federal Transit Administration.

Hordnes, E. (2019). *Race to Electrification – Norway in a Pole Position.* Retrieved from Urban Insight: https://www.swecourbaninsight.com/urban-energy/race-to-electrification--norway-in-pole-position/.

Howell, M. (2021). *Vancouver Pushes City-wide Parking Permit Program.* Retrieved from Vancouver is Awesome: https://www.vancouverisawesome.com/vancouver-news/vancouver-pushes-city-wide-parking-permit-program-3300740#:~:text=Vancouver%20is%20pushing%20ahead%20with,up%20to%20%2445%20a%20year.

Hughes, I. and Huo, R. (2018). *Autonomy-level Classification for Robots in an IIoT World.* Retrieved from 451 Research: https://go.451research.com/MI-Robots-in-IIoT-World.html.

Hull, G.J., Roberts, C. and Hillmansen, S. (2008). Energy efficiency of a railway power network with simulation. *International Conference on Energy Technologies and Policy.* Birmingham, United Kingdom: Univerisity of Birmingham.

ICAU. (2014). *Scaling Infrastructure.* Retrieved from MIT School of Architechture and Planning: https://lcau.mit.edu/conference/scaling-infrastructure.

IDTP. (2011). *Europe's Parking U-Turn: From Accommodation to Regulation.* Rome: IDTP.

IISD. (2015). *The End of Coal: Ontario's Coal Phase-out.* Winnipeg, Canada: International Institute for Sustainable Development.

Im, J. (2019). Green streets to serve urban sustainability: Benefits and typology. *Sustainability*, 11(6483): 1–22.

Institute, R.M. (2019). *Electric Mobility: Best Practices.* Rocky Mountain Institute, Government of India and Smart City.

IPCC. (2018). *Global Warming of 1.5°C.* New York: Intergovernmental Panel on Climate Change.

Islam, A.S. and Ahiduzzaman, M. (2012). Biomass energy: Sustainable solution for greenhouse gas emission. *American Inst. Phys. Conf. Proc.*, 1441(1): 23–32. American Institute of Physics.

ISO. (2020). *Road Vehicles — Human Performance and State in the Context of Automated Driving – Part 2: Considerations in Designing Experiments to Investigate Transition Processes.* ISO/TR 21959-2: 2020.

ITE. (2021). *Curbside Management Tool User Guide.* Washington, D.C.: Institute of Transportation Engineers.

ITF. (2022). *Streets That Fit: Re-allocating Space for Better Cities.* Paris: The International Transport Forum.

Itoh, M.H. and Kitazaki, S. (2018). What may happen or what you should do? Effects of knowledge representation regarding necessity of intervention on driver performance under level 2 automated driving. *ICPS'18: Proceedings of the 2018 IEEE Industrial Cyber-Physical Systems* (pp. 621–626). Saint Petersburg, Russia: IEEE.

J2954. (2019). *Wireless Power Transfer for Light-Duty Plug-in/Electric Vehicles and Alignment Methodology.* SAE International.

J3068. (2018). *Electric Vehicle Power Transfer System Using a Three-Phase Capable Coupler.* SAE International.

J3105. (2020). *Electric Vehicle Power Transfer System Using Conductive Automated Connection Devices.* SAE International.

Jameson, F. (2002). *A Singular Modernity: Essay on the Ontology of the Present.* London & New York: Verso.

Jayasuriya, D. (1994). Street food vending in Asia: Some policy and legal aspects. *Food Control, Elsevier*, 5(4): 222–226.

Jefferies, I. (2019, November 20). Retrieved from Association of American Railroads: https://www.aar.org/article/freight-rail-highly-automated-vehicles/.

Jettanasen, C., Songsukthawan, P. and Ngaopitakkul, A. (2020). Development of micro-mobility based on piezoelectric energy harvesting for smart city applications. *Sustainability*, 1–16.

Jordan, Z.A. (1967). *The Evolution of Dialectical Materialism.* London: Macmillan.

Jorna, A. (2012). *Synthetic Fuel Costs.* Stanford, California: Stanford University.

Joshi, N. (2019). *7 Types of Artificial Intelligence.* Retrieved from Forbes: https://www.forbes.com/sites/cognitiveworld/2019/06/19/7-types-of-artificial-intelligence/.

Junkin, K. (2013). *Regional Rapid Rail: A Vision for the Future.* Toronto: Transport Actione, Ontario.

Kachlík, D., Varga, I., Báča, V. and Musil, V. (2020). Variant anatomy and its terminology. *Medicina (Kaunas)*, 56(12): 713.

Kalra, N. and Paddock, S.M. (2016). *How Many Miles of Driving Would it Take to Demonstrate Autonomous Vehicle Reliability? Driving to Safety.* Santa Monica, California: RAND Corporation.

Kane, M. (2019). *Chile Launches Latin America's First 100% Electric Bus Corridor.* Retrieved from Inside EVs: https://insideevs.com/news/377241/chile-first-100-electric-bus-corridor/.

Kant, E. (1781). *Critique of Pure Reason.* Riga: Johann Friedrich Hartknoch.

KAPSARC. (2016). *Mobility-on-demand: Understanding Energy Impacts and Adoption Potential.* Riyadh: KASARC.

Karatani, K. (2011). *History and Repetition.* New York: Columbia University Press.

Karim, D. and Bennett, S. (2022). Vision Zero Vs. Zero Vision: Framework of Systematic and Scientific Approach to Vision Zero. Annual Conference, Canadian Institute of Transportation Engineers, Vancouver, June 4, 2022.

Karim, D.M. (2017). *Disrupting Mobility Ecosystem: Combining Multimodal, Innovation, and Creative Design.* Toronto: City of Toronto.

Karim, D.M. (2017). Innovative Mobility Master Plan – Connecting Multimodal Systems with Smart Technologies. *Disrupting Mobility* (p. 1). Boston: MIT Media Lab and University of California, Berkeley.

Karim, D.M. (2019). Integrating smart urban mobility and city planning for livable cities. *International Automobile Association* (pp. 1–23). Frankfurt: International Automobile Association.

Karim, D.M. and Shallwani, T. (2010). Toward a clean train policy: Diesel versus electric. *Ontario Centre for Engineering and Public Policy* (OCEPP), 3: 18–22.

Keeble, L. (1961). *Town Planning at the Crossroads.* London: The Estates Gazette Limited.

Khayal, O. (2019). The history of Bajaj rickshaw vehicles. *Global Journal of Engineering Sciences*, 3(2): 1–8.

Kleinman, M.T. (2000). *The Health Effects of Air Pollution on Children.* Irvine, California: South Coast Air Quality Management District (SCAQMD).

Kour, R. and Charif, A. (2016). Piezoelectric roads: Energy harvesting method using piezoelectric technology. *Innovative Energy & Research*, 5(1).

Kwon, D. (2018). Self-taught robots. *Scientific American*, 26–31.

Kwon, H., Ryu, M.H. and Carlsten, C. (2020). Ultrafine particles: Unique physicochemical properties relevant to health and disease. *Experimental & Molecular Medicine*, 52: 318–328.

Lacan, J. (1960–61). *Le Séminaire. Livre VIII. Le transfert.* Paris: Seuil.

Lacan, J. (1973). *The Four Fundamental Concepts of Psycho-analysis.* Paris: Le Seuil.

Lambert, F. (2020). *Uber and Hyundai Unveil New Electric Air Taxi with 60-mile Range.* Retrieved from Electrek: https://electrek.co/2020/01/07/uber-hyundai-electric-air-taxi-evtol/.

Layton, B.E. (2008). A comparison of energy densities of prevalent energy sources in units of houles per cubic meter. *International Journal of Green Energy*, 5: 438–455.

Le Vine, S., Lee-Gosselin, M., Sivakumar, A. and Polak, J. (2014). New approach to predict the market and impacts of round-trip and point-to-point carsharing systems: case study of London. *Transportation Research Part D*, 32(C): 218–229.

Le Vine, S., Zolfaghari, A. and Polak, J. (2014). *Carsharing: Evolution, Challenges and Opportunities.* London: Centre for Transport Studies, Imperial College London.

Ledsham, T. and Savan, B. (2017). *Building a 21st Century Cycling City: Strategies for Action in Toronto.* Toronto: Metcalf Foundation.

Lee-Shanok, P. (2017). *Ontario Condo Act a Roadblock for Electric Vehicle Owners.* Retrieved from CBC News: https://www.cbc.ca/news/canada/toronto/ontario-hopes-revised-condo-act-ev-friendly-1.4155747.

Lefebvre, H. (1947). *The Critique of Everyday Life.* London: Verso.

Lenton, T.M., Held, H., Kriegler, E., Hall, J.W., Lucht, W., Rahmstorf, S. and Schellnhuber, H.J. (2008). Tipping elements in the Earth's climate system. *PNAS*, 105(6): 1786–1793.

Lenton, T.M., Rockström, J., Gaffney, O., Rahmstorf, S., Richardson, K., Steffen, W. and Schellnhuber, H.J. (2019). *Climate Tipping Points –Too Risky to Bet Against.* Retrieved from Nature: https://www.nature.com/articles/d41586-019-03595-0#ref-CR2.

Lessing, H. (2001). What led to the invention of the early bicycle? *Cycle History 11, San Francisco*, 11: 28–36. Retrieved from New Scientist: https://www.newscientist.com/article/mg18524841-900-brimstone-and-bicycles/.

Levin, S. (1998). Ecosystems and the biosphere as complex adaptive systems. *Ecosystems*, 1(5): 431–436.

Li, L. and Loo, B.P. (2014). Alternative and transitional energy sources for urban transportation. *Current Sustainable/Renewable Energy Reports*, 1: 19–26.

Li, X. and Strezov, V. (2014). Modelling piezoelectric energy harvesting potential in an educational building. *Energy Conversion and Management*, 85: 435–442.

Li, X., Gorghinpour, C., Sclar, R. and Castellanos, S. (2018). *How to Enable Electric Bus Adoption in Cities Worldwide.* Berlin: World Resources Institute, WRI and German Federal Ministry.

Liao, Y., Gil, J., Pereira, R.H., Yeh, S. and Verendel, V. (2020). Disparities in travel times between car and transit: Spatiotemporal patterns in cities. *Nature*, 10: 4056.

Lima, M. (2015). *The Bicycle in the 21st Century.* Retrieved from Theprotocity: http://theprotocity.com/the-bicycle-in-the-21st-century/.

Listokin, D., Voicu, I., Dolphin, W., Camp, M., Jay, D., Leavey, M. and Sherry, J. (2007). *Infill Development Standards and Policy Guide.* New Jersey: Center for Urban Policy Research, Rutgers University for New Jersey.

Litman, T. (2011). Can smart growth policies conserve energy and reduce emissions? *Cent. Real Estate Quarterly Journal*, 1–4.

Litman, T. (2017). *The Future of Mobility in Cities –Multimodal and Integrated.* Retrieved from Planetizen: https://www.planetizen.com/news/2017/10/95204-future-mobility-cities-multimodal-and-integrated.

Litman, T. (2018). Retrieved from Carsharing: Vehicle Rental Services that Substitute for Private Vehicle Ownership: https://www.vtpi.org/tdm/tdm7.htm.

Litman, T. (2022). *Parking Requirement Impacts on Housing Affordability.* Victoria: Victoria Transport Policy Institute.

Little, A. (2015). *The Future of Urban Mobility 2.0: Towards Networked, Multimodal Cities of 2050.* Rome, Italy: International Association of Public Transport (UITP).

Lu, Z., Happe, R., Cabrall, C.D., Kyriakidis, M. and Winter, J.C. (2016). Human factors of transitions in automated driving: A general framework and literature survey. *Transportation Research Part F*, 43: 183–198.

Lucas, A., Prettico, G., Flammini, M.G., Kotsakis, E., Fulli, G. and Masera, M. (2018). Indicator-based methodology for assessing EV charging infrastructure using exploratory data analysis. *Energies*, 11(1869): 1–18.

Mao, B., Chen, H. and Chen, S. (2002). Sustainability assessment of speed regulation of urban traffic. *IATSS Research*, 26(2): 18–24.

Marchetti, C. (1994). *Anthropological Invariants in Travel Behavior.* Laxenburg: IIASA Research Report.

MaRS Discovery District. (2016). *Microtransit: An Assessment of Potential to Drive Greenhouse Gas Reductions.* Toronto: MaRS Discovery District and Richmond Sustainability Initiatives.

Martinson, R. (2017). *Resilience in a Transportation System: A Whole System Approach, Ttransportation Ssystems Resilience.* Washington D.C.: Transportation Research Circular E-C226.

Martret, O. (2020). *Electric Vehicles – Cleaner, Greener and On-Demand?* Retrieved from Shotl: https://shotl.com/news/electric-vehicles-cleaner-greener-and-on-demand.

Masoumi, H. (2019). A discrete choice analysis of transport mode choice causality and perceived barriers of sustainable mobility in the MENA region. *Transport Policy*, 79: 37–53.

Matuka, R. (2014). *The History of the Electric Car.* Retrieved from US Department of Energy.

Matyas, M. (2020). Opportunities and barriers to multimodal cities: Lessons learned from in-depth interviews about attitudes towards mobility as a service. *European Transport Research Review*, 12(7): 1–11.

Maybee, J.E. (2020). *Hegel's Dialectics.* Retrieved from the Stanford Encyclopedia of Philosophy: https://plato.stanford.edu/entries/hegel-dialectics/.

McCormack, D.P. (2013). *Refrains for Moving Bodies: Experience and Experiment in Affective Spaces.* Oxford: Due University Press.

McMahon, J. (2019). *9 Shared-Mobility Startups Eager to Disrupt Transportation.* Retrieved from Forbes: https://www.forbes.com/sites/jeffmcmahon/2019/03/06/9-shared-mobility-startups-eager-to-disrupt-transportation/.

McNabb, M. (2019). *DRONEII: Tech Talk – Unraveling 5 Levels of Drones.* Drone Talk.

Meadows, D. (2008). *Thinking in Systems: A Primer* (Wright, D. ed.). Hartford: Chelsea Green Publishing.

Medina-Tapiaa, M. and Robusteb, F. (2018). Exploring paradigm shift impacts in urban mobility: Autonomous vehicles and smart cities. *Transportation Research Procedia*, 33: 203–210.

Melaina, M., Bush, B., Muratori, M., Zuboy, J. and Ellis, S. (2017). *National Hydrogen Scenerios: How Many Stations, Where, and When?* Washington, D.C.: National Renewable Energy Laboratory for the H2USA.

Menon, M. (2015). *Indifference to Difference: On Queer Universalism.* Minneapolis: University of Minnesota Press.

Metrolinx. (2008). *The Big Move: Transforming Transportation in the Greater Toronto and Hamilton Area.* Toronto: Metrolinx.

Metrolinx. (2011). *Mobility Hub Guidelines for the Greater Toronto and Hamilton Area.* Toronto: Metrolinx.

Millard-Ball, A. (2019, March). The autonomous vehicle parking problem. 75: 99–108.

Millennium Ecosystem Assessment Board. (2005). *Ecosystems and Human Well-being: A Framework for Assessment.* New York: Island Press.

Miller, E. (2017, October 25). Big Data, Better Transportation Planning (S. Paikin, Interviewer).

MIT Media Lab. (2019). *Persuasive Electric Vehicle (PEV).* Retrieved from MIT Media Lab City Science Group: https://www.media.mit.edu/projects/pev/overview/.

Mitchell, A. (2013). *Risk and Resilience: From Good Idea to Good Practice. OECD Development Assistance.* Paris: OECD Development Assistance.

Mitchell, W.J., Borroni-Bird, C.E. and Burns, L.D. (2015). *Reinventing the Automobile.* Cambridge, USA: The MIT Press.

Mohorčich, J. (2020). Energy intensity and human mobility after the anthropocene. *Sustainability*, 12: 2376–2389.

Molloy, J., Schatzmann, T., Schoeman, B., Tchervenkov, C., Hintermann, B. and Axhausen, K.W. (2021). Observed impacts of the Covid-19 first wave on travel behaviour in Switzerland based on a large GPS panel. *Transport Policy*, 104: 43–51.

Morawska, L., Moore, M.R. and Ristovski, Z.D. (2014). *Health Impacts of Ultrafine Particles: Desktop Literature Review and Analysis.* Canberra: Australian Government Department of the Environment and Heritage.

Mostashari, A., Omer, M. and Nilchiani, R. (2013). Assessing resilience in a regional road-based transportation network. *International Journal of Industrial and Systems Engineering*, 13(4): 389–408.

MotionTag. (2022). *AI for Mobility Research: Towards Fully Automated Travel Diaries.* Retrieved from MotionTag: https://app.livestorm.co/motion-tag/ai-for-mobility-research/live?s=255c294a-f6e3-431f-bd44-5afab5e5fcdc#/chat.

Movmi. (2018). *Carsharing Market Analysis: Growth and Industry Analysis.* Retrieved from Movmi.net: https://movmi.net/carsharing-market-growth/.

Muheim, P. and Partners. (1996). *Car Sharing Studies: An Investigation.* Dublin, Ireland: Graham Lightfoot.

Müller, V.C. (2020). *Stanford Encyclopedia of Philosophy.* Retrieved from Stanford University: https://plato.stanford.edu/entries/ethics-ai/.

Münzel, K.W., Boon, K., Frenken, J. and van der Blomme, D. (2019). Explaining carsharing supply across Western European cities. *International Journal of Sustainable Transportation*, 1–12.

NACTO. (2013). *Urban Street Design Guide*. New York: National Association of City Transportation Officials.

NACTO. (2017). *Designing to Move People*. Retrieved from NACTO: https://nacto.org/publication/transit-street-design-guide/introduction/why/designing-move-people/.

Najini, H. and Muthukumaraswamy, S.A. (2017). Piezoelectric energy generation from vehicle traffic with technoeconomic analysis. *Journal of Renewable Energy*, 1–16.

Namazu, M. (2017). *The Evolution of Carsharing: Heterogeneity in Adoption and Impacts*. Vancouver: The University of British Columbia.

NCCHPP. (2014). *A 30-km/h Speed Limit on Local Streets*. Montreal: National Collaborating Centre for Healthy Public Policy.

Nelson, R.G. (2022). A microbe proved that individualism is a myth. *Scientific American*, 32–33.

Network Rail Infrastructure Limited. (2020). *Network Statement 2020*. London, UK: Network Rail.

Newswire. (2010). *Vancouver First City in the World to Endorse the Fossil Fuel Non-Proliferation Treaty*. Retrieved from Fossil Fuel Non-Proliferation Treaty: https://www.newswire.ca/news-releases/vancouver-first-city-in-the-world-to-endorse-the-fossil-fuel-non-proliferation-treaty-843699223.html.

NHTSA. (2016). *Federal Motor Vehicle Safety Standards: Minimum Sound Requirements for Hybrid and Electric Vehicles*. Washington D.C.: National Highway Traffic Safety Administration, NHTSA.

Nilsson, N.J. (1982). *Principles of Artificial Intelligence*. Elsevier Inc.

NTSB. (2020). *Tesla Crash Investigation Yields 9 NTSB Safety Recommendations*. National Transportation Safety Board.

OECD. (2014). *Guidelines for Resilience Systems Analysis*. Paris: OECD Publishing.

Ohta, K. (1998). TDM measures toward sustainable mobility. *IATSS Research*, 22(1).

Oldenburg, R. (1999). *The Great Good Place: Cafes, Coffee Shops, Bookstores, Bars, Hair Salons, and Other Hangouts at the Heart of a Community*. Boston: Marlowe & Company.

Omi, K. (2018). *Alternative Energy for Transportation*. Retrieved from Issues in Science and Technology: https://issues.org/omi/.

Ongel, A., Loewer, E., Roemer, F., Sethuraman, G. and Chang, F. (2019). Economic assessment of autonomous electric microtransit vehicles. *Sustainability*, 2–18.

Ontario Medical Association. (2005). *The Illness Costs of Air Pollution: 2005–2026 Health and Economic Damage Estimates*. Toronto: OMA.

Orenstein, M. (2020). *COVID-19's Effect on Energy and Emissions – and Implications for the Future*. Retrieved from Canawest Foundation: https://cwf.ca/research/publications/what-now-covid-19s-effect-on-energy-and-emissions-and-implications-for-the-future/.

Pagliaro, J. and Rider, D. (2018). *Tory and Keesmaat Disagree about the Gardiner Expressway. Here's a Close Look at Their Claims*. Retrieved from The Toronto Star: https://www.thestar.com/news/toronto-election/2018/10/05/tory-and-keesmaat-disagree-about-the-gardiner-expressway-heres-a-close-look-at-their-claims.html.

Panchal, D.U. (2015). *Two and Three Wheeler Technology*. PHI Learning Pvt. Ltd., ISBN 9788120351431.

Parasuraman, R. (1992). Adaptive function allocation effects on pilot performance. *NASA/FAA Workshop on Artificial Intelligence and Human Factors*. Daytona Beach, Florida, USA: NASA and FAA.

Parasuraman, R., Sheridan, T. and Wickens, C. (2000). A model for types and levels of human interaction with automation. *IEEE Transactions on Systems, Man, and Cybernetics –Part A: Systems and Humans*, 30(3): 286–297.

PBS. (2009). *Timeline: History of the Electric Car*. Retrieved from PBS.Org: https://www.pbs.org/now/shows/223/electric-car-timeline.html.

Perner, J., Unteutsch, M. and Lövenich, A. (2018). *The Future Cost of Electricity-based Synthetic Fuels*. Berlin: Agora Energiewende.

Pete. (2015). *Electric Cargo Bike Guide*. Retrieved from Electric Bike Report: https://electricbikereport.com/electric-cargo-bike-guide/.

Pichère, P. (2015). *The Law of Diminishing Returns: Understand the Fundamentals of Economic Productivity*. pp. 9–12. ISBN 978-2806270092. Web only: 50Minutes.com.

Pope III, C.A., Burnett, R.T., Thun, M.J., Calle, E.E., Krewski, D., Ito, K. and Thurston, G.D. (2002). Lung cancer, cardiopulmonary mortality, and long-term exposure to fine particulate air pollution. *The Journal of the American Medical Association*, 287(9): 1132–1141.

Porru, M., Serpi, A., Mureddu, M. and Damiano, A. (2020). A multistage design procedure for planning and implementing public charging infrastructures for electric vehicles. *Sustainability*, 2889(12): 1–17.

Pratt, R.H. (1970). A utilitarian theory of travel mode choice. *Highway Research Record*, 40–53.

Priemus, H. (2007). Dutch Spatial Planning between Substratum and Infrastructure Networks. *European Plannning Studies*, 15(5): 667–686.

Puchalsky, C.M. (2005). Comparison of emissions from light rail and bus rapid transit. *Transportation Research Record*, 1927(1): 31–37.

Qiu, C., Chau, K.T., Ching, T.W. and Liu, C. (2014). Overview of wireless charging technologies for electric vehicles. *Journal of Asian Electric Vehicles*, 12: 1679–1685.

Raad Voor Verkeer en Waterstaat. (2001). *Van modal split naar modal merge, Advies over de toekomst van hetregionaal verkeer en vervoer.* Den Haag: Dutch Advisory Council for Transport, Public Works, and Watermanagement.

Rajvanshi, A.K. (2002). Electric and improved cycle rickshaw as a sustainable transport system for India. *Current Science*, 83(6): 703–707.

Ram, G., Mouli, C., Duijsen, P.V., Grazian, F., Jamodkar, A., Bauer, P. and Isabella, O. (2020). Sustainable E-bike charging station that enables AC, DC, and wireless charging from solar energy. *Energies*, 13(3549): 1–21.

Ratti, C. (2018). *The Dynamic Street.* Retrieved from Carlo Ratti Associati: https://carloratti.com/project/the-dynamic-street/.

Reddy, T. (2008). *Synthetic Fuels Handbook: Properties, Process, and Performance.* McGraw-Hill.

Regnier, E. (2007). Oil and energy price volatility. *Energy Economic*, 29(3): 405–427.

Richard, F. and Cooper, H. (2005). Richard and cooper. "Why electrified rail is superior". *21st Century Science & Technology*, 18: 26–29.

Rickstrom, J. and Klum, M. (2015). *Big World, Small Planet: Abundance within Planetary Boundaries.* New Haven and London: Yale University Press.

Rideamigos. (2018). *What is Transportation Demand Management?* Retrieved from Rideamigos: https://rideamigos.com/transportation-demand-management-tdm/.

Rider, D. (2020). *Toronto Adds Electric Bicycles to Bike-share Fleet — at no Extra Cost to Users.* Retrieved from Toronto Star: https://www.thestar.com/news/city_hall/2020/08/19/toronto-adds-electric-bicycles-to-bike-share-fleet-at-no-extra-cost-to-users.html.

Rieti, J. (2017). *CBC News.* Retrieved from Toronto discourages electric car use by denying on-street chargers, driver says: https://www.cbc.ca/news/canada/toronto/electric-vehicles-blocked-1.4368014.

Ritchie, H. (2020). *What are the Safest and Cleanest Sources of Energy?* Retrieved from Our world in data: https://ourworldindata.org/safest-sources-of-energy.

Rodenbach, J., Mathis, J., Chicco, A., Diana, M. and Nehrk, G. (2017). *Car Sharing in Europe: A Multidimensional Classification and Inventory.* European Union: STARS and AUTON.

Rosenzweig, C., Solecki, W. and Slosberg, R. (2006). Mitigating New York city's heat island with urban forestry, living roofs, and light surfaces. a report to the new york state energy research and development authority. *NYSERDA*, 06(06): 133.

SAE. (2014). *Taxonomy and Definitions for Terms Related to On-Road Motor Vehicle Automated Driving Systems.* USA: SAE International.

SAE. (2018). *Taxonomy and Definitions for Terms Related to Shared Mobility and Enabling Technologies.* USA: SAE International.

SAE International. (2014). *Ground Vehicle Standards.* USA: SAE International.

SAE International. (2019). *A Dictionary of Terms for the Dynamics and Handling of Single Track Vehicles (Motorcycles, Scooters, Mopeds, and Bicycles).* Warrendale, PA, USA: J1451_201909. Society of Automotive Engineers.

SAE International. (2019). *J3194 –Taxonomy and Classification of Powered Micromobility Vehicles.* Warrendale, PA, USA: Society of Automotive Engineers.

Saunders, K. (2017). *Where's the Hype for Automated Trains? Part 1: History and Background.* Automation.

Sawilla, Schütt and Oskar. (2018). *Ipt-technology.* Retrieved from Wireless Opportunity Charging Buses in Madrid: https://ipt-technology.com/case-opportunity-charging-madrid/.

SCAQMD. (2000). *Multiple Air Toxics Exposure Study.* San Francisco: South Coast Air Quality Management District.

Schneider, C.G. and Hill, L.B. (2007). *No Escape from Diesel Exhaust: How to Reduce Commuter Exposure.* Boston: Boston: Clean Air Task Force.

Sclar, R., Gorghinpour, C., Castellanos, S. and Li, X. (2018). *Barriers to Adopting Electric Buses.* Berlin: World Resources Institute, WRI and German Federal Ministry.

Scott, A.J. (2014). Beyond the creative city: Cognitive–cultural capitalism and the new Urbanism. *Regional Studies*, 48(4): 565–578.

Shaheen, S. and Cohen, A. (2019). *Shared Micromobility Policy Toolkit: Docked and Dockless Bike and Scooter Sharing.* Schmidt Family Foundation.

Shaheen, S., Cohen, A. and Zohdy, I. (2016). *Shared Mobility: Current Practices and Guiding Principles.* Washington D.C.: Federal Highway Administration.

Shared-Use Mobility Center. (2017). *Shared-use Mobility Referrence Guide.* Chicago, USA: Shared-Use Mobility Center.

Sharpe, M. (2008). *Slavoj Žižek.* Retrieved from Internet of Encyclopedia of Philosophy: https://iep.utm.edu/zizek/.

Sheldrake, R. (2009). *Morphic Resonance: The Nature of Formative Causation.* Rochester, Vermont: Park Street Press.

Shepertycky, M. and Li, Q. (2015). Generating electricity during walking with a lower limb-driven energy harvester: Targeting a minimum user effort. *Plos ONE,* 1–16.

Shladover, S.E. (2016). The truth about "self driving" cars. *Scientific American,* 52–57.

Shoup, D. (1999). The trouble with minimum parking requirements. *Transportation Research Part A Policy and Practice,* 33(7): 549–574.

Siegenfeld, A. and Bar-Yam, F.Y. (2020). An introduction to complex systems science and its applications. *Complexity,* 1–16.

Siemens Mobility. (2015). *Sustainable Urban Infrastructure: Vienna Edition – Role Model for Complete Mobility.*

Smart Growth. (2017). *What is Gentle Density and Why Do We Need It?* Retrieved from Smart Growth: https://www.smartergrowth.ca/what-gentle-density-and-why-do-we-need-it.

Smith, J.E. (2019). *Irrationality: A History of the Dark Side of Reason.* Princeton: Princeton University Press.

Smith, R.A. (2008). Enabling technologies for demand management: Transport. *Energy Policy,* 36(12): 4444–4448.

Society of Automobile Engineers, SAE. (2018). *Shared Mobility: Taxonomy and Definitions in SAE J3163™.*

Sousa, D. (2011). Freudian theory and consciousness: A conceptual analysis. *Mens Sana Monogr.,* 9(1): 210–217.

Spaen, B. (2019). *This All-Electric Water Taxi Could Revolutionize Green Transportation.* Retrieved from Green Matters: https://www.greenmatters.com/news/2018/06/25/qSvID/water-taxis-transportation.

Sperling, D. and Shaeen, S. (1999). Carsharing: Niche market or new pathway? *ECMT/OECD Workshop on Managing Car Use for Sustainable Urban Travel* (pp. 1–25). Dublin, Ireland: OECD.

Spulber, A., Dennis, E.P. and Wallace, R. (2016). *The Impact of New Mobility Services on the Automotive Industry.* Ann Arbor, Michigan: Cargroup.Org.

Staffell, I., Scamman, D., Abad, A.V., Balcombe, P., Dodds, P.E., Ekins, P., Shah, N., and Ward, K.R. (2019). The role of hydrogen and fuel cells in the global energy system. *Energy & Environmental Science,* 12(463-491).

STAPPA and ALAPCO. (2000). *Cancer Risk from Diesel Particulate: National and Metropolitan Area Estimates for the United States.* San Francisco: State and Territorial Air Pollution Program Administrators and the Association of Local Air Pollution Control Officials.

Steer Davies Gleave. (2009). *GO Transit Lakeshore Express Rail Benefit Case, Interim Report.* Toronto: Metrolinx.

Steffen, W., Richardson, K., Rockström, J., Cornell, S., Fetzer, I., Bennett, E., Bennett, E.M., Biggs, R., Carpenter, S.R., Vrie, W.D., Wit, C.A.D., Folke, C., Gerten, D., Heinke, J., Mace, G.M., Perssson, L.M., Ramanathan, V., Reyers, B. and Sörlin, S. (2015). Planetary boundaries: Guiding human development on a changing planet. *Science,* 15: 1–10.

Stohler, W. and Giger, P. (1989). *Cost-Benefit Analysis of the Electrification of the Beira Alta Line in Portugal.* London: Institution of Electrical Engineers.

Stone, T. (2017). *Lessons Learned from the History of Car Sharing.* Retrieved from https://tiffanydstone.com/: https://tiffanydstone.com/2013/08/23/lessons-learned-from-the-history-of-car-sharing/.

Stone, T. (2018). *Siemens to Demonstrate World's First Autonomous Tram Running in Real Traffic in German City.* Retrieved from traffictechnology.com: https://www.traffictechnologytoday.com/news/autonomous-vehicles/siemens-to-demonstrate-worlds-first-autonomous-tram-running-in-real-traffic-in-german-city.html.

Strompen, F., Litman, T. and Bongardt, D. (2012). *Reducing Carbon Emissions through Transport Demand Management Strategies: A Review of International Examples, Final Report.* GIZ China, Transport Demand Management in Beijing.

Sugarman, A. and Kanner, K. (2002). Topographic theory: IV. System preconscious. pp. 835–839. *In*: Sledge, M.H. (ed.). *Encyclopedia of Psychotherapy.* Cambridge: Academic Press.

Sumar, F., Mallon, S., Landgarden and Schaer, J. (2014). *Who Really Owns Public Spaces?* Retrieved from Bloomberg News: https://www.bloomberg.com/news/articles/2014-06-30/who-really-owns-public-spaces.

SUMC. (2015). *Shared Use Mobility: Reference Guide.* Chicago: Shared-use Mobility Center (SUMC).

SUMC. (2017). *Build Your Own Mobility Hub –7 Lessons for Cities from Bremen Germany.* Retrieved from Shared Mobility Center: https://sharedusemobilitycenter.org/build-your-own-mobility-hub-7-lessons-for-cities-from-bremen-germany/.

Swenson, R. (2016). The solar evolution: Much more with way less, right now—the disruptive shift to renewables. *Energies,* 9(9): 676.

Takefuji, Y. (2008). And if public transport does not consume more energy? (PDF). *Le Rail,* 31–33.

Tao, P., Stefansson, H. and Saevarsdottir, G. (2014). Potential use of geothermal energy sources for the production of Li-ion batteries. *Renewable Energy*, 61.

Teodorescu, B. and Calin, R.A. (2015). The base articulations of the liminality concept. *Review of European Studies*, 7(12): 97–101.

The Economist. (2017). A world turned upside down. *Renewable Energy*, pp. 18–20.

The Guardian. (2011). *19th Century Cyclists Paved the Way for Modern Motorists' Roads.* Retrieved from The Guardian: https://www.theguardian.com/environment/bike-blog/2011/aug/15/cyclists-paved-way-for-roads.

The Guardian. (2017). *Smaller, Lighter, Greener: Are Micro EVs the Future of City Transport?* Retrieved from The Guardian: https://www.theguardian.com/sustainable-business/2017/may/11/micro-evs-city-transport-suemens-renault-green-air-pollution.

The TEV project. (2017). *Tracked Electric Vehicle System. Reference Technical Booklet.* Retrieved from The TEV project: http://tevproject.com/.

Toole Design Group and Pedestrian and Bicycle Information Center. (2012). *Bike Sharing in the United States.* USDOT, Federal Highway Administration.

Transport Canada. (2009). *Bike Sharing Guide.* Ottawa: Transport Canada.

Trigg, T. (2015). *Cities Where It's Faster to Walk than Drive.* Retrieved from Scientific American: https://blogs.scientificamerican.com/plugged-in/cities-where-it-s-faster-to-walk-than-drive/.

TuSimple. (2020). *TuSimple Launches World's First Autonomous Freight Network with UPS, Penske, U.S. Xpress, and McLane Company, Inc.* Retrieved from stockhouse.com: https://stockhouse.com/news/press-releases/2020/07/01/tusimple-launches-world-s-first-autonomous-freight-network-with-ups-penske-u-s.

UITP. (2013). *Press Kit: Metro Automation Facts, Figures, and Trends.* International Association of Public Transport.

UITP. (2014). *Metro Automation Facts, Figures and Trends.* International Association of Public Transport (UITP).

US Bureau of Transportation Statistics. (2020). *Energy Intensity of Passenger Modes.* Retrieved from US Energy Consumption by the Transportation Sector: https://www.bts.gov/content/energy-intensity-passenger-modes.

US Department of Energy. (2018). *Alternative Fuel Vehicles.* Retrieved from US Department of Energy: https://www.energy.gov/public-services/vehicles/alternative-fuel-vehicles#/find/nearest?country=US.

US Environmental Protection Agency. (2008). *Heat Island Compendium.* US EPA.

USGS. (2003). *Effects of Urban Development on Floods.* Washington D.C.: US Geological Survey. Retrieved from U.S.Ggeological Survey.

Valença, G., Moura, F. and Sá, A.M. (2021). Main challenges and opportunities to dynamic road space allocation: From static to dynamic urban designs. *Journal of Urban Mobility*, 1: 1–9.

Varoufakis, Y. (2020). *Another Now: Dispatches from an Alternative Present.* London: Bodley Head.

Venugopal, P., Shekhar, A., Visser, E. and Scheele, N. (2018). Roadway to self-healing highways with integrated wireless electric vehicle charging and sustainable energy harvesting technologies. *Applied Energy*, 212: 1226–1239.

Vuchic, V.R. (2005). *Urban Transit: Operations, Planning, and Economics.* New York: John Wiley & Sons.

*Watch: Toronto's Surge in E-bike Ownership Creates Concerns over Safety.* (2018). Retrieved from Iheartradio: https://www.iheartradio.ca/newstalk-1010/news/watch-toronto-s-surge-in-e-bike-ownership-creates-concerns-over-safety-1.3726810.

Weichenthal, S., Ryswyk, K., Goldstein, A., Shekarrizfard, M. and Hatzopoulou, M. (2015). *Characterizing the Spatial Distribution of Ambient Ultrafine Particles in Toronto, Canada: A Land-use Regression Model. Environmental Pollution*, 47(PT A): 1–8.

Weir, L. (2018). *Pina Bousch's Dance Theatre: Tracing the Evolution of Tanz Theatre.* Edinburgh: Edinburgh University Press.

Weißbach, D., Ruprecht, G., Hukeac, A., Czerski, K., Gottlieb, S. and Hussein, A. (2013). Energy intensities, EROIs (energy returned on invested), and energy payback times of electricity generating power plants. *Energy*, 52: 210–221.

West, G. (2017). *Scale.* New York: Penguin.

Wiener, E.L. and Curry, R.E. (1980). Llight deck automation: Promise and Problems. *Ergonomics*, 995–1011.

Wilson, K. (2018). *An Overview of SAE International: Standards Activities Related to Charging of Hybrid/Electric Vehicles.* Ground Vehicles Standards, SAE International.

Wilson, L. (2013). Shades of green: Electric cars' carbon emissions around the globe. *Shrink That Footprint*, pp. 1–28.

Wolverton, T. (2016). *Wolverton: Elon Musk's Hyperloop Hype Ignores Practical Problems.* Retrieved from The Mercury News: https://www.mercurynews.com/2013/08/13/wolverton-elon-musks-hyperloop-hype-ignores-practical-problems/.

World Commission on Environment and Development. (1987). *Our Common Future.* Oxford: Oxford Univeristy Press.

Xiong, H., Wang, L., Linbing, D., Wang and Druta, C. (2011). Piezoelectric energy harvesting from traffic induced deformation of pavements. *International Journal of Pavement Research and Technology*, 5(5): 333–337.

Zadra, J.R. and Clore, G.L. (2011). Emotion and perception: The role of affective information. *Wiley Interdiscip. Rev. Cogn. Sci.*, 2(6): 676–685.

Zavestoski, S. and Agyeman, J. (2015). *Incomplete Streets: Processes, Practices, and Possibilities.* New York: Routledge.

Zhang, W. and Guhathakurta, S. (2016). Parking spaces in the age of shared autonomous vehicles: How much parking will we need and where? *Sustainable Cities and Society*, 19: 34–45.

Zielinski, S. (2006). New mobility: The next generation of sustainable urban transportation. *National Academy of Engineering*, 36(4).

Žižek, S. (1997). *The Abyss of Freedom/Ages of the World.* Ann Arbor: University of Michigan Press.

Žižek, S. (2009). *First as Tragedy, Then as Farce.* London: Verso Books.

Žižek, S. (2012). *Less Than Nothing: Hegel and the Shadow of Dialectical Materialism.* London: Verso Books.

# Section III

# Shifting to Local and Low-carbon Energy Systems

# CHAPTER 5

# Energy Transformation
## Feeding the New Mobility Ecosystem

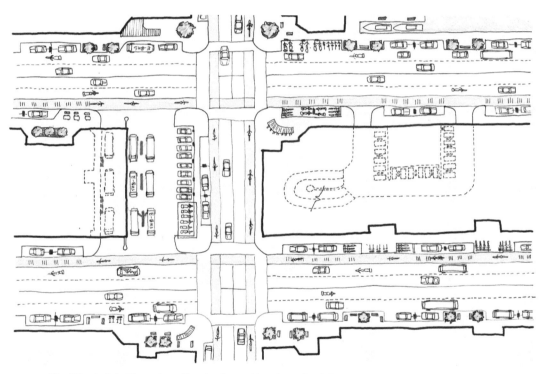

**Fig. 5.0:** Artistic illustration of local, micro-grid, and non-fossil fuel urban mobility energy ecosystem.

*"While the 20th century was marked by the class of ideologies, embodied by fascist, communist, and capital societies, the 21st century will be shaped by…a diminishing supply of fossil fuels and other crucial resources."*

—Peter Berg, *The Finite Planet*

## Introduction

In city plans for new human development the demand for energy generated by driving alone comes with excessive energy waste and unsustainable use of limited natural resources. Despite immense technological progress and development, our economies and societies still fundamentally depend on natural ecosystems to provide a hospitable climate, clean water, food, fibres, and numerous other goods and services. Two planetary processes, auto-oriented urban sprawl and fossil fuel emissions by long-distance private vehicle driving, are gradually pushing us over the safe thresholds of "planetary boundaries" (Steffen et al., 2015). By 2050, urban mobility systems will use 17.3% of the planet's bio capacities, five times more than in 1990 (Little, 2015).

Non-renewable and one-time use fossil fuel comes with enormous cost to society. Following the global trend of the consuming nearly 30% of energy in the mobility sector, the transportation sector in the City of Toronto has grown exponentially to become the largest source (41%, excluding rail, plane, and boat) of greenhouse-gas (GHG) emissions (GTA Clean Air Council, 2017). Linking mobility patterns, energy usage and GHG emissions, a Greater Toronto Area study (Weichenthal et al., 2015) concluded that most emissions are caused by "extreme commuters", i.e., people who work in downtown Toronto but live in the outer suburbs and commute by private vehicle, predominantly using fossil fuel energy. In this book, unlike last century's city planning, the approach to new mobility energy is to create a low-carbon "urban ecosystem" (Priemus, 2007) by mixing land-use with appropriate density, addressing the depletion of natural and financial resources, and managing a sustainable growth within "planetary boundaries". The shift in mobility patterns will gradually achieve GHG emissions reduction targets instead of unnecessarily pushing poor urban residents who are currently trapped by "vehicle necessity".

Alternative mobility, including a major focus on electrification of all forms of mobility, emerged as a critical element of future mobility planning and design. While electric vehicles are at the forefront of the discussion, the electrification of transit, bicycles, micromobility, and other mobility modes are quietly advancing. Electrification of regional or intercity travel, goods movement, and rail corridors have become the centre of a system upgrade in Canada and parts of the USA. The rest of the developed world has already acted and advanced alternative energy by replacing their fossil-fuel-dependent private vehicles, trucks, trains, rail, buses, and surface transit systems.

The enduring benefits of alternative energy for all mobility sectors present an enormous opportunity to develop a low-carbon or carbon-neutral society that preserves our environmental equilibrium. Electric public transit and rail, or other energy source systems such hydrogen, solar, nuclear, or wind energy should become the fundamental responsibility of the public sector. Electric bicycles and new micromobility vehicles pushed network-wide system changes due to their high potential to replace short distance vehicles trips. Unfortunately, private vehicle policy often left with federal, state, or provincial governments created a void in cities addressing what to do with private vehicles that consume most of the fossil fuels. Energy systems left with hydro authorities, who typically work in isolation, blocking alternative energy transition. Due to the lack of a systematic approach to alternative energy of all mobility modes, user confusion remains about the types, configurations, system changes, and policy requirements even through a small segment of demography leaning toward fossil-free mobility modes for various personal or environmental awareness reasons.

This chapter offers a future urban mobility energy ecosystem approach from a city building perspective. It explores an overall approach to a stable, affordable, and sustainable energy source for future urban mobility. The chapter is designed as a mobility innovation plan with design concept guidance on E-Mobility and alternative energy challenges faced by city planners every day, including operational and design barriers blocking the path of independence from fossil fuel. The overall strength and weakness of each non-fossil fuel energy profile, and their respective evolution, will need to be clearly understood to develop policies, process changes, and new approaches to public or private space design. The fundamentals of a mobility energy planning framework and high-level estimation infrastructure quantification are described to quantify city building energy targets and mitigation or implementation measures. A series of strategic concepts, using practical models for energy access, accessibility, location, space, urban design solutions or approaches to street redesign that link all mobility modes, are recommended to achieve mobility energy targets and associated city planning policies while introducing new urban design perspectives. These ideas and concepts hope to fill the current void in mobility planning processes and implication tools that often lack an energy solution for the future mobility ecosystem.

> *"If you want to find the secrets of the universe, think in terms of energy, frequency, and vibration."*
>
> —Nikola Tesla

## Evolution of Alternative Energy in Mobility

Humans are an energy-hungry species, and the evolution of energy is as old as the planet's age. But the evolution of mobility energy has only evolved in the last three centuries, particularly during the modern industrial age. Like all mobility inventions, the earlier history of mobility was surprisingly cleaner compared to the post WW II era. Mobility energy starts with human, or animal powered energy and wind assisted mediums. Electrification followed, flourished, and died. Then we entered the dark era of dirty energy sources like animal fat or coal in the 19th century and crude oil in the 20th century. As history repeats itself, recent efforts to transform mobility energy are focused on clean, greener energy sources again at the beginning of this century, hoping to avoid volatile, unreliable, and increasingly harder to find oil energy that has literally blackmailed urban mobility systems. Evolution periods described here are not rigid but rather an interpretation of different energy and technology rises and falls through urban mobility energy history.

*Early prototypes (early 19th century):* Whether a prototype vehicle, a train, airship or water transport, early mobility ideas all evolved around electrification or spotty applications of fuel cell technology. In the 18th and early 19th centuries, the burst of a new mobility system powered by electricity led to mass production of goods for people during the early industrial era. But there was a dark side. Electricity sources were heavily polluted using coal in UK and the rest of Europe.

*First mass adoption of E-Mobility (late 19th century):* Early E-Mobility prototypes quickly become common mass mobility systems in cities, through the brains and hands of a few pioneering geniuses. Germany and the UK led with the electric streetcar and the first high-speed rail prototype. William Morrison, from Des Moines, Iowa, created the first successful electric vehicle in the USA. It resembled little more than an electrified wagon, but it sparked an interest in electric carriages. Compared to the gas- and steam-powered mobility, electric or hybrid vehicles (notably taxis in New York) were quiet, easy to drive, and didn't emit smelly pollutants, leading to become a popular mobility mode among urban residents, especially women (Matuka, 2014). From the electric garbage truck to Porsche's hybrid vehicle, to the electric helicopter, E-Mobility become one-third of total mobility production in large US cities, a level of E-Mobility penetration was achieved only by Norway in 2019.

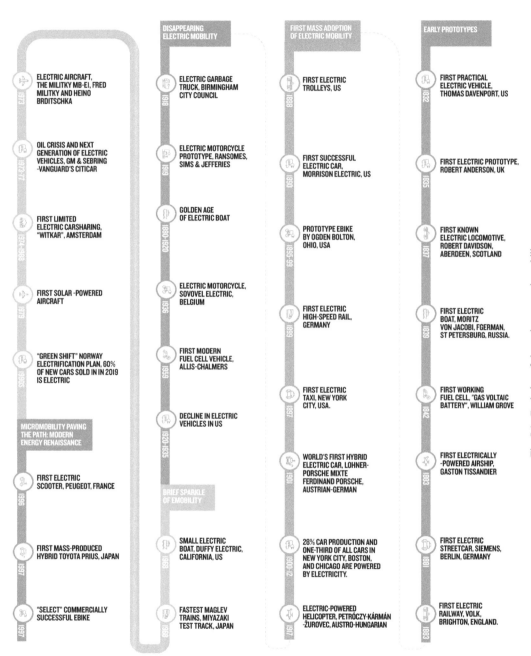

**DISAPPEARING ELECTRIC MOBILITY**

**FIRST MASS ADOPTION OF ELECTRIC MOBILITY**

**EARLY PROTOTYPES**

1973 — ELECTRIC AIRCRAFT, THE MILITKY MB-EI, FRED MILITKY AND HEINO BRDITSCHKA

1972-77 — OIL CRISIS AND NEXT GENERATION OF ELECTRIC VEHICLES, GM & SEBRING -VANGUARD'S CITICAR

1974-1988 — FIRST LIMITED ELECTRIC CARSHARING, "WITKAR", AMSTERDAM

1979 — FIRST SOLAR -POWERED AIRCRAFT

1990S — "GREEN SHIFT" NORWAY ELECTRIFICATION PLAN, 60% OF NEW CARS SOLD IN IN 2019 IS ELECTRIC

**MICROMOBILITY PAVING THE PATH: MODERN ENERGY RENAISSANCE**

1996 — FIRST ELECTRIC SCOOTER, PEUGEOT, FRANCE

1997 — FIRST MASS-PRODUCED HYBRID TOYOTA PRIUS, JAPAN

1997 — "SELECT" COMMERCIALLY SUCCESSFUL EBIKE

1918 — ELECTRIC GARBAGE TRUCK, BIRMINGHAM CITY COUNCIL

1919 — ELECTRIC MOTORCYCLE PROTOTYPE, RANSOMES, SIMS & JEFFERIES

1880-1920 — GOLDEN AGE OF ELECTRIC BOAT

1936 — ELECTRIC MOTORCYCLE, SOVOVEL ELECTRIC, BELGIUM

1959 — FIRST MODERN FUEL CELL VEHICLE, ALLIS-CHALMERS

1920-1935 — DECLINE IN ELECTRIC VEHICLES IN US

**BRIEF SPARKLE OF EMOBILITY**

1968 — SMALL ELECTRIC BOAT, DUFFY ELECTRIC, CALIFORNIA, US

1990 — FASTEST MAGLEV TRAINS, MIYAZAKI TEST TRACK, JAPAN

1888 — FIRST ELECTRIC TROLLEYS, US

1890 — FIRST SUCCESSFUL ELECTRIC CAR, MORRISON ELECTRIC, US

1895-99 — PROTOTYPE EBIKE BY OGDEN BOLTON, OHIO, USA

1899 — FIRST ELECTRIC HIGH-SPEED RAIL, GERMANY

1897 — FIRST ELECTRIC TAXI, NEW YORK CITY, USA.

1901 — WORLD'S FIRST HYBRID ELECTRIC CAR, LOHNER-PORSCHE MIXTE FERDINAND PORSCHE, AUSTRIAN-GERMAN

1900-12 — 28% CAR PRODUCTION AND ONE-THIRD OF ALL CARS IN NEW YORK CITY, BOSTON, AND CHICAGO ARE POWERED BY ELECTRICITY.

1917 — ELECTRIC-POWERED HELICOPTER, PETRÓCZY-KÁRMÁN -ŽUROVEC, AUSTRO-HUNGARIAN

1832 — FIRST PRACTICAL ELECTRIC VEHICLE, THOMAS DAVENPORT, US

1835 — FIRST ELECTRIC PROTOTYPE, ROBERT ANDERSON, UK

1837 — FIRST KNOWN ELECTRIC LOCOMOTIVE, ROBERT DAVIDSON, ABERDEEN, SCOTLAND

1839 — FIRST ELECTRIC BOAT, MORITZ VON JACOBI, FGERMAN, ST PETERSBURG, RUSSIA.

1842 — FIRST WORKING FUEL CELL, "GAS VOLTAIC BATTERY", WILLIAM GROVE

1883 — FIRST ELECTRICALLY -POWERED AIRSHIP, GASTON TISSANDIER

1881 — FIRST ELECTRIC STREETCAR, SIEMENS, BERLIN, GERMANY

1883 — FIRST ELECTRIC RAILWAY, VOLK, BRIGHTON, ENGLAND.

**Fig. 5.1:** Evolution of alternative energy in mobility.

*Disappearing era of E-Mobility* (*early 20th century*): This early burst of alternative mobility crash landed with the discovery of oil in Poland, Russia, and Canada and particularly Spindletop oilfield in the USA in 1901 (Berg, 2011). The race to become the fossil fuel superpower colluded with the discovery of the diesel engine, and its mass production in the USA followed by Europe in the early 20th century. During the 1920s the electric car ceased to be a viable commercial product, often attributed to the desire for longer distance vehicles with more horsepower, and the ready availability of gasoline. While electric automobiles lost traction, others continued the alternative mobility energy quest, as electric powered motorcycles, small boats, aircraft, and the most notable electromagnetic-powered high-speed trains flourished outside of the USA.

There was one notable exception: Rail Electrification. It flourished during the energy crisis and remained a bright spot during the dark nights of the fossil fuel takeover. The superiority of electric traction over steam and other hybrid-diesel locomotives is undeniable, yet it remains the most controversial among all electrified mobility modes, particularly in North America. Rapid growth in urban areas at the beginning of the 20th century, fuelled by the continuing industrial revolution, created an increasing demand for public transit. Short-range, steam powered rapid transit systems were replaced by faster and efficient electric systems that absorbed the rising demand (Duffy, 2003). Electric trains operate with quick acceleration, which is ideal for urban metro transit systems. Similarly, long-range electrified commuter rail service has the advantages of air-quality benefits, high-speed capability, and additional carrying capacity compared with diesel trains.

Despite these inherent advantages, the North American rail industry remained unmoved. According to Richard Freeman and Hal Cooper (Richard and Cooper, 2005), the "bank-oil cartel-automotive" alliance successfully led the resistance to electrification. In the 1950s, it lobbied for the US National Interstate and Defense Highways Act (1956), which encouraged the petroleum consuming system that still dominates the nation's mobility landscape.

Much of the electrified rail that existed was dismantled and replaced by diesel-powered hybrid locomotives that now comprise 99% of the North American rail fleet. In sharp contrast to both developed and developing nations in Asia and Europe that followed the electrification track, especially after the mid-1970s energy crisis. While 42% of rail corridors in India were electrified, the electrification rate in North America is less than 1% (Karim and Shallwani, 2010). Despite recent electrification of hydrogen fuel possibilities for intercity and regional train services in Canada and the USA, there appears to be no fundamental policy shift among decision makers to realize rail electrification's potential. The barriers to electrification in Canada appear to be psychological rather than technical or financial (Benjamin and Richards, 1981).

*Brief re-emergence of E-Mobility* (*1970 Oil Crisis*): E-Mobility and other alternative energies regained momentum briefly during the energy crisis of the 1970s. Enthusiasm produced the first practical, full-powered, and full-sized hybrid vehicle by the "Godfather of the Hybrid", Victor Wouk, in 1972. The Buick Skylark was developed by General Motors (GM) for the Federal Clean Car Incentive Program in 1970 (PBS, 2009). These vehicles sparked a shared imagination in Amsterdam with the introduction of the electric Witkar carsharing prototype. Most notable nationwide success was the Norway-produced "Green Shift" electrification plan, using, ironically, national sovereign funds generated by fossil fuel sales.

*Micromobility paving the way to alternative energy (Last decade of 20th century)*: It was little vehicle use, now known as micromobility, that next revived interest in alternative energy in mobility. A series of electric scooters, skateboards, and electric bicycles energized progressive thinkers to develop mass produced hybrid vehicles, for instance, in Japan by Toyota, electric small vehicles like Smart Car in Germany, and solar powered cars in Australia.

One might argue the influence of micromobility on alternative energy evolution, but there are some clear trends. Electric bicycles, commonly known as e-bikes, have seen a prolific rise in use and rapid sales growth since 1998. Early adopters of bicycles, such as the Netherlands and Germany, experienced the fastest adoption of e-bikes, particularly in 2009 and onward. Regular bicycle production is gradually being replaced by the electric bicycle market. Rapid growth is generally attributed to the simple redesign of traditional bicycles with an on-board battery, efficient motor, and easy controls. Nearly half of the electric bicycles were sold in China, followed by Europe and North America. Little or no harmful emissions by the electric bicycle (8–13 times more efficient than the automobile, six times more than rail transit, and the same environment impact as the traditional bicycle) was the primary force behind its fast adoption from a pollution perspective. Electric cargo-bikes emerged during this period as a practical solution to goods movement needs (Pete, 2015), particularly in dense urban areas, by overcoming the weakness of pedal-powered bicycles in steep terrain or geography. Electric cargo bike demand exploded in western and northern Europe, and became popular in North America, realizing its potential to replace the car as a cheaper and more practical option.

*Strategic reemergence of E-Mobility (first decade of 21st century)*: This short period is marked by a massive push toward a commercial model and success of alternative energy products. Whether loved or hated, Tesla's electric vehicle attempt threw a practical challenge at the automobile industry. Google's autonomous electric cars pushed alternative mobility and cleaner energy sources into the new era. And by the end of the first decade of the 21st century, Daimler mass-produced electric "smart cars" for two and started to offer a new shared vehicle service in Ulm, Germany, now famously known as Car2Go. While this era was brief, it produced a paradigm shift in the mobility industry toward a mass produced and commercially successful alternative mobility system in cities.

*Race to alternative energy (2007–2012)*: Competition to reinvent mobility, independent of fossil fuel, began a fierce race between traditional OEMs (original equipment manufacturers) and new players. And the emergence of startups with commercially successful formulas for electric or alternative energy vehicles or devices steered the automobile industry in the direction of a new reality. Alternative energy mobility was not just a pilot project anymore, it could replace fossil-fuel-based mobility in the next few decades. Electric transit buses found their first pilot project formula for success across China. Ethanol-based biofuel mobility was mass produced in Brazil. Electric trucks become common in many cities' vehicle fleets in Europe. And electric scooters and many more new mobility devices, not using fossil fuel, popped up all over the world. Even GM, often blamed as a negative dragging force to E-Mobility, joined the race with hybrid vehicles.

*New era of mass-produced sustainable energy (second decade of 21st century)*: No other decade has seen so many dramatic changes in mobility than the current one. Almost all mobility modes and energy systems moved toward a new sustainable and shared mobility path following groundbreaking steps taken at the end of the first decade. After years of frustration and failure, the electrification of city transit buses is the new normal. To improve local air quality, Shenzhen, China showed the way in 2009 and became the first city in the world to have an entirely electric fleet of more than 16,000 public buses (Institute, 2019). Electrifying its entire taxi fleet was another success. Electrification of Shenzhen's bus and taxi fleet was credited with significantly reducing local air pollution, and their success spread like wildfire. The Chilean city of Santiago launched Latin America's first electric bus corridor (Kane, 2019), with a range of up to 250 km (155 miles), in collaboration with local operators Enel X and Metbus. Solar buses and electrified age-old school buses are the next frontier.

Electrification of micro-transit also become a focus of transformation to new, flexible mobility to reduce emissions during the early days of this century's second decade. Conventional and hybrid micro-transit vehicles, such as minibuses, shuttles, or vans are common with some service providers, but switching to electric mode is still too expensive for some transit authorities. More micro-transit vehicles in circulation will, however, eventually require electrification to offset zero or low occupancy during off-peak hours and reduce overall GHG emissions (MaRS Discovery District, 2016). The majority of micro or city transit vehicles travel roughly 200 km a day, well within the typical range anxiety (usually 330 km) of electric micro-transit vehicles such as high occupancy nine-seater passenger vans (Martret, 2020). The autonomous option is expected to further optimize charging, in-between and in-vehicle travel times in the long-term, making micro-transit a truly viable option for low-density suburban or exurb or rural areas, or for simply replacing inefficient conventional bus systems (Ongel et al., 2019).

The era began with another form of mobility, now known as micromobility. Small electric vehicles swept through the heart of urban mobility, experiencing surprising acceptance from users, public agencies, and among service providers, in less than a decade. Some popular modes such as shared e-scooters, e-bikes, and e-mopeds now have a presence in over 600 cities and more than 50 countries, representing a healthy 25% market share of two-wheelers globally (Martret, 2020). China is leading the majority share of electric micromobility due to their current ban on combustion two-wheelers in many cities.

Electrification of skateboards and motorcycles was the next frontier. And micro electric vehicle (EV) cars, micro/pod cars (The Guardian, 2017) were next in line following the innovative but unfortunate management failure attempt of Citycar by MIT (Frayer and Cater, 2015). Some age-old paratransit in Asia followed suit with three-wheeled motorized rickshaws, the tuk-tuk, produced its electric version (Driving, 2015) to transform the loud, pollution-spewing vehicles that are common in Asia and South America. Electric rickshaw's have transitioned, with phenomenal growth in China, India, and other south and southeast Asian countries (Rajvanshi, 2002), evolving from a market entrant in the automobile segment of the country to a leading short distance transport solution. However, immature products are banned for safety reasons.

Inspiration from this decade's success has seeped through the remaining mobility industry. Hydrogen fuel vehicles and infrastructures was another technology that matured during the last decade. Toyota's mass produced Mirai (Cooper, 2018) was the most notable hydrogen success, akin to its hybrid vehicle Prius' success in the first decade. The first intercontinental flight by a solar plane, the Solar Impulse, was completed from Madrid, Spain to Rabat, Morocco in 2012. Electric trucks including autonomous options are not news anymore. Carsharing pioneer Zipcar added the first electric vehicles to its fleet, although it was the last choice among users (Gilpin, 2017). A French startup, SeaBubbles, launched the new electric shared water taxi service (Spaen, 2019) inspired by the 200-hundred-year-old dream of German inventor Moritz von Jacobi in 1839 in St. Petersburg, Russia. Even electric aircraft such as the new eVTOL, with a 60-mile (100 km) range and a cruising speed of up to 180 mph (290 km/h), is currently being collaborated on between Uber and Hyundai (Lambert, 2020). Daimler has invested in their all-electric air taxi startup 'Volocopter', which already has working prototypes. And with Porsche announcing that it is building an electric vertical takeoff and landing aircraft with Boeing, no doubt a series of new mobility without fossil fuel innovations will continue in the next decade. Conflict between public and new mobilities will rise and subside. And fossil fuel perceived as a favourite personal passion will gradually disappear.

*Complete energy transformation – Vision for low-carbon, and zero emissions (next decades)*: While paradigm shifts in alternative mobility prompted long-term serious planning initiatives, random pilot projects with glittering claims in social hyperactivity cannot transform mobility systems. Norway is showing the world the path to energy freedom with the step-by-step decarbonization of Norway's transport system and one of the main goals of its National Transport Plan 2018–2029. Bhutan has become the only carbon negative country, mainly through avoiding fossil fuel needs for mobility. And Costa Rica, recorded as the first country whose 99% of energy comes from renewable inland wind and solar energy systems without noticeable impact on their rich wildlife, has banned fossil fuel for mobility, making solar and electric city buses and vehicles, and renewable energy as a key source of mobility energy.

These successes are often "brushed off" with claims that clean energy does not work for large cities or for highly developed countries to run their economies. Large cities however, such as

Montréal, Seattle, Portland, San Francisco, Oslo, and a few cities in Sweden, have adopted zero-emission bus fleets and are reaching overall fossil fuel reduction targets with practicable action plans. What works in Norway may not work in Canada, even though both have low population densities, and tar sands and offshore fossil fuel remain their main funding sources. Each country and each city need to customize their plans to avoid or minimize social unrest. A "Silent Revolution" works better by gradually, but consistently, introducing new transformation.

Regardless of past energy failures, there is a renewed interest in alternative energy for urban mobility systems as planners increasingly focus on achieving a sustainable society. Recent fossil fuel phase-out plans (particularly coal), energy system upgrades, and climate change initiatives are expected to grow renewable energy sources and produce a surplus of "green electricity", creating an ideal foundation for mobility electrification. In addition to the benefits of stimulating the local and regional economies through employment opportunities for energy systems, future transitions to alternative energy powering urban mobility could forge a new geography of hope.

> *"No free energy device will ever be allowed to reach the market."*
> —Nikola Tesla

## Ups and Downs: Alternative Energy and Climate Change

Electric vehicles or other alternative fuel vehicles are often regarded as a silver lining solution to address environmental, energy, safety, and health issues affixed to the intensive fossil fuel mobility system. Reality is different. Without thoughtful application, electric vehicles still require wide roads, wasteful parking, even produce higher collision rates due to lower noise, and have other negative impacts just like fossil fuel mobility. Worst of all, electrification may shift the problem to dirty sources of electricity or alternative energy generation, increasing emissions and pollution associated with manufacturing and distribution. At their source, raw materials extraction for electric vehicles comes with water and toxicity problems, material scarcity (Xu et al., 2020), and remote locations of mining, labour abuse, and environmental damage. Markets for raw materials are equally volatile, and production countries could sabotage material prices, creating similar instability as the oil and gas industry.

Like the fossil fuel system, electric vehicles maintain the same vehicle-oriented land-uses creating urban sprawl while encouraging higher vehicle usage due to energy savings. While minimal noise is praised for reducing noise pollution, quieter electric vehicles pose serious risks, particularly for pedestrians and cyclists in cities (NHTSA, 2016). Despite electrification, Norway recently reported electric vehicle users drive more, reaching the completely opposite objective of the reduction of vehicles usage, and countering the benefits of emissions and GHG reduction.

The environmental efficiency of electric vehicles comes with several caveats. Given that most of the world's power generation is grid-tied, the carbon reduction potential of an electric car depends largely on where it is charged. Electric vehicles must be used in tandem with low carbon power to maximize carbon emission reductions (Wilson, 2013). Vehicles powered by the present European electricity mix offer a 10%–24% decrease in global warming potential (GWP) relative to conventional diesel or gasoline vehicles, assuming lifetimes of 150,000 km. However, electric vehicles exhibit the potential for significant increases in human toxicity, freshwater eco-toxicity, freshwater eutrophication, and metal depletion impacts, largely emanating from the vehicle supply chain. Results are sensitive to assumptions regarding electricity source, use phase energy consumption, vehicle lifetime, and battery replacement schedules. However, it is counterproductive to promote electric vehicles in regions where electricity is produced from oil, coal, and lignite combustion. Concentrated carbon from coal usage accounts for 39% of annual emission of $CO_2$ from fossil fuels (Beddoes, 2020). Whether we like it or not, we are gradually transitioning toward less

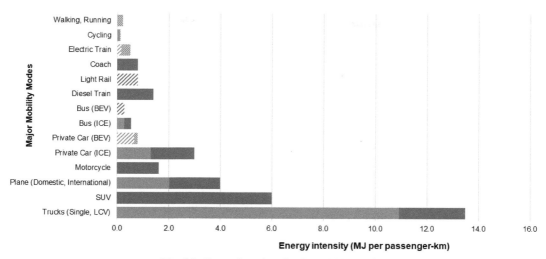

**Fig. 5.2:** Energy intensity of major mobility modes.
**Notes:** Meta research on energy intensity was conducted by the authors using various sources. (US Bureau of Transportation Statistics, 2020), (Mohorčich, 2020), (Berg, 2011) and (European Commision, 2020).

energy availability, particularly after the Anthropocene era.[1] Energy intensity of fossil fuel sources are seven to ten times more than their electric mobility modes (Fig. 5.2). The post-Anthropocene era mobility energy landscape will likely be dominated by cycling, walking, buses, and rail or metro transit systems, although battery electric vehicles are still not feasible under a highly energy-constrained scenario (Mohorčich, 2020). To counter potential setbacks in terms of water pollution and toxicity, the electrification of transportation should be accompanied by a sharpened policy focus on life cycle production, storage, and fuel transport management.

Hydrogen fuel technology suffers similar issues like electrification. Energy loss is extremely high, saddled by financially unsustainable production costs, and lack of proper regulation to watch out for the safety, operating, and maintenance issues of hydrogen-powered vehicles. Applications in rail are however more promising, but the technology is yet to mature.

Other cleaner and greener sources of power mobility come with similar concerns and issues. Nuclear energy is cheaper and safer, but waste disposal has its hidden dark side. Renewables are our best hope, but they must be produced with 100% recyclable materials to avoid massive energy, water and materials needs. Manufacturing wind or solar energy still requires intensive material resources, many to be exhausted within the next 30–50 years (Rickstrom and Klum, 2015), and mining dumps toxic residue into local bodies of water and causes health problems such as quartz needed to make silicon causes lung diseases.

Biofuels become a choice between food and fuel. Bio ethanol proving, for example, to have low energy content, often changing fertile and natural ecosystem land into monoculture fields of raw materials. Other sources of biomass remain as scarce as finding oil, or their raw material collection, conversion, and production inflict additional environmental damages.

Does this mean we abandon alternative mobility energy? Or do we deliberately plan to avoid the negative sides of sustainable energy? The obvious answer is the latter. Alternative fuel mobility will generate greater benefits if vehicle demand is limited through smart land-use, shared trips, and occupant numbers are higher when we use sustainable mobility modes.

---

[1] According to *Encyclopaedia of National Geography*, the "Anthropocene Epoch" is an unofficial unit of geologic time, used to describe the most recent period in Earth's history when human activity started to have a significant impact on the planet's climate and ecosystems.

> *"Energy cannot be created or destroyed. It can only be changed from one form to another."*
>
> —Albert Einstein

## So Why Alternative Mobility Energy[2]

Despite the challenges with alternative energy, we have greater benefits if fossil fuel is discontinued as the power of our urban mobility systems. As with any planning and engineering problems, all mobility concept and design decisions must undergo a trade-off analysis. The solution that creates the greatest benefit to the public, for each dollar spent, should be adopted.

The following discussion examines the various considerations of alternative mobility energy projects to shape a sustainable transportation policy. The factors examined include the following:

- Emissions from mobility operations and the fuel life cycle of their energy systems;
- Health and safety implications;
- Technical and economic feasibility; and
- Social and overall perceptions.

### *Emissions and fuel life cycle*

Transportation is the largest single human-produced source of outdoor air pollution (Smith, 2008) including one-third of the globe's GHG emissions (Haywood, 2006) in developed nations and the bulk of its energy comes from burning petroleum products typically used by road transport (68%). Among these products, diesel technology carries the stigma of being a 'dirty' fuel. Unlike the gasoline engine, the primary residue of diesel consumption is not a gas but charred particles that are airborne through the exhaust pipe. Diesel exhaust's principal air pollutants are nitrogen oxides and microscopically fine particles, often referred to as "particulate matter" or soot. Large, heavy-duty diesel engine vehicles are significant contributors to emissions of particulate matter, nitrogen oxides, carbon monoxide, and hydrocarbons, all of which produce poor air-quality conditions. Therefore, a clear and definite mandatory pollution mitigation policy that improves air quality to an acceptable level would set the stage for alternative energy for mobility systems. Exposure to diesel exhaust is part of our everyday lives, especially during commuting by private vehicle, shared mobility, diesel bus, and train. Although commuters spend only 6% of the day commuting to and from work, more than half of their exposure to these particles occurs during that time (Schneider and Hill, 2007). Indeed, diesel particle levels are four to eight times higher inside commuter vehicles, buses, and trains than in the ambient outdoor air. In some cases, the ultra-fine particulate matter (less than 0.1 μm) levels during commutes are so high they are comparable to driving with a smoker due to the high surface area and a capacity to adsorb a substantial amount of toxic organic compounds. High ultra-fine particulate levels are even more harmful on meteorological processes and the hydrological cycle, aggravating global climate change (Kwon et al., 2020). Emissions attributable to electric rail transport are highly variable and depend on the electricity source used to power the train. Electric light rail consistently performs better environmentally than bus rapid transit, despite recent advances in bus technology (Puchalsky, 2005). Future US Tier 4 emission standards and other recent advances in diesel engine technology will make diesel fuel almost 'clean' by removing soot and converting tailpipe emissions into harmless gases. However, diesel emission is, in fact, dirty when compared to the "life cycle emission" of electric mobility, and therein lies a significant policy gap that leads to the misinterpretation of air pollution standards.

---

[2]  This section was modified from the authors own transport and rail electrification research conducted in Toronto to scrutinize the reginal electrification. The content was revised here for all other mobility modes and other energy sources.

## Health and safety

Air pollution takes a great toll on human health and the environment. Exposure to air pollution can increase the risk of lung and heart disease and causes an estimated 5,800 premature deaths and more than 16,000 hospitalizations annually in Ontario (Ontario Medical Association, 2005). Twenty-one thousand Canadians died in 2008 at a cost of $8 billon to country's economy, and air quality related deaths are expected to rise to 90,000 by 2031 (CMA, 2008). Diesel exhaust, which includes more than 40 hazardous substances listed by the US Environmental Protection Agency, 15 of them also named as probable or possible human carcinogens because of the toxicity of its fine particles by the International Agency for Research on Cancer (IARC). In the U SA, particulate matter from diesel engines is said to be responsible for 125,000 cancer cases annually (STAPPA and ALAPCO, 2000). Apart from the overall health risk of diesel exhaust, its fine particles, generally referred to as diesel particulate matter (DPM), are toxic in few areas. (1) The elevated "fine particulate" air pollution is associated with significant increases in all causes of lung-cancer and cardiopulmonary mortality (Pope and Burnett, 2002), and DPM contributed about 70% of the cancer risk from airborne pollution (SCAQMD, 2000). (2) The deadly effects of even smaller, ultra-fine particles (UFP) matter appear to affect health outcomes such as respiratory and cardiovascular morbidity (Morawska et al., 2014) and the major contributors of nano-size pollutants from vehicles can lead to plaque buildup in the arteries (Araujo et al., 2008). (3) Pollutants abundant in urban areas, although less than 0.18 micrometres in size, cause four times more artery buildup than particles four times larger. (4) The most vulnerable victims of diesel exhaust are children whose lungs are still developing, individuals with airway obstruction, and the elderly who may have other serious health problems. As a result, such susceptible populations may experience the greater health impact even at lower particulate matter levels than the general population (Morawska et al., 2014). Young people with asthma who live near roadways with high amounts of diesel truck traffic have more asthma attacks and use more asthma medication (Kleinman, 2000). Health regulation bodies need to create a policy that protects the most vulnerable in society, and mandates alternative and clean source electrification as a viable potential solution to lower DPM and UFP counts. Finally, electric trains and buses are quieter, as noise from electric locomotives is said to be 5–10 decibels lower than from diesel powered ones (CPCS and Hatch Associates, 1992). Like emission standards, health regulation bodies need to create a nation-wide "noise reduction" policy to protect residents living close to transportation corridors.

## Technical and economic aspects

The technical, operational, maintenance, and economic benefits of alternative energy mobility modes far outweigh the initial capital costs of new energy investment in technology and infrastructure.

- *Operational and passenger benefits*
  Electric vehicles can accelerate or decelerate faster. Similarly, electric rail can typically accelerate and decelerate faster due to lighter weight than heavier diesel trains on steep grades (Stohler and Giger, 1989), and they can handle far more station stops to result in 17% shorter travel times for both passenger (for express service) and freight services (Steer Davies Gleave, 2009). Faster acceleration coupled with upgraded signalling systems allow for improved headway, which accommodates increased ridership and customer satisfaction with decreased travel time, more seating, improved station ambience with open-air stations not required, and overall higher full system on time reliability.

- *Engineering aspects of alternative energy*
  Despite its clear necessity, there are inherent risks in proceeding with an alternative energy that has no national precedent. Hydrogen fuel is riskier without a national plan. All electric vehicles, buses, and trains are not as effective in winter, compared to a warmer climate. Shared

mobility vehicles typically require frequent charging, and high mileage degrades batteries more quickly resulting in frequent battery replacement needs (KAPSARC, 2016). Utility costs, often underestimated, and overhead clearance for electrical wires might dramatically increase the cost of rail or transit electrification projects. Higher driving ranges for electric vehicles will require heavier batteries, although parts are lower in number and less heavy than the gasoline counterpart. Buses carry heavy passenger loads. Aviation and maritime shipping or long-haul trucking travel longer distances without refuelling. Electric trains have a high power-to-weight ratio compared to diesel vehicles, which carry their own power sources on board (Gross, 2020). The energy density advantage of fossil fuel counters the continuous or alternate supply of clean energy. On an average, fuel costs tend to be lower for electric vehicles or trains. But if electricity is produced from conventionally expensive energy sources, then the overall operational cost could be higher, creating a trap of increased reliance on 'dirty' power sources such as coal in India as opposed to nuclear powered electricity reliance in Canada that lowers overall environmental costs. The use of regenerative braking and coasting as a driving strategy in electric trains (for dense areas where trains stop frequently) and in vehicles and buses further reduces energy demands, noise levels, and wear on mechanical brakes, because kinetic energy is recovered and converted to electrical energy without friction (Hull et al., 2008). High-density corridors provide even more justification for railway electrification. And the busiest highways should be considered first for hydrogen and electric infrastructure and fast charging facilities.

- *Economic considerations*

Fossil fuel energy systems have been used in North America and worldwide because of their relatively low initial costs and commissioning times. These relative short-term benefits are offset by long-term re-occurring costs such as the required daily inspection of the fuel tank coolant, electrical connections close to the moving parts, and additional space for fuel storage before using, and require more time and fuel to warm up. For an electrified system, in contrast, the initial installation costs are higher and commissioning time is longer. High upfront capital costs for electrification are however offset by reduced daily maintenance (50% lower), increases in vehicle or bus rolling stock availability (3% higher), lower leasing costs (22% lower) and operational activities (15% lower) that typically consist of remote monitoring of the power utility and overhead wires. Given that electricity's renewable costs are following downward trends, and tending to be more stable than oil prices, the operation of an alternative energy system can be profitable and avoid volatile fossil fuel prices for a foreseeable time after the infrastructure costs have been incurred.

> "Electric power is everywhere present in unlimited quantities and can drive the world's machinery without the need of coal, oil, gas, or any other of the common fuels."
>
> —Nikola Tesla

## Profiles of Alternative Mobility Energy

A lack of a basic profile of each mobility mode, and their path to electrification or alternative energy transition, often fuels confusion and sometimes intense opposition to mobility energy needs. Energy configurations, requirements, and consistent polices vary widely across the mobility modes. Before developing an implementation plan, adopting a new energy approach, and establishing an energy policy, a systemwide understanding is a first requirement for mobility electrification. Even though the benefits of electric mobility (referred herein as E-Mobility) as a more efficient energy source is critical and broadly encouraged, a lack of a systemwide network of facilities, plugins and availability may deter the initial enthusiasm of alternative mobility users.

With the transportation system consuming nearly 30% of the world's energy, oil and gas remain the top energy suppliers for mobility systems in cities and rural areas. Unfortunately, the history of energy used by human civilization generally moved toward less-carbon intensive and richer in hydrogen sources while they gained more energy density (Berg, 2011). To compare efficient and environmentally friendly energy sources, few common parameters are used. Energy density, along with remaining availability, cost and safety of production, transportation and storage, and emission or GHG reductions from well-to-wheel are a more comprehensive way to look at the best, most suitable energy to move ourselves in cities.

We often say we want clean and green energy. Yet, after a century of fossil fuel use, oil and gas still dominate the mobility energy landscape and are getting more economical, cheaper, and efficient. With hidden mechanisms of energy often misunderstood, glossy and toothless sustainable energy or mobility plans often ignore energy basics. It is crucial for city builders to understand the few energy basics, not as a physicist but from a layman's viewpoint.

Energy is produced when one of four known forces (gravity, electromagnetism, and strong and weak nuclear forces) move certain things to certain distance. Since Maxwell defined energy and Boltzmann revealed the probabilistic nature of energy that undermines its certainty, we became aware of basic energy components to understand the strengths and weaknesses of different energy.

For instance, energy density (joules per unit of mass or unit of volume) is the common method used to compare different energy. One-time-use fossil fuel, the most efficient source of energy density, is also the most polluted source of energy. On the contrary, renewable sources are the most clean sources, in infinite abundance, but contain very low energy density per unit. For instance, gasoline is 10 quadrillion times more energy-dense than solar radiation, one billion times more energy-dense than wind and hydro power, and 10 million times more energy-dense than human power (Layton, 2008). By comparison, humans, who use 2,500–4,500 calories per day, are much less efficient than modern fossil fuel energy sources, which might have, for instance, brought an end to slavery even without civil war in the US. Today energy demand for every individual is equivalent to keeping 53 slaves in the 19th century (Berg, 2011). And the demand keeps rising, making it very difficult for alternative energy to succeed with its lower energy content, raw material shortages, lowering of other energy prices (Energy Innovation, 2015), and ultimately the cannibalization of its own tail of sustainable energy sources (The Economist, 2017).

Whether renewable energy would succeed or fail, Energy Return on Investment (EROI) is a crude way to understand the different energy systems (Charles et al., 2014). EROI, a ratio of the amount of energy (exergy) obtained from an energy resource to the amount of energy (exergy) expended to produce that energy or simply EROI = Energy Output/ Energy Input, means EORI is the amount of energy expended to produce a certain amount of energy, and determine the price. Lower EORI simply means energy becomes scarcer and more difficult to extract or produce (Weißbach et al., 2013). Fossil fuel increased EORI through technology but its value is decreasing as it gets harder to dig deeper into the ground or go out to the middle of the ocean to find a profitable fossil fuel source. Renewable EORIs are currently low but are contrarily reaching a higher value as technology

| **The Energy Basics** |
| --- |
| **3a**: Energy density, |
| $$E_d = E_i/V_i$$ |
| where: |
| $E_i$ = Energy type i |
| $V_i$ = Volume pf specific energy type i |
| **3b**: Energy return on investment, |
| $$EORI_i = EO/EI$$ |
| where: |
| EO = energy output of energy type i |
| EI = Energy input |

improves. Finally, renewable energy including nuclear power remains the safest source of energy, when its life assessment includes fatalities from production, storage, distribution, and pollution (Ritchie, 2020).

Today, as renewable energy still struggles to gain momentum due to low energy content and current lower EORI , the reality is making us ponder whether we need to cover all the earth's surface with solar panels and wind turbines (Berg, 2011), or do we address reducing energy use instead

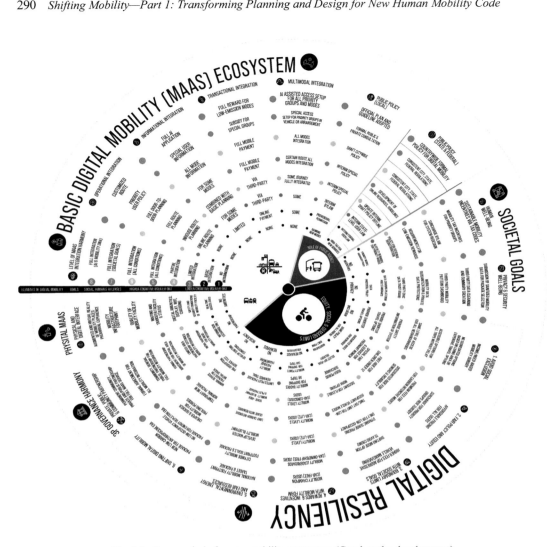

**Fig. 5.3:** Energy circle for new mobility ecosystem (Graph under development).

of trying to match ever increasing energy demand. Case in point, in 2020 during the Covid-19 pandemic's first full lockdown, energy use was reduced by 25%, while the partial lockdown reduced energy use by 18% and GHG emissions by 5% (Orenstein, 2020). Working from home and online shopping, often neglected as travel demand reduction measures, were able to reduce roughly half of vehicle usage, and 50– 75% of road transportation activities during the pandemic's first lockdown period. Demand reduction is the only to achieve alternative mobility energy success.

## Alternative Mobility Energy: Ecosystem Framework

Despite the widespread recognition of the negative impact of fossil fuel, alternative energy for urban mobility still faces monumental barriers due to multilayered challenges. Besides the transition of extensive infrastructures and vehicle technology maturity, financial, cultural, and political or public opinion stigma associated with fossil fuel industry remains an invisible psychological barrier. Various forms of mobility system alternative energy emerged in the last two decades. Electrification and biofuels are the most recognized alternative sources of mobility energy (Li and Loo, 2014) despite their potential failure to reduce emission if production and distribution system efficiency and energy loss are not properly addressed. This section describes potential alternative and transitional energy sources in the urban mobility landscape to understand current or future applications, and to identify potential planning, policy, and design changes to achieve a successful energy transition.

Confusion lingers over a practical definition of alternative energy as well as electrification. The US Energy Department defines alternative fuel vehicles as *"From electric cars and propane vehicles to natural gas-powered buses and trucks that run on biodiesel, today's options for alternative fuel vehicles are vast. Increasing the use of alternative fuels and vehicles will help reduce consumers' fuel costs, minimize pollution, and increase the nation's energy security"* (US Department of Energy, 2018). But it does not clarify how alternative energy vehicles will access fuel, nor what are those strategies and their implications on city planning perspectives.

Similar problems arose with electrification. For instance, the electrification process is defined as *"Becoming fully electrified ('electrification') is the process of converting a machine, process, system, or sector to use electricity where it did not do so before. Examples include going from a petrol- or diesel-driven passenger vehicle to an electric vehicle and connecting an oil platform previously powered by fossil fuel generators to an electric cable connected to the onshore power system"* (Hordnes, 2019). The term 'electrification' does not clarify the energy source of electricity or pathways to emission reduction or implementation strategies. In a true definition, electrification should refer simply to the phasing out of fossil source usage, generation, and processes that block the electrification path.

The next step is to define sustainable energy elements and systems to maintain consistency. To avoid multiple configurations, several regulatory bodies are working to define safety, and different aspects related to charging, security, communication, and processes of new mobility energy. For instance, new, ongoing, or planned standards will deal with electric, hybrid, and fuel cell vehicles (Wilson, 2018). A charging standard for electric buses was recently developed for infrastructure-mounted, pantograph, and socket connections for regular charging locations (J3105, 2020), depots (J3068, 2018), on-street or station charging and innovative wireless charging facilities (J2954, 2019). Some standards and regulations are yet to be produced, particularly relative to new fuel cell technology for mobility, harvesting energy, and cleaner cousins of fossil fuels such as synthetic or biofuels.

A few energy systems are well established and getting better, linking energy systems to placement, to implementation, and to appropriate redesign, planning, or policy establishment.

## *Electrification or E-Mobility*

The first option to provide alternative energy to the mobility system is easily accessible electricity sources. If electricity is produced, and transferred less or without fossil fuel, E-Mobility's transition would be faster. Recent trends appear that all mobility vehicles are gradually moving toward electrification, following the success of the electrification of automobile and bicycle modes. Charging all vehicles and mobility devices simultaneously could however destabilize the entire power system. Intelligent energy management, reducing trip demand in peak hours, and vehicle-to-grid connectivity are potential solutions.

Automobile and transit systems would need to be transitioned toward various forms of electric vehicles. Applications in urban automobile mobility include hybrid plugins (HEV), plug-in hybrid EVs (PHEVs), battery EVs (BEVs), and fuel-cell EVs (FCEVs).

- *Hybrid electric vehicle (HEV)*

  The first attempt to mainstream electrified automobiles was the HEV at the end of the last century. Initial acceleration of electricity is created with a small electric motor and battery, which replenishes itself via energy generated by the Internal Combustion Engine (ICE) as well as regenerative braking. There is no plugin charging system to recharge the battery.

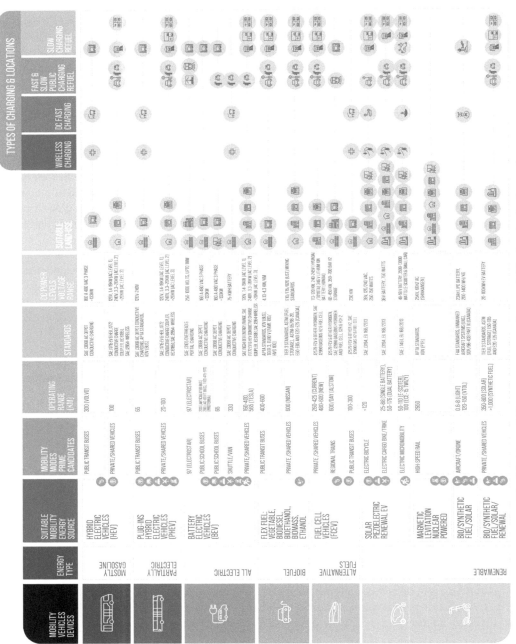

**Fig. 5.4:** New mobility energy ecosystem framework (Graph under development).

- *Plugin hybrid electric vehicle (PHEV)*

  The hybrid is a short-term hope to help transition toward an all-electric mobility system, particularly transit buses and shared mobility vehicles. PHEVs depend on both diesel/gasoline and electricity through plugins to recharge the battery and have been in use for the last 50 years without major challenges.

- *Battery electric vehicle (BEV), i.e., all electric*

  BEVs use electricity directly to charge their batteries, produce less vibration and noise, and do not have an ICE, fuel tank, or exhaust pipe, i.e., no air pollutants in operation.

- *Hydrogen fuel cell technology*

  Fuel cell vehicles are powered by hydrogen, which is produced using electricity. Hydrogen contains three times more energy per kilogram than kerosene, a common fuel for aviation. Fuel cell vehicles produce electricity by refilling with fuels such as hydrogen, alcohols, or ethers instead of recharging. One of the key merits of fuel cell vehicles is their high power-generation efficiency, because unlike a normal generation system, the system does not depend on the Carnot efficiency of thermal motors. However, hydrogen is bulky and awkward to store on board and has no established infrastructure for manufacturing and distribution.

## Renewable energy

The rise of renewable energy to power mobility systems has become a source of hope, and conflict. The intermittent nature of renewable energy is typically considered a downside, but a blessing for spotty use during the daytime. Current renewable energy capacity, however, is not built with a storage capacity that could supply reliable sources of energy for mobility in cities. The mobile nature of mobility however matches perfectly with different sources of renewables, when renewables for mobility are chemical (oxidization, geothermal, or hydrogen fusion), gravitational forces like tidal waves, or simply using elevation differences such as gravity, solar, wind, and biomass through photosynthesis.

## Solar energy and photovoltaic technology

Where traditional energy access is difficult or expensive, solar energy could replace fossil fuel with greater success. While the placement of photovoltaic technology is easier almost everywhere if the space is designed properly, the application of solar energy in mobility is still limited except for a few solar prototype vehicles and the production of electricity for charging mobility vehicles and devices. Solar vehicles are limited to solar buses (Tindo, Australia), boats (PlanetSolar) and light aircraft (Solar Impulse), while rooftop solar energy and larger off-grid solar systems are spreading slowly and remain as a major source of charging for electric vehicles, particularly in isolated or remote places where conventional hydro is unavailable. Generating power from solar energy for mobility support systems is gaining some ground in urban areas. For instance, solar panels generating power to light up promotional panels and bus information boards during evenings/nights. Low energy devices such as mobility kiosks, additional lights, digital signage, or payment systems are frequently supported by solar cells since traditional hydro was not originally provided or solar was simply cheaper than conventional energy sources. Potential solar energy applications are solar-powered rail corridors or elevated urban transit (Swenson, 2016), continuously chargeable highway or trails support by overhead solar panels (The TEV project, 2017). If solar energy solutions are customized through urban planning systems and incorporated into the urban design fabric, solar energy could provide affordable and stable sources of alternative mobility energy (Deluchhi and Jaconson, 2009).

## Wind

Dense urban areas limit the opportunity for continuous wind energy sources. But they could provide a stationary, cleaner energy source if distribution is linked to home, work, and other common land-uses from a nearby wind plant location. As energy storage gets more efficient using electrochemical processes, including those found in photoelectrochemical devices, batteries, fuel cells, and supercapacitors, the storage and distribution of wind energy could be simplified and become a cheaper, reliable energy source for urban mobility systems.

## Geothermal

Abundant sources (in the main western part of North America, Iceland, Indonesia, Philippines, Turkey, New Zealand, and Mexico) and all-time availability gives geothermal an advantage over other renewable sources of energy (Center for Sustainable Systems, 2020). Since it does not require transportation or storage or needs only a small area to produce energy at lower costs, geothermal would be ideal as a slow and stationary energy source to power mobility vehicles at home, work, or small industrial, large industrial, or commercial centres. To avoid chemical or salt damage for roads and bridges in winter months, potential application of geothermal snow melting and/or geothermal de-icing is showing promise for cold climate counties (Eugster, 2007). The potential use of geothermal energy sources to produce Li-ion batteries for electric vehicles is proposed to reduce emission and avoid the thermal hazards of the Li-ion battery (Tao et al., 2014). Enhanced geothermal systems using manmade reservoirs make it an easily available source where the lack of continuous rock heat capacity is a concern, particularly in eastern North America.

## Electromagnetic or magnetic levitation

The discovery of electromagnetism's enormous application in high-speed mobility led to today's maglev train technology, with Germany, Japan, and China becoming leaders in harnessing new energy to solve long-distance travelling needs. Despite sufficient nuclear energy availability, USA and Canada failed to capture its potential due to political disputes, and lack of skills and knowledge in high-speed rail technology (Karim and Shallwani, 2010). The gigantic electricity production needed to power maglev trains is entirely dependent on nuclear energy (both renewable and non-renewable). However, low speed urban maglev trains which require manageable amounts of energy are gaining popularity and becoming a cost-effective, reliable, and environmentally-sound transit option for urban mass transportation around the world (Hoopengardner and Thompson, 2012). Despite enormous potential, however, challenges remain, with urban maglev requiring a new form of hydro, a practical urban design approach, and consistent system management and risk implementation procedures.

## Energy harvesting and piezoelectric

Converting mechanical stress into electrical energy has been a dream since its first demonstration by the brothers Pierre Curie and Jacques Curie in 1880 (Curie and Pierre, 1880). However, storing the energy in a battery remained a challenge. So called "free energy", converting cycling, walking, and mobility mechanical devices into electricity gained traction recently. To generate piezoelectricity, the alternative energy source used is a mechanical energy by piezoelectric material, which can convert mechanical energy into electrical energy. It can convert mechanical energy from pressure forces and vibrations during activities such as walking, cycling, and travel into electrical energy (Jettanasen et al., 2020). The most successful example is the "Copenhagen Wheel", produced by Superpedestrian Inc. USA, using regenerative braking which is becoming the easiest way to capture energy. Massive pedestrian flow at transit stations has also been successfully converted into energy and reverted into transit vehicle usage (Takefuji, 2008). Major pedestrian flow, such as at educational institutions, could be connected to backpack or knee device (Shepertycky and Li, 2015) technologies to harvest walking energy into other micro-mobility and bicycle charging needs (Li and Strezov, 2014). The largest source of "Piezoelectric Energy" could be harvested from heavy vehicle traffic (Najini and Muthukumaraswamy, 2017) or traffic induced deformed pavements (Xiong et al., 2011) by creating energy for sustainable mobility modes through in-motion charging such as electric travel lanes for buses or carpools (Kour and Charif, 2016).

### Regenerative braking

Regenerative braking, another vast potential reusable energy source method, is the process of recapturing energy that would otherwise be lost during a vehicle's braking event. Most prevalent in the vehicles or train systems, it can be applied to all mobility vehicles. Instead of waste, the energy can be recycled to use and accelerate the vehicle again or to power some other electrical load. By recuperating braking energy, hybrid cars and buses could be up to 30% more fuel efficient than conventional combustion vehicles in urban settings (Cook, 2014). As energy storage of lithium-ion batteries improves, this energy capture could further reduce the consumption cost of electricity for E-Mobility systems.

### Alcohol and biofuels

Biomass could be the short-term transitional energy route before renewable energy finds its natural way to become more efficient and cheaper than fossil fuel. Biomass, plant materials such as leaves, stalks, and wood, can be burned directly or processed to create biofuels, like ethanol. Non-crop-based biofuels are promising to avoid food vs. energy competition and can be produced from wood residues, bagasse, rice husks, agro-residues, animal manure, and municipal and industrial waste (Islam and Ahiduzzaman, 2012). Soil fertility, the high costs of production, transportation, and storage (Li and Loo, 2014) and very low energy return (EORI) remain biomass' fundamental barriers to the easy replacement of fossil fuel. However, combined with synthetic and biofuel, short-term transition could be achieved due to compatibility with existing policy and infrastructure needs.

### Synthetic fuels

Synthetic fuel is the closest cousin to fossil fuel, and considered as a short-term sustainable transition energy source for urban mobility due to its lower GHG emissions (Christensen and Petrenko, 2017) and compatibility with existing infrastructure if production cost is lower (Jorna, 2012). Synthetic fuels are still crude-oil or crude-oil-processed-fuel equivalents and produced from other sources such as coal, natural gas, and biomass (Reddy, 2008). They can be manufactured, via chemical conversion processes from 'de-fossilized' carbon dioxide sources such as point source capture from the exhausts of industrial processes, and direct capture from air or from biological sources. Trains, buses, short-haul trucks, long-haul trolley trucks and buses, cars, motorcycles, and inland waterway transport vehicles would be the best candidate for synthetic fuel (Perner et al., 2018). In another way, GHG can become a raw material, from which gasoline, diesel, and substitute natural gas can be produced with the help of electricity from renewable sources. This also avoids the food vs. fuel debate. Finally, policy requirement for synthetic fuel land-use planning and mobility operations would be like fossil fuel operations.

### Nuclear energy

Once believed to be the cheapest, safest, and hugest quantity of transport energy suppliers, nuclear still dominates as the cleaner but riskiest energy source. Huge transmission costs, public resistance, the hidden costs of nuclear waste, and the long-term usability of its land once a nuclear plant ceases operation remain monumental barriers despite its enormous energy density and EORI advantage. Thus, the importance of power generation using nuclear energy, premised on the '3Ss' of safeguards, safety, and security, is clear and indisputable (Omi, 2018). Climate change and escalating oil prices have persuaded some countries such as Germany to adopt a cautious stance toward nuclear energy and change their minds and seriously consider it as an alternative. In Canada, nuclear provides the largest source of clean energy to power mobility electricity needs.

### *Gravitational energy*

Often considered a fairy tale, the relatively unknown but high potential application of gravity could soon become reality where conditions exist. Steep terrain, the ideal candidate, if transport guideways are properly developed, gravity powered acceleration or deceleration could move people or goods in tubular module shaped vehicles (Bojji, 2011). The most famous application that is sweeping the mobility industry over the last few years is the pod-based transit module or hyperloop tube train. However, practical application remains a huge question for the overhyped technology (Wolverton, 2016). Small pod-modules have the highest potential due to their manageable scale, lower cost, and minimal impact on the urban landscape.

## Conceptual Modelling of Mobility Energy Ecosystem

Mobility energy planning is still it its infancy stage, and a scarcity of a strategic framework and model has led to random and sporadic energy planning without any real outcomes. Developing future scenarios for future mobility is a multistage task involving multidisciplinary experts. Available literature provides the basic concepts but focuses on specific issues instead of taking broader city planning perspectives. This section attempts to combine specific concepts while broadening their application to city-wide planning and design issues. Conceptual design and implementation scenarios through various concepts are provided in the next sections, while qualitative and quantitative approaches are developed in this section. Mobility planning stages and scale are illustrated in Fig. 5.5.

### *Overall planning stages*

Mobility energy quantification is a multistage process. Each stage requires specific information, from an initial broader city-wide level to granular details in every stage. Each subsequent stage then requires specific information (Porru et al., 2020), and professional expertise to understand the dynamics of mobility energy planning. Considering area context, mobility modes, the nature of each mode, and planning and policy developments, seven stages are proposed:

1. Macro-scale area planning;
2. Sub-area scale planning;
3. Micro area detail planning;
4. Energy demand planning;
5. Mode-specific planning;
6. Prerequisite for infrastructure types planning and design; and
7. Implementation staging and policy/bylaw development.

### *Macro-scale area planning*

Mobility energy modelling would look at broader, city-wide areas or neighbourhoods, and considering their context, subdivide cities into additional subzones. It roughly follows a city's

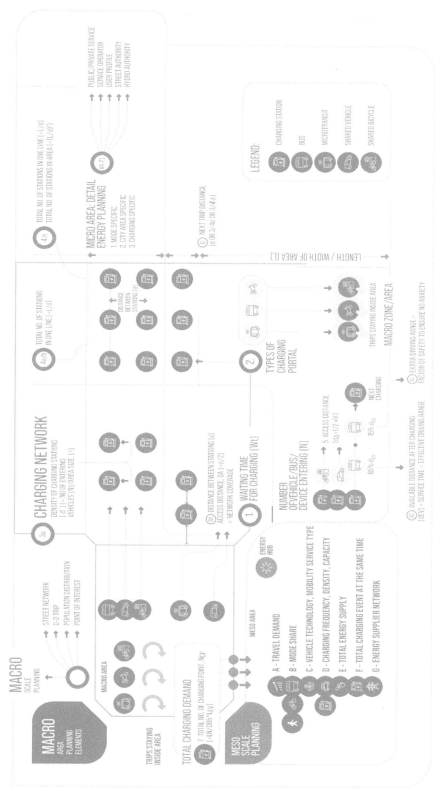

**Fig. 5.5:** Illustration of city-wide mobility energy planning concept for long-range plans (Graph under development).

planning districts or area plans, but it may or may not align with traditional traffic zones for travel demand modelling. At this stage, city-wide information would be needed to understand the mobility usage and associated high level energy needs:

- Population density and distribution, to understand where the majority of land-use related activity would occur;
- Origin-destination trips, to understand where people are going to or coming from between the different communities or neighbourhoods;
- Identifying trips that stay internal, and incoming trips that would need energy to recharge or refuel in that neighbourhood; and
- Points of interest, to identify energy demand hotspots while servicing or waiting between trips.

### *Sub-area scale planning*

Once a macro pattern is established, specific sub-areas or zones would be brought into focus to understand the types of land-use and energy needs to customize energy infrastructures and match the context of the area. Downtown areas' needs higher and frequent or faster energy usage compared to residential neighbourhoods where energy demand is high during the late afternoon or evening hours. Besides the macro energy area, input from resident, business and operator would provide context-sensitive specific energy details:

- The scale of travel demand within the area, and energy needs for the entire area;
- Types of mobility modes, their share, and the nature of vehicle and driver usage;
- The mechanical nature of vehicle or device technology that determines refuel or recharge frequency, density, and capacity;
- Assessing the total energy supply and availability for mobility systems, in addition to other sectors that use energy at the same time;
- Collaboration with hydro and utility agencies to understand potential changes and future demand for different energy; and
- Energy usage patterns and possible options of spreading the energy demand.

### *Micro area detail planning*

Careful detail is the central objective of this stage to address deeply rooted problems. For instance, driving-range anxiety, and stagnation of the number of new electric vehicle users, refueling station locations, and access for hydrogen fuel vehicle users, frequent and quick access to energy access portals in public spaces for both active and micro-mobility modes, and continuous and fast charging to reduce battery replacement or battery size for transit operators. In the initial stage of introducing electric vehicles, the allocation of charging stations is difficult to determine due to the uncertainty of candidate sites for stations and unidentified charging demands, which are determined by diverse factors (Ahn and Yeo, 2015). Quantifications of energy demand are based on these key principles:

- Servicing time or waiting time between trips = Charging time;
- Refuelling frequency = Total vehicle driving distance/Distance covered after refuelling;
- Charging or refuelling demand = Number of charging points;
- Density of charging stations = Number of charging stations, $(N_{cs})$/Area, $(L^2)$;
- Density of refuelling stations = Number of refuelling stands * Number of stations $(N_{cs})$/Area, $(L^2)$;

- Distance to next charging point should be reduced by 15% to make sure vehicle can reach next station before it runs out of energy;
- Distance after charging or refuelling = 85% of distance after recharging or refuelling; and,
- The proportion of peak time demand and ways to reduce peak demand.

## Energy demand planning

The network structure of future energy remains relatively unknown. As charging infrastructure or hydrogen fuel stations are being rolled out in North America, Japan, Europe, and China, common building blocks of these network structures need to be clearly defined. This stage requires energy experts to work with a city's energy and environment department, and for the hydro authority to collaborate with major industry partners, operators, and service providers. Basic building blocks or parameters proposed include energy demand from electric vehicles, energy use intensity, a charger's intensity distribution, their use-time ratios, energy-use ratios, the nearest distance between chargers and availability, the total service ratio, and the carbon intensity as an environmental impact indicator (Lucas et al., 2018). The mass supply of hydrogen is not possible in urban areas (Melaina et al., 2017), however hydrogen supplied by reforming city gas to supply hydrogen to nearby stations may be a cost-effective option for establishing a hydrogen refuelling infrastructure (Bae et al., 2020). Urban solar integration is also a new energy concept and still under development. A few ideas have emerged. One concept offers city districts and neighbourhoods to be turned into solar power stations that behave like atoms, and the division of the city turns into "cellular units" according to four fundamental criteria (Amadoa and Poggi, 2014): the construction timeline, population density, urban morphologies, and land-use patterns.

## Mode-specific planning

Energy demand for e-bikes, and micromobility, public transit, and shared mobility remain unexplored areas of city planning. Most energy plans often take an invisible approach to multimodal needs other than electric vehicles or buses. Clean and green energy options in public transit is the utmost priority but there are few known alternative energy adoptions. Transit operations are gradually moving into solar and electric or hybrid technology, but with few successes. Barriers and paths to success have been established in the last two years.

- Common obstacles identified a lack of operational knowledge on electric bus systems, unfamiliar procurement and financing schemes, and institutional deficiencies in terms of authority, funding and land needed for the changes (Sclar et al., 2018).
- Common success factors that enable electric bus adoption are structured and flexible pilot programmes, well-informed and methodical cost-benefit analyses, and actionable and timebound targets for scaling-up adoption from a small number of buses to entire fleets (Li et al., 2018).
- Energy demand for bicycles and smaller vehicles like scooters and kick-scooters can be managed on boulevards or on outside posts on building walls or driveways that are easily visible and where storage space is available. Buildings/institutions can easily provide level-1 (110v) vehicle charging facilities where secure bicycle facilities are provided and subsidized by vehicle charging revenue.
- The solar micro grid and 48V DC nano grid are ideal in public spaces or campus locations, for active and micromobility (e-scooter, pod car) energy needs, since charging can be done in 3–5 hrs (Ram et al., 2020).
- Rail electrification is generally shrouded in a mystery of assumptions and misperceptions. Despite broad agreement of the importance of rail electrification, the threshold criteria

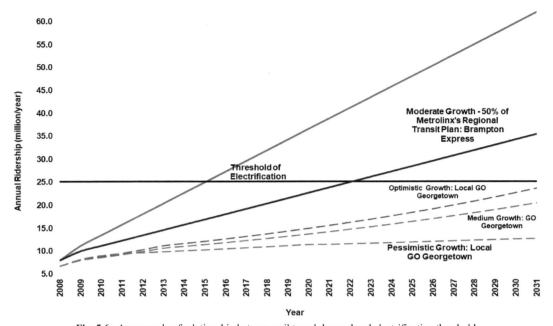

**Fig. 5.6:** An example of relationship between rail travel demand and electrification threshold.

**Notes:** Rail electrification threshold technique was developed by the author independently after the author's initial work was published by West Toronto PEO chapter (Karim and Shallwani, 2010). Rail growth data was used from Regional Transportation Plan: The Big Move 1.0 by Metrolinx for Greater Toronto area region (Metrolinx, 2008).

when a system will be electrified remains undefined or generally vague among rail transit agencies. European and Asian rail electrification, however, tells a very different story. Rail electrification is particularly justified for the high-density corridors. The electrified lines in UK (Network Rail Infrastructure Limited, 2020) tend to serve the busiest parts of the network and consequently carry a greater density of traffic than the non-electrified parts of the network. Electric trains tend to be operated in longer formations than diesel trains, reflecting the demand in the markets they serve. Figure 5.6 illustrates an example of how passenger rail demand driven by a city's growth plan establishes a general criterion when a certain corridor would be approaching the electrification threshold. This process establishes a clear path of rail electrification for the entire rail's network-wide energy transformation using scientific process and priority-based paths for energy independence. Given capricious fuel prices, and the greater dependency for transportation of people and goods on these volatile fuel sources, fossil fuel dependent nations face grave economic consequences if they continue to be dependent on oil and diesel.

## Prerequisite for infrastructure types planning and design

Types of energy and associated technology needs to be identified once energy demand, density, and configurations are known from the micro area, and mode-specific details have been sorted out. This stage needs collaboration between the hydro/utility authority and infrastructure planning to identify high-level details including:

- Types of charging portals suitable for various vehicle or devices;
- Types of energy supply stations clustered to create eco-energy hubs (see next section);
- Types of charging power needs, and the best suitable vendor in the market;

- Customized energy supply outlets to match different modes frequency and nature of service usage; and
- Identified space redesign needs and options, while addressing urban design issues and keeping the best possible and safest conditions for all types of users in the public space (see next section).

### *Implementation staging and policy/byelaw development*

In many ways, it is always too easy to plan in paper. Reality is different. But not impossible if targets for initial energy transformation and replacement are set properly. At each stage, a list of easier implementable items could be targeted. Examples of low-hanging items to begin a long list of energy transition would be:

- Targeting new development with incentives to instal a new energy system, or keeping an option open for a new energy system to be installed;
- Identifying active and micromobility hotspots, and providing electric and solar powered options at ground level;
- Retrofitting transit stations and stops at the locations frequently used by electric or hybrid buses, and micro-energy needs for specific transit services at stops for transit users;
- Electrifying bikeshare fleets and adding solar charging hotspots for personal e-bikes for bikeshare and e-bike users combined;
- Allowing electric bicycle or cargo bike users to charge at work or commercial places;
- Retrofitting downtown hotspots with fast DC chargers and wireless charging at general hydro or solar stands to reduce demand on the energy grid.
- Allowing micro grid, solar nano grid, and location substations for alternative energy as public-private businesses to feed mobility energy systems without dipping into the general grid.
- Opening the door, with guidance and regulation, for third party vendors to instal new energy services and equipment such as new charging stations and new apps to save on costs and combine pricing, linking energy access to other mobility modes through mobility-as-a-service.

## Alternative Energy Mobility: Planning and Design Concepts

The slow and frustrating progress of an energy shift from dirty fossil fuel to alternative cleaner and greener energy sources is often attributed to the lack of a systemwide approach. A city's energy policy design and planning are rarely successful in achieving alternative energy freedom, but a few cities in China and Norway have achieved remarkable success despite challenges. Previous political and experimental projects in the mobility sector, albeit some failures, provide a glimpse to the future pathway. Answers to common barriers to energy transformation are known but not fully practised through system-wide polices and the regulatory framework. Public and private entities should fully understand these barriers to alternative energy transformation to surmount the obstacles.

Each time an alternative energy success had been accomplished, the system achieved a critical mass of density of cleaner vehicles or devices, achieved energy infrastructure transition, closely followed user needs and patterns, while removing energy supply 'anxiety' with reliable and continuous sources. Range anxiety caused by a limited driving range and the low availability of charging stations discouraged acceptance by new consumers and limited the economic benefits of electric vehicles (Ahn and Yeo, 2015). The few lessons learned from past successful or failed attempts at alternative energy mobility have common underlying features: an energy ecosystem approach combining short- and long-term achievable action plans, space redesign, and network-wide energy access, including overall policy incentives for clean energy and disincentives for dirtier fuel sources.

The following are the proposed elements of a grand energy ecosystem to reinvent a city's mobility energy source:

1. Gradual phase out of dirty energy sources;
2. Mandatory energy policy implementation through the city's development, permit and capital plan for mobility services;
3. Redesigning of space for new low-carbon energy;
4. Easily accessible alternative energy within reasonable walking distance;
5. Variety and diversity in energy supply infrastructures, as practically as possible, for all types of vehicles with proper standardization;
6. Continuous supply of alternative energy to provide sufficient options for different types of mobility and nature of vehicle or device usage;
7. Creating energy hubs to develop a distribution of alternative energy network; and,
8. Alternative energy for all multimodal mobility modes.

Figure 5.7 illustrates a systematic planning and design approach to the alternative mobility energy supply. Seven basic principles are applied to capture the essence of the variety of energy sources, the diversity of mobility devices, or vehicle and equal energy transformation for all mobility modes through supply locations and infrastructures.

### *Fossil fuel exit plan*

An alternative mobility energy plan can succeed only when there is a mandatory exit plan for dirty fossil fuel-based mobility. Keeping fossil fuel as a core energy supply will ultimately lead to 'additional' nice-to-have or feel-good alternative energy for sustainable 'show-off'. The exit plan would start at the national or provincial level. The Canadian coal-phase out plan was among the most notable national plans, achieving a real reduction in the most inefficient and polluting energy used to generate electricity (Canada Energy Regulator, 2020), and the last coal energy source in the Province of Ontario was retired in 2014 (IISD, 2015). China, the EU, Japan, and the UK are leading major initiatives to phase out fossil fuels. Vancouver has committed to exit fossil fuel use and endorsed the Fossil Fuel Non-Proliferation Treaty (Newswire, 2010). As cities consume 70–80% of the world's energy, leading cities, for instance Tokyo, Houston, Stockholm, Sydney, Cape Town, are developing renewable energy plans (Appleby, 2015). An "ecosystem approach" E-Mobility strategic plan, for instance, the one developed by the Norwegian EV association, is now widely seen as the most effective way to stimulate quicker electric vehicle adoption. By putting a city's goals, objectives, policies, and efforts together into a city-wide action map, the variety of alternative energy needs could be developed for the entire mobility ecosystem (Haugneland et al., 2017).

However, these plans are not going to see the light at the end of the tunnel if they aim for very lengthy periods have no action plans embedded into the city or organization's policy, a gradual implementation process, and provide proper guidance and skills to achieve the goal.

### *Mandatory energy policy*

One of the key features of all successful energy transformation examples is consistent government policy, regulations, positive and practical attitudes toward alternative energy while developing guidance for 'future-ready' conditions, and a clear message on space and system redesign. Random alternative energy projects create urban nuisance that ultimately leads to scrapping the new energy system. A comprehensive approach to integrate a new energy system into new or retrofit projects generally incorporates street or space reconstruction, and mandatory replacement requirements of the fossil fuel dependent system.

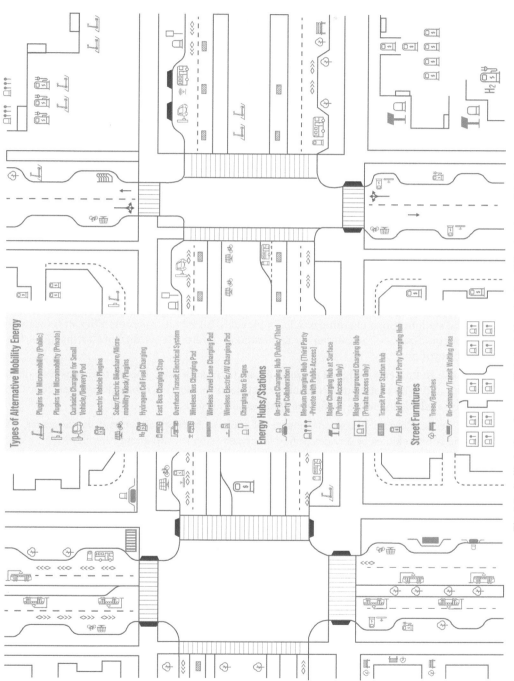

**Fig. 5.7:** An illustration of energy efficient neighbourhood mobility planning and design.

A few shining examples, however, provide a glimpse of possible energy transformation:

- *Electric-ready city*: Mandatory policy for electric vehicle fleets, charging facilities, and EV-ready conduits emerged as a successful trend, including:
  - ○ Government incentives for new construction zoning byelaws, to allow the extension of the electricity grid and the installation of EV-ready wiring in the walls, floors, or ceilings akin to California, London, and EU requirements (Fishbone et al., 2017).
  - ○ Mandatory EV charging parking: Recently adopted by Vancouver (City of Vancouver, 2019) and Toronto as part of Toronto Green standards (City of Toronto, 2018) which require 20–50% spaces to be fitted with conduits for electrical charging.
  - ○ Sustainable energy modelling: Toronto requires an "Energy efficiency" report, which includes options for renewable energy (City of Toronto, 2020).
  - ○ Mandatory fleets: Greening the government vehicle fleet, including public transit, bikeshare, carshare, and rideshare, could be imposed as a mandatory multi-phase implementation policy (Akndi, 2020) to gradually increase the electric vehicle fleet.
  - ○ Urban design for electrical boxes, charging and waiting area would provide practical solutions for integrating new energy features into the urban fabric.
- *Solar-ready city*: Rooftop solar cells are becoming common in large urban areas, however, surface mobility applications in urban setups remain unanswered. A few innovative approaches emerged as a path forward:
  - ○ Public solar charging stations: Systematic policy for solar rooftop bus stops/stations is low hanging fruit to provide energy for transit displays, payment, or kiosks.
  - ○ Pointed stations: Solar charging points for bicycles, bikeshare, micromobility, or information kiosks could reduce the burden on conventional hydro that is difficult to install in busy public corridors.
  - ○ Solar sheds: Properly designed pergolas or sheds could provide energy for pedestrian shelter heating and e-bike stations. Practice would need to identify urban design aesthetics and shadow analysis to ensure sufficient lights to solar panels.
  - ○ Solar fleets: Remain uncertain because of their technological immaturity, however, like electric solar vehicles or devices policy is the next step toward energy freedom.
- *Urban magnetic levitation for elevated and light urban transit*: The viability of magnetic or electric powered light transit depends entirely on a combination of change in hydro power, and detailed urban design and street planning policy to accommodate impending change in urban linear transit.
- *Urban design guidance*: An aesthetically pleasing urban planning and design concept is a critical step to develop professional practice. Additional space will be required for pedestrians and parking due to charging stands, safe wiring distances, and signage. Guidance and an "energyscape manual" would be vital to design transit and power substations in an urban context, the proper placement of facilities on public sidewalks or in public spaces, design assistance for third-party installation of charging stations, and installation procedures for hydro authorities to redesign or replace the old system in the public space.
- *Options for all sustainable energy*: Mandatory policy needs to offer several levels of development, financial or faster or priority implementation incentives to balance additional cost of transmission, personal and maintenance and operational changes that require successful energy transformation. Beside policy changes, additional guidance is needed for space redesign, signage, coloured pavement marking and wayfinding.

### Mobility and energy continuum and eco-energy hubs are conceived to Energy and Space continuum – Redesign for new energy

Spaces design and planning are key to success when it comes to future city building. If plans provide details for the gradual redesign of space or facilities through a continuous development process of city building and leave scope for adding new energy systems when technology matures, sustainable energy will achieve a natural success. Big approaches of grand redesign for entire areas or streets are unreal and ignore ongoing small opportunities. But it's where we start the process that's the major conundrum. Some easy targets are:

- *Around the building*: Retrofitting setbacks would provide easy energy access to energy for residents and visitors, or opportunity to rent energy for active and micromobility modes. Redesigning driveways would provide shared, delivery, and visitor vehicles access to new energy, sometimes through third party vendors. Reclaiming abandoned frontage, unused entrance areas, or dead building corners to create mobility parks would provide semi-private access to solar energy or electrical energy, including people's activities converted into energy storage.

- *Energy curb*: Coding the curb for serving vehicle passengers, while providing fast contact or induction is guaranteed to transform shared mobility success. Often called a "smart curb", the underside of cars become the natural charging points (Mitchell et al., 2015). However, the other side of the boulevard curb should be extended to reduce the unused wide travel lane and make it a wider space for pedestrians, additional storage space, and energy connections for e-bikes and electric micromobility.

- *Compatible urban hydro*: Conventional hydro often focuses on a single energy supply for specific types of users, the single largest barrier to alternative energy. Multiple types of energy supply with a diversity of charging ports are critical to accommodate the variety of urban land-use and user needs. Besides energy supply, the hydro authority needs to consider or be part of the street or space redesign and extend design options to not just buildings but to a variety of energy options for the curb lane, smart curbs, magnetic transit street curb or median options, and take inaccessible places for conventional energy and replace them with wireless or solar or other urban context-sensitive energy supply mediums. Once a diverse energy system is available, third-party suppliers of alternative energy would be allowed to instal their facilities through regulated processes, service agreements, and payment options.

- *Urban energy lane*: A continuous energy supply could greatly extend clean energy needs for mobility systems. A continuous supply reduces vehicle energy needs, lowers cost, and increases successful energy transfer. But it requires extensive planning of an "energy lane" in all possible locations. Wireless spots or continuous energy systems could be embedded in transit lanes, high-occupancy travel lanes, trails, or smart sidewalks and highways, while capturing solar or energy harvest techniques, or supplying electric energy using wind, solar, nuclear, or hydroelectric sources.

### Easily accessible alternative energy

Access to alternative energy vehicles, systems, or devices within a reasonable walking distance, and equal access to energy supply is vital for initial system survival. Extensive and dense coverage of energy infrastructures ensures public trust, user convenience, and the nudging of continuous habits toward cleaner mobility energy sources. The density of charging points will be generally greater than fossil fuel due to the greater frequency of charging, and the density of alternative energy vehicles and charging facilities should be available within a 3–5-min walking distance. To ensure critical density and easy access, an energy charging facility should be available at all possible locations such as public streets or lands, publicly accessible semi-private spots or within residential or commercial private locations. Private residential or commercial properties need to instal additional common access to charging locations, while inviting a third party to operate and maintain supply infrastructures. The latter needs to be recognized as energy policy by city building, energy, and planning sections to provide easy retrofit for the property owners.

## *Variety and diversity*

A variety of charging facilities and types of alternative energy emerged as a crucial challenge to diversify the mobility energy system. Charging facilities with proper power sources should be available for a variety of vehicles such as transit buses or rails, delivery trucks or vans, shared mobility vehicles, delivery bots or other smaller or micromobility vehicles and bicycles. The standardization of ground vehicle systems and associated charging facilities are currently underway (SAE International, 2014). Electrification is a common alternative energy, other viable alternative energy sources such as solar and hydrogen fuel are gaining ground due to their additional advantages over electrification. Types of alternative energy will depend on public agency policies and could vary from country to country. Germany and Japan, for instance, are advanced in hydrogen fuel cell technology while other countries including the US and Canada remain skeptical toward full cell technology (Staffell et al., 2019). Solar energy is the more appropriate source for smaller energy demands such as kiosks, payment stations, and on-street facilities. Magnetic levitation is becoming an increasingly popular urban tubular transit system. The combination of energy sources gives a diversity of energy sources options during a volatile price crisis (Regnier, 2007) and provides flexible options to continue critical mobility services during disruptions.

## *Continuous supply*

Mobility services that are constantly operating rely on continuous sources of energy to avoid "range anxiety". A continuous energy supply should cover all mobility activities, such as longer duration storage facilities, service, or usage points, charging while waiting, or even when vehicles or service devices are continuously moving (Sawilla et al., 2018). A continuous energy supply should be located on both public or private lands, while inviting third party vendors to provide pay-per-usage facilities to ensure and recover the cost of continuous supply (Fig. 5.8). A continuous supply of energy sources may include but is not limited to:

- *Slower charging*: Roughly 80% of energy supply is needed for charging at home and 95–97% energy supply could cover both at home and at work locations. Charging facilities (more than 6 hr of charging time, with minimum 6–11 kW and maximum 22 kW charging ports, for 15–20 km of driving using one-hour charging) should be deployed at source, for instance for longer distance mobility vehicles, or for device storage locations like bus depots, overnight residential or employment buildings, and transit vehicles at stations.

- *Slow and fast charging*: Most public places and private commercial facilities have high turnover of vehicles or devices. Users spend roughly between an hour to a few hours at these shopping centres and street retail outlets, hotels, cafés or restaurants, coffee shops, business centres, hospitals, sports or recreation centres, major government centres, or visiting friends and family. These places require a combination of fast and slow charging options. Charging facilities (roughly 2 hr charging time with minimum 3–11 kW, but ideally at least 22 kW charging port to provide 40–50 km of driving range for per hour of charging) would continue to charge or refuel mobility vehicles or devices while users continue their activities.

- *Opportunity charging*: Opportunity charging is typically outside of a longer storage facility and distributed throughout the network. This strategy results in smaller batteries requirements on large vehicles or buses. Opportunity charging could be provided using a traditional fast charging facility or the wireless charging option.

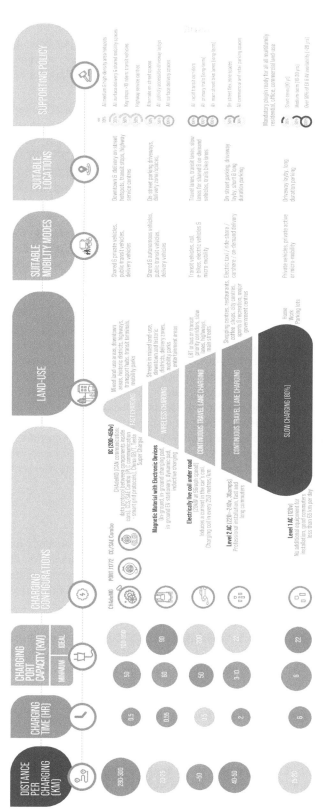

**Fig. 5.8:** Diversity and variety of energy charging (Graphic under development).

○ Fast charging: Fast DC charging facilities (30-min charging time with minimum 50 kW but ideally 100–350 kW charging port for 280–3,000 km of driving range for per hour of charging) at frequent usage points are critical for continuous services like transit, at stops/stations, and highways during layover or resting periods, in delivery vehicle loading zones, and at utility service vehicle working areas.

○ Wireless at service points: The need for wireless charging is vital for the survival of shared mobility, public transit, and autonomous electric vehicles. Wireless power transfer technology brings enormous benefits from reduced battery size and extending driving range, while reducing vehicle pricing that may stimulate the electric vehicle market (Qiu et al., 2014). An inductive power transfer, IPT, wireless charging facility (30–35 min charging time during downtime of vehicle service with minimum 60 kW, but ideally 90kW charging port for 20–25 km of driving range for per hour of charging) provides convenient options for charging during the delivery of goods, passenger loading or unloading periods, or while waiting for autonomous or share mobility services (Barry, 2013) without looking for traditional energy sources. In public transit, induction relies on magnetic charging plates beneath roadways and a counterpart inside the bus. When an induction-capable bus passes over the charging plate, the two magnets become 'tuned', and current flows to charge the on-board battery. Wireless facilities could be embedded into travel lanes or into sidewalks to allow easier access to track or lane supply for maintenance.

• *In-Motion charging on travel lane or path*: Public transit buses or rails, delivery trucks, or vans and other continuous supply services require a constant supply of energy, particularly in the city centre or downtown areas. Combining energy harvesting methods, overhead solar energy, and contactless wireless changing technology, self-healing highways or streets or bicycle trails could further reduce in-vehicle energy storage or charging needs (Venugopal et al., 2018). Continuous supply could be achieved by installing electric vehicle travel lanes and solar bicycle trails (roughly 30 min of charging time while driving 50km distance with a minimum 50 kW but ideally a 200 kW charging port) like electric rail or tram or magnetic levitation corridors. Charging during motion ensures the state of charge (SOC) is always high enough to reach the next power lane or charging point. These facilities should be carefully chosen for busy routes or a high number of alternative energy vehicles passing the streets or areas.

### Eco-energy mobility hubs

Extensive energy coverage depends on a dense network of infrastructures. Coverage depends on the type of land-use, energy demand, and the nature of energy usage. Arbitrary implementation of alternative energy facilities could lead to system failure, particularly in dense urban areas, while systematic and practical success of alternative energy is intimately linked to density of alternative energy vehicles, density of charging facilities, peak demand, and charging rate technology. These common features define the framework and configuration of mobility hubs, supported by energy hubs or stations, and linked through energy interconnectors (Geidl et al., 2007). The combination of an "energy hub" (transformation, conversion, and storage of various forms of energy in centralized units) with energy interconnectors (the combined transportation of different energy carriers over longer distances in single transmission devices) would enable multiple sources of energy to convert into the diverse needs of mobility systems. Mobility energy hubs should be context-sensitive, i.e., land-use and environment conditions would inform different levels of hub categories.

• *Major mobility energy hubs (large property)*: This would be generally located inside large residential, commercial, institutional or government complexes, in collaboration with public and private sectors. All mobility modes and all types of energy and charging facility would be available at a major mobility energy hub. Users are mainly facility residents, employees, or visitors. These facilities are mostly underground or a dedicated structured facility.

- *Medium mobility energy hubs* (*medium density private property*): Third parties would be invited to instal common access, secure charging facilities, underground in denser urban areas. Only prearranged booking or membership basis users would be able to access this energy source.

- *Surface energy hubs* (*semi-private*): These facilities will be generally located in public laneways, driveways, and small corner storage locations, and installed via third party vendors while property management signs a long-term agreement. These locations could be public. And all users would be able to access the facilities regardless of their trip origin or destination.

- *On-street energy hubs* (*public only*): Public agencies and hydro authorities would instal, operate and maintain these curbside or extended boulevard facilities, on street or on public lands. Operation and maintenance could be supplied by private entrepreneurs while public agencies collaborate to redesign the street elements to accommodate new alternative energy infrastructures.

- *Transit energy hubs*: Transit authorities would instal, operate, and maintain these facilities at major stations or stops. Operation and maintenance could be supplied by private entrepreneurs while public agencies oversee the alternative energy system.

- *Micro energy hubs* (*third-party*): City policy could open the door for a reliable third-party to instal alternative energy facilities on public or private lands and always accessible to any users.

## Multimodal energy approach

The current approach to electric mobility generally focuses on vehicle mobility, and major policy is directed toward energy supply and charging facilities in traditional surface, underground, or structured parking lots. While this approach, partially useful for private vehicles, spells potential trouble for shared mobility, public transit, active, micromobility, and other sustainable modes. There are solutions to multimodal energy needs:

1) Shared and active mobility modes mostly stay at ground level, and mostly operate on public streets or publicly accessible spaces or special corridors. Public charging with designated vehicle or devices storage should be available at these locations;

2) Public energy policy should include mandatory micromobility or active mobility facility;

3) Storage space and charging must be planned carefully and designed at all possible ground level locations, including building frontage, setback areas, driveways, or privately owned but publicly accessible lands;

4) Planning and redesign strategies could be embedded into redevelopment or street reconstruction policies. Once opportunity is lost, it is prohibitively expensive for hydro and third parties to instal alternative energy facilities and infrastructures;

5) Shared and active modes usually serve short trips and are continuously used by users. The need for energy supply and charging, including security, payment and accessibility issues should be an integral part of sustainable energy plans undertaken by public agencies;

6) Planning for urban rail stations for alternative energy often generates controversy, and planning mistakes for alternative energy are common. A newly built rail shed and facilities in Toronto's Union Station are incompatible with an electric rail fleet (Gee, 2016), and exclude vertical clearance, tunnels, bridges, and an environment for rail electrification in GO Transit's long-range infrastructure plans (Junkin, 2013, 2020); and

7) Shared vehicles and micromobility need compatible energy supply at the optimum location. Mistakes are common, including lack of home-vehicle charging for on-street users (Rieti, 2017) or carshare charging, legislative barriers to vehicle charging at condominiums (Lee-Shanok,

2017), lack of travel space considerations (Watch, 2018), and e-bike charging (Rider, 2020) for electric bicycles. These mistakes could be easily avoided by having an alternative energy plan that covers all mobility modes and energy supply or user needs. Successful energy transition plans, such as Norway's or Sweden's, addressed the demand for multimodal modes and relevant energy facilities and charging needs in both national and local levels.

## Summary: Resourceful Mobility Energy Planning

Urban quality of life could be dramatically improved if cities are carefully designed to open possibilities for a new, clean, and green renewable energy system. Planning and design for new mobility energy is too often the afterwork of mobility plans. Instead, a mobility energy framework could be easily developed, knowing the strengths, weaknesses, and suitability of all possible alternative energy system to avoid the pitfalls of past failed plans. Determining demand, identifying the scale, and funding for gradual implementation is possible if practical steps and guidelines are provided. Strategic concepts could serve to develop proper and meaningful energy policy as part of the city building process. Variety and diversity of energy supply challenges for all multimodal modes could be solved through easy access to energy, continuous supply, and redesign strategies for all possible spaces through eco-energy hubs, particularly public space through private and public collaboration. Of course, no careful planning can solve energy problems without a complete community that reduces the need for long-distance travel with the availability of sustainable multimodal options at our fingertips.

## References

Ahn, Y. and Yeo, H. (2015). An analytical planning model to estimate the optimal density of charging stations for electric vehicles. *PLoS ONE*, 1–26.

Akndi. (2020). *Greening Government Fleets: A Helpful Guide to Understanding.* Ottawa: Natural Resources Canada.

Albert, A. and Gonzalez, M.C. (2017). Using convolutional networks and satellite imagery to identify patterns in urban environments at a large scale. *Proceedings of the 23rd ACM SIGKDD International Conference on Knowledge Discovery and Data Mining*, (pp. 1357–1366).

Amadoa, M. and Poggi, F. (2014). Solar energy integration in urban planning: GUUD model. *Energy Procedia*, 50: 277–284.

Anderson, J.M., Kalra, N., Stanley, K.D., Sorenson, P., Samaras, C. and Oluwatola, O.A. (2016). *Autonomous Vehicle Technology: A Guide for Policymakers.* Santa Monica, California: RAND Corporation, RR-443-2-RC.

Appleby, K. (2015). *Five Cities Proving that We Can Quit Fossil Fuels.* Retrieved from City Monitor: https://citymonitor.ai/horizons/five-cities-proving-we-can-quit-fossil-fuels-1444.

Araujo, J.A., Barajas, B., Kleinman, M., Wang, X., Bennett, B.J., Gong, K.W., Navab, M., Harkema, J., Sioutas, C., Lusis, A.J. and Nel, A.E. (2008). Ambient particulate pollutants in the ultrafine range promote early atherosclerosis and systemic oxidative stress. *Circular Research*, 102(5): 589–596.

Bae, S., Lee, E. and Han, J. (2020). Multi-period planning of hydrogen supply network for refuelling hydrogen fuel cell vehicles in urban areas. *Sustainability*, 12(4114): 1–23.

Barry, K. (2013). *Wired.* Retrieved from In South Korea, Wireless Charging Powers Electric Buses: https://www.wired.com/2013/08/induction-charged-buses/.

Becic, E., Zych, N. and Ivarsson, J. (2018). *Vehicle Automation Report.* Washington, USA: National Transportation Safety Board, HWY18MH010.

Becky, P.Y., Lo, O. and Banister, D. (2016). Decoupling transport from economic growth: Extending the debate to include environmental and social externalities. *Journal of Transport Geography*, 57: 134–144.

Beddoes, Z.M. (2020). Time to make coal history. *The Economist.*

Benjamin, L. and Richards, D. (1981). Electrification is the way to move Canada in the 1980s. *Canadian Public Policy*, 7(81).

Berg, N. (2020). *This AI-powered Parking Grage Rewards You for Not Driving.* Retrieved from Fast Company: https://www.fastcompany.com/90575914/this-ai-powered-parking-garage-rewards-you-for-not-driving#:~:text=With%0a%20new%20test%20program,in%20to%20work%20at%20all.

Berg, P. (2011). *The Finite Planet: How Resource Scarcity will Affect our Environment, Economy, and Energy Supply.* Oshawa, Canada: Island Press.

Bhat, C. (2017). *Travel Modeling in an Era of Connected and Automated Transportation Systems: An Investigation in the Dallas-Fort Worth Area.* Austin, USA: Technical Report 122. Center for Transportation Research. The University of Texas at Austin.

Bhat, R.V. and Waghray, K. (2000). *Profile of Street Foods in Asian Countries.* Basel, Karger: World Rev. Nutr. Diet.

Billings, C.E. (1980). *Human-centered Aircraft Automation; A Concept and Guidelines.* Moffet Field, CA: NASA Technical Memorandum, NASA Ames Research Center.

Bojarski, M., Testa, D.D., Dworakowski, D., Firner, B., Flepp, B., Goyal, P., Jackel, L.D., Monfort, M., Muller, U., Zhang, J., Zhang, X., Zhao, J., and Zieba, K. (2016). End-to-End learning for self-driving cars. *Computer Vision and Pattern Recognition, Cornell University*, pp. 1–9.

Bojji, R. (2011). Gravity powered transport systems for rail, road, water, and airport use. *13th International Conference on Automated People* (pp. 22–25). Paris, France: American Society of Civil Engineers.

Borzino, N., Chng, S., Mughal, M.O. and Schubert, R. (2020). Willingness to pay for urban heat island mitigation: A case study of Singapore. *Climate*, 8: 82.

Botsman, R. (2010). *What's Mine is Yours: The Rise of Collaborative Consumption.* Harper Business.

Bourdieu, P. and Wacquant, L.D. (1992). *An Invitation to Reflexive Sociology.* Cambridge, UK: Polity Press and Blackwell Publishers.

Britton, E. (2000). Carsharing 2000: Sustainable transport's missing link. *Journal of The Commons*, 1–351.

Canada Energy Regulator. (2020). *Market Snapshot: Canada's Retiring Coal-fired Power Plants will be Replaced by Renewable and Low-carbon Energy Sources.* Retrieved from Canada Energy Regulator: https://www.cer-rec. gc.ca/en/data-analysis/energy-markets/market-snapshots/2020/market-snapshot-canadas-retiring-coal-fired-power-plants-will-be-replaced-renewable-low-carbon-energy-sources.html.

*Carsharing.Org.* (2017). Retrieved from What is carsharing?: https://carsharing.org/what-is-car-sharing/.

Carter, C. (2019). *Autonomous Passenger Ferries: Congestion-buster or Hype on the High Seas?* Retrieved from Smart Cities World: https://www.smartcitiesworld.net/special-reports/special-reports/autonomous-passenger-ferries-congestion-buster-or-hype-on-the-high-seas.

Center for Sustainable Systems. (2020). *Geothermal Energy.* Detroit, Michigan: University of Michigan. Retrieved from Geothermal Energy.: http://css.umich.edu/sites/default/files/Geothermal%20Energy_CSS10-10_e2020. pdf.

Charles, A.S., Lambert, H.G. and Balogh, S.B. (2014). EROI of different fuels and the implications for society. *Energy Policy*, 64: 141–152.

Chellapilla, K. (2018). *Rethinking Maps for Self-Driving.* Medium.

Christensen, A. and Petrenko, C. (2017). *CO2-Based Synthetic Fuel: Assessment of Potential European Capacity and Environmental Performance.* Brussels: European Climate Foundation and the International Council on Clean Transportation.

City of Toronto. (2018). *Toronto Green Standard Version 3.* Toronto, Canada: City of Toronto.

City of Toronto. (2020). *Energy Efficiency Report Submission & Modelling Guidelines: For the Toronto Green Standard (TGS) Version 3.* Toronto, Canada: Environment and Energy Division & City Planning Division, City of Toronto.

City of Vancouver. (2019). *EV Charging Infrastructure Requirements for New Residential Buildings Guidance.* Vancouver, Canada: City of Vancouver.

Civitas. (2016). *Cities towards Mobility 2.0: Connect, Share, and Go!* Brussels, Belgium: CIVITAS WIKI consortium.

CMA. (2008). *No Breathing Room National Illness Costs of Air Pollution.* Ottawa: Canadian Medical Association.

Cook, C. (2014). *Transforming the Transportation Industry with Renewable Energy.* Retrieved from Renewable Energy World: https://www.renewableenergyworld.com/2014/09/18/transforming-the-transportation-industry-with-renewable-energy/#gref.

Cooper, D. (2018). *It's tooEearly to Write off Hydrogen Vehicles.* Retrieved from Engadget: https://www.engadget. com/2018-05-29-hydrogen-fuel-cell-toyota-mirai-evs.html.

CPCS and Hatch Associates. (1992). *Commuter Rail Services: Electrification Study.* Toronto: GO Transit.

Curie, J. and Pierre, C. (1880). Développement, par pression, de l'électricité polaire dans les cristaux hémièdres à faces inclinées. *Comptes Rendus* (in French), 9: 294–295.

Dan, K. (2007). Flight of the pigeon. *Bicycling, Rodale, Inc.*, 48: 60–66.

Dave. (2018). *Car-Sharing vs. Private Vehicle Ownership Costs.* Retrieved from Carsharing US: https://arlingtonva. s3.amazonaws.com/wp-content/uploads/sites/19/2017/03/DES-Carshare-CarShare_vs_PrivateCarOwnership_ Cost_Analysis.pdf.

David, H. (2004). *Bicycle: The History.* Yale University Press. ISBN 0-300-10418-9.

Debhia, P. (2019). *The History of Electric Scooters.* Retrieved from LinkedIn: https://www.linkedin.com/pulse/history-electric-scooters-prashant-dedhia-negotiation-ninja-/.

Deluchhi, M.A. and Jaconson, M.Z. (2009). A path to sustainable energy by 2030. *Scientific American*, 58–65.

DeMaio, P. (2009). Bike-sharing: Impacts, models of provision, and future. *Journal of Public Transportation*, 12(4): 41–56.

DeMaio, P.J. (2003). Smart bikes: Public transportation for the 21st century. *Transportation Quarterly*, 57(1): 9–11.

Driving. (2015). *Company Wants to Bring Rickshaws to North America.* Retrieved from Driving: https://driving.ca/auto-news/news/company-wants-to-bring-rickshaws-to-north-america.

Duffy, M.C. (2003). *Electric Railways: 1880–1990.* London: The Institution of Engineering and Technology.

Endsley, M.R. and Kiris, E.O. (1995). The out-of-the-loop performance problem and level of control in automation. *Human Factors The Journal of the Human Factors and Ergonomics Society*, 2: 27.

Energy Information Administration (EIA). (2017). *Study of the Potential Energy Consumption Impacts of Connected and Automated Vehicles.* Washington, D.C. 20585: US Department of Energy.

Energy Innovation. (2015). *Comparing The Costs of Renewable and Conventional Energy Sources.* Retrieved from Energy Innovation: https://energyinnovation.org/2015/02/07/levelized-cost-of-energy/.

Eugster, J.W. (2007). Road and bridge heating using geothermal energy. Overview and examples. *Proceedings European Geothermal Congress* (pp. 1–5). Unterhaching, Germany: European Geothermal Congress.

European Commision. (2020). *Energy Efficiency Indicator.* Retrieved from European Commision: https://ec.europa.eu/transport/themes/energy-efficiency-indicator_en.

Fishbone, A., Shahan, Z. and Badik, P. (2017). *Electric Vehicle Charging Infrastructure: Guidelines for Cities.* Warsaw, Poland: CleanTechnica.

Fishman, E. (2014). Bikeshare: A review of recent literature. *Transport Reviews*, 92–113.

François-Lavet, V., Henderson, P., Islam, R., Bellemare, M.G. and Pineau, J. (2018). An introduction to deep reinforcement learning. *Foundations and Trends in Machine Learning*, 11-3-4: 1–102.

Frayer, L. and Cater, F. (2015). *How a Folding Electric Vehicle Went from Car of The Future to 'Obsolete'.* Retrieved from NPR: http://www.npr.org/sections/alltechconsidered/2015/11/05/454693583/how-a-folding-electric-vehicle-went-from-car-of-the-future-to-obsolete.

Furman, B., Fabian, L., Ellis, S., Muller, P. and Swenson, R. (2014). *Automated Transit Networks (ATN): A Review of the State of the Industry and Prospects for the Future.* San José: Minata Transportation Institute.

Galatoulas, N.F., Genikomsakis, K.N. and Loakimidis, C.S. (2020). Spatio-temporal trends of e-bike sharing system deployment: a review in Europe, North America and Asia. *Sustainability*, 12: 4611.

Gawron, V.J. (2019). *Automation in Aviation –Definition of Automation.* McLean, VA: The MITRE Corporation.

Gee, M. (2016). *Raise the Roof? Union Station Reno Runs into Problem: New Trains won't Fit.* Retrieved from The Globe and Mail: https://www.theglobeandmail.com/news/toronto/union-station-shed-renovation-stalled-by-low-arches-and-an-electrified-future/article28448568/.

Geidl, M., Koeppel, G., Favre-Perrod, P., Klöckl, B., Andersson, G. and Fröhlich, K. (2007). The energy hub – a powerful concept for future energy systems. *Third Annual Carnegie Mellon Conference on the Electricity Industry* (pp. 2–10). Pittsburgh: Carnegie Mellon University.

Gilpin, L. (2017). *Can Car-Sharing Culture Help Fuel an Electric Vehicle Revolution?* Retrieved from Insideclimate: https://insideclimatenews.org/news/07122017/car-rental-sharing-electric-vehicles-zipcar-evs-uber-lyft-green-commuter.

Global Union. (2020). *Top 10 principles for Ethical Atifical Intelligence.* Nyon, Switzerland: The Future World of Work.

Gomes, L. (2014). *Hidden Obstacles for Google's Self-Driving Cars: Impressive Progress Hides Major Limitations of Google's Quest for Automated Driving.* Cambridge, USA: MIT Technology Review.

Gross, S. (2020). *Why are Fossil Fuels so Hard to Quit?* Retrieved from Brookings Institution: https://www.brookings.edu/essay/why-are-fossil-fuels-so-hard-to-quit/#:~:text=We%20understand%20today%20that%20humanity's,climate%20of%20our%20entire%20planet.

GTA Clean Air Council. (2017). *Climate Action for a Healthy, Equitable and Prosperous Toronto.* Toronto: City of Toronto.

Harms, S. and Truffer, B. (1998). *The Emergence of a Nationwide Carsharing Co-operative in Switzerland: A Case Study for the Project "StrategicNiche Management as a Tool for Transition to a Sustainable Transportation System.* 1998: EAWAG-Eidg. Anstalt fur Wasserversorgung und Gewasserschutz.

Haugneland, P., Lorentzen, E., Bu, C. and Hauge, E. (2017). Put a price on carbon to fund EV incentives – Norwegian EV policy success. *EVS30 Symposium* (pp. 1–8). Stuttgart, Germany: Norwegian EV Association.

Haywood, J.B. (2006). Fueling our transportation future. *Scientific American.*

Hess, A. and Schubert, I. (2019). Functional perceptions, barriers, and demographics concerning E-cargo bike sharing in Switzerland. *Transportation Research Part D: Transport and Environment*, 71: 153. Retrieved from Science daily: https://www.sciencedaily.com/releases/2019/07/190710121536.htm.

Hoopengardner, R. and Thompson, M. (2012). *FTA Low-Speed Urban Maglev Research Program: Updated Lessons Learned.* Arlington, USA: US Federal Transit Administration.

Hordnes, E. (2019). *Race to Electrification – Norway in a Pole Position.* Retrieved from Urban Insight: https://www.swecourbaninsight.com/urban-energy/race-to-electrification--norway-in-pole-position/.

Hughes, I. and Huo, R. (2018). *Autonomy-level Classification for Robots in an IIoT World.* Retrieved from 451 Research: https://go.451research.com/MI-Robots-in-IIoT-World.html.

Hull, G.J., Roberts, C. and Hillmansen, S. (2008). Energy efficiency of a railway power network with simulation. *International Conference on Energy Technologies and Policy.* Birmingham, United Kingdom: University of Birmingham.

IISD. (2015). *The End of Coal: Ontario's Coal Phase-out.* Winnipeg, Canada: International Institute for Sustainable Development.

Institute, R.M. (2019). *Electric Mobility: Best Practices.* Rocky Mountain Institute, Government of India and Smart City.

Islam, A. and Ahiduzzaman, M. (2012). Biomass energy: Sustainable solution for greenhouse gas emission. *American Inst. Phys. Conf. Proc.*, 1441(1): 23–32. American Institute of Physics.

ISO. (2020). *Road Vehicles –Human Performance and State in the Context of Automated Driving - Part 2: Considerations in Designing Experiments to Investigate Transition Processes.* ISO/TR 21959-2: 2020.

Itoh, M., Zhou, H. and Kitazaki, S. (2018). What May Happen or What You Should Do? Effects of Knowledge Representation Regarding Necessity of Intervention on Driver Performance under Level 2 Automated Driving. *ICPS'18: Proceedings of the 2018 IEEE Industrial Cyber-Physical Systems* (pp. 621–626). Saint Petersburg, Russia: IEEE.

J2954. (2019). *Wireless Power Transfer for Light-Duty Plug-in/Electric Vehicles and Alignment Methodology.* SAE International.

J3068. (2018). *Electric Vehicle Power Transfer System Using a Three-Phase Capable Coupler.* SAE International.

J3105. (2020). *Electric Vehicle Power Transfer System Using Conductive Automated Connection Devices.* SAE International.

Jayasuriya, D.C. (1994). Street food vending in Asia: Some policy and legal aspects. *Food Control, Elsevier*, 5(4): 222–226.

Jefferies, I. (2019, November 20). Retrieved from Association of American Railroads: https://www.aar.org/article/freight-rail-highly-automated-vehicles/.

Jettanasen, C., Songsukthawan, P. and Ngaopitakkul, A. (2020). Development of Micro-mobility based on Piezoelectric energy harvesting for smart city applications. *Sustainability*, 1–16.

Jorna, A. (2012). *Synthetic Fuel Costs.* Stanford, California: Stanford University.

Joshi, N. (2019). *7 Types Of Artificial Intelligence.* Retrieved from Forbes: https://www.forbes.com/sites/cognitiveworld/2019/06/19/7-types-of-artificial-intelligence/#48c88ca9233e.

Junkin, K. (2013). *Regional Rapid Rail: A Vision for the Future.* Toronto: Transport Action, Ontario.

Kalra, N. and Paddock, S.M. (2016). *How Many Miles of Driving Would It Take to Demonstrate Autonomous Vehicle Reliability? Driving to Safety.* Santa Monica, California: RAND Corporation.

Kane, M. (2019). *Chile Launches Latin America's First 100% Electric Bus Corridor.* Retrieved from Inside EVs: https://insideevs.com/news/377241/chile-first-100-electric-bus-corridor/.

KAPSARC. (2016). *Mobility-on-demand: Understanding Energy Impacts and Adoption Potential.* Riyadh: KASARC.

Karim, D.M. and Shallwani, T. (2010). Toward a clean train policy: Diesel versus electric, the Ontario Centre for Engineering and Public Policy. *Ontario Centre for Engineering and Public Policy (OCEPP)*, 3: 18–22.

Khayal, O. (2019). The history of Bajaj rickshaw vehicles. *Global Journal of Engineering Sciences*, 3(2): 1–8.

Kleinman, M.T. (2000). *The Health Effects of Air Pollution on Children.* Irvine, California: South Coast Air Quality Management District (SCAQMD).

Kour, R. and Charif, A. (2016). Piezoelectric roads: Energy harvesting method using piezoelectric technology. *Innovative Energy & Research*, 5(1).

Kwon, D. (2018). Self-taught robots. *Scientific American*, 26–31.

Kwon, H., Ryu, M.H. and Carlsten, C. (2020). Ultrafine particles: Unique physicochemical properties relevant to health and disease. *Experimental & Molecular Medicine*, 52: 318–328.

Lambert, F. (2020). *Uber and Hyundai Unveil New Electric Air Taxi with 60-mile Range.* Retrieved from Electrek: https://electrek.co/2020/01/07/uber-hyundai-electric-air-taxi-evtol/.

Layton, B.E. (2008). A comparison of energy densities of prevalent energy sources in units of houles per cubic meter. *International Journal of Green Energy*, 5: 438–455.

Le Vine, S., Lee-Gosselin, M., Sivakumar, A. and Polak, J. (2014). New approach to predict the market and impacts of round-trip and point-to-point carsharing systems: case study of London. *Transportation Research Part D*, 32(C): 218–229.

Le Vine, S., Zolfaghari, A. and Polak, J. (2014). *Carsharing: Evolution, Challenges and Opportunities*. London: Centre for Transport Studies, Imperial College London.

Ledsham, T. and Savan, B. (2017). *Building a 21st Century Cycling City: Strategies for Action in Toronto*. Toronto: Metcalf Foundation.

Lee-Shanok, P. (2017). *Ontario Condo Act a Roadblock for Electric VehicleOowners*. Retrieved from CBC News: https://www.cbc.ca/news/canada/toronto/ontario-hopes-revised-condo-act-ev-friendly-1.4155747.

Lessing, H. (2001). What led to the invention of the early bicycle? *Cycle History 11, San Francisco*, 11: 28–36. Retrieved from New Scientist. https://www.newscientist.com/article/mg18524841-900-brimstone-and-bicycles/.

Li, L. and Loo, B.P. (2014). Alternative and transitional energy sources for urban transportation. *Current Sustainable/Renewable Energy Reports*, 1: 19–26.

Li, X. and Strezov, V. (2014). Modelling piezoelectric energy harvesting potential in an educational building. *Energy Conversion and Management*, 85: 435–442.

Li, X., Gorghinpour, C., Sclar, R. and Castellanos, S. (2018). *How to Enable Electric Bus Adoption in Cities Worldwide*. Berlin: World Resources Institute, WRI and German Federal Ministry.

Lima, M. (2015). *The Bicycle in the 21st Century*. Retrieved from Theprotocity: http://theprotocity.com/the-bicycle-in-the-21st-century/t.

Litman, T. (2018). Retrieved from Carsharing: Vehicle Rental Services that Substitute for Private Vehicle Ownership: https://www.vtpi.org/tdm/tdm7.htm.

Little, A. (2015). *The Future of Urban Mobility 2.0: towards Networked, Multimodal Cities of 2050*. Rome, Italy: International Association of Public Transport (UITP).

Lu, Z., Happe, R., Cabrall, C.D., Kyriakidis, M. and de Winter, J.C. (2016). Human factors of transitions in automated driving: A general framework and literature survey. *Transportation Research Part F*, 43: 183–198.

Lucas, A., Prettico, G., Flammini, M.G., Kotsakis, E., Fulli, G. and Masera, M. (2018). Indicator-based methodology for assessing EV charging infrastructure using exploratory data analysis. *Energies*, 11(1869): 1–18.

MaRS Discovery District. (2016). *Microtransit: An Assessment of Potential to Drive Greenhouse Gas Reductions*. Toronto: MaRS Discovery District and Richmond Sustainability Initiatives.

Martret, O. (2020). *Electric Vehicles – Cleaner, Greener and... On-Demand?* Retrieved from Shotl: https://shotl.com/news/electric-vehicles-cleaner-greener-and-on-demand.

Matuka, R. (2014). *The History of the Electric Car*. Retrieved from Department of Energy, USA.

McMahon, J. (2019). *9 Shared-Mobility Startups Eager to Disrupt Transportation*. Retrieved from Forbes: https://www.forbes.com/sites/jeffmcmahon/2019/03/06/9-shared-mobility-startups-eager-to-disrupt-transportation/#79ca1bf5177e.

McNabb, M. (2019). *DRONEII: Tech Talk – Unraveling 5 Levels of Drones*. Drone Talk.

Medina-Tapiaa, M. and Robusteb, F. (2018). Exploring paradigm shift impacts in urban mobility: Autonomous vehicles and smart cities. *Transportation Research Procedia*, 33: 203–210.

Melaina, M., Bush, B., Muratori, M., Zuboy, J. and Ellis, S. (2017). *National hydrogen scanarios: How Many Stations, Where, and When?* Washington. D.C.: National Renewable Energy Laboratory for the H2USA.

Metrolinx. (2008). *The Big Move: Transforming Transportation in the Greater Toronto and Hamilton Area*. Toronto: Metrolinx.

Millard-Ball, A. (2019, March). The autonomous vehicle parking problem. 75: 99–108.

MIT Media Lab. (2019). *Persuasive Electric Vehicle (PEV)*. Retrieved from MIT Media Lab City Science Group: https://www.media.mit.edu/projects/pev/overview/.

Mitchell, W.J., Borroni-Bird, C.E. and Burns, L.D. (2015). *Reinventing the Automobile*. Cambridge, USA: The MIT Press.

Mohorčich, J. (2020). Energy intensity and human mobility after the anthropocene. *Sustainability*, 12: 2376–2389.

Morawska, L., Moore, M.R. and Ristovski, Z.D. (2014). *Health Impacts of Ultrafine Particles: Desktop Literature Review and Analysis*. Canberra: Australian Government Department of the Environment and Heritage.

Movmi. (2018). *Carsharing Market Analysis: Growth and Industry Analysis*. Retrieved from Movmi.net: https://movmi.net/carsharing-market-growth/.

Muheim, P. and Partners. (1996). *Car Sharing Studies: An Investigation*. Dublin, Ireland: Graham Lightfoot.

Müller, V.C. (2020). *Stanford Encyclopedia of Philosophy*. Retrieved from Stanford University: https://plato.stanford.edu/entries/ethics-ai/.

Münzel, K., Boon, W., Frenken, K. and van der Blomme, D.J. (2019). Explaining carsharing supply across Western European cities. *International Journal of Sustainable Transportation*, 1–12.

Najini, H. and Muthukumaraswamy, S.A. (2017). Piezoelectric energy generation from vehicle traffic with technoeconomic analysis. *Journal of Renewable Energy*, 1–16.

Namazu, M. (2017). *The Evolution of Carsharing: Heterogeneity in Adoption and Impacts*. Vancouver: The University of British Columbia.

Network Rail Infrastructure Limited. (2020). *Network Statement 2020*. London, UK: Network Rail.

Newswire. (2010). *Vancouver First City in the World to Endorse the Fossil Fuel Non-Proliferation Treaty*. Retrieved from Fossil Fuel Non-Proliferation Treaty: https://www.newswire.ca/news-releases/vancouver-first-city-in-the-world-to-endorse-the-fossil-fuel-non-proliferation-treaty-843699223.html.

NHTSA. (2016). *Federal Motor Vehicle Safety Standards: Minimum Sound Requirements for Hybrid and Electric Vehicles*. Washington D.C.: National Highway Traffic Safety Administration, NHTSA.

Nilsson, N.J. (1982). *Principles of Artificial Intelligence*. Elsevier Inc.

NTSB. (2020). *Tesla Crash Investigation Yields 9 NTSB Safety Recommendations*. National Transportation Safety Board.

Ohta, K. (1998). TDM measures toward sustainable mobility. *IATSS Research*, 22(1).

Omi, K. (2018). *Alternative Energy for Transportation*. Retrieved from Issues in Science and Technology: https://issues.org/omi/.

Ongel, A., Loewer, E., Roemer, F., Sethuraman, G. and Chang, F. (2019). Economic assessment of autonomous electric microtransit vehicles. *Sustainability*, 2–18.

Ontario Medical Association. (2005). *The Illness Costs of Air Pollution: 2005–2026 Health and Economic Damage Estimates*. Toronto: OMA.

Orenstein, M. (2020). *COVID-19's Effect on Energy and Emissions – and Implications for the Future*. Retrieved from Canawest Foundation: https://cwf.ca/research/publications/what-now-covid-19s-effect-on-energy-and-emissions-and-implications-for-the-future/.

Panchal, D.U. (2015). *Two and Three Wheeler Technology*. PHI Learning Pvt. Ltd. ISBN 9788120351431.

Parasuraman, R. (1992). Adaptive function allocation effects on pilot performance. *NASA/FAA Workshop on Artificial Intelligence and Human Factors*. Daytona Beach, Florida, USA: NASA and FAA.

Parasuraman, R., Sheridan, T.B. and Wickens, C. (2000). A model for types and levels of human interaction with automation. *IEEE Transactions on Systems, Man, and Cybernetics-Part A: Systems and Humans*, 30(3): 286–297.

PBS. (2009). *Timeline: History of the Electric Car*. Retrieved from PBS.Org: https://www.pbs.org/now/shows/223/electric-car-timeline.html.

Perner, J., Unteutsch, M. and Lövenich, A. (2018). *The Future Cost of Electricity-based Synthetic Fuels*. Berlin: Agora Energiewende.

Pete. (2015). *Electric Cargo Bike Guide*. Retrieved from Electric Bike Report: https://electricbikereport.com/electric-cargo-bike-guide/.

Pope III C.A. and R.T. and Burnett, M.J. (2002). Lung cancer, cardiopulmonary mortality, and long-term exposure to fine particulate air pollution. *The Journal of the American Medical Association*, 287(9): 1132–1141.

Porru, M., Serpi, A., Mureddu, M. and Damiano, A. (2020). A multistage design procedure for planning and implementing public charging infrastructures for electric vehicles. *Sustainability*, 2889(12): 1–17.

Priemus, H. (2007). Dutch spatial planning between substratum and infrastructure networks. *European Plannning Study*, 15(5): 667–686.

Puchalsky, C.M. (2005). Comparison of emission from light rail transit and bus rapid. *Transportation Research Record*, 1927(1): 31–37.

Qiu, C., Chau, K.T., Ching, T.W. and Liu, C. (2014). Overview of wireless charging technologies for electric vehicles. *Journal of Asian Electric Vehicles*, 12: 1679–1685.

Rajvanshi, A.K. (2002). Electric and improved cycle rickshaw as a sustainable transport system for India. *Current Science*, 83(6): 703–707.

Ram, G., Mouli, C., Duijsen, P.V., Grazian, F., Jamodkar, A., Bauer, P. and Isabella, O. (2020). Sustainable E-bike charging station that enables AC, DC, and wireless charging from solar energy. *Energies*, 13(3549): 1–21.

Reddy, T. (2008). *Synthetic Fuels Handbook: Properties, Process, and Performance*. McGraw-Hill.

Regnier, E. (2007). Oil and energy price volatility. *Energy Economic*, 29(3): 405–427.

Richard, F. and Cooper, H. (2005). Freeman and cooper. "Why Electrified Rail is Superior". *21st Century Science & Technology*, 18: 26–29.

Rickstrom, J. and Klum, M. (2015). *Big World, Small Planet: Abundance within Planetary Boundaries*. New Haven and London: Yale University Press.

Rideamigos. (2018). *What is Transportation Demand Management?* Retrieved from Rideamigos: https://rideamigos.com/transportation-demand-management-tdm/.

Rider, D. (2020). *Toronto Adds Electric Bicycles to Bike-share Fleet — at No Extra Cost toUusers.* Retrieved from Toronto Star: https://www.thestar.com/news/city_hall/2020/08/19/toronto-adds-electric-bicycles-to-bike-share-fleet-at-no-extra-cost-to-users.html.

Rieti, J. (2017). *CBC News.* Retrieved from Toronto discourages electric car use by denying on-street chargers, driver says: https://www.cbc.ca/news/canada/toronto/electric-vehicles-blocked-1.4368014.

Ritchie, H. (2020). *What are the Safest and Cleanest Sources of Energy?* Retrieved from Our world in data: https://ourworldindata.org/safest-sources-of-energy.

Rodenbach, J., Mathis, J., Chicco, A., Diana, M. and Nehrk, G. (2017). *Car Sharing in Europe: A Multidimensional Classification and Inventory.* European Union: STARS and AUTON.

SAE. (2014). *Taxonomy and Definitions for Terms Related to On-road Motor Vehicle Automated Driving Systems.* USA: SAE International.

SAE. (2018). *Taxonomy and Definitions for Terms Related to Shared Mobility and Enabling Technologies.* USA: SAE International.

SAE International. (2014). *Ground Vehicle Standards.* USA: SAE International.

SAE International. (2019). *A Dictionary of Terms for the Dynamics and Handling of Single Track Vehicles (Motorcycles, Scooters, Mopeds, and Bicycles).* Warrendale, PA, USA: J1451_201909. Society of Automotive Engineers.

SAE International. (2019). *J3194 –Taxonomy and Classification of Powered Micromobility Vehicles.* Warrendale, PA, USA: Society of Automotive Engineers.

Saunders, K. (2017). *Where's the Hype for Automated Trains? Part 1: History and Background.* Automation.

Sawilla, S. and Schütt Oskar. (2018). *Ipt-technology.* Retrieved from Wireless Opportunity Charging buses in Madrid: https://ipt-technology.com/case-opportunity-charging-madrid/.

SCAQMD. (2000). *Multiple Air Toxics Exposure Study.* San Francisco: South Coast Air Quality Management District.

Schneider, C.G. and Hill, L.B. (2007). *No Escape from Diesel Exhaust: How to Reduce Commuter Exposure.* Boston: Boston: Clean Air Task Force.

Sclar, R., Gorghinpour, C., Castellanos, S. and Li, X. (2018). *Barriers to Adopting Electric Buses.* Berlin: World Resources Institute, WRI and German Federal Ministry.

Scott, A.J. (2014). Beyond the creative city: cognitive–cultural capitalism and the new Urbanism. *Regional Studies*, 48(4): 565–578.

Shaheen, S. and Cohen, A. (2019). *Shared Micromobility Policy Toolkit: Docked and Dockless Bike and Scooter Sharing.* Schmidt Family Foundation.

Shaheen, S., Cohen, A. and Zohdy, I. (2016). *Shared Mobility: Current Practices and Guiding Principles.* Washington D.C. USA: Federal Highway Administration.

Shared-Use Mobility Center. (2017). *Share-use Mobility Reference Guide.* Chicago, USA: Shared-Use Mobility Center.

Sheldrake, R. (2009). *Morphic Resonance: The Nature of Formative Causation.* Rochester, Vermont: Park Street Press.

Shepertycky, M. and Li, Q. (2015). Generating electricity during walking with a lower limb-driven energy harvester: Targeting a minimum user effort. *PLoS ONE*, 1–16.

Shladover, S.E. (2016). The truth about "Self Driving" cars. *Scientific American*, 52–57.

Siemens Mobility. (2015). *Sustainable Urban Infrastructure: Vienna Edition – Role Model for Complete Mobility.*

Smith, R.A. (2008). Enabling technologies for demand management: Transport. *Energy Policy*, 36(12): 4444–4448.

Society of Automobile Engineers, SAE. (2018). *Shared Mobility: Taxonomy and Definitions in SAE J3163™.*

Spaen, B. (2019). *This All-Electric Water Taxi Could Revolutionize Green Transportation.* Retrieved from Green Matters: https://www.greenmatters.com/news/2018/06/25/qSvID/water-taxis-transportation.

Sperling, D. and Shaeen, S. (1999). Carsharing: Niche market or new pathway? *ECMT/OECD Workshop on Managing Car Use for Sustainable Urban Travel* (pp. 1–25). Dublin, Ireland: OECD.

Spulber, A., Dennis, E.P. and Wallace, R. (2016). *The Impact of New Mobility Services on the Automotive Industry.* Ann Arbor, Michigan: Cargroup.Org.

Staffell, I., Scamman, D., Abad, A.V., Balcombe, P., Dodds, P.E., Ekins, P., Shah, N. and Ward, K.R. (2019). The role of hydrogen and fuel cells in the global energy system. *Energy & Environmental Science*, 12: 463–491.

STAPPA and ALAPCO. (2000). *Cancer Risk from Diesel Particulate: National and Metropolitan Area Estimates for the United States.* San Francisco: State and Territorial Air Pollution Program Administrators and the Association of Local Air Pollution Control Officials.

Steer Davies Gleave. (2009). *GO Transit Lakeshore Express Rail Benefit Case, Interim Report.* Toronto: Metrolinx.

Steffen, W., Richardson, K., Rockström, J., Cornell, S., Fetzer, I., Bennett, E., Bennett, E.M., Biggs, R., Carpenter, S.R., Vrie, W.D., Wit, C.A.D., Folke, C., Gerten, D., Heinke, J., Mace, G.M., Psersson, L.M., Ramanathan, V.,

Reyers, B. and Sörlin, S. (2015). Planetary boundaries: Guiding human development on a changing planet. *Science*, 15: 1–10.

Stohler, W. and Giger, P. (1989). *Cost-benefit Analysis of the Electrification of the Beira Alta Line in Portugal.* London: Institution of Electrical Engineers.

Stone, T. (2017). *Lessons Learned from the History of Car Sharing.* Retrieved from https://tiffanydstone.com/: https://tiffanydstone.com/2013/08/23/lessons-learned-from-the-history-of-car-sharing/.

Stone, T. (2018). *Siemens to Demonstrate World's First Autonomous Tram Running in Real Traffic in German City.* Retrieved from traffictechnology.com: https://www.traffictechnologytoday.com/news/autonomous-vehicles/siemens-to-demonstrate-worlds-first-autonomous-tram-running-in-real-traffic-in-german-city.html.

Strompen, F., Litman, T. and Bongardt, D. (2012). *Reducing Carbon Emissions through Transport Demand Management Strategies: A Review of International Examples.* Final Report. GIZ China, Transport Demand Management in Beijing.

Swenson, R. (2016). The solarevolution: Much more with way less, right now—the disruptive shift to renewables. *Energies*, 9(9): 676.

Takefuji, Y. (2008). And if public transport does not consume more energy? (PDF). *Le Rail*, 31–33.

Tao, P., Stefansson, H. and Saevarsdottir, G. (2014). Potential use of geothermal energy sources for the production of Li-ion batteries. *Renewable Energy*, 61.

The Economist. (2017). A world turned upside down. *Renewable Energy*, 18–20.

The Guardian. (2011). *19th Century Cyclists Paved the Way for Modern Motorists' Roads.* Retrieved from The Guardian: https://www.theguardian.com/environment/bike-blog/2011/aug/15/cyclists-paved-way-for-roads.

The Guardian. (2017). *Smaller, Lighter, Greener: Are micro EVs the Future of City Transport?* Retrieved from The Guardian: https://www.theguardian.com/sustainable-business/2017/may/11/micro-evs-city-transport-suemens-renault-green-air-pollution.

The TEV Project. (2017). *Tracked Electric Vehicle System. Reference Technical Booklet.* Retrieved from The TEV project: http://tevproject.com.

Toole Design Group and Pedestrian and Bicycle Information Centre. (2012). *Bike Sharing in the United States.* USDOT, Federal Highway Administration.

Transport Canada. (2009). *Bike Sharing Guide.* Ottawa: Transport Canada.

TuSimple. (2020). *TuSimple Launches World's First Autonomous Freight Network with UPS, Penske, U.S. Xpress, and McLane Company, Inc.* Retrieved from stockhouse.com: https://stockhouse.com/news/press-releases/2020/07/01/tusimple-launches-world-s-first-autonomous-freight-network-with-ups-penske-u-s.

UITP. (2013). *Press Kit: Metro Automation Facts, Figures, and Trends.* International Association of Public Transport.

UITP. (2014). *Metro Automation Facts, Figures, and Trends.* International Association of Public Transport (UITP).

US Bureau of Transportation Statistics. (2020). *Energy Intensity of Passenger Modes.* Retrieved from U.S. Energy Consumption by the Transportation Sector: https://www.bts.gov/content/energy-intensity-passenger-modes.

US Department of Energy. (2018). *Alternative Fuel Vehicles.* Retrieved from US Department of Energy: https://www.energy.gov/public-services/vehicles/alternative-fuel-vehicles#/find/nearest?country=US.

US Environmental Protection Agency. (2008). *Heat Island Compendium.* US EPA.

Venugopal, P., Shekhar, A., Visser, E. and Scheele, N. (2018). Roadway to self-healing highways with integrated wireless electric vehicle charging and sustainable energy harvesting technologies. *Applied Energy*, 212: 1226–1239.

*Watch: Toronto's Surge in E-bike Ownership Creates Concerns over Safety.* (2018). Retrieved from Iheartradio: https://www.iheartradio.ca/newstalk-1010/news/watch-toronto-s-surge-in-e-bike-ownership-creates-concerns-over-safety-1.3726810.

Weichenthal, S., Ryswyk, K., Goldstein, A., Shekarrizfard, M. and Hatzopoulou, M. (2015). Characterizing the spatial distribution of ambient ultrafine particles in Toronto, Canada: A land-use regression model. *Environmental Pollution*, 47(PT A): 1–8.

Weir, L. (2018). *Pina Bousch's Dance Theatre: Tracing the Evolution of Tanz Theatre.* Edinburgh: Edinburgh University Press.

Weißbach, D., Ruprecht, G., Hukeac, A., Czerski, K., Gottlieb, S. and Hussein, A. (2013). Energy intensities, EROIs (energy returned on invested), and energy payback times of electricity generating power plants. *Energy*, 52: 210–221.

Wiener, E.L. and Curry, R.E. (1980). Light deck automation: Promise and problems. *Ergonomics*, 995–1011.

Wilson, K. (2018). *An Overview of SAE International: Standards Activities Related to Charging of Hybrid/Electric Vehicles.* Ground Vehicles Standards, SAE International.

Wilson, L. (2013). Shades of Green: Electric Cars' Carbon Emissions around the Globe. *Shrink That Footprint*, pp. 1–28.

Wolverton, T. (2016). *Wolverton: Elon Musk's Hyperloop Hype Ignores Practical Problems.* Retrieved from The Mercury News: https://www.mercurynews.com/2013/08/13/wolverton-elon-musks-hyperloop-hype-ignores-practical-problems/.

World Commission on Environment and Development. (1987). *Our Common Future.* Oxford: Oxford Univeristy Press.

Xiong, H., Wang, L., Linbing, Wang, D. and Druta, C. (2011). Piezoelectric energy harvesting from traffic induced deformation of pavements. *International Journal of Pavement Research and Technology*, 5(5): 333–337.

Xu, C., Dai, Q., Gaines, L., Hu, M., Tukker, A. and Steubing, B. (2020). Future material demand for automotive lithium-based batteries. *Nature*, 99: 1–9.

Zhang, W. and Guhathakurta, S. (2016). Parking spaces in the age of shared autonomous vehicles: How much parking will we need and where? *Sustainable Cities and Society*, 19: 34–45.

Zielinski, S. (2006). New mobility: The next generation of sustainable urban transportation. *National Academy of Engineering*, 36(4).

# Section IV

# Implementation of New Mobility Code

# CHAPTER 6

# Physical Mobility(-as-a-Place)
# for Everyday
## Reinventing Public Realm

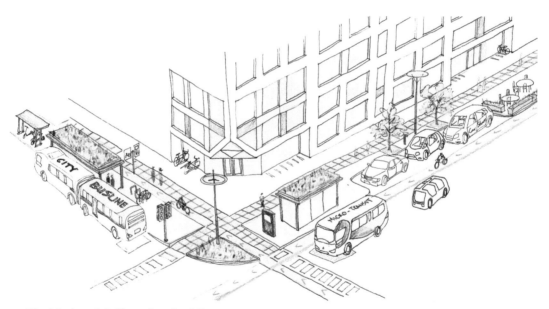

**Fig. 6.0:** An artistic illustration of mobility-as-a-place through reinvention of place, policies, and implementation.

*"Space is not a scientific object removed from ideology or politics."*
—Henri Lefebvre

## Introduction to Public Spaces for a New Mobility Ecosystem

Most of human experiences are learned behaviour. Our most primitive and fundamental experience comes from living in a manmade or natural built environment. This intimate relation between human and space originates from a sense of community and the subjectivity that emerges when our bodies interact with a myriad of spaces. During our everyday life, we pass through these physical spaces and as our body interacts consciously or unconsciously, it builds our memories, affinity, and feelings through hedonistic and sensorial effects. Thus, the human body and mind become the archive of our living experience in the world. Today we live in cities which are a result of a social, political, and cultural transformation that mutated through imperialism and colonialism, to scientific discovery and industrialization, to arrival of the technologically "advanced society" in the 21st century. Our living experience is now forced to adjust to the man-made environment built with an ideological and rigid rational philosophy. In some places, particularly mobility spaces, we feel welcoming and harmonious. Often, this is on narrower streets with touches of cultural, green, and human-focused places. All ages and abilities of people feel a different way but our experience with human-scale environment is similar. In other places we feel uncomfortable, tense, and intimidated. Often, negative experiences are associated with mega streets and highway interchanges or in gigantic parking lots. For city builders, planners, designers, and mobility service operators, the connection between the human body, feelings, and the mobility space design remains unknown. This chapter proposes to reconnect our primitive affinity to mobility public spaces which is now mostly mobility space due to difficult access to isolated green and open spaces.

One of the fundamental premises of why humans move, and how to build a city around the inherent nature of mobility, remains today a great omission in urban mobility. Prevalent assumptions that humans move mainly for economic or purpose-oriented reasons created a tendency to build megastructures to satisfy linear travel demand movement. With the mega mobility approach, urban planners, architects, and traffic engineers have created a gendered environment that predominantly suits the needs of "white European" men and the heteronormative family (Beebeejaun, 2017). Often vehemently denied and institutionally suppressed, 21st century women rejected this dogma (Hayden, 1980) and imminently shook-up the unavoidable deceptive principles of city building. In an era of changing demography and lifestyles, the awakening of human rights, and major disruptions in working culture, these urban mobility principles are facing existential validity. To the contrary, places for staying or lingering that do not move are based on assumptions that most people access public places by vehicle, so they're centralized in locations far away from common neighbourhoods. Additionally, instead of focusing on why and what humans enjoy through our daily activities, placemaking assumes standard activity and installs limited facilities. Thus, public places look too structured and manicured when devoid of the organic nature of human activities and natural environment in everyday life. The lack of connectivity and unfair ideologies about human mobility and activities have created an invisible Berlin Wall between megastructures for linear moving and gigantic open or public spaces that are located far away from living spaces.

Unfortunately, mobility space and placemaking are often considered segregated processes. As a matter of fact, they are just two sides of the moon. Mobility spaces by default are assumed to be consumed by the automobile. Everyone can 'see' the clearly visible spaces. Public spaces, particularly small spaces where city residents spend their daily lives, remain invisible like the other side of the moon's surface. This segregation was not accidental, but rather intentional.

Urban space, particularly public space, is the heart of our daily life. Every moment we are out of our home we interact with urban space for different purposes in life. When we move, we interact with streets, trees, wildlife, cultural destinations, people on sidewalks, bike lanes, transit lanes. When we stay, we intermingle in public squares, on street corners, and in open spaces besides our living spaces. Although modern traffic engineers wrongly assumed urban mobility spaces had to be immense in scale to satisfy demand, humans never felt comfortable in disproportionately large spaces. Large and barren spaces reflect the structured plans of organizing bodies such as governments, corporations, and other institutional bodies (Certeau, 2011). On the contrary, we have limited capacity and can only interact with facility sizes that are built on our scale (Gehl and Svarre, 2013). Humans always spontaneously search for the lowest energy path while walking. They create a feeling about urban spaces (McCormack, 2013) through unsanctioned and unscripted activities, and tactically prefer the small parts of urban spaces that become default social interaction places for all residents. Trivial sensations, small feelings, and local understandings that arise within the realm of our mind and body come from the meaningless interactions in small public spaces in everyday urban life. This is a baleful omission in understanding urban space. Resistance has grown to a rigid and institutionalized process of city planning, and tactical urbanism was born out of the needs of small spaces in everyday life (Hou, 2020). Underutilized space, particularly parking spaces, building sides or frontages, became the target of guerrilla urbanism. However, streets and major vehicle infrastructures remained untouchable places until recently. Since every inch of street space is treated as a sacred place and needed for seemingly infinite vehicle usage, most urbanism boundaries stopped behind the invisible wall between building frontage and the street. There are no such walls between mobility space and everyday urban spaces. This imaginary "Berlin Wall" which was originally created through a "European white" male colonization philosophy and a utilitarianism approach in traffic engineering needs to come down. Despite its wrongful existence, it might be a more difficult and monstrous task than bringing down the real Berlin Wall.

An idea is useless if it is never implemented. Many ideas proposed in this book will not become a reality if the path to implementation is not enriched with knowledge, skills, and changes in practice and policies.

This chapter proposes a few powerful processes of implementing the mobility DNA concept to rebuild all our mobility spaces slowly over time, avoiding the spectacle of a handful of streets made over. This chapter also focuses on the systematic understanding of how to find the invisible space, making it visible, developing reclaiming practices, and finally bringing about the transformation process to become human space. While the approaches will provide clues to reclaiming and recreating invisible spaces, the intention is to not make rigid new professional practices, but rather to allow creative thinking that would open the door to the infinite possibilities of new livable spaces in urban areas.

> *"The trouble with traffic engineers is that when there's a problem with a road, they always try to add something. To my mind, it's much better to remove things."*
> —Hans Mondermann

## Everyday Mobility Spaces: Mobility-as-a-Place (MAAP)

The creation of urban mobility spaces for all genders, races, ethnicities, ages, and abilities remains an unachievable dream despite its recent awakening. One of the underlying failures is the continuing ignorance of the small activities and sensations in everyday life that build our city. Our life is deeply connected to the small sentiments we experience every day. Most of them are in public mobility spaces. But the mega mobility world ignores the needs of everyday life and views every mobility facility building principle through the capitalistic discourse of infrastructure and the sole purpose is economic gain. Removing our rose-coloured sunglasses on how we perceive mobility facilities would mean changing the underlying institutional practices, principles, and assumptions of city building. The underlying philosophy of changing design principle is simple. At the heart of changing course is understanding the daily, minute needs of mobility space.

The key principles of mobility space redesign are fundamentally different from the existing traffic engineering discourse. While many basic tools from traffic planning are useful, this chapter avoids the rigid approach of thinking every space around the private vehicle. The first principle is the shifting capability of redesigned places when conditions change. Flexible elements and space reallocation techniques via physical or digital assignment would reopen closed doors for all mobility users, prioritizing zero- or low-emission mobility. The invisible street space concept introduced in this book reflects how all small elements of mobility space can be reclaimed from their unused state and reused concurrently with shifting usage among all active and low-emission but high-occupancy shared mobility users. The second principal is inclusion of all gender, ability, and ethnic background members of the community to select suitable design elements to meet the greater community benefit. This principle aligns with the "indifference to difference" (Menon, 2015) concept that reinforces thinking of the different needs, feelings, and experiences of community members in terms of their social, physical, and cultural background, subsequently creating a consistent process that reflects a common design outcome. The human space concept introduced herein incorporates every possible space used by different kinds of people in the community. The third principle is creating harmony with nature. The green mobility concept is developed to bring back wildlife, the natural environment, water management and trees, and a child- and women-friendly landscape with congenial lingering space for senior citizens. The fourth principle, bringing down the barrier between public, private, and community members is proposed to create a collaborative process for creation, shared operation, and maintenance principles to reduce the burden on public caring of spaces where the community lives and explores. The fifth principle is shared equity and well-being for all residents or visitors in the neighbourhood. Instead of overemphasizing areas around key transit nodes, the eco-mobility multimodal hub concept proposes to redesign mobility access for all people and spread the benefits to every small corner of the community. The sixth principle is the equal distribution of spaces for all human activities, mobility users, and green places. Mega mobility structures partially or fully discard human rights by allocating the most public space to only wealthy and privileged private vehicle owners. The space reallocation principle introduced in Chapter 4 is reinserted as an element of redesign to make sure human rights are respected in the appropriate manner. The final principle is keeping the mobility landscape and supply at an affordable size and level that reduces or eliminates the financial, social, and systematic discriminatory burdens currently imposed by mega mobility structures.

In the past we barely made a conscious acknowledgement of the corporeal experience of our spaces, but now these previously ignored spaces are hard to avoid. This new heightened awareness of everyday space that our human bodies' activities invade daily offers a new horizon of critical discussion of the human body and mind and the space, in anticipation of incorporating that knowledge into design processes such as urban planning, urban design, and architectural representation, and traffic engineering processes and practices.

The following section provides a few silent and gradual but most powerful changes that focus less on mobility identity and embrace a playful view of all possibilities to reinvent urban mobility spaces. The intention is to build a practice of noticing small and gradual changes, rather than today's dramatic diversity and inclusivity talk about urban mobility space that takes us nowhere. The gradual approach is built on our unconscious desire for quality space while integrating fundamental human rights and mobility equity instead of using a 'patchwork' approach to fixing the problem afterwards.

> "The street is the river of life of the city, the place where we come together, the pathway to the center."
> —William H. Whyte

## Creation of Multimodal Eco-mobility Hubs

Mobility equity has become a burning issue in the last decade. There are a lot of high-level ideas, rankings, and indices proposed to address mobility inequality problems. But none have established the link between ideas and a real implementation process. Equity is not a fantasy or a talk show topic for users who face systematic discrimination every time mobility services are offered or used. Equity must be built into a mobility system that automatically takes on the foundational issues in every layer of mobility planning and design. This chapter address those implementation issues head-on with a fresh new concept of fair access to mobility services or locations.

The mobility equity concept using the eco-mobility multimodal hub proposed earlier in this book needs a detail planning and implementation process. The creation of these spaces is not easy, but a comprehensive understanding process makes practitioners and decision makers' paths easier. Despite various proposals of mobility hubs and policies, no systematic understanding and process is available to planners on how to implement these ideas. The first problem is a combination of making low-emission modes more attractive as per the local mobility culture and keeping options open for future changes. A multimodal ecosystem approach for each area solves this issue when there is no land-use or transit service changes anticipated in the subject planning area. The second issue is managing and integrating the complex layers of multimodal mobility modes using land-use changes as the catalyst to increase the attractivity of a low-emission mobility ecosystem. With land-use changes and the full completion/adoption of new transit, the mobility mix and the overall demand change over time. Some mobility modes are more popular in one area, and some technology or services are more mature in other areas due to land-use diversity. The true multimodal mode share that each person experiences in a single trip around a neighbourhood mobility hub solves mobility access and equity problems and increases the use of low-emission multimodal mobility options to avoid single vehicle trips. The third step is understanding the scale of demand for each mobility mode using the emerging mobility mix from step two. No facility can be built, or no services can be provided until we know the quantity, intensity, and scale of demand for the short, interim, or long-term situation. Quantification of space, facility size, service frequency, and mode services availability are the ingredients of a successful neighbourhood oriented multimodal eco-mobility hub. The final step is developing the eco-mobility hub location, influence zones and policy tools for implementation. This step distributes the overall supply equally among the eco-mobility hubs using the mobility form concept. This ensures increasing mobility access to all community destinations within a very short walking distance. This process leads to the creation of the final shape and form of eco-mobility hubs, provides principles for detailed design, and sets the stage for evidence-based policies to ensure the facilities are built by both private and public entities over time at an appropriate scale with a proper design oriented toward human scale instead of the current practice of throwing mobility facilities randomly as the need arrives. The following sections provide a brief overview of the eco-mobility hub planning and design process.

### *Step 1: Local multimodal mobility mix (without land-use or mobility changes)*

The preferred mobility solutions for a local area or a part of the city depends on existing culture and future adaptation of new mobility technology. The concept of a "multimodal ecosystem" (introduced in Chapter 4), i.e., a combination of modes, would be customized for existing, interim, and ultimate future mobility solutions. Existing or initial multimodal combinations would represent the primary mode of transportation, predominantly transit, walking, cycling, and automobile modes. Interim mode share would incorporate the anticipated shift in travel behaviour such as the opening of new light rail, other potential higher-order transit, the maturity of new mobility nodes or technologies to a roughly 10% threshold and shifting conditions of demography or energy or environmental conditions that may influence the mobility shift. These new mobility nodes would include the potential introduction of shared or micro-transit for special services, the imminent introduction of micromobility modes such as shared scooters, personal mobility devices, mini or pod cars, and other new mobility modes. The impact of new technology such as mobility-as-a-service and the impact of automation technology particularly on vehicles and transit are expected to shift the current automobile-oriented paradigm toward shared multimodal options among area users. Finally, ultimate mode share would consider the "mobility boundary" limits introduced early in this book, while creating policies, plans, and incentives (disincentives) to increase the modal shift toward sustainable, high-occupancy, and low-emission options. If there is no land-use or significant mobility services changes (such as a new transit line), practitioners could skip step two and continue from step three. These decisions are primarily set by a city's strategic directions such as future mobility energy, infrastructure, financial constraints, environmental objectives, and maximum benefits, community wishes, and quality of life of city residents.

### *Step 2: Change of land-use and mobility mix*

Despite widespread use of mobility demand, particularly mode share usage in mobility planning, the realistic approach of understanding the link between land-use changes and their effect on local mobility culture and induced mobility demand remains on hollow ground. Increasing internal trips that are usually short and stay local would be the basic guiding principle to create a new ecosystem with the help of mixed-use and new-built environment or transit service changes. However, this is a slow and lengthy process. Initially land-use may not alter the mobility mix, but the introduction of rapid transit in interim and full redevelopment with high- or mid-rise land-use changes, with sufficient non-residential mix, would trigger a second layer of the mobility ecosystem within and outside the eco-mobility hub area. Chapter 4 of this book provides the theoretical foundation of the true multimodal mobility merge concept, and a fresh approach to mode share as combined in the same journey instead of a separated one. Applying these concepts into a real project such as the creation of multimodal eco-mobility needs improvization improvisation that comes from local knowledge and the mobility culture.

However, it can be accomplished in a different way compared to traditional mode share uses. The micro version of the multimodal concept introduced in Chapter 4 is reutilized to quantify the multimodal demand for each mobility mode.

- *Initial hub area mobility supply conditions*: An inventory of existing and planned facility is the starting point of this initial step before land-use changes are introduced. The next step is observing each area on the human scale (walkable distance) and identifying the quality of service and mobility service gaps of the place. Subsequently, existing traced personal mobility data around certain selected nodes are the real measurements of true multimodal mode share. However, the success of the eco-mobility hub mechanism is hidden in land-use and mobility interaction. If the mixed-use of land is low, trips that stay internally in each hub area will be low. These internal trips would provide vital information to land-use planners to increase the proportion of mixed-use, particularly in non-residential uses through anticipated or planned redevelopment.

- *Interim mode share for hubs*: These hubs change during interim periods due to immediate land-use changes or the introduction of new developments. The first step is to inform land-use planners about the appropriate share and right mix of land-use policies, that are tested against shared internal and external trips to find the maximum proportion that generates the highest possible internal trips within the eco-hub area. This will reduce longer trips and maximize less expensive mobility services that connect hub-to-hub within the same neighbourhood. Secondly, through iteration and testing, internal trips of an entire area are estimated against the optimum share of non-residential use, and intensity of land-use diversity. The entire process will generate interim mobility demand, multimodal mode share, and the potential scale of future mobility needs. For instance, interim mode share was developed for an area plan in Toronto assuming an initial minimal adoption of shared and micromobility modes that would be available to area residents when redevelopment is completed in the decade after the opening of the Eglinton Crosstown (ECLRT) light rail (Fig. 6.1a).

- *Ultimate mode share for hubs*: The final mode share would be establishing the maximum possible users accessing the hubs or mobility services and introducing incentives or design changes toward the modal shift. This is based on available local resources, limiting negative impacts, and finding balances with the least resource-oriented objectives of each mobility mode. The final layer is the previously introduced idea of mode share tweaks that consider the inter-dependence of modes and mode diversion between the modes, to create true local multimodal mode share. This stage will also create or align with strategic objectives. The mobility combo (Step 1), changes in Step 2, and mobility boundaries and the city's overall strategic directions will determine the ultimate, complex multimodal mode share for each eco-hub area. An illustration of the iterative process of developing ultimate mode share shows (Fig. 6.1b) how vehicle demand could be gradually reduced as active, light rail (ECLRT) and mixed-use development is completed over a decade.

## Step 3: Overall area multimodal facility and service demand

Once mode share and other travel demand is established for an entire planning area, the demand for each mobility mode and effect of modal merge or diversion is determined using simple trip generation, distribution, and trip assignment for new mobility modes. While some new modes create new mobility demand, most of the new modes of mobility compliment transit, walking, and cycling and enable a significant portion of residents and visitors to live or work without automobile usage. The following two-step analysis quantifies the potential modal shifts and subsequent mobility supply quantity for new mobility modes for each eco-mobility hub.

*3.a: Trip merging and diversion toward a new mobility ecosystem*: The ultimate target for a new mobility mode's introduction is to reduce vehicle demand. This is a primary policy target for all cities but the path to achieve this policy is often lost in a detailed implementation process. Estimated demand for new mobility modes can be utilized to determine the scale of new facilities and how and what level of vehicle infrastructure, parking, and spaces can be reduced reasonably over the next few decades as a step-by-step process.

To estimate vehicle reduction, the trip merging between the modes and diversion rate from automobile modes by various modes can be estimated. For instance, the attractiveness of carshare and shared/micro-transit among the vehicle users is relatively stronger. On the contrary, bikeshare, or micro-mobility predominantly diverts trips from transit, rideshare, walking, or cycling. Shared transit is emerging as a complementary service to traditional fixed-route systems for specific markets such as campuses, business parks, and large neighbourhoods. New mobility modes will also provide a new way to merge different modes to complete a single trip. For instance, a few new mobility modes such as shared micromobility typically act as a supplement travel mode, i.e., access or secondary support to main modes (typically transit) especially among specific demography. Shared scooters, motorbikes, kick-skaters, pod-cars, velocars[1] and many others producers are preparing entries into the mobility market depending on city policy and restrictions. These new emerging modes of the ecosystem are expected to provide an alternative mode of transportation and may change the concept of vehicle ownership. Using new mobility modes, models, and a local database, trip diversions from automobiles for a planning area in Toronto are estimated and summarized in Fig. 6.2.

*3.b: Estimating multimodal demand for each mode*: Like automobile or transit demand estimating methods, travel demand for new mobility modes can be derived from local data sources, existing mobility ecosystem transportation models, published results and a comprehensive database or tools developed by the Shared Mobility Center (SMC, 2018). The demand for each major shared

---

[1] Generally known as velo (bicycle) cars.

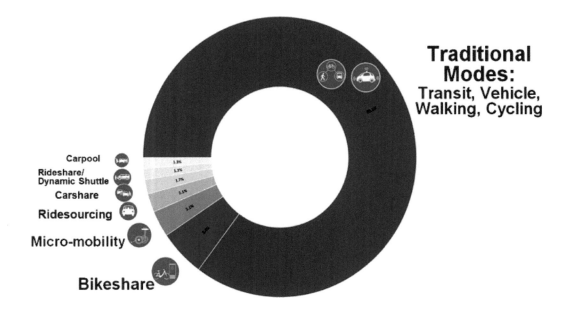

## a) Interim multimodal mode share

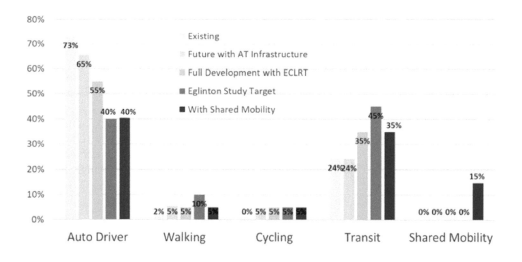

## b) Ultimate multimodal mode share

**Fig. 6.1:** An illustration of an eco-mobility hub area mode share.

and new mobility mode can be estimated by analysing the existing trends from available data and a moderate increase of demand under future conditions.

However, unlike the traditional guessing game method of estimating travel demand for new mobility modes, these estimated demands were verified and validated in several ways. Checks were done for multiple reasons. For starters too, few supplies led to a decline of new mobility mode usage. Oversupply led to underutilized systems. The business model for new technologies or shared

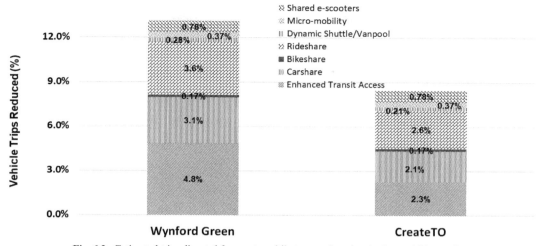

**Fig. 6.2:** Estimated trips diverted from automobile to new shared and micromobility modes.

modes has a limited supply capacity, especially with the restrictions imposed by public agencies. Secondly, operators service and operations parameters could be utilized to estimate the potential capacity of specific modes. Limitations such as space constraints (i.e., the number of stations per square kilometre, or acceptable walking distances to service points) lead to the specific size of the new system of mobility modes. Finally, estimating trip rates per person and usage rates per single unit provides a further modification to the estimated travel demand of new mobility modes. An illustration of multimodal mobility mode demand for the largest landowners is provided in Table 6.1 for two planning areas in Toronto. Combining supply limits or restrictions, operators service parameters and usage rates, by trial-and-error in several rounds, led to practical, achievable mobility demand, and supply equilibrium for each eco-hub area.

### Step 4: Implementation process of an eco-mobility hub

Area-wide demand and scale provides an overall framework of the eco-mobility hub. Once overall demand for an area is estimated, the final step would be to develop the details of eco-mobility that would translate into a real facility scale and quantity of mobility services for potential eco-mobility hub locations. This can be accomplished in three simple steps. Initially key areas would be identified for ideal hub locations. An influence zone would subsequently define an area around each eco-hub node. Total mobility demand and supply would now be distributed for each eco-mobility hub to determine the scale of facility and services for all neighbourhood eco-mobility hubs. Finally, needs and future funding and resources of the eco-mobility area would be identified for each landowner and operator to maintain these facilities in collaboration with city services and private operators.

- *Identifying an eco-mobility node*: Figure 6.3 depicts overall locations of multimodal infrastructure including eco-mobility hubs in the core planning area. Service area was estimated first using an ArcGIS "Service Area" tool, as part of the Network Analyst extension with 'non-overlapping', toggled to provide 13 discrete service area shapes. These were then manually adjusted to account for certain aspects now accounted for in the Service Area allocation algorithm, for instance, the greater weight of a transit stop over small or large scale multimodal eco-mobility hubs.

- *Creation of an eco-mobility zone*: Based on the multimodal framework described in previous sections, Table 6.2 elaborates on summaries of multimodal facilities, location, catchment areas,

**Table 6.1:** Estimated demand for emerging new mobility modes.

| Area Name | Bikeshare | | | Carshare | | | | Traditional & Smart Carpool | | | | Rideshare | | | | Shared Transit/Smart Vanpool | | | | Micromobility | | | |
|---|---|---|---|---|---|---|---|---|---|---|---|---|---|---|---|---|---|---|---|---|---|---|---|
| | Residents per bicycle | | Commercial | Residential | | Commercial/Office/ Retail | | Estimated Carpool Trips Demand | | Estimated Carpool Spaces | | Estimated Rideshare Trips Demand | | Estimated Rideshare Space | | Estimated Shared Transit Trips Demand | | Estimated Rideshare Space | | Estimated Micro-mobility Trips Demand | | Estimated Micro-mobility Space (Each space for 8-10 vehicles) | |
| | Number of Bicycles | Number of Stations | Number of Bikeshare Bicycles | Total Fleet Demand (Total # carshare vehicle) | Stations | Total Fleet Demand (Total # carshare vehicle) | Number of Vehicles | AM | PM | AM | PM | AM | PM | AM | PM | AM | PM | AM | PM | AM | PM | AM | PM |
| Allen District | 55 | 3.67 | 8.60 | 17 | 6 | 0 | 0 | 136 | 167 | 61 | 75 | 0 | 0 | 17 | 20 | 68 | 83 | 2 | 2 | 0 | 0 | 0 | 0 |
| Wynford Green | 69 | 4.6 | 37.8 | 21 | 7 | 3 | 1 | 190 | 209 | 85 | 94 | 0 | 0 | 21 | 25 | 95 | 104 | 3 | 3 | 199 | 243 | 5 | 6 |
| CreateTO + Other Softsites | 50 | 3.4 | 28.3 | 15 | 5 | 1 | 0 | 139 | 153 | 63 | 69 | 0 | 0 | 15 | 19 | 69 | 76 | 2 | 2 | 146 | 178 | 3 | 4 |

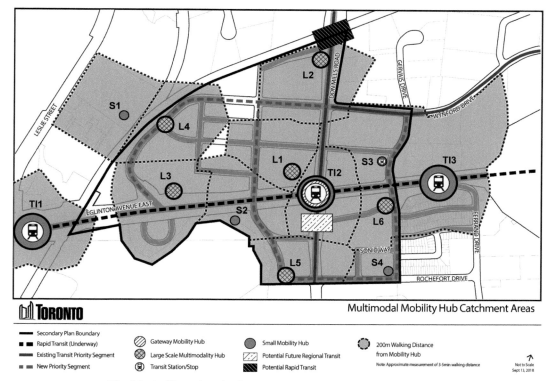

**Fig. 6.3:** An illustration of policy analysis for a multimodal eco-mobility hub.

and multimodal hubs that would facilitate mobility demand generated by the future residents and visitors to Toronto's Don Mills Crossing area. It should be noted that additional demand at light-rail transit (LRT) stations or bus terminals will be higher than multimodal facilities estimated for this planning study. Table 6.2 provides comprehensive examples of multimodal supply process for each eco-mobility hub. This is vital information for planners to create policies that will achieve installation of these mobility facilities, and the correct scale of services and space needs for transportation service agencies to plan and design facilities and spaces for construction. This process solves all questions of how many new multimodal facilities will be needed, built, and used by future residents.

- *Creation of an eco-mobility policy*: Once the eco-mobility hub area (i.e., influence zone) and central node are known, the imaginary boundary is removed through three layers of policy making (Fig. 6.3). First, central nodes give a rough estimate of the proposed eco-mobility hub for implementation purposes where various multimodal facilities will be located. Second, a policy zone or area provides a tool to policy makers to provide a detailed policy direction for relevant landowners to deliver land and built spaces, provide funding, and construct the facilities. This opens the door to city and private operations installing facility and services without any headache during the implementation stage.

Multimodal eco-mobility hub planning and implementation may appear insignificant compared to mega mobility structures, however, we will never achieve vehicle alternatives if we don't plan carefully and earlier in the process of ecosystem maturity. Unlike typical mobility facility, multimodal area planning involves active participation with multiple private, community and public agency contributions. At the end, the eco-mobility hub policy provides a powerful tool to measure equitable mobility access for all residents and ways to improve their quality of life regardless of social status.

**Table 6.2:** An illustration of multimodal infrastructure and service for new eco-mobility hubs.

| Type of Hubs | Land-use or Policy Context | Name of Multimodal Hubs | Approximate Location | Bikeshare | | | Long-term Bicycles (Tier 1) | Short-term Shareable Bicycles (Tier 2) | Carshare | | Traditional & Smart Carpool | | Rideshare | | Shared Transit/Smart Vanpool | | Micro-mobility | |
|---|---|---|---|---|---|---|---|---|---|---|---|---|---|---|---|---|---|---|
| | | | | No of Trips (Peak Hour Demand) | Number of Stations | No. of Bike Repair Stands | | | No of Trips (Peak Hour Demand) | Number of Vehicles | No of Trips (Peak Hour Demand) | No. of Carpool Spaces | No of Trips (Peak Hour Demand) | No. of Rideshare Spaces | No of Trips (Peak Hour Demand) | No. of Spaces | No of Trips (Peak Hour Demand) | No. of Spaces Equivalent to Vehicles |
| **Transit Interchange (T) Hub** | Major Transit Station Area | Transit Interchange (T1): Sunnybrook Park Station | Eglinton Avenue and Leslie Street | 120 | 1 | 1 | - | 30 | 20 | 2 | - | - | 23 | 2 | 37 | 1 | 83 | 2 |
| | Major Transit Station Area and Gateway Mobility Hub | Transit Interchange (T2): Science Centre Station | Eglinton Avenue and Don Mills Road | 120 | 1 | 2 | 60 | 37 | 40 | 4 | - | - | 46 | 4 | 37 | 1 | 125 | 3 |
| | Major Stansit Station Area | Transit Interchange (T3): Aga Khan Park and Museum Stop | Eglinton Avenue and East of Gervais Drive | 120 | 1 | 1 | - | 30 | 20 | 2 | - | - | 23 | 2 | 37 | 1 | 83 | 2 |
| **Large Scale Multimodal Hub** | Wynford Green: Block 1, 4 and 7 | L1 | Northwest Corner of Eglinton Avenue and Don Mills Road | 189 | 2 | 8 | 1,199 | 99 | 102 | 10 | 157 | 70 | 81 | 7 | - | - | 52 | 1 |
| | Future Community/Recreational Centre: Wynford Green | L2 | Northwest Corner of Wynford Drive and Don Mills Road | 130 | 1 | 4 | | 37 | 37 | 4 | 52 | 23 | 44 | 4 | 35 | 1 | 32 | 1 |
| | Wynford Green: Block 12 | L3 | Northeast Corner of Wynford Drive Extension at Eglinton Avenue | 205 | 2 | 4 | 1,174 | 102 | 68 | 7 | - | - | 79 | 7 | 35 | 1 | 107 | 2 |
| | Wynford Green: Block 9 and 11 | L4 | Active Rail Crossing at Wynford Drive Extension | 55 | 0 | 4 | 424 | 38 | 32 | 3 | - | - | 29 | 3 | 35 | 1 | 14 | 1 |
| | Science Centre and CreateTO Southwest Block | L5 | Northwest Corner of Future Street A Southern Extension and Don Mills Road | 101 | 1 | 1 | 881 | 238 | 37 | 4 | 90 | 41 | 126 | 11 | 45 | 1 | 106 | 3 |
| | CreateTO Southeast Block | L6 | Southwest Corner of Ferrand Road and Eglinton Avenue | 101 | 1 | 1 | 2,066 | 142 | 37 | 4 | 62 | 28 | 87 | 8 | 31 | 1 | 73 | 2 |
| **Small (Neighbourhood) Multimodal Hub** | North Side of Active Rail Crossing Near Leslie | S1 | North Side of Active Rail Crossing Near Leslie Neighbourhood | 74 | 1 | 1 | - | 30 | 7 | 1 | - | - | 11 | 1 | - | - | 70 | 2 |
| | Future Park at CreateTO Southwest Block | S2 | Southwest Corner of Street A and Eglinton Avenue East | 101 | 1 | 1 | - | 20 | 10 | 1 | - | - | 11 | 1 | - | - | 42 | 1 |
| | Don Mills Bus Terminal | S3 | Northwest Corner of Gervais Drive and Eglinton Avenue | 120 | 1 | 1 | - | 30 | 20 | 2 | - | - | 23 | 2 | 37 | 1 | 83 | 2 |
| | Dennis Trimble Community Centre | S4 | Northwest Corner of Ferrand Road and Rochefort Drive | 101 | 1 | 1 | - | 50 | 37 | 4 | - | - | 23 | 2 | 37 | 1 | 42 | 1 |
| **Total** | | | | 1,537 | 13 | 30 | 5,804 | 883 | 468 | 47 | 362 | 163 | 605 | 53 | 364 | 9 | 911 | 21 |

*"Only he who can see the invisible can do the impossible."*
—Frank L. Gaines

## Invisible and Illusive Unused Vehicle Spaces

When we live and consume in a world of cars, it makes it harder for us to see the hidden world. City streets are designed to mimic expressways. Higher speed highways require a lot more space than city streets. Speeds in urban areas rarely exceed the 30–40 kmph range, making many core vehicle spaces a waste in the form of unused or underutilized conditions. Our habits of 'highway-like' design make those unused vehicle spaces invisible. Even though the places are right in front of our eyes, we've become used to saying, "but those spaces are needed for rush hours or trucks or buses" whenever a proposal is raised to remove these unnecessary and unused items from the street. Indeed, a comprehensive review of unused vehicle traffic space by the author revealed one-quarter of pavement surface for vehicles is unused by traffic users on urban streets and over 60% of vehicle parking spaces remain empty, yet budget and resources are continuously burnt to maintain those unused places. For instance: roughly 163 km of roads are resurfaced or reconstructed every year (Transportation Services, 2020) and if just one metre of asphalt space remains unused, a city wastes at least $8.1 million every year. The reality is, total unused space is typically 2–3 m of space that remains unused by any road user, wasting roughly $16–$24 million every year or $160–$240 million in a 10-year timeframe. This is a staggering waste of public tax revenue but is rarely raised neither by public servants nor professionals. While we are all part of an excess wealth economy which generates enormous waste as a byproduct of Ford's mass consumerism (Cross, 1993), questions remain why such a monumental waste remains undetected. It is the result of a deeply ingrained belief system and delusion among infrastructure planning professionals that "every inch of pavement space is used by cars and is needed for road capacity and safety reasons". None of these infrastructure folklores have been proven nor has any evidence ever been found through scientific scrutiny. The wide streets built predating modern standards are treated as an 'untouchable' object, much like a bible. New approaches like complete streets or Vision Zero have developed a new design philosophy of narrower and safer urban streets. These new design approaches are putting old and pre-standard mega structure folklores and ideologies under the microscope. Through new knowledge of street design and new safety findings, we can now see most of the invisible mobility space that remains unused or underutilized. If reclaimed, these places will still incur cost, but green space and active mobility facilities cost one-sixth to a tenth of that of vehicle infrastructures (Gössling and Choi, 2015), hence, net societal, well-being, and financial benefits are much higher to society.

To find that illusive but unused and wasted space, we need to perform an xray of current street design elements and scrutinize them under a microscope.

This section (and the next few sections) takes on a difficult but much needed careful look to find those illusive and invisible spaces on our streets. These spaces are not underutilized travel lanes but invisible corners, turnings, and ghost spaces that can be reutilized for transit or active mobility infrastructure. Taking a travel lane away from vehicles would be a very bold and comprehensive space reclaim, a move that rarely happens, but is the obvious next step after reclaiming the first layer of invisible places. Some approaches, such as "Tactical Urbanism" (Tactical Urbanism Guide, 2012), deal with these spaces using temporary change, which is a vital stage for experimenting and figuring out the details and challenges. The process described here is for permanent changes that should be embedded into all stages of city building, from official plan policy to secondary plans, mandatory standards, practice guidelines, and finally inserting change into every department's work plans, process, and funding allocation.

Figure 6.4 attempts through public space x-ray to visually display those invisible spaces that remain hidden from public and professional eyes.

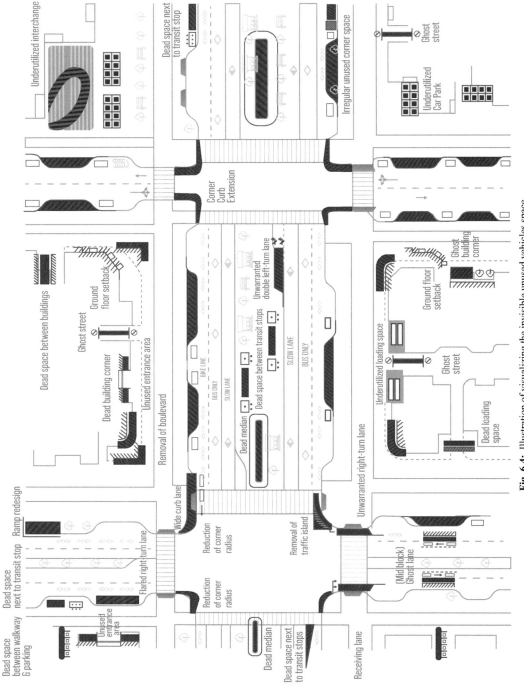

**Fig. 6.4:** Illustration of visualizing the invisible unused vehicles space.

*"In modern time, our sensitivity was dominated by time but in post-modern time it is by space."*

—Frederic Jameson

## Urban Mobility Design: Codes for Green (Mobility) Spaces

Once an x-ray finds those illusive spaces, we need to search for a systematic approach and build practice process, knowledge, and skills to reutilize these spaces. The following performs the x-ray and explains the detailed process to expose why those spaces are redundant, recategorize them into reusable public space, and integrate them into our green space and human activity needs. Sustainable mobility modes described in this book predominantly use the language of urban design and landscape knowledge to see through the city's visual mobility surface and landscapes. Small spaces and resources can be integrated into old or new public spaces and avoid adding additional space for new mobility modes. Systematic planning also helps to declutter public space when these mobility facilities are added on the top of human needs or for greening the hard space in a symbiotic manner.

The most common inquiries are the location of these illusive places and what mindset makes them invisible. This space visibility exercise is to uncover common unused places. But depending on country and practice there will be many more and types or categories of unused places. Most places are in the public street or within a city's right-of-way. However, many other mobility places immediately adjacent to the street and considered 'essential' for vehicles are underutilized, or wrongly used. Once a proper standard is utilized, innovative minds can come together and these new spaces can create the much needed green and human places while reclaiming roughly 30–40% of public streets, half of private streets, and 60% of vehicle storage space from cars. The new spaces are categorized using a "mobility park" concept, a critical integration of mobility needs, and green and human space into a city's small, extensive, and connected public realms.

This attempt at finding invisible space is not the end, but the beginning of multiple stages of planning and design. City planners need to incorporate systematic process and practice to search for these places every time there is a new development or pavement resurfacing or minor or major construction that touches a street or mobility space. Capital works should include a new work plan and funding process to reclaim these spaces whenever there is a construction planned through the yearly infrastructure plan. City master plans need to recognize the approach and rewrite the practice guidelines on how to search for these spaces and reuse these illusive spaces. Urban designers will need to develop innovative "urban mobility design" ideas and creative policies to incorporate and integrate landscaping and streetscaping that typically starts at the front of the building and stops at an invisible wall before the boulevard. Architects need find ways to design these places with innovative space planning and reorient their thinking to suggest a new form of mobility connection network. Traffic engineering and mobility service providers will need to come together and work with the rest of the city builders to create mobility facilities in between new green and human spaces. Strategists and thinkers will need to bring an innovative approach, and build 'human' cities instead of 'smart' cities for corporations.

### (*Green*) *Mobility Parks*

Public Park creation has become a nightmare for city planners due to the scarcity of land, particularly in dense urban areas. And yet large unused vehicle space remains hidden in front of our eyes. Removing redundant interchanges, widening large and unsafe highways ramps, normalizing high-speed ramps, converting, or reclaiming unused large or small off-street parking, and converting abandoned private loading spaces could create a standard city park without major effort or the need to purchase new expansive lands for city parks. Some stunning examples remind us how such large spaces are often wrongfully claimed as 'essential' space for vehicles which is never used. This section proposed six potential types of green space, their hidden location, shapes and forms, and their high-level design strategies to reclaim the space for the green and human space envisioned in this book.

i. *Large invisible mobility space*: Large, spiralling interchange ramps or simply normalizing ramps (roughly perpendicular to the street instead of a long-angled ramp) would reclaim such large spaces that a standard city park would be created from each "much needed" but unused ramp coming off urban highways or expressways. For instance, a typical 'loop-shaped' urban highway ramp occupies roughly 1.0 hectare of land, an equivalent to the average parkland space per 306 residents in Toronto[2] (Toronto, 2017) or minimum open green space needed for 950 residents as per WHO recommendations[3] (Kuchelmeister, 1998) or 430 residents as per LEED standards[4] (Govindarajulu, 2014). Sadly, developing nations such as Dhaka has only 0.052 sq m of green space per person (Bari and Efroymson, 2009) where hundreds of gigantic highway loop ramps were built in the last decade alone (RAJUK, 1995) without assessing green space needs for residents. This is a direct violation basic human rights, yet no engineering ethics prevented building excessive and unnecessary mega-sized vehicle infrastructures (WBB Trust, 2015). Similarly, when some urban interchanges were redesigned with linear ramps instead of loop ramps, no traffic delays were reported even though each ramp trapped green space for 306 residents in Toronto. An entire secondary plan neighbourhood was uncovered when the City of Toronto decided to reconstruct one of its large highway interchanges, known as the Six Points Interchange Reconfiguration (City of Toronto, 2018). The York ramp removal at the

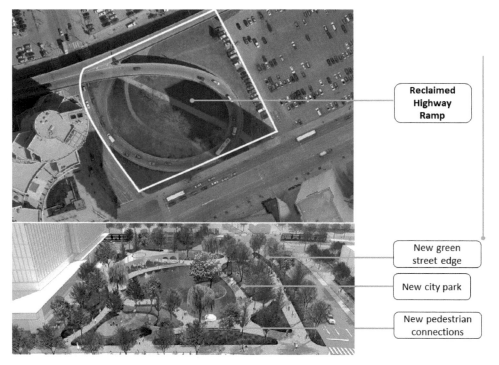

**Supplementary Fig. 6.1:** Reclaiming interchange ramps.
Image location: York Street and Queens Quay, Toronto, Ontario
Image source : City of Toronto York Street Park Plan web site

---

[2] 2.8 hectares (6.9 acres) of parkland per 1,000 residents.
[3] At least 9 sq m of open green space per urban dweller.
[4] Minimum 20 sq m per capita.

Toronto waterfront reclaimed an entire standard-sized city park (City of Toronto, 2017) from what had been a dark, ugly, and unsafe place for the last five decades. High-speed highway exit ramps were found to be unsafe for vehicles and active users, thus the Ministry of Transportation of Ontario recently redesigned them into 'normalized' ramps. The author developed a "complete interchange" concept (City of Toronto, 2017) making it a common practice to remove or redesign highway interchanges in Toronto and reclaiming roughly 2–5 ramps to create "soccer field sized" green spaces for city residents particularly in green space deprived areas.

ii. *Ugly parking to green space*: Often the misunderstood demand for parking was wrongly built by removing precious green space in the city centre. Severely underutilized and in a high-transit and active mobility city centre created a golden opportunity for its removal. Many small- or medium-sized unused or underutilized parking spaces are now being converted into the original public squares that existed in the beginning of the 20th century before vehicle culture forcefully took over our precious public spaces. A few cornerstone examples of new public squares were created from off-street and sometimes neglected parking space in old farmer's market locations in Stratford, Welland, and Brantford, and Toronto's new Berczy Park. The limited parking demand was easily replaced by using the green curb extension concept that creates parking layby between tree islands.

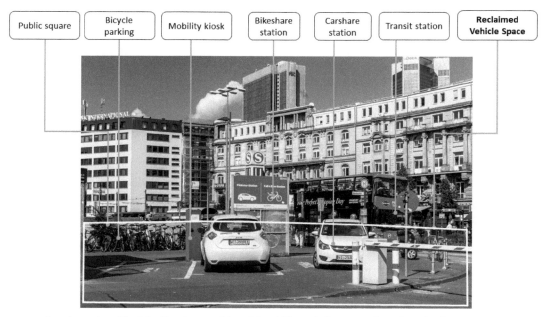

**Supplementary Fig. 6.2:** Creating a multi-modal mobility park from unused transit station frontage area.
Image location: Frankfurt Main Rail Station, Germany
Image source: The Author

iii. *Large private space*: Unused or misplaced loading space in front of or on the side of a building generally occupies small city park sizes. Loading space remains an eyesore in the public realm. Many loading activities can be served from an on-street loading space. Shared loading, curbside loading, or simply using smaller vehicles makes these spaces redundant. No business service suffered any losses nor was any delivery interrupted when these spaces were reclaimed and converted into green frontage space or children's play areas.

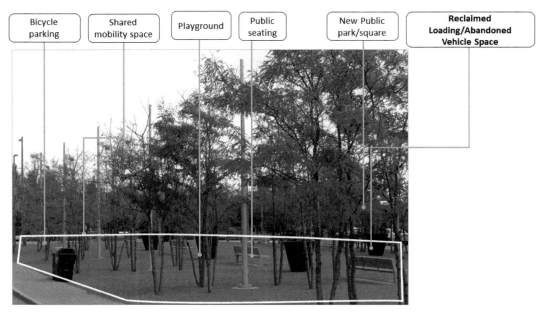

**Supplementary Fig. 6.3:** Reusing abandoned loading space.
Image location: Canary District
Image source: The Author

## Island Parks

Popularized in Latin American cities, creating an island in the middle of the street from a dead or hidden median has become common and the most frequently form of linear green places for urban residents. Since an island runs parallel to streets and is easily accessible by residents, it has become the most equitable way to provide green space access to all city residents and visitors instead of concentrated or isolated in traditional park lands.

i.  *Dead zone in the middle of street*: The possibility of creating a green street median is often misunderstood. The space in between the two left-turn lanes at intersections remains unused or badly designed, making these spaces invisible or abandoned on most city streets. Many Latin American cities, including Havana, Quito, Mexico City, Lima, Santiago, and Buenos Aires created large island or median parks that facilitate street vendors, art displays, performances, comfortable walking corridors, festival spaces, children's play areas, social gatherings, or lingering spaces for city residents. The most iconic island park is Paseo De Marti in Havana, created by a French architect and planners with local artists' and neighbourhood residents' help, and is almost a one kilometre long and 15 m, wide. A roughly 8-km long double island park (on both sides of a bus rapid transit route) on Avenue 9 de Julio in Buenos Aires is another shining example of green mobility space on a street island. Recently, island park creation has become the new inspiration for small cities such as City of El Monte, California (Powell, 2022) that plan to create island mobility parks including separated bikeways, planted buffers, and a median with a linear park and path. The island mobility park concept could transform many suburban traffic infested wide streets into quality public streets as demand for vehicle reduces gradually overtime.

ii. *Around transit service points*: Transit facilities running in the middle of the street often pay little attention to the space between two transit stops, and it remains unused or abandoned. Instead of leaving this dead concrete space, the Spadina streetcar in Toronto recently installed

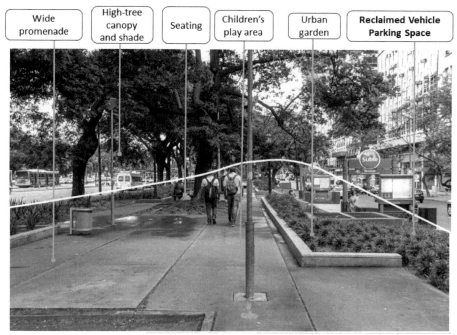

Wide promenade | High-tree canopy and shade | Seating | Children's play area | Urban garden | **Reclaimed Vehicle Parking Space**

**Supplementary Fig. 6.4:** Creating median Island Park on street.
Image location: Avenue 9 de Julio, Buenos Aires, Argentina
Image source: The author

green space including medium size tress between stops. Space immediately next to transit stops often becomes orphaned land even though transit riders need comfort and protection from weather, pollution, and buffer from cars running in the adjacent travel lane. The new St. Clair streetcar line in Toronto has installed small green spaces around stops, and most bus rapid

New promenade | Local wildlife sanctuary | New public seating | Green street edge | New bike counter | New bike lane | **Reclaimed Vehicle Space**

**Supplementary Fig. 6.5:** Green Transit Park on street.
Image location: Métro Laurier Station, Montréal, Québec
Image source: The Author

transit systems in Latin America, particularly Quito, Buenos Aires, Lima, and Santiago, have developed a practice of creating tree covered transit shelter spaces. This mimics the island park concept although it is mostly just spotted around transit stops.

iii. *Between the buildings*: Between two building faces, both public or private alleyways are often abandoned or used as illegal or unofficial parking space. Access to such locations is often not possible, and undesirable, nor does it satisfy any parking demand. These spaces are being reclaimed around the world as small connecting paths, narrow social gathering spaces, and additional green island parks between buildings.

**Supplementary Fig. 6.6:** Green Pedestrian Space between the Buildings.
Image location: Rue Prince-Arthur East, Montreal, Quebec
Image source: The Author

iv. *Green surface parking lots*: Small surface parking spaces can be retrofitted with green islands between parking aisles. Green islands including a pedestrian path can be created instead of a continuous asphalt surface. Green surface parking implementation in Toronto is one of the best examples of green parking lots (City of Toronto, 2007). It is now common practice in many other Canadian cities, originally inspired by the European green parking concept (Kodransky and Hermann, 2011), especially in The Netherlands and Germany. Treed islands between walkways and parking rows are another example of unused areas that can instead be used as a buffer between vehicles and pedestrians.

v. *Unwarranted left-turn lane*: One of the most extreme examples of excessive vehicle space addiction can be detected when double or even triple left-turn lanes were introduced with very little capacity or safety gains. These oversized turning lanes require a dedicated light phase and steal away time from the traffic signal cycle while increasing delays in all directions for all users. The worst of double or triple left-turns are linked to very high walking and cycling crash rate when crossing the street. The hazardous nature of double left-turn lanes on city streets led to their banning or active discouragement by many municipalities, such as a recent policy developed by York Region (Region, 2007) in the Greater Toronto Area. If reclaimed, this unwarranted space can be converted to a green island park to increase trees and other lingering amenities between the two signalized intersections.

| Local wildlife sanctuary | New public square | New playground | Green street edge | **Reclaimed Vehicle Parking Space** |

**Supplementary Fig. 6.7:** Reclaiming Underutilized Parking Lots.
Image location: Berczy Park, Toronto
Image source: The Author

## *Mobility Parkette*

Lack of standards for city parks forced planners to create small parks or parkettes to provide at least the bare minimum breathing room for park-deficient areas in dense neighbourhoods. If reclaimed properly, unused pavement for vehicles would be of sufficient size to create a small park. These spaces are widely available on every city block and street corner. Reclaiming these abandoned or unused vehicle spaces would create the most equitable access to green and lingering space, particularly where park land is severely deficient. Generally pedestrian amenities, end-use facility for cycling including bike parking and bikeshare, and micromobility space could be integrated to create a truly functional mobility parkette.

i.  *Unwarranted traffic island*: Often used as a tool to speed up right turning traffic in slower urban streets, the traffic island, commonly known as a 'pork-chop island', is directly linked to increasing crashes, particularly among pedestrians and vulnerable users. To hang on to the seemingly hazardous traffic island concept, an attempt was made to make it a smart "right-turn channel" (Sacchi et al., 2013). However, the "smart island" turned out to be unsmart for pedestrian safety. Borrowed from high-speed turning on highways, traffic islands occupy a huge amount of land that often equates the size of a city parkette. After a few right-turn islands were converted to small corner parks in Toronto, including the author's involvement in several locations (City of Toronto, 2017), the city eventually decided to remove all right-turn islands and slip lanes including whenever there is reconstruction or opportunities exist as part of the City's Vision Zero programme (City of Toronto, 2017). The City of Montreal banned right-on-red turning and other cities, particularly in Latin America, are actively removing all traffic islands as part of truck hazard removals and improving pedestrian safety while converting the places into parkettes where opportunities exist.

ii. *Redundant connecting streets*: Frequent midblock connections between main streets remain underutilized most of the time due to the multiple options given to vehicles. On the contrary, midblock streets are vital for pedestrians, cyclists, and micromobility to reduce delays, but are useless for vehicles as travel time gain is insignificant. Montreal, Ottawa, and many university

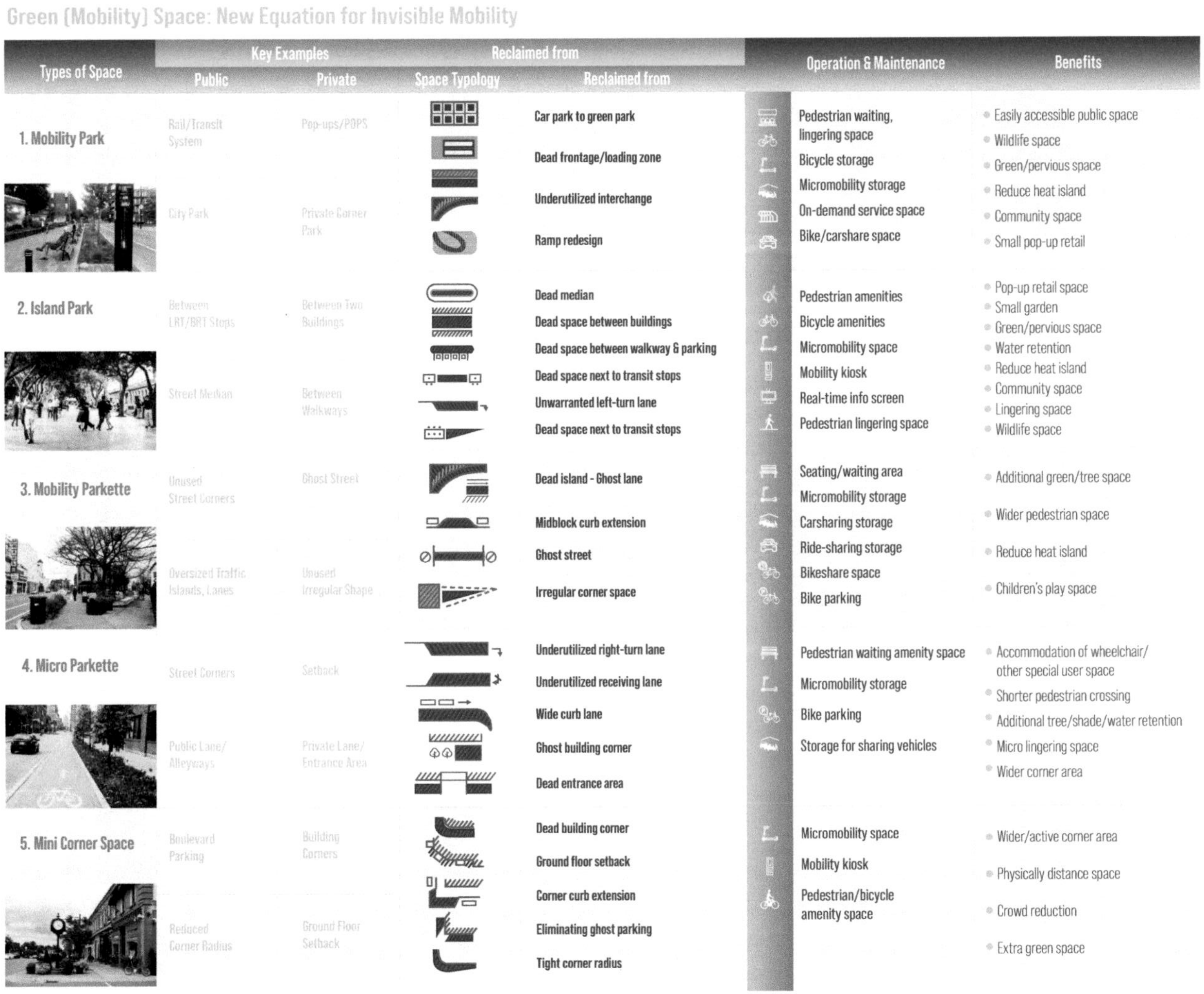

Green (Mobility) Space: New Equation for Invisible Mobility
Types of Space
Key Examples
Public
Private
Reclaimed from
Space Typology
Reclaimed from
Operation & Maintenance
Benefits
1. Mobility Park
Rail/Transit System
Pop-ups/POPS
City Park
Private Corner Park
Car park to green park
Dead frontage/loading zone
Underutilized interchange
Ramp redesign
Pedestrian waiting, lingering space
Bicycle storage
Micromobility storage
On-demand service space
Bike/carshare space
Easily accessible public space
Wildlife space
Green/pervious space
Reduce heat island
Community space
Small pop-up retail
2. Island Park
Between LRT/BRT Stops
Between Two Buildings
Street Median
Between Walkways
Dead median
Dead space between buildings
Dead space between walkway & parking
Dead space next to transit stops
Unwarranted left-turn lane
Dead space next to transit stops
Pedestrian amenities
Bicycle amenities
Micromobility space
Mobility kiosk
Real-time info screen
Pedestrian lingering space
Pop-up retail space
Small garden
Green/pervious space
Water retention
Reduce heat island
Community space
Lingering space
Wildlife space
3. Mobility Parkette
Unused Street Corners
Ghost Street
Oversized Traffic Islands, Lanes
Unused Irregular Shape
Dead island - Ghost lane
Midblock curb extension
Ghost street
Irregular corner space
Seating/waiting area
Micromobility storage
Carsharing storage
Ride-sharing storage
Bikeshare space
Bike parking
Additional green/tree space
Wider pedestrian space
Reduce heat island
Children's play space
4. Micro Parkette
Street Corners
Setback
Public Lane/ Alleyways
Private Lane/ Entrance Area
Underutilized right-turn lane
Underutilized receiving lane
Wide curb lane
Ghost building corner
Dead entrance area
Pedestrian waiting amenity space
Micromobility storage
Bike parking
Storage for sharing vehicles
Accommodation of wheelchair/ other special user space
Shorter pedestrian crossing
Additional tree/shade/water retention
Micro lingering space
Wider corner area
5. Mini Corner Space
Boulevard Parking
Building Corners
Reduced Corner Radius
Ground Floor Setback
Dead building corner
Ground floor setback
Corner curb extension
Eliminating ghost parking
Tight corner radius
Micromobility space
Mobility kiosk
Pedestrian/bicycle amenity space
Wider/active corner area
Physically distance space
Crowd reduction
Extra green space

**Fig. 6.5:** Green (mobility) space: A new equation for invisible mobility space.

**Supplementary Fig. 6.8:** Reclaimed Green Parkette from Right-turn Island.
Image location: Fairford Avenue and Coxwell Avenue, Toronto
Image source: The Author

campus streets or short block connections in Ryerson or the University of Toronto were converted into pedestrian zones, temporary squares, green space or small linear parks, or other human activity or active mobility storage uses. Most of the time, vehicle drivers did not even notice any impact after the short distance street conversions.

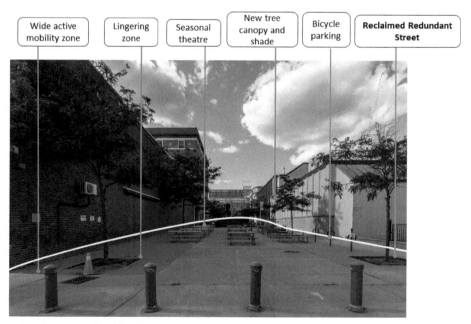

**Supplementary Fig. 6.9:** Converting Redundant and Underutilized Streets to Active Mobility Zones.
Image location: Victoria Street, Downtown Oshawa
Image source: The Author

iii. *Ghost lanes*: When highway-sized travel lanes were introduced to city streets, a portion of the travel lane turned into a ghost space and remained unused due to slower speeds on urban streets. A narrower travel lane width was introduced recently by professional standard associations including the author's extensive research results (Karim, 2015), resulting in an almost double lane-sized portion becoming redundant. This creates an opportunity to reclaim space for other usage particularly for wide sidewalks, landscaped buffers, micromobility and bicycle lanes, and storage space. Since almost every city street lane is wide, this is the longest and largest invisible, unused vehicle space in the city. During Covid-19, many cities rushed hastily to reclaim the wide curb travel lane spaces, including a long-sought-after programme envisioned by the author since turned into an official process that is now named 'ActiveTO' (City of Toronto, 2020). Designating reclaimed ghost travel lane space for "edge-line cycling" (City of Toronto, 2017) also spread like wildfire during the pandemic, extending cycling facility onto suburban streets as originally proposed by the author in 2013.

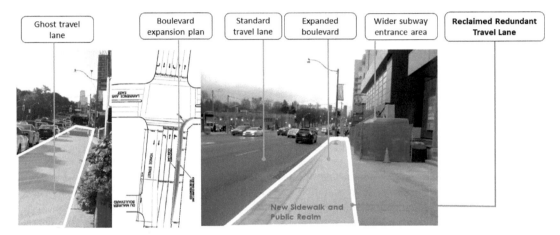

**Supplementary Fig. 6.10:** From Ghost Lane to Wide Boulevard.
Image location: North-east corner of Yonge Street and Lawrence Avenue, Toronto, Canada
Image source: The Author

iv. *Unused curb spaces*: Space between parking spaces remains another hidden location that has never caught the eye of place makers. Sidewalk curb extensions at midblock locations can easily extend the boulevard space to create seating, trees, waiting or lingering spaces in addition to art installations or street vendors, or performance space for local artists. This also creates a very short street crossing opportunity. The same amount of parking space could remain, although it should be questioned whether reducing 10–20% of on-street parking is sufficient or should more on-street or curb space be converted to green and human space. After numerous successfully reclaimed spaces with the author's involvement in city projects, and other successes, many small, extended curbs and widened boulevards are now a common engineering practice in the Toronto region (City of Toronto, 2017) and across Canada. Many of these attempts were converted to 'CurbTO' (City of Toronto, 2020), a programme long-envisioned and originally developed by the author seven years before the Covid-19 pandemic. "Reimagining Yonge Street" was finally approved by the City of Toronto and includes the author's vision for curb extensions and abandoned invisible space reclaims at every intersection in North York, making it the largest small space systematically reclaimed in Toronto. The City of Montreal went one step further, by greening the extended curb space for outdoor dining, flowery streetscapes, and water retention or small garden features on every street of all neighbourhoods.

**Supplementary Fig. 6.11:** Creating a Midblock Street Parkette.
Image location: Farmer's market, downtown Welland, Canada
Image source: The Author

v. *Irregular corner space*: Skewed intersections often create irregular shaped corner spaces that remain abandoned or unused by vehicles. These corner spaces can be reclaimed and integrated into the city system's palette. Many progressive North American cities, such as Montreal, Boston, and Peterborough have systematically reclaimed skewed intersection corners and converted them into small urban green spaces.

## *Micro Parkettes*

Besides the first three categories of typical space, there are still many opportunities to create micro parkettes along the city street, making a continuous green corridor for environmental, urban animal spaces, and additional human activity or amenities or mobility storage spaces. These smaller spaces are harder to see but exist more frequently than any other of the invisible spaces on our streets.

i. *Unused turning lanes*: A dedicated right-turn lane is another space added by a traffic engineering practice that has never properly explained why it is needed nor when it is warranted. Generally, more than a 900-vehicle demand for a right turn requires a dedicated right-turn lane. This amount of turning traffic can only exist at exit points off an expressway. There is resistance to removing the right-turn, even though they are used only 3% of the time in a day, nearly useless to vehicle traffic, and mostly used by aggressive drivers. Unfortunately, these turning lanes are often created by taking away more needed areas for pedestrians waiting at traffic signals or intersection corners. After removing several right-turn lanes in Toronto, it became apparent the elimination of the ghost turning lane had no significant impact on traffic operations. The spaces reclaimed created the much needed wider waiting areas, larger transit stops, landscaped buffers, and active or micromobility storage space.

ii. *Unused receiving travel lanes*: Predominantly used on highways to receive vehicles turning onto intersecting highways, city traffic engineers were mistakenly used to receiving vehicle

| Reclaimed On-street Parking Space | New tree space | Water retention space | Micro green space | Bicycle parking | Wide sidewalk |

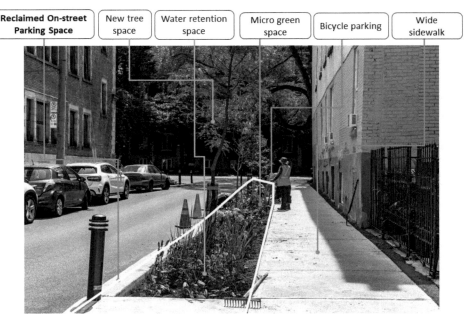

**Supplementary Fig. 6.12:**  Creating Micro Parkettes on Street.
Image location: Nepoleon Street, Montreal, Quebec
Image source: The Author

lanes in slow traffic conditions. However, these lanes are often used as aggressive passing lanes on the far side of intersections and have no operational benefit besides inspiring unsafe, speeding, and dangerous driving behaviours. Many receiving lanes in suburban streets could now be reclaimed from these spaces to add space to narrow and substandard boulevards or to convert them into small green parkettes.

iii. *Undefined travel lanes*: Widening travel lanes near intersections, often referred to as "flared turning space", is another mysterious rural highway application mistakenly applied to busy and slow urban intersections. This space encourages aggressive turning, cannot be officially defined as a lane or a turning lane, and basically remains a mysterious space to traffic engineers. These narrow triangular shapes could be reclaimed with tighter corners to reduce speed and create a wider boulevard space, giving more area to pedestrians who are generally placed too close to speeding travel lanes.

iv. *Ghost building corners and entrance areas*: Building entrance areas often remain abandoned without paying attention to how the space can be better used. These spaces are often misused with the most notorious and ugly form of parking (boulevard parking). Removing boulevard parking is becoming common in many cities and entrance areas are turning into green landscapes and the remaining spaces are being used for wide pedestrian lingering space, micromobility, or cycling storage spaces.

## *Mini Corner Space*

The space typology is the smallest of unused and invisible vehicle spaces in cities. Most of these spaces are linked to incorrect vehicle turning space related assumptions found among old school traffic engineering practice predating professional engineering manuals or guidelines. New urban street and mobility space concepts are revealing the unscientific and invalid assumptions often referred to by traffic technicians or analysts without proper investigation of actual turning space needs These spaces may not seem too big but are the most frequent candidates and widely available for reclaimed space. Small green spaces cumulatively add comfort and vital human space for street and building users, particularly for ground floor retail and commercial establishments.

i. *Private setback space*: Setback is often required by city planners to provide minimum distance from the property line to the building wall which adds extra publicly accessible land next to a public street. Often seen as a nuisance request by the developers, it has been proven vital during sidewalk space crises in Covid-19 pandemic periods. Indeed, Paris famously required all building owners to provide mandatory setback for retail frontage usage, additional space to pedestrians in addition to the city's regular sidewalks. This space is often used by senior citizens or children or pregnant women or persons with physical limitations as a slow-moving pedestrian zone. Additional pedestrian amenities, cycling, and micromobility storage are additional benefits for sustainable mode users. Double-rowed tree boulevards include the possibility of a narrow and long continuous linear green corridor for wildlife. Urban gardens and shade in extreme weather are added benefits of reclaiming private setback for public usage.

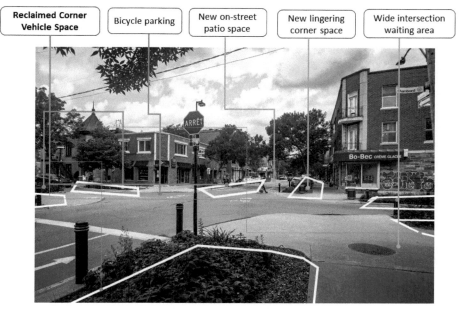

**Supplementary Fig. 6.13:** Creating Mini Corner on Street.
Image location: Laurier Avenue, Montreal, Quebec.
Image source: The Author

ii. *Around building corners*: Additional green space at the ground floor is often created or reclaimed by extending balconies or upper floors over setback areas. This, a compromise solution for full setback is particularly relevant for small development on narrow streets. When both curb spaces are extended using corner bump outs (see next section), the combined space creates an almost circular shaped wide pedestrian area at street corners. Akin to setback, this extra space at ground level could be used for mini urban gardens, flowery landscaping, additional seating, or wider pedestrian waiting areas.

iii. *Extended street corners*: Comparable to reducing corners, intersection corner curbs can be extended to reclaim remaining curb spaces by extending the corner radius that is never used by any vehicles. The extra corner radius provides win-win solutions for both large vehicles and pedestrians in addition to a mini greening opportunity. It is one of the oldest of urban resident habits to gather at the closest, most lovable street corners to meet with friends, neighbours, or acquaintances, and remain the most popular lingering spaces in the neighbourhood. Extended intersections often provide extra waiting areas for pedestrians, wider outdoor dining or retail viewing areas and additional greening at every street corner.

iv. *Ghost parking in boulevard*: Even though public lands end at private property, the vehicle invasion has occupied every surface of city land. One of the ugliest and strangest of parking practices is known as "boulevard parking", allowing vehicles to drive over sidewalks and park between a building and the sidewalk. Boulevard parking often causes the most unfortunate collisions with children due to severe driver visibility issues. It's an extreme example of wasted space and of completely unnecessary vehicle usage. Many cities banned boulevard parking to remove unnecessary, unsafe, and haphazard presence of cars along building frontage. Once reclaimed, green and lingering space in the boulevard could become a most pleasing human interaction space between building users and passers-by.

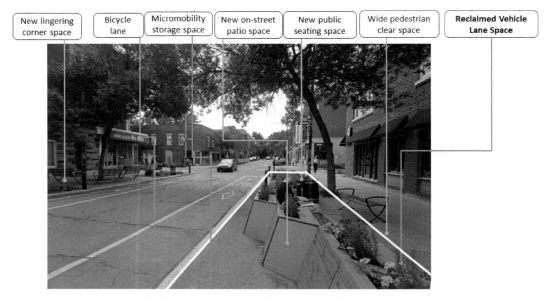

**Supplementary Fig. 6.14:**  Creating Extended Street Corners.
Image location: Laurier Avenue, Montreal, Quebec.
Image source : The Author

v. *Overdesigned street corners*: To accommodate trucks, everywhere, a generous turning corner radius has become another source of wasted space at every intersection. When multiple lanes are available, wide radius corners are unnecessary for trucks or large vehicles. Even on one-way streets where vehicles are not allowed to turn in a specific direction, a wide radius squeezes pedestrian space into a mockingly narrow and substandard waiting area where two pedestrians have difficulty passing each other. After using them for over a century, a few one-way street corners were finally reclaimed in downtown Toronto. And re-sized delivery vehicles and tightened corner area redesigns and knowledge are now common practices with the introduction of specific corner radius guidelines through a collaboration between the public realm and the (City of Toronto, 2017).

This is not an attempt to redefine urban design or the urban planning process. The idea is to inform and bring new urban mobility designs into previously 'untouchable' core traffic areas of urban public and private space close to the street, transit stations, or other public mobility spaces. The fundamental premise is to increase the awareness among planners and designers when they search for better and wider active mobility, green and human space which has become a nightmare during the city building process. The core concept is to inform and ask traffic engineering and infrastructure planning professionals to scrutinize these 'unused' vehicle spaces and adopt new and progressive urban streets and a people-oriented approach. Once culture has changed, the practitioners will develop and apply innovative design and bring in creative minds using the most progressive standards and guidelines to release these seemingly 'essential' vehicle spaces for the greater good of people, and to make our streets vibrant or improve the public realm, increase social well-being, and increase our quality of life.

> *"Kerbs are public spaces and should be put to use to benefit the greatest number of people."*
>
> —Dr. Tomothy F. Welch

## Scaling, Reusing, and Redesigning Invisible Space

How big are those invisible spaces? What can we fit into the reclaimed space? How should we redesign these spaces? Why do we need to clutter public space again, even if it is to be used for active and sustainable mobility facilities?

The author frequently receives these questions once those invisible spaces are visualized or truly reclaimed through various projects in the Greater Toronto Area and South or Southeast Asia. The answers are sometimes intriguing, sometimes too simple.

The size of some unused vehicle spaces is astounding, although they vary with neighbourhood character, land-use context, and infrastructure type. Unused spaces are larger in wide suburban streets and near old highway interchange areas. In old parts of the city where streets remained untouched for more than a century, wide travel lanes with overdesigned corners are now common. Postmodern era neighbourhoods built after WW II have the largest volumes of unused vehicle spaces in streets and highways. These areas also present a great opportunity to reclaim and rebuild urban spaces that work for people. To provide a sense of scale to the enormous sizes of unused vehicles space, each type of space typology was compared with a soccer field and green space needed for each person. Green and human space needs are the most fundamental rights to city space access by each resident. By combining a few of these reclaimed spaces a soccer-field-sized public space can be created in every district or neighbourhood in the city. Redesigning the space so that every person will have breathing room for their daily dose of green and activity space keeps away physical and mental health problems.

Due to its sheer size, it is also astonishing how many placemaking features, landscape elements, and mobility facilities could fit into those reclaimed spaces. To visualize the scale, this section provides overall visual tools to instal daily life necessities such as large and medium trees, planting beds, amenities such as benches, public art, planters, and all possible sustainable mobility facilities. Large spaces could literally fit all human needs, whereas medium-sized space should be carefully examined for selected facilities that are the most useful for most of the area residents. Suitable mobility facilities will also vary depending on practicality or local mobility culture.

Are we decluttering with these new public spaces? The simple answer is no. However, new mobility facilities have been carefully examined, local partners consulted including the public, and most importantly, all design elements are properly designed within local context, culture, and a balance between green, human, and mobility needs. The logic behind using a new public space is very basic: most of the sustainable mobility stays on the surface, provides easy access, and needs only small amounts of land that are equally distributed across the street or neighbourhoods.

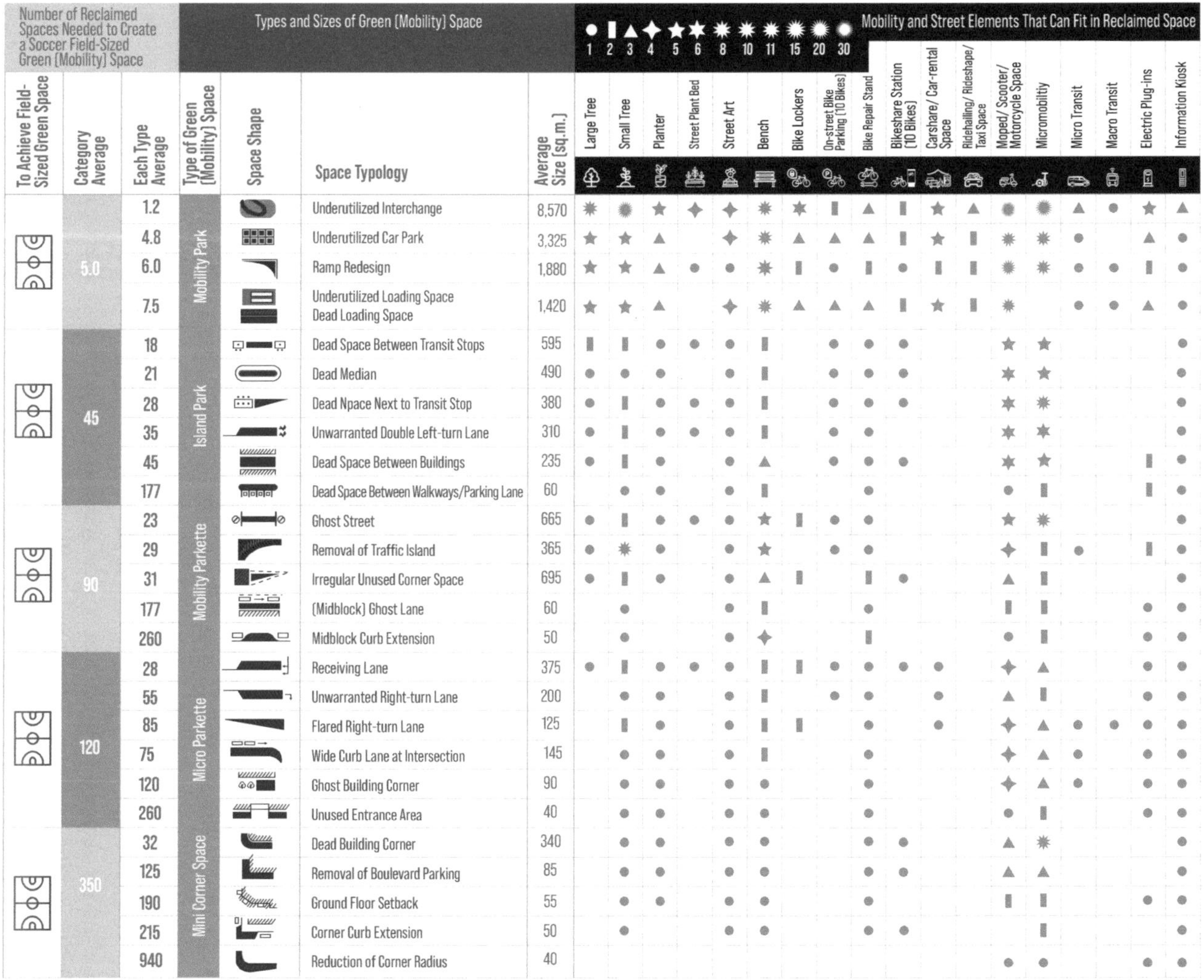
Number of Reclaimed Spaces Needed to Create a Soccer Field-Sized Green (Mobility) Space
Types and Sizes of Green (Mobility) Space
1 2 3 4 5 6 8 10 11 15 20 30
Mobility and Street Elements That Can Fit in Reclaimed Space
To Achieve Field-Sized Green Space
Category Average
Each Type Average
Type of Green (Mobility) Space
Space Shape
Space Typology
Average Size (sq.m.)
Large Tree
Small Tree
Planter
Street Plant Bed
Street Art
Bench
Bike Lockers
On-street Bike Parking (10 Bikes)
Bike Repair Stand
Bikeshare Station (10 Bikes)
Carshare/ Car-rental Space
Ridehailing/ Rideshape/ Taxi Space
Moped/ Scooter/ Motorcycle Space
Micromobility
Micro Transit
Macro Transit
Electric Plug-ins
Information Kiosk
5.0
Mobility Park
1.2 Underutilized Interchange 8,570
4.8 Underutilized Car Park 3,325
6.0 Ramp Redesign 1,880
7.5 Underutilized Loading Space Dead Loading Space 1,420
45
Island Park
18 Dead Space Between Transit Stops 595
21 Dead Median 490
28 Dead Npace Next to Transit Stop 380
35 Unwarranted Double Left-turn Lane 310
45 Dead Space Between Buildings 235
177 Dead Space Between Walkways/Parking Lane 60
90
Mobility Parkette
23 Ghost Street 665
29 Removal of Traffic Island 365
31 Irregular Unused Corner Space 695
177 (Midblock) Ghost Lane 60
260 Midblock Curb Extension 50
120
Micro Parkette
28 Receiving Lane 375
55 Unwarranted Right-turn Lane 200
85 Flared Right-turn Lane 125
75 Wide Curb Lane at Intersection 145
120 Ghost Building Corner 90
260 Unused Entrance Area 40
350
Mini Corner Space
32 Dead Building Corner 340
125 Removal of Boulevard Parking 85
190 Ground Floor Setback 55
215 Corner Curb Extension 50
940 Reduction of Corner Radius 40

**Fig. 6.6:** Scale invisible street and reuse for new public realm and mobility spaces.

Since these spaces are found almost everywhere, it is also a great opportunity to provide sustainable mobility access and equitable options to all residents. This is where the traditional rigid transit approach failed, giving vital access to areas that become 'posh' neighbourhoods. This is the same reason car culture succeeded by giving people access to cars anywhere and everywhere. To compete against easy access to cars, sustainable options must be available within very short walking distances.

The basic principles of reinventing and redesigning space are kept simple for illustration purposes. For this visual tool the following principles are used, however, it would be up to the urban designers, planners, landscape and building architects to respond with how these principles should be developed to make the best use of precious new space.

- *Green and human space is a priority*: Most of the reclaimed space is assumed to be converted into green space, depending on an area's needs or a city's parks and recreation programme. Larger spaces, roughly 80% of space, is assumed to be utilized for green or human usage. Medium-sized areas are more suitable for a balance between green and human space, roughly 50– 70%, and the rest used for mobility facilities. Smaller spaces would be difficult to fit large elements, hence 80% of small space was considered for amenities, active mobility, and small green spaces.

- *Green and shared curb lane*: Greening and humanizing the curb lane is now critical as people need to wait for accessed shared mobility vehicles to arrive whether it is transit, flexible transit, high occupant rideshare, carshare, or bikeshare facilities. Curb lanes are assumed to be redesigned having a maximum three standard vehicles or two transit shuttles space or the standard length of a bikeshare station, or bike corrals, while breaking up curb lane parking by reclaiming at least two vehicle spaces for green or waiting areas within a block. Curbs near intersections should be extended to reduce crossing distances while reclaiming those spaces for human activity or additional green space. This process recovers at least 40% of curb lane parking while increasing the remaining space for higher efficient mobility modes, hence, escalating the total capacity and usage of the curb lane.

- *Active middle street and transit corridors*: Transit islands are assumed to be repurposed for additional green space or to add additional space from adjacent wide travel lanes to create recreational space for residents. Simply adding at least 10–20 m of green space after a transit stop makes the entire corridor look green and creates a less stressful transit journey.

- *Micro space for micro or active mobility*: Active and micromobility users are predominantly assumed to access extended curbs or reclaimed private spaces such as setback or residential driveways while incorporating amenities and small trees or planting beds next to these facilities.

- *Shared, sustainable first, private mobility last*: Space reallocation criteria assumed as a priority for the highest efficiency and lowest carbon generating mobility modes. The second priority would be flexible or traditional fixed route transit and high-occupancy shared vehicles. Private vehicles could use the leftover public mobility only if owners pay higher fees and it subsidizes the other users.

- *Space for invisibles*: Children's space, lingering space for senior citizens, additional landscaping and amenities for women was assumed at the highest level of priority while allocating reclaimed or regular public space. This vision roughly follows recent NACTO guidelines that added children's and gathering space for people, including basic principles for autonomous urbanism (NACTO, 2020).

- *Easy walk, easy access*: The reallocation of mobility space was based on short walking distances for sustainable mode users. On-street, building frontage, driveways, and corner areas are easily accessible by nearby residents to meet their instant demand for short trips. Roughly

5 min. walking distance access was assumed for shared vehicles and 2–3 min for active and micromobility modes.

- *Coverage and network density*: Network density is vital for transit, active, and shared mobility to survive and thrive to replace vehicle usage. Using an eco-mobility hub concept, each hub area was assumed to be accessible within 3–5 min walking distance and to contain all mobility mode facilities to ensure equal coverage is provided for all citizens.

- *Private and public collaboration*: For users or residents, the line between private and public is invisible. Space reclaiming and repurposing of mobility space needs both private and public entities to work together. Space for bikeshare could be allowed between setback and the public boulevard. Reversely, private operators would pay a surcharge for using public space that was reclaimed and redesigned for shared or micromobility vehicles. The cost of reclaiming the operations and maintenance of these spaces will be covered by the surcharge collected through the payment process on shared mobility platforms.

- *Space for future mobility changes*: The most common mistake is not keeping an option open for future mobility modes and associated facilities. This fatal mistake led to a space crunch for bikeshare or micromobility storage, and the denial of other high-occupant shared mobility services. If green curb lanes were redesigned properly, the boulevard was widened for multilevel users, setback was asked for public usage, additional connectivity was secured through the development stage, policies were required for alternative energy, and the reconstruction process reclaimed or redesigned century old public spaces, any new mobility arrival would have been easier to accommodate. Many European cities kept future-ready design changes in mind when major reconstruction was to be done for mobility infrastructures. Once new mobility modes such as micromobility arrived, it already had extra or a wider space to accommodate it.

Using these principles, the illustration has proven a soccer-field-sized public space could be reclaimed every year during the initial periods. Every space typology size was compared to provide a scale of these invisible places, and several green parking and human design elements to complement new mobility ecosystem facilities to fit in new reclaimed areas. This would avoid a typical pushback from all sides and provide clear evidence that there is sufficient space for green, human activity, or space for new mobility if systematic process, knowledge, and skill is available.

> *"I don't want traffic behaviour, I want social behaviour."*
> —Hans Monderman

## Scale of Human Activity in Invisible Mobility Space

Many planners remain suspicious of shared mobility's power to make an active city. This is a valid concern. However, shared mobility is high occupancy, and combined with active mobility can transform city space. It cannot be done though without reclaiming the invisible spaces. The additional, recovered space from unused lanes and invisible spaces would accommodate the higher level of people's activity in the city's public space.

At the end of the invisible planning and design process, an obvious question would arise: How many person trips will be generated by the shared and sustainable mobility services? And most importantly how many mobility services and users could fit into the new reclaimed spaces? To answer this inquiry, an illustrative example is provided in Fig. 6.7 depicting how to estimate users coming out of each shared and sustainable mobility services. This estimation is a combination of person rate for each mobility vehicle or service and finding the size of the recovered spaces to accommodate these users during the busiest times on the street.

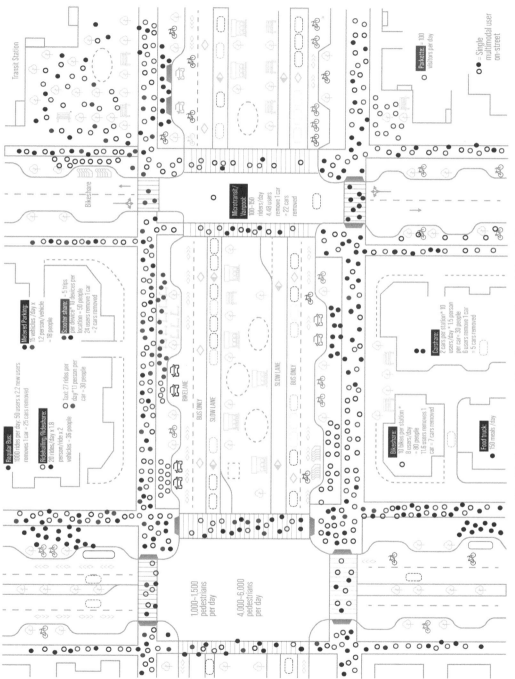

**Fig. 6.7:** Scale of human acidity after converting invisible mobility spaces.

The first step is estimating the rate of person trips coming out of active and micro-mobility, transit, and other shared vehicles. Figure 6.7 illustrates a typical example rate of each mobility service. Once a user comes out of new mobility ecosystem services, an equivalent of a human (a dot in a circle in the figure) demonstrates the hotspots of human activity (distinguished by colour in the circle). Using overall area demand and mobility services, it is clear the new mobility ecosystem generates much higher person trips demand than a typical transit and active mobility system. It also activates every corner or dead space, creating Jane Jacob's public "eye on the street" that makes city systems safe without the need of enforcement services.

The second step is to find whether the reclaimed spaces are sufficient for the reasonable amount of space needed for heightened human activity. The last section provided an approximate size of human space in reclaimed invisible spaces. Using the level of service concept per person in public space (Fruin, 1971) and a pedestrian comfort threshold (Gehl, 2011), the number of pedestrians in a public space can be estimated. This process provides sufficient clarity to predict the comfort level of users when a space will be reclaimed and reused in the real world. Figure 6.7 illustrates people's activity at different mobility services locations. Without reclaimed and sufficient spaces, users will face crowded conditions which generally lead to numerous incidents and problems when an area is rebuilt. Toronto's downtown area is a classic example of planning mistakes after residential density was increased over the last two decades, but sufficient vehicle space was not reclaimed through the redevelopment process. Eventually sidewalks and street corners became crowded, and then an embarrassingly visible space problem during the Covid-19 pandemic. The practice of understanding demand, checking for sufficient space, and reclaiming those spaces will ensure future residents will have comfortable and sufficient space for daily life activity without incident and problems.

> *"The walls between art and engineering exist only in our minds."*
> —Theo Jansen

## Urban Mobility Design: Code for Designing Human Space

People are merely classified as 'traffic' in the street design stage. But a human is more than just traffic. We have emotions, cherish our culture, love food, and like to interact with other people. We linger in spaces for various human activities. Humans need to interact with at least 10 different items when we pass through a built environment to avoid physical and mental boredom. Moving with or without tangible utility reason is in our mobility DNA. And our life is ingrained into our public places, streets, and city squares. Affinity to public places and streets will remain the heart of public life, and it may take decades or sometimes centuries to grow a street culture that is synchronized with local identity. But what makes public mobility space an organic element of our species remains undefined and unexplored territory.

Human activity is rarely accounted for in public street planning. Streets can be designed for all mobility modes, but without a strategy of how to bring people out with daily and enjoyable activities, a street will remain lifeless with or without progressive design ideas. Inspired by Jane Jacobs' pioneering pedestrian space planning practice in "the social life of small urban spaces" (Whyte, 1980), iconic 20th century thinking, "cities for people" (Gehl, 2010), a pioneer of 21st century public space design, introduced us to the importance of human scale and social activity while designing city life. But placemaking is still confined to squares, the streetscape, or behind the invisible wall, and stops right before the public boulevard. Core traffic areas remain 'untouchable' and many cities' restrictions reduce every inch of vehicle flow space to a "sacred place". Many progressive approaches such as the "complete street" concept fall short of incorporating human activities into the sterile definition of placemaking (Toth, 2011). In recent years, NACTO, hand-in-hand with another modern 'streetfighter' Janette Sadik-Khan, introduced the concept of planning streets for human rights protests, outdoor dining, nighttime or off-peak markets, and space planning for pandemics and evolving crises (Sadik-Khan, 2020). This is a step in the right direction. Reclaiming unused and underutilized vehicle spaces should be the standard practice, not a rapid response to a crisis. The German practice of coding urban space for human activity is a vital source of inspiration (Mikoleit and Purckhauer, 2011). These precedents inspired the idea of the "human space" concept described here but on a different level and from different perspectives. The first objective is to make invisible or underutilized space visible. The second is the creation of space through the city building process. However, just creating space may leave it empty or useless or boring if space for organic activity and improvization opportunity does not exist. Thirdly, even after reclaiming the invisible core traffic areas, questions remain about how to deliberately design and plan for human activity, and what a human does and how they connect life and public places in everyday life. Finally, human activity, performance, and cultural activity in mobility public space will gradually make its way to become part of everyday life. These spaces should not be 'spectacles' or tourist destinations or places just for social media bonanzas. These spaces should be designed, planned, and used for everyday life. Every human activity is a real-life performance and space binds them together (Halprin Conservancy, 2021) in a natural 'human-space' harmony. Human activity in a proposed space is expected to create an invisible vibration and waves of feeling through space that create a wonderful urban life.

> *"Design is not just what it looks and feels like. Design is how it works"*
> —Steve Jobs

## Human-space Approach

If done with careful thought, street design, planning, and policies could act as the catalyst to encourage these activities by default. "Human space" is introduced here to reflect at least six major types that touch most of a human's social life and culture on our streets and in our public places. All these activities need special sizes, shapes, and a few common criteria. This is the core idea of the human space concept in addition to the preceding complete street approach. The idea is simple: deliberately create space to give an option for human activities rather than just adding 'typical' walkable or bikeable features to 'complete' our urban streets and other mobility spaces. This is not a comprehensive list of human activity, rather, an attempt to invoke design thoughts beyond concrete, asphalt, or the typical streetscape.

1. Streets for street vendors, commerce, and economic activity. This is not supporting off-street retail, rather deliberately creating flexible space beyond just for food trucks.
2. Space for the social life that creates our identity through public space.
3. Space for art and culture activities that preserve our heritage, on public outdoor spaces instead of hiding behind the walls of inaccessible museums or galleries, making art and culture open to every citizen at any time.
4. Space for street theatre and performance to activate static and dead space with signs of human life.
5. Space for street organics to bring urban food, the natural environment, and wildlife to our urban doorsteps.
6. Space for knowledge, awareness, and interaction to increase our connectivity between people, neighbours, and different cultures to address our inequality and invisible divisions.

### *Space for street vendors and economic activity*

One of the most ancient forms of retail since the beginning of human civilization is selling goods in a public place. During the last 10,000 years of human history, street vendors have occupied local streets or alleyways, and open-air public squares to exchange homemade or commercial goods. Beginning in Asia Minor, near the Middle East, it spread everywhere humans ever lived and inhabited. Street food is the most common of street vendor activities in addition to clothing, skilled artisans, metal products, leather workers, and other daily life needs (Gharipour, 2012). Street food represents a nation's heart, identity, and cultural heritage. And the proliferation of street food in Asia, Latin America, and other culturally vibrant places is interlinked with daily urban life. To make way for car-oriented big-box shopping malls and keeping streets clear for cars, pedestrians, or bicycles, the street vendors are often referred to as a 'parasites' despite their immense contributions to our greatest cultural treasures. Car-oriented big-box mega malls and chain stores never aligned with people's daily habits and began to collapse in less than two decades. Covid-19 intensified the retail collapse into freefall, increasing social inequality (Pueyo, 2022) and loss of a vibrant traditional street environment. To the contrary, well planned street vendor systems became desirable destinations with the democratic sharing of public space (Bhat and Waghray, 2000), a source of revenue by generating more financial gain than wasteful parking space (Jaffe, 2021), and a catalyst for social and cultural exchange. Managing these spaces required an organic approach and a challenging path (Jayasuriya, 1994). Typically, a street vendor needs 5–6 sq m of square or rectangular space on an extended curb, facing the sidewalk or on-street parking, in between double-rowed trees, and a wide boulevard, on a wide median or in a public square. At least 3 m of pedestrian clearway should be maintained in all formats. These layouts, size, and space configurations should be part of the street construction plan to facilitate temporary, daily, or permanent activities including provisions for benches, shelters, and other amenities. Separate operation and maintenance administrations generally manage these areas, supplying security, proper lighting at night and toilets, while integrating mobility modes and information systems inside these street vendor areas. Asian countries have developed organized

**Supplementary Fig. 6.15:** Small Business Space.
Image location: Phra Sumen Road, Bangkok, Thailand
Image source: The Author

night markets and there are daily or weekly market systems in Latin America. Revenue and taxes come from street economic activities. Free space and operational support for street vendors is often provided by public agencies that usually collaborate with local businesses, NGOs, and cultural or artistic organizations.

## Space for social life

There is no greater place in the city other than on the street or in the square to inject and harbour the social activities of human life. Following Adolf Loos's failed ideology to remove aesthetics (Loos, 1910), traffic engineers gradually removed all traces of human ornaments of the local community's social and cultural identity from mobility spaces. Subsequently, space for social and cultural life gradually disappeared from urban streets inside the aggressive mouth of our hunger for meaningless road widening. The rough edges and hard surface of lifeless high-capacity streets did not work at all for children, women, and senior citizens. Ignorance of human rights through mega mobility structures left these demographics invisible on most suburban streets in North America. Streets that should have been stimulating children's creativity imagination and knowledge (Ekawati, 2015). Recognizing the issue, Norway created a national child research centre, the Norwegian Centre for Child Research, and Toronto recently initiated a similar path creating a planned vertical community for children (City of Toronto, 2020) and child-friendly guidelines. The social effects of cars on cities were put under the spotlight by livable street pioneer Donald Appleyard in the 1980s, showing how wide streets reduced social activities, and friends (Appleyard, 1972). His glaringly detailed work on street size and social-network analysis gave birth to modern livable street movements (Vasconcellos, 2004) including complete streets. Staying longer on the street or spending time there with family or friends produces overall mental health benefits, particularly for women who generally suffer depression three times more often than men. Mobility of the elderly on city streets came into the

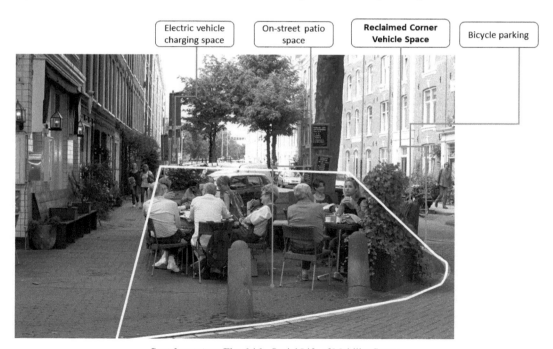

**Supplementary Fig. 6.16:** Social Life of Mobility Space.
Image location: Amsterdam, Holland
Image source: The Author

spotlight after many seniors were hit by cars in recent years, in North America, particularly in the last decade in Toronto. Interactions with people or friends while walking on the street will remain one of the greatest activities for healthy aging (Pei et al., 2019). Playing with friends on the island median of Paseo De Marti in Havana is a common scene among senior citizens. Protest in mobility spaces, particularly on streets, used to be commonplace for political rights and to exercise democracy. Against this democratic right, street marches or protests have been officially banned by public authorities in the name of moving cars. Through the invisible "space reclaiming" method, this book proposes to create new spaces and the ability to set up for quick street closure when a citizen demand arises. These new spaces are now often used for human rights protests such as Black Lives Matter or climate change awareness. Recently NACTO proposed innovative ways to accommodate healthy street protests through new shifting street design principles (Sadik-Khan, 2020). Many Asian cities intentionally include space for exercise and recreation on a city's right-of-way or shared private setback, generally maintained by private-public collaboration. Creating neighbourhood identity through street banners with local business collaboration has become commonplace in recent decades. Temporary shelter space on streets for the homeless is a bold idea but a reality only in Asian cities. The possibility of combining possible street vendor spaces to be used systematically as shelter has its challenges but is a better option than sleeping on the street or sidewalk without any care at all. Reclaimed curb, boulevard, and median spaces are major candidates for this activity if it is provided and managed in systematic way.

### *Space for cultural and art*

Culture and art are often pushed inside the buildings and become a product for wealthy and fortunate citizens in the city. This is not sustainable nor is it desirable to create another layer of inequality. Over 10 millennia, human culture was nurtured and flourished in public squares and on city streets. This display of human culture and art was systematically almost wiped out by road space aggression with vehicles in the last century. But these are innovative ways to turn our back on the destruction

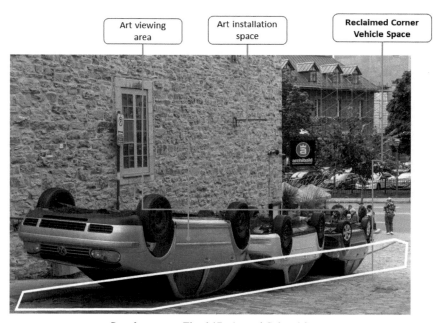

**Supplementary Fig. 6.17:** Art and Cultural Space.
Image location: Rue Notre-Dame, Quebec City, Quebec
Image source: The Author

of public art and culture. For instance, simply installing art in reclaimed setback or on a boulevard along a city street was one of the major initiatives that became a citywide mandatory per cent funding policy through the development process in Toronto (City of Toronto, 2010). Turning street graffiti into official art was another recent success through art painted on lifeless street walls, traffic signal or utility boxes in Toronto (City of Toronto, 2012) following the street art movement worldwide, particularly in Latin America and Montreal. Reclaiming curb space using curb extensions, reusing setback, or redesigning medians made these programmes possible. Regular art vendors or pop-up art shows would have free but organized space, if median or wide boulevard or street corner spaces were created systematically. Seasonal cultural activity or yearly festivals require larger spaces, such as closing streets. A street or mobility space redesign or reconstruction would incorporate extra space and the necessary facilities for festivals. An urban movie program became popular when Montreal experimented with the possibility on street corners and in squares or abandoned parking lots. Mobility amenities such as artistic seats (Rife and Andrews, 2018) and benches started in Europe (Dovery, 2014). Creative bike parking started in a small city in the Yukon in Canada and become popular (Transport Canada, 2010) around the world. These ideas require a long, rectangular, or small square shaped space (roughly 30 sq m) that can be reclaimed from wide travel lanes or unused parking space and redesigned into a wider boulevard, promenades, street medians, or curb extensions at street corners.

> *"We experience ourselves as dancers through awareness of our movements and our city through awareness of our movements within it."*
>
> —Anna Halprin

### Space for street performance

Like cultural activity, performance and theatre on the street is often seen as a nuisance, yet many flock to these activities out of curiosity and just to enjoy time with family or friends or groups. Street

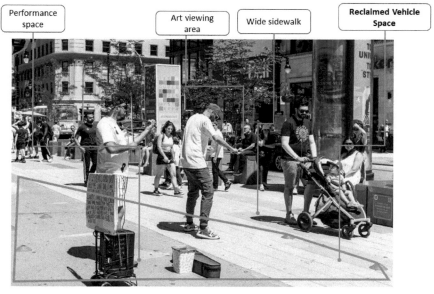

**Supplementary Fig. 6.18:** Space for Public Performance.
Image location: Saint-Catherine Street West, Montreal, Quebec, Canada
Image source: The Author

performances became an illegal activity and were squeezed onto the narrow substandard sidewalk. Flocks of people in a circle, rectangular, or square shape on a public street or in a street corner square would be a better candidate to accommodate these activities in deliberately designed spaces. Wider pedestrian crossings were deliberately planned in Santiago to accommodate the city's famous red-light performers (Fison, 2013). While it has become a common practice to accommodate small performance like music at an extended corner or extended sidewalk or boulevard, dance, acrobatics, and theatre require special care in designing a space in a wide street median, with combination setback, chamfered and extended street corners to create a large circle space for atmospheric shows. Teaching painting or dance on the street is a common scene on the medians of Havana and many Latin American cities. Planning and designing for street theatre and performance remained a neglected area until its much-needed revival helped rebuild city life during the Covid-19 pandemic.

## *Space for organics*

Over time traffic engineering nearly eliminated all the natural system that would have existed for over ten millennia of human history. Road widening, especially near the curb, has taken down all natural systems mercilessly under the cover of an "environmental assessment" study. Not a single environmental study for road widening ever concluded that taking out the natural organic system would be detrimental to the environment or human settlement. Over time however, innovative ideas have grown to keep our public spaces as organic as possible (Register, 2006). The green streets concept (Im, 2019) was later adopted by many cities including Toronto (City of Toronto, 2017) and many US cities adopted a low-impact development approach. Linear parks along the street are a popular concept in Latin American cities to maintain a continuous green corridor (Crewe, 2001). Linear long and wide rectangular green space can be created by taking out underutilized two travel

**Supplementary Fig. 6.19:** Spaces for Organic Life.
Image location: Rain station front square, Paris, France
Image source: The Author

lanes from six-lane mega streets, particularly in suburban areas. A continuous and connected green corridor is vital for wildlife and plant growth. Through the revival of urban or on street micro gardening, and combining street flower beds at busy, vibrant and tourism attraction destinations, micro gardening and street green spaces can counter our monumental water problems resulting from climate change. However, the creation of these systems remains a challenge. Buying land to create a park or green system is nearly impossible in dense cities. But reclaiming all curbside and boulevard space from very wide street lanes (usually 3–4 m of reclaimable space on main streets) is one of the most practical ways to achieve continuous green space. Rebuilding a streetscaped island is popular in Latin America and became a must have street element in Asia. Wider setback or small squares are ideal for urban micro community gardening in dense areas. After Paris allowed anyone to plant an urban garden (Cooke, 2016), vegetable gardens began to grow in reclaimed space in front of many transit stations. Creating a pervious layer and a water retention system on the curbside often requires the reclaiming of unused curb space and supporting a plant system in the reclaimed space with natural water. Toronto's wet weather flow and stormwater system (City of Toronto, 2017) was another successful formula that was combined with the street redesign efforts. Many invisible space recoveries were led by the water department, an unexpected ally in the redesigning of unused vehicles space. Besides a linear system, spotted green space in the setback, an extended curb for street planting beds, and street corners in the boulevard could be reclaimed for additional green space.

### *Space for education, learning, awareness, and social connectivity*

Street design is rarely considered a space for knowledge, human rights, or social equity. Yet it's by looking at a street environment that we try to guess the character of a neighbourhood and the local culture of people living nearby. Traffic engineering and the mobility design process typically excludes

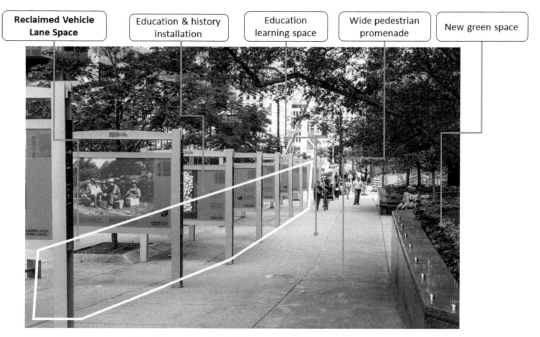

**Supplementary Fig. 6.20:** Learning and Connecting Space.
Image location: Avenue McGill College, Montreal, Quebec, Canada.
Image source: The Author

thin inclusive building concepts and is left to planners, decision makers, or members of the public to figure out later as an add-on item. These community building concepts should be part of deliberate street and mobility space design work plans. Places for social connection can be deliberately designed (CTB, 2017) through a systematic programme of mobility placemaking. Precedents already exist. Creating a meeting place with seating and a green landscape needs a small round or small square space which could be created by a combination of double curb extensions and building chamfer. These little meeting places provide social gathering and lingering space, particularly for seniors and women, including refuge space to take a short break for employees working from home. Combining a social balcony (Jordahn, 2019) and wide boulevard with additional small lingering space creates an environment to observe people from home or for chatting with acquaintances on the sidewalk. The Covid-19 pandemic intensified the lack of children places for spending time on the streets or on neighbourhood corners, since all kids' places were banned and intentionally removed in the traffic engineering world. But it needs serious revisiting, this micro-ethics approach. Reclaiming unused travel or parking lanes as linear space with a low-height buffer could be created for children's nature, climate, and local culture learning space or simply to get to know their same-age friends in the same neighbourhood. Various forms of direct or indirect learning and education happens on mobility public space. "Little free library" stands on street sides or alleyways have become popular in North America (Little Free Library, 2009) for the free sharing of books among neighbourhood residents or visitors. These spaces need only a small square space (2 × 2 sq m) and green buffer to feel safe and comfortable. Telling local history through plaques, murals, or organized graffiti has become a part of street design around the world. Many innovative Asian or African ideas generated a concept of occasionally holding outdoor school classes or tours for real-life learning and local cultural awareness. These activities need a wide double-rowed tree boulevard or a wide median with trees and amenities, generous private setback, and building façades or walls that display the local stories or raise environmental awareness. Besides physical design, digital access can also be part of street or space redesign. Digital equity through mobility screens or payment through kiosks, which can act as a neighbourhood news medium, in reclaimed boulevard or corner space is another way to reduce inequality. Digital screens that provide real-time mobility information can also display local stories or the history of street activity. A small rectangular space (1.5 ~ 2.0 sq m) around or in front of an area can be redesigned to accommodate digital engagement in mobility space. Collaboration between education, local businesses, historic societies, startups, and digital service providers and the city is vital to creating and bringing these activities to our streets.

> *"Because safe streets that succeed for children will succeed for people of every age and ability."*
>
> —Janette Sadik-Khan

## Playful Space, Playful Participation

Playful street and space design needs playful participation from the community. But the current public consultation model is badly broken and favours the dominant voice over the silent majority. Before giving any chance to the people who know their area and have basic human rights to public space, predetermined planning assumptions and traffic ideology have already been built into future street or mobility space redesign scenarios when they are first presented to the public. Isolated and inaccessible public meetings and rigid planning approval processes restrict people from providing meaningful input into a space where they are going to spend the rest of their life.

There is a simple and meaningful way to fix this age-old community participation problem. But it is not going to be easy, given the current paradigm of imposing rules and procedures, practised by practitioners for over a century. The most logical place to reach out to community members is

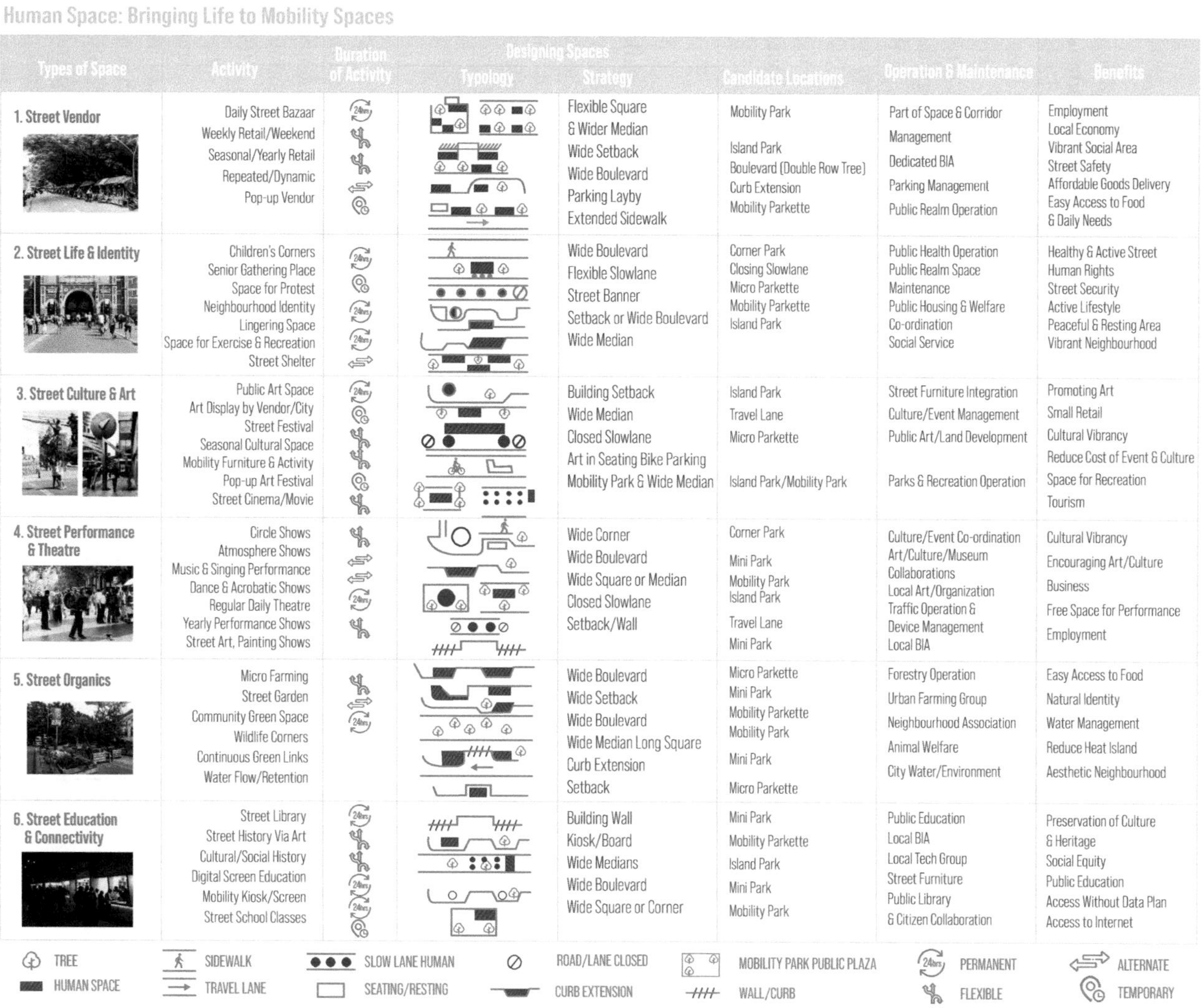

## Human Space: Bringing Life to Mobility Spaces

| Types of Space | Activity | Duration of Activity | Designing Spaces (Typology) | Strategy | Candidate Locations | Operation & Maintenance | Benefits |
|---|---|---|---|---|---|---|---|
| 1. Street Vendor | Daily Street Bazaar; Weekly Retail/Weekend; Seasonal/Yearly Retail; Repeated/Dynamic; Pop-up Vendor | | | Flexible Square & Wider Median; Wide Setback; Wide Boulevard; Parking Layby; Extended Sidewalk | Mobility Park; Island Park; Boulevard (Double Row Tree); Curb Extension; Mobility Parkette | Part of Space & Corridor Management; Dedicated BIA; Parking Management; Public Realm Operation | Employment; Local Economy; Vibrant Social Area; Street Safety; Affordable Goods Delivery; Easy Access to Food & Daily Needs |
| 2. Street Life & Identity | Children's Corners; Senior Gathering Place; Space for Protest; Neighbourhood Identity; Lingering Space; Space for Exercise & Recreation; Street Shelter | | | Wide Boulevard; Flexible Slowlane; Street Banner; Setback or Wide Boulevard; Wide Median | Corner Park; Closing Slowlane; Micro Parkette; Mobility Parkette; Island Park | Public Health Operation; Public Realm Space Maintenance; Public Housing & Welfare Co-ordination; Social Service | Healthy & Active Street; Human Rights; Street Security; Active Lifestyle; Peaceful & Resting Area; Vibrant Neighbourhood |
| 3. Street Culture & Art | Public Art Space; Art Display by Vendor/City; Street Festival; Seasonal Cultural Space; Mobility Furniture & Activity; Pop-up Art Festival; Street Cinema/Movie | | | Building Setback; Wide Median; Closed Slowlane; Art in Seating Bike Parking; Mobility Park & Wide Median | Island Park; Travel Lane; Micro Parkette; Island Park/Mobility Park | Street Furniture Integration; Culture/Event Management; Public Art/Land Development; Parks & Recreation Operation | Promoting Art; Small Retail; Cultural Vibrancy; Reduce Cost of Event & Culture; Space for Recreation; Tourism |
| 4. Street Performance & Theatre | Circle Shows; Atmosphere Shows; Music & Singing Performance; Dance & Acrobatic Shows; Regular Daily Theatre; Yearly Performance Shows; Street Art, Painting Shows | | | Wide Corner; Wide Boulevard; Wide Square or Median; Closed Slowlane; Setback/Wall | Corner Park; Mini Park; Mobility Park; Island Park; Travel Lane; Mini Park | Culture/Event Co-ordination; Art/Culture/Museum Collaborations; Local Art/Organization; Traffic Operation & Device Management; Local BIA | Cultural Vibrancy; Encouraging Art/Culture; Business; Free Space for Performance; Employment |
| 5. Street Organics | Micro Farming; Street Garden; Community Green Space; Wildlife Corners; Continuous Green Links; Water Flow/Retention | | | Wide Boulevard; Wide Setback; Wide Boulevard; Wide Median Long Square; Curb Extension; Setback | Micro Parkette; Mini Park; Mobility Parkette; Mobility Park; Mini Park; Micro Parkette | Forestry Operation; Urban Farming Group; Neighbourhood Association; Animal Welfare; City Water/Environment | Easy Access to Food; Natural Identity; Water Management; Reduce Heat Island; Aesthetic Neighbourhood |
| 6. Street Education & Connectivity | Street Library; Street History Via Art; Cultural/Social History; Digital Screen Education; Mobility Kiosk/Screen; Street School Classes | | | Building Wall; Kiosk/Board; Wide Medians; Wide Boulevard; Wide Square or Corner | Mini Park; Mobility Parkette; Island Park; Mini Park; Mobility Park | Public Education; Local BIA; Local Tech Group; Street Furniture; Public Library; & Citizen Collaboration | Preservation of Culture; & Heritage; Social Equity; Public Education; Access Without Data Plan; Access to Internet |

Legend: Tree · Human Space · Sidewalk · Travel Lane · Slow Lane Human · Seating/Resting · Road/Lane Closed · Curb Extension · Mobility Park · Public Plaza · Wall/Curb · Permanent · Flexible · Alternate · Temporary

**Fig. 6.8:** Framework of human space implementation.

where they live and the places they pass by every day. The street is the most widely used space by every member of the community. Technology is also available now for online and interactive participation. The following is a brief overview of the playful participation concept, combing in-person interaction with maintaining a comfortable distance and rightful use of technology in a playful way for meaningful and real-world participation from community members.

### Part 1: Go to an everyday place

Instead of forcing everyone to go and comment in a boring and interactive way, the most logical place to start asking people questions and surveying them would be by going to key community meeting points or places. And the most unbiased citizens who would provide input are children since they have not developed an ideological mindset and say whatever is in their heart. The second important member is women who know the short cuts to people-friendly places by default. Seniors know the history and evolution of the community. The next step is finding unscripted input through pop-ups. Toronto started a unique unscripted process of public participation under the guidance of a former chief planner.[5] The process is commonly known as Planners in Public Spaces or PiPS (Toronto, 2013). Planners typically pop-up on streets, in transit stations, community centres, sports centres, neighbourhood squares, markets, or key destination locations and inquire about upcoming changes and projects in the community to receive their input. An interactive online process including GISenabled (Geographic Information System Mapping) public comment around the exact location of a facility would likely bring changes to help solve current mobility problems.

### Part 2: Use GIS and AI for input analysis

Analysing and summarizing vast input becomes a challenge. Several technologies are now available to rescue planners from the cumbersome process. Natural language process (NLP) is a special machine learning algorithm and has the capacity to analyse, categorize, and summarize vast data input. A dashboard can be created to summarize existing concerns, anticipated changes, and a wish list of items to be reflected in plans of the future. This exercise will be the foundation of future changes instead of top-down assumptions about the place or the community.

### Part 3: Revamp the traditional proposal

A rigid and broken process of hiring consulting expertise emerged as a major barrier to the future planning and design process. With laidback knowledge and resistant to changes, local practitioners often develop a professional dogma and impose an ideological mindset through a vehicle-oriented or stenotype gentrification process of city building. In developing nations, large companies manipulate government's laidback conditions and capture multimillion dollar processes despite having little or no background in local areas. Giving a large project to one single firm or company created a sure-fire path to failure. A single company can never possess all experts. Splitting the project process among all possible contributors and community partners ensures no single entity dominates with a hidden ideological mindset. Small cities such as Guelph in Ontario started a unique public procurement process (Cassie, 2017) following these principles. It opened the door for local associations, community partners, local artists, and organizations to insert themselves into the future planning and design change process. Several boroughs in the City of Montreal have already fully established an extensive public and community input process while building in-house mobility expert teams to reduce the baleful influence of the consulting process (Roggema, 2014). External interests only get involved in clearing the site and the construction process when the planning process is complete. Redesign ideas are established by the city, public, and community.

---

[5] Former chief planner Jennifer Keesmaat in the City of Toronto.

### Part 4: Select inspiring mobility places

While an existing issues wish list is compiled, community and practitioners won't be given enough visual and physical possibilities of accomplishments elsewhere in a similar neighbourhood form. At this point, practitioners and selected community members will find inspiring mobility projects, streets, or places around the city, in neighbouring cities or around the world. Through careful examination, a series of similar characteristic streets or places will be selected for the next step.

### Part 5: Virtual planning and design interaction

When inspiring streets or places are selected, the city or expert will connect with those places and create a 3D street model of the vibrant places for computer simulation. Once ready, the scanned 3D map will be placed on the first segment of the closed street that will go through the reconstruction process. Community members and residents who will pass through the street will interact and choose the lovable parts of the design elements they like from the inspiring places. Children will have the opportunity to play with design elements that worked somewhere else. Women will select the design features and make them comfortable and feel safe. Seniors will choose which elements they would like to see in their future street.

### Part 6: Augmented playful design

The second part of the same street will keep existing conditions while moving and adding preferred elements from selected vibrant streets. Preferred and selected items will be placed by the community or visitors with the help of city staff or experts. This stage needs augmented reality assistance to insert, place, and trial-and-error the process of bringing selected or loved inspiring features into existing streets to play or interact with them. Typically, this process is known as a design charrette[6] (Lennertz and Lutzenhiser, 2006) but technological additions are new. Key participants of this process area are typically students, government, developers, industry, children, scientists, designers, general citizens, and experts and specialists (Roggema, 2014). This team will carefully gather, document and analysze the input for the future implementation stage.

### Part 7: Augmented playful design

This stage is usually skipped in the typical planning process. Once community members or visitors select their lovable elements of change, they could invite their friends and families through the augmented reality setup. They will play, feel, express emotions. This will ensure the broadening of the validity of selected design elements to a larger audience, mimicking real-life conditions. Augmented reality technology will provide the opportunity of interaction in a real existing street with virtual elements of lovable design features.

### Part 8: Analyse and create conceptual design

Both segments, street and input will now go back to the drawing board. City staff, practitioners, and experts will assess, analyse, rebuild, and develop a final conceptual design. If time and budget is available, the final conceptual design could be displayed on a closed existing street in a final augmented reality setup for the last opportunity for residents to review and play with their future street. The project will summarize all input from the public and sort out feasible options that can

---

[6] A design charrette is a collaborative design and planning workshop that occurs over four to seven consecutive days, is held on-site, and includes all affected stakeholders at critical decision-making points.

be established given budget, space, and resources. At this stage, the selected future design has community input and is verified by experts. It would be ready for a detail analysis, design detail, construction steps, and scheduling before it goes to tender for actual construction.

This seven-step gameplan of participation fills the gap in the current process's exclusion from all members of the community. It opens the door for contextualizing every project or mobility place as per the local culture, needs, and for fulfilling their wish lists. It avoids a rigid copy-and-paste mentality and expert's forceful ideological input to replicate and remove all aesthetics from mobility facilities. If mobility facilities are built for people, people should take part and control their living space for future changes.

## Summary

Our human memory and life are built around the spaces where we live. Mobility spaces are common, frequently accessible, and shape our everyday life. These spaces give us feelings, emotions, and perceptions about our living conditions. Most of these spaces are now occupied by the automobile, and that has created a disconnect between human and living spaces. Despite our cultural identity and social life being intricately linked to everyday mobility spaces, we still don't have the in-depth knowledge, skills, and systematic planning and design process to allocate our scarce urban spaces according to true human needs. This chapter provides several intriguing concepts, a detailed framework, and a practical mechanism to identify these seemingly invisible and unused vehicle spaces, and a detailed implementation process of how to recover them gradually as the city rebuilds itself with the urbanization process. Mobility equity and easy access is ensured through the fresh new concept of one-stop multimodal eco-mobility hubs that are equally distributed in every corner of every neighbourhood. This concept fills the mobility access gap created by vehicular approach of transit-oriented design and offers multiple mobility options contrary to the vehicle-only paradigm. The process of performing an x-ray to identify invisibles spaces, space reallocation science and unique redesign strategies including typology, shape, form, scale, and design elements gives a practical process and the right tools to decision makers and practitioners to reclaim unused and underutilized vehicle spaces. The chapter highlights the new concept of building green and human activity space deliberately instead of adding them later after a facility is built. Finally, the chapter briefly touches upon the process of playful participation and getting meaningful input from city residents who often feel isolated from the city building process. The main objective of this chapter was to reclaim and rebuild mobility spaces for people and give back their right to public spaces. The continuous and easy access to vibrant streets and active mobility public spaces on every corner of the city neighbourhood is the best treatment for mental and physical conditions for all residents of cities.

## References

Adams, J. (1995). *Risk*. London: Ruthledge, University College.
Ahn, Y. and Yeo, H. (2015). An analytical planning model to estimate the optimal density of charging stations for electric vehicles. *PLoS ONE*, 10(11): 1–26.
Akndi. (2020). *Greening Government Fleets: A Helpful Guide to Understanding*. Ottawa: Natural Resources Canada.
Albert, A. and Gonzalez, M.C. (2017). Using convolutional networks and satellite imagery to identify patterns in urban environments at a large scale. *Proceedings of the 23rd ACM SIGKDD International Conference on Knowledge Discovery and Data Mining*, (pp. 1357–1366).
Amadoa, M. and Poggi, F. (2014). Solar energy integration in urban planning: GUUD model. *Energy Procedia*, 50: 277–284.
Anderson, J.M., Kalra, N., Stanley, K.D., Sorensen, P., Samaras, C. and Oluwatola, O.A. (2016). *Autonomous Vehicle Technology: A Guide for Policymakers*. Santa Monica, California: RAND Coportation, RR-443-2-RC.
Appleby, K. (2015). *Five Cities Proving that We Can Quit Fossil Fuels*. Retrieved from City Monitor: https://citymonitor.ai/horizons/five-cities-proving-we-can-quit-fossil-fuels-1444.

Appleyard, D. (1972). The environmental quality of city streets: The resident's viewpoint. *Journal of the American Planning Association*, 35: 84–101.

Bae, S., Lee, E. and Han, J. (2020). Multi-period planning of hydrogen supply network for refuelling hydrogen fuel cell vehicles in urban areas. *Sustainability*, 12(4114): 1–23.

Baldwin, E. (2022). *10 Actions to Improve Streets for Children*. Retrieved from Arcdaily News: https://www.archdaily.com/945350/10-actions-to-improve-streets-for-children.

Bari, M. and Efroymson, D. (2009). *Detailed Area Plan (DAP) for Dhaka Metropolitan Development Plan (DMDP): A Critical Review*. Dhaka: Work for a Better Bangladesh.

Barry, K. (2013). *Wired*. Retrieved from In South Korea, Wireless Charging Powers Electric Buses: https://www.wired.com/2013/08/induction-charged-buses/.

Bartholomew, R. (2015). *Understanding Impact: Research and Policy Development*. London: Centre for Longitudinal Studies Strategic Advisory Board.

Batty, M. (2009). *Cities as Complex Systems: Scaling, Interaction, Networks, Dynamics and Urban Morphologies*. New York: Springer.

Becic, E., Zych, N. and Ivarsson, J. (2018). *Vehicle Automation Report*. Washington, USA: National Transportation Safety Board, HWY18MH010.

Becky, P., Lo, O. and Banister, D. (2016). Decoupling transport from economic growth: Extending the debate to include environmental and social externalities. *Journal of Transport Geography*, 57: 134–144.

Beddoes, Z.M. (2020). Time to make coal history. *The Economist*.

Beebeejaun, Y. (2017). Gender, urban space, and the right to everyday life. *Journal of Urban Affairs*, 39(3): 323–334.

Benjamin, L. and Richards, D. (1981). Electrification is the way to move Canada in the 1980s. *Canadian Public Policy*, 7(81).

Berg, N. (2020). *This AI-powered Parking Garage Rewards You for Not Driving*. Retrieved from Fast Company: https://www.fastcompany.com/90575914/this-ai-powered-parking-garage-rewards-you-for-not-driving.

Berg, P. (2011). *The Finite Planet: How Resource Scarcity will Affect Our Environment, Economy and Energy Supply*. Oshawa, Canada: Island Press.

Bhat, C. (2017). *Travel Modeling in an Era of Connected and Automated Transportation Systems: An Investigation in the Dallas-Fort Worth Area*. Austin, USA: Technical Report 122. Center for Transportation Research. The University of Texas at Austin.

Bhat, R.V. and Waghray, K. (2000). *Profile of Street Foods in Asian Countries*. Basel, Karger: World Rev. Nutr. Diet.

Billings, C.E. (1980). *Human-centered Aircraft Automation; A Concept and Guidelines*. Moffet Field, CA: NASA Technical Memorandum, NASA Ames Research Center.

Bochner, B.S., Hooper, K., Sperry, B. and Dunphy, R. (2011). *Enhancing Internal Trip Capture Estimation for Mixed-Use Developments*. Washington D.C.: Transportation Research Board.

Bojji, R. (2011). Gravity powered transport systems for rail, road, water, and airport use. *13th International Conference on Automated People* (pp. 22–25). Paris, France: American Society of Civil Engineers.

Borzino, N., Chang, S., Mughal, M.O. and Schubert, R. (2020). Willingness to pay for urban heat island mitigation: A case study of Singapore. *Climate*, 8: 82.

Botsman, R. (2010). *What's Mine is Yours: The Rise of Collaborative Consumption*. Harper Business.

Bourdieu, P. and Wacquant, L.D. (1992). *An Invitation to Reflexive Sociology*. Cambridge, UK: Polity Press and Blackwell Publishers.

Britton, E. (2000). Carsharing 2000: Sustainable transport's missing link. *Journal of The Commons*, 1–351.

Burden, D. (2021). *Building the Healthy City: Inciting the Healthy Choice*. Retrieved from Healthy City Design: https://healthycitydesign2019.salus.global/uploads/media/conference_lecture_presentation/0001/20/2459bb881e47ab6c074662a39832376707619a43.pdf.

Canada Energy Regulator. (2020). *Market Snapshot: Canada's Retiring Coal-fired Power Plants will be Replaced by Renewable and Low-carbon Energy Sources*. Retrieved from Canada Energy Regulator: https://www.cer-rec.gc.ca/en/data-analysis/energy-markets/market-snapshots/2020/market-snapshot-canadas-retiring-coal-fired-power-plants-will-be-replaced-renewable-low-carbon-energy-sources.html.

*Carsharing.Org*. (2017). Retrieved from What is carsharing?: https://carsharing.org/what-is-car-sharing/.

Carter, C. (2019). *Autonomous Passenger Ferries: Congestion-buster or Hype on the High Seas?* Retrieved from Smart Cities World: https://www.smartcitiesworld.net/special-reports/special-reports/autonomous-passenger-ferries-congestion-buster-or-hype-on-the-high-seas.

Cassie, C. (2017). *The Guelph Civic Accelerator: A Public Procurement Experiment—A Case Study*. Guelph: Brookfield Institute.

Cecco, L. (2021). *Toronto Swaps Google-backed, Not-so-Smart City Plans for People-centred Vision*. Retrieved from The Guardian: https://www.theguardian.com/world/2021/mar/12/toronto-canada-quayside-urban-centre.

Center for Sustainable Systems. (2020). *Geothermal Energy.* Detroit, Michigan: University of Michigan. Retrieved from Geothermal Energy. http://css.umich.edu/sites/default/files/Geothermal%20Energy_CSS10-10_e2020.pdf.

Certeau, M.D. (2011). *The Practice of Everyday Life.* Berkeley: University of California Press.

Charles, A., Lambert, H.G. and Balogh, S.B. (2014). EROI of different fuels and the implications for society. *Energy Policy*, 64: 141–152.

Chellapilla, K. (2018). *Rethinking Maps for Self-Driving.* Medium.

Christensen, A. and Petrenko, C. (2017). *CO2-Based Synthetic Fuel: Assessment of Potential European Capacity and Environmental Performance.* Brussels: European Climate Foundation and the International Council on Clean Transportation.

Cinty of Toronto. (2018). *Six Points Interchange Reconfiguration.* Retrieved from City of Toronto: https://www.toronto.ca/wp-content/uploads/2017/11/91d0-pcu-Six-Points-Enviornmental-Assessment-Study.pdf.

City of Toronto. (2007). *Design Guidelines for 'Greening' Surface Parking Lots.* Toronto: City of Toronto.

City of Toronto. (2010). *Percent for Public Art Program Guidelines.* Toronto: City of Toronto.

City of Toronto. (2012). *StreetARToronto.* Retrieved from City of Toronto: https://www.toronto.ca/services-payments/streets-parking-transportation/enhancing-our-streets-and-public-realm/streetartoronto/.

City of Toronto. (2015). *Dufferin Street Avenue Study City Initiated Official Plan Amendment.* Toronto: City of Toronto.

City of Toronto. (2015). *Tippett Road Area Regeneration Study – Final Report.* Toronto: City of Toronto.

City of Toronto. (2017). *Chapter 9: Street Design for Intersections.* Toronto: City of Toronto.

City of Toronto. (2017). *Corner Radii Guideline.* Toronto: City of Toronto.

City of Toronto. (2017). *Curb Extensions Guideline.* Toronto: City of Toronto.

City of Toronto. (2017). *Intersection Improvements at Millwood Road and Laird Drive.* Toronto: City of Toronto.

City of Toronto. (2017). *Lower-Simcoe Ramp, Gardiner Expressway.* Toronto: City of Toronto.

City of Toronto. (2017). *Street Design for Cycling: Toronto Complete Street Guidelines.* Toronto: City of Toronto.

City of Toronto. (2017). *The City's Wet Weather Flow Master Plan.* Retrieved from City of Toronto: https://www.toronto.ca/services-payments/water-environment/managing-rain-melted-snow/the-citys-wet-weather-flow-master-plan/.

City of Toronto. (2017). *Toronto Green Streets Technical Guidelines.* City of Toronto: Toronto.

City of Toronto. (2017). *Toronto's Road Safety Plan.* Toronto: City of Toronto.

City of Toronto. (2018). *Toronto Green Standard Version 3.* Toronto, Canada: City of Toronto.

City of Toronto. (2020). *COVID-19: ActiveTO.* Retrieved from City of Toronto: https://www.toronto.ca/home/covid-19/covid-19-protect-yourself-others/covid-19-reduce-virus-spread/covid-19-activeto/.

City of Toronto. (2020). *COVID-19: CurbTO.* Retrieved from City of Toronto: https://www.toronto.ca/home/covid-19/covid-19-protect-yourself-others/covid-19-reduce-virus-spread/covid-19-curbto/.

City of Toronto. (2020). *Energy Efficiency Report Submission & Modelling Guidelines: For the Toronto Green Standard (TGS) Version 3.* Toronto, Canada: Environment and Energy Division & City Planning Division, City of Toronto.

City of Toronto. (2020). *Growing Up: Planning for Children in New Vertical Communities: Urban Design Guidelines.* Toronto: City of Toronto.

City of Vancouver. (2019). *EV Charging Infrastructure Requirements for New Residential Buildings Guidance.* Vancouver, Canada: City of Vancouver.

Civitas. (2016). *Cities towards Mobility 2.0: Connect, Share and Go!* Brussels, Belgium: CIVITAS WIKI consortium.

CMA. (2008). *No Breathing Room National Illness Costs of Air Pollution.* Ottawa: Canadian Medical Association.

Cook, C. (2014). *Transforming the Transportation Industry with Renewable Energy.* Retrieved from Renewable Energy World: https://www.renewableenergyworld.com/2014/09/18/transforming-the-transportation-industry-with-renewable-energy/#gref.

Cooke, C. (2016). *Paris Allows Anyone to Plant an Urban Garden.* Retrieved from Inhabitat: https://inhabitat.com/paris-allows-anyone-to-plant-an-urban-garden-anywhere/.

Cooper, D. (2018). *It's Too Early to Write off Hydrogen Vehicles.* Retrieved from Engadget: https://www.engadget.com/2018-05-29-hydrogen-fuel-cell-toyota-mirai-evs.html.

CPCS and Hatch Associates. (1992). *Commuter Rail Services: Electrification Study.* Toronto: GO Transit.

Crewe, K. (2001). Linear parks and urban neighbourhoods: A study of the crime impact of the boston South-west Corridor. *Journal of Urban Design*, 6(3): 245–264.

Cross, G. (1993). Time, money, and labor history's encounter with consumer culture. *International Labor and Working-Class History*, 43: 2–17.

CSL. (2013). *Skills and Knowledge Framework.* London: Civil Service Learning.

CTB. (2017). *Section 8. Creating Good Places for Interaction.* Retrieved from Community Tool Box: https://ctb. ku.edu/en/table-of-contents/implement/physical-social-environment/places-for-interaction/main.

Curie, J. and Pierre, C. (1880). Développement, par pression, de l'électricité polaire dans les cristaux hémièdres à faces inclinées. *Comptes Rendus* (in French), 9: 294–295.

Dan, K. (2007). Flight of the pigeon. *Bicycling, Rodale, Inc.*, 48: 60–66.

Dave. (2018). *Car-Sharing vs. Private Vehicle Ownership Costs.* Retrieved from Carsharing US: https://arlingtonva. s3.amazonaws.com/wp-content/uploads/sites/19/2017/03/DES-Carshare-CarShare_vs_PrivateCarOwnership_ Cost_Analysis.pdf.

David, H. (2004). *Bicycle: The History.* Yale University Press. ISBN 0-300-10418-9.

Debhia, P. (2019). *The History of Electric Scooters.* Retrieved from LinkedIn: https://www.linkedin.com/pulse/ history-electric-scooters-prashant-dedhia-negotiation-ninja-/.

Deluchhi, M.Z. and Jaconson, M.A. (2009). A path to sustainable energy by 2030. *Scientific American*, 58–65.

DeMaio, P. (2009). Bike-sharing: Impacts, models of provision, and future. *Journal of Public Transportation*, 12(4): 41–56.

DeMaio, P.J. (2003). Smart bikes: Public transportation for the 21st century. *Transportation Quarterly*, 57(1): 9–11.

Dovery, R. (2014). *Public Art Projects Made These 7 Amazing Bus Stops.* Retrieved from Next City: https://nextcity. org/daily/entry/public-art-bus-stops-photos.

Driving. (2015). *Company Wants to Bring Rickshaws to North America.* Retrieved from Driving: https://driving.ca/ auto-news/news/company-wants-to-bring-rickshaws-to-north-america.

Duffy, M.C. (2003). *Electric Railways: 1880–1990.* London: The Institution of Engineering and Technology.

Ekawati, S.A. (2015). Children-friendly streets as urban playgrounds. *Social and Behavioral Sciences*, 179: 94–108.

Endsley, M.R. and Kiris, E.O. (1995). The out-of-the-loop performance problem and level of control in automation. *Human Factors The Journal of the Human Factors and Ergonomics Society*, 2: 27.

Energy Information Administration. (2017). *Study of the Potential Energy Consumption Impacts of Connected and Automated Vehicles.* Washington, D.C. 20585: US Department of Energy.

Energy Innovation. (2015). *Comparing the Costs of Renewable And Conventional Energy Sources.* Retrieved from Energy Innovation: https://energyinnovation.org/2015/02/07/levelized-cost-of-energy/.

Eugster, J.W. (2007). Road and bridge heating using geothermal energy. overview and examples. *Proceedings European Geothermal Congress* (pp. 1–5). Unterhaching, Germany: European Geothermal Congress.

European Commision. (2020). *Energy Efficiency Indicator.* Retrieved from European Commision: https://ec.europa. eu/transport/themes/energy-efficiency-indicator_en.

Fishbone, A., Shahan, Z. and Badik, P. (2017). *Electric Vehicle Charging Infrastructure: Guidelines for Cities.* Warsaw, Poland: CleanTechnica.

Fishman, E. (2014). Bikeshare: A review of recent literature. *Transport Reviews*, 92–113.

Fison, M. (2013). *Santiago's Red Light Jugglers.* Retrieved from BBC News: https://www.bbc.com/news/ magazine-23896316.

François-Lavet, V., Henderson, P., Islam, R., Bellemare, M.G. and Pineau, J. (2018). An introduction to deep reinforcement learning. *Foundations and Trends in Machine Learning*, 11(3-4): 1–102.

Frayer, L. and Cater, F. (2015). *How a Folding Electric Vehicle Went from Car of The Future to 'Obsolete'.* Retrieved from NPR: http://www.npr.org/sections/alltechconsidered/2015/11/05/454693583/how-a-folding- electric-vehicle-went-from-car-of-the-future-to-obsolete.

Fruin, J. (1971). *Pedestrian Planning and Design.* New York: Metropolitan Association of Urban Designer and Environmental Planners, Inc.

Furman, B., Fabian, L., Ellis, S., Muller, P. and Swenson, R. (2014). *Automated Transit Networks (ATN): A Review of the State of the Industry and Prospects for the Future.* San José: Minata Transportation Institute.

Galatoulas, N.F., Genikomsakis, K.N. and Loakimidis, C.S. (2020). Spatio-temporal trends of E-bike sharing system deployment: a review in Europe, North America, and Asia. *Sustainability*, 12: 4611.

Gawron, V.J. (2019). *Automation in Aviation –Definition of Automation.* McLean, VA: The MITRE Corporation.

Gee, M. (2016). *Raise the Roof? Union Station Reno Runs into Problem: New Trains Won't Fit.* Retrieved from The Globe and Mail: https://www.theglobeandmail.com/news/toronto/union-station-shed-renovation-stalled-by- low-arches-and-an-electrified-future/article28448568/.

Gehl, J. (2010). *Cities for People.* Copenhagen: Island Press.

Gehl, J. (2011). *Danish Architect Jan Gehl on Good Cities for Walking.* Retrieved from Streetsblog: https:// sf.streetsblog.org/2011/06/14/danish-architect-jan-gehl-on-good-cities-for-walking/.

Gehl, J. and Svarre, B. (2013, Novenmber 12.). *How to Study Public Life: Methods in Urban Design.* New York, Ontario, Canada: Island Press.

Geidl, M., Koeppel, G., Favre-Perrod, P., Klöckl, B., Andersson, G. and Fröhlich, K. (2007). The energy hub – a powerful concept for future energy systems. *Third Annual Carnegie Mellon Conference on the Electricity Industry* (pp. 2–10). Pittsburgh: Carnegie Mellon University.

Geng, J., Long, R. and Chen, H. (2016). Impact of information intervention on travel mode choice of urban residents with different goal frames: A controlled trial in Xuzhou, China. *Transportation Research Part A: Policy and Practice*, 91: 134–147.

Gharipour, M. (2012). *The Culture and Politics of Commerce in The Bazaar in the Islamic City: Design, Culture, and History.* New York: The American University in Cairo Press.

Gilpin, L. (2017). *Can Car-sharing Culture Help Fuel an Electric Vehicle Revolution?* Retrieved from Insideclimate: https://insideclimatenews.org/news/07122017/car-rental-sharing-electric-vehicles-zipcar-evs-uber-lyft-green-commuter.

Global Union. (2020). *Top 10 Principles for Ethical Artifical Intelligence.* Nyon, Switzerland: The Future World of Work.

Gomes, L. (2014). *Hidden Obstacles for Google's Self-Driving Cars: Impressive Progress Hides Major Limitations of Google's Quest for Automated Driving.* Cambridge, USA.: MIT Technology Review.

Gormley, W.T. (2007). Public policy analysis: Ideas and impacts. *Annu. Rev. Polit. Sci.*, 10: 297–313.

Gössling, S. and Choi, A.S. (2015). Transport transitions in Copenhagen: Comparing the cost of cars and bicycles. *Ecological Economics*, 113: 106.

Govindarajulu, D. (2014). Urban green space planning for climate adaptation in Indian cities. *Urban Climate*, 10(1): 35–41.

Griloa, F., Pinho, P., Aleixo, C., Catita, C., Silva, P., Lopes, N., Freitas, C., Santos-Reis, M., Timon McPhearsond, T., and Branquinho, C. (2020). Using green to cool the grey: Modelling the cooling effect of green spaces with a high spatial resolution. *Science of The Total Environment*, 1–10.

Gross, S. (2020). *Why are Fossil Fuels so Hard to Quit?* Retrieved from Brookings Institution: https://www.brookings.edu/essay/why-are-fossil-fuels-so-hard-to-quit/.

GTA Clean Air Council. (2017). *Climate Action for a Healthy, Equitable, and Prosperous Toronto.* Toronto: City of Toronto.

Hallsworth, M., Parker, S. and Rutter, J. (2011). *Policy Making in Real World: Evidence and Analysis.* London: Institute for Government.

Halprin Conservancy. (2021). *Anna Halprin: The Origin of Form.* Retrieved from Halprin Conservancy: https://www.halprinconservancy.org/anna-halprin.

Harms, S. and Truffer, B. (1998). *The Emergence of a Nationwide Carsharing Co-operative in Switzerland: A Case Study for the Project "StrategicNiche Management as a Tool for Transition to a Sustainable Transportation System".* 1998: EAWAG-Eidg. Anstalt fur Wasserversorgung und Gewasserschutz.

Haugneland, P., Lorentzen, E., Bu, C. and Hauge, E. (2017). Put a price on carbon to fund EV incentives – Norwegian EV policy success. *EVS30 Symposium* (pp. 1–8). Stuttgart, Germany: Norwegian EV Association.

Hayden, D. (1980). What would a non-sexist city be like? Speculations on housing, urban design, and human work. *Signs*, 5(Suppl. 3): S170–S187.

Haywood, J.B. (2006). Fueling our transportation future. *Scientific American.*

Hess, A. and Schubert, I. (2019). Functional perceptions, barriers, and demographics concerning e-cargo bike sharing in Switzerland. *Transportation Research Part D: Transport and Environment*, 71: 153. Retrieved from Science daily: https://www.sciencedaily.com/releases/2019/07/190710121536.htm.

Hoopengardner, R. and Thompson, M. (2012). *FTA Low-Speed Urban Maglev Research Program: Updated Lessons Learned.* Arlington, USA: Federal Transit Administration, USA.

Hordnes, E. (2019). *Race to Electrification – Norway in a Pole Position.* Retrieved from Urban Insight: https://www.swecourbaninsight.com/urban-energy/race-to-electrification--norway-in-pole-position/.

Hou, J. (2020). Guerrilla urbanism: Urban design and the practices of resistance. *Urban Design International*, 25: 117–125.

Hughes, I. and Huo, R. (2018). *Autonomy-level Classification for Robots in an IIoT World.* Retrieved from 451 Research: https://go.451research.com/MI-Robots-in-IIoT-World.html.

Hull, G.J., Roberts, C. and Hillmansen, S. (2008). Energy efficiency of a railway power network with simulation. *International Conference on Energy Technologies and Policy.* Birmingham, United Kingdom: University of Birmingham.

Iannelli, V. (2021). *When is an Accident a Crime and When Should Parents Be Charged?* Retrieved from Very Well Family: https://www.verywellfamily.com/charging-parents-kids-accident-3969696.

IISD. (2015). *The End of Coal: Ontario's Coal Phase-out.* Winnipeg, Canada: International Institute for Sustainable Development.

Im, J. (2019). Green streets to serve urban sustainability: Benefits and typology. *Sustainability*, 11: 6483–6505.

Islam, A. and Ahiduzzaman, M. (2012). Biomass energy: Sustainable solution for greenhouse gas emission. *American Inst. Phys. Conf. Proc.*, 1441(1): 23–32. American Institute of Physics.

ISO. (2020). *Road Vehicles — Human Performance and State in the Context of Automated Driving – Part 2: Considerations in Designing Experiments to Investigate Transition Processes.* ISO/TR 21959-2.

Itoh, M., Zhou, H. and Kitazaki, S. (2018). What may happen or what you should do? Effects of knowledge representation regarding necessity of intervention on driver performance under level 2 automated driving. *ICPS'18: Proceedings of the 2018 IEEE Industrial Cyber-Physical Systems* (pp. 621–626). Saint Petersburg, Russia: IEEE.

J2954. (2019). *Wireless Power Transfer for Light-duty Plug-in/Electric Vehicles and Alignment Methodology.* SAE International.

J3068. (2018). *Electric Vehicle Power Transfer System Using a Three-Phase Capable Coupler.* SAE International.

Jaffe, E. (2021). *The Future of Curb Space is about Much More than Parking.* Retrieved from Medium: https://medium.com/sidewalk-talk/the-future-of-curb-space-is-about-much-more-than-parking-46ced028b74d.

Jayasuriya, D.C. (1994). Street food vending in Asia: Some policy and legal aspects. *Food Control, Elsevier*, 5(4): 222–226.

Jefferies, I. (2019, November 20). Retrieved from Association of American Railroads: https://www.aar.org/article/freight-rail-highly-automated-vehicles/.

Jettanasen, C., Songsukthawan, P. and Ngaopitakkul, A. (2020). Development of micro-mobility based on piezoelectric energy harvesting for smart city applications. *Sustainability*, 1–16.

Jordahn, S. (2019). *Social BalconiesCconnects Existing Balconies to Encourage Social Interaction.* Retrieved from Dezeen News: https://www.dezeen.com/2019/01/14/video-social-balconies-edwin-van-capelleveen-mini-living-movie/.

Jorna, A. (2012). *Synthetic Fuel Costs.* Stanford, California: Stanford University.

Joshi, N. (2019). *7 Types Of Artificial Intelligence.* Retrieved from Forbes: https://www.forbes.com/sites/cognitiveworld/2019/06/19/7-types-of-artificial-intelligence/#48c88ca9233e.

Junkin, K. (2013). *Regional Rapid Rail: A Vision for the Future.* Toronto: Transport Action, Ontario.

Kalra, N. and Paddock, S.M. (2016). *How Many Miles of Driving Would it Take to Demonstrate Autonomous Vehicle Reliability? Driving to Safety.* Santa Monica, California: RAND Corporation.

Kane, M. (2019). *Chile Launches Latin America's First 100% Electric Bus Corridor.* Retrieved from Inside EVs: https://insideevs.com/news/377241/chile-first-100-electric-bus-corridor/.

KAPSARC. (2016). *Mobility-on-demand: Understanding Energy Impacts and Adoption Potential.* Riyadh: KAPSARC.

Karim, D.M. (2015). Narrower lanes, safer streets. *Annual General Meeting, Canadian Institute of Transportation Engineers* (pp. 1–22). Regina: Canadian Institute of Transportation Engineers.

Karim, D.M. (2017). Creating an innovative mobility ecosystem for urban planning areas. pp. 21–47. *In*: G.M. Shaheen (ed.). *Disrupting Mobility: Impacts of Sharing Economy and Innovative Transportation on Cities.* Cham: Springer.

Karim, D.M. and Shallwani, T. (2010). Toward a clean train policy: Diesel versus electric. *Ontario Centre for Engineering and Public Policy (OCEPP)*, 3: 18–22.

Khayal, O. (2019). The history of Bajaj rickshaw vehicles. *Global Journal of Engineering Sciences*, 3(2): 1–8.

Kleinman, M.T. (2000). *The Health Effects of Air Pollution on Children.* Irvine, California: South Coast Air Quality Management District (SCAQMD).

Knoflacher, H. (1981). *Human Energy Expenditure in Different Modes: Implications for Town Planning.* Washington D.C.: International Symposium on Surface Transportation System Performance, US Department of Transportation.

Knoflacher, H. (2017). Understanding professionals, politicians, and the society in the motorized World – and how to help them. *International Journal of New Technology and Research*, 3(8): 60–65.

Kodransky, M. and Hermann, G. (2011). *Europe's Parking U-turn: From Accomodation to Regulation.* Munich: ITDP.

Kour, R. and Charif, A. (2016). Piezoelectric roads: Energy harvesting method using piezoelectric technology. *Innovative Energy & Research*, 5(1).

Kubiszewski, I., Costanza, R., Franco, C., Lawn, P., Talberth, J., Jackson, T. and Aylmer, C. (2013). Beyond GDP: Measuring and achieving global genuine progress. *Ecological Economics*, 93: 57–68.

Kuchelmeister, G. (1998). *Asia-Pacific Forestry Sector Outlook Study: Urban Forestry in the Asia-Pacific Region –Situation and Prospects (Working Paper No. APFSOS/WP/44).* Rome: United Nations Food and Agriculture Organization.

Kwon, D. (2018). Self-taught Robots. *Scientific American*, 26–31.

Kwon, H., Ryu, M.H. and Carlsten, C. (2020). Ultrafine particles: Unique physicochemical properties relevant to health and disease. *Experimental & Molecular Medicine*, 52: 318–328.

Lambert, F. (2020). *Uber and Hyundai Unveil New Electric Air Taxi with 60-mile Range.* Retrieved from Electrek: https://electrek.co/2020/01/07/uber-hyundai-electric-air-taxi-evtol/.

Layton, B.E. (2008). A comparison of energy densities of prevalent energy sources in units of houles per cubic meter. *International Journal of Green Energy*, 5: 438–455.

Le Vine, S., Lee-Gosselin, M., Sivakumar, A. and Polak, J. (2014). New Approach to predict the market and impacts of round-trip and point-to-point carsharing systems: Case study of London. *Transportation Research Part D*, 32(C): 218–229.

Le Vine, S., Zolfaghari, A. and Polak, J. (2014). *Carsharing: Evolution, Challenges, and Opportunities.* London: Centre for Transport Studies, Imperial College London.

LeCorbusier. (1929). *The City of Tomorrow and its Planning.* New York: Urbanisme, Payson & Clarke Ltd.

Ledsham, T. and Savan, B. (2017). *Building a 21st Century Cycling City: Strategies for Action in Toronto.* Toronto: Metcalf Foundation.

Lee-Shanok, P. (2017). *Ontario Condo Act a Roadblock for Electric Vehicle Owners.* Retrieved from CBC News: https://www.cbc.ca/news/canada/toronto/ontario-hopes-revised-condo-act-ev-friendly-1.4155747.

Lennertz, B. and Lutzenhiser, A. (2006). *The Charrette Handbook. The Essential Guide for Accelerated Collaborative Community Planning.* Chicago: The American Planning Association.

Lessing, H. (2001). What Led to the Invention of the Early Bicycle? *Cycle History 11, San Francisco*, 11: 28–36. Retrieved from New Scientist. https://www.newscientist.com/article/mg18524841-900-brimstone-and-bicycles/.

Li, L. and Loo, B.P. (2014). Alternative and transitional energy sources for urban transportation. *Current Sustainable/ Renewable Energy Reports*, 1: 19–26.

Li, X. and Strezov, V. (2014). Modelling piezoelectric energy harvesting potential in an educational building. *Energy Conversion and Management*, 85: 435–442.

Li, X., Gorghinpour, C., Sclar, R. and Castellanos, S. (2018). *How to Enable Electric Bus Adoption in Cities Worldwide.* Berlin: World Resources Institute, WRI and German Federal Ministry.

Lima, M. (2015). *The Bicycle in the 21st Century.* Retrieved from Theprotocity: http://theprotocity.com/the-bicycle-in-the-21st-century/.

Litman, T. (2018). Retrieved from Carsharing: Vehicle Rental Services that Substitute for Private Vehicle Ownership: https://www.vtpi.org/tdm/tdm7.htm.

Little Free Library. (2009). *Little Free Library Book Exchanges.* Retrieved from Little Free Library: https://littlefreelibrary.org/about/.

Little, A. (2015). *The Future of Urban Mobility 2.0: Towards Networked, Multimodal Cities of 2050.* Rome, Italy: International Association of Public Transport (UITP).

Loos, A. (1910). *Ornement et Crime.* Vienna: Les Cahiers d'aujourd'hui.

Lu, Z., Happe, R., Cabrall, C.D., Kyriakidis, M. and Winter, J.C. (2016). Human factors of transitions in automated driving: A general framework and literature survey. *Transportation Research Part F*, 43: 183–198.

Lucas, A., Prettico, G., Flammini, M.G., Kotsakis, E., Fulli, G. and Masera., M. (2018). Indicator-based methodology for assessing EV charging infrastructure using exploratory data analysis. *Energies*, 11(1869): 1–18.

MaRS Discovery District. (2016). *Microtransit: An Assessment of Potential to Drive Greenhouse Gas Reductions.* Toronto: MaRS Discovery District and Richmond Sustainability Initiatives.

Martret, O. (2020). *Electric Vehicles – Cleaner, Greener, and... On-Demand?* Retrieved from Shotl: https://shotl.com/news/electric-vehicles-cleaner-greener-and-on-demand.

Matuka, R. (2014). *The History of the Electric Car.* Retrieved from US Department of Energy.

McCormack, D.P. (2013). *Refrains for Moving Bodies: Experience and Experiment in Affective Spaces.* Oxford: Duke University Press.

McMahon, J. (2019). *9 Shared-Mobility Startups Eager To Disrupt Transportation.* Retrieved from Forbes: https://www.forbes.com/sites/jeffmcmahon/2019/03/06/9-shared-mobility-startups-eager-to-disrupt-transportation/#79ca1bf5177e.

McNabb, M. (2019). *DRONEII: Tech Talk – Unraveling 5 Levels of Drone.* Drone Talk.

Medina-Tapiaa, M. and Robusteb, F. (2018). Exploring paradigm shift impacts in urban mobility: Autonomous vehicles and Smart cities. *Transportation Research Procedia*, 33: 203–210.

Melaina, M., Bush, B., Muratori, M., Zuboy, J. and Ellis, S. (2017). *National Hydrogen Scenerios: How Many Stations, Where, and When?* Washington D.C.: National Renewable Energy Laboratory for the H2USA.

Menon, M. (2015). *Indifference to Difference: On Queer Universalism.* Minneapolis: University of Minnesota Press.

Metrolinx. (2008). *The Big Move: Transforming Transportation in the Greater Toronto and Hamilton Area.* Toronto: Metrolinx.

Metrolinx. (2011). *Mobility Hub Guidelines for the Greater Toronto and Hamilton Area.* Toronto: Metrolinx.

Mikoleit, A. and Purckhauer, M. (2011). *100 Lessons for Understandng the City.* Zurich: The MIT Press.

Millard-Ball, A. (2019, March). The autonomous vehicle parking problem. 75: 99–108.

MIT Media Lab. (2019). *Persuasive Electric Vehicle (PEV).* Retrieved from MIT Media Lab City Science Group: https://www.media.mit.edu/projects/pev/overview/.

Mitchell, W.J., Borroni-Bird, C.E. and Burns, L.D. (2015). *Reinventing the Automobile.* Cambridge, USA: The MIT Press.

Mohorčich, J. (2020). Energy intensity and human mobility after the anthropocene. *Sustainability*, 12: 2376–2389.

Morawska, L., Moore, M.R. and Ristovski, Z.D. (2014). *Health Impacts of Ultrafine Particles: Desktop Literature Review and Analysis.* Canberra: Australian Government Department of the Environment and Heritage.

Movmi. (2018). *Carsharing Market Analysis: Growth and Industry Analysis.* Retrieved from Movmi.net: https://movmi.net/carsharing-market-growth/.

Muheim, P. and Partners. (1996). *Car Sharing Studies: An Investigation.* Dublin, Ireland: Graham Lightfoot.

Müller, V.C. (2020). *Stanford Encyclopedia of Philosophy.* Retrieved from Stanford University: https://plato.stanford.edu/entries/ethics-ai/.

Münzel, K., Boon, W., Frenken, K. and van der Bloome, J.D. (2019). Explaining carsharing supply across Western European cities. *International Journal of Sustainable Transportation*, 1–12.

NACTO. (2020). *Blueprint for Autonomous Urbanism*, (2nd Edn.) New York: NACTO.

NACTO. (2020). *Designing Streets for Kids.* New York: NACTO.

Najini, H. and Muthukumaraswamy, S.A. (2017). Piezoelectric energy generation from vehicle traffic with technoeconomic analysis. *Journal of Renewable Energy*, 1–16.

Namazu, M. (2017). *The Evolution of Carsharing: Heterogeneity in Adoption and Impacts.* Vancouver: The University of British Columbia.

Network Rail Infrastructure Limited. (2020). *Network Statement 2020.* London, UK: Network Rail.

Newswire. (2010). *Vancouver First City in the World to Endorse the Fossil Fuel Non-Proliferation Treaty.* Retrieved from Fossil Fuel Non-Proliferation Treaty: https://www.newswire.ca/news-releases/vancouver-first-city-in-the-world-to-endorse-the-fossil-fuel-non-proliferation-treaty-843699223.html.

NHTSA. (2016). *Federal Motor Vehicle Safety Standards: Minimum Sound Requirements for Hybrid and Electric Vehicles.* Washington D.C.: National Highway Traffic Safety Administration, NHTSA.

Nilsson, N.J. (1982). *Principles of Artificial Intelligence.* Elsevier Inc.

North District, C.o. (2015). *Sheppard East Corridor: Transportation Review.* Toronto: Transportation Planning, City of Toronto.

NTSB. (2020). *Tesla Crash Investigation Yields 9 NTSB Safety Recommendations.* National Transportation Safety Board.

Ohta, K. (1998). TDM measures toward sustainable mobility. *IATSS Research*, 22(1).

Omi, K. (2018). *Alternative Energy for Transportation.* Retrieved from Issues in Science and Technology: https://issues.org/omi/.

Ongel, A., Loewer, E., Roemer, F., Sethuraman, G. and Chang, F. (2019). Economic assessment of autonomous electric microtransit vehicles. *Sustainability*, 2–18.

Ontario Medical Association. (2005). *The Illness Costs of Air Pollution: 2005–2026 Health and Economic Damage Estimates.* Toronto: OMA.

Orenstein, M. (2020). *COVID-19's Effect on Energy and Emissions – and Implications for the Future.* Retrieved from Canawest Foundation: https://cwf.ca/research/publications/what-now-covid-19s-effect-on-energy-and-emissions-and-implications-for-the-future/.

ORF. (2011). *Integrated Transport Policy – A Vision which Doesn't Work Today – How to Make it a Reality (Part II).* Retrieved from Observer Research Foundation: https://www.orfonline.org/research/integrated-transport-policy-a-vision-which-doesnt-work-today-how-to-make-it-a-reality-part-ii/.

Panchal, D.U. (2015). *Two and Three Wheeler Technology.* PHI Learning Pvt. Ltd., ISBN 9788120351431.

Parasuraman, R. (1992). Adaptive function allocation effects on pilot performance. *NASA/FAA Workshop on Artificial Intelligence and Human Factors.* Daytona Beach, Florida, USA: NASA and FAA.

Parasuraman, R., Sheridan, T.B. and Wickens, C.D. (2000). A model for types and levels of human interaction with automation. *IEEE Transactions on Systems, Man, and Cybernetics – Part A: Systems and Humans*, 30(3): 286–297.

PBS. (2009). *Timeline: History of the Electric Car.* Retrieved from PBS.Org: https://www.pbs.org/now/shows/223/electric-car-timeline.html.

Pei, X., Sedini, C. and Zurlo, F. (2019). Building an age-friendly city for elderly citizens through co-designing an urban walkable scenario. *Proceedings of the Academy for Design Innovation Management* (pp. 69–80). London: Academy for Design Innovation Management.

Perner, J., Unteutsch, M. and Lövenich, A. (2018). *The Future Cost of Electricity-Based Synthetic Fuels.* Berlin: Agora Energiewende.

Pete. (2015). *Electric Cargo Bike Guide.* Retrieved from Electric Bike Report: https://electricbikereport.com/electric-cargo-bike-guide/.

Policy Profession. (2019). *Policy Profession Standards: A Framework for Professional Development.* London: Policy Profession.

Pope III, C.A., Burnett, R.T., Thun, M.J., Calle, E.E., Krewski, D., Ito, K. and Thurston, G.D. (2002). Lung cancer, cardiopulmonary mortality, and long-term exposure to fine particulate air pollution. *The Journal of the American Medical Association*, 287(9): 1132–1141.

Porru, M., Serpi, A., Mureddu, M. and Damiano, A. (2020). A multistage design procedure for planning and implementing public charging infrastructures for electric vehicles. *Sustainability*, 2889(12): 1–17.

Powell, J. (2022). *How One City's Pavement Repair Project Became a Community-Focused Linear Park.* Retrieved from Alta Planning Blog: https://blog.altaplanning.com/how-one-citys-pavement-repair-project-became-a-community-focused-linear-park-e014ad3a554c.

Priemus, H. (2007). Dutch spatial planning between substratum and infrastructure networks. *European Plannning Study*, 15(5): 667–686: .

Puchalsky, C.M. (2005). Comparison of Emission from Light Rail and Bus Rapid Transit. *Transportation Research Record*, 1927(1): 31–37.

Pueyo, T. (2022). *How to Fight the Retail Apocalypse.* Retrieved from Uncharted Territories: https://uncharted territories.tomaspueyo.com/p/retail-apocalypse/.

Qiu, C., Chau, K.T., Ching, T.W. and Liu, C. (2014). Overview of wireless charging technologies for electric vehicles. *Journal of Asian Electric Vehicles*, 12: 1679–1685.

RAJUK. (1995). *Dhaka Metropolitan Development Plan (1995–2015).* Dhaka: RAJUK.

Rajvanshi, A.K. (2002). Electric and improved cycle rickshaw as a sustainable transport system for India. *Current Science*, 83(6): 703–707.

Ram, G., Mouli, C., Duijsen, P.V., Grazian, F., Jamodkar, A., Bauer, P. and Isabella, O. (2020). Sustainable E-bike charging station that enables AC, DC, and wireless charging from solar energy. *Energies*, 13(3549): 1–21.

Reddy, T. (2008). *Synthetic Fuels Handbook: Properties, Process, and Performance.* McGraw-Hill.

Region, Y. (2007). *Access Guidelines: Section 5.* Newmarket: Transportation and Works Department, York Region.

Register, R. (2006). *Ecocities: Rebuilding Cities in Balance with Nature.* Gabriola Island, British Columbia: New Society Publishers.

Regnier, E. (2007). Oil and energy price volatility. *Energy Economic*, 29(3): 405–427.

Richard, F. and Cooper, H. (2005). Why electrified rail is superior. *21st Century Science & Technology*, 18: 26–29.

Rickstrom, J. and Klum, M. (2015). *Big World, Small Planet: Abundance within Planetary Boundaries.* New Haven and London: Yale University Press.

Rideamigos. (2018). *What is Transportation Demand Management?* Retrieved from Rideamigos: https://rideamigos.com/transportation-demand-management-tdm/.

Rider, D. (2020). *Toronto Adds Electric Bicycles to Bike-share Fleet — at No Extra Cost to Users.* Retrieved from Toronto Star: https://www.thestar.com/news/city_hall/2020/08/19/toronto-adds-electric-bicycles-to-bike-share-fleet-at-no-extra-cost-to-users.html.

Rieti, J. (2017). *CBC News.* Retrieved from Toronto discourages electric car use by denying on-street chargers, driver says: https://www.cbc.ca/news/canada/toronto/electric-vehicles-blocked-1.4368014.

Rife, E. and Andrews, M. (2018). *Street Seats: Urban Placemaking in Portland.* Retrieved from Design Museum Everywhere: https://designmuseumfoundation.org/street-seats/.

Ritchie, H. (2020). *What are the Safest and Cleanest Sources of Energy?* Retrieved from Our world in data: https://ourworldindata.org/safest-sources-of-energy.

ROAMEF. (2016). *ROAMEF Cycle.* Retrieved from ROAMEF: http://www.roamef.com/what-we-do/roamef-cycle.

Rocky Mountain, I. (2019). *Electric Mobility: Best Practices.* Rocky Mountain Institute, Government of India and Smart City.

Rodenbach, J., Mathis, J., Chicco, A., Diana, M. and Nehrk, G. (2017). *Car Sharing in Europe: A Multidimensional Classification and Inventory.* European Union: STARS and AUTON.

Roggema, R. (2014). *The Design Charrette: Ways to Envision Sustainable Futures.* Dordrecht: Springer Science + Business Media.

Ryerson Urban Analytics Institute. (2019). *How Parking Regulations Need to Evolve for High-Rise Buildings.* Toronto: Residential and Civil Construction Alliance of Ontario.

Sacchi, E., Sayed, T. and de Leur, P. (2013). A comparison of collision-based and conflict-based safety evaluations: The case of right-turn smart channels. *Accident Analysis and Prevention*, 59: 260–266.

Sadik-Khan, J. (2020). *Streets for Pandemic Response and Recovery.* New York: Global Designing Cities Initiative.

SAE. (2014). *Taxonomy and Definitions for Terms Related to On-road Motor Vehicle Automated Driving Systems.* USA: SAE International.

SAE. (2018). *Taxonomy and Definitions for Terms Related to Shared Mobility and Enabling Technologies.* USA: SAE International.

SAE International. (2014). *Ground Vehicle Standards.* USA: SAE International.

SAE International. (2019). *A Dictionary of Terms for the Dynamics and Handling of Single Track Vehicles (Motorcycles, Scooters, Mopeds, and Bicycles).* Warrendale, PA, USA: J1451_201909. Society of Automotive Engineers.

SAE International. (2019). *J3194 – Taxonomy and Classification of Powered Micromobility Vehicles.* Warrendale, PA, USA: Society of Automotive Engineers.

SAE International, J. (2020). *Electric Vehicle Power Transfer System Using Conductive Automated Connection Devices.* SAE International.

Saunders, K. (2017). *Where's the Hype for Automayed Trains? Part 1: History and Background.* Automation.

Sawilla, S. and Schütt, O. (2018). *Ipt-technology.* Retrieved from Wireless Opportunity Charging Buses in Madrid: https://ipt-technology.com/case-opportunity-charging-madrid/.

SCAQMD. (2000). *Multiple Air Toxics Exposure Study.* San Francisco: South Coast Air Quality Management District.

Schneider, C.G. and Hill, L.B. (2007). *No Escape from Diesel Exhaust: How to Reduce Commuter Exposure.* Boston: Clean Air Task Force.

Sclar, R., Gorghinpour, C., Castellanos, S. and Li, X. (2018). *Barriers to Adopting Electric Buses.* Berlin: World Resources Institute, WRI and German Federal Ministry.

Scott, A.J. (2014). Beyond the creative city: Cognitive–cultural capitalism and the new Urbanism. *Regional Studies*, 48(4): 565–578.

Shaheen, S. and Cohen, A. (2019). *Shared Micromobility Policy Toolkit: Docked and Dockless Bike and Scooter Sharing.* Schmidt Family Foundation.

Shaheen, S., Cohen, A. and Zohdy, I. (2016). *Shared Mobility: Current Practices and Guiding Principles.* Washington D.C.. USA: Federal Highway Administration.

Shared-Use Mobiltiy Center. (2017). *Share-Use Mobility Referrence Guide.* Chicago, USA: Shared-Use Mobiltiy Center.

Sheldrake, R. (2009). *Morphic Resonance: The Nature of Formative Causation.* Rochester, Vermont: Park Street Press.

Shepertycky, M. and Li, Q. (2015). Generating electricity during walking with a lower limb-driven energy harvester: Targeting a minimum user effort. *PLoS ONE*, 1–16.

Shladover, S.E. (2016). The truth about "Self Driving" cars. *Scientific American*, 52–57.

Siemens Mobility. (2015). *Sustainable Urban Infrastructure: Vienna Edition – Role Model for Complete Mobility.*

Smart Growth America. (2021). *Dangerous by Design.* Washington, D.C.: Smart Growth America.

SMC. (2018). *Shared Transportation Modes Dramatically Reduce Greenhouse Gases.* Retrieved from Shared-use Mobility Center: https://learn.sharedusemobilitycenter.org/benefitcalculator/.

Smith, R.A. (2008). Enabling technologies for demand management: Transport. *Energy Policy*, 36(12): 4444–4448.

Society of Automobile Engineers, SAE. (2018). *Shared Mobility: Taxonomy and Definitions in SAE J3163™.*

Spaen, B. (2019). *This All-Electric Water Taxi Could Revolutionize Green Transportation.* Retrieved from Green Matters: https://www.greenmatters.com/news/2018/06/25/qSvID/water-taxis-transportation.

Sperling, D. and Shaeen, S. (1999). Carsharing: Niche market or new pathway? *ECMT/OECD Workshop on Managing Car Use for Sustainable Urban Travel* (pp. 1–25). Dublin, Ireland: OECD.

Spulber, A., Dennis, E.P. and Wallace, R. (2016). *The Impact of New Mobility Services on the Automotive Industry.* Ann Arbor, Michigan: Cargroup.Org.

STAPPA and ALAPCO. (2000). *Cancer Risk from Diesel Particulate: National and Metropolitan Area Estimates for the United States.* San Francisco: State and Territorial Air Pollution Program Administrators and the Association of Local Air Pollution Control Officials.

Steer Davies Gleave. (2009). *GO Transit Lakeshore Express Rail Benefit Case, Interim Report.* Toronto: Metrolinx.

Stohler, W. and Giger, P. (1989). *Cost-Benefit Analysis of the Electrification of the Beira Alta Line in Portugal.* London: Institution of Electrical Engineers.

Stone, T. (2017). *Lessons Learned from the History of Car Sharing.* Retrieved from tiffanydstone: https://tiffanydstone.com/2013/08/23/lessons-learned-from-the-history-of-car-sharing/.

Stone, T. (2018). *Siemens to Demonstrate World's First Autonomous Tram Running in Real Traffic in German City.* Retrieved from traffictechnology.com: https://www.traffictechnologytoday.com/news/autonomous-vehicles/siemens-to-demonstrate-worlds-first-autonomous-tram-running-in-real-traffic-in-german-city.html.

Strompen, F., Litman, T. and Bongardt, D. (2012). *Reducing Carbon Emissions through Transport Demand Management Strategies: A Review of International Examples, Final Report.* GIZ China, Transport Demand Management in Beijing.

Swenson, R. (2016). The solarevolution: Much more with way less, right now—the disruptive shift to renewables. *Energies,* 9(9): 676.

Tactical Urbanism Guide. (2012). *Tactical Urbanism.* Retrieved from Tactical Urbanist's Guide: http://tacticalurbanismguide.com/about/.

Takefuji, Y. (2008). And if public transport does not consume more energy? (PDF). *Le Rail,* 31–33.

Tao, P., Stefansson, H. and Saevarsdottir, G. (2014). Potential use of geothermal energy sources for the production of Li-ion batteries. *Renewable Energy,* 61.

The Economist. (2017). A world turned upside down. *Renewable Energy,* pp. 18–20.

The Guardian. (2011). *19th Century Cyclists Paved the Way for Modern Motorists' Roads.* Retrieved from The Guardian: https://www.theguardian.com/environment/bike-blog/2011/aug/15/cyclists-paved-way-for-roads.

The Guardian. (2017). *Smaller, Lighter, Greener: Are micro EVs the Future of City Transport?* Retrieved from The Guardian: https://www.theguardian.com/sustainable-business/2017/may/11/micro-evs-city-transport-suemens-renault-green-air-pollution.

The TEV Project. (2017). *Tracked Electric Vehicle System. Reference Technical Booklet.* Retrieved from The TEV project: http://tevproject.com/.

Toole Design Group and Pedestrian and Bicycle Information Centre. (2012). *Bike Sharing in the United States.* USDOT, Federal Highway Administration.

Toronto. (2017). *Dufferin Wilson Regeneration Area: Interim Control Bylaw, Final Report.* Toronto: City of Toronto.

Toronto. (2018). *ConsumersNext: Planning for People and Business at Sheppard & Victoria Park –Final Report.* Toronto: City of Toronto.

Toronto. (2019). *Don Mills Crossing Secondary Plan, Offiical Plan Amendment.* Toronto: City of Toronto.

Toronto. (2019). *Laird in Focus, Official Plan Amendment.* Toronto: City of Toronto.

Toronto, C.o. (2013). *About Planners in Public Spaces (PiPS).* Retrieved from City of Toronto: https://www.toronto.ca/city-government/planning-development/outreach-engagement/planners-in-public-spaces/.

Toronto, C.o. (2017). *Parkland Strategy: Preliminary Report.* Toronto: City of Toronto.

Toth, G. (2011). *Are Complete Streets Incomplete?* Retrieved from Project for Public Places: https://www.pps.org/article/are-complete-streets-incomplete.

Transport Canada. (2009). *Bike Sharing Guide.* Ottawa: Transport Canada.

Transport Canada. (2010). *Bicycle End-of-trip Facilities: A Guide for Canadian Municipalities and Employers.* Ottawa: Public Works and Government Services Canada.

Transportation Services. (2020). *2020 Operating Budget & 2020 –2029 Capital Plan.* Toronto: City of Toronto.

TuSimple. (2020). *TuSimple Launches World's First Autonomous Freight Network with UPS, Penske, U.S. Xpress, and McLane Company, Inc.* Retrieved from stockhouse.com: https://stockhouse.com/news/press-releases/2020/07/01/tusimple-launches-world-s-first-autonomous-freight-network-with-ups-penske-u-s.

UITP. (2013). *Press Kit: Metro Automation Facts, Figures, and Trends.* International Association of Public Transport.

UITP. (2014). *Metro Automation Facts, Figures, and Trends.* International Association of Public Transport (UITP).

University of Toronto. (2015). *School of Cities.* Retrieved from University of Toronto: https://www.schoolofcities.utoronto.ca/.

US Bureau of Transportation Statistics. (2020). *Energy Intensity of Passenger Modes.* Retrieved from US Energy Consumption by the Transportation Sector: https://www.bts.gov/content/energy-intensity-passenger-modes.

US Department of Energy. (2018). *Alternative Fuel Vehicles.* Retrieved from US Department of Energy: https://www.energy.gov/public-services/vehicles/alternative-fuel-vehicles#/find/nearest?country=US.

US Environmental Protection Agency. (2008). *Heat Island Compendium.* US EPA.

Vasconcellos, E.A. (2004). The use of streets: A reassessment and tribute to Donald Appleyard. *Journal of Urban Design,* 9(1): 3–22.

Venugopal, P., Shekhar, A., Visser, E. and Scheele, N. (2018). Roadway to self-healing highways with integrated wireless electric vehicle charging and sustainable energy harvesting technologies. *Applied Energy,* 212: 1226–1239.

*Watch: Toronto's Surge in E-bike Ownership Creates Concerns over Safety.* (2018). Retrieved from Iheartradio.: https://www.iheartradio.ca/newstalk-1010/news/watch-toronto-s-surge-in-e-bike-ownership-creates-concerns-over-safety-1.3726810.

WBB Trust. (2015). *Parks and Playgrounds in Dhaka: Taking Stock and Moving Forward.* Dhaka: Work for a Better Bangladesh.

Weichenthal, S., Ryswyk, K., Goldstein, A., Shekarrizfard, M. and Hatzopoulou, M. (2015). Characterizing the spatial distribution of ambient ultrafine particles in Toronto, Canada: A land-use regression model. *Environmental Pollution*, 47(PT A): 1–8.

Weir, L. (2018). *Pina Bousch's Dance Theatre: Tracing the Evolution of Tanz Theatre.* Edinburgh: Edinburgh University Press.

Weißbach, D., Ruprecht, G., Hukeac, A., Czerski, K., Gottlieb, S. and Hussein, A. (2013). Energy intensities, EROIs (energy returned on invested), and energy payback times of electricity generating power plants. *Energy*, 52: 210–221.

Whyte, W.H. (1980). *The Social Life of Small Urban Places.* Ann Arbor: Edwards Brothers.

Wiener, E.L. and Curry, R.E. (1980). Light deck automation: Promise and Problems. *Ergonomics*, 995–1011.

Wilson, K. (2018). *An Overview of SAE International: Standards Activities Related to Charging of Hybrid / Electric Vehicles.* Ground Vehicle Standards. SAE International.

Wilson, K. (2021). *Bill Would Finally Give Bikeshare Transit Dollars.* Retrieved from Streetblog USA: https://usa.streetsblog.org/2021/02/02/bill-would-finally-give-bikeshare-transit-dollars/.

Wilson, L. (2013). Shades of Green: Electric Cars' Carbon Emissions Around the Globe. *Shrink That Footprint*, pp. 1–28.

Wolverton, T. (2016). *Wolverton: Elon Musk's Hyperloop Hype Ignores Practical Problems.* Retrieved from The Mercury News: https://www.mercurynews.com/2013/08/13/wolverton-elon-musks-hyperloop-hype-ignores-practical-problems/.

Woo, L. (2019). *Transit Oriented Development Implementation.* Toronto: Metrolinx.

World Commission on Environment and Development. (1987). *Our Common Future.* Oxford: Oxford University Press.

Xiong, H., Wang, L., Linbing, D., Wang, and Druta, C. (2011). Piezoelectric energy harvesting from traffic induced deformation of pavements. *International Journal of Pavement Research and Technology*, 5(5): 333–337.

York Region. (2015). *Transportation Master Plan: Recommended Policy Principles.* Newmarket: York Region.

Zhang, W. and Guhathakurta, S. (2016). Parking spaces in the age of shared autonomous vehicles: How much parking will we need and where? *Sustainable Cities and Society*, 19: 34–45.

Zielinski, S. (2006). New mobility: The next generation of sustainable urban transportation. *National Academy of Engineering*, 36(4).

# Section V
# Implementation of New Mobility

# CHAPTER 7

# Shifting Flexible Policies for a New Mobility Ecosystem

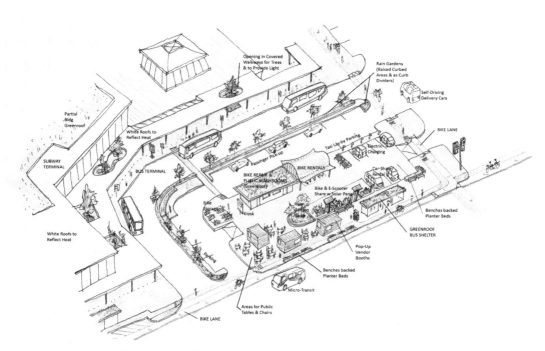

**Fig. 7.0:** An artistic illustration of shifting mobility policy implementation for a new multi-modal ecosystem.

> *"As the city filled with mobile strangers, even next-door neighbours became*
> *strangers. This is the story of the motorcar, and it has not much longer to run."*
> —Marshall McLuhan (1964)

## Introduction—Flexible and Shifting Policies

Regulations are perceived as a double-edged sword. The delicate balance of the adaptation of a new philosophy, new technology, new mobility modes, and public safety and security is a difficult task. The fast pace of new mobility entries, rapid development of new technologies, and disruptive moves by operators is pushing policy and decision makers toward blank, empty walls. Strains are now visible in new entities entering the market without permission and public agency attempts to ban new travel modes or technologies. None have prevailed. In the end, the best city building philosophy is apparent when everyone leaves the policy room with an unhappy face.

One of the root causes of poor multimodal mobility facility is intimately linked to weak policy structures and requirements by the public agency. Weak policy language and virtually no mandatory requirements for sustainable mobility modes leads to poor conditions for users. To the contrary, vehicle policies come with enormous detail. The extent of vehicle-oriented detailed policies and their mandatory requirements for infinite amounts of infrastructures through the growth or development process is overwhelming and often confuses planners and practitioners seeing a hardline contradiction between official principles and implementation tools. In contrast, the link between city growth and sustainable facility is nearly nonexistent. Multimodal is often pushed aside inferring sustainable mobility facilities are covered under the development charges or fees. This act is often referred to as 'double-dipping' even though it's allowed to 'dip' 10–15-fold for vehicle-oriented infrastructures through various planning processes. In reality, except for concrete sidewalks or basic trails, most sustainable mobility items are intentionally excluded from development charge assessment and the implement process. Even the items included in development charges are estimated without quantitative facility estimates since they were never part of the modelling or assessment process. For instance, standard minimum width is applicable in remote suburban locations where demand is low but transit corridors or centres or downtown areas need wider sidewalks. This extra sidewalk width and associated cost is not part of the development or growth estimate. Similarly, transit-oriented policy principles rarely connect the dots between city growth and transit supporting infrastructures, operations, and maintenance. Cash strapped transit agencies struggle to survive to cover basic operation and maintenance and remain empty-handed against user facilities, comfort, safety, and placemaking elements that contribute to higher ridership. The same is true for cycling and pedestrian facilities. New mobility systems are rarely even recognized in city plans. Therefore, they rarely showing up as policy language.

The policy gap between a city's vision and its implementation process is not accidental. It is an act of the Cartesianism principles of separating city building needs and ecology from mobility systems. Under Fordism culture, every little and seemingly useless vehicle facility is perceived as a must-have or necessary element for city growth and economic prosperity. Sustainable principles are used as cover but underneath considered only "nice to have" or "feel good" items. Late capitalism with the help of social media heightened this completely contradictory practice in normal social behaviour. To avoid these seemingly endless policy black holes, this book (and Part 2 of the series) includes sustainable mobility in every layer of mobility system development. This helps us to identify when, where, and how many things are needed for sustainable mobility when it is time to write effective policies.

The rewriting of legislation to bring the various laws covering different modes of transport into harmony holds genuine promise. But it will require a collaborative partnership between the different mobility agencies and service providers. None of the current mobility policies are inclusive to collaboration between partners. Fortunately, pilot tests are laying the groundwork for new federal, provincial/state, and local interim policies and byelaws. Proven policies could be applied in regeneration planning to scope out its strengths and weaknesses in the real world. Once tested and verified, citywide changes in official plans and policies to integrate positive benefits, new street design process, and mandatory requirements for developments would pave the way toward widespread acceptance of a new mobility ecosystem. Changes in capital plans because of new mobility ecosystem master plans are gradually showing how to incorporate new mobility ecosystem facilities and gradually remove excessive or unused vehicle spaces in our public realm. Learning from leading-city experiences, professional standards, and guidelines would gradually develop new standards for new mobility ecosystems. Adopting new practices, however, remains painfully slow due to a lack of institutional recognition and the near non-existence of training and learning resources. While social media and conferences are full of future mobility project examples and buzzwords, the shallow understanding of new mobility and its complex implementation layers should be addressed soon to avoid the default philosophical mistakes that led to the automobile-oriented city building paradigm that we live in today.

Effective and successful policy implementations are rare. The inclusion of the mobility ecosystem for all multimodal mobility however has started recently, with baby steps. The flexible mobility policy examples incorporated in this chapter for each layer of city building are a series of collections from real life policy examples written and assisted by the author for several Canadian cities and around the world. Resources like this book, and a new curriculum, is the simple answer to today's stagnant old-school mobility practices. The introduction and adaptation of these new applications through appropriate regulations, policies and the hard and/or soft infrastructures in the proposed ecosystem will likely eliminate current mobility gaps.

> *"If you've got to be evidence-based, and inclusive, and joined up, and consultative, and outward-looking, you can't deliver a policy in a week."*
> —Unknown civil servant mentioned in *Policy Making in the Real World*

## Complex Layers of Mobility Ecosystem Policy

City policies are often blamed as a bureaucratic barrier to creative city building. The blame is partially valid. The rest is the wild imagination of the unbridled capitalist view of city building. Traditional policy-making process is rigid, isolated, and mostly written or created by a one-sided view of city building. On the contrary, it takes time to create an effective policy that minimizes the negative impact on human, society, and environment. Policy effects are often indirect, navigate complex layers of ecosystem, and span over a long timeframe (Hallsworth et al., 2011). Effective policy is a combination of society, art, and science.

Private, non-government, and public agency policymakers suffer from a poor policymaking process, lack of skills, and the misunderstanding of the policy-making process throughout their entire professional lives. Policymaking is often referred to as "leaning on the job" without any systematic knowledge, training, or skills. It is common among policymakers to never go through skills and knowledge training in their entire career even though the impact of those polices can literally inflict a serious negative (Bartholomew, 2015) but often unintentional impact on a community or city, sometimes even at the countrywide level. Without skills and the knowledge of policymaking, policy becomes victim of a utilitarian ideology that is linear, rigid, and fragile in the face of changing conditions. The controllable sequence[1] of policymaking (ROAMEF, 2016) based on only 'rationality' avoids flexibility and treats fundamental values, events, and politics as external 'noise' that should be minimized. Evidence, fact checking, careful process, and implementation difficulties or challenges are often overlooked or not considered at all. These "common sense" approaches to public policy creation are often distorted by professional dogma, political ideology, and interest groups (Gormley, 2007). The influence of this policy- making culture eventually made its way into the urban mobility policy world. Its impact is now obvious, and clearly visible today is its one-sided vehicle-oriented policy view that has created our deteriorating city living conditions.

There are other meaningful ways to make successful mobility policy. This section provides overall highlights and examples of mobility policymaking examples from the author's past experiences and other resources that avoided the rigid, linear, and controlled process.

> *"Why are all the measures of transport scientist and traffic engineers to solve these problems not successful or generate even more problems?"*
>
> —Hermann Knoflacher

## *Fundamental contradictions of mobility policymaking and practices*

Every city develops its own future mobility vision. Policy is the measurable steps to achieve the vision. Effective and realistic action plans with funding and public works process makes it a reality. When policy falls short of understanding the city's vision (ORF, 2011), human and community needs, futile policy ends in status quo despite a 'spectacle' start of a new great vision.

Multimodal mobility acts as an ecosystem very similar to a natural ecosystem. Every mode and its elements are linked and depend on each other. This requires a 'system' knowledge (Hudson and Lowe, 2009). Most importantly interaction between the modes is complex and almost unknown to modern policymakers. On the contrary, the unimodal vehicle system only imposes limits on other modes and takes over other mode user spaces without considering interaction between the modes. Lack of system and interaction knowledge makes it impossible for policy and decision makers to create a new policy that addresses the growing negative influence of vehicles in cities.

Mobility policymaking suffers the same consequence. The relationship between science or engineering professionals and broader society remains[2] weak (Colombo and Karney, 2009) and convoluted by conflict of interest, bias in scientific advising, and limited perceptions (McComas, 2005) of new technology or infrastructure risks. This fundamental gap leads to the negative impact of policy or lack of making a real difference to greater society. Policy is supposed to change the process, approach, and affect real change in implementation. Instead, often mobility policies are full of shiny promises, buzzwords, fuzzy priority objectives with extremely ineffective goals or purposes. Almost all city policies refer to ineffective and meaningless policies for sustainable mobility, for instance, "encourage walking for all mobility infrastructures", "improve cycling facility", "create transit-oriented environment", "implement complete streets", "promote less vehicle usage". To the contrary, vehicle related policies are very precise, direct and provide every possible detail and direction for every planning process, implementation, monitoring, and funding the allocation process. The central reason behind ineffective policies for sustainable mobility systems is the underlying bias toward the vehicle-oriented system even though strategic visions explicitly aim to reduce the usage

---

[1] Linear policymaking that form government policies are commonly known as "ROAMEF Cycle" which consists of "Rationale, Objectives, Appraisal, Monitoring, Evaluation, Feedback". The UK Government recently abandoned this rigid making process in favour of a flexible, inclusive, and research-oriented policymaking process.

[2] Typically, in the field of sociology of scientific knowledge (SSK).

of vehicles in cities. If vehicle reduction is the fundamental policy, why do city policies provide the details of how to achieve the opposite and remain as vague as possible toward sustainable mobility targets. This rigid form of policymaking, in isolation and by a monoculture, around vehicles is a longtime practice of ignoring the possible the other sides and separating the policy from society (Maybee, 2009). The policy failure is a combination of lack of skills, experience, and systematic bias toward a unimodal vehicle system.

There is another dimension of ineffective multimodal policies. 'Modern' traffic scientists, engineers. and planners are very protective of the vehicle-oriented system built over the 70 years of the automobile invasion (Knoflacher, 2017). Any time a detail of a non-vehicle-oriented street design element and sustainable mobility planning makes its way to draft a policy, it is taken out almost every time by old-school traffic engineers. The logic is that only engineers know the system and they are not bound by the 'non-engineers' policy. Whenever there was a definitive target, in measures to reduce vehicle usage drafted in new policy, traffic planners always aggressively erased those measures or tried every possible way to block them citing they do not help achieve their vehicle-oriented performance measures. Logic was that the vehicle system can't be restricted by measurable targets, sustainable mobility can't have a better performance than vehicles, and sustainable mobility policy should be vague to feel like "nice to have items when possible" and so on. When a new experiment for walking, cycling, or transit became successful, traffic scientists and academics instantly pointed out the lack of research confirmation by an 'established' vehicle-oriented experts in the community. Even now with over two decades of scientific findings on sustainable mobility success established through repeated confirmation, it is still blocked by traditional practitioners inferring that "academic findings have no practical usage in the real mobility system". These numerous myths and folklore reflect the reality of a lack of evidence-based and scientific approach to sustainable mobility that typically exists in vehicle-oriented ideology.

> *"Successful policy is produced when evidence, politics, and delivery all come together."*
>
> —Policy Skills Framework, UK

### *Hidden layers of successful policymaking*

Creating policy that works for residents remains an enigma in cities. There are no sets of rules toward a desired end. But one issue is certain that most policy that treats only the symptoms ends in failure. Policy that treats the root causes of a structural system problem and lays out a plan to accomplish change gradually will always become successful. This is the only "magic wand" of policymaking. which comes only with the painful learning of the complex layers of the policymaking process.

A few skills are essential for good policymaking. It takes time, training, and practical understanding of the actual subject. Policy creation by professionals completely unrelated or with distant knowledge in the field invariably ends in absolute failure. The fundamentals of policymaking depend on key skills, for instance, an outward and forward-looking approach, evidence-based process, inclusivity, innovation, collaboration, and evaluation (Hallsworth et al., 2011). The last three layers of policy learning remain perennially poor skills attainment among public policy and decision makers.

Although every layer of policymaking is complex, some basic skills are simple. Three basic skills are suggested toward attaining policymaking knowledge: (1) analysis and use of evidence, (2) complex politics and a public decision-making process such as democratic path, and (3) delivering policy (Policy Profession, 2019). The policy competence framework is also very simple – professional skills, behaviour skills, and knowledge must come with working experience, deeper subject knowledge, and having qualifications in the same field. Finally, levels of policymaking start from developing knowledge, applying it in the real field to become an effective policymaker, and developing a strong policy crafting process, after successful policymaking from years of success in mobility planning and design (CSL, 2013). This is usually rare, particularly in mobility planning. Most mobility policymakers are politically appointed and come from completely outside of the mobility system planning. Often, they are a bureaucratic appointee from a "project management, finance or environmental management" background. All these skills are essentials for any system. However, just managing projects, whether successfully or running from one position to another position, is not an absolute proven path to good mobility policymaking.

> *"It's suggestion that policy can be made through a series of logical, sequential steps, with a clear beginning and end within a finite period, is a dangerous over-simplification."*
>
> —Michael Hallsworth

## Making Resilient and Effective Mobility Policies

Overcoming the ideological fantasy of today's ineffective multimodal ecosystem policy remains one of the fundamental barriers to creating an effective and meaningful policy for a low-emission system. Even if this barrier is removed, we lack the basic steps of a creative and neutral policymaking process that can reduce bias against non-vehicle mobility modes. Since the policy will be imposed upon a greater society, all forms of its impact and open discussion about its potential impact should be explored before creating it. Policy writing is not being an expert or good at writing English or the mastery of a language, but this policymaking dogma often leads to giving the job to a person who is good at writing but has very little knowledge or shallow experience in the relevant subject field. This situation is often exploited by external entities who have self-serving interests and twist the policy toward their own agenda. If all relevant formats, contexts, possible knowledge, and boundaries are given, actual policy writing can be written by anyone.

Successful policy is navigating the waters while touching every aspect of the policy connected to human or natural or social environment. There is the magical formula of connecting the greater society to the mobility policy except getting inputs from all sides, opposing views, different philosophical grounds, and considering all possible future scenarios. The policy should be tested against potential future conditions that may arise from resource depletion and environmental changes. Dialectic philosophy could resolve some barriers if an effective and practical process is adopted. As introduced earlier in this book, the dialectic process creates a debate using Socrates' style, brings in opposite philosophies using Hagel and finds contradictions based on Marx's dialectic approach to vetting new or old systems. But the objective is not absolute policy, rather applying a Lacanian approach to search for new equilibrium conditions in a society where the new policy could fit and will leave the door open for flexible planning, design, and facilities that can adapt to new shifting conditions. This book refers to the approach as "shifting policies". The fundamental elements of a shifting policy are not new, but rather a forgotten approach and buried under the utilitarian manufactured vehicle-focused era. From the author's real-world policymaking experiences, a few common principles emerged as a foundation for a successful policy making process.

### Precise and targeted policy

Unlike urban design or land-use policies, mobility policies come with only vague references to sustainable mobility modes, except the automobile. Precise goals with set targets worked well to build vast amounts of an unnecessary scale of vehicle systems due to policy's unscientific and lobby-driven nature. But despite its failure, detailed policymaking can be used for a better multimodal ecosystem. Policy for a new ecosystem needs to be specific and precise, with easily understandable targets to increase low-emission and sustainable mobility facilities, and gradually reduce or remove vehicle-focused unused or underutilized infrastructures or spaces.

## *Mandatory policy*

The rigid walls of today's vehicle system often resist a mandatory policy that targets vehicle reduction in various forms. If policy language keeps it as a voluntary requirement, it will never be seen as a priority. The elements of a mobility ecosystem that have been tested and successfully implemented need to be codified as a mandatory policy. Trial projects and piloted area success measurements, findings, and formats should assist in formulating policies while opening the dialogue with various departments and in a public forum.

## *Mandatory incentives*

A mandatory policy will require resources and funding for implementation parties or agencies. If the policy brings greater societal and financial gains, they should be able to come up with policy incentives. Various forms of incentives such as parking reduction, density bonusing, development fee relief, or priority in process are a few examples. It's counterintuitive and theoretically unfounded to create a rigid vehicle requirements policy then counters it with an incentive that is perceived as a false policy incentive.

## *Fair exchange of carrots and sticks*

One-sided regulations never work well. The receiving end of the regulations needs an alternative incentive to avoid perceiving new policies as punitive measures. Both mandatory policy and effective one to one incentive should be investigated under all possible impacts as well as checking the process before making it a formal policy programme.

## *Implementable green policy*

Social media has created endless and false chat rooms which perceive the green city in the wrong way. The most progressives planners and designers should shy away from them while writing mobility energy policy. Many cities (including Toronto and other large Canadian cities) developed green streets but very little found its way into a mandatory policy. It was created as an isolated and a one-off 'feel-good' fantasy. Instead, the mandatory greening of mobility spaces should be part of the "minimum one-third" policy rule to be achieved when streets, parking, and other mobility spaces are going through major reconstructions. Toronto and many other cities recently created mandatory development standards to enforce these mobility tools, but contents and extents are still insufficient toward the full application of a mobility ecosystem.

## *Implementable human activity policy*

The existence of human activity space and relevant policy is nearly non-existent. The past assumption that parks and isolated open spaces are sufficient created the reality of no-human activity space in many corners of neighbourhoods. A formal policy framework should identify the creation of one-third of human activity space between mobility flow and green space. Shaped and formed human space needs to be outlined in official plans to contemplate the numerous requirements for genders, children, seniors, and the countless divisions among humans.

### Policy evidence and transparency

The creation of a policy needs to come from sound evidence while combing art, culture, social, and environmental aspects of city life. Many vehicle policies were inserted with isolated and selfish beliefs of personal greed and labelled basic needs, but falsely. Ignoring additional separated lanes or storage space in suburbia for autonomous vehicles is the best example. Evidence and findings would assist decision makers in identifying the scale of new facility or services needed and apply mobility boundary limits where it becomes harmful to greater society.

### Policy detail and proof

Writing empty, buzzword-filled policy language by sustainable mobility supporters and planners has become the most difficult barrier to real progress. New multimodality needs to be identified clearly in each element with their intended scale, shape, form, facility size, safety, and comfort items. Often it is claimed to be "not possible", but it's because we do not have the knowledge, skills, and practical experience. The following lays out numerous examples of detailed policy that clearly spell out the details.

### Scientific principles and validity

Many vehicle-related policies include the completely unscientific approach to level-of-service measures that create a vicious cycle of oversized and wasteful vehicle infrastructure that cities cannot afford in the 21st century. Park-and-ride is another baseless policy that has no underlying logic or principles of increasing transit ridership. The same is true for the new mobility ecosystem. Electric mobility policies should not reply to industry direction to limit plug-in vehicle space and limit shared vehicles usage. Arguing both sides of a new policy will bring us closer to true policy language if the dialectic method is applied appropriately.

### Policy mapping

Policy remains invisible to the public despite the fact it's behind literally everything in cities. Some cities are making policies more visible with open data and interactive mapping systems. But it is still unfinished. All elements of a system need to be visually represented and clicking on those elements should show you where and how policy requires or restricts some mobility facilities or services. This will assist practitioners, consultants, experts, planners, or citizens in understanding more clearly in an interactive visual and typical facility or system illustration. Boston, Singapore, and some other small cities found new visual policy tools to make it easier to create or search for relevant mobility policies instead of having to read through thousands of pages.

> *"The philosophers have only interpreted the world in various ways; the point is to change it."*
>
> —Theses on Feuerbach

## The Mobility Shopping List

The theory only makes sense if it changes the city in "meaningful way", which is implementation when the ideas get tested, verified, and modified. The implementation of a multimodal ecosystem is not new. It started with the voluntary and ineffective travel demand management (TDM) concept. Despite every city having TDM programmes and policies, it has archived very little and has barely put a dent into single occupancy vehicle usage. Most successful programmes reached 5% or less reduction of vehicle usage. The key failure was a multicultural ideology that keeps adding infinite layers to the "alphabet soup" of mobility issues or items on top of the basic automobility systems which remain intact. Like multiculturism that repeatedly reproduced the basic inequality in the economy, these ineffective TDM multimodal programmes and policies tried to patch the damage inflicted by the underlying vehicle system that remains untouched. Faced with new low-occupant ride hailing and future autonomous vehicles that will increase vehicle usage, these gains will be wiped out and turned into another 'feel-good' effort to fix vehicle usage in cities.

Instead of a toothless travel demand policy, the author created a new tool to identify, quantify, and implement mobility facility requirements, policy, incentives, and restrictions into an extensive mobility shopping list. It identifies every little detail needed for all small or medium mobility facilities as part of typical development requirements or infrastructure reconstruction process. Table 7.1 illustrates an example of a detail of elements of the multimodal mobility ecosystem that needs a strong foundation to defeat dominant vehicle usage, but at the same time systematically and gradually reduces single-vehicle usage over two or three decades. Many of these items were originally proposed as part of a revision to the Toronto Green Standards. Some were adopted in modified form, a few in voluntary form, and most others remain under scrutiny and waiting for cultural change to realize their new mobility potential. Key principles on this shopping list are:

1. Expanding new mobility ecosystem ideas into specific elements including its context, needs, and implementation path.

2. Aligning overall city policies, and connecting the operational, maintenance, and implementation process for smooth integration into an overall ecosystem.

3. Matching with land-use context, built form, and mobility forms. All previous TDM programmes failed to connect with the context which became the root cause of failure.

4. It includes all possible existing, emerging, potential, and future mobility modes into the ecosystem.

5. It includes mandatory, voluntary, and balanced carrots and sticks, with fairness for both sides, i.e., mobility services' providers and public guardians of mobility systems.

6. The list provides equivalent incentives to entice practitioners, developers, and participants to consider multimodal options instead of vehicle options.

7. The list proposes gradual and systematic estimation of vehicle usage reduction instead sudden spectacular changes that often lead to backlash.

8. It quantifies with a proposed scale of development or construction changes to find the appropriate scale of vehicle replacement which keeps new systems in proper scale and size and avoids oversupply or undersupply of new multimodal facilities.

9. It provides application rates by linking land-use density to built or mobility form.

10. It connects to design options and creative ways of reclaiming space where the new mobility facility will be located.

11. It provides detailed tools for any practitioner to realize the process, quantify, create policy, develop a meaningful implementation process, and alter the current ineffective form of TDM programmes.

12. It includes both digital and physical mobility systems to create a 'physical' mobility ecosystem.

13. It gives detail tools and information to incorporate resiliency and the shifting mobility concept into every stage of the mobility building process.

14. It provides evidence and quantifies from scientific findings instead of playing guessing games with facility scope, scale, and size.

**Table 7.1:** The shopping list of multimodal ecosystem needs and requirements.

| SUSTAINABLE MODE CHOICE | INNOVATIVE MOBILITY OPTION | INNOVATIVE/ CONNECTED TECHNOLOGY | Current TGS Standards — Tier 1 (Mandatory) | Tier 2 (Voluntary) | Potential Strategies | Information Sharing — Real-time/Digital | Wayfinding/Information Package |
|---|---|---|---|---|---|---|---|
| BICYCLE | SHARED RENTAL (OR PRIVATE) SYSTEMS | Bike-share | Provide a public bike share location at-grade and program for visitors on the site. Specifications: Bike share stations must include a minimum of 11 docking points. Bike share stations may be provided on private property or within the public boulevard. Location and size criteria must be approved by Transportation Services, Cycling Infrastructure and Programs | | | Realtime Display | Signage/ Wayfinding |
| | | E-bike | | A9.2.5 (Optional) Enhanced Bicycle parking rates (Mid-Rise) Residential: Bicycle Zone 1 (1.2 per unit) Provide a minimum of 1.08 long-term and 0.12 short-term bicycle parking spaces per dwelling unit. Bicycle Zone 2: (1.0 per unit) Provide a minimum of 0.9 long-term and 0.1 short-term bicycle parking spaces per dwelling unit. | A9.2.1 Potential Strategies (Mid-Rise) Dedicated bicycle storage racks, bicycle lockers or cages | Realtime Display | |
| | SHARED/ SEMI-SHARED FACILITIES (PUBLICLY ACCESSIBLE) | 1. Secured Bicycle Parking or Bike-station 2. Shelter/Weather Protection 3. Enhanced Bike parking | | | | | |
| | | Shared/Pop-up Bike Parking | | | | Realtime Display | |
| | | Bike-corral (On-street Bicycle Parking in Public Right-of-way) | | | | | |
| | TRIP END AMENITIES/ROUTE FACILITIES | Shower/Change facilities | A9.2.4 Shower & Change facilities (Mid-Rise) Non-residential uses. Provide shower and change facilities for each gender consistent with the rate identified in Chapter 230 of the City-wide Zoning Bylaw | | | | |
| | | Bike Repair Station | | | | | |
| | | Bicycle Kiosk/Display/Signage (Route Information, Counter, Parking Signals/Signage) | | | | | |
| | | Bicycle ramps on stair/ramps, dedicated elevator, separate entrances | | | A9.2.1 Potential Strategies (Mid-Rise) Bicycle ramps on staircases Dedicated entrances to indoor bicycle parking facilities. Dedicated bicycle elevator | | |
| | PARKING | Bicycle Parking Rates | A9.2.1 Bicycle parking rates (Mid-Rise) Residential: Bicycle Zone 1: (1 per unit) Bicycle Zone 2: (0.75 per unit) All other users: Bicycle Zone 1 and Bicycle Zone 2: Provide long-term and short-term bicycle parking spaces consistent with the non-residential bicycle parking rates identified in Chapter 230 of the City-wide Zoning Bylaw | | | | |
| | | Long-term Bike Parking | A9.2.2 Long-term bicycle parking (Mid-Rise) Residential, long-term bicycle parking must be provided in a secure location, long-term bicycle parking facility or purpose-built bicycle locker controlled-access in the following locations: (i) on the first storey of the building; (ii) on the second storey of the building; (iii) on levels of the building below-ground commencing with the first level below-ground and moving down, in one level increments when at least 50% of the area of that level is occupied by bicycle parking spaces, until all required bicycle parking spaces have been provided | | | | |
| | | Short-term Bike Parking | A9.2.3 Short-term bicycle parking location (Mid-Rise) Locate short-term bicycle parking in a highly visible and publicly accessible location at-grade or on the first parking level of the building below grade. | | | | |

*Column groups in the original: OFFICIAL PLAN POLICY AND OTHER BYLAW REQUIREMENTS (Toronto Example); APPLICATION/GUIDANCE — DEVELOPMENT PROJECTS (Residential: Low-Rise, Mid/High-Rise; Non-Residential); SPACE/RESOURCE REQUIREMENTS (Publicly Accessible; Within Public ROW Dedicated; Shared Spaces/Lanes; Staffing/Funding; PUDO (Semi-Public); Private/Offstreet); INFORMATION SHARING (Real-time/Digital; Wayfinding/Information Package); DESIGN CHANGES (Bump-out/Bulb-out; Lay-by; Landscaped Parking; Pick-up/Drop Off; On-street Service Location).*

**OFFICIAL PLAN POLICY AND OTHER BYLAW REQUIREMENTS (Toronto Example)**

| SUSTAINABLE MODE CHOICE | INNOVATIVE MOBILITY OPTION | INNOVATIVE/CONNECTED TECHNOLOGY | Tier 1 (Mandatory) | Tier 2 (Voluntary) | Potential Strategies | Application/Guidance (bullets) |
|---|---|---|---|---|---|---|
| PEDESTRIAN | Demand-Only | Accessible pedestrian routes | **AG 1.1 Connectivity (Both)** Provide safe, direct, universally accessible pedestrian routes, including crosswalks and midblock crossings, that connect the buildings onsite to the off-site pedestrian network and priority destinations. **Specification # 1** Off-site pedestrian networks and priority destinations include: sidewalks, transit stops/stations, parking areas (bikes and cars), surrounding parks and open space, mid-block walkways, underground concourses, primary building entrances or other key pedestrian access | | | Low-Rise; Non-Residential; Publicly Accessible; Within Public ROW; Dedicated; Shared Spaces/Lanes; Funding/Staffing; Private/Offstreet; Wayfinding; Pick-up/Drop Off; Landscaped Parking |
| | | Walkway through the sites/blocks | | | | Low-Rise; Non-Residential; Publicly Accessible; Within Public ROW; Dedicated; Shared Spaces/Lanes; Funding/Staffing; Private/Offstreet; Realtime Display; Wayfinding; Bump-out/Bulb-out; Lay-by; Landscaped Parking; Pick-up/Drop Off |
| | SIDEWALK AND PEDESTRIAN SPACE | Sidewalk Width | **AG 3.2 Sidewalk space (Both)** Provide a pedestrian clearway at least 2.1 m wide, to safely and comfortably accommodate pedestrian flow. **Specification #2** The pedestrian clearway is the universally accessible, unobstructed, direct and continuous path of travel within the sidewalk zone. *A clearway greater than 2.1 m wide may be required at corners, transit nodes or other locations with high pedestrian volumes or pedestrian activity (e.g. at grade patios and retail uses). **Specifications #3** A sidewalk zone at least 6.0 m wide, measured from curb to buildings face, is recommended to support a variety of streetscape elements including the pedestrian clearway, trees, furniture, lighting, utilities, cafes, etc. that contribute to a vibrant and complete street. | | | Low-Rise; Non-Residential; Publicly Accessible; Within Public ROW; Dedicated; Shared Spaces/Lanes (○); Funding/Staffing; Landscaped Parking |
| | | Pedestrian Amenities | | | | Non-Residential; Publicly Accessible; Within Public ROW; Dedicated; Wayfinding |
| | | Tree/Streetscape Buffer (between curb and sidewalk) | | | | Non-Residential; Publicly Accessible; Within Public ROW; Realtime Display |
| | | Curb Extension, Green Bump Outs | | | | Non-Residential; Publicly Accessible; Within Public ROW |
| | | Median and streetscape | | | | Low-Rise; Non-Residential; Publicly Accessible; Within Public ROW; Dedicated; Shared Spaces/Lanes; Funding/Staffing; Private/Offstreet; Bump-out/Bulb-out; Lay-by; Landscaped Parking; Pick-up/Drop Off; On-Street Service Location |
| | CROSSINGS | Highly Visible Crossings | | | | Non-Residential; Publicly Accessible; Within Public ROW; Funding/Staffing |
| | | Midblock Street Crossings | **AG 1.1 Connectivity (Both)** Provide safe, direct, universally accessible pedestrian routes, including crosswalks and midblock crossings, that connect the buildings onsite to the off-site pedestrian network and priority destinations. **Specification # 1** Off-site pedestrian networks and priority destinations include: sidewalks, transit stops/stations, parking areas (bikes and cars), surrounding parks and open space, mid-block walkways, underground concourses, primary building entrances or other key pedestrian access | | | Non-Residential; Within Public ROW; PUDO (Semi-Public); Funding/Staffing; Realtime Display; Wayfinding |
| | | Pedestrian Waiting Areas | | | | Non-Residential; Within Public ROW; Funding/Staffing; Realtime Display; Wayfinding |
| | WEATHER PROTECTION | Covered Outdoor Waiting Area/Canopy/Awnings | **AG 3.1 Weather protection (Mid Rise)** Provide covered outdoor waiting areas for pedestrian comfort and protection from inclement weather. **Specification # 4** Outdoor waiting areas must include the primary entrance to the building or any entrance adjacent to a lobby. Coverings such as canopies and awnings should be capture for shade and weather protection and to mitigate bird collisions. | | | Non-Residential; Publicly Accessible; Within Public ROW; Dedicated; Funding/Staffing; Private/Offstreet; Bump-out/Bulb-out; Lay-by; Landscaped Parking; Pick-up/Drop Off; On-Street Service Location |
| | AMENITIES | Benches | **AG 3.2 Sidewalk space (Both)** Provide a pedestrian clearway at least 2.1 m wide, to safely and comfortably accommodate pedestrian flow. **Specification # 1** A sidewalk zone at least 6.0 m wide, measured from curb to buildings face, is recommended to support a variety of streetscape elements including the pedestrian clearway, trees, furniture, lighting, utilities, cafes, etc. that contribute to a vibrant and complete street. | | | Non-Residential; Publicly Accessible; Within Public ROW; Dedicated; Wayfinding; Bump-out/Bulb-out; On-Street Service Location |
| | | Patio Space | | | | Non-Residential (○); Publicly Accessible; Dedicated (○); Shared Spaces/Lanes (○); Funding/Staffing (○); PUDO (○); Private/Offstreet (○); Landscaped Parking (○) |

| SUSTAINABLE MODE CHOICE | INNOVATIVE MOBILITY OPTION | INNOVATIVE/ CONNECTED TECHNOLOGY | Tier 1 (Mandatory) | Tier 2 (Voluntary) | Potential Strategies | LOW-RISE | MID/HIGH-RISE | NON-RESIDENTIAL | PUBLICLY ACCESSIBLE | WITHIN PUBLIC ROW | DEDICATED | SHARED SPACES/LANES | FUNDING/ STAFFING | PUDO (SEMI-PUBLIC) | PRIVATE/OFFSTREET | REALTIME/ DIGITAL | WAYFINDING/INFORMATION PACKAGE | BUMP-OUT/ BULB-OUT | LAY-BY | LANDSCAPED PARKING | PICK-UP/DROP OFF | ON-STREET SERVICE LOCATION |
|---|---|---|---|---|---|---|---|---|---|---|---|---|---|---|---|---|---|---|---|---|---|---|
| | | Bollards | | | | | | • | • | • | | ○ | ○ | ○ | ○ | | | • | • | ○ | | • |
| | LIGHTING | Street Lights | AQ 3.4 Pedestrian specific lighting (Both). Provide pedestrian-scale lighting... | | | • | • | • | • | • | | | | • | • | | | | ○ | • | • |
| SHARED VEHICLE SYSTEM | CAR-SHARING | One-way Car-share | AQ 1.1 LEV spaces (Mid-Rise)... | | | • | • | • | • | • | • | • | • | | Realtime Display | Signage/ Wayfinding | | • | • | | |
| | | Two-way Car-share | | | AQ 1.1 Potential Strategies (Mid-Rise). Designated and marked parking spaces for LEV, carpool or car-sharing. | • | • | • | • | • | • | • | | | | | | | • | • | | |
| | | Peer-to-peer Carsharing | | | | • | • | • | | | | ○ | | ○ | • | | | | | | | |
| | | Fractional Ownership | | | | • | • | | | | | ○ | | ○ | • | | | | | | | |
| | RIDESHARING | Traditional Carpool | AQ 1.1 LEV spaces (Mid-Rise)... | | | | • | ○ | ○ | • | • | • | • | | | | | • | • | | |
| | | Dynamic/Social Carpool | | | AQ 1.1 Potential Strategies (Mid-Rise). Designated and marked parking spaces for LEV, carpool or car-sharing. | | • | • | ○ | ○ | • | • | | • | | | | | • | • | | |
| | | Vanpool/Shuttle | | | | • | • | • | • | • | • | | | • | | | | | | | • | • |
| | RIDESOURCING | Traditional Taxi | | | | • | • | • | • | • | • | | | • | | | | | | | • | • |
| | | App-based Ridesourcing Se | | | | • | • | • | • | • | • | | | • | | | | | | | • | • |
| | | Ridesharing/Ridesplitting | | | | • | • | • | • | • | • | | | • | | | | | | | | |
| | HIGH OCCUPANY VEHICLE (HOV) LANES | | | | | | | | | | | | | • | | | | | | | | • |
| | SHARED PARKING PROVISION (SHARED OCCUPANCY) | | | | AQ 1.1 Potential Strategies (Mid-Rise). Shared Parking | • | • | • | • | • | | | | • | | | | | | | | |
| SUSTAINABLE SHARED/PRIVATE VEHICLE USER | LOW EMISSION VEHICLES | Electric Vehicle and Plug-ins | AQ 1.1 LEV spaces (Mid-Rise)... | AQ 1.2 Enhanced LEV spaces (Mid-Rise)... | AQ 1.1 Potential Strategies (Mid-Rise). Designated and marked parking spaces for LEV, carpool or car-sharing. | ○ | ○ | ○ | ○ | ○ | ○ | ○ | | | ○ | Realtime Display | Signage/ Wayfinding | | | | | |
| | | Small Vehicle | AQ... Specification #6... | | | ○ | ○ | ○ | | | ○ | ○ | | | ○ | | | | | | | |

**OFFICIAL PLAN POLICY AND OTHER BYLAW REQUIREMENTS (Toronto Example)**

| SUSTAINABLE MODE CHOICE | INNOVATIVE MOBILITY OPTION | INNOVATIVE/ CONNECTED TECHNOLOGY | Current TGS Standards — Tier 1 (Mandatory) | Tier 2 (Voluntary) | Potential Strategies | DEVELOPMENT PROJECTS — RESIDENTIAL LOW-RISE | MID/HIGH-RISE | NON-RESIDENTIAL | SPACE/RESOURCE REQUIREMENTS — PUBLICLY ACCESSIBLE | WITHIN PUBLIC ROW | DEDICATED SPACE/LANES | SHARED SPACE/LANES | FUNDING/ STAFFING | PUDO (SEMI-PUBLIC) | PRIVATE/OFFSTREET | INFORMATION SHARING — REAL-TIME/ DIGITAL | WAYFINDING/INFORMATION PACKAGE | DESIGN CHANGES — BUMP-OUT/ BULB OUT | LAY-BY | LANDSCAPED PARKING | PICK-UP/DROP OFF | ON-STREET SERVICE LOCATION |
|---|---|---|---|---|---|---|---|---|---|---|---|---|---|---|---|---|---|---|---|---|---|---|
| DYNAMIC/SHARED TRANSIT | MaaS (transit) | Dynamic Transit Service (no fixed route) | | | | • | • | • | • | • | • | | • | | | Realtime Display | Signage/ Wayfinding | • | • | | • | • |
| | | Dynamic Transit Service (semi-fixed route) | | | | • | • | • | • | • | • | | • | | | | | • | • | | • | • |
| | Subscription (Paratransit) | Static Paratransit Transit Service (no fixed route) | | | | • | • | • | • | • | • | | | | | | | • | • | | • | • |
| MICRO-MOBILITY | PERSONAL TRANSPORTATION | Motorbike | | | | ◦ | ◦ | ◦ | ◦ | ◦ | ◦ | ◦ | | | ◦ | Signage/ Wayfinding | Signage/ Wayfinding | | | | | |
| | | Personal Mobility Devices | | | | ◦ | ◦ | ◦ | ◦ | ◦ | ◦ | ◦ | | | | | | | | | | |
| | SHARED/PRIVATE | Shared E-Scooter | | | | ◦ | ◦ | ◦ | ◦ | ◦ | ◦ | ◦ | | | ◦ | | | | | | | |

**OFFICIAL PLAN POLICY AND OTHER BYLAW REQUIREMENTS (Toronto Example)**

| Group | Innovative Mobility Option | Innovative/Connected Technology | Current TGS Standards — Tier 1 (Mandatory) | Tier 2 (Voluntary) | Potential Strategies | Dev. Residential Low-Rise | Residential Mid/High-Rise | Non-Residential | Publicly Accessible | Within Public ROW | Dedicated Spaces/Lanes | Shared Spaces/Lanes | Funding/Staffing | PUDO (Semi-Public) | Private/Off-Street | Info Sharing: Digital Real-time | Wayfinding/Info Package | Bump-out/Bulb-out | Lay-by | Landscaped Parking | Pick-up/Drop off | On-Street Service Location |
|---|---|---|---|---|---|---|---|---|---|---|---|---|---|---|---|---|---|---|---|---|---|---|
| **TRAVEL DEMAND MANAGEMENT** — Mobility Service Provider | | Transportation Management Associations (TMA), Smart Commute Program | | | | • | • | • | | | | | • | | | Realtime Display | Metrolinx Program | | | | | |
| | | Automobile occupancy rate increase, peak trip reduction, staggered work schedule/zone | | | | | | • | | | | | | | | | | | | | | |
| | Employer Travel Program | Compressed Work Week | | | | | | • | | | | | • | | | | | | | | | |
| | | Flexible work hours | | | | | | • | | | | | • | | | | Employee information package | | | | | |
| | | Telecommuting | | | | | | • | | | | | • | | | | | | | | | |
| | | Diverse travel programs (e.g. caregivers, shift workers, other vulnerable groups) | | | | | | • | | | | | • | | • | | | | | | | |
| | Financial | Road Pricing | | | | | | • | | | • | • | • | | | Realtime Display / Realtime Display | Signal/Wayfinding | | | | | |
| **GOODS MOVEMENT** — Shared Services | | Delivery Services, Courier | | | | • | • | • | • | • | • | • | | | | | | | | | | |
| | Transportate/Private Delivery Service | Accessible Loading (Special Assistance/Medical Services) | | | | • | • | • | • | • | • | • | | | • | | | | | | | |
| | | Courier/Service Vehicle | | | | • | • | • | • | • | • | • | | | | | | | | | | |
| | | Motor coach/temporary operator | | | | • | • | • | ○ | ○ | | | | | | | | | | | | |
| | | Off-peak Delivery | | | | | | | | | | | | | | | | | | | | |
| **TRAVEL INFORMATION SYSTEM** | | Real-time Display | | | | • | • | • | • | • | | • | | | | Realtime Display | Signal/Wayfinding | | | | | |
| | | Transit Map | | | | • | • | • | • | • | | • | | | | | | | | | | |
| | | Information Booklet | | | | • | • | • | • | • | | • | | | | | | | | | | |
| | | Trip Planner/App service | | | | • | • | • | ○ | ○ | | • | | | | | | | | | | |

*"COVID-19 has been likened to an X-ray, revealing fractures in the fragile skeleton of the societies we have built."*

—UN Secretary-General António Guterres

## Making Resilient and Effective Mobility Ecosystem Policies

The core belief of the vehicle system was that "not the science" but the new vehicle technology in the early 20th century would replace the "flawed and unhealthy" system that used to exist in dense urban neighbourhoods, particularly in downtown and heritage areas. And it promised a better life. Therefore, an artificial and structured system was forcefully imposed with a utilitarian ideology to deliver the "dream city of tomorrow" (LeCorbusier, 1929). As discussed throughout this book, along with logical and scientific findings, human mobility has very little or nothing to do with the artificial system that's been imposed over a century. Movement is one of our basic human rights and intricately linked to our simple and natural daily life in cities. When a human needs to find multiple ways, they use their primal features of species and utilize multiple tools for different kinds of tasks. Humans have been good at using multiple mobility options to travel geographically in varied environments since ancient times. It's still true today but lost under our unimodal automobile defaults. Despite a machine induced artificial environment, human intelligence is naturally inclined toward a multimodal mobility environment if mobility facilities and services are available. Multimodality is our basic movement identity which needs to be reflected in new city building policies and practices while reviving the old and ancient knowledge of human movement.

The vehicle made its way everywhere because of its abundance. Multimodal mobility must do the same with easy and convenient access through new policies. Unlike rigid and hard infrastructure approach to automobility, the multimodal mobility needs softer mobility landscape that reflects our social and cultural conditions. To make the multimodal policy the norm, it needs to reinvent the mobility supply process, find new partners outside of public agencies (like community, private companies, collaborators), practice new policies with targeted measures, test policies in new areas or locations, and finally adopt new practices through policy, and acquire new skills and knowledge including fresh new resources. This sometimes requires forceful and mandatory policies, sometimes innovative design, sometimes new experiments. And on the way to finding the right tools and policies, we ought to go through a rigorous testing, trial, and discovery process. This section highlights those successful experimental trials and later officially adopted official policies and explains the process of making those policies.

*"Use only that which works and take it from any place you can find it."*

—Bruce Lee

### Street network policies

The creation of human scale public streets and connection networks is a forgotten skill in mobility planning. Typically, architects draw random lines as 'streets' to make is it easy for vehicles. These disconnected, curvilinear, and circuitous routes work for vehicles, but do not work for mobility modes that usage "body energy" (Knoflacher, 1981). Humans need the shortest energy path while walking, cycling, or using a public transit system. Two policy examples of a fine-grained multimodal network are provided from Toronto's "area planning" success. At the heart of the first example is the light rail station at Don Mills and Eglinton Avenue. The new four corners "opened up" the system by increasing the number of access points and connectivity to the fine-grained street network. A combination of narrow local streets, pedestrian-only paths, cycling connections, narrower private streets, and station connections were utilized to develop a new fine-grained network. Systematic barriers such as rail corridors and grade separated interchanges were resolved with the innovative replacement of vehicle ramps with a multiuse trail or creating an active mobility bridge to overcome the grade separated barrier.

The second example contains a very dense street network with a focus on breaking the barrier of a cul-de-sac street and solving the absence of subway connections to the immediate neighbourhoods with a series of active mobility connections instead of typical vehicle-dominated street connections. Mandatory setback for Highway 401 had typically become a dead space but this area plan replaced it with a multi-use trail system to separate the polluted highway from residential neighbourhoods. Except for one street (Tippett Road), all other new street space was predominantly for pedestrian, cycling, or micro-mobility usage, with occasional local access for vehicles at selected locations. Both networks came out of the initial vehicle-based network proposed by developers and their consultants as the default choice, and were eventually completed through intense multimodal analysis, land-use and urban design scrutiny, a multimodal mobility ecosystem approach, extensive public consultation, and the eventual collaboration of all landowners in the planning area. Finally, instead of fancy toothless policy language, a fine-grained mobility network was intentionally developed and inserted as a mandatory multimodal network requirement into the bylaws of the area's urban structure system to transfer lands, instal these connections or links, or contribute funds as part of the entire area's redevelopment process.

---

**Multimodal Mobility Network Example**

**Creation of fine-grained street network**: "8.4. The planned public street network shown on Map 40.4 [see map below] Street Network will provide a fine grain of public streets and a high level of permeability for pedestrian, cycling and vehicular circulation, improving access to and from the Secondary Plan Area while creating new blocks that will be appropriately scaled for redevelopment." (Don Mills Crossing Secondary Plan, Toronto)

**Visual Illustration of Street Network**

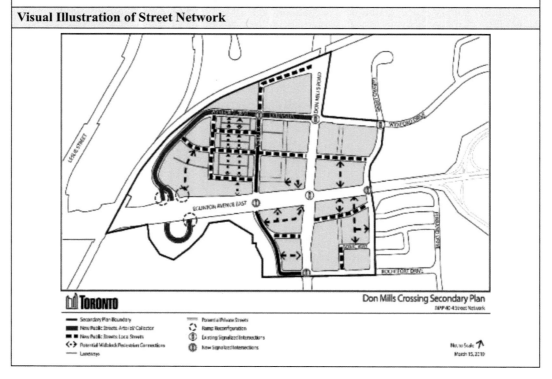

**Multimodal Mobiltiy Network Connectivity**:

"5.1. Transportation

5.2. Multiple connections for all transportation modes, particularly for walking and cycling south of Wilson Avenue, will be provided to avoid dependency on a single access to Wilson Avenue;

5.3. Pedestrian and cycling opportunities will be prioritized by securing east-west connections through the area to connect the Wilson Subway Station entrance south of Wilson Avenue to Champlain Boulevard and other local destinations;

5.4. Three north-south connections through the area south of Wilson Avenue to connect Wilson Avenue to the southern extents of the area will be pursued as shown on Map 3 [see below]". (Tippett Road Area Regeneration, Toronto)

**Visual Illustration of Subway Access Centred Street Network**

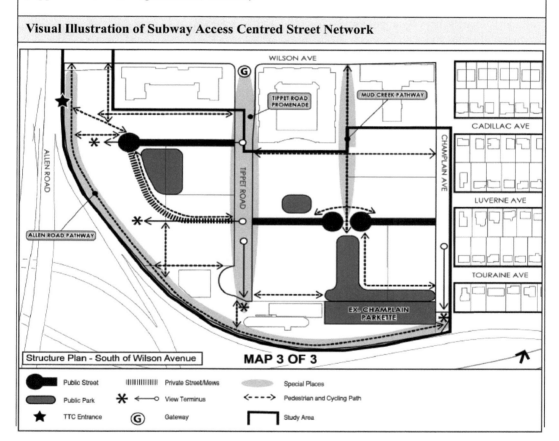

## *Multimodal ecosystem policies*

The common starting point of typical and toothless multimodal policies begins with tweaking minor elements or things to promote multiple mobility options without touching the existing vehicle system. True multimodal planning must start with reducing vehicle usage and replacing it with multimodal facilities. No one plan followed provides the facility as a voluntary charity or vague policy language changes the development requirements, therefore it should be mandatory but with practical, gradual, and consistent approaches. In the following example of a mandatory vehicle reduction policy, such as the 1970s Dutch approach, the author proposed mandatory vehicles reduction standards for new (re)development requirements. The idea was eventually adopted in modified form as part of Toronto's new green standards (City of Toronto, 2018). Based on six experimental multimodal mobility master planning projects in Toronto, two layers of mandatory and one voluntary target for vehicle reduction were estimated and inserted as a quantified reduction target. But other sustainable modes needed to replace vehicle reductions or total travel demand wouldn't reduce. Multimodal facility and travel demand management requirements would need to replace the vehicle reduction. However, this required a process change, so a requirement of multimodal assessment enforcing how to determine the scale, quality

| Policy to Mandate Multimodal Mobility Ecosystem |
|---|
| **Vehicle reduction standards** |
| **Mandatory requirements:** "AQ 1.1. Single-Occupant Auto Vehicle Trips Reduce single occupancy auto vehicle trips generated by the proposed development by 15% through a variety of multimodal infrastructure strategies and Transportation Demand Management (TDM) measures." |
| **Additional voluntary requirements:** "AQ 1.4. Single-Occupant Auto Vehicle Trips (Optional) Reduce single occupancy vehicle trips generated by proposed development by 30% through a variety of multimodal infrastructure strategies and Travel Demand Management (TDM) measures." (Toronto Green Standard Version 3) |
| **Multimodal assessment and facility assessment**: "5.1. Quantitative multimodal transportation assessments and site-related mitigation measures with functional designs shall be prepared for all development applications and future studies within the area that demonstrates sufficient and safer transportation infrastructure to service the proposed development." (Tippett Road Area Regeneration, Toronto) |
| **Mandatory development requirements for facility installation**: "5.10. New developments will provide transportation-related amenities including on-street parking and other street improvements and shared mobility spaces and programs for retail uses on all streets and in the vicinity of Wilson Subway Station including, but not limited to, pick-up/drop-off areas, on-street bicycle parking, publicly accessible spaces for shared vehicles or bicycle systems, digital mobility information technologies and transit supportive infrastructures/services." (Tippett Road Area Regeneration, Toronto) |
| **Hold development until rapid transit and multimodal facilities are built**: "1.1.3 – Development of residential uses may be controlled through the use of a Holding (H) symbol and permitted following the fulfillment of criteria to allow removal of the Holding (H) symbol as it relates to the provision of new public streets, infrastructure construction, implementation of higher order transit, provision of non-residential floor area and/or dedication of parkland." (Consumers Next Secondary Plan, Toronto) |

and resources was developed as part of initial area plans (City of Toronto, 2015) by the author. Once multimodal mobility assessment is done, additional policy is inserted to require mandatory, conditionally necessary, and additional facility installation by various stakeholders, especially city agencies and developers (City of Toronto, 2015). These steps in various forms, process, and assessment ensure all multimodal facility identified in the planning process will be eventually delivered by the area's development stakeholders.

## *Transportation and land-use interaction policies*

Mobility is a direct outcome of land-use policies. Yet the link between the two vital parts of city building remains out of the policy realm. Despite the known and established link between higher vehicle use due to sprawling land-use, land-use practitioners are extremely reluctant to connect these two worlds through effective land-use policy that would produce shorter lengths, local and greater amounts of internal trips. However, it's a completely fruitless effort to create sustainable mobility policy if vehicle-oriented land-use policies remain untouched. as a matter of fact, similar policies have been successfully transformed to eliminate vehicle usage at its root. While a few well-known vehicle-oriented developments such as big-box retail and car-dependent retail are harming area residents' quality of life, it is extremely rare to restrict such usage particularly in mixed-use areas. Prohibiting this toxic usage through city policies and byelaws (City of Toronto, 2015) provides a clear signal to developers what alternate mixed-use community they should be looking at for their land redevelopment. Subsequently, relatively restrictive land-use policy could prevent further

| Land-use and Multimodal Mobility Ecosystem Policy |
|---|
| **Prohibition automobile-oriented usage**: "3.2.4. New auto-oriented and large format retail uses are discouraged." (Dufferin Street Secondary Plan, Toronto) |
| **Banning vehicle-oriented land-usage**: "For the lands within the Dufferin Wilson Regeneration Area shown within the heavy lines on the attached Schedule '1' to this Byelaw, for a period of one year the following uses shall be prohibited: car washing establishment, gasoline station, motor vehicle body repair shop and dealership, manufacturing, contractor's establishment, custom workshop, car rental agency, parking lot, public self-storage warehouse, retail over 5,000 sq. m., service station, transportation terminal and warehouse." (Dufferin Wilson Regeneration Study, Toronto) |
| **Banning parking structure land-uses**: "3.1. Above grade parking structures are prohibited as stand-alone uses. Above grade parking structures must be ancillary uses on sites which contain employment uses. Where they are ancillary uses, above grade parking structures may not be located in the front yard of existing or proposed buildings and be designed to support and define the public realm. Active uses on the ground floor of ancillary parking structures are encouraged to support and provide amenity to the business park along the building edges defined by the Structure Plan on Map 38.2." (Consumers Next Secondary Plan, Toronto) |
| **Retail at grade at pedestrian priority area**: "3.2.2. To ensure Dufferin Street performs its role as a main street and focal point for the local community, as well as a meeting place for local neighbourhoods and the wider community, retail at grade will be required for new development at key intersections identified in the Priority Retail Areas Plan (Map 8). These priority areas coincide with a high order pedestrian zone, where pedestrian traffic is generally higher than the rest of the Secondary Plan Area, or where there is a concentration of existing retail. Retail at grade, although not required, will be encouraged on all other blocks." (Dufferin Street Secondary Plan, Toronto) |
| **Mandatory small blocks for active mobility environment:** "3.1.3. The large lots indicated on Map 2 will be divided into smaller scaled parcels with a fine grain of public streets to ensure a high level of permeability for public circulation and to encourage an appropriate scale of development for those blocks." (Dufferin Street Secondary Plan, Toronto) |
| **Mandatory setbacks for wider activity mobility facility**: "3.4.1. Consistent building setback will contribute to a vital retail main street environment and will assist in improving the civic and pedestrian experience. Building setback on Dufferin Street will allow for new consistent built edges with a more generous public sidewalk area and will reinforce the goals of the Transportation Master Plan in encouraging walking and cycling and will be no less than five metres." (Dufferin Street Secondary Plan, Toronto) |

deterioration of environmental quality and pollution and the most toxic forms of vehicle-oriented usage such as car wash, car rental, and surface parking related usage (Toronto, 2017). Stand-alone parking structures that break down urban fabric should be prohibited through policies. As a compromise, the specific policy in the ConsumersNext business park (Toronto., 2018.) allows a parking structure only if the ground floor provides active retail usage. An active ground floor parking structure was built in 2019, although this example of compromise may not survive the era of work-from-home. However, this compromise formula could temporarily transform all park-and-rides at reginal rail stations such as GO Transit's or along rail corridors in California. However, the recent transit-oriented approach (Woo, 2019) quietly skipped the possibility of lesson learning from the ConsumersNext case for activating the dead landscape surrounding GO Transit stations across the Greater Toronto region. Even the best mobility will be powerless if mixed-use policies remain vague due to a taboo culture of "not instructing" the development community on how the city would like to see greater community benefits by linking land-use and mobility performance on the same table. Mixing transit and associated land usage with retail, commercial, and other daily necessities would increase 'self-sustained' trips (Bochner et al., 2011) that remain within the same community. While planners often argue for a mixed-use community through citywide "mixed-use zone" policies, the policy requirements for an appropriate proportion of non-residential usage are still an unknown science. Grade-level retail policy requirement, particularly in pedestrian priority areas (see policies in the next sections) should be good place to start (City of Toronto, 2015). The requirement of small block sizes that by default increase pedestrian trips is another unique policy tool that should be part of any new area development. Pedestrian areas are often squeezed between buildings and the paved portion of the roadway. Besides reducing vehicle-oriented land-uses, an alternate way to widen the pedestrian space would be requiring setback without harming the human-scale size of the street. The success of these policies, particularly in North America where pedestrian mode shared rarely exceeds 10% outside of downtown, is a clear indication of how land-use policies linking mobility produce a better result rather than fixing mobility problems after everything is built.

### Eco-mobility hub policies

A new theory of neighbourhood mobility access using eco-mobility hubs developed by the author has been tested on a few planning areas in Toronto. This innovative concept of new neighbourhood planning, where policy requires mobility services or facilities around multimodal hubs, has emerged as a new planning form that addresses mobility inequality while eliminating mobility access deserts. A few policy examples illustrated in this section provide a sense of the implementation process that could be established through mainstream planning tools and process. The first example provides an eco-mobility hub in a business park (Toronto, 2018) where residential and other mixed land-uses were introduced. Due to unacceptable distances from future rapid transit at Sheppard Road, an innovative approach was essential to address the mobility access gaps. This process also ensures where and how future multimodal hubs would be located, and what scale of facility is needed. Once identified, it was easy to define policy and set up the requirements for development and collaborate and instal these new multimodal hubs. The idea was later applied to mixed-use residential neighbourhoods in the Don Mills Crossing area (Toronto, 2019) to test whether the same concept could be modified and whether eliminating mobility inequality could be addressed through a systematic planning process. The policy identifies a location that is attached to a new development and identifies types of mobility services that could be integrated into the new multimodal hub location. The third example is an illustration of an eco-mobility hub at the city's existing famous landmark museum that lacked mobility access from adjacent neighbourhoods. It provides directions regarding how a new multimodal mobility hub could be placed and planned, and how external development would provide the most effective multimodal options and vibrant placemaking through the benefits of new development process. Planning incentives such as a density bonus, process incentives such parking reduction and other benefits were identified though the Planning Act and the city's new green standards process. The impact of the new connection between the novel form of mobility access such as neighbourhood multimodal eco-hubs and land-use theory and associated policies that address social equity will emerge in the next decade when these planning areas are fully built in a new mobility form.

| Eco-mobility Hub Policy Example |
| --- |

**Creation of business park multimodal eco-mobility hub**: "6.21. To promote shared mobility and alternative modes of travel to reduce single-occupant automobile trips, "Eco-Mobility Hubs" will establish one-stop service points for multimodal systems including bikeshare, rideshare, and carshare facilities at locations identified on Map 38.11 [see map below] and as defined by the Transportation Master Plan." (Consumers Next Secondary Plan. Toronto)

**Creation of neighbourhood multimodal eco-mobility hub**: "At locations conceptually identified on Map 40.12 [see map below] development will incorporate multimodal hubs that include a mix of elements such as bikeshare stations, carshare spaces, high-occupancy vehicle parking, and ride hare hailing points. The exact locations, appropriate concentration and mix of multimodal elements will be determined and secured through the development review process." (Don Mills Crossing Secondary Plan, Toronto)

**Integration of multimodal hub with existing facility**: "4.4.6. (e) District Connector: "The District Connector will provide an opportunity to cross Eglinton Avenue East at the Aga Khan Park and Museum LRT stop, where opportunities for establishing a transportation hub could be integrated with the public realm to support pedestrian movement and provide access to bikeshare and other cycling-related amenities." (Don Mills Crossing Secondary Plan, Toronto)

| Visual Illustration of Business Park Multimodal Hub Policy |
| --- |

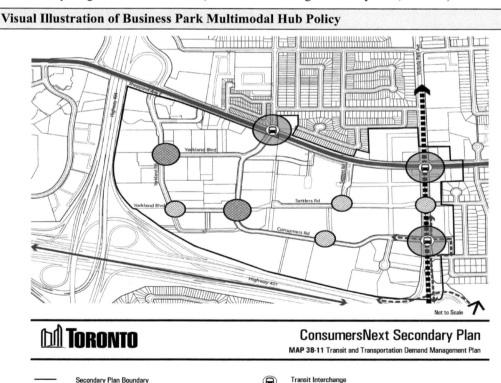

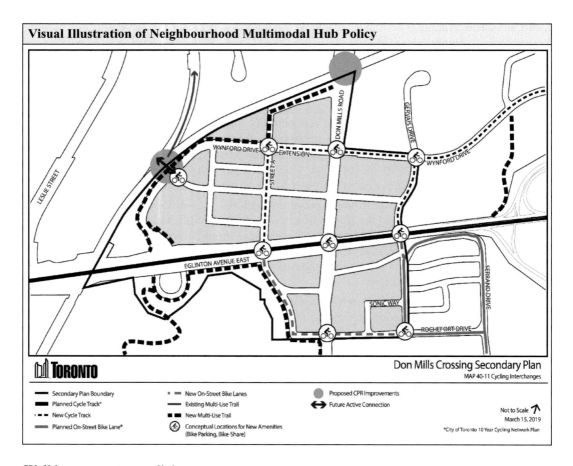

**Visual Illustration of Neighbourhood Multimodal Hub Policy**

*Don Mills Crossing Secondary Plan*
MAP 40-11 Cycling Interchanges

Legend:
— Secondary Plan Boundary
▬ Planned Cycle Track*
▪ ▪ ▪ New Cycle Track
— Planned On-Street Bike Lane*
▪ ▬ New On-Street Bike Lanes
— Existing Multi-Use Trail
▪ ▪ New Multi-Use Trail
Ⓢ Conceptual Locations for New Amenities (Bike Parking, Bike-Share)
● Proposed CPR Improvements
⬄ Future Active Connection

Not to Scale
March 15, 2019
*City of Toronto 10 Year Cycling Network Plan

### Walking ecosystem policies

The ecosystem of walking facilities and actual pedestrian needs, through policy, remains vague. This policy gap is one of the major causes of the lack of any walkable facility after a new development project is completed. To avoid these policy gaps, a new pedestrian planning process was developed and applied by the author. A few examples in this section provide how pedestrian facility, access, and safety can be achieved through specific policy requirements. One of the key concepts was developing a 'pedestrian-priority' area and identifying an associated facility that would make a place pedestrian-friendly. The first application was the Dufferin Street corridor (City of Toronto, 2015) where a higher-order pedestrian zone was identified in the mandatory mixed-use development areas to eliminate the possibility of surface parking lots and to instal pedestrian-friendly innovative and creative designs, particularly at priority intersection areas. Previously these specifics were omitted in fear of backlash from transportation engineers. However, engineers lacked planning and local knowledge, leading to a serious lack of communication while new projects were being completed without changing or improving pedestrian conditions. These new policy concepts highlighted creative design connections and provided clear directions to engineers and technicians as to how they should redesign the street when there are redevelopment projects or during major or minor road reconstructions that typically occur every 5–7 years. They also guided development either to instal these new design features or provide funding toward future street reconstructions. These specifics were later inserted into the City's new mandatory requirements for pedestrian improvements to make sure all new medium-high density developments build and maintain new higher quality pedestrian facilities. These polices resulted in numerous wider sidewalks, promenades, shorter crossings, pedestrian refuge islands, streetscapes, furniture, amenities, numbers of connections and walkways in addition to the City's minimum sidewalk only standards.

---

### Pedestrian Priority Policy Example

**Pedestrian priority and specific facility needs**: "7.4.2. High Order Pedestrian Zones are areas with high volumes of pedestrian traffic and where a fine-grained walking network is required to provide key connections for pedestrians. Locations where high volumes of pedestrian activity exists and/or are anticipated, shown on Map 7a as High Order Pedestrian Zones, will be provided with high quality facilities and amenities for pedestrians to:

a) Increase pedestrian safety at offset intersections;

b) Shorten pedestrian crossing with curb bulb-outs and intersection radius reduction;

c) Increase the width of sidewalk, pedestrian boulevard space at intersections, and pedestrian crossing to maintain acceptable pedestrian services; and,

d) Enhance street furniture, streetscape treatments, and pedestrian amenities to improve pedestrian and TTC user experience." (Dufferin Street Secondary Plan, Toronto)

**Pedestrian facility specifics**: "8.24. Along key pedestrian routes and pedestrian priority locations identified on Map 40.10 [see map below] Pedestrian Connections, the design of public streets will secure amenities for pedestrians such as wide sidewalks, protected crossings, pavement markings, seating areas, curb extensions, and bump-outs. Where pedestrian priority locations are identified along streets that include centre medians, these medians should be extended into the marked pedestrian crossing refuge spaces, where possible." (Don Mills Crossing Secondary Plan, Toronto)

**Sufficient number of pedestrian connections**: "5.4. Three north-south connections through the area south of Wilson Avenue to connect Wilson Avenue to the southern extents of the area will be pursued as shown on Map 3." (Tippett Road Area Regeneration, Toronto)

**Pedestrian facility specifics and standards**

**Mandatory Requirements**

"AQ 3.1. Connectivity: Provide safe, direct, universally accessible pedestrian routes, including crosswalks and midblock crossings that connect the buildings on-site to the off-site pedestrian network and priority destinations.

AQ 3.2. Sidewalk Space: Provide a context-sensitive pedestrian clearway that is a minimum of 2.1 m. wide, to accommodate pedestrian flow safely and comfortably.

AQ 3.3. Weather Protection: Provide covered outdoor waiting areas for pedestrian comfort and protection from inclement weather.

AQ 3.4. Pedestrian Specific Lighting: Provide pedestrian-scale lighting that is evenly spaced, continuous, and directed onto sidewalks, pathways, entrances, outdoor waiting areas, and public spaces." (Toronto Green Standard Version 3)

**Policy Illustration of Pedestrian Pirority (Dufferin Street Secondary Plan, Toronto)**

## *Transit ecosystem policies*

While all cities are encouraging transit development, policy specifics remain fuzzy with not clearly defined basic elements of transit-oriented principles. Many cities identify transit as the backbone of their mobility systems but turn their back on the supportive infrastructure and facilities that make transit successful. Transit lacks a link to the planning process, and to eventually capturing opportunities to build critical supportive infrastructure or secure necessary lands, resources, and financing. Even with development and growth generated by new transit demand, the lack of policy has resulted in no associated improvements for transit users or systems. As mentioned earlier, planners often deceptively argue that transit facility is covered under development charges and cannot be asked of because that would mean "double dipping" toward facility requirements from externals sources. Ironically, higher levels of transit usage and additional future density proposed by developers are not part of the growth estimate nor included in the development charges. Long term facility replacements, maintenance, and associated needs for last-mile connections are also omitted or ignored in the funding formula. This planning discrimination against transit systems ultimately comes up empty for transit authorities with very limited budgets or subsidized operations rendering them unable to provide comfortable, safe, and vibrant facilities or places for transit users. These policy gaps

---

**Transit Priority Policy Example**

**Transit priority measures**: "Transit priority measures such as HOV lanes may be implemented along Victoria Park Avenue to improve transit experience and reliability. Queue jump lanes will not be used to implement surface transit priority." (ConsumersNext Secondary Plan, Toronto)

**Interim transit priority measures**: "8.16. Prior to the implementation of higher order transit along the Don Mills Road corridor, incremental improvements to surface transit will be pursued including potential enhanced express service, bus-only lanes or other surface transit priority measures." (Don Mills Crossing Secondary Plan, Toronto)

**Bikeshare for transit**: "8.13. The expansion of the bike share network to areas around transit stations and public facilities will be prioritized to facilitate connectivity to and from these locations." (Don Mills Crossing Secondary Plan, Toronto)

**Access to fare-free zones**: "8.15. Development in the area should protect for the future extension of higher order transit along the Don Mills Road Corridor and future interchanges between the LRT and potential higher order transit extensions, including, where feasible, connection to fare-free zones and provision of amenities for pedestrians and cyclists." (Don Mills Crossing Secondary Plan, Toronto)

**Requirements for transit supportive measures**: "7.3.4. Transit supportive infrastructure, such as pavement markings at key stops, seating, street furniture and security features, will be incorporated into the design of such infrastructure where possible to support existing and growing ridership." (Dufferin Street Secondary Plan, Toronto)

**Mandatory connections for rapid transit station**: "5.3. Pedestrian and cycling opportunities will be prioritized by securing east-west connections through the area to connect the Wilson Subway Station entrance south of Wilson Avenue to Champlain Boulevard and other local destinations." (Tippett Road Area Regeneration, Toronto)

eventually lead to deteriorating conditions and declining transit usage. However, there is a remedy through a proper policy framework. This section illustrates a few successful and meaningful transit supportive facilities that were achieved through a difficult but strong and specific policy framework. Many cities are struggling to fix mega six-lane streets. Some cities such as York Region started a new policy realm that the region will accept or operate six-lane streets only if two of the lanes are dedicated to transit systems (York Region, 2015). Toronto added new policies to instal bus-only lanes through area planning policies. In some cases, interim bus-only policies were instructed before any light-rail facility would be built in the long term to make sure interim conditions enjoy transit priority measures (Toronto, 2018). A lack of policies for transit supporting facilities persisted over four decades of subway operations while no mandatory new connections, new sidewalks/walkways to stations were required from new city growth or development process. A few specific policies forced new developments to make underground and fare-free connections to ensure pedestrians could cross between neighbourhoods without having to pay transit fare again to just cross the street or access retail around stations, and to support new transit signals, shelters, amenities, associated bikeshare, bicycle parking, pedestrian crossing, and other connected facilities (Toronto, 2019). The purpose of these policies is to ensure adjacent development and future mobility projects recognize and identity facility gaps and collect funding before reconstruction starts.

### Bicycle ecosystem policies

Policy requirements for bicycle infrastructure often spark an outcry among practitioners. Even through vehicle policy requires almost infinite list of facilities to be installed, bicycle requirements have always been seen as 'additional' and 'unfair' as an external entity of city supply systems. Ironically, the development community and other agencies are regularly inquiring about bicycle facilities realizing they are always a cheap, easy, and quick way to reduce project costs and provide something sustainable through developments. Several new innovative policy innovations were proposed by the author in various forms to address this systemic mobility bias. Akin to pedestrian policy, a cycling priority area known as a "cycling interchange" was developed to identify priority locations and associated safety and design features to be built by operations, securing space, and funding from adjacent developments (City of Toronto, 2015). Additional bicycle demand is always observed in front of a building adjacent to station areas, key destinations, or trip attraction areas, however, bicycle parking rates and supply have not increased as per demand, in addition to high level bicycle parking or micromobility storage demand at rapid transit stations. Since these areas are not typically covered in the city's byelaw requirements, innovative policy can specifically provide directions to instal shared bicycles with enhanced bicycle parking rates (Toronto, 2019). Similar approaches are suggested for cycling interchange locations. Left-turning facility, safety protection barriers, and protected bicycle lane policies are added to clarify the types of cycling priority areas (Toronto, 2019). Some of these specific policy details were later formalized in the City's mandatory development standards (City of Toronto, 2018). Similar weather protected features, such as shelters, through additional bikeshare funding from the development process, were added to citywide standards. These new policy innovations changed bicycle culture and took the understanding of cycling user needs to a higher level of awareness. However, proper implementation of these policies and their application during real projects still has a long way to go.

## Cycling Priority Policy Example

**Defining cycling priority with specific facility needs**: "7.4.1. (c) Bicycle infrastructure and facilities will be appropriately planned and provided with all site developments as identified in Map 7b. Bikeshare facilities will be encouraged at all proposed cycling interchanges identified in Map 7b." (Dufferin Street Secondary Plan, Toronto)

**Bicycle infrastructure with specifics**: "8.25. Bicycle infrastructure and facilities will be appropriately planned and provided as identified on Map 40. 11, Cycling Interchanges [see map below]. At the identified intersection of cycling routes and near transit stations, bike share facilities and bicycle parking spaces are encouraged to be integrated into the design of the public realm." (Don Mills Crossing Secondary Plan, Toronto)

**Specific bicycle facility policy**: "10.10. Cycling interchanges, as shown on Map 4, Mobility Plan, will have seamless and continuous transfer for cyclists across streets by providing bike boxes and other infrastructure to secure appropriate turning movements for cyclists; 10.11. Cycling infrastructure and facilities, including bicycle parking and shared bike facilities, should be provided along cycling routes and at cycling interchanges." (Laird in Focus, Toronto)

**Additional bicycle parking above parking rates:** "AQ 2.6. Publicly Accessible Bicycle Parking (Optional): For all uses within 500 m of a transit station entrance, provides at least 10 publicly accessible, short-term bicycle parking spaces, at-grade on site or within the public boulevard in addition to parking required under AQ 2.1. Bicycle parking must be weather protected except when located in the public boulevard; OR, provide a publicly accessible bicycle shelter at-grade along the site frontage." (Toronto Green Standard Version 3)

**Additional shared bicycle parking**

"AQ 2.7. Bicycle Shelter (Optional): Provide a public bike share location at-grade on the site or within the public boulevard." (Toronto Green Standard Version 3)

## Visual Illustration of Bicycle Policy

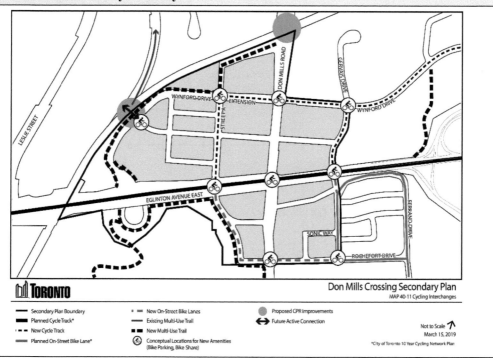

**Don Mills Crossing Secondary Plan**
MAP 40-11 Cycling Interchanges

Legend:
— Secondary Plan Boundary
▬ Planned Cycle Track*
▪ ▬ New Cycle Track
▬ Planned On-Street Bike Lane*
▪ ▬ New On-Street Bike Lanes
— Existing Multi-Use Trail
▪ ▪ New Multi-Use Trail
Ⓖ Conceptual Locations for New Amenities (Bike Parking, Bike Share)
● Proposed CPR Improvements
⟷ Future Active Connection

Not to Scale
March 15, 2019
*City of Toronto 10 Year Cycling Network Plan

## Shared micromobility policies

Active and micromobility facilities bring the highest possible benefits to a city and its residents. Full public agency support and collaboration with external or private entities is, however, key to its success. While walking and cycling policies are relatively widespread, micromobility policy intervention is rare. Policy interventions should be designed to improve public transit and shared bicycle or micromobility systems in general (Geng et al., 2016) rather than focusing only on restricting vehicles usage. Tailored policies should be targetted to specific groups or entities with a different mobility goal framework in mind. This section proposes a few effective and proven measures. Policy mechanism through

| Bikeshare Funding Policy Example |
|---|
| **Development funding for bikeshare** |
| "The owner shall pay to the City of Toronto $100,000.00, indexed upwardly in accordance with the Statistics Canada Non-Residential Construction Price Index for Toronto for the period from the date of the execution of the Section 37 Agreement to the date of payment to the City of Toronto, for bicycle share stations within Ward 19, as may be determined by the Chief Planner and Executive Director, City Planning Division, in consultation with the Ward Councillor." (Typical development funding requirement example from City of Toronto) |

the various layers of the planning process is one of the easiest venues to address this gap. For instance, secondary or area plans shall strengthen the bikeshare policies for funding and create space within the right-of-way as part of multimodal and travel demand measures. Identical to how bike parking is provided under the City's planning Act, the dockless scooter, moped, bikeshare space, operational, maintenance and funding requirements are common planning mechanisms. A few planning mechanisms are: (1) community benefits sections under the city planning Act (e.g., Section 37 or 45 in Toronto); (2) inclusion of conditions in development disputed court rulings; (3) replacing vehicle parking with micromobility or shared bicycle space and facilities in "committee of adjustment" decisions; (4) site plan requirements for travel demand measures policy; and (5) mandatory citywide standards. One of the common constraints of micro-mobility is new funding sources. Through the development review process funding requirements can be added (see example in box). The financial department would act as a liaison between departments, collect and deposit micro-mobility funds into accounts like community benefits funds (such as Section 37 funds in Toronto). And later the micro-mobility/bikeshare/cycling unit would be notified to coordinate with the planning department and release the funding for citywide improvements. Similar process is currently underway in the US for a countrywide funding mechanism for shared bicycle and micromobility facilities (Wilson, 2021). These funds could be used for existing or future facility expansion. After the funds sit for a few years and collect interest, they are made available to bike share/micromobility systems when the active mobility operations unit implements a project. It can be used for purchasing new bicycles or scooters or to develop or modify facilities for public-private collaboration projects. These processes, policies, and mechanisms ensure an entire active mobility ecosystem is built through future city projects and access to sufficient resources are available to implement those projects.

## Space reclaiming policies

Reclaiming space usually faces harsh criticism from traffic operations and the old-school traffic engineering community. However, area needs tell a different story. Unused space in different mobility facilities can be identified (as described in the last chapter) but specific policy would provide directions as to how to redesign those places. A couple of policy examples are provided in this section. Many old highway interchanges built with outdated engineering standards, and the need for those facilities will disappear when a mixed-use community is built. Instead of leaving setback areas as abandoned spaces along highway corridors or interchanges, reclaimed areas could be used for wider and safer multi-use trails and converted into linear public parks. Similarly, many residential intersections and streets were built using highway standards in the 1960s. Right-turn lanes and islands, oversized lanes, and unused curb space are common examples. Through appropriate policies, traffic operations would remove these unused and expensive vehicle spaces to recover them for wider sidewalks, bike lanes, and for additional green spaces or mini parks for the disadvantaged community who has suffered greater negative impact of vehicles over the last few decades. These policies are

---

**Vehicle Spaces Reclaim Example**

**Highway interchange reclaim**: "4.4.4. (e) Wynford Drive Extension: The existing ramps at Eglinton Avenue East will be reconfigured with redundant ramps removed to provide space for pedestrians and cyclists while facilitating safe movements of vehicles to and from the Wynford Drive Extension." (Don Mills Crossing Secondary Plan, Toronto)

**Unused vehicle space reclaim**: "4.4.5. (d) District Connector: improvements to pedestrian and cycling facilities along the District Connector will provide a safer environment for these users, including but not limited to the removal of channelized turning lanes; the addition of cycling lanes; the widening of sidewalks; the provision of public art; and, consistency in lighting, paving and street furniture." (Don Mills Crossing Secondary Plan, Toronto)

---

fiercely opposed by traditional traffic operations but it's time to override our outdated street design elements and practices with safer, better, and cheaper active mobility facilities.

## Shared vehicle and parking policies

Policy conflict between private vehicle parking space for high-occupant shared vehicles or ride facilities are gradually intensifying as new mobility usage and demand are maturing toward a greater share of modes. Parking policies for vehicles were the most corrosive and discriminatory policies ever devised by cities (ORF, 2011) when 95% of these spaces remain unused while city residents have no human activity space left to enjoy urban life. The first step to reversing this outdated parking policy is reducing demand especially for ancillary land-uses and introducing shared parking policy. The second step is to create or redesign curb space using greening techniques introduced earlier in this chapter, since on-street space is utilized multiple times a day, is open for shared vehicles, and is close to adjacent land-use, easily

---

**Shared Vehicle Policy Example**

**Parking reduction**: "7.5.5. Parking requirements for development which includes at-grade retail on Typical Avenue Blocks identified in Map 2, may be reduced at the City's discretion. Reductions in parking will be considered based on contributions to the implementation of the TDM measures identified in the Dufferin Street Transportation Master Plan and other sustainable transportation mobility options and facilities." (Dufferin Street Secondary Plan, Toronto)

**Parking reduction for TDM measures**: "8.30. Parking requirements may be reduced at the City's discretion. These reductions will be considered on a site-by-site basis including a review of how reductions in parking requirements could contribute to advancing TDM measures identified in TDM plans." (Don Mills Crossing Secondary Plan, Toronto)

**On-street parking and pedestrian safety buffer requirements for retail**: "7.5.4. On- street parking will be permitted, where appropriate, to enhance street activity, serve at-grade retail uses, provide a buffer between vehicular traffic and sidewalks, create a desirable pedestrian environment, and contribute to the neighbourhood parking supply." (Dufferin Street Secondary Plan, Toronto)

maintained, and accessible to locations. The creation of curbside management was proposed by the author, and initially rejected, but later a full unit was born during the Covid-19 pandemic in Toronto. One of the earliest ideas was proposed through area plan policies to create curbside management to reuse curb spaces, make them greener and safer and at the same time generate new revenue sources that won't evaporate as shared mobility usage increases. Replacement of general parking for shared vehicles, bicycles and micromobility through public parking authority mandate initially faced fierce opposition but is gradually being implemented now in Toronto and many other North American and European cities. Since shared vehicle and shared ride facilities reduce parking demand, typical parking spaces can be drastically reduced, and the remaining could be used for the storage of shared vehicles. These alternate uses of parking spaces or parking structures finally attracted mainstream development's attention (Ryerson Urban Analytics Institute, 2019) following many successes in North York and elsewhere in the city. Finally, citywide development standards were adopted to formalize these

**Creation of curbside management**: "8.32. Where on-street parking is permitted, curbside management strategies will be pursued, where appropriate, to reserve space for bike sharing stations and/or on-street parking of car sharing." (Don Mills Crossing Secondary Plan, Toronto)

**Shared vehicle and carpool requirements**:

"7.5.3. New parking facilities will generally be provided below-grade as part of new development and will be organized to reflect sustainable transportation goals, such as providing designated carsharing spaces and priority parking for eco-friendly and carpooling vehicles." (Dufferin Street Secondary Plan, Toronto)

**Replace parking for shared vehicles**: "8.31. New parking facilities, provided below-grade as part of new development, will be organized to reflect TDM Plan measures and sustainable transportation goals such as providing designated priority spaces for carshare vehicles, car-pool vehicles, or bike share stations." (Don Mills Crossing Secondary Plan, Toronto)

**Creation of shared vehicle spaces:** "AQ 1.2. LEV and Sustainable Mobility Spaces: If providing more than the minimum parking required under the Zoning Byelaw, the excess spaces must be dedicated priority parking spaces for low-emitting vehicles (LEV), carpooling/ridesharing or for publicly accessible spaces dedicated to shared vehicle systems such as carsharing, ridesharing, or micromobility systems." (Toronto Green Standard Version 3)

**Public parking for shared vehicle and bicycle**: "10.16. Integrate, where appropriate, Toronto Parking Authority facilities in development below-grade near the Eglinton Crosstown LRT Station and implement TDM and shared mobility elements such as carshare and shared bike facilities to reduce parking demand." (Laird in Focus, Toronto)

shared vehicle and active mobility facilities to replace private vehicle spaces in Toronto and inspired many other cities around the world. But parking elimination and its replacement with shared and low-emission mobility has a long way to go to overturn more than 40% of city land dedicated to unused, underutilized, and empty parking spaces.

## Street redesign policies

Akin to traffic operations, the old-school engineering profession initially resisted instructions to redesign streets toward greater public benefits. However, narrow professional dogma has no place in the 21st century's intense urbanization and space-constrained era. Several new approaches were developed by the author for Toronto areas in addition to typical and sometimes ineffective complete street approaches that lacked detail in the implementation process. The first step is to provide overall guidance on how to redesign new public streets or modify existing streets into complete streets and apply the green mobility and human space concepts introduced in his book. The second step is making consistent designs for narrow alleyways, private streets, driveways, and walkways like public streets, so everyone benefits from the new design changes. The third idea is to provide specific creative design elements for specific streets, including locations, particularly maintaining design consistency with rapid transit routes. Identifying additional invisible space and redesigning those places specifically would force engineers to rethink how the future street should look like. Median and landscape redesign is the next step of street design transformation. This list is long, but these examples illustrate why streets and mobility public space designing should not be left only with engineers or technicians who do not always have the vision, know the needs, nor listen to the horrifying safety stories from local communities.

---

**Street Redesign Policy Example**

**Street redesign policy for all users**: "8.7. Existing and new streets will include facilities for pedestrians, cyclists, transit users, and shared mobility users within the public right-of-way as well as landscaping as guided by the policies of this Secondary Plan." (Don Mills Crossing Secondary Plan, Toronto)

**Direction for design private streets/laneways:** "8.9. Private streets and laneways, where appropriate, will be publicly accessible, and will be designed to function as public streets and provide connections with the public realm." (Don Mills Crossing Secondary Plan, Toronto)

**Street tree requirements**: "4.4. Trees will be planted on both sides of all new or existing streets in the Secondary Plan Area as part of a development proposal and will be designed consistently with the Dufferin Street Urban Design Guidelines." (Dufferin Street Secondary Plan, Toronto)

**Median landscape requirements**: "4.2. Landscaped medians will be implemented to facilitate vehicular access and regress at appropriate locations to improve overall traffic flow. Transit priority measures will be provided where possible and appropriate to enhance transit users' experience." (Dufferin Street Secondary Plan, Toronto)

**Invisible space and elements for street redesign**: "5.7. Laird Drive will be an enhanced main street to accommodate: (i) safe and separated cycling facilities; (ii) gateways with public realm enhancements within the right-of-way to achieve high quality civic outdoor amenity spaces; and (iii) curb extensions on local streets adjacent to Laird Drive will provide additional space for pedestrians and landscaping." (Laird in Focus, Toronto)

**Travel lane and street narrowing policy**: "10.6 - The planned street network will connect to the surrounding street system to: (i) provide safe and convenient pedestrian and cycling routes; (ii) link key destinations within and beyond the area and provide direct connections to the Eglinton Crosstown LRT Station; and (iii) narrow existing and planned roadway lane widths to minimize pedestrian crossing distances." (Laird in Focus, Toronto)

## *Mobility energy policies*

Mobility energy remains outside of the typical mobility demand and supply process as cities develop master plans or future operational or infrastructure strategies. However, because electrification and alternate energy have now come into the city's priorities and vision, mobility practitioners cannot stay silent. One of the most common examples of mobility energy policy emerged recently with the replacing of private vehicle space with electric shared vehicle space. Several North American cities such as Vancouver and Seattle, have pioneered the mobility energy policy following widespread success in Europe and East Asia. The author introduced a new mobility energy policy as a new development standard for citywide policy that provides specific guidance to the proportion of spaces needed to be 'plugged-in' and provided options through a mandatory and additional voluntary policy mechanism. However, the many mobility energy policy mechanisms proposed in Chapter 9 of this book remain to be implemented through future city policy changes.

| Mobility Energy Policy Example |
| --- |
| **Electric vehicle standards** |
| **Mandatory requirements:** "AQ 1.3. Electric Vehicle Infrastructure: Design the building to provide 20% of the parking spaces with electric vehicle supply equipment (EVSE). The remaining parking spaces must be designed to permit future EVSE installation." |
| **Mandatory requirements** "AQ 1.5. Electric Vehicle Infrastructure (Optional): Design the buildings to provide 25% of the parking spaces with electric vehicle supply equipment (EVSE). The remaining parking spaces must be designed to permit future EVSE installation." (Toronto Green Standard Version 3) |

## Street culture policies

Street culture is an entirely new policy realm for many city building practitioners. Like mobility energy, mobility planners remain silent about the cultural and social needs of street space while writing new mobility policies. However, urban designers, landscape architects, and planners are pioneering street culture policies through city plans and planning mechanisms. The requirement of local cultural display and heritage preservation is one of the finest examples in Toronto. Requiring mandatory installation and funding for public art in building setback or public space is a unique policy creation in Toronto but gaining ground across other adjacent municipalities. But it needs to go still further to incorporate the human space concept detailed in this book.

| Street Culture Policy Example |
| --- |
| **Cultural space on mobility facilities**: "5.24. Any required rail safety, air quality and noise/vibration mitigation structures or other measures such as berms and noise walls must be of a high design quality. Berms should be landscaped and maintained and opportunities for murals and community artwork should be pursued on the face of noise walls and other structures which are visible from the public realm." (Don Mills Crossing Secondary Plan, Toronto) |
| **Public art on street requirements**: "4.3. Public art is highly encouraged as part of the Dufferin Landscape Gateway, in parks, urban plazas, street boulevards, and other private open spaces." (Dufferin Street Secondary Plan, Toronto) |

## Mobility access and safety policies

Mobility safety remains one of the most controversial sources of intense conflicts between the old-school traffic engineering community and those who have lost loved family members because of traffic operation and design violence (Smart Growth America, 2021). Despite the nations-wide outcry and thousands of safety reports that identified severely flawed and outdated street and highway design elements, policy to reverse safety outcomes remains relatively scarce. Vision Zero is progressing slowly but its fundamental principles are rarely inserted into the systematic planning and city building process. This section illustrates how to reverse outdated and flawed design principles and assumptions of typical old-school engineering practice with creative design principles. Intersection safety becomes the centre of the first safety policy changes. During area planning review, the author and many progressive planners came to realize the severe safety consequences of families of those communities. Hence, direct design and modification was proposed with funding requirement from the development process to fix the decade-old safety problems. Minimizing conflict between vehicle and active mobility users particularly inside and around buildings is another policy area that was enforced by mandatory safety changes. Similarly, the policy was tested in several communities to address age-old problems of traffic infiltration through creative design elements. Goods' delivery often induces additional safety problems to vulnerable users, so general goods movement and mobility delivery policies were tested to address common safety problems. Like safety, improving physical and digital access remains another vague area in mobility policies. Following the Seattle example of digital information and real time display, the author introduced multiple mobility options display requirements in Toronto that are now receiving widespread recognition and being applied elsewhere in Canada and the US. However,

---

**Mandatory Mobility Safety Policy Example**

**Location of vehicle to minimize conflict for pedestrians:** "7.2.6. A system of public laneways, shared private driveways and mews should be introduced to ensure service vehicles and parking access, to facilitate internal block circulation for vehicles and pedestrians and minimize impact to the Dufferin Street streetscape and cycling infrastructure." (Dufferin Street Secondary Plan, Toronto)

**Minimize conflict with service vehicle:** "7.2.5. Access and servicing to development from new or existing local and collector streets will be encouraged. The impact of driveways, garages, and parking areas will be minimized by locating them at the side or back of buildings, or underground." (Dufferin Street Secondary Plan, Toronto)

**Mandatory intersection safety policy:** "5.6. Safety and public realm improvements including the provision of shorter crossing distances for pedestrians at the intersection of Tippett Road and Wilson Avenue will be identified for all developments on lands designated Mixed Use Areas." (Tippett Road Area Regeneration, Toronto)

**Traffic infiltration and safety requirements:** "5.8. All new developments on Champlain Boulevard will contribute to pedestrian and cycling improvements by providing appropriate landscaped medians, highly visible and shorter crossings, on-street parking with planted buffers or curb extensions and wider sidewalks, sufficient intersection capacity and design features to reduce negative impacts of vehicles on existing residential communities east of Champlain Boulevard." (Tippett Road Area Regeneration, Toronto)

**Intersection safety policy:** "10.8. At key pedestrian connections, and at other intersections as necessary, the intersections should provide high quality facilities and amenities, including but not limited to the following: (i) removal of channelized traffic islands where possible; (ii) shortened pedestrian crossings with curb extensions and intersection radius reduction; (iii) wider crosswalks at the crossings where anticipated high pedestrian volumes will occur; and (iv) the provision of enhanced street furniture, streetscape treatments, and pedestrian amenities." (Laird in Focus, Toronto)

**Real-time travel information policy:** "10.17. Encourage transit usage through development by providing development-related transit benefits such as real-time arrival display boards and direct connections to the Eglinton Crosstown LRT Station." (Laird in Focus, Toronto)

**Good delivery and safety policy:** "10.20. (iii) Locate goods and service access for development along Laird Drive at the rear of the property from local streets, public lanes, and/or shared private driveways." (Laird in Focus, Toronto)

these are preliminary illustrations only. Extensive policy intervention for the many mobility access concepts introduced in this book will hopefully address our numerous mobility access gaps through future policy efforts.

*"A man can do as he wills, but not will as he wills."*
—Arthur Schopenhauer (1788–1860)

## Continuous Progress and Resiliency for the New Mobility Ecosystem

Automobility was promoted as a symbol of "free will", an illusionary marketing product of freedom. Unlike feudalism when a product was produced for a purpose, the product produced under Fordism ideology targets manipulated desire under the cover of freedom as an ultimate of a human's everyday life (Bernays, 1928). Ford's toxic homogenous consumptions culture become a parasite of desire (Bean, 2020). Our desire is, however, conditioned (Schroeder, 2020). The manipulated conditions are unsustainable and disappear once market campaign ends. Natural and environment changes eventually take over manmade conditions. The philosophy of writing practically new and effective policies is simply adjusting to shifting the mobility ecosystem that can adjust itself when condition changes. Since the effect of policy is a painfully slow process, it is vital to avoid the ideology of short-lived manipulated desire. And as the new mobility system progresses gradually, it will need reality checks. Original goals and mobility boundary limits that would need to be checked periodically to evaluate the successes and gaps of the new system. With evaluation will come new inquiries. Once the initial stage of the new ecosystem matures, continuous system monitoring, and instant evaluation opportunities would provide a clear understanding of where the new mobility system is going. A city's plans and policies define what will be the evaluation process, and target objectives and the gradual improvement of the quality life of residents and visitors. This section briefly discusses the yet to be established three processes to check mobility ecosystem resiliency.

### *Progress of mobility boundary limits*

When an ecosystem matures, it provides an indication when it reaches a dynamic equilibrium state. New scientific data from cities provides us the opportunity to measure changes in the system. Key performance criteria established through the mobility boundary concept (Karim, 2017) as a genuine progress indicator (Kubiszewski et al., 2013) would be the most meaningful and practical step to evaluate the new ecosystem performance and resiliency. New ecosystem indicators that include social, cultural, and environmental wellbeing for greater society benefits provide the outcomes of the mobility ecosystem. By comparing the status quo with new changes, we can estimate the incremental changes for each of the six boundary limits (safety, land-use, mobility access, quality of mobility infrastructures, social life and wellness, and health and energy) and their sub-elements. Figure 7.1 summarizes the incremental changes to mobility boundary elements for a planning area in Toronto.[3] Compared to typically low-density suburban land-use, the proposed mixed-use with a new mobility ecosystem is expected to reduce by over one-fifth parking demand and by more than half people's travel distance. At the same time internal trips within the area will increase by one-fifth due to more daily needs now available within the same community and the fast improvement

---

[3] Preliminary results were published earlier in Chapter 2 of *Disrupting Mobility*, a book written by the author (Karim, 2017). This illustration provides an update of the original results.

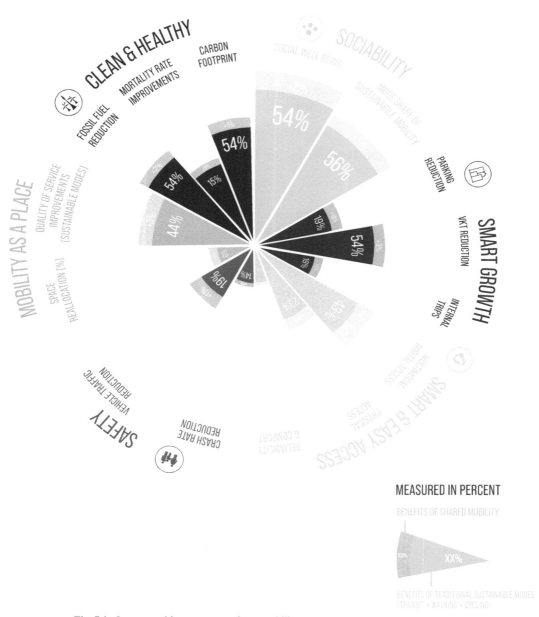

**Fig. 7.1:**  Incremental improvement of new mobility ecosystem to mobility boundary limits.

of easier and comfortable access for transit and active mobility supported by new shared and micro-mobility modes. With vehicle demand reduction, the carbon footprint per person and reduction in use of fossil fuel will improve by more than half while reducing pollutants compared to previous low-density and vehicle-oriented land-uses. Area residents are expected to see health impacts improve by one-fifth compared to existing conditions. With vehicle reduction, sustainable modes are expected to improve by 56% which assumes improved social well-being and a higher level of social interactions through placemaking. Both digital and physical access to mobility services are expected to improve 56% and 38% due to mandatory real-time information, multiple connections, to rapid transit stations, and multimodal access for daily needs. These changes expect to improve reliability of sustainable modes and encourage higher usage. As vehicle usage reduces and conflict is reduced through specific intersection and street design changes, residents can expect a roughly a one-third overall vehicle traffic reduction and an 18% reduction in crash rates. As vehicle usage is reduced, at least an additional 20% of space will be reclaimed through the invisible space detection and redesigning techniques introduced in this book. Sustainable and shared mobility mode users are expected to experience close to a half more service improvements with the new mobility ecosystem. Once these results are converted to mobility boundary limits, all six elements are expected to stay within a safe boundary zone, reducing the threat to overall natural boundary elements for small neighbourhoods. However, one small block in the city is not enough to see overall citywide or large regional benefits. All city areas need to achieve a similar performance for meaningful impact and maintain the mobility boundary limits to stay within the safe zone. These approaches and results demonstrate the possibilities of this ultimate objective.

> *"Standards always are out of date. That is what makes them standards."*
> —Alan Bennett

## *Preparing the future city builders*

Breaking barriers and reinventing city planning plans and process are not silver lining solutions. Without transferring knowledge, skills, and training, progressive planning or policies will never reach the light at the end of the tunnel. Recent trends of hiring renowned planning practitioners or strong leaders in cities or mobility sectors is one of the encouraging signs where staff is conditioned with a culture of progressive and creative process. Progressive planners are rare but do occasionally rise to the occasion. Once they have left the position however, because of political pressure or simply resistance to new city building ideas, their knowledge and skills disappear over time. While recent leadership changes are encouraging, the reinvention of a citywide mobility culture is slow and painful. There is a long list of critical elements that can turn visions or plans or policies into reality. A short list of series of meaningful cultural changes would be:

- Starting a conversation, sharing, or learning new knowledge or skills or creative mobility ideas.
- Developing initial training for selected individuals by pioneers in the field, gathering background knowledge, applicability, and transferability of new ideas for each specific city.
- Identifying how to customize or improvize new mobility culture as an application to identify the modified form of local cultural alignment or difficulties.
- Developing training processes, platforms for knowledge sharing, debating regularly between different fields, and engaging experts to break silos between special knowledge holders.
- Developing a new group of practitioners to test new knowledge and skills for new mobility approaches.
- Selecting an area or projects and applying newly acquired knowledge and skills.
- Carefully customizing plans and developing strategies that could be applied or customized for test areas or projects.
- Performing new travel demand practices, identifying new mobility ecosystems of supply, and adopting an implementable approach using real human mobility data and findings. It is vital to avoid or resist the pressure to use flawed static mobility data or models that impose structural barriers. As a side benefit, the outcome of this process will develop new resources for future projects.

- Verifying the process with a person with prior knowledge, and testing and debating the new approach, its merits, and demerits. However, it is critical not to get bogged down by the "infinite no" answers from old-school mobility practitioners against adopting new knowledge, skills, and mobility culture process. At the same time, there is no reason to develop a rivalry against old-school professionals. They have obligations and a process to follow. If they do take time to change however, eventually all practitioners will change their mindsets since the new ideas will be proven to be safer, more affordable, and easier, and to solve real-life problems instead of creating new ones.

- Present new plans and policies to the public, approach previously experienced individuals, and approach the professional community to make sure a new ecosystem built has the legs, hands, head, heart, and all vital organs to sustain itself on its own.

- This stage also needs rigorous checks of service operations, maintenance and implementation, verification, funding sources, and other challenges to overcome.

- Find implementation pioneers, collaborators, and partners from private, public, and technology sectors for all layers of the city buildings process and anticipate challenges from internal and externals sources.

- Adopt new plans and policies, insert mandatory, different layers of necessary, optional, and voluntary requirements, along with meaningful incentives for partners and collaborators.

- Once adopted or completed, share, train, and present to internal and external venues and platforms. Develop processes for new knowledge, skills, and training using the results from new areas and projects.

- Adopt as a permanent programme and process for creative and innovative new mobility ecosystem approaches, processes, and programmes to make a new decision making, practice, and established process at every layer of mobility planning, design, implementation, and continuous service or programmes for everyday culture.

- This stage needs major changes for all city builders, institutions to adopt the new education curriculum, professional associations, and communities to develop new knowledge and documents.

- It's time to change citywide and state/province wide or even countrywide plans, policies, and practices with requirements for new mobility ecosystems, with sufficient flexibility for variations of process.

- Obviously, it's also time to identify who or what is still resisting just for the sake of ideology, and the professional dogma that iteratively produced repeated problems and system breakdown. Whether it's human, old process, or the system, it's time to respectively retire those impractical and unreasonable barriers. This is a difficult decision, but necessary to avoid spoiling the entire new process that was established through a lengthy series of steps.

- By the time new approaches were implemented, a new mobility culture most likely arrived. Very likely another, more creative, new process has matured, and been tested and implemented elsewhere. It's time to begin a new cycle of continuous changes.

## *Mapping the future city*

Changing the course of a city is most complex. Complex systems need to find balance between all elements to reach a stable equilibrium status (Batty, 2009.) that improves quality of life for all. Balance does not come from a utilitarian approach or just rigid rational culture. City building needs all urban expertise to come together. Despite more than 80% of people living in cities, city building remains a random, sporadic, ideological, or dogma-driven system. We have been building cities for thousands of years yet there are no schools or process to understand what city building is. Schools for cities, for instance, at the University of Toronto (University of Toronto, 2015) only developed among academic institutions in the last decade, albeit in limited scale or resources. To reinvent the city, we need a mental map of the city to understand where and how things are linked, interact, and eventually stabilize. But what would a mental map of the city look like? There is no clear answer, but it could start with few ideas on what is causing the recurring problems, inequality, and degradation in quality of life.

One idea would be to literally develop a new complex city mapping system alike when Google replaced the old paper mapping system. But we've learned that Google system disruptions can disrupt numerous elements of our daily life. So, can we literally develop something like the Google system for cities? The starting point would obviously not be Google itself. We know how miserably Google's idea of the "smart city" failed (Cecco, 2021). It would not be done in the mayor's office nor the corporate boardroom, or under a civic feudalism structure either. It must come from a collaborative place for all city builders, expertise, and platforms coming together in a dynamically changing system.

Instead of talking and deceiving ourselves with promises, all future city elements, plans, and improvements can be mapped out in future layers of potential changes. This includes all the future changes to any street or place due to redevelopment or city projects, other planned improvements, or future capital works. These systems are in place already such as those partially covered by open data systems. But crowdsourced input remains missing. Instead of the project-only public input process, this would be a continuous public and external source input process. Many residents know where the unsafe places are, why some areas or designs connect with their emotions, places of cultural attachments, their lovable neighbourhood corners, and which areas need improvements. General planners and non-public interest groups can insert their ideas into the different information layers of the overall "city dashboard". This democratizes the city building process by giving equal opportunity for residents' input about their surrounding areas and how to improve those areas. A review body would analyse all inputs and recommend to the city or project team where to incorporate citizen or crowdsourced ideas and make real transformative changes.

## Summary

Regulation has worked as a double-edged sword for mobility systems. Regulation and policy are two sides of same coin. One-sided and biased policy stifles innovations, and banning and restrictions miss golden opportunities. A Weak policy leads to public harm and a negative impact on the quality of life. Achieving a fine-line balance is a delicate task and needs a strong policy development culture and sound practices. Currently vital organs of policymaking are missing for multimodal mobility options. A weak and ineffective policy is directly linked to the poor state of multimodal mobility. Writing policies without prior experience or knowledge remains a key barrier to maturity of the multimodal mobility ecosystem. This final chapter addresses the regulation and policymaking culture, basic foundations and practices that create conditions for a strong, precise, and effective governing environment that would lead to a resilient multimodal ecosystem. Golden rules and pitfalls in the policy-making and regulation process are illustrated to overcome initial barriers and developing resiliency and the ability of shifting mobility systems come from a fundamental list of skills and processes of the organizational path. Some details illustrate successful examples from the Greater Toronto Area and provide a glimpse at difficult but creative approaches to multimodal mobility policy development that led to successful system implementation. The identification of system scale, size, and all elements of vital organs of the new mobility ecosystem are key to policy implementation. But writing and developing does not guarantee success. Policy-making is more about developing culture, creating conditions, and a collaborating mindset to open the door to all key partners of city building. The last section provides some secret rules, processes, and steps to developing a good policy-making culture and collaborative environment. It also provides visualization and policy access tools to find the way to citizens without dumping thousands of processes and documents on the public. Ultimately the goal is to increase the capacity of regulation and the policy-making process for decision makers and practitioners involved in multimodal mobility systems.

# References

Akndi. (2020). *Greening Government Fleets: A Helpful Guide to Understanding.* Ottawa: Natural Resources Canada.

Albert, A. and Gonzalez, M.C. (2017). Using convolutional networks and satellite imagery to identify patterns in urban environments at a large scale. *Proceedings of the 23rd ACM SIGKDD International Conference on Knowledge Discovery and Data Mining*, (pp. 1357–1366).

Amadoa, M. and Poggi, F. (2014). Solar energy integration in urban planning: GUUD mode. *Energy Procedia*, 50: 277–284.

Anderson, J.M., Kalra, N., Stanley, K.D., Sorensen, P., Samaras, C. and Oluwatola, O.A. (2016). *Autonomous Vehicle Technology: A Guide for Policymakers.* Santa Monica, California: RAND Coportation, RR-443-2-RC.

Appleby, K. (2015). *Five Cities Poving that We Can Quit Fossil Fuels.* Retrieved from City Monitor: https://citymonitor.ai/horizons/five-cities-proving-we-can-quit-fossil-fuels-1444.

Appleyard, D. (1972). The environmental quality of city streets: The resident's viewpoint. *Journal of the American Planning Association*, 35: 84–101.

Bae, S., Lee, E. and Han, J. (2020). Multi-period planning of hydrogen supply network for refuelling hydrogen fuel cell vehicles in urban areas. *Sustainability*, 12(4114): 1–23.

Barry, K. (2013). *Wired.* Retrieved from In South Korea, Wireless Charging Powers Electric Buses: https://www.wired.com/2013/08/induction-charged-buses/.

Bartholomew, R. (2015). *Understanding Impact: Research and Policy Development.* London: Centre for Longitudinal Studies Strategic Advisory Board.

Batty, M. (2009). *Cities as Complex Systems: Scaling, Interaction, Networks, Dynamics, and Urban Morphologies.* New York: Springer.

Bean, T. (2020). *Capitalism Gone Wild: The Ending of 'Parasite' Explained.* Retrieved from Forbes: https://www.forbes.com/sites/travisbean/2020/01/30/capitalism-gone-wild-the-ending-of-parasite-explained/.

Becic, E., Zych, N. and Ivarsson, J. (2018). *Vehicle Automation Report.* Washington, USA: National Transportation Safety Board, HWY18MH010.

Becky, P.Y., Lo, O. and Banister, D. (2016). Decoupling transport from economic growth: Extending the debate to include environmental and social externalities. *Journal of Transport Geography*, 57: 134–144.

Beddoes, Z.M. (2020). Time to make coal history. *The Economist.*

Beebeejaun, Y. (201). Gender, urban space, and the right to everyday life. *Journal of Urban Affairs*, 39(3): 323–334.

Benjamin, L. and Richards, D. (1981). Electrification is the way to Move Canada in the 1980s. *Canadian Public Policy*, 7(81).

Berg, N. (2020). *This AI-powered Parking Garage Rewards You for Not Driving.* Retrieved from Fast Company: https://www.fastcompany.com/90575914/this-ai-powered-parking-garage-rewards-you-for-not-driving#:~:text=With%20a%20new%20test%20program,in%20to%20work%20at%20all.

Berg, P. (2011). *The Finite Planet: How Resource Scarcity will Affect Our Environment, Economy, and Energy Supply.* Oshawa, Canada: Island Press.

Bernays, E. (1928). Manipulating public opinion: The why and the how. *American Journal of Sociology*, 33(6): 958–971. Retrieved from Bombay Institute for Critical Analysis and Research: https://stayhappening.com/e/capitalism-history-logic-limit-E2ISU60HUMH.

Bhat, C. (2017). *Travel Modeling in an Era of Connected and Automated Transportation Systems: An Investigation in the Dallas-Fort Worth Area.* Austin, USA: Technical Report 122. Center for Transportation Research. The University of Texas at Austin.

Bhat, R.V. and Waghray, K. (2000). *Profile of Street Foods in Asian Countries.* Basel, Karger: World Rev. Nutr. Diet.

Billings, C.E. (1980). *Human-centered Aircraft Automation; A Concept and Guidelines.* Moffet Field, CA: NASA Technical Memorandum, NASA Ames Research Center.

Bochner, B.S., Hooper, K., Sperry, B. and Dunphy, R. (2011). *Enhancing Internal Trip Capture Estimation for Mixed-Use Developments.* Washington D.C.: Transportation Research Board.

Bojji, R. (2011). Gravity powered transport systems for rail, road, water, and airport use. *13th International Conference on Automated People* (pp. 22– 25). Paris, France: American Society of Civil Engineers.

Borzino, N., Chang, S., Mughal, M.O. and Schubert, R. (2020). Willingness to pay for urban heat island mitigation: A case study of Singapore. *Climate*, 8: 82.

Botsman, R. (2010). *What's Mine is Yours: The Rise of Collaborative Consumption.* Harper Business.

Bourdieu, P. and Wacquant, L.D. (1992). *An Invitation to Reflexive Sociology.* Cambridge, UK: Polity Press and Blackwell Publishers.

Britton, E. (2000). Carsharing 2000: Sustainable transport's missing link. *Journal of The Commons*, 1– 351.

Burden, D. (2021). *Building the Healthy City: Inciting the Healthy Choice.* Retrieved from Healthy City Design: https://healthycitydesign2019.salus.global/uploads/media/conference_lecture_presentation/0001/20/2459bb881e47ab6c074662a39832376707619a43.pdf.

Canada Energy Regulator. (2020). *Market Snapshot: Canada's Retiring Coal-fired Power Plants will be Replaced by Renewable and Low-carbon Energy Sources.* Retrieved from Canada Energy Regulator: https://www.cer-rec.gc.ca/en/data-analysis/energy-markets/market-snapshots/2020/market-snapshot-canadas-retiring-coal-fired-power-plants-will-be-replaced-renewable-low-carbon-energy-sources.html.

*Carsharing.Org.* (2017). Retrieved from What is carsharing?: https://carsharing.org/what-is-car-sharing/.

Carter, C. (2019). *Autonomous Passenger Ferries: Congestion-buster or Hype on the High Seas?* Retrieved from Smart Cities World: https://www.smartcitiesworld.net/special-reports/special-reports/autonomous-passenger-ferries-congestion-buster-or-hype-on-the-high-seas.

Cecco, L. (2021). *Toronto Swaps Google-backed, Not-so-smart City Plans for People-centred Vision.* Retrieved from The Guardian: https://www.theguardian.com/world/2021/mar/12/toronto-canada-quayside-urban-centre.

Center for Sustainable Systems. (2020). *Geothermal Energy.* Detroit, Michigan: University of Michigan. Retrieved from Geothermal Energy.: http://css.umich.edu/sites/default/files/Geothermal%20Energy_CSS10-10_e2020.pdf.

Certeau, M.D. (2011). *The Practice of Everyday Life.* Berkeley: University of California Press.

Charles, A.S., Lambert, H.G. and Balogh, S.B. (2014). EROI of different fuels and the implications for society. *Energy Policy*, 64: 141– 152.

Chellapilla, K. (2018). *Rethinking Maps for Self-Driving.* Medium.

Christensen, A. and Petrenko, C. (2017). *CO2-based Synthetic Fuel: Assessment of Potential European Capacity and Environmental Performance.* Brussels: European Climate Foundation and the International Council on Clean Transportation.

City of Toronto. (2007). *Design Guidelines for 'Greening' Surface Parking Lots.* Toronto: City of Toronto.

City of Toronto. (2010). *Percent for Public Art Program Guidelines.* Toronto: City of Toronto.

City of Toronto. (2012). *StreetARToronto.* Retrieved from City of Toronto: https://www.toronto.ca/services-payments/streets-parking-transportation/enhancing-our-streets-and-public-realm/streetartoronto/.

City of Toronto. (2015). *Dufferin Street Avenue Study City Initiated Official Plan Amendment.* Toronto: City of Toronto.

City of Toronto. (2015). *Tippett Road Area Regeneration Study – Final Report.* Toronto: City of Toronto.

City of Toronto. (2017). *Chapter 9: Street Design for Intersections.* Toronto: City of Toronto.

City of Toronto. (2017). *Corner Radii Guideline.* Toronto: City of Toronto.

City of Toronto. (2017). *Curb Extensions Guideline.* Toronto: City of Toronto.

City of Toronto. (2017). *Intersection Improvements at Millwood Road and Laird Drive.* Toronto: City of Toronto.

City of Toronto. (2017). *Lower-Simcoe Ramp, Gardiner Expressway.* Toronto: City of Toronto.

City of Toronto. (2017). *Street Design for Cycling: Toronto Complete Street Guidelines.* Toronto: City of Toronto.

City of Toronto. (2017). *The City's Wet Weather Flow Master Plan.* Retrieved from City of Toronto: https://www.toronto.ca/services-payments/water-environment/managing-rain-melted-snow/the-citys-wet-weather-flow-master-plan/.

City of Toronto. (2017). *Toronto Green Streets Technical Guidelines.* City of Toronto: Toronto.

City of Toronto. (2017). *Toronto's Road Safety Plan.* Toronto: City of Toronto.

City of Toronto. (2018). *Six Points Interchange Reconfiguration.* Retrieved from City of Toronto: https://www.toronto.ca/wp-content/uploads/2017/11/91d0-pcu-Six-Points-Enviornmental-Assessment-Study.pdf.

City of Toronto. (2018). *Toronto Green Standard Version 3.* Toronto, Canada: City of Toronto.

City of Toronto. (2020). *COVID-19: ActiveTO.* Retrieved from City of Toronto: https://www.toronto.ca/home/covid-19/covid-19-protect-yourself-others/covid-19-reduce-virus-spread/covid-19-activeto/.

City of Toronto. (2020). *COVID-19: CurbTO.* Retrieved from City of Toronto: https://www.toronto.ca/home/covid-19/covid-19-protect-yourself-others/covid-19-reduce-virus-spread/covid-19-curbto/.

City of Toronto. (2020). *Energy Efficiency Report Submission & Modelling Guidelines: For the Toronto Green Standard (TGS) Version 3.* Toronto, Canada: Environment and Energy Division & City Planning Division, City of Toronto.

City of Toronto. (2020). *Growing Up: Planning for Children in New Vertical Communities: Urban Design Guidelines.* Toronto: City of Toronto.

City of Vancouver. (2019). *EV Charging Infrastructure Requirements for New Residential Buildings Guidance.* Vancouver, Canada: City of Vancouver.

Civitas. (2016). *Cities towards Mobility 2.0: Connect, Share, and Go!* Brussels, Belgium: CIVITAS WIKI consortium.

CMA. (2008). *No Breathing Room National Illness Costs of Air Pollution.* Ottawa: Canadian Medical Association.

Colombo, A. and Karney, B. (2009). Why engineers need public policy training and practice. *The Journal of Policy Engagement*, 1(1): 9– 12.

Cook, C. (2014). *Transforming the Transportation Industry with Renewable Energy.* Retrieved from Renewable Energy World: https://www.renewableenergyworld.com/2014/09/18/transforming-the-transportation-industry-with-renewable-energy/#gref.

Cooke, C. (2016). *Paris Allows Anyone to Plant an Urban Garden.* Retrieved from Inhabitat: https://inhabitat.com/paris-allows-anyone-to-plant-an-urban-garden-anywhere/.

Cooper, D. (2018). *It's Too Early to Write off Hydrogen Vehicles.* Retrieved from Engadget: https://www.engadget.com/2018-05-29-hydrogen-fuel-cell-toyota-mirai-evs.html.

CPCS and Hatch Associates. (1992). *Commuter Rail Services: Electrification Study.* Toronto: GO Transit.

Crewe, K. (2001). Linear parks and urban neighbourhoods: A study of the crime impact of the boston south-west corridor. *Journal of Urban Design*, 6(3): 245–264.

CSL. (2013). *Skills and Knowledge Framework.* London: Civil Service Learning.

Curie, J. and Pierre, C. (1880). Développement, par pression, de l'électricité polaire dans les cristaux hémièdres à faces inclinées. *Comptes Rendus* (in French), 9: 294–295.

Dan, K. (2007). Flight of the pigeon. *Bicycling, Rodale, Inc.*, 48: 60–66.

Dave. (2018). *Car-Sharing vs. Private Vehicle Ownership Costs.* Retrieved from Carsharing US: https://arlingtonva.s3.amazonaws.com/wp-content/uploads/sites/19/2017/03/DES-Carshare-CarShare_vs_PrivateCarOwnership_Cost_Analysis.pdf.

David, H. (2004). *Bicycle: The History.* Yale University Press. ISBN 0-300-10418-9.

Debhia, P. (2019). *The History of Electric Scooters.* Retrieved from LinkedIn: https://www.linkedin.com/pulse/history-electric-scooters-prashant-dedhia-negotiation-ninja-/.

Deluchhi, M.A. and Jaconson, M.Z. (2009). A path to sustainable energy by 2030. *Scientific American*, 58–65.

DeMaio, P. (2009). Bike-sharing: Impacts, models of provision, and future. *Journal of Public Transportation*, 12(4): 41–56.

DeMaio, P.J. (2003). Smart bikes: Public transportation for the 21st century. *Transportation Quarterly*, 57(1): 9–11.

Dovery, R. (2014). *Public Art Projects Made These 7 Amazing Bus Stops.* Retrieved from Next City: https://nextcity.org/daily/entry/public-art-bus-stops-photos.

Driving. (2015). *Company Wants to Bring Rickshaws to North America.* Retrieved from Driving: https://driving.ca/auto-news/news/company-wants-to-bring-rickshaws-to-north-america.

Duffy, M.C. (2003). *Electric Railways: 1880–1990.* London: The Institution of Engineering and Technology.

Ekawati, S.A. (2015). Children-friendly streets as urban playgrounds. *Social and Behavioral Sciences*, 179: 94–108.

Endsley, M.R. and Kiris, E.O. (1995). The out-of-the-loop performance problem and level of control in automation. *Human Factors The Journal of the Human Factors and Ergonomics Society*, 2: 27.

Energy Information Administration EIA. (2017). *Study of the Potential Energy Consumption Impacts of Connected and Automated Vehicles.* Washington, D.C. 20585: US Department of Energy.

Energy Innovation. (2015). *Comparing the Costs of Renewable and Conventional Energy Sources.* Retrieved from Energy Innovation: https://energyinnovation.org/2015/02/07/levelized-cost-of-energy/.

Eugster, J.W. (2007). Road and bridge heating using geothermal energy. Overview and examples. *Proceedings European Geothermal Congress* (pp. 1– 5). Unterhaching, Germany: European Geothermal Congress.

European Commision. (2020). *Energy Efficiency Indicator.* Retrieved from European Commision: https://ec.europa.eu/transport/themes/energy-efficiency-indicator_en.

Evans, M. (2001). Understanding policy networks: Towards a dialectical approach. *Political Studies*, 49: 542–550.

Fishbone, A., Shahan, Z. and Badik, P. (2017). *Electric Vehicle Charging Infrastructure: Guidelines for Cities.* Warsaw, Poland: CleanTechnica.

Fishman, E. (2014). Bikeshare: A review of recent literature. *Transport Reviews*, 92–113.

Fison, M. (2013). *Santiago's Red Light Jugglers.* Retrieved from BBC News: https://www.bbc.com/news/magazine-23896316.

François-Lavet, V., Henderson, P., Islam, R., Bellemare, M.G. and Pineau, J. (2018). An introduction to deep reinforcement learning. *Foundations and Trends in Machine Learning*, 11(3-4): 1–102.

Frayer, L. and Cater, F. (2015). *How a Folding Electric Vehicle Went from Car of The Future to 'Obsolete'*. Retrieved from NPR: http://www.npr.org/sections/alltechconsidered/2015/11/05/454693583/how-a-folding-electric-vehicle-went-from-car-of-the-future-to-obsolete.

Fruin, J. (1971). *Pedestrian Planning and Design.* New York: Metropolitan Association of Urban Designer and Environmental Planners, Inc.

Furman, B., Fabian, L., Ellis, S., Muller, P. and Swenson, R. (2014). *Automated Transit Networks (ATN): A Review of the State of the Industry and Prospects for the Future.* San José: Minata Transportation Institute.

Galatoulas, N.F. (2020). Spatio-temporal trends of e-bike sharing system deployment: A review in Europe, North America and Asia. *Sustainability.*, 12: 4611.

Gawron, V.J. (2019). *Automation in Aviation – Definition of Automation.* McLean, VA: The MITRE Corporation.

Gee, M. (2016). *Raise the Roof? Union Station Reno Runs into Problem: New Trains won't Fit.* Retrieved from The Globe and Mail: https://www.theglobeandmail.com/news/toronto/union-station-shed-renovation-stalled-by-low-arches-and-an-electrified-future/article28448568/.

Gehl, J. (2010). *Cities for People.* Copenhagen: Island Press.

Gehl, J. (2011). *Danish Architect Jan Gehl on Good Cities for Walking.* Retrieved from Streetsblog: https://sf.streetsblog.org/2011/06/14/danish-architect-jan-gehl-on-good-cities-for-walking/.

Geidl, M., Koeppel, G., Favre-Perrod, P., Klöckl, B., Andersson, G. and Fröhlich, K. (2007). The energy hub – A powerful concept for future energy systems. *Third Annual Carnegie Mellon Conference on the Electricity Industry* (pp. 2–10). Pittsburgh: Carnegie Mellon University.

Geng, J., Long, R. and Chen, H. (2016). Impact of information intervention on travel mode choice of urban residents with different goal frames: A controlled trial in Xuzhou, China. *Transportation Research Part A: Policy and Practice*, 91: 134–147.

Gharipour, M. (2012). *The Culture and Politics of Commerce in The Bazaar in the Islamic City: Design, Culture, and History.* New York: The American University in Cairo Press.

Gilpin, L. (2017). *Can Car-Sharing Culture Help Fuel an Electric Vehicle Revolution?* Retrieved from Insideclimate: https://insideclimatenews.org/news/07122017/car-rental-sharing-electric-vehicles-zipcar-evs-uber-lyft-green-commuter.

Global Union. (2020). *Top 10 Principles for Ethical Artifical Intelligence.* Nyon, Switzerland: The Future World of Work.

Gomes, L. (2014). *Hidden Obstacles for Google's Self-Driving Cars: Impressive Progress Hides Major Limitations of Google's Quest for Automated Driving.* Cambridge, USA: MIT Technology Review.

Gormley, W.T. (2007). Public policy analysis: Ideas and impacts. *Annu. Rev. Polit. Sci.*, 10: 297–313.

Gross, S. (2020). *Why are Fossil Fuels so Hard to Quit?* Retrieved from Brookings Institution: https://www.brookings.edu/essay/why-are-fossil-fuels-so-hard-to-quit/.

GTA Clean Air Council. (2017). *Climate Action for a Healthy, Equitable, and Prosperous Toronto.* Toronto: City of Toronto.

Hallsworth, M., Parker, S. and Rutter, J. (2011). *Policy Making in Real World: Evidence and Analysis.* London: Institute for Government.

Halprin Conservancy. (2021). *Anna Halprin: The Origin of Form.* Retrieved from Halprin Conservancy: https://www.halprinconservancy.org/anna-halprin.

Harms, S. and Truffer, B. (1998). *The Emergence of a Nationwide Carsharing Co-operative in Switzerland: A Case Study for the Project "StrategicNiche Management as a Tool for Transition to a Sustainable Transportation System.* 1998: EAWAG-Eidg. Anstalt fur Wasserversorgung und Gewasserschutz.

Haugneland, P., Lorentzen, E., Bu, C. and Hauge, E. (2017). Put a price on carbon to fund EV incentives – Norwegian EV policy success. *EVS30 Symposium* (pp. 1–8). Stuttgart, Germany: Norwegian EV Association.

Hayden, D. (1980). What would a non-sexist city be like? Speculations on housing, urban design, and human work. *Signs*, 5(Suppl. 3): S170–S187.

Haywood, J.B. (2006). Fueling our transportation future. *Scientific American.*

Hess, A. and Schubert, I. (2019). Functional perceptions, barriers, and demographics concerning e-cargo bike sharing in Switzerland. *Transportation Research Part D: Transport and Environment*, 71: 153. Retrieved from Science daily: https://www.sciencedaily.com/releases/2019/07/190710121536.htm.

Hoopengardner, R. and Thompson, M. (2012). *FTA Low-Speed Urban Maglev Research Program: Updated Lessons Learned.* Arlington, USA: Federal Transit Administration, USA.

Hordnes, E. (2019). *Race to Electrification – Norway in a Pole Position.* Retrieved from Urban Insight: https://www.swecourbaninsight.com/urban-energy/race-to-electrification--norway-in-pole-position/.

Hou, J. (2020). Guerrilla urbanism: Urban design and the practices of resistance. *Urban Design International*, 25: 117–125.

Hudson, J. and Lowe, S. (2009). *Understanding the Policy Process.* Bristol, UK: The Policy Press.

Hughes, I. and Huo, R. (2018). *Autonomy-level Classification for Robots in an IIoT World.* Retrieved from 451 Research: https://go.451research.com/MI-Robots-in-IIoT-World.html.

Hull, G.J., Roberts, C. and Hillmansen, S. (2008). Energy efficiency of a railway power network with simulation. *International Conference on Energy Technologies and Policy.* Birmingham, UK: University of Birmingham.

IISD. (2015). *The End of Coal: Ontario's Coal Phase-out.* Winnipeg, Canada: International Institute for Sustainable Development.

Im, J. (2019). Green streets to serve urban sustainability: benefits and typology. *Sustainability*, 11: 6483–6505.

Institute, R.M. (2019). *Electric Mobility: Best Practices.* Rocky Mountain Institute, Government of India and Smart City.

Islam, A. and Ahiduzzaman, M. (2012). Biomass energy: Sustainable solution for greenhouse gas emissions. *American Inst. Phys. Conf. Proc.*, 1441(1): 23–32. American Institute of Physics.

ISO. (2020). *Road Vehicles — Human Performance and State in the Context of Automated Driving – Part 2: Considerations in Designing Experiments to Investigate Transition Processes.* ISO/TR 21959-2: 2020.

Itoh, M., Zhou, H. and Kitazaki, S. (2018). What may happen or what you should do? Effects of knowledge representation regarding necessity of intervention on driver performance under level 2 automated driving. *ICPS'18: Proceedings of the 2018 IEEE Industrial Cyber-Physical Systems* (pp. 621–626). Saint Petersburg, Russia: IEEE.

J2954. (2019). *Wireless Power Transfer for Light-Duty Plug-in/Electric Vehicles and Alignment Methodology.* SAE International.

J3068. (2018). *Electric Vehicle Power Transfer System Using a Three-Phase Capable Coupler.* J3068. SAE International.

J3105. (2020). *Electric Vehicle Power Transfer System Using Conductive Automated Connection Devices.* SAE International.

Jaffe, E. (2021). *The Future of Curb Space is about Much More than Parking.* Retrieved from Medium: https://medium.com/sidewalk-talk/the-future-of-curb-space-is-about-much-more-than-parking-46ced028b74d.

Jayasuriya, D.C. (1994). Street food vending in Asia: Some policy and legal aspects. *Food Control, Elsevier*, 5(4): 222–226.

Jefferies, I. (2019, November 20). Retrieved from Association of American Railroads. https://www.aar.org/article/freight-rail-highly-automated-vehicles/.

Jettanasen, C., Songsukthawan, P. and Ngaopitakkul, A. (2020). Development of micro-mobility based on Piezoelectric energy harvesting for smart city applications. *Sustainability*, 1–16.

Jordan, Z.A. (1967). *The Evolution of Dialectical Materialism.* London: Macmillan.

Jorna, A. (2012). *Synthetic Fuel Costs.* Stanford, California: Stanford University.

Joshi, N. (2019). *7 Types of Artificial Intelligence.* Retrieved from Forbes: https://www.forbes.com/sites/cognitiveworld/2019/06/19/7-types-of-artificial-intelligence/#48c88ca9233e.

Junkin, K. (2013). *Regional Rapid Rail: A Vision for the Future.* Toronto: Transport Action, Ontario.

Kalra, N. and Paddock, S.M. (2016). *How Many Miles of Driving Would it Take to Demonstrate Autonomous Vehicle Reliability? Driving to Safety.* Santa Monica, California: RAND Corporation.Kane, M. (2019). *Chile Launches Latin America's First 100% Electric Bus Corridor.* Retrieved from Inside EVs: https://insideevs.com/news/377241/chile-first-100-electric-bus-corridor/.

KAPSARC. (2016). *Mobility-on-demand: Understanding Energy Impacts and Adoption Potential.* Riyadh: KASARC.

Karim, D.M. (2015). Narrower lanes, safer streets. *Annual General Meeting, Canadian Institute of Transportation Engineers* (pp. 1–22). Regina: Canadian Inststitute of Transportation Engineers.

Karim, D.M. (2017). Creating an innovative mobility ecosystem for urban planning areas. pp. 21–47. *In*: G.M. Shaheen, (ed.). *Disrupting Mobility: Impacts of Sharing Economy and Innovative Transportation on Cities.* Cham: Springer.

Karim, D.M. and Shallwani, T. (2010). Toward a clean train policy: Diesel versus electric. *Ontario Centre for Engineering and Public Policy (OCEPP)*, 3: 18–22.

Khayal, O. (2019). The history of Bajaj rickshaw vehicles. *Global Journal of Engineering Sciences*, 3(2): 1–8.

Kleinman, M.T. (2000). *The Health Effects of Air Pollution on Children.* Irvine, California: South Coast Air Quality Management District (SCAQMD).

Knoflacher, H. (1981). *Human Energy Expenditure in Different Modes: Implications for Town Planning.* Washington D.C.: International Symposium on Surface Transportation System Performance, US Department of Transportation.

Knoflacher, H. (2017). Understanding professionals, politicians and the society in the motorized World – and how to help them. *International Journal of New Technology and Research*, 3(8): 60–65.

Kodransky, M. and Hermann, G. (2011). *Europe's Parking U-turn: From Accomodation to Regulation.* Munich: ITDP.

Kour, R. and Charif, A. (2016). Piezoelectric roads: Energy harvesting method using piezoelectric technology. *Innovative Energy & Research*, 5(1).

Kubiszewski, I., Costanza, R., Franco, C., Lawn, P., Talberth, J., Jackson, T. and Aylmer, C. (2013). Beyond GDP: Measuring and achieving global genuine progress. *Ecological Economics*, 93: 57–68.

Kwon, D. (2018). Self-taught robots. *Scientific American*, 26–31.

Kwon, H., Ryu, M.H. and Carlsten, C. (2020). Ultrafine particles: Unique physicochemical properties relevant to health and disease. *Experimental & Molecular Medicine*, 52: 318–328.

Lacan, J. (1960–61). *Le Séminaire. Livre VIII. Le transfert.* Paris: Seuil.

Lambert, F. (2020). *Uber and Hyundai Unveil New Electric Air Taxi with 60-mile Range.* Retrieved from Electrek: https://electrek.co/2020/01/07/uber-hyundai-electric-air-taxi-evtol/.

Layton, B.E. (2008). A comparison of energy densities of prevalent energy sources in units of houles per cubic meter. *International Journal of Green Energy*, 5: 438–455.

Le Vine, S., Lee-Gosselin, M., Sivakumar, A. and Polak, J. (2014). New approach to predict the market and impacts of round-trip and point-to-point carsharing systems: Case study of London. *Transportation Research Part D*, 32(C): 218–229.

Le Vine, S., Zolfaghari, A. and Polak, J. (2014). *Carsharing: Evolution, Challenges, and Opportunities.* London: Centre for Transport Studies, Imperial College.

Le Corbusier. (1929). *The City of Tomorrow and its Planning.* New York: Urbanisme, Payson & Clarke Ltd.

Ledsham, T. and Savan, B. (2017). *Building a 21st Century Cycling City: Strategies for Action in Toronto.* Toronto: Metcalf Foundation.

Lee-Shanok, P. (2017). *Ontario Condo Act A Roadblock for Electric Vehicle Owners.* Retrieved from CBC News: https://www.cbc.ca/news/canada/toronto/ontario-hopes-revised-condo-act-ev-friendly-1.4155747.

Lessing, H. (2001). What led to the invention of the early bicycle? *Cycle History 11, San Francisco*, 11: 28–36. Retrieved from New Scientist: https://www.newscientist.com/article/mg18524841-900-brimstone-and-bicycles/.

Li, L. and Loo, B.P. (2014). Alternative and transitional energy sources for urban transportation. *Current Sustainable/Renewable Energy Reports*, 1: 19–26.

Li, X. and Strezov, V. (2014). Modelling piezoelectric energy harvesting potential in an educational building. *Energy Conversion and Management*, 85: 435–442.

Li, X., Gorghinpour, C., Sclar, R. and Castellanos, S. (2018). *How to Enable Electric Bus Adoption in Cities Worldwide.* Berlin: World Resources Institute, WRI and German Federal Ministry.

Lima, M. (2015). *The Bicycle in the 21st Century.* Retrieved from Theprotocity: http://theprotocity.com/the-bicycle-in-the-21st-century/.

Litman, T. (2018). Retrieved from Carsharing: Vehicle Rental Services that Substitute for Private Vehicle Ownership: https://www.vtpi.org/tdm/tdm7.htm.

Little Free Library. (2009). *Little Free Library Book Exchanges.* Retrieved from Little Free Library: https://littlefreelibrary.org/about/.

Little, A. (2015). *The Future of Urban Mobility 2.0: Towards Networked, Multimodal Cities of 2050.* Rome, Italy: International Association of Public Transport (UITP).

Lu, Z., Happe, R., Cabrall, C.D., Kyriakidis, M. and Winter, J.C. (2016). Human factors of transitions in automated driving: A general framework and literature survey. *Transportation Research Part F*, 43: 183–198.

Lucas, A., Prettico, G., Flammini, M.G., Kotsakis, E., Fulli, G. and Masera, M. (2018). Indicator-based methodology for assessing EV charging infrastructure using exploratory data analysis. *Energies*, 11(1869): 1–18.

MaRS Discovery District. (2016). *Microtransit: An assessment of Potential to Drive Greenhouse Gas Reductions.* Toronto: MaRS Discovery District and Richmond Sustainability Initiatives.

Martret, O. (2020). *Electric Vehicles – Cleaner, Greener, and... On-Demand?* Retrieved from Shotl: https://shotl.com/news/electric-vehicles-cleaner-greener-and-on-demand.

Matuka, R. (2014). *The History of the Electric Car.* Retrieved from Department of Energy, USA.

Maybee, J.E. (2009). *Picturing Hegel: An Illustrated Guide to Hegel's "Encyclopaedia Logic".* Lanham, MD: Lexington Books.

Maybee, J.E. (2020). *Hegel's Dialectics.* Retrieved from The Stanford Encyclopedia of Philosophy: https://plato.stanford.edu/entries/hegel-dialectics/.

McComas, K.A., Tuite, L.S. and Sherman, L.A. (2005). Conflicted scientists: The 'shared pool' dilemma of scientific advisory committees. *Public Understanding of Science*, 14: 285–303.

McCormack, D.P. (2013). *Refrains for Moving Bodies: Experience and Experiment in Affective Spaces.* Oxford: Due University Press.

McMahon, J. (2019). *9 Shared-Mobility Startups Eager to Disrupt Transportation.* Retrieved from Forbes: https://www.forbes.com/sites/jeffmcmahon/2019/03/06/9-shared-mobility-startups-eager-to-disrupt-transportation/#79ca1bf5177e.

McNabb, M. (2019). *DRONEII: Tech Talk – Unraveling 5 Levels of Drones.* Drone Talk.

Medina-Tapiaa, M. and Robusteb, F. (2018). Exploring paradigm shift impacts in urban mobility: Autonomous vehicles and smart cities. *Transportation Research Procedia*, 33: 203210.

Melaina, M., Bush, B., Muratori, M., Zuboy, J. and Ellis, S. (2017). *National Hydrogen Scenerios: How Many Stations, Where, and When?* Washington D.C.: National Renewable Energy Laboratory for the H2USA.

Metrolinx. (2008). *The Big Move: Transforming Transportation in the Greater Toronto and Hamilton Area.* Toronto: Metrolinx.

Metrolinx. (2011). *Mobility Hub Guidelines for the Greater Toronto and Hamilton Area.* Toronto: Metrolinx.

Mikoleit, A. and Purckhauer, M. (2011). *100 Lessons for Understandng the City.* Zurich: The MIT Press.

Millard-Ball, A. (2019, March). The autonomous vehicle parking problem. 75, 99–108.

Miller, A.V. (1977). *Hegel's Phenomenology of Spirit.* Oxford: Oxford University Press.

MIT Media Lab. (2019). *Persuasive Electric Vehicle (PEV).* Retrieved from MIT Media Lab City Science Group: https://www.media.mit.edu/projects/pev/overview/.

Mitchell, W.J., Borroni-Bird, C.E. and Burns, L.D. (2015). *Reinventing the Automobile.* Cambridge, USA: The MIT Press.

Mohorčich, J. (2020). Energy intensity and human mobility after the anthropocene. *Sustainability*, 12: 2376–2389.

Morawska, L., Moore, M.R. and Ristovski, Z.D. (2014). *Health Impacts of Ultrafine Particles: Desktop Literature Review and Analysis.* Canberra: Australian Government Department of the Environment and Heritage.

Movmi. (2018). *Carsharing Market Analysis: Growth and Industry Analysis.* Retrieved from Movmi.net: https://movmi.net/carsharing-market-growth/.

Muheim, P. and Partners. (1996). *Car Sharing Studies: An Investigation.* Dublin, Ireland: Graham Lightfoot.

Müller, V.C. (2020). *Stanford Encyclopedia of Philosophy.* Retrieved from Stanford University: https://plato.stanford.edu/entries/ethics-ai/.

Münzel, K., Boon, W., Frenken, K. and van der Blomme, J.D. (2019). Explaining carsharing supply across Western European cities. *International Journal of Sustainable Transportation*, 1–12.

NACTO. (2020). *Blueprint for Autonomous Urbanism* (2nd Edn.). New York: NACTO.

Najini, H. and Muthukumaraswamy, S.A. (2017). Piezoelectric energy generation from vehicle traffic with technoeconomic analysis. *Journal of Renewable Energy*, 1–16.

Namazu, M. (2017). *The Evolution of Carsharing: Heterogeneity in Adoption and Impacts.* Vancouver: The University of British Columbia.

Network Rail Infrastructure Limited. (2020). *Network Statement 2020.* London, UK: Network Rail.

Newswire. (2010). *Vancouver First City in the World to Endorse the Fossil Fuel Non-Proliferation Treaty.* Retrieved from Fossil Fuel Non-Proliferation Treaty: https://www.newswire.ca/news-releases/vancouver-first-city-in-the-world-to-endorse-the-fossil-fuel-non-proliferation-treaty-843699223.html.

NHTSA. (2016). *Federal Motor Vehicle Safety Standards: Minimum Sound Requirements for Hybrid and Electric Vehicles.* Washington D.C.: National Highway Traffic Safety Administration, NHTSA.

Nilsson, N.J. (1982). *Principles of Artificial Intelligence.* Elsevier Inc.

North District, C.o. (2015). *Sheppard East Corridor: Transportation Review.* Toronto: Transportation Planning, City of Toronto.

NTSB. (2020). *Tesla Crash Investigation Yields 9 NTSB Safety Recommendations.* National Transportation Safety Board.

Ohta, K. (1998). TDM measures toward sustainable mobility. *IATSS Research*, 22(1).

Omi, K. (2018). *Alternative Energy for Transportation.* Retrieved from Issues in Science and Technology: https://issues.org/omi/.

Ongel, A., Loewer, E., Roemer, F., Sethuraman, G. and Chang, F. (2019). Economic assessment of autonomous electric microtransit vehicles. *Sustainability*, 2–18.

Ontario Medical Association. (2005). *The Illness Costs of Air Pollution: 2005–2026 Health and Economic Damage Estimates.* Toronto: OMA.

Orenstein, M. (2020). *COVID-19's Effect on Energy and Emissions – and Implications for the Future.* Retrieved from Canawest Foundation: https://cwf.ca/research/publications/what-now-covid-19s-effect-on-energy-and-emissions-and-implications-for-the-future/.

ORF. (2011). *Integrated Transport Policy A Vision which Doesn't Work Today –How to Make it a Reality (Part II).* Retrieved from Observer Research Foundation: https://www.orfonline.org/research/integrated-transport-policy-a-vision-which-doesnt-work-today-how-to-make-it-a-reality-part-ii/.

ORF. (2011). *Integrated Transport Policy: A Vision which Doesn't Work Today – How to Make it a Reality*. Retrieved from Observer Research Foundation: https://www.orfonline.org/research/integrated-transport-policy-a-vision-which-doesnt-work-today-how-to-make-it-a-reality/.

Panchal, D.U. (2015). *Two and Three Wheeler Technology*. PHI Learning Pvt. Ltd., ISBN 9788120351431.

Parasuraman, R. (1992). Adaptive function allocation effects on pilot performance. *NASA/FAA Workshop on Artificial Intelligence and Human Factors*. Daytona Beach, Florida, USA: NASA and FAA.

Parasuraman, R., Sheridan, T.B. and Wickens, C.D. (2000). A model for types and levels of human interaction with automation. *IEEE Transactions on Systems, Man, and Cybernetics-Part A: Systems and Humans*, 30(3): 286–297.

PBS. (2009). *Timeline: History of the Electric Car*. Retrieved from PBS.Org: https://www.pbs.org/now/shows/223/electric-car-timeline.html.

Pei, X., Sedini, C. and Zurlo, F. (2019). Building an age-friendly city for elderly citizens through co-designing an urban walkable scenario. *Proceedings of the Academy for Design Innovation Management* (pp. 69-80). London: Academy for Design Innovation Management.

Perner, J., Unteutsch, M. and Lövenich, A. (2018). *The Future Cost of Electricity-based Synthetic Fuels*. Berlin: Agora Energiewende.

Pete. (2015). *Electric Cargo Bike Guide*. Retrieved from Electric Bike Report: https://electricbikereport.com/electric-cargo-bike-guide/.

Policy Profession. (2019). *Policy Profession Standards: A Framework for Professional Development*. London: Policy Profession.

Pope III, C.A., Burnett, R.T., Thun, M.J., Calle, E.E., Krewski, D., Ito, K. and Thurston, G.D. (2002). Lung cancer, cardiopulmonary mortality, and long-term exposure to fine particulate air pollution. *The Journal of the American Medical Association*, 287(9): 1132–1141.

Porru, M., Serpi, A., Mureddu, M. and Damiano, A. (2020). A multistage design procedure for planning and implementing public charging infrastructures for electric vehicles. *Sustainability*, 2889(12): 1–17.

Priemus, H. (2007). Dutch spatial planning between substratum and infrastructure networks. *European Plannning Study*, 15(5): 667–686.

Puchalsky, C.M. (2005). Comparison of emission from light rail and bus rapid transit. *Transportation Research Record*, 1927(1): 31–37.

Qiu, C., Chau, K.T., Ching, T.W. and Liu, C. (2014). Overview of wireless charging technologies for electric vehicles. *Journal of Asian Electric Vehicles*, 12: 1679–1685.

Rajvanshi, A.K. (2002). Electric and improved cycle rickshaw as a sustainable transport system for India. *Current Science*, 83(6): 703–707.

Ram, G., Mouli, C., Duijsen, P.V., Grazian, F., Jamodkar, A., Bauer, P. and Isabella, O. (2020). Sustainable E-Bike charging station that enables AC, DC, and wireless charging from solar energy. *Energies*, 13(3549): 1–21.

Reddy, T. (2008). *Synthetic Fuels Handbook: Properties, Process, and Performance*. McGraw-Hill.

Regnier, E. (2007). Oil and energy price volatility. *Energy Economic*, 29(3): 405–427.

Richard, F. and Cooper, H. (2005). Freeman, richard, and cooper. "Why electrified rail is superior". *21st Century Science & Technology*, 18: 26–29.

Rickstrom, J. and Klum, M. (2015). *Big World, Small Planet: Abundance within Planetary Boundaries*. New Haven and London: Yale University Press.

Rideamigos. (2018). *What is Transportation Demand Management?* Retrieved from Rideamigos: https://rideamigos.com/transportation-demand-management-tdm/.

Rider, D. (2020). *Toronto Adds Electric Bicycles to Bike-share Fleet — at No Extra Cost to Users*. Retrieved from Toronto Star: https://www.thestar.com/news/city_hall/2020/08/19/toronto-adds-electric-bicycles-to-bike-share-fleet-at-no-extra-cost-to-users.html.

Rieti, J. (2017). *CBC News*. Retrieved from Toronto discourages electric car use by denying on-street chargers, driver says: https://www.cbc.ca/news/canada/toronto/electric-vehicles-blocked-1.4368014.

Rife, E. and Andrews, M. (2018). *Street Seats: Urban Placemaking in Portland*. Retrieved from Design Museum Everywhere: https://designmuseumfoundation.org/street-seats/.

Ritchie, H. (2020). *What are the Safest and Cleanest Sources of Energy?* Retrieved from Our world in data: https://ourworldindata.org/safest-sources-of-energy.

ROAMEF. (2016). *ROAMEF Cycle*. Retrieved from ROAMEF: http://www.roamef.com/what-we-do/roamef-cycle.

Rodenbach, J., Mathis, J., Chicco, A., Diana, M. and Nehrk, G. (2017). *Car Sharing in Europe: A Multidimensional Classification and Inventory*. European Union: STARS and AUTON.

Ryerson Urban Analytics Institute. (2019). *How Parking Regulations Need to Evolve for High-Rise Buildings*. Toronto: Residential and Civil Construction Alliance of Ontario (RCCAO).

Sacchi, E., Sayed, T. and Leur, P.d. (2013). A comparison of collision-based and conflict-based safety evaluations: The case of right-turn smart channels. *Accident Analysis and Prevention*, 59: 260–266.

Sadik-Khan, J. (2020). *Streets for Pandemic Response and Recovery*. New York: Global Designing Cities Initiative.

SAE. (2014). *Taxonomy and Definitions for Terms Related to On-road Motor Vehicle Automated Driving Systems*. USA: SAE International.

SAE International. (2014). *Ground Vehicle Stanadards*. USA: SAE International.

SAE International. (2019). *A Dictionary of Terms for the Dynamics and Handling of Single Track Vehicles (Motorcycles, Scooters, Mopeds, and Bicycles)*. Warrendale, PA, USA: J1451_201909. Society of Automotive Engineers.

SAE International. (2019). *J3194 –Taxonomy and Classification of Powered Micromobility Vehicles*. Warrendale, PA, USA: Society of Automotive Engineers.

Saunders, K. (2017). *Where's the Hype for Automated Trains? Part 1: History and Background*. Automation.

Sawilla, Schütt and Oskar. (2018). *Ipt-technology*. Retrieved from Wireless Opportunity Charging buses in Madrid: https://ipt-technology.com/case-opportunity-charging-madrid/.

SCAQMD. (2000). *Multiple Air Toxics Exposure Study*. San Francisco: South Coast Air Quality Management District.

Schneider, C.G. and Hill, L.B. (2007). *No Escape from Diesel Exhaust: How to Reduce Commuter Exposure*. Boston: Boston: Clean Air Task Force.

Schroeder, T. (2020). *Desire*. Retrieved from The Stanford Encyclopedia of Philosophy: https://plato.stanford.edu/archives/sum2020/entries/desire/.

Sclar, R., Gorghinpour, C., Castellanos, S. and Li, X. (2018). *Barriers to Adopting Electric Buses*. Berlin: World Resources Institute, WRI and German Federal Ministry.

Scott, A.J. (2014). Beyond the creative city: Cognitive–cultural capitalism and the new Urbanism. *Regional Studies*, 48(4): 565–578.

Shaheen, S. and Cohen, A. (2019). *Shared Micromobility Policy Toolkit: Docked and Dockless Bike and Scooter Sharing*. Schmidt Family Foundation.

Shaheen, S., Cohen, A. and Zohdy, I. (2016). *Shared Mobility: Current Practices and Guiding Principles*. Washington D.C.: Federal Highway Administration.

Shared-Use Mobility Center. (2017). *Shared-Use Mobility Referrence Guide*. Chicago, USA: Shared-Use Mobility Center.

Sheldrake, R. (2009). *Morphic Resonance: The Nature of Formative Causation*. Rochester, Vermont: Park Street Press.

Shepertycky, M. and Li, Q. (2015). Generating electricity during walking with a lower limb-driven energy harvester: Targeting a minimum user effort. *PLoS ONE*, 1–16.

Shladover, S.E. (2016). The truth about "Self Driving" cars. *Scientific American*, 52–57.

Siemens Mobility. (2015). *Sustainable Urban Infrastructure: Vienna Edition – Role Model for Complete Mobility*.

Smart Growth America. (2021). *Dangerous by Design*. Washington D.C.: Smart Growth America.

SMC. (2018). *Shared Transportation Modes Dramatically Reduce Greenhouse Gases*. Retrieved from Shared-use Mobility Center: https://learn.sharedusemobilitycenter.org/benefitcalculator/.

Smith, R.A. (2008). Enabling technologies for demand management: Transport. *Energy Policy*, 36(12): 4444–4448.

Society of Automobile Engineers, SAE. (2018). *Shared Mobility: Taxonomy and Definitions in SAE J3163™*.

Spaen, B. (2019). *This All-Electric Water Taxi Could Revolutionize Green Transportation*. Retrieved from Green Matters: https://www.greenmatters.com/news/2018/06/25/qSvID/water-taxis-transportation.

Sperling, D. and Shaeen, S. (1999). Carsharing: Niche market or new pathway? *ECMT/OECD Workshop on Managing Car Use for Sustainable Urban Travel* (pp. 1–25). Dublin, Ireland: OECD.

Spulber, A., Dennis, E.P., and Wallace, R. (2016). *The Impact of New Mobility Services on the Automotive Industry*. Ann Arbor, Michigan: Cargroup.Org.

STAPPA and ALAPCO. (2000). *Cancer Risk from Diesel Particulate: National and Metropolitan Area Estimates for the United States*. San Francisco: State and Territorial Air Pollution Program Administrators and the Association of Local Air Pollution Control Officials.

Steer Davies Gleave. (2009). *GO Transit Lakeshore Express Rail Benefit Case, Interim Report*. Toronto: Metrolinx.

Steffen, W., Richardson, K., Rockström, J., Cornell, S., Fetzer, I., Bennett, E., Bennett, E.M., Biggs, R., Carpenter, S.R., Vrie, W.D., Wit, C.A.D., Folke, C., Gerten, D., Heinke, J., Mace, G.M., Persson, L.M., Ramanathan, V., Reyers, B. and Sörlin, S. (2015). Planetary boundaries: Guiding human development on a changing planet. *Science*, 15: 1–10.

Stohler, W. and Giger, P. (1989). *Cost-Benefit Analysis of the Electrification of the Beira Alta Line in Portugal*. London: Institution of Electrical Engineers.

Stone, T. (2017). *Lessons Learned from the History of Car Sharing*. Retrieved from https://tiffanydstone.com/: https://tiffanydstone.com/2013/08/23/lessons-learned-from-the-history-of-car-sharing/.

Stone, T. (2018). *Siemens to Demonstrate World's First Autonomous Tram Running in Real Traffic in German city*. Retrieved from traffictechnology.com: https://www.traffictechnologytoday.com/news/autonomous-vehicles/siemens-to-demonstrate-worlds-first-autonomous-tram-running-in-real-traffic-in-german-city.html.

Strompen, F., Litman, T. and Bongardt, D. (2012). *Reducing Carbon Emissions through Transport Demand Management Strategies: A Review of International Examples, Final Report.* GIZ China, Transport Demand Management in Beijing.

Swenson, R. (2016). The solarevolution: Much more with way less, right now—The disruptive shift to renewables. *Energies*, 9(9): 676.

Tactical Urbanism Guide. (2012). *Tactical Urbanism*. Retrieved from Tactical Urbanist's Guide: http://tacticalurbanismguide.com/about/.

Takefuji, Y. (2008). And if public transport does not consume more energy? (PDF). *Le Rail*, 31–33.

Tao, P., Stefansson, H. and Saevarsdottir, G. (2014). Potential use of geothermal energy sources for the production of Li-ion batteries. *Renewable Energy*, 61.

SAE. (2018). *Taxonomy and Definitions for Terms Related to Shared Mobility and Enabling Technologies.* USA: SAE International.

The Economist. (2017). A world turned upside down. *Renewable Energy*, pp. 18–20.

The Guardian. (2011). *19th Century Cyclists Paved the Way for Modern Motorists' roads*. Retrieved from The Guardian: https://www.theguardian.com/environment/bike-blog/2011/aug/15/cyclists-paved-way-for-roads.

The Guardian. (2017). *Smaller, Lighter,Ggreener: Are Micro EVs the Future of City Transport?* Retrieved from The Guardian: https://www.theguardian.com/sustainable-business/2017/may/11/micro-evs-city-transport-suemens-renault-green-air-pollution.

The TEV project. (2017). *Tracked Electric Vehicle System. Reference Technical Booklet*. Retrieved from The TEV project: http://tevproject.com/.

Toole Design Group and Pedestrian and Bicycle Information Centre. (2012). *Bike Sharing in the United States.* USDOT, Federal Highway Administration.

Toronto. (2017). *Dufferin Wilson Regeneration Area: Interim Control Bylaw, Final Report.* Toronto: City of Toronto.

Toronto. (2018). *ConsumersNext: Planning for People and Business at Sheppard & Victoria Park –Final Report.* Toronto: City of Toronto.

Toronto. (2019). *Don Mills Crossing Secondary Plan, Offiical Plan Amendment.* Toronto: City of Toronto.

Toronto. (2019). *Laird in Focus, Official Plan Amendment.* Toronto: City of Toronto.

Toth, G. (2011). *PPS.org.* Retrieved from Project for Public Places: https://www.pps.org/article/are-complete-streets-incomplete.

Transport Canada. (2009). *Bike Sharing Guide.* Ottawa: Transport Canada.

Transport Canada. (2010). *Bicycle End-of-trip Facilities: A Guide for Canadian Municipalities and Employers.* Ottawa: Public Works and Government Services Canada.

Transportation Services. (2020). *2020 Operating Budget & 2020–2029 Capital Plan.* Toronto: City of Toronto.

TuSimple. (2020). *TuSimple Launches World's First Autonomous Freight Network with UPS, Penske, U.S. Xpress, and McLane Company, Inc.* Retrieved from stockhouse.com: https://stockhouse.com/news/press-releases/2020/07/01/tusimple-launches-world-s-first-autonomous-freight-network-with-ups-penske-u-s.

UITP. (2013). *Press Kit: Metro Automation Facts, Figures, and Trends.* International Association of Public Transport.

UITP. (2014). *Metro Automation Facts, Figures and Trends.* International Association of Public Transport (UITP).

University of Toronto. (2015). *School of Cities.* Retrieved from University of Toronto: https://www.schoolofcities.utoronto.ca/.

US Bureau of Transportation Statistics. (2020). *Energy Intensity of Passenger Modes.* Retrieved from U.S. Energy Consumption by the Transportation Sector: https://www.bts.gov/content/energy-intensity-passenger-modes.

US Department of Energy. (2018). *Alternative Fuel Vehicles.* Retrieved from US Department of Energy: https://www.energy.gov/public-services/vehicles/alternative-fuel-vehicles#/find/nearest?country=US.

US Environmental Protection Agency. (2008). *Heat Island Compendium.* US EPA.

Vasconcellos, E.A. (2004). The use of streets: A reassessment and tribute to Donald Appleyard. *Journal of Urban Design*, 9(1): 3–22.

Venugopal, P., Shekhar, A., Visser, E. and Scheele, N. (2018). Roadway to self-healing highways with integrated wireless electric vehicle charging and sustainable energy harvesting technologies. *Applied Energy*, 212: 1226–1239.

*Watch: Toronto's Surge in E-bike Ownership Creates Concerns over Safety.* (2018). Retrieved from Iheartradio: https://www.iheartradio.ca/newstalk-1010/news/watch-toronto-s-surge-in-e-bike-ownership-creates-concerns-over-safety-1.3726810.

Weichenthal, S., Ryswyk, K., Goldstein, A., Shekarrizfard, M. and Hatzopoulou, M. (2015). Characterizing the spatial distribution of ambient ultrafine particles in Toronto, Canada: A land-use regression model. *Environmental Pollution*, 47(PT A): 1–8.

Weir, L. (2018). *Pina Bousch's Dance Theatre: Tracing the Evolution of Tanz Theatre*. Edinburgh: Edinburgh University Press.

Weißbach, D., Ruprecht, G., Hukeac, A., Czerski, K., Gottlieb, S. and Hussein, A. (2013). Energy intensities, EROIs (energy returned on invested), and energy payback times of electricity generating power plants. *Energy*, 52: 210–221.

Whyte, W.H. (1980). *The Social Life of Small Urban Places*. Ann Arbor: Edwards Brothers.

Wiener, E.L. and Curry, R.E. (1980). Light deck automation: Promise and Problems. *Ergonomics*, 995–1011.

Wilson, K. (2018). *An Overview of SAE International: Standards Activities Related to Charging of Hybrid/Electric Vehicles*. Ground Vehicles Standards, SAE International.

Wilson, K. (2021). *Bill Would Finally Give Bikeshare Transit Dollars*. Retrieved from Streetsblog USA: https://usa.streetsblog.org/2021/02/02/bill-would-finally-give-bikeshare-transit-dollars/.

Wilson, L. (2013). Shades of Green: Electric Cars' Carbon Emissions around the Globe. *Shrink That Footprint*, pp. 1–28.

Wolverton, T. (2016). *Wolverton: Elon Musk's Hyperloop Hype Ignores Practical Problems*. Retrieved from The Mercury News: https://www.mercurynews.com/2013/08/13/wolverton-elon-musks-hyperloop-hype-ignores-practical-problems/.

Woo, L. (2019). *Transit Oriented Development Implementation*. Toronto: Metrolinx.

World Commission on Environment and Development. (1987). *Our Common Future*. Oxford: Oxford University Press.

Xiong, H., Wang, L., Linbing, H., Wang, D. and Druta, C. (2011). Piezoelectric energy harvesting from traffic- induced deformation of pavements. *International Journal of Pavement Research and Technology*, 5(5): 333–337.

York Region. (2015). *Transportation Master Plan: Recommended Policy Principles*. New Market: York Region.

Zhang, W. and Guhathakurta, S. (2016). Parking spaces in the age of shared autonomous vehicles: How much parking will we need and where? *Sustainable Cities and Society*, 19: 34–45.

Zielinski, S. (2006). New mobility: The next generation of sustainable urban transportation. *National Academy of Engineering*, 36(4).

# Index